The Origins of Christian Democracy

The Origins of Christian Democracy

Politics and Confession in Modern Germany

MARIA D. MITCHELL

THE UNIVERSITY OF MICHIGAN PRESS
Ann Arbor

Published in the United States of America by
The University of Michigan Press
Manufactured in the United States of America
⊗ Printed on acid-free paper

2015   2014   2013   2012   4   3   2   1

A CIP catalog record for this book is available from the British Library.

Library of Congress Cataloging-in-Publication Data

Mitchell, Maria D., 1965–
     The origins of Christian democracy : politics and confession in modern Germany /
   Maria D. Mitchell.
        p.   cm.
   Includes bibliographical references and index.
   ISBN 978-0-472-11841-0 (cloth : alk. paper) — ISBN 978-0-472-02854-2 (e-book)
     1. Christian democratic parties—Germany—History.   2. Christian democracy—
   Germany—History.   3. Christianity and politics—Germany—History.   I. Title.
   JN3971.A979M56   2012
   324.243'04—dc23   2012025924

Dedicated to
Paul and Carolyn Mitchell
and
Dietrich and Maria Orlow

Acknowledgments

If all books have long lives, this book has led a number of them. Along the way, I have accumulated many debts of gratitude. At the University of Michigan Press, sincere thanks go to Ellen Bauerle, Alexa Ducsay, Geoff Eley, Mary Hashman, and Susan Whitlock for their patience and assistance. For institutional support, I am very grateful to the Fulbright Commission; the Quadrille Ball Committee of the Germanistic Society of America; the Friedrich-Ebert-Stiftung; the Institut für die Wissenschaften vom Menschen; the German Historical Institute; the American Institute for Contemporary German Studies; the Deutscher Akademischer Austauschdienst; the American Council of Learned Societies; Franklin & Marshall College; the Max-Planck-Institut für Geschichte; the Abigail Quigley McCarthy Center for Women's Research, Resources, and Scholarship; the Gerda Henkel Stiftung; and the Graduate Institute of International and Development Studies. I owe my deepest appreciation to Heinz Duchhardt, Ulrike Kretzschmar, Jutta Ries, Karl Otmar Freiherr von Aretin, Christine Weil, and especially Stefana Dascalescu, Ralph Melville, Claus Scharf, and Martin Vogt, for making the Institut für Europäische Geschichte the remarkable place that it is. I will always treasure my time and relationships forged there and the home that Mainz provided me.

I was fortunate to work with highly professional staff at the Bundesarchiv Koblenz; Historisches Archiv der Stadt Köln; Archiv für Christlich-demokratische Politik, St. Augustin; Archiv der Stiftung Bundeskanzler-Adenauer-Haus, Rhöndorf; Dom- und Diözesanarchiv Mainz; Hauptstaatsarchiv Düsseldorf; Landeshauptarchiv Koblenz; Institut für Zeitgeschichte München; Geheimes Staatsarchiv Merseburg; the Deutsche Bibliothek; and the National Archives and Records Administration. I am also grateful to Angela Stirken of the Haus der Geschichte der Bundesrepublik Deutschland.

Friends and fellow historians have played crucial roles in the development and completion of this project. It is my pleasure to thank Doris Bergen, Drew Bergerson, Volker Berghahn, Gerhard Besier, Frank Biess, David Blackbourn,

Rebecca Boehling, Dirk Bönker, Frank Bösch, Carl Caldwell, Noel Cary, Roger Chickering, John Conway, Martin Conway, Susanne Dickfeld-Teichmann, Ellen Evans, Antoine Grange, Ron Granieri, Michael Gross, Jussi Hanhimäki, Lisa Heineman, Dagmar Herzog, Maria Höhn, Michael Hughes, Paul Jaskot, Stathis Kalyvas, Tom Kselman, Hartmut Lehmann, Jay Locke-nour, Alf Lüdtke, Helga Lüdtke, Fred McKitrick, Paul Misner, Bob Moeller, Michael Phayer, Uta Poiger, Susan Porter, Diethelm Prowe, Gerhard Rings-hausen, Mark Ruff, Holli Schauber, Hanna Schissler, Greg Schroeder, Helmut Walser Smith, Julie Sneeringer, Tony Steinhoff, Patty Stokes, Till van Rahden, and Jonathan Wiesen. I am especially grateful to Aleksandar-Saša Vuletić for, among other things, locating Helmut Kohl's dissertation. Tony Judt was very helpful when our paths crossed in Vienna; his death remains a profound loss for many.

As an undergraduate and graduate school student, I took one course with a female professor, Kristin Bumiller. For her inspiration by example, I thank her. At Franklin & Marshall College, Alexis Castor has been an enthusiastic word counter, Annette Aronowicz an engaging interlocutor, and Cecile Zorach a treasured fellow Germanist. Special thanks go to her and to Richard March for their contribution to this project through the Franklin & Marshall College Hackman Scholarship program. In Europe, the de Syon family has offered a headquarters and many a delicious *repas. Je vous en remercie.* I am also grate-ful to Chee Chia and James Spicher for their professionalism and care.

My mother taught me respect for the influence of organized religion and community. My father taught me to value politics and history. Both modeled the importance of family and fortitude while encouraging my ambitions. In a sense, this book lies at the intersection of all their life lessons. Dietrich Orlow was my best academic mentor. From Boston to Gmunden to Geneva, he and Maria Orlow have provided unflagging support over many years. It is an honor to express my gratitude to them.

Only one other person has lived with this project from its inception. From sharing a *Bundesarchiv Kabine* to health challenges and parenting, Guillaume de Syon has offered invaluable companionship, comfort, and assistance. Corinne and Lucie de Syon have not yet visited Germany, and Christian De-mocracy means nothing to them. They do know that their mother missed many a play hour to complete her book. I hope that someday they will feel proud of my efforts as they pursue their own goals.

Portions of this book have appeared previously, in different form, as "Ma-terialism and Secularism: CDU Politicians and National Socialism, 1945–1949," *Journal of Modern History* 67.2 (1995): 278–308; and "'Antimaterialism' in Early German Christian Democracy," in *European Christian Democracy: Historical Legacies and Comparative Perspectives,* ed. Thomas Kselman and Joseph A. Buttigieg (Notre Dame, 2003). They are reprinted here with permission.

Geneva, Switzerland
June 2011

Contents

Abbreviations

Archives

ACDPStA   Archiv für Christlich-demokratische Politik, St. Augustin
BAK   Bundesarchiv Koblenz
DDAM   Dom- und Diözesanarchiv Mainz
GStM   Geheimes Staatsarchiv Merseburg
HAStK   Historisches Archiv der Stadt Köln
HStAD   Hauptstaatsarchiv Düsseldorf
IZG   Institut für Zeitgeschichte München
LHA   Landeshauptarchiv Koblenz
NA   National Archives and Records Administration
OMGUS   Office of Military Government, United States
StBKAH   Archiv der Stiftung Bundeskanzler-Adenauer-Haus, Rhöndorf

Printed Sources

DdB   Wolfgang Löhr, *Dokumente deutscher Bischöfe,* vol. 1,
         Hirtenbriefe und Ansprachen zu Gesellschaft und Politik, 1945–
         1949 (Würzburg, 1985).
DGG   Helmuth Pütz, ed., *Konrad Adenauer und die CDU der*
         britischen Besatzungszone, 1946–1949: Dokumente zur
         Gründungsgeschichte der CDU Deutschlands (Bonn, 1975).
Briefe, 1945–1947   Hans Peter Mensing, ed., *Adenauer Briefe, 1945–1947*
         (Berlin, 1983).
Briefe, 1947–1949   Hans Peter Mensing, ed., *Adenauer Briefe, 1947–1949*
         (Berlin, 1984).
Briefe über Deutschland   Mensing, Hans Peter, ed., *Konrad Adenauer Briefe*
         über Deutschland, 1945–1955 (Berlin, Munich, 1999).

GvG	Peter Löffler, ed., *Bischof Clemens August Graf von Galen: Akten, Briefe und Predigten, 1933–1946,* vol. 2, *1939–1946* (Mainz, 1988).
LNWSB	Landtag Nordrhein-Westfalen, Stenographischer Bericht
PBV	Günter Buchstab, ed., *Adenauer: "Wir haben wirklich etwas geschaffen": Die Protokolle des CDU-Bundesvorstand, 1953–1957* (Düsseldorf, 1990).
PRSB	Parlamentarischer Rat, Stenographischer Bericht
PRSU	Rainer Salzmann, ed., *Die CDU/CSU im Parlamentarischen Rat: Sitzungsprotokolle der Unionsfraktion,* vol. 2, *Die CDU/CSU im Parlamentarischen Rat* (Stuttgart, 1981).

Parties, Institutions, Organizations

AEK	Working Group of Engaged Catholics (Arbeitskreis Engagierter Katholiken)
BVP	Bavarian People's Party (Bayerische Volkspartei)
CDA	Christian Democratic Workers' Association (Christlich-Demokratische Arbeitnehmerschaft)
CDP	Christian Democratic Party (Christlich-Demokratische Partei)
CDU	Christian Democratic Union (Christlich-Demokratische Union)
CDUD	Christian Democratic Union of Germany (Christlich-Demokratische Union Deutschlands)
CGD	Christian Trade Unions of Germany (Christliche Gewerkschaften Deutschlands)
CSP	Christian Social Party (Christlich-Soziale Partei)
CSVD	Christian Social People's Service (Christlich-Sozialer Volksdienst)
CSVP	Christian Social People's Party (Christlich-Soziale Volkspartei)
CSU	Christian Social Union (Christlich-Soziale Union)
CVP	Christian People's Party (Christliche Volkspartei)
DDP	German Democratic Party (Deutsche Demokratische Partei)
DEK	German Protestant Church (Deutsche Evangelische Kirche)
DGB	German Trade Union Federation (Deutscher Gewerkschaftsbund)
DKF	German Kolping Family (Deutsche Kolpingsfamilie)
DNVP	German National People's Party (Deutschnationale Volkspartei)
DP	German Party (Deutsche Partei)

DVP	German People's Party (Deutsche Volkspartei)
DStP	German State Party (Deutsche Staatspartei)
EAK	Protestant Working Group (Evangelischer Arbeitskreis)
EKD	Protestant Church in Germany (Evangelische Kirche in Deutschland)
FDP	Free Democratic Party (Freie Demokratische Partei)
GVP	All-German People's Party (Gesamtdeutsche Volkspartei)
KAB	Catholic Workers' Movement (Katholische Arbeiterbewegung)
KPD	Communist Party of Germany (Kommunistische Partei Deutschlands)
LDP	Liberal Democratic Party of Germany (Liberal-Demokratische Partei Deutschlands)
MRA	Moral Re-Armament Movement
NSDAP	National Socialist German Workers' Party (Nationalsozialistische Deutsche Arbeiterpartei)
SED	Socialist Unity Party of Germany (Sozialistische Einheitspartei Deutschlands)
SPD	Social Democratic Party of Germany (Sozialdemokratische Partei Deutschlands)
SRP	Socialist Reich Party (Sozialistische Reichspartei Deutschland)
USPD	Independent Social Democratic Party of Germany (Unabhängige Sozialdemokratische Partei Deutschlands)
ZdK	Central Committee of German Catholics (Das Zentralkomittee der deutschen Katholiken)

Introduction

In 1945, small numbers of Protestants joined former members of the Catholic Center Party throughout occupied Germany to found the country's first avowedly interconfessional political party, the Christlich-Demokratische Union (Christian Democratic Union [CDU]). Their intention to fashion a new form of politics was part of a larger project to rechristianize defeated Germany. Together with its Bavarian counterpart, the Christlich-Soziale Union (Christian Social Union [CSU]), the CDU soon dominated the postwar German political landscape. As the state's leading party until 1969, the CDU and its policies influenced West Germany's formation and early character so completely that, for many Germans, the party became psychologically identified with the postwar state.[1] More than any other political movement, Christian Democracy forged the state of West Germany and, after 1989, German unification.

The ascendant form of post–World War II Catholic politics, Christian Democracy represented the transformation of German political Catholicism. Marked by the embrace of democracy and interconfessional anti-Marxism, postwar Christian politics contributed substantially to the stabilization of the Federal Republic, not least through the integration of conservative voters.[2] Labeled a people's party (*Volkspartei*) and "corporatist catch-all party," the CDU both laid an indispensable foundation for West German democracy and, by integrating diverse constituencies, provided a model of internal democracy.[3]

In the 1950s and 1960s, Christian Democratic policies, including NATO membership, European economic integration, and social market economics, dictated more than a West German political identity. West German anticommunism represented a linchpin of Western Cold War strategy, as the division of Europe rested to a significant degree on disavowal of the German Democratic Republic. Economically, Christian Democratic policies facilitated a rapid recovery that reinforced trans-Atlantic antisocialism, while interstate integration anchored West Germany in a peaceful and prosperous postwar Western Europe. Socially and culturally, the CDU set the tone for, among other issues, engagement with the Nazi past; the place of the family, children, and women in West German society; and the role of the churches, particularly the Catholic Church, in a postwar German democracy.

At the same time, the CDU embodied one of the most striking developments in twentieth-century German history, the transformation of confessional relations. Following World War II, West German society experienced a marked diminution of intra-Christian tension; by the late 1960s, the Protestant-Catholic cleavage so long characteristic of German life had largely faded from public view. Politically, democratic German politics shifted definitively from a system marked by self-evident confessionalism to one inhospitable to a confessionally based party. As Germany's first professed pan-Christian party, the CDU represented both an active agent and a reflection of this process.

This book focuses on the origins of German Christian Democracy in occupied Germany, when Protestants and Catholics, against the backdrop of decades of political animosity, first cooperated in the name of Christian politics. In the early postwar years, Germany remained a society defined by religious identity and suspicion. Despite the CDU's commitment to Christian cooperation, Protestant-Catholic tensions as well as divisions within each confessional camp roiled the new movement. In answer to his question, "How did the Germans succeed in rising out of the physical destruction and moral degradation created by the war of annihilation and Holocaust for which they were to blame?" Konrad H. Jarausch suggests a "collective learning process."[4] An important element of that learning process was the defusing of confessional hostilities inherited from pre-1945 German society. Their continuance and resolution within the CDU shed important light on the dynamics of postwar German history.

Confessional Milieus in Germany

This study locates Christian Democracy's origins in the context of German nineteenth- and twentieth-century politics and religion. Enemies or at best uneasy allies since the founding of the German *Reich*, religious Protestants and Catholics shared limited experience in political cooperation. Despite the lack of Catholic consensus on elemental principles of political and social organization, most German Catholics exhibited before 1945 what Wilfried Loth has labeled a "specific Catholic consciousness."[5] In his study of the Catholic worldview in Bamberg, Werner Blessing included not only Catholics of deep religious conviction but also those attached to the Catholic community through church attendance, organizations, gatherings, the Catholic press, and Catholic-organized political parties, primarily the German Center Party (Deutsche Zentrumspartei, Zentrum).[6] Bourgeois Protestants forged an equally distinct identity in nineteenth-century Germany, a cultural Protestantism (Kulturprotestantismus) infused with anti-Catholicism and linked to German nationalism.[7] On the basis of these competing utopian visions of a confessionally homogenous Germany, Olaf Blaschke has christened the German nineteenth century a "second confessional era," following the first of the sixteenth and seventeenth centuries.[8]

How best to characterize these confessional communities has been the subject of considerable scholarly energy. National literatures have employed a variety of terms, including the Dutch "pillar" and the Swiss "ghetto."[9] M. Rainer Lepsius's description of the German party system after 1871 as one of four social-moral milieus—the Catholic, the conservative, the socialist, and the bourgeois Protestant—has influenced many students of modern Germany.[10] Karl Rohe's related model posits three major political camps (*Lager*)—the socialist, nationalist, and Catholic.[11] In recent years, milieu analyses have been criticized as too static, ahistorical, and hierarchical to capture the diversity of German society. Historians have increasingly rejected the notion of a milieu within which all German Catholics (or Protestants or Jews, for that matter) would behave—and vote—in similar ways.

Indeed, an exclusive focus on distinct milieus would make impossible the kind of comparative history of religion and religious culture in Germany for which Helmut Walser Smith and Chris Clark have called.[12] In this regard, the term *Teilkultur* may offer an alternative by implying a nonsubordinate social group or culture, the voting patterns of which are directly related to its distinct assumptions and beliefs. Open to and influenced by national trends even as it cultivated its own expressions of them, a Teilkultur has boundaries, but they are permeable.[13] Karl Rohe's reminder that all such terminology is theoretically slippery is welcome, however.[14] I use the term *Teilkultur* interchangeably with *milieu,* aware of the weaknesses of both but nonetheless recognizing their value.

Though Margaret Lavinia Anderson argues that Blaschke's "second confessional era" thesis goes too far, she agrees that, "for a century and more, nothing could be said or done in Germany that was not said or done by a Protestant, a Catholic, or a Jew."[15] The two separate and competing Christian constructs of Germanness coexistent in Wilhelmine Germany did not disappear during the Weimar Republic or the Nazi era. Christians' adherence to a single political program after 1945 therefore required the adaptation of two distinct traditions, each defined to a significant degree in opposition to the other. As the literature on modern Germany makes clear, the socialist, Catholic, and conservative milieus that originated in the nineteenth century endured well into the 1960s;[16] the Catholic milieu was especially culturally and politically powerful.[17]

Interconfessional Affinities

The process of Protestant-Catholic adaptation did not begin in 1945, of course, nor did interconfessionalism take shape within a vacuum. Germany's Christian division was necessarily and consistently differentiated, privately as well as publicly. This was especially true of Germany's most religiously active Protestants and Catholics. Though separated fundamentally by practice and doctrine, the faithful of both confessions shared a commitment to Christian party politics. Crucial for the construction of Christian Democracy, this ideological affinity took concrete form in the late nineteenth century, when devout and conservative Protestants joined Catholics in rejecting modernism and such materialist phenomena as liberalism, capitalism, and socialism. This mutual opposition to materialism—a conservative trope encompassing all that challenged Christianity, including Judaism—and a corresponding embrace of an organic, patriarchal societal order united Catholics and Protestants when much else divided them.

While this Christian consonance in no way overcame confessional hostility (and in many ways was colored by it), ideological accord between the confessions did give rise to cooperative political action. In 1906, Catholic Center Party members undertook the first concerted attempt to organize an interconfessional party. Though weak and doomed to failure, this and similar initiatives highlighted both a Catholic focus on pious Protestants and a pan-Christian hostility to materialism's most potent expressions. In the wake of World War I, antimaterialism and antisecularism emerged as coherent, pervasive Christian critiques of a Germany consumed by societal turmoil. During the Weimar Republic, certain policies of social conservatism found support among religiously active Protestants and Catholics. In particular, practicing Protestants and Catholics joined to support confessional schools and to preserve traditional gender relations; in the Weimar Republic's later years, Catholic politicians sought political alliance with the German National People's Party (Deutschnationale Volkspartei [DNVP]) based primarily on Christian-inspired social and cultural politics.

At the same time that religious Protestants and Catholics made common cause on conservative social issues, the threat of German socialism united them. For those committed to Christian politics, interconfessionalism represented the only apparent means of combating the threat from the left. By 1901, in the face of the dramatic success of the Social Democratic Party of Germany (Sozialistische Partei Deutschlands [SPD]) and Marxist-inspired trade unions, Catholics and some Protestants endorsed interconfessional trade unions. Driven by the desire to forge a united Christian front against apparent agents of atheism, interconfessionalism was from its origins animated by anti-Marxism.

While Protestant-Catholic tensions eased during the Weimar Republic, ideological, economic, and cultural differences within the Christian community continued to fragment Germany's public and private spheres. Despite the Center Party's coalitions with a number of Protestant parties, its election of a clergyman as leader as late as 1928 highlighted the still palpable confessionalism of the German party system. Intra-Christian conflict, evident in the Rhineland separatist movement and the 1925 presidential election, continued to shape fundamentally German political life. As the halfhearted attempts in 1918 and 1920 to organize an interconfessional party made clear, German Christianity entered the Nazi era still deeply divided.

The National Socialist dictatorship may have masked the confessionalized character of German life but it failed to transform it. Despite Protestant-Catholic cooperation in resistance and oppositional groups, on the one hand, and widespread cross-confessional support for National Socialism, on the other, Protestants and Catholics stood no closer to interconfessional harmony at the end of the Nazi era than they had at the beginning. Seemingly unaffected by Nazi efforts to bridge the confessional gap, religious identities were in some ways reinforced by Nazi persecution.[18] Moreover, Protestant-Catholic tensions were exacerbated by the population dislocations of the late war and immediate postwar years. This aggravation of religious conflict was accompanied by a dramatic increase in church-related activity; of crucial importance to the fortunes of early Christian Democracy, the organization of the CDU took place in an atmosphere of heightened religious consciousness and confessional sensibility.

The Organization of Christian Democracy

Though shaped profoundly by the inheritance of confessional conflict and the unique circumstances of occupied Germany, the CDU's organization was also clearly indebted to reconciliatory traditions of German politics. As Noel Cary has shown, cooperation with conservative, religious Protestants had been a long-standing if rhetorical goal of Catholic politics, associated most closely with liberal Catholicism and the Christian Trade Unions.[19] In particular, clergy, former trade unionists, and Center Party members bound by anti-Nazi networks emerged in 1945 to facilitate the CDU's organization. Well aware of the collapse of political Catholicism in the face of National Socialism, these Catholics resolved that the hour of interconfessionalism had arrived.

Consistent with existing patterns of Protestant-Catholic cooperation, Catholics sought out those Protestants they deemed adequately religious and socially conservative for Christian politics. Of those, Protestant ministers and especially former members of the Confessing Church and the Christian Social People's Service (Christlich-Sozialer Volksdienst [CSVD]) would play prominent roles in bringing Christian Democracy to life. That this new party was a Catholic project was hardly lost on German Protestants. Not only was the CDU's early leadership overwhelmingly Catholic, but—as they had since the Center Party's founding in 1870—Catholic priests were key organizers of Catholic politics. Hindered by institutional weakness and internal divisions, Protestants found it difficult to chart a distinctively Protestant political path. The fate of their pre-1933 parties left conservative, religious, and anti-Marxist Protestants—despite reservations about crossing the confessional line—few alternatives to cooperation with Catholics.

Indeed, for many Protestants and Catholics, there was little love or passion in this marriage of reason. As the party's history demonstrates, early Christian Democracy was rife with confessional misunderstanding and suspicion. At the same time, first-hour Christian Democrats drew inspiration from their experiences under the Third Reich, particularly the blood-soaked bond they believed Protestants and Catholics had forged through shared resistance to National Socialism. The CDU's depiction of a church struggle (*Kirchenkampf*) pitting Nazis against unified Christians bears historical scrutiny. But in occupied Germany, it not only salved raw confessional wounds but provided moral and political validation for the party's postwar rechristianizing mission.

The CDU's legitimacy rested not simply on a cross-confessional indictment of Nazism or the (now obligatory) embrace of democracy but also on the construction of a functioning consensus on the meaning of Christian Democracy. Although the goal of rechristianizing Germany appealed to both Protestants and Catholics, it offered little practical guidance for the new party. Even as they declared the dawn of a new politics, party leaders reclaimed the ideological categories of Protestant-Catholic cooperation dating to the nineteenth century. By equating Christian Democracy with antimaterialism, early CDU leaders invested Christian Democracy with the outlines of a political agenda—

opposition to Nazism, liberalism, female emancipation, secularism, and last but not least Marxism—that would sustain it through the Federal Republic's founding years.

The bounds of antimaterialism were by no means clearly set, however, and Protestants and Catholics did not agree on the concept's roots and implications, either with each other or respectively. Intrinsically malleable as an ideological construct, materialism underwent a period of crucial redefinition in occupied Germany, above all else through the CDU's debate about Christian Socialism. After an intense intraparty battle fought largely along class and confessional lines, Catholic support for Christian Socialism was sacrificed to the coherency of antisocialism and ultimately the adoption of Ludwig Erhard's social market economy. Marking the triumph of bourgeois Catholicism's alliance with party Protestants at the expense of the Christian Trade Unionists, this delineation of antimaterialism defined interconfessionalism for the new Germany as it had been imagined since the late nineteenth century—as an antisocialist Christian alliance.

Even as CDU politicians succeeded in forging common antisocialist cause and achieving political hegemony, the CDU's interconfessional project remained incomplete. If Protestant and Catholic Christian Democrats agreed on the need to reinscribe patriarchy on postwar Germany, the question of religiously segregated public schools reminded Germans in and outside the party of the legacies of confessional animosity. At the same time, despite increasing Protestant electoral support across the postwar decades, the CDU remained an indisputably Catholic-dominated party. In 1952, when CDU Protestants established an intraparty organization, their disgruntlement made clear interconfessionalism's failings. Cross-confessional opposition to the Soviet Union, East Germany, and West German Social Democracy and support for economic recovery would enable Christian Democrats to paper over internal differences, but the confessional gap still yawned.

The situation would alter decisively by the 1960s, however, as West German society underwent a complicated process of modernization. Propelled by the success of the social market economy, consumerism and individualism began to undermine traditional authority and structures in German society. The dechristianization of everyday life, the diminished role of the clergy in Catholic politics, and the rise of Protestant Cold War liberals combined to secularize Christian Democratic rhetoric and policies. This transformation of confessional culture, complicated and uneven, had broad and profound implications for German life while encouraging and reflecting major shifts in CDU internal party politics, electoral support, campaign strategies, rhetoric, and even policy.

The CDU of the 1960s was far removed from the party of the late 1940s, and Christian Democracy represents an important element of any account of West German modernization.

The history of the CDU demonstrates that religion and confessional culture were conspicuous features of Germany's postwar landscape. In the immediate postwar era, the involvement of Protestant and especially Catholic clergy bespoke Christian Democracy's links to the churches, while the CDU's leadership, ideology, and membership derived directly from political Catholicism. At the same time, the palpable distrust between Protestants and Catholics, even those committed to interconfessional cooperation, underscored the degree to which post–Nazi Germany remained fundamentally divided by religion. For all of these reasons, the CDU's origins testify to the importance of Christian traditions—in political as well as social life and after as well as before 1945.

Histories of Christian Democracy

The years 1945–65 have been described as "a golden age for the 'Christian Democratic' parties in many parts of Europe," when Christian Democrats oversaw economic recovery and charted the path to European unity.[20] While this study focuses on the German Christian Democratic Party's early history, the CDU was but one of a number of influential Christian Democratic parties, including Italy's Democrazia Cristiana and France's Mouvement républicain populaire, that pursued politics as a postwar religious mission; in this regard, the CDU was an intrinsically European as well as German phenomenon.[21] That "political manifestations of the Catholic faith" such as European Christian Democracy have failed to attract scholarly attention equal to their Marxist, fascist, liberal, or even Green counterparts has long been a truism.[22] While there is now a substantial historiography on Christian Democracy, it cannot compete with that on other major political movements. The extant literature makes clear, however, that German political Catholicism and Christian Democracy fit into broader patterns of European development dictated by the struggle between tradition and modernity.[23]

The CDU's place in German history is evolving. The rediscovery of Christianity, especially Catholicism, by historians of modern Germany has been under way for some time now and is part of a growing recognition of the significance of religion to European and American history.[24] Although it has not yet produced an alternative master paradigm, a "religious turn" in Euro-

pean historiography has challenged standard narratives of a secularizing continent since the late eighteenth century.[25] But while confession has emerged as a
defining feature of the nineteenth century, religious identity and difference figure less prominently in histories of an apparently dechristianizing twentieth
century.[26] The place of Christianity in twentieth-century Europe certainly has
not escaped scrutiny; the role of the churches, particularly the Vatican, in the
Third Reich and the Holocaust has been the subject of a sustained and controversial historiography[27] and there is a burgeoning literature on the cultural history of Catholicism after World War II.[28] But, as Samuel Moyn has remarked,
the "recasting of the relationship between Christianity and the 'Occident' of
the postwar era" is as important as it has been ignored.[29] To a regrettable degree, the dominant picture of recent German history remains a largely areli-
gious one, undergirded not least by statistical evidence of declining religious
practice over the past half century.[30]

But church attendance is a questionable measure of the depth and influence of religious belief and culture, and modern Germany resists a pattern of
linear religious loss.[31] The religious renewals of the 1920s and 1940s and
heightened confessional conflict after World War II point to the continued relevance of religious identity across the twentieth century,[32] while recent studies
highlight the shifts in individual religious practice with age.[33] The continuance
of confessionally segregated public schools in the Federal Republic into the
1960s clearly signals the salience of post–1945 religious identity. Yet religion
as a category of analysis has not yet been fully integrated into narratives of
West German history,[34] and even accounts of Christian Democracy have
downplayed or dismissed the party's religious connections and content.[35] At
the same time, a number of studies of German political Catholicism reveal a
fundamental sympathy toward their subject;[36] in keeping with Martin Conway's observation that Christian Democracy writes its "own history," this has
also been the case for the historiography of the CDU.[37] Perhaps not surprisingly, those who offered the first competing interpretations of the party's
history—Gerhard Kraiker and A. R. L. Gurland—did so with their own ideological fervor.[38]

More recent literature has marked a welcome departure from these patterns. Noel Cary's survey of twentieth-century interconfessional initiatives is
sweeping in scope, persuasive in detail, and free of the ideological weight of
earlier scholarship on the topic.[39] Frank Bösch also offers a valuable corrective,
especially in his focus on the Protestant conservatives so crucial to the establishment of early Christian Democracy.[40] While Cary's concern is the battle
within the Catholic milieu between the refounded Center Party and the CDU

and Bösch focuses more on party organization than ideology, together they have contributed greatly to our understanding of a political movement that hitherto has been "taken for granted as part of the political furniture."[41]

By exploring the early dynamics and ideologies of Christian Democracy, I offer another perspective on German political and social development. Because I seek to situate the origins of Christian Democracy in the history of Catholic and Protestant politics, I devote the first chapter to tracing political Catholicism and varieties of Protestant politics from the nineteenth century through World War II. In the second chapter, I examine the organization of Christian Democracy in the British zone of occupation, paying special attention to the role of former trade unionists, those in resistance, and the clergy. The British zone, including the Rhineland and Westphalia, which were strongholds of political Catholicism, would produce the leading organ of early Christian Democracy; it is no coincidence that Konrad Adenauer called the Rhineland home. In the third chapter, I trace the founding of Christian Democratic parties in the American, French, and Soviet zones, where we see similar patterns of organization to those evident in the British zone, albeit with notable regional variations. I also explore the role of Protestants and female politicians in organizing the CDU.

The book's fourth chapter treats the broad ideological foundations of Christian Democracy, focusing on discrepancies inherent in the interconfessional commitment to an antimaterialist rechristianization of the Abendland (Occident). These basic ideological assumptions serve as the springboard for chapter 5's survey of specific CDU approaches to gender, confessional schools, and economic questions. In the sixth chapter, I examine Christian Democratic economic policy, specifically the intraparty debate over Christian Socialism that informed CDU policy in the North Rhine-Westphalian Landtag. In the seventh chapter, I chart the party's path through the Parliamentary Council and to the social market economy. The CDU's alliance with Ludwig Erhard would determine the public face and legacy of early Christian Democracy, and how a political party dominated by Catholics came to embrace a Protestant economics minister is one of the defining questions of West German history. This chapter also examines CDU policy in the Parliamentary Council on issues of women, family, and confessional schools to shed light on Christian Democracy's relationship to political Catholicism and negotiation of Protestant-Catholic tensions. In the final chapter, I discuss the evolution of Christian Democracy following the Federal Republic's first federal elections, as West German society and with it the CDU underwent a process of deconfessionalization that fundamentally reshaped the party's relationship to materialism and the Abendland.

Grounded in an interconfessional alliance after centuries of religious dissension, the CDU overturned a destructive legacy of the Reformation to become West Germany's first mass democratic party. In so doing, Christian Democracy offered a dramatic departure in twentieth-century politics and Christian relations, a break necessarily informed by confessional history and culture. The origins of the Christian Democratic Union represent an important chapter in German and European history. This book seeks to contribute to an understanding of that past.

CHAPTER I

Confessional Conflict in German History

Cast in the extraordinary conditions of occupied Germany, Christian Democracy was nonetheless an outgrowth of complex developments extending into the German and European past. Though a diffuse political movement with profound national variations, Christian Democracy was clearly rooted in the parties that helped reinvent Catholic identity in post–French Revolutionary Europe.[1] As the politicization of Enlightenment ideals rendered traditional Catholicism a leading target of intellectual and governmental critique, devout Catholics' adherence to traditional beliefs during a period of nation building and aggressive modernization set them at odds with almost every scientific, intellectual, and social innovation of the century.[2] The result was the emergence of "two Europes"—the clerical and the anticlerical—and, especially in the second half of the nineteenth century, a series of "culture wars" across the continent.[3]

The Kulturkampf

The confrontation between Catholics and their opponents was well under way by the 1840s, as liberals battled political Catholicism on a terrain of nationalism, civil liberties, antisemitism, and sexuality.[4] But for Catholics in Germany, the Kulturkampf realized modernization's greatest threat. Catalyzed by Protestant hostility to the 1864 Syllabus of Errors and the 1870 declaration of papal infallibility, the Kulturkampf sought to impose state control over the Catholic Church through, among other measures, the requirement of civil marriage, the imposition of state control over Catholic education and Prussian clergy appointments, and the expulsion of the Jesuit order.[5] Designed to forge a unified German nationalist culture based on Protestant values, the Kulturkampf fed on long-standing German Protestant stereotypes about and hostility to German Catholics;[6] for many middle-class Germans, it represented an opportunity for societal reform that would stem challenges to liberal hegemony.[7] The ultimate modern European conflict between liberalism and Catholicism,[8] the Kulturkampf had a dramatic impact on Catholic practices and long-lasting effects.[9] While the Kulturkampf sought to forge one nation, it codified two separate German national identities, one Protestant and one Catholic,[10] and according to Olaf Blaschke inaugurated Germany's "second confessional century."[11]

Arguably the most significant immediate legacy of the Kulturkampf was the solidification of a process already under way—the formation of the Catholic Teilkultur. Defined by its cohesive value system and daily rituals, this network of Catholic associations connected church groups, a thriving Catholic press, theater and reading clubs, and organizations for children, mothers, and workers.[12] At the same time, Catholicism continued a popular ultramontane revival in motion since the 1848 revolution, expressing itself in the forms most antipathetic to liberals: processions, new monastic orders, pilgrimages, worship of saints and the Virgin Mary. Perceived as backward by critics, Catholic responses to the Kulturkampf, including mass and female mobilization, the development of voluntary associations, and the use of emergent media, were in many ways in fact definitively modern.[13]

Indeed, by bringing Catholics, especially rural Catholics, into the public sphere and political process, the Kulturkampf ultimately contributed to the expansion of political participation in Germany.[14] With the founding of the Center Party in 1870 in Soest, the Kulturkampf forged a strong and cohesive Catholic party that would serve as a model for other national Catholic movements.[15] Dedication among German Catholics to organizations of the Catholic milieu was so strong that Center leaders felt little need to develop an independent party structure.[16] Leaders of the laity's struggle with the state, especially in the Rhine Province, Westphalia, and Hesse,[17] clergymen now proved essential to maintaining the Teilkultur's infrastructure and symbolic forms.[18] Significantly for the party's future, twenty-one of the original fifty-two signers of the program in Soest identified themselves as clerics.[19]

Propelled by clerical agitation and Catholic insecurity, the Center Party quickly emerged as the Reichstag's largest party.[20] Undermined by Catholic political and social assimilation in the wake of the Kulturkampf, however, the Center Party's support slid gradually and unevenly.[21] In response, beginning early in the twentieth century, Center Party leaders—many of whom would play leading roles in party organization after 1945—participated in a series of impassioned exchanges about dismantling the *Turm,* or tower, of German political Catholicism. These debates, challenging the legitimacy of an exclusively Catholic party, constitute important chapters in the history of Catholic political organization. They also provide a valuable perspective on the emergence of Christian Democracy after World War II.

Catholic Battles: The Romantic versus Realist Schools

The question of interconfessionalism stood at the heart of deliberations over the nature of German Catholic organization. Despite the cohesiveness resulting from the Kulturkampf, the Zentrum had been divided internally from its first days on a number of issues, including relations with the Vatican.[22] Largely united during the 1870s and 1880s by the undisputed champion of Catholic parliamentary resistance to the Kulturkampf, Ludwig Windthorst, the party nonetheless split on such questions as Jewish rights and Bismarck's antisocialist law.[23] After the Kulturkampf's resolution in the 1880s and Windthorst's death in 1891 unraveled the party's fragile solidarity, tensions within the Zentrum—especially those between agrarian and urban representatives[24]—soon became so severe that one prominent party member questioned the party's ability to survive.[25]

Windthorst's leadership of the party during its formative years was crucial to the Zentrum's development in a number of ways, among them Windthorst's commitment of the Center Party to what has been labeled the realistic, realist, secular, or liberal tradition of political Catholicism.[26] Liberal Catholics such as Windthorst, while by no means favorably disposed toward secularism, Prussianism, capitalism, or any other form of materialism or modernism they associated with Protestant-dominated Germany, nevertheless acknowledged the social, economic, and political realities of contemporary society.[27] By choosing to accept the modern state structure, the social changes of industrialization, the value of the written constitution (especially as a tool for defending Catholic rights), and the potential merit of select aspects of political liberalism,[28] realist Catholics advocated a synthesis of traditional religious belief and seemingly modern political behavior.[29]

Most important for the future of Catholic organization, liberal Catholics supported a secularized vision of political Catholicism, including freedom from clerical control and the prospect of interconfessionalism. While Catholics on the local level exhibited enormous hostility to Protestants, German Catholics did not, in contrast to German Protestants, adopt a confessionally antagonistic national discourse. Catholics may well have imagined a Germany without Jews or Social Democrats, but they never excluded religious Protestants from their vision, and for its part the Center Party never codified enmity to Protestants.[30]

Liberal Catholics were by no means hegemonic within Catholic Germany, however, and the corporatist, integralist, reactionary, sectarian, ultramontane, or romantic tradition of Catholicism remained influential well into the twentieth century.[31] Often portrayed as fundamentally opposed, these two traditions in fact shared fundamental suspicions of non-Catholic historical developments, yet important differences remained. First codified in 1838 by Joseph Görres, among others, romantic Catholicism equated the spiritual integrity of Catholic dogma with that of German romanticism;[32] it consequently rejected rationalist thought and Protestant- and Prussian-led manifestations, including democracy, liberalism, and the organization of a powerful state.[33] In opposition to the modern social order, romantic Catholics developed a cult of the Abendland modeled on the medieval Reich as a natural, God-given hierarchy founded in a decentralized, Aquinian order, in which guilds and commercial and agrarian agencies directed economic policy and guaranteed societal harmony.[34] Romantic Catholics prioritized Catholic internationalism over German nationalism and argued for an exclusively Catholic party tied closely to the church.[35]

Ultramontane Catholicism was deeply rooted in Silesia, the Rhineland, Westphalia, and Bavaria, although the geographic differences in political Catholicism explain why Bavarian Catholic organization receives little mention here. A bastion of Catholic political activity, Bavaria harbored a different confessional Teilkultur and understanding of political Catholicism than did its provincial counterparts.[36] Bavaria's historic concern for states' rights and its overwhelmingly rural constituency lent all Bavarian politics a distinctive and dogmatically conservative character. With the founding of a separate Catholic party after World War I and the CSU after World War II, Bavarian political Catholicism assumed concrete forms beyond the scope of our consideration.

The contrast between Bavarian and Rhenish-Westphalian political Catholicism became especially pronounced as the Catholic working class of the Rhineland and the Ruhr expanded,[37] and the Catholic Rhineland served as the primary stage for battles between romantic and liberal Catholicism.[38] Indeed, while active throughout Baden and Württemberg, liberal Catholics found their real nucleus in Westphalia and especially in the Rhine Province, two of Germany's leading industrial centers.[39] Centuries of exposure to French intellectual currents and culture, the Napoleonic occupation, and Prussian state modernization after 1815 all influenced the political culture of German territory west of the Rhine.[40] While nineteenth-century Cologne, the "German Rome," represented the heart of Rhenish liberal Catholicism,[41] Westphalia was less affected by the Industrial and French Revolutions. In particular, Westphalian clergy and nobility retained greater sway than did their Rhenish counterparts, a difference that would influence Catholic politics through the Weimar Republic and the founding of the CDU.[42]

Westphalia nonetheless served as an incubator of liberal Catholicism, and the prominence of Rhineland-Westphalia runs as a leitmotif through the history of political Catholicism.[43] The significance of Rhenish-Westphalian liberal Catholicism was clearly evident in the late nineteenth-century bourgeoisification of the party's leadership and the subsequent rise of a predominantly Prussian Catholic workers' movement,[44] which denied Social Democracy the strength it enjoyed in other industrial regions.[45] Ideologically, the Center's Rhenish-dominated leadership categorically rejected romantic Catholicism and accepted, for all practical purposes, the economic and social order of modern capitalism.[46] In the Rhineland and at the behest of liberal Catholics, then, the first battles over interconfessionalism would be waged.

Inventing Interconfessionalism

Encouraged by Leo XIII's 1891 papal encyclical *Rerum Novarum* (On the Condition of Workers) and in response to the growing Catholic working class and spread of socialism,[47] liberal Catholics built on the initiatives of Adolf Kolping and the 1848 Katholikentag (Catholic Assembly) to develop a sizable network of labor organizations.[48] The recognition of workers as members of a class as well as of a confession marked a watershed in Catholic political history. First, it presaged one of the strongest tensions within the Center Party, the conflict between the party's labor wing and its more conservative majority and leadership.[49] Second, by presupposing common Catholic and Protestant labor concerns that called for a coordinated Christian response, it represented a major step on the path toward interconfessionalism.[50] Thus, without endorsing the ideologies, such as bourgeois liberalism, that underlay social and economic change, Liberal Catholics nonetheless contributed to the modernization of Catholic life.[51]

For advocates of interconfessionalism, the impetus toward political and trade union cooperation with Protestants was both strategically and ideologically motivated. Proponents saw in Christian cooperation the only apparent means of combating socialism's lure for Catholic and Protestant workers.[52] Dogmatically, antisocialism had deep theological roots in Catholic teachings: Not only did Marxism—like liberalism—envision a world in which specifically Christian values played no part, but Marxism's failure to recognize humanity's God-given freedoms subordinated the individual to the state and violated Christian property rights. At the same time, Marx's utopia of egalitarianism denied the value Catholics invested in the suffering of inequality.[53]

Based in the Rhenish-Westphalian industrial areas and tradition of realist Catholicism, the Volksverein für das katholische Deutschland, an educational workers' organization founded in 1890, and the Christian Trade Unions, founded in 1901 under Adam Stegerwald, represented Catholics' initial steps toward interconfessionalism.[54] Testifying to the embeddedness of the Center Party in the Catholic Teilkultur, these developments were soon followed by the Zentrum's first major initiative. In his famous 1906 article, "We Must Come out of the Tower! [Wir müssen aus dem Turm heraus!]," Cologne journalist and Center Party leader Julius Bachem drew directly on the example of the Christian Trade Unions to argue for Catholic support of Protestant candidates sympathetic to Catholic religious principles. By invoking the Christian Trade Unions as a model, Bachem's cri de coeur reflected and prefigured the Catholicity of interconfessional proposals: While the Christian Trade Unions organized independently from the clergy, adhered to a strictly interconfessional program, and eschewed the general meetings of Catholic organizations, their origins, membership, and ideological groundings remained overwhelmingly Catholic.[55]

At the same time, Bachem made clear that Catholics had no interest in fully fledged interconfessional cooperation. By restricting his offer to religious Protestants with whom Catholics shared certain precepts—he cited in particular members of the Christian Social Party (Christlich-Soziale Partei [CSP]) and two devout and prominent Lutherans affiliated with the Zentrum[56]—Bachem unmistakably limited his cross-confessional appeal. In this way, too, Bachem's call would predesign interconfessional politics. By defining their potential future colleagues in religious—not political or class—terms, Catholics contradicted their stated goal of appealing to Protestant laborers. In the juxtaposition of Christian and labor politics, Christian values would clearly be determinate.

Spotlighted by Bachem's petition, practicing Protestants had in fact long demonstrated ideological commonalities with Catholics. While the Pietists and their successors opposed secularism, modernism, liberalism, and socialism as passionately as members of the Catholic Teilkultur, bourgeois conservatives had called since the 1870s for an antiliberal, anti-Jewish Christian state.[57] Well into the twentieth century, moreover, many of these religiously devout Protestants rejected capitalism and technology as materialistic while endorsing an organic, family-centered corporative societal order.[58] Such Protestants had even, on occasion, regarded Catholics as natural allies in the ongoing battle against secularism.[59] Baden Catholics and Pietist Protestants forged political alliances in the 1860s,[60] for example, and Protestant conservatives had refused to support several of the Kulturkampf measures.[61]

By the twentieth century, however, the pious represented a distinct minority within Protestant Germany.[62] Throughout the nineteenth century, German Protestants had demonstrated diminishing loyalty to institutional churches and dogmas, resulting in declining rates of participation in church rituals.[63] Inherent in Bachem's emphasis on religious Protestants was the widespread assumption that most Protestants had in fact secularized.[64] Seeking to distinguish between religious Protestants and those who had strayed from the church, Catholics favored devout Protestants who were also politically conservative.[65]

Catholic Clergy and Catholic Politics

Such interconfessional initiatives, tentative and contradictory though they were, marked a major departure in Catholic politics, and the resulting debates about working-class organizations and interconfessionalism—first concerning the trade unions (the Gewerkschaftsstreit) and then the Center Party (the Zentrumsstreit)—demonstrated the tensions inherent in political Catholicism's adjustment to new social and economic conditions.[66] From their debut, the liberal-romantic battles highlighted the continued prominence of clergy both in promoting and combating interconfessionalism. While the Volksverein, despite its ostensible interconfessionalism, was represented primarily by clergymen and Center Party members,[67] other priests recognized that partnering with Protestants threatened ecclesiastic control over a party once dubbed "an association of pastors."[68] Indeed, the attenuation of clerical influence was already evident in the Center Party's distancing from church-controlled networks with the expressed purpose of weaning the party from priests.[69]

The clergy nevertheless retained a determinative influence on Center Party affairs, and even the geographic designations for the warring factions in the Gewerkschaftsstreit and the Zentrumsstreit—the Cologne line versus the Berlin line—reflected priestly involvement.[70] While the Cologne line articulated liberal Catholicism, the Berlin line clergy's call for the Zentrum to remember its religious character implied close clerical control of the party and a rejection of interconfessionalism, hallmarks of romantic Catholicism.[71] That the Vatican associated the Bachem wing of the Center Party with reform Catholicism and consequently supported interconfessionalism's integralist opponents reminds us that interconfessionalism, while very much a German affair, was nonetheless part of the larger confrontation between Catholic modernity and tradition.[72]

Political Catholicism in the Weimar Republic

When the Zentrumsstreit ended in 1914 with the death of a leading Berlin line clergyman, it left the Center Party considerably divided on the eve of World War I.[73] Interconfessionalism soon became buried by the exigencies of uniting the party during war, revolution, and the founding of a new government.[74] In many ways, the Center Party well captured all the complexities and contradictions of the Weimar era. On one hand, the Catholic party represented a bastion of support for the republic. Between 1919 and 1932, the Center provided the chancellor more often and for a longer period of time than did any other party.[75] On the other hand, the Center's ambivalent support for the republic, its ideological and class divides, and its confessional character all testified to serious weaknesses that would contribute to the republic's collapse.

Although of declining appeal, confession still constituted sufficient basis for an exclusively Catholic party.[76] The Center Party's electoral strength remained regionally as well as religiously determined, with centers in Württemberg and Hesse and its strongest representation in the Prussian provinces of the Rhineland, Westphalia, and Lower Silesia.[77] The social composition of the Center's support nonetheless altered during the Weimar Republic in several notable ways. After securing the franchise in the fall of 1918, German women disappointed socialist advocates of female suffrage by voting disproportionately for Weimar's religious parties; the Center would soon be particularly beholden to female voters, who by the end of the republic constituted 60 percent of its electoral support, the highest percentage of female votes of any Weimar party.[78]

Throughout the Weimar Republic, the party also reflected the shifts in Germany's industrializing Catholic population—increasingly lower middle class and, by 1933, fully half working class.[79] Beginning in the last decade of the Kaiserreich, the SPD succeeded in attracting Catholic workers, and during the Weimar Republic, the Center Party would lose yet more laborers to the Marxist parties, especially to the Communist Party of Germany (Kommunistische Partei Deutschlands [KPD]).[80] Most Catholic workers remained loyal to the Center Party, however, and with support from priests such as Oswald von Nell-Bruening, Gustav Gundlach, and Theodor Brauer, workers' committees in the Center Party would supply some of Catholic politics' most important leaders, including Adam Stegerwald, Heinrich Brüning, and Joseph Joos.[81]

Tensions among the Zentrum's agrarian-based, conservative wing, bourgeoisie, and workers remained potent, however.[82] One of the most threatening divisions within the party—Bavarians' discontent with the Rhineland's domination of the Zentrum—led to the 1920 founding of the Bavarian People's Party (Bayerische Volkspartei [BVP]), the first schism in German Catholic politics. The seriousness of this split was made clear in the 1925 presidential election, when the BVP supported Paul von Hindenburg over Center Party candidate Wilhelm Marx, making Hindenburg's victory possible.[83]

The most profound division within the Center Party after the war, however, pegged supporters of the republic against their conservative if not authoritarian opponents.[84] The Zentrum went to great lengths in the early years of Weimar to bridge the differences between "republicans of the heart" and avowed monarchists such as Heinrich Brüning.[85] Above all else, governing with the SPD tested the Center's commitment to republicanism.[86] The Prussian coalition proved the benefits of a tactical alliance with the SPD, as the Prussian Center's cooperation with the SPD until July 1932 contributed significantly to the "unlikely rock" of Prussian democracy.[87] Despite the fact that the Center shared with the SPD constituent political positions, including respect for the constitution, democracy, and a conciliatory foreign policy,[88] the party's right wing argued that a socialist alliance would compel conservative Catholics and tradesmen to join the DNVP.[89]

Among the conservative Catholics who made good on this threat by following Martin Spahn to the Catholic Committee of the DNVP were clergymen;[90] for the first time in Center Party history, a number of priests—protesting the party's support for democracy, the republic, and political cooperation with the SPD—abandoned the Zentrum tower.[91] Grounded in their conviction that state power could be derived solely from God, conservative priests rejected the republic's constitutional invocation of "power from the people"; they were further dismayed by the republic's failure to produce a concordat or a confessional school law.[92] One of the most dramatic demonstrations of clerical hostility to the republic took place at the 1922 Katholikentag, where the conflict between monarchists and republicans came to a head in the clash between the Bavarian Cardinal Faulhaber and the president of the Prussian Staatsrat and of the Katholikentag, Konrad Adenauer.[93] Among other things, Faulhaber's response to Adenauer's plea to abandon the Catholic ghetto testified to the continuing rejection by romantic Catholics of interconfessionalism.[94]

Post–World War I Interconfessional Initiatives

Especially in the wake of the Great War, certain members of the party's leadership attempted to pressure the Zentrum to act on Julius Bachem's call to dismantle the Catholic tower. The most noteworthy of these attempts—that by Heinrich Brauns following the 1918 revolution and Adam Stegerwald's 1920 speech at the Tenth Congress of the Christian Trade Unions in Essen—revealed both the potential and limits of politics grounded in religious exclusivity. From the republic's earliest days, Catholics believed they had good reason to safeguard the Center's confessional character. In November 1918, Adolph Hoffmann, an Independent Social Democratic Party of Germany (Unäbhängige Sozialdemokratische Partei Deutschlands [USPD]) member and the new Prussian minister of education and cultural affairs, proclaimed the separation of church and state, including an end to confessional schools, a ban on religious instruction, and the threat to deny churches state financial support.[95] In the wake of the so-called Hoffmann Commandments, Catholics rallied in ways reminiscent of the Kulturkampf.[96] Indeed, the clergy's successful direction of the campaigns—first against Hoffmann and the Protestant Prussian government and then for the Center Party in the January 1919 elections—reinforced the Zentrum's reliance on politically active priests and consequently the party's confessionalism.[97]

In fact, members of the priesthood had already demonstrated their influence by rebuffing fellow clergy member and Volksverein leader Heinrich Brauns's initiative toward confessional integration. Following the revolution, Brauns argued that the Center Party should change its name to attract Protestant bourgeois antisocialists.[98] Faced with determined clergy opposition and the prospect of losing new female and traditionally reliable farmers' votes,[99] Center politicians agreed only to add the appellation "Christian People's Party."[100] After the Center's election results appeared to vindicate the rejection of a new course—together, the Zentrum and BVP received almost 20 percent of the total vote, representing close to 63 percent of the Catholic electorate—the churchmen's importance to the election campaign appeared confirmed.[101]

Less than two years later, opposition on the part of clerical and conservative party members rendered Stegerwald's appeal for interconfessional organization equally ineffectual. Stegerwald renewed Bachem's 1906 petition with a plea for interconfessionalism cowritten by Brauns and Heinrich Brüning.[102] Directed not only at the Center Party but also to the German People's Party (Deutsche Volkspartei [DVP]) and the DNVP's Christian nationalist workers and civil servants, Stegerwald's speech underscored the link between the trade unions and interconfessionalism. His address proposed no concrete means to realize the ideal of interconfessional political cooperation, however, and did little more than occasion a new round of heated discussion.[103]

While the debate over interconfessionalism highlighted the clergy's continued importance to Catholic politics, the position of priests in the party during the Weimar years remained paradoxical. On the one hand, clergymen continued to play a crucial role in reconciling the Center Party's various factions, especially those divided on the question of accepting the republic.[104] On the other hand, the Zentrum sought consistently to reduce its reliance on clerics;[105] it ceased, for example, using Katholikentage as substitute party congresses.[106] Although the Weimar Zentrum depended less openly on clergy in the day-to-day administration of party affairs, the Center's adherence to traditional Catholic cultural policies continued to grant the clergy significant authority over Center Party policy.[107] It is not surprising in that regard that the only federal school law the Center Party would accept satisfied church demands for confessional schools.[108]

Cultural Policy and Coalition Politics

As a traditional priestly priority and issue of uncontested Center Party consensus, cultural policies had always played an important role in cementing the party's commonalities; for most Center members, *Kulturpolitik* embodied best what they understood under Christian politics.[109] After the republic's constitution secured other Catholic demands, including an end to governmental influence over church appointments and state financial support for the church, the defense of confessional schools assumed especial importance for many Catholics;[110] indeed, by 1928, confessional schools—enshrined by the 1929 papal encyclical *Divini illius Magistri* (On the Christian Education of Youth)— represented the sole issue on which all Center Party factions could agree.[111] While the Organization of Catholic Germans for Defense and Promotion of Christian Schools and Education (Organisation der Katholiken Deutschlands zur Verteidigung und Förderung der christlichen Schule und Erziehung), under the direction of Canon Wilhelm Böhler, claimed complete independence from the Center Party, the common members among the organization, BVP, and Zentrum belied that profession.[112]

Although identified most closely with the Catholic Church and Center Party,[113] the defense of confessional schools also attracted religious Protestants opposed to secularism and materialism. Certain policies of social conservatism had consistently enjoyed support among practicing Protestants and Catholics;[114] cultural commonalities between the Center and the conservative Protestant parties were by no means limited to the school issue.[115] Indeed, reflecting their grounding in religious doctrine, both the Center Party and Protestant parties on the right understood women as agents of Christian morality with distinctly female and maternal responsibilities. Center Party and DNVP propaganda directed at women stressed God, family, and culture, including the parties' commitment to confessional schools, traditional marriage (through opposition to divorce reforms or the rights of children born outside marriage), and the criminalization of abortion.[116] Like the Catholic Center Party, the DNVP and the DVP also won an above average share of female support.[117]

In a foreshadowing of the post–1945 consensus that would emerge within the CDU, the Center Party joined conservative, religious Protestant parties such as the DNVP—and less consistently the DVP—to resist SPD attempts to codify the "formalistic equalization" of men and women.[118] In addition to their shared resistance to liberalizing divorce and revising the 1900 Civil Code's guarantee of patriarchal privilege,[119] the Center Party and DNVP agreed on specific issues of birth control and abortion.[120] Some of this commonality was evident in Protestant and Catholic denunciations of the 1938 National Socialist legislation loosening divorce requirements; Christians also criticized what they perceived as the Nazis' encouragement of pornography and premarital sex.[121]

Throughout the Weimar years, the Center remained divided between those open to a coalition with the DNVP and those who opposed it on principle. Although the Center entered the Weimar Republic allied with the SPD in Prussia, Reich party leaders emphasized that this by no means signaled an unconditional commitment to left-of-center coalitions; many members of the Center Party regarded alliance with the SPD as a tactical measure necessary only until the DNVP agreed to a coalition.[122] In the later years of the Weimar Republic, when faced with the quandary of establishing agreements to the left or the right, the Center repeatedly allowed cultural issues to dictate its final decision. Coalition with the right did not bring about what the Center had anticipated, however, as became dramatically clear with the failure of the 1927 school bill. Indeed, Zentrum leaders were continually disappointed that the DNVP failed to advocate for Protestant interests as energetically as did the Zentrum for Catholic concerns, and the Prussian Center Party especially resented the DNVP's 1929 refusal to support the Prussian concordat.[123]

Political Catholicism Reaffirmed: The 1928 Center Party Chairship

The Center Party's continued reliance on specifically Catholic issues and the importance of clergy members to bridging internal party differences were arguably demonstrated most dramatically by the December 1928 battle over the party's chairship between the Center's bourgeoisie and its workers. Almost all Christian Trade Unionists agreed with the fundaments of Center Party economic policy—the natural law right to property and essentially free competition with social welfare policies, including support for codetermination.[124] While attempts to reconcile Catholicism and socialism had been especially widespread in the wake of World War I,[125] most Christian socialists during the Weimar years were theoreticians or academics,[126] and only in Frankfurt did a critical mass of Center Party members support Christian socialism, including Walter Dirks and others associated with the *Rhein-Mainische Volkszeitung* who would be active in the early CDU.[127] Instead, Center Party workers largely embraced Jesuit teachings closely associated with the Cologne line, in particular the doctrine of solidarism codified by Cologne scholar Heinrich Pesch, which accepted a liberal and individualistic societal order with a commitment to social justice.[128] It was less a theoretical objection, then, that inspired Christian Trade Unionists' unrest than the belief that the party never truly had their interests at heart.

The 1927 confrontation between the party's leaders and its labor representatives, under the leadership of Stegerwald, over the issue of civil servant pay raises produced a near crisis.[129] One year later, when Stegerwald and Joseph Joos vied for the party leadership, they were roundly rejected by the party's more conservative majority, which backed clergyman Ludwig Kaas. At a point when internal divisions prevented even the semblance of a unified policy, the Zentrum resorted to its traditional conflict-resolution mechanism and chose a clerical figure ostensibly hostage to no specific socioeconomic faction. By naming a priest head of the party for the first time, the Center Party reinforced the tower of German Catholic politics and its distance from interconfessionalism.[130]

Political Catholicism and National Socialism

Kaas's election signaled not only the reassertion of clerical authority over Catholic politics but also the Center Party's shift to the right.[131] Under Kaas and Brüning, who would become chancellor in 1930, the Zentrum and the Weimar Republic found themselves under the rule of men who had never accepted republican democracy.[132] The Center Party also found itself electorally reliant on female, older, and conservative voters; together with the BVP, it polled at best half of German Catholics.[133] After the National Socialist breakthrough in the September 1930 elections, Center Party leaders debated forming a coalition with the Brown Shirts in an attempt to control them. These calculations were not without ideological considerations; both Brüning and his even more authoritarian successor, Franz von Papen (who left the Center Party after becoming chancellor in June 1932), supported cooperation with the National Socialist German Workers' Party (Nationalsozialistische Deutsche Arbeiterpartei [NSDAP]) based on the two parties' presumed rejection of communism, liberalism, and "excessive" parliamentary democracy. That the Center did not participate in the negotiations for the January 30, 1933 coalition was no reflection of its aversion to cooperation with the Nazis but the result of its intentional exclusion.[134]

Indeed, the Center Party offered no clear alternative to antidemocratic forces during the Weimar Republic's waning years.[135] In the terror-influenced March 5, 1933 elections, the Center received just over 11 percent of the vote, and the BVP fell below 3 percent for the first time, while the Nazis enjoyed an increase of support in Catholic areas, especially among farmers and the commercial middle class.[136] By voting for the Enabling Law later that month, the Center Party forever associated political Catholicism with abetting the Nazis' legal seizure of power; although heatedly debated within the party's ranks[137] and initially opposed strongly by the Center's labor wing, the Zentrum's decision and its widely perceived link to the Vatican's successful concordat negotiations did little to enhance the party's image as a defender of democracy.[138]

While the Center Party appeared generally accommodating to the new head of state, some Catholics went even farther; in April 1933, von Papen founded Cross and Eagle, a Catholic organization dedicated to an authoritarian, corporative order and romantic vision of a German Reich.[139] In May 1933, in a last-ditch effort to salvage a party torn by the Enabling Law debate and Kaas's departure to Rome to help negotiate a concordat, party leaders named Brüning, fashioned as "Our Führer" in the 1932 Reichstag elections, the Zentrum's new chair.[140] Brüning's term was short-lived: In early July 1933, the Center Party dissolved itself; later that month, Hitler signed the concordat.

Protestant Politics in the Weimar Republic

The Center Party's role in the Weimar Republic's downfall was decisive in Catholic debates about the post–Nazi path of political Catholicism, resulting in the decision to abandon the Zentrum tower for interconfessional cooperation.

Although the Center Party had joined in coalitions with the SPD, its heart, as demonstrated by Kulturpolitik considerations, lay with conservative, religious Protestants. Those commonalities could not erase a fundamental difference between political Catholicism and Protestant politics, however. While political Catholicism generally supported the Weimar Republic until its demise, non-Marxist Protestant parties were more clearly antidemocratic.

For religious Protestants, the end of World War I seemed to herald a new era of Catholic domination. As the Catholic nations of France, Belgium, and Italy emerged victorious, other European Catholics—Poles, Lithuanians, and the Catholic Slavs of the former Habsburg monarchy—appeared to benefit from the postwar settlement.[141] The Catholic Center Party's new prominence underscored Protestants' loss of the privileges they had enjoyed since 1871,[142] while the republic's equal recognition of the Catholic Church inspired fears of Catholic proselytizing.[143] Many Catholics themselves believed that the collapse of the Protestant Prussian empire provided a first real opportunity to achieve Catholic ideological hegemony.[144]

Fear concerning diminished Protestant influence in the new republic reinforced Protestant hostility to the new state form. Religious Protestants for the most part remained monarchists who subsumed loyalty to the Kaiser and the Hohenzollern dynasty into fealty to the nation.[145] In this, Protestants were influenced by nationalist and conservative church leaders, who did much to conflate the powerful concepts of Kaiser, Reich, nation, and Protestantism.[146] Symbolically, Lutheran ministers designed their own church flag rather than display the republic's black, red, and gold colors.[147]

Politically, most religious Protestants rejected the German Democratic Party (Deutsche Demokratische Partei [DDP]) and DVP for their anticlericalism while abhorring the KPD and SPD for their atheism and ideology of class conflict. Not surprisingly, church leaders and many devout Protestants supported the DNVP, one of the most antagonistic parties to the early republic. Although its policies were rarely explicitly Protestant in nature, the DNVP invoked Christian rhetoric, supported church causes, and produced school legislation with which most Protestant Church leaders were satisfied.[148] The church therefore believed it enjoyed a reliable ally in the DNVP, at least until Alfred Hugenberg became chair in October 1928 and steered the party in an increasingly authoritarian direction that nevertheless failed to prevent the DNVP's loss of one-third of its voters to the NSDAP between 1928 and 1930.[149]

Of the numerous consequences of Hugenberg's leadership of the DNVP, the one of perhaps greatest consequence for Christian Democracy was the founding of the CSVD. Organized in 1929 specifically in opposition to Hugenberg's politics, the CSVD filled with former DNVP members,[150] many of whom had supported the CSP before it dissolved in 1918.[151] The only explicitly Protestant party in the Weimar Republic, the CSVD, based in Württemberg, Nassau, and the Siegerland, was colored by its inheritance from the Pietist movement; its creed of political Protestantism held little appeal for adherents to Luther's doctrine of two kingdoms.[152] Although the CSVD never won more than 3 percent of the vote in a Reichstag election, its articulation of political Protestantism was significant, and its membership would wield disproportionate influence on the Christian Democratic movement.[153]

In sharp contrast to the DNVP, the CSVD recognized the Weimar Republic's legitimacy and supported Chancellor Brüning and the Christian Trade Unions. Like the Center Party, it embraced the state's role in addressing social problems as well as perceived threats to German morality (so-called *Schmutz und Schund*). Primarily lower middle- and middle-class, CSVD members shared with Catholics a hostility to those forces seen as destabilizing Germany—materialism, atheism, liberalism, and Marxism.[154] It was no surprise, then, that the CSVD and the Center Party publicly embraced cooperation.[155] While some members, led by Paul Bausch, distanced themselves from National Socialism, the CSVD as a party struggled to draw a clear line between itself and the Nazis and in March 1933 voted without reservation for the Enabling Law. As the Protestant tradition of state loyalty overcame any inclination to resistance, chair Wilhelm Simpfendörfer (1929–32) declared that every Protestant was obligated to support the new government. After the CSVD's forced dissolution in June 1933, the party largely divided between those who joined the Confessing Church and those who became parliamentary independents hosted by the NSDAP (*Hospitanten*).[156]

While CSVD members showed sympathy for Brüning and the Christian Trade Unions, liberal politicians also signaled an opening to Catholic politics during the late Weimar years.[157] In the July 1932 Reichstag elections, some Protestant and Jewish voters abandoned the DDP for the Center Party,[158] while isolated members of the DDP declared the Center the only eligible party for democratic voters.[159] The general picture of liberals toward the end of Weimar, however, reflected rightward drift amid dissolution. The DDP's reconstitution in 1930 as the German State Party (Deutsche Staatspartei [DStP]) failed to stem its electoral decline, while the DVP, which had never regarded parliamentary principles as more than tactical, became increasingly authoritarian and politically impotent following Gustav Stresemann's death in 1929. Ultimately, one quarter of those who had voted for the DVP or DDP between 1928 and 1930 supported the NSDAP.[160]

This limited phenomenon of Protestants attracted to the Center Party and the CSVD on the eve of the republic's collapse presaged what would be a larger movement of Protestants toward interconfessional politics after 1945. Like most practicing Protestants, however, many of these forerunners welcomed the Nazi takeover, and in general, a clear correlation existed between support for Nazism and religious Protestantism.[161] Drawing on a long-standing Protestant understanding of a national church and the particular conflation of Protestantism and German nationalism, the NSDAP infused National Socialism with reverence for Jesus and Martin Luther to become the first German party to attract a plurality of Protestant support.[162]

Protestant Church leaders certainly sympathized with the National Socialists, who appealed to the church's nationalism as well as to its hostility to Jews and liberals; a striking one-third of Protestant ministers joined the NSDAP or other Nazi organizations.[163] The Nazis, for their part, invested considerable energy in shoring up Protestant institutions to create a bulwark against German Catholicism; the most prominent of these institutions was the German Christian movement (Glaubensbewegung Deutsche Christen).[164] With more than half a million members and control of Germany's regional bishoprics, the German Christians had, by September 1933, accepted the Führer principle and Hitler's candidate, Ludwig Müller, as *Reichsbischof* of the German Protestant Church (Deutsche Evangelische Kirche [DEK]).[165]

Martin Niemöller and Karl Barth began to organize in response to the motion by the General Synod of the Old Prussian Union in September 1933 to adopt the Aryan Paragraph.[166] Led by Protestants in the Rhineland and Westphalia, dissidents would issue the May 1934 Barmen Declaration rejecting Nazi teachings and would soon thereafter found the Confessing Church. The Confessing Church would itself split in short order between an accommodationist wing, led by Bishop Marahrens, and the more anti-Nazi Dahlemites, led by Karl Barth, a division that would continue into the postwar era with consequences for the CDU.[167] For all that it symbolized Protestant resistance to National Socialism, the Confessing Church failed to pose a fundamental threat to the Nazi regime or to protest Jewish persecution. Unlike the Catholic Church, which mobilized its faithful to oppose Nazi ordinances on crucifixes in schools, for example, the Confessing Church leadership was never able to expand its influence beyond the minority clergy.[168]

Confessing Church leaders would play prominent roles in post–World War II Germany, including in politics and economics. Of significance for the future of Christian Democracy was the 1942 gathering of Confessing Church members in Freiburg, where Carl Goerdeler, Franz Böhm, Helmut Thielicke, and Otto Dibelius met to debate Protestant theology and democracy. Their discussions concerning the economic organization of a post–Nazi state led them to embrace a Christian-influenced free market with a strong social system, a program similar to that developed during the war by Alfred Müller-Armack and Ludwig Erhard in their own Freiburg meetings.[169] The Freiburg-based Erwin von Beckerath Study Group, which included Böhm, Erhard, Walter Eucken, and Adolf Lampe, had ties to both the Goerdeler and the Kreisau resistance circles as well as to the Confessing Church; indeed, Goerdeler appeared to have approved of at least elements of Erhard's economic program, which he reviewed shortly before July 20, 1944.[170] At the same time, Wilhelm Röpke and Alexander Rüstow published and spoke extensively in exile of a "third way" between laissez-faire capitalism and Marxism.[171] Though clearly Protestant in origin, these economic deliberations would ultimately be embraced by Catholic politicians and come, as the social market economy, to symbolize West German Christian Democracy. First, however, former members of the Center Party would need to experience twelve years of brutal dictatorship to persuade them that the hour of interconfessional politics had come.

Christian Opposition to National Socialism

The question of the Center Party and more broadly the Catholic relationship to National Socialism is complex and controversial.[172] Proportionately, devout Catholics voted for the Nazis before 1933 to a lesser degree than did Protestants,[173] although other aspects of the Nazis' origins, rise, and practice suggest indispensable Catholic participation.[174] The bishops' March 28, 1933, revocation of their September 1930 prohibition against Nazi Party membership and exhortation to Catholics to support the state powers—as well as the absence of church protest against Jewish persecution—suggest a collaborative relationship between organized Catholicism and National Socialism.[175]

Ideologically, however, Catholicism offered many Catholic Germans a defense shield against Nazi ideological coordination.[176] Whether this constituted cultural resistance, passive resistance, or inner emigration—and whether these terms even warrant the designation of resistance—is open to debate; significantly for postwar political Catholicism, Catholic consciousness indisputably survived National Socialist rule.[177] Throughout the Nazi era, the Catholic cultural networks imbedded in the Catholic Teilkultur not only remained unbroken but in some cases reacted to oppression by binding more tightly together, particularly as Catholics rallied around their priests.[178] In the second half of the Third Reich, the Nazis regarded devout Catholics as their greatest internal threat; indeed, fully half of the priests in Germany (including Danzig and the Sudetenland but excluding Austria) came into contact with Hitler's terror.[179] At the same time, reflecting the paradoxical role of the Catholic Church in the Third Reich, not one German bishop (either Protestant or Catholic) was arrested during the Nazi years for political reasons.[180]

Representing an important chapter in the history of political Catholicism, limited pockets existed of active Catholic opposition to the Nazi regime. Obviously, one cannot consider a Center Party resistance network—either in Germany or in exile—on the scale of the SPD or KPD, nor can one speak of a Catholic resistance against Hitler per se: After 1933, all Catholic political activity directly violated the Vatican-sanctioned concordat. Nevertheless, members of the Center Party tied primarily to the Christian Trade Unions formed close-knit anti-Nazi circles that would serve as important mediating stages for the postwar transformation of political Catholicism. That these "Catholics in resistance"[181] later became undisputed banner carriers for the CDU was not surprising. They were, above all else, the only former Zentrum members to have maintained connections throughout the Nazi years; furthermore, members of the Center Party's labor wing had traditionally provided the organizational initiatives toward interconfessional cooperation.[182]

Catholic oppositional activities highlighted other characteristics of Catholic political organization as well. Underground groupings were predominantly based in the Rhineland, reflecting that area's historic leadership of political Catholicism and foreshadowing its postwar significance. At the same time, individual clergymen—despite the concordat's explicit ban on clerical political involvement and contrary to church hierarchy wishes—participated in discussions on the nature of political Catholicism and its future. Priests' influence in these gatherings testified to their continued stature in the Catholic milieu and positioned them to help organize Christian Democracy following Nazism's demise.

The oppositional networks in question represented a complicated intersection of men and women from almost every conceivable ideological and political camp in Germany. By July 20, 1944, contacts had been made between such unlikely political partners as communists, Christian Trade Unionists, monarchists, and the old Junker elite. Though most of these relationships would fall victim to Nazi persecution or postwar political pressures, the bridging of the fundamental confessional divide remained a powerful experience for some future Christian Democrats. In this way, and again as forums for political debate, resistance networks came to play a crucial role in the CDU's founding history.

Of the different ex-Zentrum and Christian Trade Union members involved in conspiratorial activity, Jakob Kaiser, former state secretary of the Christian Trade Unions in the Rhineland and Westphalian Reichstag Center Party deputy, was by far the most prominent. Convinced that a stronger union movement would command more respect from the Nazis, Kaiser became in April 1933 the driving force in the Christian Trade Unions for a unified trade union. As the concordat negotiations came to an end and the Christian Trade Unions were dissolved, their delegates were expelled from the German Labor Front but not arrested, leaving them free to organize illegally.[183]

While the standing of former Centrists and Christian Trade Unionists in Goerdeler's proposed cabinet testified to Catholic links with Goerdeler,[184] former Centrists' and Christian Trade Unionists' contacts included other prominent Weimar politicians as well. In late 1933, a Düsseldorf circle of Protestants and Catholics developed around Franz Etzel, Paul Franken, Maximilian Freiherr von Gumppenberg, and Karl Arnold, former secretary of the Christian Trade Unions. In 1935, longtime Düsseldorf mayor, DNVP member, and Protestant Robert Lehr joined the group; after 1940, Catholics and Protestants gathered at Lehr's house to continue their oppositional discussions.[185] At the other end of Germany, the Kreisau circle in Silesia brought together Protestants and Catholics, Jesuit priests, trade unionists, and large landholders, including Christian socialists and Christian conservatives, to organize against Hitler.[186]

Within the Catholic Teilkultur, former Christian Trade Unionists maintained close contact with erstwhile members of the Catholic Workers' Movement (Katholische Arbeiterbewegung [KAB]) through meetings at the Ketteler House in Cologne.[187] Participants included clerics active in Catholic politics before 1933, including Otto Müller, who would die following his September 1944 arrest, and those who would direct political Catholicism in occupied Germany, among them Dominicans Laurentius Siemer and Eberhard Welty of the Walberberg monastery.[188] The KAB was also connected to the German Kolping Family (Deutsche Kolpingsfamilie [DKF], previously the Katholischen Gesellenverein) and the illegal Catholic student organization Unitas.[189] Although overwhelmingly Catholic, this broader Cologne circle of clerics, academics, and former members of the Christian Trade Unionists, Center Party, and KAB included several Protestants—conservatives and Social Democrats.[190]

In their deliberations concerning the fate of political Catholicism, these Nazi opponents agreed that the German party system had disintegrated as the result of a surfeit of minor parties. Significantly and in sharp contrast to resisters in the KPD and SPD, members of neither the Center Party nor the Christian Trade Unions maintained a clear commitment to refounding their pre-1933 organizations.[191] At the end of 1943, the KAB sponsored a conference at which Kaiser envisioned a "party for all working people" to succeed the Center Party, an idea that attracted, among others, Walter Dirks, Adam Stegerwald, Wilhelm Elfes, Karl Spiecker, and Joseph Wirth.[192] What sort of party this implied was not altogether clear: Discussions centered on a Christian party modeled on Britain's Labour Party or an interconfessional union designed to fulfill Stegerwald's 1920 Essen program.[193] What remained beyond debate was that confessional politics as they had hitherto existed would have no place in a post–Nazi Germany.[194] Less than two years later, Catholic politicians would begin translating these deliberations into action.

CHAPTER 2

Politics in Defeat: The Organizational Beginnings of Christian Democracy

In 1945, former members of the Center Party intent on founding a Christian Democratic party confronted a society seemingly on the verge of total collapse. Whether the war's aftermath would induce interconfessional politics or democracy in general was anything but certain. For the vast majority of Germans, party politics were as abstract as daily needs were pressing. Shortages of food, water, electricity, housing, medical care, and heat were profound, and desperate want led to desperate measures, some—such as the theft of coal—with clerical approval.[1] Widespread population transfers further strained the country's battered infrastructure. That the Soviet zone initially absorbed the most evacuees and refugees exacerbated the postwar migration crisis, as the refugee tide would ultimately sweep westward.[2] Although more than four million Germans died during the war, the population of the future Federal Republic of Germany increased from some forty-four million in 1946 to almost fifty million four years later.[3]

Germany's Religious Topography

These demographic upheavals would necessarily have long-lasting effects, among them the creation of the first confessionally balanced German state. Politically, the approximate balance of Protestants and Catholics in the three western occupation zones helped lay the groundwork for the dissolution of Germany's intra-Christian barrier and the political success of Christian Democracy. Within that future state, moreover, such large-scale population transfers redrew Germany's confessional map, reconfiguring mid-seventeenth-century patterns that had largely persisted.[4] As sizable numbers of Protestants and even more Catholics moved into areas populated by their Christian counterparts, the newcomers inadvertently destroyed the "closed village" topography of much of the German countryside.[5]

This phenomenon hardly produced a fully confessionally integrated West Germany. Many traditional strongholds of Center Party support, including the administrative districts of Trier, Cologne, and Münster, remained more than two-thirds Catholic, while predominantly Protestant areas in northern Germany such as Schleswig-Holstein, Hamburg, Berlin, and Lower Saxony (with the exclusion of the administrative district of Osnabrück) were left more than two-thirds Protestant.[6] Nonetheless, the effects of this forced immigration were dramatic. While in 1939, fifty-seven German districts had been more than 95 percent Catholic, in 1946, there was only one (in the Upper Palatinate); likewise, while thirteen districts before World War II had been more than 85 percent Protestant, no such district existed after 1946. In Bavaria alone, only 9 of the prewar 1,424 purely Catholic municipalities remained monoconfessional, while none of the 140 previously Protestant-only municipalities was intact.[7] In addition, in large areas of future West Germany, including Franconia, the Palatinate, Hesse, and North Rhine-Westphalia, neither Protestants nor Catholics commanded a two-thirds majority.[8]

Throughout Germany, refugees stood out for their dialects, value systems, and daily practices, including cooking and worship.[9] Expellees were stereotyped as uneducated, inflexible, and enthusiastic Nazis.[10] While considerable tension existed within religious communities,[11] greater hostility emerged along the Protestant-Catholic divide.[12] Indeed, sudden and forced integration of the two confessional groups by no means engendered confessional harmony.[13] In some cases, native Protestants interpreted Catholic religious services as outwardly hostile political acts;[14] in others, the replacement of Protestant Nazi officeholders by less blemished Catholics antagonized confessional relations.[15] In this regard, the concerns Konrad Adenauer shared with Catholic chaplain Johannes Weber regarding "eastern refugees" planting "the Prussian spirit" in Rhenish youth were typical.[16] Over the next years, a significant number of expellees would relocate to regions where their own religion dominated.[17]

Although this unforeseen desegregation hardly eased confessional tensions, the war-related population transfers did alter structurally the relationship between Protestants and Catholics, with profound implications for political and religious life in the Federal Republic.[18] By mixing populations that had previously known little of each other, war refugees set in motion processes that would contribute significantly to the dissolution of old milieus and the success of interconfessional politics.[19] Within the Catholic Teilkultur, resistance to expellees' differing practices hindered their integration into church communities, promoting secularization; at the same time, the newcomers' ways undermined the authority of indigenous traditions.[20] None of these effects was immediately apparent in 1945, however, as the war's end appeared to herald a new era of religiosity.

The "Hour of the Church" in Occupied Germany

Even as confessional identities were being rearticulated, Protestants and Catholics engendered one of the most significant social phenomena of the immediate postwar era, the return to the churches. This divine renaissance was hardly limited to Germany, as Christianity enjoyed an enormous upswing of approbation across the continent in the aftermath of World War II.[21] Contemporary observers, including the occupying powers, reported "a religious revival like none Europe had seen in a hundred years," rendering religion, "outside of hunger," the "most powerful force in Germany."[22] The sources of the Christian resurgence varied. With almost every other societal institution discredited by Nazi collaboration, the spiritual authority and administrative continuity of especially the Catholic Church conferred enormous prestige on church leaders.[23] The persecution of Catholic priests as well as the outspokenness on Catholic issues—what Beth Griech-Polelle has called "selective opposition"—by bishops such as von Galen and Faulhaber contributed considerably to the church's image as a bastion of anti-Nazism.[24] That the Allies utilized church leaders as intermediaries and advisers in the earliest days of occupation reinforced this impression,[25] as did the Nuremberg war crimes tribunal's classification of Nazi treatment of the Catholic Church as a "crime against humanity."[26]

Faith certainly played a role. In Jerry Z. Muller's estimation, the "return to religion" represented a prominent feature of postwar German culture.[27] For untold Germans, especially devout National Socialists now bereft of belief, the churches offered moral direction.[28] Religion also provided emotional comfort to those suffering extreme deprivation, including expellees,[29] while yet others sought a sense of community and familiarity in an atomized society.[30] Recognizing the poisoned legacy of nationalist and conservative thought, many educated Germans identified in Christianity a new ideology of respectability.[31] That religious leaders offered the only voices critical of Allied occupation and denazification policies also encouraged many Germans who had left the churches to regard the clergy as spokesmen,[32] especially as the churches consciously adopted the role of "mouthpiece of those who have no voice in public life."[33]

Moreover, of perhaps unparalleled importance in a country absent a government, political parties, unions, and educational and economic institutions, the churches were the sole German organizations capable of grappling with the population's immediate needs.[34] While both churches had suffered considerable material losses[35] and Catholic officials complained of a postwar priest shortage,[36] the Protestant Evangelical Relief Organization and especially Catholic Caritas provided lifesaving relief throughout the occupied zones.[37] The only organizations in Germany with legal contacts to the outside world, the churches solicited aid from foreign churches, organized the import of raw materials, distributed care packages, and provided primary services for youth, POWs, expellees, and refugees.[38]

The "Hour of the Church" was indeed a moment in time. Despite the fact that 1945 was the first year in decades that saw more people joining the Catholic Church than leaving it,[39] the church's membership, even in its hour of revival, did not equal its pre-Nazi numbers.[40] Nonetheless, the revitalization of the Catholic Church in the wake of the war testifies to the strength of a Catholic Teilkultur that survived the Third Reich intact. Under National Socialism, the Catholic world sustained vigorous assaults that both weakened and strengthened it. On one hand, Nazism took a toll by interrupting the transmission of milieu ideals to the next generation and propagating a mythical interconfessional *Volksgemeinschaft*.[41] On the other hand, Hitler's appeal for Catholic-Protestant unity[42] and Nazi efforts to bridge the confessional gap through the replacement of confessional with community schools enjoyed limited success.[43] At the same time, German Christians' dream of a "people's church" floundered in large part because of members' anti-Catholicism;[44] the neo-pagan German Faith Movement's efforts to overcome Germany's confessional divide were no more successful.[45]

Moreover, the church's response to Nazi persecution—to transfer Catholic life from lay organizations to clerical jurisdiction[46]—actually intensified laity loyalty to the church and its beliefs.[47] Although the church would fail to reestablish its rich pre-Nazi organizational life for a number of reasons, including the hierarchy's decision to retain the organizational control claimed during the Nazi years, the immediate postwar years gave little indication of this future weakness.[48] In contrast to German Protestantism, Catholicism had made no doctrinal concessions to National Socialism; the few pro-Nazi theologians who sought formally to reconcile Catholic and Nazi teachings remained marginalized.[49] As a result, the Catholic Teilkultur arguably provided a stronger foundation for the organization of the CDU than did the socialist milieu, battered by Nazi oppression, for the reorganization of the SPD.[50]

If the Catholic milieu emerged from the Nazi period emboldened by its survival,[51] the Protestant Church was clearly less unified. Although the Württemberg state bishop, Theophil Wurm, succeeded at the Treysa Church Conference in forging out of the intact Lutheran state churches and the Confessing Church Council of Brethren what would become the Protestant Church in Germany (Evangelische Kirche in Deutschland [EKD]), Protestants struggled in the aftermath of the war to bridge the profound divisions of the Nazi years. While conservative, Lutheran state churches in Württemberg, Bavaria, and Hanover sought to cooperate with former German Christians and reorganize the Protestant Church in a traditionally hierarchical way, the more liberal Council of Brethren associated with Karl Barth and Martin Niemöller called for radical reform.[52]

Crucial to these debates was a reassessment of traditional Protestant theology. In contrast to Catholicism, which posited that man was created in God's image and was therefore obligated to work toward a moral society, Protestant convictions of original sin implied that human society was inevitably flawed; individuals were therefore to pursue ethically pure lives, but the sacred and the secular were intrinsically separate and were to remain so. Although hardly orthodox within Protestantism—CSVD founders advocated Protestant political engagement—the legacy of Luther's two kingdom theory for post–1945 Protestant engagement in politics remained palpable, even as Barthians and Lutherans largely concurred after 1945 on Protestants' duty to participate in the public sphere.[53] Consequently, Protestants would be divided not only theologically and on how best to reorganize the church but also politically.[54] In 1945, this disunity meant that Protestant Church leaders would play a less active and coherent role in the reorganization of postwar German politics than would their Catholic counterparts.

Allied Occupation

Religious Germans were naturally not the only Germans committed to rebuilding a post–Nazi Germany. In early May 1945, former Social Democrats established a local association in Hanover under the leadership of Kurt Schumacher, who would serve as chair of the SPD until his death in 1952. The Communist Party, which merged with the SPD in the Soviet zone in April 1946 to form the Socialist Unity Party of Germany (Sozialistische Einheitspartei Deutschlands [SED]), was founded in Berlin on June 11, 1945; it would retain the name KPD in the western zones until its ban in 1956. In contrast, the Free Democratic

Party (Freie Demokratische Partei [FDP]) emerged slowly out of a series of smaller party centers; led by Theodor Heuss, it would not be founded officially until December 1948.[55] At the same time, antifascist committees, or *Antifas,* sprang up throughout Germany, often propelled by workers whose visions of an alternate society garnered little sympathy from the Western Allies.[56]

All politically interested Germans faced extraordinary circumstances in 1945. From the unconditional surrender of May 8, 1945, until the proclamation of the Occupation Statute on September 21, 1949, the Allied-created zones constituted an entity without legal status. Foreign soldiers and administrators controlled almost every aspect of German public life. Above all else, the Allies designed the new political stage: Occupying officers determined which parties could campaign under which leaders, the scheduling of elections, and the content of publications and political speeches.[57] Although their control over German politics diminished steadily, the Allies retained final say over any important German decision until the occupation's end.[58]

The Allied presence was so central to the development of German postwar politics that early CDU history is best analyzed according to zonal boundaries. While the Soviets authorized party activity in June, the Americans in August, and the British in September, the French waited until December 1945 to sanction political parties.[59] Soviet policies, of course, had the most dramatic impact: By eliminating the Berlin-based CDU as a power within the larger German Christian Democratic scene, Soviet policy would inadvertently shape future CDU personnel and policy to Konrad Adenauer's advantage. Of the Christian Democratic organizations founded after World War II, those under British occupation would prove the most influential. The transformation of political Catholicism in the British zone was dictated above all by the zone's inclusion of the Rhineland and Westphalia.[60] In keeping with the history of the Center Party, western Prussians dominated the metamorphosis of political Catholicism and the course of the CDU thereafter; at the same time, the Rhineland was a center of Protestant CDU political activity.

In particular, Cologne CDU organizers led the entire west German area, both in terms of program and personnel. Followed by the Westphalian state association, the Rhenish state association quickly emerged as the most organized of the new party groupings, and the Rhineland and Westphalia soon boasted by far the strongest organizations in Germany.[61] Not only in retrospect were those steps taken in the Rhineland and especially Cologne paradigmatic; politicians of the day were well aware of their significance.[62] As Konrad Adenauer wrote in December 1946, "The decision over the future destiny of Germany will be taken in the British zone and, within the British zone, in the state North Rhine-Westphalia."[63]

The ascendancy of British zone Christian Democracy was also a function of the relatively favorable conditions of the British occupation. While CDU leaders complained that British occupation policy discriminated against the CDU to favor the SPD,[64] Christian Democrats also reported evidence of British openness to an interconfessional party and enthusiasm for the CDU's Christianity.[65] As in the U.S. zone, individual local officers allowed or even encouraged German political activity when it was still officially forbidden, while the British concern with excluding extremist parties worked in Christian Democrats' favor.[66] Of considerable importance, the British were the only occupation power to authorize committees of representatives from the zone's leading parties, a step that did much to reinforce the British zone CDU's preeminence vis-à-vis other CDU parties.[67]

Christian Democracy in the Rhineland

As the polestar of German Christian Democracy, the Rhenish CDU exuded influence far beyond the Rhineland and the immediate postwar years; as the archetype of Christian Democratic organization, it deserves closer examination.[68] The founding of the Rhineland CDU in Cologne was led by a small group of former Center Party members. In January 1945, as Leo Schwering fled the Allied bombing of the concentration camp in which he had been imprisoned, he encountered Wilhelm Warsch, another erstwhile Zentrum man who had also taken refuge in Königswinter on the Rhine.[69] After canvassing fellow former Center Party members, Schwering and Warsch gathered a group of interested colleagues at the home of Schwering's close friend, Catholic dean Josef Ibach.[70] Making direct reference to the Center's previous attempts to interconfessionalize, these men resolved that it was time to realize the promise of Stegerwald's 1920 initiative.[71]

Although the Catholic milieu had emerged from the Nazi years intact, its members harbored serious concerns about the stability of its political institutions. Most of this weakness, they believed, had been inherited from the Weimar Republic, which had seen a steady diminution of Center Party support. Likely to remain small, a purely Catholic party could only continue to fragment the political system, they imagined.[72] Furthermore, as diligently as former members of the Center Party worked to rebut accusations of Nazi collaboration,[73] they could not deny that political Catholicism had been irrevocably sullied by its actions in 1933;[74] indeed, as the coming years would demonstrate, political opponents would not hesitate to exploit the Center Party's vote for the Enabling Law.[75] On the basis of these arguments, then, Warsch and Schwering concluded that the Center Party was finished.[76]

Their early efforts to organize a new political movement faced considerable hurdles. Because the Americans would not authorize political activity until late August 1945 (the British occupation of Cologne began officially on June 21),[77] all of the Rhenish CDU's early organizational meetings violated occupation statutes.[78] Moreover, Warsch and Schwering were routinely denied permission to travel to Cologne to meet with fellow Center Party veterans. Despite such logistical setbacks, the nucleus of the Cologne and then Rhenish CDU expanded throughout the spring. As it did so, opposition within the Catholic community began to coalesce.[79]

Former Catholic political leaders resisted Schwering and Warsch's lead for a variety of reasons. First and foremost, there existed an enormous emotional, sentimental attachment to the Zentrum. The Center Party had never been simply a political party for Catholics but one body within the network of Teilkultur organizations—"a kind of second 'Church'"—into which Catholics were born and to which they belonged their entire lives.[80] The Center Party and the Catholic Church, according to one prominent member, had been "married";[81] for "old Center people," explained another, abandoning the Center Party was a "tremendous sacrifice."[82] As Konrad Adenauer later explained, "I don't begrudge any earlier adherent of the Center Party for not at first being able to decide on coming to the CDU. I have been a devoted adherent of the Center Party my entire life long, and I admit to you, it also took me very serious deliberations and a certain inner effort to say farewell to the *Zentrum.* I did not do it with a light heart."[83]

In addition to the emotional sanctuary the Center Party had offered its members, organizers feared reenacting the failed post–World War I attempts to interconfessionalize the Zentrum, disadvantaging the Center Party vis-à-vis other parties reorganizing in 1945.[84] Moreover, suspicion and prejudice concerning Protestants was deep-seated; even Catholics well-disposed toward cooperation worried that they would need to sacrifice constituent elements of their platform on the altar of interconfessionalism.[85] Nevertheless, by late May, Schwering and Warsch had secured enough converts to move forward.[86] Because political meetings of more than six people were forbidden, organizers could not send out postcard invitations (the only kind of mail permitted), leading to delays in scheduling a founding assembly.[87] When the meeting finally took place on June 17 in the Kolping House in Cologne, it was attended exclusively by Catholic former members of the Center Party.[88]

After declaring their intention to found a Christian Democratic party, those present designated a smaller group to draft a party program and extended invitations to select Protestants for a subsequent gathering one week later.[89] As religious anti-Nazis, Fritz Fuchs and Pastor Hans Encke corresponded precisely to Catholic priorities in selecting Protestant political partners: The latter was a theologian, and both men had been members of the Confessing Church.[90] For the most part, however, those at the late June session differed little from attendees of the June 17 meeting, where the composition was approximately one-third academics, one-third workers, and one-third civil servants, white-collar employees, and tradesmen. Shortly thereafter, Protestant prelate Karl Eichen would join the program commission, as would Johannes Albers, former Center Party and Christian Trade Union leader in Cologne.[91]

The influence of the Catholic clergy was more pronounced than it had been at the earlier June assembly: Not only did the meeting take place in the Dominican monastery at Walberberg, but the monastery's head, Laurentius Siemer, joined Eberhard Welty in directing the proceedings.[92] In drafting a party program, those present drew on the early June 1945 address by Pope Pius XII, Schwering's June 17 speech, and a collection of Welty's anti-Nazi sermons in a brochure, *What Now?* Following the Walberberg gathering, a subcommittee, in which Welty played a central role, edited the final version of the program, which began circulating in early July as the *Cologne Guiding Principles: A Summons to the German Volk to Come Together.*[93]

After the late June session, Schwering and other party organizers continued to solicit clergy blessing for their young enterprise. Schwering met in Cologne with the head of the German Bishops' Conference, then Archbishop (later Cardinal) Josef Frings. Frings, whom Schwering had known since he was a child, had helped Schwering financially during the Nazi years by arranging lectures for him at Cologne churches. While delaying the party's founding in part due to Frings's objections to the program's treatment of confessional schools,[94] Schwering, Theodor Scharmitzel, and Peter Josef Schaeven devoted several weeks to canvassing former Westphalian colleagues.[95] The Cologne group led by Schwering then met again in the Kolping House. On August 20, 1945, they wrote to the headquarters of the Allied military government to request permission to found a Christian Democratic party in Cologne, explaining that influential members of the former Center Party had decided to forgo the reestablishment of a traditional Catholic party—"which mainly had no contact with the Protestant population"—in favor of founding a new, interconfessional union.[96]

The Rhineland as Paradigm

Party Founders

Beyond their resurrection of the long-standing question of interconfessionalism, these earliest steps on the part of Rhenish Catholics were representative in numerous ways. Although the wide-ranging series of separate Christian Democratic parties founded in 1945 and 1946 bore a variety of names—not until mid-December 1945 would a concerted effort be made to establish one common name for an interzonal party—the vast majority of the groups identifying themselves as Christian Democratic shared assumptions about the party's future direction. This programmatic resemblance was a product of the personnel continuity of these groups with pre-1933 political Catholicism: Almost invariably, the CDU's organization across Germany was led by former Center Party members, Christian Trade Unionists, and priests, many of whom had been involved in anti-Nazi circles. With the exception of scattered Protestant-led foundings, the decision to establish a Christian Democratic party was made by men and small numbers of women who had belonged to the Catholic Teilkultur all their lives.

Schwering, who would head the Rhenish CDU until he was succeeded by Adenauer in February 1946, had not only been a Center Party deputy in the Prussian Landtag but had served as chair of the Volksverein in Cologne.[97] The other organizers were equally involved in Catholic life and politics: A leading member of the Center Party, Warsch had been mayor of Krefeld-Uerdingen before the Nazis deposed him in 1933, while both Schaeven and Scharmitzel had been involved with the Windthorstbünde, the Center Party's youth organization.[98] Albers had long served as secretary of the Christian Trade Unions in Cologne; he also chaired the Cologne Center Party from 1924 to 1933. Beginning in November 1945, he would cochair the Cologne CDU with Schaeven.

Beyond their rootedness in the Catholic milieu, a striking number of these men had actively opposed the Nazis. Schwering, for example, was imprisoned in 1944 by the Gestapo following his participation in Kolping House discussions in Cologne.[99] Scharmitzel organized Unitas, which originally met in the Dominican monastery in Cologne,[100] while Albers was involved in the KAB circle led by Bernhard Letterhaus, Nikolaus Gross, and prelate Otto Müller before being imprisoned in August 1944.[101] Identifying a "spirit of the catacombs" coursing through the early CDU,[102] Schwering memorialized Letterhaus, Gross, and Müller—all killed by the Nazis—as "Christian witnesses [*Blutzeugen*]" for whom he served as an "executor of [their] will."[103] Distinctly prominent among anti-Nazi Christian Democrats were above all former Christian Trade Unionists, many of whom reclaimed their tradition of strong support for interconfessionalism to advocate on behalf of Christian Democracy.[104]

Priests in Politics

Consistent with the traditions of political Catholicism, the role of the clergy highlighted another central feature of Rhenish Christian Democratic organization. Schwering and his colleagues' reliance on clerics, especially upper clergy in the persons of Ibach, Siemer, and Welty, in organizing a Christian Democratic party would be symptomatic of almost all early CDU organization.[105] Essential to the new party as political helpmates, facilitators, and advisers in the Rhineland and beyond, Catholic priests would play central roles in establishing the CDU throughout occupied Germany.[106] Their influence on traditional Catholic cultural politics was especially pronounced; it was not without significance that party organizers took seriously Frings's reservations about their position on confessional schools.

A constituent if controversial feature of Catholic politics since the founding of the Center Party, ecclesiastic influence was also a product of Germany's extraordinary recent history. In the same way lay party founders drew on Nazi-era connections, some clergy laid claim to their own oppositional networks. Both Siemer and Welty were tied to the KAB in Cologne. In addition to working closely with subversive Rhenish groups, Siemer had contacts with the Kreisau and Görlitz resistance circles; imprisoned from 1935 to 1936 on the suspicion of anti-Nazism, he was sentenced to death in absentia after July 20, 1944. As a result of Siemer's and Welty's activities, the Gestapo confiscated the Dominican monastery in Walberberg in 1942.[107]

The prominence of the clergy was further a product of the Allies' accommodation of ecclesiastic authority. After Warsch and Schwering were denied permission to travel, a fellow priest and friend of Ibach free from the web of Allied restrictions visited Cologne for them.[108] Schwering also speculated that neither the Americans nor the British disturbed the (still officially illegal) political gatherings at the Walberberg monastery because respect for the Dominicans rendered the monastery "inviolable."[109] Throughout Germany, priests provided crucial means of communication—telephones, meeting rooms, messengers to Catholic politicians. As long as the ban on political gatherings was in place, Catholic masses and festivals served as valuable discussion forums.[110]

Though greatly reduced even by 1949, public engagement of the priest-hood was fundamental to the party's founding. It is of decisive importance to the early history of Christian Democracy, then, that the Catholic clergy after 1945 aided more than hindered interconfessionalism.[111] Catholic clerical sup-port for Christian Democracy emerged surprisingly quickly, as the Rhenish bishops expressed concern about refounding the Center Party as early as May 1945.[112] While the bishops made no official political pronouncement at either their June gathering in Werl or the Fulda Bishops' Conference in August, their internal discussions favored the CDU.[113]

In contrast to papal intervention in the pre–World War I Zentrumsstreit, the Catholic clergy appears to have proceeded without any direct communica-tion from the Vatican. Many former Center Party members certainly took note of Pope Pius XII's Christmas messages, especially *Benignitas et humanitas* in 1944, offering an unprecedented papal endorsement of democracy.[114] But, while Pope Pius XII made known his views on confessional schools and the concordat and there was some indication that he supported German Jesuit ad-vocates of interconfessionalism, he appears to have left the decision regarding political Catholicism to the German hierarchy.[115] Resistance to interconfes-sionalism within the Catholic Church leadership was also weakened by the severing of the traditional base of integralist Catholicism, the Breslau diocese, from western Germany after 1945.[116] At both the papal and national levels, then, opposition to interconfessionalism appeared diminished, leaving western Catholic clerics, many of whom had embraced the Cologne line before 1933, to reach their own judgments.

The bishops were not in full agreement, however, nor did they convey clear instructions to the lower clergy, a number of whom, especially in the Rhineland and Westphalia, favored refounding the Zentrum.[117] In his January 6, 1946, New Year's Message to the Diocese Clergy on Political Questions, Conrad Gröber, archbishop of Freiburg, noted with regret the sharp political differences among the churchmen in his archdiocese, urging all priests to adopt a common stance.[118] But, even as the majority of the German Catholic clergy signaled support for an interconfessional party by early 1946, a significant group of upper and especially lower clergy remained loyal to the Center Party.[119] Less educated and bound more closely to the land, lower clergy were as a rule more conservative than their superiors;[120] Center Party support was especially deep in nonurban areas and among older clergy.[121] Of those rural priests who did support Christian Democracy, at least some had pre-1933 con-tacts with the Catholic or Christian labor movements.[122]

The bulk of the German Catholic hierarchy ultimately opted to support the interconfessional initiative for a host of reasons. Fearful of increased Soviet control over Germany and of Marxism's temptations for German Protestants, Catholic clergy were also deeply concerned about limiting the number of parties to prevent a recurrence of the Weimar Republic's collapse.[123] In this regard, they embraced the CDU because it was the first Catholic party to organize; as Gröber indicated, the bishops sought above all else to avoid political divisions within the Catholic milieu.[124] Maintaining unity was especially crucial to the bishops' top domestic priority, reestablishing confessional schools.[125]

Clergy differed not only on the fate of political Catholicism but also on the appropriate ecclesiastical role in party politics.[126] While widely regarded as valid, including by the Allies, the concordat's postwar legal status was in fact uncertain (and would not, despite consideration during the Parliamentary Council, be definitively resolved until 1957). Keen to retain the agreement it had negotiated in 1933,[127] the Vatican hoped to anchor the concordat in daily practice and German law by adhering scrupulously to its terms,[128] which included state funding and control of theological faculties, a federal guarantee of confessional schools, and a ban on clerical involvement in politics.[129] In keeping with this strategy, the bishops declared in May 1945 that "the clergy should stay out of politics."[130] West German bishops meeting in November 1945 confirmed the prohibition on priests in politics, though they did acknowledge that clergy, especially in the countryside, could not simply "look on" when serious political issues arose.[131] One year later, the west German bishops formalized this position by decreeing that priests could stand as political candidates only with church permission, should give no public political speeches, and should refrain from using their church offices for political propaganda.[132]

Church promulgations notwithstanding, German clerics participated actively in early postwar politics. Indeed, while few clergy violated the concordat between 1933 and 1945, far more did so immediately following the war, when the agreement's status was less clear. On one hand, difficulties in communication within the country and with Rome fostered a degree of clerical freedom that diminished steadily until 1949,[133] when the Vatican actively enforced the prohibition on politically active priests.[134] On the other, some clergy, including Wilhelm Böhler, disagreed with the stricture on clerical participation,[135] while still others disregarded the concordat because they hoped to replace it with state concordats.[136]

In contrast to the Nazi years, few priests believed the ban on clerical involvement in politics extended to party membership or pronouncements from the pulpit at election time.[137] Many clerics seemed to adopt the position of Trier bishop Franz Rudolf Bornewasser, who in the summer of 1946 explained to Peter Altmeier, former Center Party Koblenz city councillor and co-organizer of the Rhineland-Palatinate CDU, that the concordat in no way prevented priests from supporting party politics. Clerics could be helpful in a number of ways, he explained—by giving speeches, participating in discussions and meetings, selecting candidates, and contributing to party organization and programs.[138] For his part, priest Karl Wies of Oberwesel, who would head a committee for the political orientation of clergy, argued that direct clerical participation hardly violated the concordat, as priests were not party politicians but "party crusaders."[139] The desire to honor the concordat does help to explain why, despite organizing and joining the party—in 1947, 18 percent of all Rhenish priests were registered CDU members[140]—clergymen in general eschewed leadership roles in the CDU.[141] Not unusual was the situation in Freiburg, where the CDU's founder, prelate Ernst Föhr, declined party office but selected his successor as chair while remaining involved in party work.[142]

As the history of the Center Party before 1933 had demonstrated, however, ecclesiastical engagement in political Catholicism had never been undisputed. Out of fear that church leaders would seek to dictate CDU policy, some Catholic party founders in Mainz rejected concerted clerical efforts to influence the CDU[143] and, in the early postwar months, Adam Stegerwald spoke especially forcefully about the impossibility of retaining Protestants in a party controlled by the church hierarchy.[144] In a 1946 speech, Josef André declared, "The clergy should stay out of party disputes as much as possible,"[145] a sentiment Eugen Kogon echoed in *Frankfurter Hefte* editorials in 1946 and 1947.[146] In June 1948, the district association of the Christian Democratic Party in Birkenfeld (in the Rhineland-Palatinate) reported that every politically active priest in the CDU cost the party Protestant votes and members.[147] For the most part, however, in recognition of Christian Democracy's dependence on the rank and file of the Catholic Teilkultur, party leaders actively solicited clerical participation.[148] Konrad Adenauer, who followed closely the church hierarchy's political discussions in the summer of 1945,[149] detected "strong *kulturkämpferischen* overtones" in restrictions on priests in politics[150] and complained frequently to church officials that the clergy was not sufficiently politically involved.[151] In a November 1948 letter to Cardinal Frings (who joined the CDU that month), Adenauer protested Münster bishop Michael Keller's policy of political abstinence, charging German clerics with repeating their error of 1933.[152]

Party Minorities: Women and Protestants

The prominence of clergy and former Center Party members, especially those involved in anti-Nazi and trade union activities, were not the only constituent features of early CDU organization prefigured in the Rhineland. As would be true of all other CDU foundings, the Rhenish party's establishment was largely a male affair. At the late June meetings in Cologne, just two of the eighteen organizers present were female; two more Catholic women would join when the program commission expanded.[153] Subordinate before the Nazi years in the male-dominated Center Party and the Catholic Church, female Christian Democrats would continue to struggle after World War II to influence Christian politics. Although small numbers of women participated actively in building CDU parties, few of the most influential early Christian Democrats were female.

The role of Protestants also revealed continuity with traditions of political Catholicism. As the history of interconfessional initiatives made clear, Christian Democracy, as it had existed in the minds of Center Party politicians before 1945, had never entailed unqualified Protestant-Catholic cooperation. In the same way Julius Bachem had set restrictions on his call for Catholics to "come out of the tower" almost forty years earlier, Catholics after World War II prioritized cooperation with religiously active Protestants.[154] In an "open letter" addressed specifically to "all the Catholic men and women of the Rhineland," Catholic CDU leaders stressed that the Protestants with whom they had chosen to work were "devout."[155] As Walter Dirks explained, the CDU should not accept all Protestants but only those who had grasped the "principle of the era" and the Christian "political mission."[156]

The appeal of practicing Protestants was especially great after the war as a consequence of the widespread belief that Protestants, because they were less religious, had supported Nazism to a greater degree than had Catholics.[157] Indeed, in all the Protestant regions where Christian Democrats sought to organize, party leaders complained about the difficulties of finding leading Protestants untainted by Nazi collaboration.[158] Catholics' concern with securing certifiably religious Protestants for their new, interconfessional party helps explain their continuing efforts to attract Protestant clergy members to the CDU. While CDU Catholics believed that men of the cloth played a less influential role in Protestant communities than among Catholics,[159] they nonetheless valued Protestant ministers for their spiritual authority and practical assistance. That the Rhenish CDU organizers' first Protestant contacts included clergy would prove paradigmatic for broader CDU organization.

Beyond the Protestant religious leadership, certain organizations of Protestant Germany took on heightened meaning in the eyes of Rhenish Christian Democrats as evidence of Protestants' political and religious piety. Foremost among these was the Confessing Church, to which both Fritz Fuchs and Pastor Hans Encke had belonged. Although more consistently opposed to Nazi interference in church affairs than to National Socialist ideology or policies, the

Confessing Church's refusal to support the German Christians earned it veneration as anti-Nazi in and beyond the Rhenish CDU.[160] In a speech at the founding of the Spandau CDU, Emil Dovifat, former Center Party member and editor of the Christian Trade Unions' daily newspaper, praised the Confessing Church for having defended "Christian principles" against National Socialism (*Nazitum*).[161] "The official Protestant Church," according to a Berlin CDUD publication, "did not possess the requisite clarity to recognize the danger that National Socialism posed for the Church, even Christianity in general. . . . It became a slave to the state. The Confessing Church for that reason . . . laid claim to be the lawful Protestant Church in Germany."[162]

For at least one old Zentrum man, the inspiration of Confessing Church leaders made Christian Democracy possible. Carl Bachem, an eighty-eight-year-old veteran of Center Party politics and younger cousin of Julius Bachem, wrote in November 1945, "Only the strongest alliance with devout Protestants can save us. After Pastor Niemöller has provided such a magnificent example of unshakable Christian faith, broad, Christian elements of the Protestant part of the *Volk* will surely now allow themselves to be won over as well."[163] Indeed, according to Walter Dirks, the Confessing Church had laid the groundwork for Protestants' liberation from their traditional understanding of Christianity, making possible their "political conversion."[164]

The CSVD performed a similar role in the postwar era for former Centrists soliciting Protestant partners.[165] Still anchored in their regions of pre-1933 support, these CSP successors would ultimately come to provide the bulk of engaged Protestants in the early CDU in Baden-Württemberg, the Rhineland-Palatinate, North Rhine-Westphalia, northern Hesse, and parts of Lower Saxony.[166] Former CSVD members' prominence was especially significant in the Rhenish and Westphalian CDU, where, as a result of the British zone's dominance of the new party, they would enjoy greater influence than other Protestant Christian Democrats. Like other constituent features of the CDU founding era, the Catholic strategy of identifying sufficiently religious and non-Nazi Protestants by focusing on the Confessing Church and the CSVD would hardly limit itself to the Rhineland but repeat itself across occupied Germany.

Christian Democracy beyond the Rhineland

Characterized by limited inclusion of religious Protestants and the prominence of Catholic men of the Zentrum, Christian Trade Unions, and priesthood, the first step toward Christian Democracy in the heartland of political Catholicism served as the model for a regional network of party groupings. This was true in terms of both organization and program. Following their publication, the Cologne Guiding Principles were employed immediately by party leaders as the basis for a common Rhineland-Westphalia platform and beyond.[167] The November 1945 Trier Christian Democratic Party's Guiding Principles, for example, were largely based on the Cologne Guiding Principles, while the Koblenz Guiding Principles in turn were based on Trier's.[168] Indeed, as was evident in the decision of Krefeld Zentrum veterans to found a Christian Democratic party, Cologne had fulfilled its historical task as the hub of progressive German political Catholicism by the summer of 1945.[169]

While the Cologne founding influenced Christian Democrats in smaller towns such as Dormagen, Grevenbroich, Hochneukirch, and Düren,[170] one of the most important groups encouraged by the Rhineland events was that in Düsseldorf.[171] Despite Maximilian Freiherr von Gumppenberg's efforts to win over fellow former Zentrum members, opposition to interconfessionalism was considerable, led by Wilhelm Hamacher, general secretary of the Rhenish Center Party before 1933 and future leader of the post–1945 Center Party. Hamacher, who argued that Catholics should wait to see how public opinion developed,[172] advocated a separate-parties solution, by which the two confessions would cooperate closely with each other in accordance with the Weimar model of the Zentrum and the Protestant CSVD.[173]

Its initial reluctance to abandon the Center Party notwithstanding, the Christian Democratic group in Düsseldorf exhibited a notable degree of early interconfessional cooperation, in large part due to Nazi-era alliances.[174] Düsseldorf's Catholic resistance circle had close connections with Protestant anti-Nazis; Robert Lehr participated in wartime discussions that included former Center Party and Christian Trade Unions leader Karl Arnold.[175] In addition, Düsseldorf's confessional makeup—one-third Protestant—helps explain the greater representation of Protestants and Protestant clergy in the early Düsseldorf CDU.[176]

The initial disinclination to embrace the new political movement in Düsseldorf had its parallels throughout the northern Rhineland but was strongest in the less industrialized province of Westphalia, where a more conservative tradition of political Catholicism and greater reliance on the clergy translated into broader support for refounding the Center Party. Not only were many Christian Democratic groups in Westphalia slow to form, but Zentrum loyalists would ultimately establish the postwar German Center Party there, representing a fundamental organizational split within the Catholic Teilkultur.[177] In contrast to the Rhineland, where, according to Hans Schreiber, secretary of the Düsseldorf Center Party before 1933 and of the CDU Rhenish state association, "only very few clergymen" could be considered "secret or open patrons" of the Center Party,[178] clerical support for the Center Party in Westphalia was notably stronger. As a result, Christian Democrats had difficulty organizing CDU chapters outside of areas loyal to the Christian Trade Unions.

That the majority of Westphalian Catholic political leaders eventually supported the CDU resulted at least in part from the assistance they received from Rhenish CDU organizers and Westphalian upper clergy.[179] In Münster and its environs, for example, the city's bishop, Clemens August Graf von Galen, well known in and outside of Germany for his opposition to the Nazi euthanasia program and postwar criticisms of the Allies, played a decisive role in the founding of the CDU.[180] Working closely with Georg Jöstingmeier, his legal adviser during the Nazi era, von Galen drafted a party program and helped organize the first public Christian Democratic gathering for the city and surroundings of Münster. Protestants present included former members of the Confessing Church and CSVD.[181]

In Paderborn, a traditional stronghold of Catholic youth organization, a group of Catholics gathered around Kaspar Schulte, praeses of the Catholic Workers' Associations of the Archdiocese, and prior Paul Simon. Simon, whom the Nazis had dismissed from his Tübingen professorship as a consequence of his friendship with Heinrich Brüning, worked with former leader of the Westphalian Center Party Josef Kannengießer and Christian Trade Unions cofounder Johannes Gronowski to establish a Paderborn branch of the party in November 1945.[182] Simon's influence was evident not just in Paderborn but in Westphalia as a whole;[183] based on his contacts with Protestants stemming from the Nazi era,[184] especially with Friedrich Holzapfel and praeses Karl Koch, both former Confessing Church members, Simon was instrumental in bringing together Westphalian Protestants and Catholics.[185] Schulte was active not only in Paderborn but also in Dortmund, a leading center of the Christian Trade Unions during the Weimar years, where he directed an early June meeting of former trade unionists and clergy that prompted a series of meetings among representatives from Paderborn, Essen, and Dortmund who soon formed the Wattenscheid Circle.[186] With the encouragement of Jesuit Johannes Hirschmann and under the influence of events in the Rhineland, members of this Wattenscheid Circle decided on August 13, 1945, to found a Christian Democratic party.

When a CDU party finally organized in Essen in January 1946, it was the work of former members of the Christian Trade Unions, especially Heinrich Strunk.[187] Though leading Protestants included two former members of the

CSVD, Gustav Heinemann and former Essen CSVD chair Hans Spiecker,[188] Christian Democracy in Essen, as in regions of the Wattenscheid Circle, was predominantly a Catholic affair. Indeed, Protestants organized independently in only one Westphalian town, Ravensberg,[189] although in Hagen individual Protestant clergy, CSVD, and Confessing Church members joined former Center Party members to found the CDU in September 1945.[190]

Protestant participation would be most pronounced in former CSVD strongholds—the Siegerland, East Westphalia, and Wuppertal.[191] After initially debating establishing a liberal party, a Wuppertal group dominated by former Confessing Church members opted for Christian Democracy.[192] That Otto Schmidt scheduled the early December organizational meeting at a November gathering of Wuppertal Confessing Church representatives testified to the strong connections between the Wuppertal CDU and the Confessing Church.[193] A founding member of the Confessing Church, Schmidt would play an especially prominent role in the early CDU, and the Wuppertal party would form one of the most influential Protestant centers of Christian Democracy in the early postwar era.

The Wuppertal party also cast into sharp relief a distinctive feature of early Protestant participation in Christian Democracy, its class basis. Most Protestants who joined the early CDU were religious; of enormous significance to the CDU, they were also middle-class. Indeed, in contrast to Catholic centers of Rhenish Christian Democracy, which boasted strong union representation, Protestants were far more closely associated with business groups and the middle class than with workers or their organizations.[194] Fifteen of the thirty-four organizers in the Wuppertal party's founding group, for example, were manufacturers or held leading positions in industry. The rest were academics or civil servants; only one was a worker.[195] Where Catholic party organizers succeeded in attracting devout Protestants to their ranks, they did so largely in keeping with the traditions of interconfessionalism. Religious, middle-class antisocialists, not workers, constituted the bulk of the party's Protestant population. Not surprisingly, this profile would have significant consequences for early Christian Democratic politics.

Rhenish and Westphalian Christian Democrats Advance

If Catholics were initially selective about the Protestants they recruited, they also recognized that Christian Democracy would only survive with substantial Protestant support. Catholic concern for Protestant participation was certainly evident at the official foundings of the Rhineland and Westphalian CDU parties on September 2, 1945. The result of late summer contacts between the Rhenish and the less well organized Westphalian organizations, the establishment of the Rhenish and Westphalian Christian Democratic parties represented a significant step toward asserting western Prussian leadership of the CDU. The gathering in Cologne to found the Rhenish state association brought together the Cologne party, the Düsseldorf circle, and the Protestant Wuppertal organization, each with affiliated regional groups.[196] While Cologne Catholics directed and dominated the gathering as well as the new Rhenish state association's organizational apparatus,[197] select Protestants—including Otto Schmidt— served as featured speakers.[198]

The same sort of attention to confessional representation was evident at the simultaneous founding in Bochum of a Christian Democratic party for Westphalia. Even before the meeting, Lambert Lensing had stressed, "The more truly influential Protestants who come to Bochum, the better."[199] Once again, although Catholics filled most of the executive committee's seats, Protestants—including Otto Boelitz, former DVP member and Prussian minister for science, art, and adult education, and Otto Rippel and Wilhelm Lindner, former CSVD and Confessing Church members—were disproportionally represented in the new party's leadership.[200] Indeed, Protestants and Catholics alike were aware of the symbolism of granting Protestants prominent party positions.[201] As deputy chair of the Westphalian CDU, Holzapfel stressed the importance of his appointment to achieving confessional equilibrium.[202] This concern with confessional distribution would have a long history in the party; in some cases, it guided the party's organization. After the founding of the CDU in Hamborn (near Duisburg) by both Catholic and Protestant clergy members, for example, two chairs were named—one of each confession—and an advisory board of eight Protestants and eight Catholics was established.[203]

While Rhenish and Westphalian Christian Democrats developed a common political platform, other groups formed in the British zone throughout the fall of 1945. A large majority of these organizations followed the basic patterns evident in the Rhineland and Westphalia: Predominantly led by Catholics, especially those tied to Christian labor organizations, and with priestly support, these groups sought out devout Protestants, particularly clergy members and those associated with the CSVD, to make credible their claims to Christian Democracy.[204] Notably, with some exceptions, such as Schleswig-Holstein, the initiative lay with Catholics even in Protestant areas. The Bremen CDU was founded in a Catholic rectory, while the Hanover CDU was directed by former Center Party members gathered in the home of former Hanover Center Party chair Bernhard Pfad and a nearby Franciscan cloister.[205] Pfad was joined by his wife, Martha Pfad; Anton Storch, former Christian Trade Unionist; and Wilhelm Naegel, Center Party veteran. Protestants were represented by Protestant church administrator Adolf Cillien and Arnold Fratzscher, a former member of the CSVD and the Confessing Church.[206]

Division within the Catholic Milieu: The Founding of the Center Party

As the Christian Democratic movement spread throughout the British zone in the fall of 1945, those opposed to the creation of an interconfessional party organized as well. On October 14, 1945, some sixty former Center Party members now living in the British zone gathered in Soest, the founding city of the Center Party in 1870, to reestablish the German Center Party.[207] Based primarily in rural areas where Catholics represented the large majority, the new Center Party relied especially on the support of lower clergy.[208] In keeping with the concordat, only one priest belonged to the party's governing board, but a number of other clerics assumed official advisory roles.[209]

Despite its official commitment to interconfessional cooperation, the new Center Party revealed little interest in recruiting Protestants and indeed never attracted a Protestant member.[210] Although the party was soon plagued by internecine battles, an organizational split within the Catholic Teilkultur had caused great concern for Christian Democrats since the summer of 1945.[211] Schwering and other Christian Democratic leaders initially sought to dismiss the potential importance of a refounded Zentrum. In mid-September, Schwering wrote to Lensing that the "old academics" loyal to the Center Party were not "very dangerous"; Center Party leader Hamacher, Schwering believed, "is from all appearances swinging toward us."[212] Even two weeks later, Hans Schreiber described the opposition within the Catholic camp to Christian Democracy as "for the most part emotionally based and therefore surmountable."[213] Despite his professed confidence, however, Schwering continued to fear the impact of a Westphalian Center Party on the burgeoning Christian Democratic movement in the Rhineland, a concern shared by fellow Christian Democrats.[214]

In an effort to forestall the establishment of the rival party, Christian Democrats had negotiated with their former colleagues throughout the fall of 1945.[215] Even on the eve of the Center Party's founding, Kannengießer and Prior Simon sought to prevent Johannes Brockmann, former Zentrum Prussian Landtag delegate, from moving forward.[216] After the new Center's leaders rejected additional entreaties to discussion, Schwering acknowledged that the conflict could no longer be kept from the public eye.[217] Nonetheless, Kannengießer reported in early December that Brockmann and his compatriot, Fritz Stricker, seemed more open to cooperation; negotiations therefore continued into 1946.[218] At the same time, Christian Democrats dedicated enormous time and energy to "creating necessary clarity among the clergy," whom they regarded as crucial instruments in the battle for Catholic votes.[219] Beginning in mid-October, Hans Schreiber worked to organize what he dubbed "priests' conferences" to offset Hamacher's attempts to win over the clergy.[220] Schwering, for his part, assured Josef Ibach that he was in "the closest touch with the highest clerical circles," especially the archbishop of Cologne and bishop of Aachen.[221]

The success of these CDU efforts was not always clear, although Christian Democrats initially expressed optimism. In late September 1945 and again two months later, Schwering wrote to Lensing that the Zentrum was having hardly any impact in the Rhineland and that the bishop of Münster's support, announced to great effect at the Bochum party founding, was a very encouraging sign.[222] Schreiber was also hopeful; he wrote to Kannengießer in November 1945 that, at a gathering of ecclesiastical deans from Trier in Koblenz, the German bishops present, including those from the British zone, officially disavowed Hamacher's decision.[223] A week earlier, however, Kannengießer had reported that many area clergy members, including some he had contacted personally, stood firmly behind Hamacher and the new Center Party.[224] Meanwhile, Schwering's December 1945 initiative fizzled when Prelate Heinen announced at a conference of the deans of Cologne-Kalk that his longer conversation with Hamacher made it impossible for him to advise other clerics to abandon the Center; numerous past attempts to work with Protestants, Heinen noted, had always ended in failure.[225] Nonetheless, in mid-January 1946, Schwering reported, "In general, I can say with pleasure that the counter efforts of the Zentrum have been, so far, negligible and insignificant. I am no longer afraid of this party."[226]

Indeed, well into the next year, CDU members discussed repeatedly, both among themselves and with Catholic clergymen, the clergy's role in overcoming the Catholic schism, especially as the Center Party continued to enjoy deep support in parts of Westphalia, including Münster.[227] In June 1946, Kannengießer reported that Münster vicar capitular Franz Vorwerk, whom Kannengießer had known for decades from Center Party politics, "shares our political view completely. He regrets very much, however, that the entire clergy—due to the rift—is unable to side openly with the CDU. I cannot agree with him entirely, but I do see the extraordinarily large difficulties."[228]

Already in April 1946, Adenauer had written to leading Catholic priests in Cologne to follow up on his meeting with Center Party leaders in an effort to merge the two parties. Adenauer, who had in the interim met with Frings, asked the upper clergy to inform their fellow Rhenish-Westphalian clerics about the "real character" of the Center Party in an effort to overcome the "unfortunate conflict within the Catholic clergy" on the question.[229] Over the next year, Adenauer would repeatedly urge the bishops to state publicly that the refounded Center Party should disband.[230] In late April 1947, Adenauer complained to Frings, now a cardinal, that the Center "largely owes its existence and its growth in this election to the activities of Catholic clergymen." Noting that three priests had signed a Westphalian Center Party pamphlet claiming that the CDU sought to found a new Christian church, Adenauer warned that other parties would continue to profit from Catholic division if the bishops did not clamp down on their lower clergy.[231]

That the refounding of the Center Party represented not simply political competition but a psychological blow for Christian Democrats was evident in the animosity that developed among former Zentrum colleagues as their political paths diverged.[232] In Erkrath, the Catholic priest branded the local CDU chair a "deserter" for choosing the "'so-called' Christian Democratic Party."[233] In late November 1945, Heinrich Strunk chided Hamacher for ignoring a Catholic's "responsibility" to support Christian Democracy.[234] Helene Wessel's decision to stay with the Center Party poisoned her relationship with Helene Weber, one of Germany's very few other prominent female Catholic politicians, and led to a rupture with Wessel's mentor, Johannes Gronowski, and his family.[235] In August 1945, Lensing wrote to Fritz Stricker that his support for the Center Party would mean the end of their long friendship.[236] As Lensing wrote to Schwering some years later, "I know that I made a lot of enemies with the founding of the Westphalian CDU, especially among former Center supporters."[237]

Despite the threat posed by the refounded Center Party, the British zone CDU would soon emerge as the best organized and strongest of the party groupings in occupied Germany. While the strength of the Catholic Teilkultur and the tradition of liberal Catholicism were determinative, the relatively accommodating British occupation policies facilitated the success of Christian Democracy in the British zone. This was nowhere more obvious than in the experiences of Christian Democrats in the other occupation zones.

CHAPTER 3

Christian Democratic Organization beyond the British Zone: Priests, Protestants, Patriarchy

In many ways, early Christian Democracy in the French, American, and Soviet zones bore strong resemblance to that in the British zone. Throughout defeated Germany, the CDU was organized by former members of the Center Party with strong participation from trade unionists and clergy, including many who had resisted the Nazis. Small numbers of women contributed, while Protestants largely eschewed the new party; of those who joined, religious Protestants, especially former Confessing Church and CSVD members, stood out. As in the British zone, regional variations mattered greatly. Beyond the British zone, the participation of anti-Nazi opposition figures in Berlin, the prominence of the clergy in the Palatinate, and a Bavarian emphasis on state autonomy would testify to the importance of political traditions. In a now famous quote, the French newspaper *L'Ordre* described the 1946 CDU as "socialist and radical in Berlin, clerical and conservative in Cologne, capitalist and reactionary in Hamburg, and counterrevolutionary and particularist in Munich."[1] While overstated, this description nonetheless hints at the competing impulses that shaped Christian Democracy in its founding years.

The French Zone

As had been the case in the British zone, occupation policies shaped decisively the development of Christian Democracy in the French zone. By administering their rule more directly and with proportionately more officials than the other occupying powers, the French created the most difficult conditions for German politicians in the western zones.[2] The priorities of Charles de Gaulle and his successors—joint Allied control over the Rhine's left bank, internationalization of the Ruhr, the federal organization of Germany, and the resolution of the Saarland question to French advantage—reflected France's goal of postwar security.[3] In an effort to dictate the outlines of Germany's future party system, the French forbade political parties until December 13, 1945 and regulated party activity tightly thereafter, never authorizing, for example, party zonal associations. There is no evidence, however, that the French specifically disadvantaged Christian Democracy, and some evidence indicates that they favored Catholic clergy more than did other occupying powers.[4]

Stringent occupation policies were not the only explanation for the relatively weak development of Christian Democracy in the French zone. Widespread support for refounding the Center Party combined with a strong tradition of regional autonomy to retard coordinated interconfessional organization. When Christian Democrats did organize, however, they revealed the typical characteristics of early Christian Democratic development present in the British zone. In addition to clerical influence, Christian Democratic organization in French-occupied Baden reflected the strength of networks of both Nazi opponents and the Center Party. In the southern half of Baden, party activity was focused in Baden's capital city, Freiburg. (The northern halves of both Baden and Württemberg were under American occupation; only in 1952 would Württemberg-Baden, Württemberg-Hohenzollern, and Baden merge into Baden-Württemberg.) The December 1945 founding of a Christian Democratic organization in Freiburg, the Christian Social People's Party (Christlich-Soziale Volkspartei [CSVP]), was led by Prelate Föhr, former leader of the Baden Center Party Landtag faction. Föhr had been pressured by Conrad Gröber, archbishop of Freiburg, to solicit Confessing Church support for a new interconfessional union.[5] The influence of the Confessing Church in Freiburg was apparent in the participation of Protestant ministers and members of the Freiburg School, including Franz Böhm and Adolf Lampe.

Gröber was also active in Konstanz, where he supported former Confessing Church and Protestant People's Service (the Baden CSVD) member Hermann Schneider's efforts to organize a Christian Democratic group. Although the party attracted overwhelmingly former Center Party members, leading representatives of the Confessing Church in Baden and its surrounding region moved rather seamlessly into the CDU.[6] Continuities with the CSVD were also evident in northern Württemberg, where early Christian Democratic propaganda mirrored images from a 1932 CSVD campaign poster.[7]

In Südwürttemberg-Hohenzollern, Christian Democracy revealed the influence of former Christian Trade Unionists, especially those who had established contact with fellow unionists in other zones, including Johannes Albers,

Jakob Kaiser, and Josef Ersing.[8] In Tübingen, efforts were spearheaded by a former Center Party politician referred by the local Catholic dean to Protestants associated with resistance activities and the Confessing Church, including Ulrich Steiner, Eugen Wirsching, and Paul Binder.[9] In Trier, former Center Party members orchestrated a party founding.[10]

Similarly, almost all of the organizers in the Rhineland-Palatinate had been Center Party politicians.[11] Especially striking in the Palatinate was the evidence of clerical involvement in Catholic politics. As he had during the war years, Catholic priest and former head of the Palatinate Center Party Johannes Finck argued that the era of the old parties, including an exclusively Catholic party, was over.[12] Finck enjoyed critical support from Gustav Wolff, a fellow former Palatinate Center Party leader who had conducted wartime discussions concerning a Christian Democratic Party.[13] Wolff and Finck by no means enjoyed universal support, however; Catholics determined to refound the Center Party were led by, among others, Finck's brother, Albert, former Rhenish Center Party secretary.

Indeed, support for the Christian Democratic initiative in the Palatinate was generally slow to develop. The majority of former Zentrum and BVP members (half of the Palatine had previously belonged to Bavaria) argued that an interconfessional party should retain the name Zentrum; only a minority, led by representatives from Landau, sought to organize in an avowedly interconfessional way.[14] After an October 1945 meeting with Adam Stegerwald, Wolff redoubled his efforts to spread the union message throughout the Palatinate.[15] In January 1946, following meetings with Catholic clergymen, Wolff and nine other men applied for permission to found a Christian Democratic Union.[16]

That influential members of the Catholic clergy aided in the interconfessional cause was notable in light of Wolf's estimate that some 90 percent of the Palatinate clergy opposed the founding of a Christian Democratic party.[17] Though this figure was surely high, the clergy was clearly divided; when the decision to organize a Christian Democratic party was made, it resulted in large part from the intervention of clerical leaders. In the Trier area, for example, Bishop Bornewasser played a key role in catalyzing the organization of a Christian Democratic Party,[18] while in Mainz the CSVP (soon renamed the CDU) would be founded in January 1946 after a conference of Catholic clergy and laypeople directed by the bishop of Mainz, Albert Stohr, former Hessian Center Party representative, and Lorenz Diehl, former general secretary of the Hessian Center Party.[19] Consistent with other patterns of Christian Democratic organization, priority was laid on encouraging the participation of deeply religious Protestants—specifically Protestant clergy and former members of the Confessing Church and CSVD.[20]

The American Zone

Party foundings in the American zone displayed notable parallels to those in the French and British zones, though occupying policies differed and Bavaria pursued a distinctive path. Marked initially by the JCS 1067 directive and a practice of favoring traditional elites, the American occupation policies soon proved themselves less stringent than those of the other occupiers.[21] General Lucius D. Clay, the American deputy military governor, favored instilling democracy through local self-government and electoral politics proceeded especially rapidly in 1946.[22] American officers were generally well disposed to the creation of a Christian party and their encouragement of CDU requests for party authorization provoked complaints from other parties about American favoritism.[23]

The development of Christian Democracy in the American zone was determined decisively by the zone's inclusion of Bavaria. With the important exception of Adam Stegerwald, Bavarian party organizers maintained little contact with Christian Democratic party founders in the rest of Germany.[24] Based on its unique Catholic Teilkultur and personnel networks from the BVP, Bavarian Christian Democracy evolved into a separate party organ with its own political platform. Symbolically, the party's name (initially devised by Stegerwald) would resist standardization.

The CSU's development was determined above all by an internal rivalry between Josef Müller and Alois Hundhammer. While Müller echoed the CDU's rhetoric of interconfessionalism, he was strongly opposed by the cleric Hundhammer, who advocated a particularist, Bavarian, Catholic CSU, and Fritz Schäffer, the last BVP chair, both of whom were Nazi political prisoners. Müller ultimately lost the political battle; although he maintained his own power base within the union through the occupation years, an emphasis on Bavarian autonomy with little priority on cooperating with Protestants would clearly dictate early CSU politics.[25]

In the rest of the zone, the groups to organize most quickly were led by former members of the Center Party and Christian Trade Unions. In Karlsruhe, former Zentrum politicians joined a Confessing Church representative and the erstwhile head of Baden's CSVD to found a party in mid-August 1945. A Christian Social Union was organized in Heidelberg in early November after clergy of both confessions urged the abandonment of the Center Party. In Mannheim, reflecting the traditional strength of liberalism in northern Baden and Württemberg, the CDU attracted a significant number of former DDP politicians, although the initiative for the early October founding lay with a Center Party veteran. In Stuttgart, prominent Zentrum men, led by Josef André and

Felix Walter, founded the CSVP together with former CSVD chair Paul Bausch and former CSVD chair and Confessing Church member Wilhelm Simp-fendörfer. As was the case in both Mannheim and Karlsruhe, organizers in Stuttgart were well aware of the initiatives taken in the North Rhineland and Berlin.[26]

In Hesse, Christian Democracy both adhered to traditional patterns and assumed a singular character. Although Wiesbaden and Darmstadt, the latter under the leadership of Maria Sevenich and former Zentrum member Heinrich von Brentano, saw the development of Christian Democratic groupings,[27] the most important founding in Hesse took place in Frankfurt, where Catholic in-tellectuals associated with the Weimar-era *Rhein-Mainische Volkszeitung* wrote to the military government in English on September 15, 1945, that a Christian Democratic party had been organized by "20 persons of the former *Zentrumspartei,* the former *Demokratischen Partei* and members of the pro-fessing Church further [*sic*] Roman Catholic as well as Protestant men who did not belong to one of the above mentioned parties."[28] Leading among the Frank-furt Christian Democratic organizers were Walter Dirks and Eugen Kogon, who by early 1946 would largely abandon party work to devote themselves to publishing the *Frankfurter Hefte.*[29] The gathering in Frankfurt was also charac-terized by significant participation of active anti-Nazi figures, including—in addition to Dirks and Kogon—those from Catholic People's Work (Katholische Volksarbeit) and Werner Hilpert, former head of Saxony's Center Party.[30]

The Soviet Zone

In the Soviet zone, former Christian Trade Unionists led by Jakob Kaiser orga-nized what would become, after the Rhenish-Westphalian organization, the major center of early CDU political activity.[31] The strength of the trade union network was especially obvious in the absence of a traditional Catholic Teilkul-tur; indeed, the overwhelmingly Protestant population of Berlin and the Soviet zone explains both the high representation of Protestants as well as the rela-tively limited involvement of Catholic clergy in the early Berlin CDU. In con-trast to the western zones, which by the end of the summer of 1945 had sepa-rated administratively their military government from their tactical troops, the Red Army continued to play a prominent role in the occupation. Initially seem-ingly supportive of free party organization—the Soviet zone was the first to permit German political activity—the Soviets soon revealed their true under-standing of antifascism and democracy. Following the Red Army, three groups of German Communist Party exiles arrived in Berlin armed with plans for the political organization of the Soviet zone.[32]

Berlin Christian Democrats too drew directly on Nazi-era connections to organize politically. Despite the absence of a Catholic milieu, former Center Party members and Catholic clergymen did participate in the party's organization. At the same time, former Confessing Church members, including Ferdinand Friedensburg and Theodor Steltzer, the latter of whom also belonged to the Kreisau circle and ecumenical Michaelsbruderschaft, joined early discussions concerning a Christian Democratic party. The Soviets regarded Protestant clerical support for Christian Democracy throughout the Soviet zone as decisive.[33] Most striking, however, was the influence of men and women of the Christian Trade Unions. As those who had survived the war in the Berlin area located their colleagues, discussions about founding a Christian Democratic Party, begun during the Nazi years, recommenced.[34] Although he played an active role in founding the Berlin CDU, Jakob Kaiser's initial interest lay in establishing a broad-based labor union. Motivated by the experience of the trade unions under National Socialism, supporters of a politically and religiously independent unified labor union enjoyed clear support from the British and especially American occupation powers.[35] Founded in April 1947 in the British zone under the leadership of Hans Böckler, the German Trade Union Federation (Deutscher Gewerkschaftsbund [DGB]) was led by former members of the free unions. Although committed to attracting workers identified with the free, Christian, communist, and liberal labor traditions, the DGB failed to overcome many Catholics' skepticism, and few Catholics assumed leading positions.[36]

Indeed, in the Soviet zone, the unified trade union quickly came under Soviet influence, and Kaiser and other leading trade unionists such as Karl Arnold and Johannes Albers would soon prioritize party politics over labor involvement.[37] In his earliest efforts, Kaiser sought to found a workers' party on the model of the British Labour Party, though differences with Social Democrats convinced him of the project's futility.[38] Based on a program drafted by Andreas Hermes, former Center Party Prussian Landtag and Reichstag delegate, the Christian Democratic Union of Germany (Christlich-Demokratische Union Deutschlands [CDUD]) was founded in Berlin on June 26, 1945.[39] Within a year, the Soviet zone CDUD was second only to the Rhenish-Westphalian CDU in size while claiming an unusually high proportion of women, Protestants, farmers, and workers;[40] a striking number of CDUD founders had also actively opposed the Nazis. Like Hermes, for example, Steltzer had survived because the Nazis failed to enact his death sentence before war's end. A significant group of other party founders had spent time in prison, a concentration camp, or—like Jakob Kaiser and Elfriede Nebgen—in hiding.[41]

In part as a consequence of its members' stature—no other early CDU organization claimed as many politically prominent founders—the influence of the CDUD quickly extended beyond the former capital.[42] By the late summer of 1945, Christian Democratic parties had been founded in Sachsen, Sachsen-Anhalt, Thuringia, Mecklenburg, and Mecklenburg-Vorpommern.[43] As Christian Democracy spread throughout the Soviet zone, there was clear evidence of Catholic dominance and ecclesiastical involvement.[44] In Chemnitz, for example, priest Ludwig Kirsch, former Saxon Center Party chair and Sachsenburg concentration camp inmate, gathered former members of the Center Party and CSVD to found the Christian People's Party (Christliche Volkspartei [CVP]).[45]

While Christian Democracy took root throughout the eastern occupation zone, the influence of Berlin events was apparent beyond the Soviet zone in cities as distant as Mannheim, Karlsruhe, Stuttgart, and Hanover. Otto Lenz, a former Center Party politician sentenced to four years' imprisonment by the Nazis, played an especially crucial role in facilitating communication as he traveled from the western zones to Berlin; there he met with Hermes, Kaiser, and Ernst Lemmer, former DDP and DStP man, all now denied permission to leave the Soviet zone after Steltzer failed to return from Schleswig-Holstein.[46] In addition to Lenz, former Christian Trade Unionists in western Germany used clergy members to communicate with Kaiser and others in Berlin.[47]

The relationship of Berlin to western German Christian Democrats was a central concern of Christian Democracy from the outset. Western colleagues beseeched Kaiser to visit,[48] and Kaiser for his part expressed the hope that the Berlin and Rhenish parties would pursue similar paths.[49] At the founding of the Westphalian CDU in Bochum, Lensing reported hearing of the "advanced" party organization in Berlin. Despite the two groups' differing names, he stressed that "they want exactly what we do, and the Berliners are of the same opinion as the Westphalians and the Rhinelanders, that this political movement must not remain limited to individual areas, but must develop into a great national party."[50]

Christian Democratic parties in the western and eastern zones did not develop in parallel, however. Hearing the first reports of the Berlin founding in August 1945, some Cologne Christian Democrats "perceived it as an eastern zone affair."[51] Not only did the leading western groups organize for the most part independently of Berlin, but they resented enormously Berlin's self-designation as the country's leading CDU branch. In their view, the addition of "of Germany" at the end of the Berlin party name—so that it read the Christian

Democratic Union of Germany[52]—reflected a Berlin overestimation that the Berlin program served the entire country.[53] Furthermore, Christian Democrats in western Germany suspected the Berlin organization of collaboration with the Soviet occupation forces; the Cologne CDU, for example, initially resisted using the name *Union* out of fear of association with a potentially Soviet-compromised Berlin CDU.[54]

This concern was not completely unfounded. From its earliest days, the CDUD confronted considerable restrictions on its political activity. Christian Democratic leaders initially adopted a cooperative stance, and in late July 1945 Hermes authorized the CDUD to join the antifascist bloc.[55] But the Soviets disfavored the party's connections to Christian churches, and by October 1945 Soviet harassment of CDUD deputy chair Walther Schreiber made clear that public criticism of Soviet policies would not be allowed.[56] Conflict between the Soviet authorities and CDUD leaders came to a head on December 19, 1945, when the Soviets removed Schreiber and Hermes as CDUD chairs and returned Hermes's sole surviving son to a Soviet POW camp.[57]

The specific impetus for the crisis was land reform: On November 22, Hermes had refused to sign a "Help the New Farmers!" statement endorsed by the KPD, SPD, and Liberal Democratic Party of Germany (Liberal-Demokratische Partei Deutschlands [LDP]). Following Hermes's December 11 interview with Marshall Zukov and dismissal, the Soviets named Jakob Kaiser and Ernst Lemmer the new chairs of the CDUD.[58] Over the next two years, the Soviet crackdown on all non-Marxist parties would—by restricting the most basic of CDUD activities—influence profoundly the course of Christian Democracy across Germany.

Postwar Protestantism

While Berlin Christian Democrats sought to circumvent Soviet control and western German Catholics fought an internecine battle around the Zentrum tower, German Protestant pursuits constitute a separate chapter of early Christian Democratic history. The Protestant role in the organization of Christian Democracy was paradoxical: While Catholics trumpeted interconfessional cooperation, their preference for religious Protestants restricted the pool of potential recruits. For their part, Protestants demonstrated real reserve toward the new party and in some cases toward party politics in general. Deterred by the links between the former Center Party and the new CDU, Protestants joined the CDU in relatively small numbers.

This was especially true, not surprisingly, in Catholic-dominated areas, while in majority Protestant regions two patterns emerged. In northern Germany, where there was no real tradition of Center Party organization, the CDU was founded largely by practicing Protestants. But in confessionally mixed areas, including within Protestant enclaves in Catholic regions, Protestants showed little inclination to seize the initiative,[59] and Catholic influence remained disproportionate.[60] In general, wherever there remained discernable elements of the Center Party tradition, even committed Protestants wavered.[61]

In part, the lack of coherent Protestant participation in the early CDU was a function of Protestant heterogeneity. In contrast to Catholic Germany, the country's Protestant population was characterized by tremendous religious, cultural, and political variety. Most devout in Pietist areas in Württemberg and Reformed areas of the Rhineland, Protestants were predominantly Lutheran in Westphalia and Berlin-Brandenburg; like the Rhineland, Westphalia and Berlin-Brandenburg were organized under the united churches joining the Lutheran and Calvinist (Reform) traditions. At the same time, Protestant Germany was marked by relative distance from its churches, especially in the northern German regions, considered by some as being among the "most secularized" areas in Europe.[62] Politically, Protestants had supported—with the exception of the Catholic Center Party—the entire range of parties during the Weimar Republic, with only the National Socialists attracting a Protestant plurality.

For Protestants outside the Marxist milieu, the post–World War II world presented few political options. Both the DDP/DStP and especially the DVP had been largely discredited for their roles in the rise and rule of National Socialism. Liberals maintained arguably the weakest contacts of political camps throughout the Nazi years, and the FDP, which would ultimately attract primarily former DDP members and more secular liberals, was not founded until December 1948.[63] To an even greater degree, the pre-1933 conservative parties had been discredited by collaboration with the Nazis.[64] While conservatives, especially religious conservatives, recognized the need politically to begin anew,[65] their choices were limited by the Allied ban on parties of the far right.[66] The four powers not only forbade what they deemed overly conservative or nationalistic parties but screened individual members associated with authorized parties.[67]

More broadly, Protestant prospects had been weakened fundamentally by the postwar settlement and division of Germany. The Allied-sanctioned German-Polish border severed the East Elbian Junker population from its territorial power base, while in the Soviet zone the occupiers expropriated the Junker class and destroyed the Prussian state and army. Not only did German conservatism find itself deracinated, but, as would soon become apparent, the confessional equity of the future state of West Germany would impede Protestant political domination of religious politics or the country. For the first time in modern German history, Catholics would ascend to the political elite.

Organized Protestantism clearly needed to chart new political paths. In this effort, it would be led by its clergy. In a decisive turn away from long-established Protestant suspicion of party politics, church leaders at the August 1945 Treysa Church Conference called for active Protestant political engagement and a democratic Christian state.[68] Protestants' political decisions remained colored by their traditional suspicion of democracy, however, and many church leaders continued to prefer a Lutheran-inspired Protestant aristocratic state to an ecumenical democracy.[69] Indeed, two months after Treysa, church leaders rejected the option of supporting a specific party.[70] At the same time, tension between Lutherans and Reform Protestants reasserted itself, as conflicts within Protestant theology evident in 1934 discussions about the Barmen Declaration reemerged.[71] While the majority of Lutheran clergy generally favored the Christian Democratic movement, some former Confessing Church members identified with Karl Barth, who argued that all political doctrines, including Christian Democracy, were a "form of idolatry";[72] these more liberal Protestants ultimately would pursue an alliance with Social Democracy.[73]

In part because of these divisions, the Protestant clergy's relationship to the CDU never approximated that between the party and the Catholic clergy.[74] In 1945, however, in a reflection of the CDU's broad appeal to Germany's Christians, clear signs pointed toward Protestant clerical support for Christian Democracy.[75] While Treysa participants expressed discomfort with one party or program labeling itself "Christian" to the exclusion of others, they praised "efforts to resolve political differences between Protestantism and Catholicism"; they also commended Catholic priests and laity for supporting an interconfessional rather than Catholic party.[76] Despite misgivings among some Protestant churchmen regarding clerical involvement in politics, the CDU attracted numerous Protestant ministers, including those who had never before been politically active.[77]

Although the CDU ultimately won the votes of the majority of Protestant senior clergy, including former Confessing Church member Otto Dibelius, and enjoyed particular success among older ministers, the Protestant clergy for the most part adhered to a doctrine of political neutrality, with the state churches even discouraging party membership.[78] As a result, Christian Democrats complained repeatedly in the immediate postwar years about the Protestant clergy's public reserve vis-à-vis the CDU.[79] In March 1946, for example, one Catholic

Christian Democrat identified the lack of Protestant clerical support as the "core problem for the further development of the Union in Protestant provinces."[80] Throughout the occupation, Catholics dedicated a great deal of energy toward recruiting Protestant ministers. In the fall of 1945, both the Rhenish and Westphalian parties appointed liaisons to work on securing Protestant clergy support,[81] and over the coming years, the CDU continued its efforts to attract politically disinterested Protestant ministers.[82] As in their own milieu, Catholics regarded men of cloth as rainmakers; as they committed themselves to expanding Protestant participation, they prioritized converting pastors to their cause.

Protestants in the Early CDU

Soliciting Protestants was Christian Democrats' foremost concern after the party foundings on September 2, 1945 in Westphalia and the Rhineland; organizers regarded northern Germany as the next critical area for establishing the CDU. Of those who facilitated connections among the Rhenish, Westphalian, and northern German organizations, Friedrich Holzapfel, a former member of the DNVP and the Confessing Church who later described himself as a CDU "minister without portfolio," was the key figure. Referred to Josef Kannengießer by Prior Simon, with whom Holzapfel had cooperated in the resistance movement,[83] Holzapfel had recruited other influential Protestants, including Otto Boelitz and former CSVD and Confessing Church members Otto Rippel und Wilhelm Lindner.[84] Holzapfel would also persuade leading personalities such as Hans Schlange-Schöningen and Pastor Adolf Cillien to join the Christian Democratic movement. At the same time, Holzapfel was instrumental in preventing the establishment of a new liberal party in the Hamburg area.[85] When the CDU did take hold, the majority of the early party members was Catholic, with significant representation from the Confessing Church.[86]

Among those whom Holzapfel won to the Christian Democratic cause, Schlange-Schöningen was arguably the most influential.[87] A former Prussian Landtag and Reichstag DNVP representative, Schlange-Schöningen had helped raise funds for the NSDAP and was no stranger to enemies of the republic.[88] Schlange-Schöningen was also no quick convert to Christian Democracy; as late as mid-October 1945, he expressed doubts about the feasibility of interconfessional cooperation.[89] After Adam Stegerwald's death weakened the prospects for Schlange-Schöningen's plan to divide Germany into a Catholic, southern sphere of Christian Democratic influence and a northern, Protestant zone,[90] Schlange-Schöningen led a gathering in Plön in late October 1945 with the specific objective of forming a new Christian Democratic party;[91] soon, he would play a crucial role recruiting fellow expellees and DNVP members.[92]

In general, however, Protestants in northern Germany and the rural areas of northern Lower Saxony, Hesse, and Baden-Württemberg remained wary of political cooperation with Catholics.[93] They, like Protestants throughout Germany, expressed reservations about party politics in general and about the CDU's self-designation as a Christian party in particular.[94] Reflecting their continued distrust of the old Catholic party, one of the most decisive issues for Protestants was a symbolic one. According to Holzapfel, the new party could by no means retain the appellation *Zentrum:* "The name '*Zentrum*' would have been understood in Protestant circles as a capitulation to the Catholic side and would have had the effect of renewed fragmentation on the Protestant side."[95] In late November, well after he had chosen to align himself with the Christian Democrats, Schlange-Schöningen addressed his "devoted Protestant friends" who "cannot hide . . . a certain nervousness about cooperation with Catholics in general and now especially with former *Zentrum* circles." In a strong statement, Schlange-Schöningen identified himself as "a devoted Protestant Christian" who rejected all "allegations or fears that the Christian Democratic Union is a disguised *Zentrum,* that is, the old ultramontane party."[96] That language mattered on both sides of the confessional divide was clear in Konrad Adenauer's protest that former Center Party members found "insulting" Schlange-Schöningen's description of the old Center "as ultramontane."[97]

Overcoming such confessional prejudices and sensitivities was clearly a priority for both Catholic and Protestant Christian Democrats. At an early October 1945 meeting of the Christian Democratic provisional executive committee in Westphalian Hamm, Kannengießer acknowledged that "a certain reserve in Protestant circles still must be overcome."[98] In March 1946, a Bielefeld party member noted that, "The inhibitions within Protestant circles are shocking,"[99] while Otto Schmidt wrote to Adenauer that, "Up till now, both at home and abroad, we are still regarded as the offshoot of the old Center Party that is trying to recruit Protestant circles."[100] In an effort to win over their coreligionists, party Protestants repeatedly appealed to prominent CDU Protestants to deliver speeches in non-Catholic areas.[101] Holzapfel was invited numerous times throughout the fall of 1945 and into 1946 to address Protestants who "have not yet found the way to us."[102] In August 1946, for example, a Protestant minister wrote to request that Holzapfel deliver a speech in Bochum-Hövel, where "our Protestants are becoming somewhat discontented and regard the CDU as a purely Catholic affair."[103] A May 1946 gathering of

Protestant Rhenish and Westphalian Christian Democrats highlighted the importance of achieving greater Protestant influence within the CDU, especially on personnel decisions, to counter the impression that the CDU was nothing more than the successor party of the old Zentrum.[104]

The Challenge of Integrating Protestants

If Protestants were put off by the new party's Catholicism, Catholic Christian Democrats had their own concerns, particularly regarding their Protestant colleagues' relationship to National Socialism. Convinced of a close correlation between Protestantism and Nazism, Catholic Christian Democrats distinguished explicitly between the majority of Germany's Protestants and those sufficiently religious for the CDU.[105] As Jakob Kaiser argued, under the pressure of the oppressive regime, "Only what was tied to an inner worldview— let's say this openly—to Catholicism and *devout* evangelical Christianity was also tied politically to a moral law and offered inner resistance."[106] In particular, for CDU Catholics, Protestant membership in the Confessing Church or the CSVD represented not only sufficient proof of religiosity but a guarantee of opposition to National Socialism. If the focus on these groups required a denial of the very ambiguous personal and institutional histories of Confessing Church and CSVD members,[107] their appeal nonetheless represented a bedrock of early Catholic Christian Democracy.[108]

Despite CDU Catholics' early organizational and rhetorical emphasis on "non-Nazi" Protestant Christians, by no means had all pious Protestants belonged to the Confessing Church or CSVD. The DNVP, for example, provided a relatively large reservoir of potential CDU recruits, as between 1930 and 1932 it polled twice the support of the CSVD.[109] Consequently, the CDU would ultimately accommodate many Protestants associated with antirepublican parties, including the NSDAP.[110] Although the question of dealing with former antidemocrats, especially former members of the NSDAP—Protestant or Catholic—was not widely discussed in the early party, it did not go unaddressed, especially after competing parties began to attack individual Christian Democrats for their political pasts. CDU members did call for the prosecution of those who had committed crimes during the Nazi dictatorship,[111] and most Catholic party centers agreed that active Nazis should be excluded from postwar public life. At the same time, however, practically no one wanted to deny CDU membership to those who had been members of the NSDAP.[112]

In this regard, Lambert Lensing's remarks are of particular interest. As publisher of the Dortmund Center Party newspaper *Tremonia,* which appeared until the end of the war, Lensing was banned by British occupation authorities from publishing again until 1949.[113] At the founding of the Westphalian CDU, Lensing argued that one could neither build "a new world" based on hate nor permit the guilty to escape their due punishment. It was crucial, he maintained, that the CDU not allow "disguised National Socialists" to infiltrate CDU ranks, but it "would be a big mistake" to exclude those who had joined the NSDAP out of political naïveté or under financial pressure: "We will open our doors to these fellow citizens, as far as we are persuaded of their loyalty, and offer them a political home," Lensing opined, adding that such people could not assume leadership positions for a "fairly long time."[114]

If Lensing's acceptance of those who had supported Nazism was rooted in sympathy with his own past, he was not alone among early CDU Catholics in his problematic relationship to recent history. Adolf Süsterhenn, for example, as a Center Party member of the Cologne city parliament, had initially welcomed the National Socialists,[115] while Josef Beyerle, former Center Party Landtag delegate and Württemberg minister of justice, had been a member of the SS.[116] It was rumored that Josef Albers voluntarily joined the SS in 1934 and enjoyed the special protection of the *Gauleiter.*[117] In 1946, Gustav Wolff was sentenced to a one-year ban on professional activities for his involvement in the Third Reich,[118] while Adam Stegerwald's relationship to National Socialism has been the subject of considerable debate.[119] But because far more Catholic Christian Democrats in the immediate postwar era had opposed National Socialism than collaborated with it, the question had a different resonance for Protestants.

Indeed, Protestant Christian Democrats frequently revealed greater openness to accepting former members of the NSDAP.[120] Typical in this regard was Schlange-Schöningen, who was repeatedly called on to defend his relations with the NSDAP. Arguing that the CDU needed to distinguish among various groups of former Nazis "for reasons of justice and good political sense," Schlange-Schöningen insisted that the CDU accept the overwhelming majority of NSDAP members, including "idealists and decent patriots," such as soldiers and youth, and civil servants and white-collar workers forced into party membership against their will.[121] That Schlange-Schöningen enjoyed widespread support in his views was evident in the embrace of a sympathetic portrayal of the National Socialist past, including staunch opposition to denazification efforts, by the early Schleswig-Holstein CDU.[122]

For most early Christian Democrats, more pressing than the question of accepting former Nazis were the dilemmas posed by Protestants who had been members of the DNVP, DVP, and DDP. While Catholic Christian Democrats did occasionally object to the presence of former DNVP members in their ranks—in March 1946, for example, Josef Heinrich Engel wrote to Josef Kannengießer to complain about German Nationalists who "before '33 opposed democracy, who overthrew the Weimar Republic and helped Hitler with his comrades to power"[123]—for most CDU Catholics, the DNVP's close identification with the Protestant churches overcame any reservations.[124] In a November 1946 speech, Jakob Kaiser insisted that the fact that "conservative people" had "found their way to us" did nothing to diminish Christian Democracy's "progressive" character. "Conservative is not identical to reactionary, as it is so often, extremely superficially, shouted around about. A conservative attitude seeks to preserve values that have proven themselves worthy of preservation."[125] According to speakers' guidelines for the British zone CDU, former members of the DNVP had undergone "inner change."[126] As Hermann Pünder explained in July 1946, "If our ranks include members who earlier stood elsewhere and to the right, why not? No one needs to feel ashamed about still learning something in later years, and he certainly does not need to feel ashamed that in the twelve years Hitler taught him a blood-curdling object lesson."[127]

As a consequence of his prominence in both Weimar-era politics and the early CDU, Schlange-Schöningen attracted special attention from political opponents and the Allies. The same party training guidelines suggested that, should the CDU be reproached for accepting a personality from the conservative camp, in particular Schlange-Schöningen, "Then you answer that he left the German Nationalists long before 1933 due to Hugenberg's course."[128] In December 1946, Adenauer urged Schlange-Schöningen to defend himself by legal means if necessary from attacks regarding his past launched by a Communist deputy in the North Rhine-Westphalian Landtag.[129] For his part, Schlange-Schöningen underscored his involvement in the events of July 20, 1944, insisting, "It is a wonder that I escaped the consequences. My friends, with whom I worked together closely, were hanged."[130]

In addition to Schlange-Schöningen, the legacy of Weimar-era activities created difficulties for Otto Boelitz, an erstwhile DVP member, and Friedrich Holzapfel, formerly of the DNVP. In both cases, members of the refounded Center Party called on Catholic CDU members to defend their new Protestant colleagues against charges of antidemocracy and anticlericalism.[131] As a result of his activities as Prussian minister for science, art, and adult education, Boelitz in particular was suspected both within and beyond the early CDU of anti-Catholicism,[132] and special party propaganda materials were designed to defend him, especially in areas of postwar Center Party strength.[133]

Boelitz's putative anticlericalism shed light on another front on which Protestant inclusion created difficulties for CDU Catholics—the integration of former liberals, especially from the DDP and DVP. The Catholic reaction to liberal elements in the party certainly struck a different chord from the welcome chorus for pious Protestants, especially in western Germany.[134] In describing the CDU's efforts to wean Protestants from their traditional devotion to nationalism, monarchism, and militarism, Walter Dirks stressed the greater difficulties liberal Protestants faced than their religious counterparts in beginning politically anew.[135] Only in limited cases, particularly in Berlin, did party propaganda single out Protestant liberals as founders of the CDU.[136] In a January 1946 speech, for example, Emil Dovifat expanded the political definition of *Christian* to "welcome *the* liberal in our ranks who translates his heightened individual freedom into attainment for the people at large,"[137] while Elfriede Nebgen stressed the anti-Nazi backgrounds of "men from the domain of the former democratic party" now active in the CDUD.[138]

At the same time, liberals felt themselves compelled to defend their place in a Christian party. In July 1946, Ernst Lemmer explained that Germany's Christians had become "more democratic" since the end of the Weimar Republic, while the Democrats had become "more Christian."[139] The CDU welcomed enthusiastically, then, those who might not identify themselves in the first line as Christians but who "out of moral-humanitarian inclinations demand the return of politics to the order of moral laws": "So the liberal belongs to us, too, when he accommodates his personal freedom to higher moral responsibility and devotes utterly his dogmatic individualism to brotherly help for his fellow man."[140] Theophil Kaufmann, a fellow former DDP man, struck a similar note when, in answer to his own question, "Why is the Christian Union being opposed with such fervor?" he posited the "indescribably marvelous new idea of the absolute unity of Christian and *morally oriented people* without confessional or Church boundaries."[141]

In all of these ways, Protestants and Catholics justified the inclusion of those whose political pasts or principles posed troubling questions for their new alliance. For both Protestants and Catholics, the taint of the Third Reich could be expunged for those who had not committed a crime beyond securing party membership. If Protestants were more sympathetic to Nazi sympathizers, CDU Catholics, despite their clear preference for Protestants in the pastorate, CSVD, or Confessing Church, were hard put to deny membership to any Protestant who expressed interest. From the Catholic vantage point, individual cases could be defended; more broadly, contemporary religious devotion compensated for past political misjudgment.

Women in the Early CDU

Religious conviction also characterized another minority group within the party, women. Small in number and typically Catholic, unmarried, and educated, female CDU organizers were often experienced politicians who became important players in internal CDU politics. Though influential on a number of policy questions, early CDU women were, like female German politicians before 1933, particularly interested in questions of family and social policy. This was equally true for unmarried as for married women, the latter of whom regularly joined party activities with their husbands. Protestant female activity in the party's earliest days was even rarer than that of Catholic women; most of the active Protestant women participated in the Soviet zone, where Protestants constituted the overwhelming majority of the population.[142]

Three women stand out for their involvement in early Christian Democracy. The first, Christine Teusch, was representative of Catholic women in German politics. Born into a prominent Catholic family, Teusch, a schoolteacher, founded and led the first Women's Department of the Christian Trade Unions in Cologne while serving as a Center Party representative in the National Assembly and the Reichstag. Forcibly retired in 1936 from her teaching position and placed in "protective custody" in 1944, she played an active role in organizing the Rhenish CDU.[143] Like Teusch, Helene Weber was Catholic, a teacher, and a Center Party delegate in the National Assembly and Reichstag; she enjoyed close ties to the Adenauers after having taught Adenauer's wife before World War I.[144] After her dismissal from the Prussian state government in 1933, Weber performed private Catholic welfare activities for the duration of the Third Reich. Although devoted in 1945 to reorganizing the Professional Association of Catholic Female Welfare Workers, she quickly resumed her former prominence in Catholic politics.

A third prominent woman in the early CDU had a far less typical biography.[145] Among the most colorful figures in the young party, Maria Sevenich was also one of the few Christian Democratic women who routinely engaged topics beyond family and social policy.[146] A KPD member before 1933, Sevenich was condemned to death in absentia after she fled to France, where she renounced communism, returned to Catholicism, and was arrested by the Gestapo. After the war, she worked first to establish the CDU in Darmstadt and Hesse before moving to Lower Saxony. As Heinrich von Brentano later described, "She was intelligent and passionate, and in the beginning years, she accomplished an enormous amount."[147]

Well known for her rhetorical ability[148]—party advertisements heralded her as "Germany's best female speaker"[149]—and sharp criticism of the occupation powers, which inspired both her nickname, the CDU's "enfant terrible," and a short-lived party-enacted speaking ban in 1946,[150] Sevenich initially enjoyed an excellent relationship with Adenauer, with whom she often shared the stage at political rallies.[151] As a woman in her late thirties with a strong following among party youth,[152] Sevenich came into conflict with more than a few of her male colleagues.[153] After staging a hunger strike in October 1946 to draw attention to the occupying British food policies,[154] she and her husband would leave the party in 1948 in protest of its coalition and economic policies.

Bad Godesberg: Christian Democracy's First National Conference

Sevenich's debut in broader Christian Democratic politics took place at the CDU's first interzonal meeting. After overcoming considerable practical difficulties regarding lodgings and provisions as well as Rhenish resentment of Berlin leaders' dominance of the conference's organization, the First Reich Conference of the Christian Democratic Union took place on December 14–16, 1945, in Bad Godesberg, thirty kilometers from Cologne.[155] Sevenich, who delivered a speech, "The Union as God's Work in Service to the Cross," stood out for her rhetorical abilities and her sex but not for her religious affiliation.[156] Not only was the Bad Godesberg gathering—despite CDU women's pleas for female representation[157]—dominated by men, but it continued the general pattern of Catholic ascendancy over Christian Democracy. Despite Catholics' stated concerns with ensuring adequate Protestant representation, including that of Protestant clergy,[158] the proceedings were overseen almost entirely by former Center Party men from the Rhineland and Westphalia.[159]

Although the meeting was to be held in the Rhineland, Rhenish and Berlin party organizers had agreed that Andreas Hermes would direct the conference.[160] However, the crisis between the CDUD and the Soviets peaked in mid-December, and Hermes, like all other Berlin Christian Democrats, was denied permission to leave the Soviet zone.[161] While the French military authorities also forbade Christian Democratic politicians to participate, neither the Americans nor the British enforced their own statutes prohibiting interzonal gatherings, so the overwhelming majority of the representatives present came from the British and American zones.[162] When party leaders at Bad Godesberg organized a secretary's office for the British zone in Düsseldorf and less than one month later hosted the first meeting of the CDU British Zonal Committee in

Herford (selected because it was predominantly Protestant),[163] they made clear that Hermes's goal of anchoring the new party in Berlin would remain unfulfilled.[164] Indeed, the influence of Rhenish Catholics on the early CDU was dramatically evident in the adoption of the Cologne Guiding Principles as the basis of the first official Christian Democratic program.

The organizational momentum of the British zone CDU in early 1946 brought with it the party's first decisive leadership struggle. Appointed Oberbürgermeister of Cologne by the Americans, Konrad Adenauer was dismissed on October 6, 1945 by British brigadier John Barraclough for what Barraclough described as administrative incompetence.[165] Although officially forbidden to pursue political activity, Adenauer had from the early summer worked closely with early Christian Democrats, who proposed repeatedly that he assume a leadership position; on September 2, 1945, he was elected in absentia to the advisory council for the Rhenish Christian Democratic party.[166] Throughout the late summer and early fall of 1945, Adenauer corresponded with CDU supporters and clergymen, including Laurentius Siemer and Abbot Herwegen, about party matters.[167] The British ban, which Adenauer maintained pertained only to the governing district of Cologne, was lifted entirely on December 13, 1945, the day before the Bad Godesberg conference began.[168] Reflecting the influence of Rhenish leaders within the British zone as well as Adenauer's political proficiency, the seventy-year-old Rhinelander was soon elected chair of both the Rhenish and British zone CDU.[169]

As a Cologne Center Party leader and devout Catholic, Adenauer both revealed and reinforced the prominence of Rhenish Catholics in the early CDU. Better known in the Weimar years as a municipal rather than national politician, Adenauer had nonetheless supported the Cologne line and, as was evident at the Katholikentag in 1922, the project of interconfessionalism. After refusing, as chair of the Prussian State Council, to sanction the Nazi dissolution of the Prussian Landtag (and after replacing the Nazi flag on the Deutzer suspension bridge with a Cologne city flag for Hitler's February 1933 visit), Adenauer was banished from office on March 13, 1933.[170] Feeling abandoned both by Center Party colleagues and by the Protestant politicians with whom he had hoped to forge common cause,[171] Adenauer fled to the Benedictine abbey Maria Laach before ultimately settling in the Rhenish village of Rhöndorf.[172] Although he rebuffed entreaties from fellow former Center Party members, including Jakob Kaiser, to join resistance activities,[173] Adenauer and his wife, a Catholic convert from Protestantism, would be arrested in 1944. After divulging her husband's hiding place under Gestapo interrogation, Gussie Adenauer attempted suicide; a resulting illness likely led to her 1948 death.[174]

As Adenauer asserted his authority over the CDU's future direction and came, more than any other individual, to symbolize Christian Democracy at home and abroad, his leadership of the new party attested to the CDU's deep roots in the Catholic Teilkultur. As the CDU worked to consolidate its organizational initiatives, recruiting Protestants remained essential. In keeping with past patterns of interconfessionalism, Protestants who embraced Catholic interconfessional initiatives were generally middle-class and self-consciously religious. Even as the Catholic command over early Christian Democracy remained authoritative, Protestant contributions would be decisive as the CDU turned to its next major challenge, laying the ideological foundations of Christian Democracy.

CHAPTER 4

Secularism, Materialism, and Rechristianization: The Construction of a Christian Democratic Ideology

The legacy of the prewar Center Party determined not only the organization and personnel of the CDU but also the party's programmatic development. If Protestants of varying political backgrounds and religious views played instrumental roles, the party's ideological formation was clearly dominated by Cologne line Catholics. Despite the failure of Bachem's, Brauns's, and Stegerwald's initiatives, the Center Party's attempts before 1933 to level the Catholic Turm had posited a link between Catholic political reform and interconfessionalism. If ever an opportunity for reinvention presented itself, Germany in 1945 was it.[1]

A salvific call to Christian cooperation hardly sufficed as a political program, however. In the same way the party's organization revealed profound intra-Christian suspicion, the construction of a Christian Democratic ideology would lay bare the legacy of centuries of confessional division. The legitimacy of German Christian Democracy rested not simply on the public association of Catholics and Protestants but on the party's ability to establish consensus on the broader meaning of Christian Democracy. Only after forging an intact ideological alliance would former Center Party members and Protestants realize their long-standing goal of pan-Christian politics. That a Christian political ideology emerged from the shadows of the Third Reich reflects not only the dynamics of early interconfessional politics but also the conditions of occupied Germany. This was especially true as Germans began to take stock of the rise and fall of Hitler. German history figured prominently in early Christian Democracy, both as a frame for the future and source of ideological inspiration.

National Socialism as Materialism

Under Allied control, CDU organizers had little alternative but to articulate their vision of Christian Democracy in legally permissible ways. In light of their political impotence, early Christian Democrats focused less on detailed policy prescriptions than larger, abstract questions regarding Germany's future and dramatic past. Like most public discourse in occupied Germany regarding National Socialism, the CDU contribution was framed in theoretical, even metaphysical, terms.[2] Allied censorship and widespread popular resentment of the lost war led to a virtually complete anti-Nazi consensus among German public figures; it is no surprise that a rejection of National Socialism introduced almost every CDU program and speech. Christian Democrats' focus on Nazism was not purely tactical, however. For both Protestants and Catholics in the CDU, the roots and patterns of Nazism underscored fundamental Christian commonalities. In this way, National Socialism served as an effective rhetorical and explanatory means through which Christian Democrats began to make common cause.[3]

In their programs, correspondence, and speeches in the early postwar era, CDU members consistently located Nazism in an epic battle between good and evil, specifically "between Christian and materialist convictions, between fear of God and idolization of man."[4] A stock phrase in conservative critiques of nineteenth- and early twentieth-century German society, materialism had been invoked by Christians as a catch-all locution to discredit everything they associated with Germany's modernization and secularization. In this Manichaean model of competing historical philosophies, Nazism was not simply Hitlerian dictatorship but an expression of centuries-old materialist forces hostile to Christianity. By leading these forces to their logical and ultimate conclusion, National Socialism had revealed the innate evil and impotence of the materialist age.[5]

As portrayed by the early CDU, that evil had taken a particular toll on the Christian community. While church leaders and CDU politicians by no means dominated public discourse in occupied Germany, they did contribute significantly to some of its strains, one of which—Germany's victimization—would emerge as a central trope in West German politics and life. The humiliation of defeat, the massive loss of human life, and the very real hardships of daily survival fostered a climate of hopelessness and despair in which Germans of almost all persuasions lamented losses "through no fault" of their own.[6] In staking out a specifically Christian place in this broader culture of self-concern, clergymen and politicians did not necessarily prescribe the rhetoric of average Catholics and Protestants, the majority of whom focused on their suffering as a result of bombings, evacuations, and other war-related tribulations. But by emphasizing a distinctive configuration of German adversity that stressed Christian persecution at the hands of Nazi leaders, devout Christian leaders reinforced a broader understanding of Germans as victims.[7]

Potent already during the late war years, when Catholic clerics cast the Allied advance as a final battle between salvation and rejection,[8] the Christian portrayal of the Third Reich as apocalyptic confrontation between "materialist heathens" and "Germany's true Christians" had several implications.[9] First, because the roots of Nazi evil were ascribed to large-scale societal phenomena such as individualism, secularism, and industrialism, more detailed inquiries into how Nazism came to power were rendered moot; perpetrators merged with anti-Christian materialists, and the question of who bore guilt for Nazi crimes lost any and all specificity.[10] Second, although Germans were apparently its ultimate victims, materialism was by no means a German-specific condition; as a plague on all of Christian Europe, it could have induced Nazism anywhere.[11] In the words of Karl Arnold, "Hitler was no typical and exclusively German phenomenon; he was rather the personification of the destructive spirits in Europe and in the world, and Germany was in this sense only the local place on which the European boil burst."[12] That the materialist boil burst in Germany was in fact a product of German beneficence and leadership of Christendom:[13] According to Wilhelm Elfes, Germany had suffered Nazism "*for* other peoples" in order to immunize them against it.[14]

In part because Germans bore the burden of the materialist assault on Europe for their fellow Europeans, Germans paid little heed to their neighbors as victims. Christian Democrats overwhelmingly referred to their fellow Europeans only when laying blame for Nazism's rise. Christian elites joined other Germans in recounting their misery at the hands of a variety of groups, including the World War I victors who had imposed the unjust peace of Versailles; the foreign powers who had appeased Hitler; the Poles and Czechs who had expelled ethnic Germans; and last but not least the Allies, whose war and occupation policies were routinely condemned as more inhumane than Nazi crimes.[15]

Third, in the same way that the materialist paradigm elided non-German suffering, it invalidated Nazism's non-Christian victims. From Houston Stewart Chamberlain to Hermann Goedsche, the association of Jewish Europeans with materialism had a long lineage.[16] In Germany, as the Kulturkampf revitalized Catholic anti-Talmudism, conservative Catholics joined religious Protestants in associating Jews with liberalism and materialism;[17] well into the twentieth century, antisemites would link materialism to Jewish-influenced sexual immorality.[18] Christian Democrats' conspicuous silence surrounding the fate of Jews signaled more, then, than the antisemitism and racism still so potent in occupied Germany:[19] By interpreting Nazism as the product of materialist forces committed for centuries to Christianity's subversion, Christian Democrats reserved the category of victim exclusively for Christians and by extension suggested a perverse link between Jews and their persecutors.

As a result, Christian Democrats enabled Germans to discuss the horrors of Nazism with no reference to the enslavement of fellow Europeans, the waging of racial war, or the Holocaust.[20] Indeed, it is striking how rarely Christian elites in occupied Germany touched on Jewish genocide in private correspondence, speeches, or party gatherings such as the December 1945 Bad Godesberg conference.[21] When Christian Democrats did mention the Final Solution, it was generally in defensive or misleading terms. In August 1945, for example, in describing the "events in the German concentration camps that have in the meantime become public," arousing "global outrage," Adam Stegerwald insisted that it was "predominantly foreigners who were affected by the enormous mass death in the concentration camps."[22] As one of the few party publications in occupied Germany to acknowledge Jewish death,[23] the Frankfurt CDU program nonetheless recognized first the suffering of "the large number of Germans" before listing, in descending order, "fighters of true democratic convictions, Protestant and Catholic Christians, countless Jewish fellow citizens, men and women from all levels of society."[24] This predisposition found its echo, furthermore, in party members' occasional repetitions of prewar anti-Jewish stereotypes or resentments, especially on the part of Protestants.[25]

Moreover, Christian Democrats rarely noted that a Christian political party would nominally exclude Jewish members; when mention of Jewish participation in the CDU was made, it was self-conscious.[26] Berlin party founders, for example, after listing a veterinarian, Dr. Kantorowicz, as a Jewish founding member,[27] noted, "It is no secret that Jewish fellow citizens are taking quite an active interest in the work of the Union."[28] And while early Christian Democrats reported that a handful of Jewish Germans joined their party, at least two prominent CDU Protestants had been persecuted as Jews by the Nazis,[29] and it is possible that party members counted as Jewish were in fact Christians of Jewish descent.[30] Notably, it was not until the mid-1960s that the CDU would decree officially that party members need not belong to a Christian church (although Christian church membership was still required for Bundestag candidates).[31]

In a revealing reflection of the fluid lines between religion and politics in occupation Germany, Protestant and Catholic clergymen articulated the same interpretation of Nazism as did the early CDU.[32] With the sole exception of the 1948 Katholikentag, the German Catholic leadership eschewed acknowledgment of guilt for the Holocaust.[33] Associating Jews with vengeance, communism, and scurrilousness, Cardinal Aloisius Muench, Catholic liaison between the U.S. Office of Military Government and the German Catholic Church (and later Vatican nuncio to Germany), portrayed Catholics as the leading victims of both the Third Reich and occupying Allies.[34] In a January 1946 pastoral letter, the bishop of Münster, Clemens August Graf von Galen, well known in and outside Germany for his opposition to the Nazis' euthanasia program,[35] described the Nazi dictatorship as among the "most malicious and heaviest" crosses German Catholics had to bear.[36] If others felt themselves victimized by recent events, von Galen and fellow clergymen asserted, they certainly had not suffered as much as had Christian Germans over the past twelve years:[37] "We do not deserve to be considered and handled as guilty parties," said von Galen in October 1945. "We suffered more under the Nazis than others."[38]

While Germany's Catholic bishops, despite early internal differences, soon adhered to this interpretation of National Socialism and its victims without public exception,[39] the Protestant clergy's discussion of Christianity's relationship to Nazism, in part reflecting the faiths' different theologies concerning original sin, was more differentiated.[40] In clear contrast to their Catholic colleagues, Protestant leaders used the word *guilt* in postwar pronouncements, most famously in the October 1945 Stuttgart Declaration, in which the Council of the EKD indicted all Protestants for "not having professed our faith more courageously, not having prayed more sincerely, not having believed more joyously, and not having loved more ardently."[41] Although exceptional, particularly in retrospect, for its clear acceptance of blame, the Stuttgart Declaration's statement of guilt was never intended to have direct political consequences.[42] In referring to Christians' suffering under the Nazis, the Stuttgart Declaration echoed other postwar EKD statements in its stress on Christian suffering and silence about the Jews.[43]

Indeed, the declaration, in large part the work of Martin Niemöller and his closest cohorts, was rejected by the broader German Protestant public and the majority of the church council's members.[44] Already evident at Treysa, intra-Protestant divisions on interpreting the past would not be bridged. Arguing that guilt could be absolved only through individual confession, conservative Lutheran Protestants invoked Luther's doctrine of two kingdoms to stress their spiritual, not political, defiance of Hitler. Their interpretation would outweigh, although not elide, that of the minority Dahlemites, who in August 1947 would charge Lutheran doctrine with having prevented Protestants from effectively resisting Nazism.[45] Indeed, many Protestants rejected any public acknowledgment of German guilt. Hans Schlange-Schöningen, for example, argued that it was incumbent on Germans, especially in the face of the Allies' "war psychosis," to remember the difficult circumstances of the Nazi years:[46] "This guilt question is so often discussed now. Perhaps, gentlemen, from Germans themselves far too often. That which took place in the last twelve years is so clear to the world that we need no informers in Germany, who make us look ridiculous in front of foreigners. There is also a dignity in disaster."[47]

If the Catholic hierarchy revealed less outward dissension than the Protestant leadership, a handful of prominent Catholics did articulate a more critical view of Christianity's relationship to National Socialism. In contrast to the overwhelming majority of CDU members, who rejected the notion of collective guilt,[48] anti-Nazi priest Carl Klinkhammer argued in *Neues Abendland* that although Germans did not suffer from collective guilt, Christians—in particular clerics who had preached obedience to state authority—needed to atone.[49] Catholics associated with the newspaper *Ende und Anfang* also criticized what they saw as Catholicism's affinity for corporative-authoritarian states, citing Franco, Mussolini, and Hitler. More prominently, Walter Dirks and Eugen Kogon in the *Frankfurter Hefte* called on the church to acknowledge Catholic guilt while criticizing Germans for ignoring Jewish suffering.[50]

Among the few prominent Catholics to recognize the legitimacy of the denazification proceedings and the Nuremberg war crimes trials,[51] Dirks and Kogon were joined by Jakob Kaiser, who credited the Nuremburg trials with making public Nazi crimes and added that "the occupied powers brought not the hunger, but food. Hitler's crimes brought us the hunger."[52] While Dirks's, Kogon's, and Kaiser's were minority public voices within German Catholicism, others expressed their criticisms privately.[53] In February 1946, Konrad Adenauer complained to Catholic Pastor Bernhard Custodis that "the German people and the bishops and the clergy bear considerable guilt for the occurrences in the concentration camps." That the bishops failed to unite in protest of Nazi crimes could not now be excused, Adenauer added, so it was best to keep silent about the entire matter.[54]

Catholic and Protestant religious elites' designation of Christians as Nazism's primary victims helps to explain how a Christian victim identity fit within the larger Christian worldview in the late 1940s, a worldview that—with the founding of the CDU—soon found expression in politics.[55] In a party characterized by members' religiosity, the equation of *Christian* with *victim* represented more than political propaganda: As one element of a larger antimaterialist Christian Democratic ideology, the rendering of Christian victimhood posited an important foundation of the political consensus on which the party was established. This was especially the case because the CDU did not imagine that Christians had suffered passively under Hitler's oppression. Instead, by portraying Christians as both Nazism's innocent victims and its valiant resisters, Christian Democrats made a direct claim on the moral authority of the postwar nation.

Christians as Resisters: The Kirchenkampf

The assertion that Christians had led the German resistance to Hitler and his henchmen was a common one in occupied Germany. Catholic religious leaders paid tribute to bishops who, "from the outset, seriously warned of the false teachings and errors of National Socialism"[56] as well as to clergymen imprisoned and killed during the Third Reich.[57] Christian Democrats joined in heralding Catholics' "glorious struggle" against Nazism to protect their own and especially their children's religious beliefs.[58] CDU Protestants, for their part, singled out the Confessing Church and the CSVD as exemplars of resistance. The Confessing Church, according to Hans Ludwig von Arnim, "bore the major burden of the struggle, the attack, as well as of the defense as the first organized enemy of National Socialism and its totalitarian demands,"[59] while the CSVD, according to Paul Bausch, "had, in the years between 1930 and 1933, been in the vanguard of the defensive battle against National Socialism."[60]

If focused on their own confessional records of Nazi resistance, Christian Democrats nonetheless spoke frequently of a larger Christian opposition to the Third Reich. National Socialism, according to Jakob Kaiser, endeavored to eliminate every strain of Christian influence from public life because it rightly identified Christianity as "the strongest counterweight against all aberrations and exaggerations of political extremes."[61] Writing in June 1946, Christian Democrats in Lower Saxony maintained that Christians had consistently opposed the Third Reich for its "disavowal of Christian moral law." It was therefore "no coincidence . . . when National Socialism, very early on, recognized its most powerful internal enemy in the faithful of both confessions, and called in its elite organization, the SS, against this enemy."[62]

The notion that National Socialism found in the "community of Christians"—Protestant and Catholic—its "most serious adversary"[63] soon found expression in the postwar trope of the Kirchenkampf.[64] Initially understood to connote the battle between Hitler and the Protestant churches,[65] the Kirchenkampf—adapted to signify a broader struggle between the Christian churches and the Nazis—came to represent in Christian Democratic discourse the dawn of interconfessionalism. According to Josef Kannengießer in a political pamphlet published in 1946, "In its annihilatory determination, Nazism made no distinction between Protestant and Catholic Christianity. It offered sugar instead of a lash first to one confession, then the other, in order to prevent the Christian confessions from forging a common defense. It wanted, however, to eradicate both. Christians clearly recognized this danger; they looked for help. But one hope after the other vanished. In their distress, they fled to God. This flight to God . . . was the lifeline of devout Christians of all confessions. It was the awakening to a new way of thinking. The survivors divided by belief met each other in trust in God and recognized one another as brothers. A centuries-old barrier was demolished. . . . This spiritual structural change led in the political arena to the hour of birth."[66]

Striking for its religious language and imagery, Kannengießer's Christian Kirchenkampf paradigm was echoed in numerous Christian Democratic statements.[67] In a November 1945 party program, for example, Bockum-Hövel Christian Democrats emphasized how, after "National Socialism combated both confessions with the same vileness, violence, and brutality . . . [t]he pain linked both confessions more tightly to each other; we have learned together from this ordeal."[68] According to an early Swabian party program, Christians "drew closer together" under the persecutions of the Third Reich. "They listened to each other, discovered numerous common interests, and saw above all that the causes of the unspeakable suffering that has come over us are to be sought in the drift from God."[69]

At the center of the Kirchenkampf stood necessarily National Socialism; only the experience of the Hitler dictatorship, according to CDU Catholics, had bridged the confessional divide. A cofounder of Christian Democracy in Berlin, Elfriede Nebgen, explained how, after the "misfortune" and "hate" of Hitler had overwhelmed both churches and Germany, religious and political leaders first realized the political importance of overcoming "the unholy consequences of the division of faiths."[70] As party leader Hermann Pünder stated succinctly in July 1946, "Hitler showed us where the common enemy of all Christians stands."[71]

Christian Democrats believed it was incumbent on them to realize this historic opportunity after such a breakthrough in confessional relations. As Lambert Lensing exhorted founding members of the Westphalian CDU, "Should the experience of the last twelve years already, a few months after the end of National Socialism, be forgotten again? Or should it not encourage us to make the attempt in politics to work together in one party as Christians according to Christian principles?"[72] Karl Zimmermann, a Cologne CDU organizer and first director of the CDU in North Rhineland, echoed this point: Because Catholics and Protestants had "suffered and fought together," it was now the "order of the hour" to establish together "a new Germany on the foundation of Christianity and democracy. In the twelve years of struggle and of persecution, a meeting of both confessions took place, which now in the era of peace must bear fruit." Otherwise, Zimmermann concluded, twelve years of suffering would have been in vain.[73]

The importance of this Christian "community of resistance"[74] to ending the four-century "nightmare" of confessional conflict represented a constituent element of Protestant CDU discourse as well.[75] According to Robert Lehr, a participant in interconfessional anti-Nazi discussions in wartime Düsseldorf, the cooperation of "the two big confessions everywhere in the German *Vaterland*" represented an indisputable "lesson of the past twelve years" and "one of the few rays of hope" in a devastated Germany.[76] Defending his CDU membership against charges of political expediency, Theodor Steltzer declared, "It is not about a halfhearted marriage of intellect or sober tactical considerations. The years of struggle against Hitler have given rise to a new feeling of community."[77] Protestant Christian Democrats even joined party Catholics in describing Nazi persecution as a blessing in disguise. If Walter Dirks declared, "In truth, the era of persecution became our salvation,"[78] Wilhelm Simpfendörfer, former member of the Confessing Church and CSVD and a cofounder of the North Württemberg CDU, maintained, "When this fruit of unification in the affliction of the last years matured, we want to be grateful for this blessing of affliction."[79]

That the Kirchenkampf discourse was crucial to the construction of a Christian Democratic ideology does not, of course, render it historically valid. Yet the sense of a new era in Protestant-Catholic relations was palpable beyond the CDU, as both churches proclaimed the common Christian struggle against the Nazis a breakthrough in confessional relations.[80] This was especially evident in Bishop von Galen's stress on the Catholic and Confessing Churches' shared persecution and his connections with Protestant opponents of euthanasia[81] as well as in Confessing Church members' regard for the Catholic Church as a bulwark of Christian defense against Nazism.[82] Indeed, while some Confessing Church members recounted how interconfessional experiences in oppositional circles and prison had softened their anti-Catholicism,[83] others maintained that bonds forged with Catholics during years of "shared anguish and shared suffering" could lead a "thinking member" of the Confessing Church only to the CDU.[84]

Although Protestant-dominated—the 1928 papal encyclical *Mortalium Animos* banned Catholics from joining ecumenical organizations—the ecumenical movement in the pre–World War I and especially interwar years spawned a number of Protestant-Catholic initiatives, from the coordinated denunciation of Bolshevism to the Una Sancta Brotherhood in Germany. In some cases, these initiatives continued into the war and postwar years;[85] in occupied Germany there was a concerted impetus toward cooperation, including the organization of the Ecumenical Council and the Working Group of Christian Churches.[86] Moreover, despite competing efforts to attract parishioners,[87] the churches earned public acclaim by coordinating their postwar relief efforts[88] and such joint initiatives as a local radio station.[89]

While these steps point to heightened commitment to Christian unity in the immediate postwar period,[90] the extent of this irenic spirit is less clear.[91] Nazi efforts to forge an interconfessional Volksgemeinschaft failed to transform confessional relations, while postwar population dislocations exacerbated Protestant-Catholic tensions. If the war, in Andrew Chandler's words, altered the "theological imagination of both Protestantism and Catholicism," the effects of that alteration would take years to emerge.[92] As early as May 1946, Walter Dirks lamented cracks in the newfound Nazi-era Christian alliance,[93] and even Christian Democrats who embraced interconfessionalism stressed that political cooperation in no way implied cultural or religious assimilation.[94] As Konrad Adenauer explained in 1946, "Certainly none of us, neither Catholic nor Protestant, wants to mix up the two confessions. No, each church should lead its own life. But we want to be conscious in public life that we both stand on the same Christian soil."[95]

As sincere as these proclamations of a new era in Christian relations may have been, it is difficult to overlook this rhetoric's strategic value. Recalling how Protestants and Catholics prayed and suffered together in the face of Nazi persecution and Allied bombing clearly associated Christians with the "other Germany."[96] The invocation of the Kirchenkampf served not only to associate Christianity with resistance to Nazism but also to provide the CDU with a moral rationale and historical framework. With the collapse of National Socialism, Christian Democrats declared definitive Christian triumph over materialism. As the political expression of Christian Germany, Christian Democracy's mission was to implement the Christian victory.[97] "History proved that we were right," Josef Beyerle proclaimed at a February 1946 party rally in Ulm. "Christianity has remained victorious against those who had intended its destruction."[98]

Rechristianizing Germany

For both confessions after 1945, the conquest of materialism and secularization as the roots of Nazi evil implied that Germany's path to "salvation" led necessarily to Christianity.[99] The CDU was far from alone in this stance. In Germany as in other European countries, the secularism thesis and its program for the future boosted Christianity's prestige considerably.[100] If Catholic Church officials exuded a spirit of "ecclesiastical triumphalism" after the war,[101] the rechristianization discourse was widespread, from French Protestants to British Anglicans to especially the United States.[102] Not only did German agents of rechristianization meet with enthusiasm on the part of the Anglo-American Allies,[103] but such extragovernmental groups as the Moral Re-Armament Movement (MRA) enjoyed notable support from the Western Allies.[104]

The call to rechristianize Germany certainly constituted part of almost every early CDU publication and speech, as party members urged their fellow Germans to "join us for a German rebirth of the cultural, moral, and spiritual forces of true Christianity."[105] In their earliest program, drafted in June 1945, Cologne Christian Democrats pledged fealty to "a living God" and "his commandments" as the sole foundation for "social order and community,"[106] while a summer 1945 Düsseldorf program insisted the state draw its "inner direction and strength from the values of Christianity."[107] Underscoring that recovery depended "on the effectiveness of Christian forces in the Volk,"[108] the September 1945 Guiding Principles of the Christian Democratic Party in the Rhineland and Westphalia were echoed by party organizers in Südwürttemberg-Hohenzollern, who emphasized that "only when the Christian spirit provides the supporting pillars of the reconstruction" would Germans find "life is worth living once again."[109]

Supported by Protestant theologians and church leaders, CDU Protestants joined their Catholic counterparts in portraying the goal of postwar politics as the organization of a "Christian state"[110] governed in the "spirit of Christianity."[111] Implicit in political activity, explained Paul Bausch in 1945, was the responsibility to subordinate every aspect of political life to the strictures of God's Ten Commandments. Because the "severing of political life" from Christianity had produced Adolf Hitler, "our Volk now faces the decision of whether it will carry out the reconstruction of its political life in the fear of God or in opposition to God."[112] The program of christianizing Germany, in the words of Ulrich Steiner, implied "nothing less than the Christian revolution in all branches of human life. . . . We have been called to action, and when we are not ready to organize our lives afresh and fruitfully as revolutionaries of Christian conviction, then the revolutionaries of the devil—that is to say, the revolutionaries of the materialistic idea of utilitarianism—will do it for us."[113] According to Hans Schlange-Schöningen, "That which we understand as Christian is the great declaration of war against materialism."[114]

Confessionalized Understandings of the Christian State: The Catholic CDU

Despite the frequency and passion with which Protestants and Catholics called for rechristianization, early CDU references to Christianity were not matched by the degree of clarity in the term's usage. In the land of the Reformation, *Christian* had for centuries implied profoundly different things to Protestants and Catholics. As the two communities extolled Christian norms and values, their interpretation of *Christian* was decidedly confessional.[115] Some of this was surely a function of the new Christian Democrats' age. Because the Nazi dictatorship had prevented the democratic education of a generation of potential politicians, the majority of politicians after 1945 had been politically active before 1933. While their experiences may have contradicted or moderated certain staples of their worldviews, most CDU members returned in the postwar era to nineteenth-century norms in constructing a Christian Democratic ideology.[116]

Dissonance sounded not simply between CDU Protestants and Catholics. CDU Catholics were, like party Protestants, characterized by notable ideological and political differences; as political Catholicism before 1945 had well demonstrated, religious affinity hardly ensured political harmony. Jakob Kaiser, for example, would offer dissenting economic and foreign policies based on his understanding of Catholic teachings, while Catholic intellectuals such as Walter Dirks and Eugen Kogon quickly felt themselves alienated by the party's direction.[117] Nonetheless, Catholic Christian Democrats shared far more similar political backgrounds and societal views than did most party Protestants. In a testament to the survival of the Catholic Teilkultur, CDU Catholics continued to operate on the political and ideological assumptions characteristic of pre-1933 Catholic Germany.[118]

This continuity was above all else demonstrated by the Catholic equation of a Christian state with a Catholic rendering of antimaterialism. Because most if not all forms of modernity before World War I were perceived as anti-Catholic, Catholics had consistently associated modernism and materialism with such "modern" phenomena as liberalism, atheism, Judaism, Freemasonry, and Protestantism.[119] Despite their long-fought battles with romantic Catholics and integration into the modern German state and economy, even realist Catholics, including those who endorsed interconfessionalism during the Weimar years, rejected the materialist, individualist forces they associated with non-Catholic Germany.[120] Konrad Adenauer, for example, condemned materialism and its associated "illnesses" in his 1922 speech at the Katholikentag,[121] while Weimar-era Center Party publications accused materialism of animating the party's political opposition.[122] Antimaterialism as an axiom of Christian Democracy, then, necessarily posed fundamental questions about the CDU's interconfessionalism.

Catholic depictions of materialism's essence and origins made clear its confessional character. As secularization broadened in meaning from the specific confiscation of church holdings to connote cultural, political, or spiritual emancipation from illegitimate religious rule, it retained its strong anti-Catholic connotations.[123] For centuries, German Catholics had traced secularism, modernism, and rationalization to movements that placed the individual at the center of human development—the Renaissance, the Reformation, the Enlightenment, and the French Revolution. In the wake of World War I, Catholics blamed Germany's defeat on the Reformation, the Enlightenment, and the Protestant glorification of the nation and state.[124] Even into the 1950s, some Catholics linked Protestantism to secularism and its products, including the Enlightenment, rationalism, nationalism, and Prussianism.[125]

Indeed, after World War II, CDU Catholics adhered to a traditional Catholic critique of secularism and materialism with notable uniformity. Whereas some Catholic Christian Democrats continued to associate the Reformation with Germany's secular, materialist development,[126] many Catholics, with such notable exceptions as Eugen Kogon and Walter Dirks, rejected the Enlightenment:[127] Not only had the philosophes inspired the anti-Catholic French Revolution, but as one of the leading manifestations of the materialist phenomena, Enlightenment philosophy had paved the path to National Socialism.[128] As Theodor Scharmitzel explained in a March 1946 speech, "The world view of the Enlightenment [*Aufklärertums*], Free Thinkers [*Freidenkertums*], individualism, Marxism, communism, Bolshevism, nationalism, chauvinism, militarism, and, finally . . . National Socialism, a demonic mixture of all destructive systems, undermined step by step the Christian world of ideas." For post-Nazi Germany, Scharmitzel concluded, "The forces of recovery are rooted only in the uncompromising return from this false path, which led us into the abyss, to the supremacy of the Christian body of thought in the life of individuals and the state in all of its institutions and manifestations."[129]

Scharmitzel was hardly alone in defining the project of Christian Democracy as the reversal of the dominant trends of modern European history. While CDU Catholics typically characterized materialism as a centuries-old movement, their understanding of its nature was defined primarily by the preceding two hundred years. In particular, in a testament to the continuities of the Catholic milieu, Catholic Christian Democrats echoed Center Party founders by rejecting most vehemently the spirit and political developments of the post–French Revolutionary century. The nineteenth century, according to Heinrich Krone, former Center Party deputy general secretary and Reichstag delegate, had been the "great century" or the "high point" of the *bürgerliche* world," when, as invention followed invention, "modern man" took pride in his "achievements" and began to believe he had prevailed over "space and time." After the twentieth century had demonstrated "the enormous defects of the *bürgerliche* world,"[130] however, the man of the nineteenth century, who believed passionately in his freedom and searched desperately for the "truth," was forced to recognize that he had become not "more free but less free" as a result of his search.[131] Nazism had proven false the materialistic belief in progress apart from Christianity.[132]

Man's false assumption that he had overcome the limits of "space and time" was rooted in the nineteenth century's rise of natural sciences as well as modern Germans' faith in technology. Technological progress, according to the Catholic CDU, was falsely regarded not as a means of serving God but as a societal goal in and of itself; as National Socialism's technological accomplishments had demonstrated, technology could prosper only in a soulless world infused with materialist thinking.[133] The assumption, argued Maria Sevenich in her speech at the CDU conference in Bad Godesberg, that man could overcome the natural limits of human existence with the "discovery of steam and electricity" and "the mechanization of life" had served merely to "catapult" humans into a "fateful nothingness": In the postwar era, she explained, this "false orientation . . . calls forth in people the desire and understanding to unite themselves again in an orderly world that corresponds entirely to what God truly wants."[134]

In the same way that CDU Catholics continued to reject materialistic science pursued in a spirit of secularism, they also condemned the modern era's political and economic developments. In a clear echo of nineteenth-century Center Party rhetoric and based on natural law teachings regarding the sacred nature of the individual,[135] Catholics rejected modern society's emphasis on secular individualism to stress individuals' ties and responsibility to God and the community.[136] In particular, liberals' great optimism about human progress contradicted the Catholic belief in the necessity of moral laws to control human evil stemming from original sin. Indeed, the most serious flaw inherent in political liberalism, according to Emil Dovifat, was its "overestimation of human nature as essentially good, the overvaluing of reason and freedom, and the overemphasis of human attributes." National Socialism, Dovifat asserted, had demonstrated "where this autonomy leads."[137] Founded on the delusion of rationalism, Karl Arnold explained, liberal society was in danger of dying because it had "absorbed too much rationalistic matter as nourishment."[138]

Based on the same logic that rejected the liberal belief in individual initiative, CDU Catholics also condemned the philosophy of free-enterprise capitalism, which they regarded, especially in the second half of the nineteenth century, as fully intertwined with liberalism.[139] Of the moral directives contained in Catholic social teachings, one of the most important was respect for Christian brotherhood; devotion to the welfare of one's Christian equal proscribed financial profit at his or her expense. In an August 1946 speech, Karl Zimmermann asserted that "the capitalistic economy recognizes neither God and his commandments as the guiding principle for its actions, nor is man in his natural dignity and freedom the goal of its indefatigable activities."[140] Based on a similar pretext, Josef André drew a widely held conclusion for postwar Christian politics: "No one can found a new state on the obsolete and economically outmoded liberal-democratic body of thought. . . . [T]he era of Manchester liberalism is over."[141]

While CDU Catholics dismissed liberalism as "only just a memory of old times,"[142] they condemned simultaneously the modern age's other leading political ideology, Marxism. Rooted in the nineteenth century's "natural scientific, positivistic spirit," Marxist socialism had, according to Dovifat, developed as the logical response to liberalism's "unbridled capitalism."[143] "Liberalism and Marxism," insisted Konrad Adenauer, "are two sprouts from the same root, from the root which knows only this life . . . and in whose outlook the hereafter no longer plays a role."[144] Marxism had helped to spread the materialistic worldview of the nineteenth century by supporting Darwin and Nietzsche,[145] the latter of whom came in for special critique from postwar Catholics for his support of materialism, autonomism, and relativism.[146] As one of the various representations of "materialism in modern times," explained the Schwäbisch-Gmund party program, Marxism necessarily had helped pave "the way for National Socialism, in that it created the most important prerequisite for its reprehensible methods—namely, denying the existence of God."[147] Indeed, according to Maria Sevenich, "Hitler is the one great expression of the capitalistic, mistaken way of thinking, Marx was the other. Neither can overpower it; instead, they express it in a consistently horrible, exaggerated way."[148]

In rejecting both liberal capitalism and Marxism for their materialist understandings of the individual, Catholics petitioned after 1945 for a distinctly Catholic form of societal and economic organization. As codified in March 1946 in the British zone CDU's Neheim-Hüsten Program, the "rights and duties of the individual" above all else anchored the Catholic CDU's view of society.[149] Instead of a rationalistic, mechanistic view of the individual, Catholics embraced an understanding of the Christian individual responsible to God and the community.[150] Most prominently articulated by Max Scheler, Catholic teachings about the Christian individual or *Persönlichkeit* (personalism) found a central place in almost every CDU publication or speech.[151] For the CDU, the sanctity of the Persönlichkeit and the related concept of human dignity (*Würde des Menschen*) highlighted the philosophical differences between a political movement based on Christianity and one propelled by Germany's materialist forces.[152] As the first of the Cologne Guiding Principles made clear, "The spiritual dignity of the individual person will be recognized. The individual will be valued as a self-accountable person, not as a mere member of the Gemeinschaft."[153]

As the building blocks for the construction of a Christian Democratic ideology, the correlative notions of the Persönlichkeit and human dignity undergirded the CDU's understanding of the postwar order, beginning with democracy. Following the Nazi dictatorship and under Allied occupation, political Catholicism endured none of the pre-1933 Center Party battles concerning republicanism. But even as the CDU committed itself unequivocally to the principles of democratic governance, Catholics' condemnation of modern Europe's "materialistic interpretation of history and irreligious zeitgeist"[154] invalidated the political and philosophical foundations for democracy as practiced in pre-Nazi Germany. In this, Catholic Christian Democrats echoed the ambiguities of the larger Catholic post–World War II stance on democracy: Even as Pius XII offered an unprecedented papal endorsement of democracy, he reiterated his predecessors' fear of communism and liberal democracy's empowerment of the masses.[155]

In contrast to liberals and socialists, CDU Catholics adhered to a distinctly Catholic interpretation of the origins and nature of democracy that prioritized respect for "the freedom and dignity of the Persönlichkeit" and the individual's inherent "human dignity."[156] Indeed, in a self-affirming formula that designated the conditions for democracy as uniquely Christian before concluding that only Christianity could fulfill them, Catholic CDU members rejected decades of European politics as materialistic and therefore nondemocratic: "The Christian worldview alone guarantees justice, order, and moderation, value and freedom of the individual, and with that a true and genuine democracy. . . . We consider the high regard Christianity has for human dignity—for the value of every single individual—the foundation and guiding principle of our work in the political, economic, and cultural life of our Volk."[157]

In addition to protecting the Christian individual's rights and in keeping with Catholic social teachings, democracy also entailed for CDU Catholics the recognition of individuals' responsibilities to the Gemeinschaft. In a November 1945 speech, "The Spiritual Foundations of the Christian Democratic Union," Elfriede Nebgen located the foundation for democracy in the "obligation of the individual" to the community.[158] Stressing the integrality of the community to the Catholic conception of democracy, Adam Stegerwald wrote in August 1945, "Democracy is the battle against selfishness; democracy is the battle against individual egoism and group egoism. Democracy is the happy marriage of individual freedom and community awareness."[159]

Such descriptions bore the unmistakable undertones of traditional, Catholic organic thinking, with its emphasis on unity and harmony. Invoking similar language to that Catholic republicans had employed following World War I, Catholic Christian Democrats portrayed democracy as the "dominion of the Volk, as it has grown organically in *all of its groupings,* with no preference for a *class,* a *Stand* (economic estate), [or] a party."[160] In his speech at the founding assembly of the Düsseldorf CDU in late November 1945, Karl Arnold proclaimed, "We declare our allegiance to democracy, the only possible way to bring back the spiritual vitality of our Volk and to release from fateful rigidity this spiritual vitality with the force of a newly grasped sense of life. But let us be clear about this: Democracy cannot be decreed for the Volk as a state gift. . . . Democracy cannot grow from top to bottom; it must come from the Volk and grow into governing state authority. . . . Democracy is, finally, a political atmosphere that enables forces from the moral and spiritual essence of all the strata of the Volk to grow. . . . Democracy is therefore no mechanical affair, but an organic and creative political manifestation of life."[161]

The Abendland

That democracy for CDU Catholics was grounded in the traditions of Catholic political thought was underscored by their interpretation of its geographic origins. Following World War II, Catholics consistently located democracy's roots in the romantic Catholic ideal of the religiously homogenous Abendland, a corporative order that integrated the family with other organic institutions, most importantly the church and state. If the state, according to Catholic natural law, was a moral entity forged by individuals in keeping with their God-endowed social nature, its power was to be sharply limited. As the Catholic teaching of subsidiarity, codified in the papal encyclical *Quadragesimo anno* of 1931, made clear, because the state should inherit only those tasks that lower echelons of society, from the family to the neighborhood, village, city, and regional level on up, could not manage, it necessarily respected the sanctity of the individual.[162] Democracy, Konrad Adenauer explained, was rooted in Christianity's understanding of "the dignity, the value and the inalienable rights of every single person. . . . We are Christian Democrats because we are deeply convinced that only a democracy rooted in the Christian *abendländische* worldview, in Christian natural law, [and in] the tenets of Christian ethics can fulfill the great educative mission for the German Volk and give rise to its recovery."[163]

Dating from the Reformation, the Abendland had enjoyed currency as the designation for an antimodern, culturally unified Europe since the concept's infusion with romanticism in the nineteenth century. Inspired by the 1918 publication of Oswald Spengler's *Decline of the West,* Protestant and especially Catholic academics and clerics sustained utopian visions of a conservative and even revolutionary Christian Europe reclaiming its medieval integrity from the forces of the Enlightenment, secularism, liberalism, capitalism, and individualism.[164] Invoked before and during the Nazi years to justify colonizing Eastern Europe, the Abendland served National Socialists as propaganda for the invasion of the Soviet Union as a defense against communism and an unchristian Asia. Clearly infused with antisemitism before 1945, the Abendland continued to be regarded by some post–World War II observers as anti-Jewish[165] or at least exclusionary of Jews.[166]

As the CDU's idealization of a medieval social hierarchy rather than constitutional mass democracy underscored the distinctly Catholic postwar understanding of democracy, widespread use of the term *Abendland* by journalists, intellectuals, and clergymen of both confessions testified to the postwar hegemony of Christians and conservatives.[167] That the term quickly emerged as one of the dominant discourses of the occupation years reflected not only the ascendance of the Catholic milieu but also the appeal of a motif that enabled the pariah state of Germany to nestle again in the bosom of Western Europe. Certainly, the Abendland served as a primary slogan for the CDU from the party's earliest days.[168]

According to the CDU, if Germany had represented the essence of the Abendland, materialism's assault on the idea had produced the Nazi movement and devastated Germany. As the Gelsenkirchen Christian Democrats explained in July 1945, "Since the alienation of the abendländischer spirit from the Christian foundation of its culture, materialism (in multifarious stages of development, the last of which was National Socialism) plunged the *Völker* into increasingly greater misfortune."[169] In a party program outline, Württemberg-Hohenzollern CDU members charged materialism's "renunciation of Christianity" with having destroyed "the united Abendland" and brought the German Volk "to the brink of destruction."[170] Moreover, because materialism had laid siege to all of the Abendland, guilt for Nazism could only be "a collective guilt of the entire Western world [*des gesamten Abendlandes*]."[171]

In the same way that Christian Democrats posited a unique German relationship to materialism, they saw Germany as enjoying a special connection to the Abendland. According to Karl Zimmermann, "We cannot ignore the history of our own Volk, as no European Volk is so greatly obliged to the *abendländischer* spirit as the German. The National Socialists have not always ruled us. Their thousand-year *Reich* only lasted twelve years. We want to draw from the historical abundance of our own great and splendid past."[172] Andreas Hermes was equally insistent on the organic connection between Germany and the Abendland: "We neither want to nor should forget that the magnificent flowering of the culture of the Abendland, under the centuries-long leadership of the German nation, possessed its deepest roots in the union of Christianity with Teutonism [*Germanentum*]."[173]

That the battle between Christianity and materialism had ended with the Nazis' defeat signaled the urgency of reclaiming abendländische ideals; according to the Catholic CDU, the hour of Germany's return to the Abendland had come.[174] In June 1946, Walter Dirks explained that, after "a long process of disintegration" that unfolded through the stages of "nominalism, the Reformation, absolutism, the Enlightenment, the nation state, liberalism, capitalism and materialism, imperialism and Bolshevism, [and] finally fully realized secularism, we have reached anarchy and the dehumanization of man, which finally manifested itself naked and hideous in National Socialism; salvation lies in reflecting on our own heritance, in the avowal of the spirit of the Abendland."[175] In the Cologne Guiding Principles, the CDU proclaimed that only a sincere commitment to "Christian and abendländische" values and a "social order" inspired by "Christian natural law" could renew Germany after the disaster of National Socialism.[176] Numerous party programs and politicians echoed the reference to building "a new democracy in the spirit of Christian, abendländische culture"[177] or founding the new German state to preserve the Christian culture of the Abendland.[178] According to Josef André, Christian Democrats offered the sole answer to the "abendländische culture's question of survival." Only a "crusade against the dehumanization of man through despotism in every form" could preserve the "powerful values of the abendländischen Persönlichkeit and culture."[179]

The Abendland and Protestant Prussia

In locating the ideals and program of Christian Democracy in the Abendland, Catholics underscored the religious nature of their vision of democracy and postwar political recovery. At the same time, the confessionalism of the Catholic CDU's vision of Christian Democracy was reinforced by Catholics' mapping of the Abendland and its primary enemy, materialism. While locating the roots of democratic Germany in the country's Catholic, western areas, CDU members simultaneously depicted Protestant Prussia as the physical embodiment of materialism. In this way, the Abendland and Prussia lent a religious geography to the confrontation between (Catholic) Christianity and materialism, underscoring the pronounced confessionalism of the early Catholic CDU.

Catholics had long understood the Abendland as anti-Prussian. As far back as the sixteenth century, a marked hostility had existed between Prussia as the protagonist of the Reformation and the southern German frontrunners of the Catholic Reformation; as Prussia became more powerful, tensions between it and the ecclesiastical territories accreted.[180] In the nineteenth century, some Catholics construed German unification as a deliberate violation of the abendländische integrity of the medieval Reich; during the Weimar years, Abendland theorists continued to attack Prussia as a bastion of materialistic chauvinism and militarism.[181] Especially in the wake of National Socialism, however, as CDU Catholics posited the Christian Abendland as the antithesis to materialist Nazism, materialist Prussia was rendered the antipode to the Abendland.[182]

Anti-Prussianism was by no means limited to Catholic Germans after World War II. If the Allies' denazification and deprussification programs were based on coherent if historically misinformed diagnoses of Nazism's origins, the occupiers consistently located the bastion of German militarism and political extremism in Prussia. Indeed, the simultaneous collapse of the Nazi regime and the dismemberment of the Prussian state symbolized for many, including Protestant Germans, the symbiosis between Prussianism and Nazism.[183] Catholics in postwar Germany nevertheless retained their long-standing hostility to Prussia as a godless power guilty of the cardinal sin of arrogance.[184] Especially since the Kulturkampf, southern German and Rhenish Catholics had regarded apostasy and secularization as predominantly Prussian-inspired phenomena. In particular, German Catholics had associated Prussia with such manifestations of materialism as militarism, antiquated East Elbian capitalism, the Kulturkampf, and the socialist-led Weimar coalition.[185]

In the view of Catholics, Prussia's long-standing materialism was a consequence of its powerful state's disregard for human dignity. Influenced by Catholic experiences during the Reformation, the Enlightenment, and the French Revolution, Catholic antistate sentiment directed specifically against Prussia increased dramatically in the Rhine Province and Westphalia in reaction to the 1803 Final Recess, after which millions of Catholics found themselves minorities in Protestant-ruled states.[186] The Congress of Vienna, which awarded Prussia overwhelmingly Catholic territories in western Germany, merely compounded Catholic Germany's disquiet.[187] That a confessionally colored antistate and anti-Prussian sentiment would prove a prominent impulse in the development of German political Catholicism was first demonstrated by the Cologne Turmoil of 1837.[188] In the wake of the war of 1866, Catholic hostility toward the new Prussian-dominated state catalyzed the organization of the Center Party;[189] the ostensibly national Kulturkampf focused on western Prussia only reinforced this hostility. During the Weimar Republic, the Rhineland represented the mecca of abendländische intellectual activity, especially that oriented toward Franco-German reconciliation,[190] while the so-called Hoffmann Commandments, the Rhenish separatist movements, and even the Rhineland's thousand-year anniversary in 1925 all reified anti-Prussianism by linking the Rhineland to the Abendland.[191]

In a CDU dominated by Rhenish-Westphalian Catholics, it was no surprise that this long-honed tradition of anti-Prussianism emerged in full force in the wake of Nazism's collapse. Among other points, CDU Catholics insisted that Prussia's rise marked a radical departure from the Holy Roman Empire's decentralization and protection of "German freedoms."[192] As Adenauer explained, the Prussian state, inspired by the philosophies of romanticism, Herder, and Hegel, represented an "almost God-like entity" in the German people's eyes. After German unification under Prussian domination, the state had come to resemble an inorganic "sovereign machine" inherently threatening to individuals' worth. Because materialist states inexorably prioritize power over the Persönlichkeit, National Socialism institutionalized violations of human dignity in direct contravention of "Christian natural law."[193] In a December 1946 letter, Adenauer explained that "National Socialism was nothing but a logical further development of Prussian statism."[194] "Prussia," he declared in September 1948, "is identical to centralism, and centralization is identical to depersonalization."[195]

Adenauer was by no means alone in singling out Hegel and Prussian "power politics."[196] Maria Sevenich charged the Hegelian philosophy of the state with having made inevitable National Socialism, "the last exaggerated and pathological realization of the Prussian notion of the powerful state,"[197] while Adam Stegerwald decried how, in Frederick the Great's "avowed soldiers' state," "state omnipotence" was "spiritualized" in philosophy and history at the cost of individual freedom.[198] According to Peter Altmeier, "It was a regrettably mistaken development in German history that, through the anti-*Reich* dynastic power politics of Frederick the Great and his successors on the Prussian throne, the German leadership passed to the powers of eastern Elbia, whose eventual lawful [*legitime*] successors were Hitler and his 'old guard.' This line of development of German history has become the greatest catastrophe of our people."[199]

If Prussia writ large embodied for CDU Catholics materialist evil, its capital represented that evil in concentrated form. In emphasizing Berlin's radical culture, Adenauer reflected traditional Catholic hostility to Berlin as the embodiment of materialism: socialist, liberal, and unchristian.[200] During the Weimar Republic, Adenauer contended, Berlin had become a "hedonistic [*heidnische*] city" in which political parties dedicated to the destruction of Christianity had taken root.[201] Even with the demise of National Socialism, Berlin's materialism remained undiluted. Marxists had been powerful there and would be again after World War II, when, Adenauer imagined, socialism would rule even without Soviet occupation.[202] In Adenauer's view, the number of Berliners who had voted for the Nazis was immaterial: "Berlin is still just the collective noun for "'Prussian endeavors.'"[203] For all of these reasons, Adenauer and other western Prussian Christian Democrats consistently criticized suggestions of a German postwar capital in Berlin.[204] As Adenauer opined in 1946, "We in the West reject much of what generally is called Prussian spirit. Our former war enemies have no reason to handle us particularly kindly. It is up to us to slowly destroy the distrust. As soon as Berlin becomes the capital again, however, that distrust abroad will be inextinguishable. Whoever makes Berlin the new head creates spiritually a new Prussia."[205]

Adenauer's reference to "we in the West" well captured CDU Catholics' perception of their distinct identity. While materialism had found its true expression in Protestant Germany, Catholics suggested that western, abendländische, and Catholic areas represented the real and democratic Germany.[206] At the first meeting of the Consultative Assembly for the Rhineland-Palatinate, Ernst-Albert Lotz, CDU president of the state assembly, expressed the hope that "West Germany, which has a special character and mission," would win back the influence it had lost decades before "Prussia [*Großpreussen*] estab-lished its dominion and, after 1918, consolidated it," facilitating the rise of National Socialism.[207] Peter Altmeier was equally insistent that West Germans should lead the German recovery: "The political emphasis and the leading cul-tural center of future German state life must lie here on the Rhine, where the nationalistic and centralistic authoritarian state thinking never could take root, where militarism never had a home, [where] on the contrary—during the Nazi era as well—democratic, federalistic and peace-loving thinking always re-mained alive."[208]

Inherent in these attacks on the godless state and capital of "Prussianized Germany [*verpreußten Deutschland*]" was the assumption that the materialism undergirding both Prussianism and Nazism had been limited to the eastern, Protestant area of Germany.[209] Positing a teleology from the Reformation to Prussian state power to Bismarck's anti-Catholicism to Weimar's socialism to Hitler's murderous dictatorship,[210] CDU Catholics suggested that the Refor-mation provided Prussia "the authoritarian justification and the desired deep-seated opposition to the Catholic powers" that it needed;[211] they linked in par-ticular the Reformation's emphasis on individual conscience and Luther's doctrine of two kingdoms to state absolutism.[212] Now, in the wake of World War II, Catholics suggested that Protestants had delivered on that legacy by embracing National Socialism while Catholics had, as Altmeier put it, re-mained loyal to peaceful, democratic federalism.

The association of Protestantism, Prussianism, and Nazism was hardly conducive to interconfessional cooperation and on occasion threatened alto-gether to undermine the Kirchenkampf ideology.[213] As we saw with the CDU's organization, Catholics convinced of widespread Protestant support for Hitler labored to distinguish between majority Protestants and those who had op-posed Nazism. Adenauer went so far to assert that German Catholics had of-fered more effective resistance than any Protestants, including the SPD, a claim echoed within the party.[214] Speaking on March 24, 1946, in the great hall of the University of Cologne, Adenauer opined that the Rhenish capital deserved Al-lied bombings less than any other major German city: "For nowhere was there such open resistance before 1933 and spiritual resistance after 1933 to National Socialism; nowhere were the National Socialist votes, even in the last free elec-tions in 1932, percentage-wise as low as in Cologne."[215]

In grounding so clearly their program for the CDU and postwar Germany in the Catholic and especially Rhenish Catholic worldview, CDU Catholics tes-tified to the endurance of a Catholic consciousness in German politics in the wake of the Nazi regime. They also demonstrated the still potent universalism of

Catholic thinking, as French, Dutch, and Swiss Catholic thinkers echoed their distinctive interpretation of German history and democracy.[216] That Catholics' program of antimaterialism was by no means confessionally neutral reflected clearly the animosity that had sustained an exclusively Catholic party in Germany until 1933. By revealing the weight of centuries of anti-Protestant suspicion in their vision for postwar Germany, Catholics posed vital questions regarding the construction of an interconfessional Christian Democratic ideology.

Confessionalized Understandings of Materialism: The Protestant CDU

The diversity of leading Protestant Christian Democrats' political lineage left them without easy claim to a unifying organizational tradition. Although Protestants were granted disproportional representation in the CDU's leadership ranks and played indispensable roles in the party's early organization, they by no means constituted a cohesive confessional bloc within the CDU. Because German Protestants historically shared neither a common political tradition nor a codified moral program similar to Catholic social teachings,[217] early CDU Protestants initially offered little by way of an ideological front; indeed, for lack of any other binding ideological ties, cooperation with Catholics, the imposition of a Christian state, and opposition to materialist movements coalesced to define early Protestant Christian Democracy.

If Catholics were consumed with the battle between the CDU and the refounded Center Party, CDU Protestants also found themselves plagued by intrareligious disputes. Protestant debates concerning designating a political party *Christian* first emerged at the August 1945 Treysa Church Conference.[218] Much to the disappointment of Protestant Christian Democrats, this question continued to vex.[219] Even as some Dahlemites appeared to favor the SPD, other Confessing Church veterans who rejected Luther's doctrine of two kingdoms embraced Christian Democracy: Hans von Arnim, for example, argued that Protestants should support the CDU because Christianity should not remain a private concern but belonged in the public sphere.[220] In a November 1947 speech, Hans Schlange-Schöningen, acknowledging continuing objections to the party's name from those he believed would otherwise join the CDU, hastened to assure his fellow Protestants: "1. We are not a confessionally tied party in any way. We welcome every decent German without regard to confession. 2. We reject every religious despotism in the party and leave each party member to determine his relationship to God himself. 3. We do not want politics to be carried out from the pulpit."[221] Despite Schlange-Schöningen's and other CDU Protestants' best efforts, however, theological objections to naming a party "Christian" would remain a troubling issue for the Protestant CDU.[222]

While many religiously devout and conservative Protestants shared Catholic apprehensions about modernity, of the utmost importance for the construction of a Christian Democratic ideology was the Protestant conviction of a connection between secularism, materialism, and Nazism.[223] "National Socialism," in the words of Wilhelm Simpfendörfer, "is not the root, but the fruit; it is not the cause of a disease, but a symptom. It is only *one* expression of the mentality of one who has released himself from the ties to God and the transcendence, and made himself the measure of all things, and [who] is only interested in this life. National Socialism is in other words only *one* expression of the secularized mentality, although probably the most thoroughgoing. . . . The mentality of the purely worldly and purely secular man is the sickness of the world in our epoch."[224] If Protestants associated with the Confessing Church were especially vocal on this topic,[225] Protestants from the nationalist parties also linked directly the ascent of materialism and the rise of National Socialism. In answer to the question, "How could it have happened?" Otto Boelitz cited "materialism before 1933" and declared, "We had become a Volk that no longer searched for God with all its heart, a Volk alienated from God, that went astray."[226]

Like their Catholic party partners, Protestants held late eighteenth- and nineteenth-century materialist manifestations, including the French Revolution, responsible for Germany's catastrophe.[227] In a speech at the founding of the Düsseldorf CDU, Robert Lehr condemned strongly the "meteoric rise of the natural sciences in the last centuries"; by having repressed the humanities and religion for the goal of scientific progress, the "mechanistic view of life" encouraged man to seek to establish human rule over nature. Human energy, Lehr continued, should be dedicated not to achieving technical progress but to the "spiritual perfection of humanity. We must orient our private affairs and our state apparatus toward a supernatural, an ultimate goal in God."[228] In a September 1946 pamphlet, the Wuppertal Protestants condemned the nineteenth century's blind belief in "progress" and called for a "new meeting of religion, spirit, and politics."[229]

Despite these important commonalities, Catholic and Protestant critiques of modernity and their accompanying understandings of Christian Democracy nevertheless continued to rest on two divergent worldviews. Theologically based differences were evident in Protestants' and Catholics' calls to rechristianization, as conservative Protestants loyal to Luther's two kingdoms doctrine emphasized the acts of individual Protestants—prayer, loyalty to the church, social engagement—over Christian political commitment.[230] Moreover, while both confessions embraced the Christian notion of man created in God's image, Protestants differed on the origins of human rights, tracing individualism and classical humanism variously to the Stoics, Renaissance, Enlightenment, and eighteenth-century North America.[231] According to Wilhelm Simpfendörfer, religious sects during the Reformation had inspired the world in their battle against the state on behalf of God-given human dignity.[232] Otto Heinrich von der Gablentz, former Confessing Church member and cofounder of the Berlin CDUD, concurred: Only the Reformation's revolt against the intolerant medieval hierarchy of clerical rulers (*Priesterherrschaft*) had righted the balance between individual freedom and the community.[233]

In a similar rejection of the Catholic, abendländische interpretation of German history, numerous CDU Protestants contested the association of Prussianism with the materialist evil underlying National Socialism. Consistent with the broader postwar discourse concerning Prussia, which found the most hostile opponents to Prussia in the Catholic and Marxist camps, defenders of Prussia both within and beyond the CDU were almost exclusively Protestant.[234] Perhaps the most eloquent speaker on this topic was von der Gablentz, who after the war proudly defended Prussia against those wreaking their "cowardly revenge."[235] In "The Tragedy of Prussia," a speech delivered numerous times throughout occupied Germany, von der Gablentz declared, "Prussia belongs to Germany and has, for Germany and from the home base of Germany, an unfulfilled mission in Europe."[236] In his explicit rejection of the equation of materialism and Prussianism, von der Gablentz was echoed by Theodor Steltzer, who, while conceding that the overweening power of the Prussian state had served Germany badly, equated Prussian statism with "Bavarian authoritarian state bureaucracy."[237]

Consistent with their defense of Prussia, Protestants operated with a different understanding of its countermodel, the Abendland. During the Weimar Republic, small numbers of leading Protestant academics embraced an avowedly ecumenical, utopian vision of a unified Europe inspired by a medieval German empire; both Theodor Steltzer and von der Gablentz, for example, decried secularism's assaults on the Abendland.[238] Protestants and Catholics nevertheless differed profoundly on the Abendland's origins, boundaries, and demography: While Protestants argued that Britain had spread Christianity to Europe, Catholics looked to Ireland;[239] more broadly, they located the Abendland in France, Germany, and Italy north of Rome, with its heart in the Rhineland.[240]

As for the East, Catholics associated the "Baltic-Slavic mixed Volk [*Misch-volkes*]" and "East Elbian brutality" with the Hohenzollern family, the Refor-mation, and Prussia, not the Abendland.[241] According to Hans-Peter Schwarz, Adenauer's understanding of the Abendland excluded the German tribes, Byz-antium, the Eastern Orthodox Church, and the Reformation.[242] In contrast, for Protestants both in and beyond the CDU, the Abendland was traditionally char-acterized by nationalism or a broader pan-Europeanism that looked east to Cen-tral Europe, conjuring up German-colonized Slavic Eastern Europe and the Teutonic Knights' Christianization.[243] Von der Gablentz was well aware of this discrepancy when he insisted that all Germans "must confess to having a bit of Prussianness in us, even when we are passionate enemies of Prussia." It was, in his view, essential to healing rifts between the East and the West to "make clear to the West that it alone does not come close to constituting the Abendland, that the Slavs belong to Europe just as the Teutons and Romans do."[244]

It is perhaps not surprising, then, that Protestants, including those in the CDU, spoke more often of *Europa, das christliche Europa,* or *das christliche Abendland,*[245] terms that had their roots in Weimar, when the "Christian Abend-land" explicitly implied classical Greek and Roman culture as well as medieval Christianity.[246] While conservative Protestants, particularly Lutherans, more easily adopted the Abendland discourse than did liberal Protestants, Protestant Church leaders and Christian Democrats stayed somewhat distant from the Abendland.[247] Catholic intellectuals served as the leading advocates of the Abendland, as evident in the Catholic journal *Neues Abendland* and Catholic-dominated organizations such as Abendländische Aktion and the Abendlän-dische Akademie,[248] and the geographic center of Abendland discourse re-mained distinctly western; in the Soviet zone of occupation, only Christian Democratic politicians spoke of the Abendland.[249]

That the term *Abendland* would continue to carry confessional weight was obvious in 1953, when Eugen Gerstenmaier, a prominent Protestant Chris-tian Democrat, felt compelled to insist that a diverse "Christian Abendland" did not equate with a "Catholic Abendland."[250] As late as 1964, Walter Dirks would explain that Catholic and Protestant paths to Christian Democracy, in-cluding their understanding of the Abendland, were based on two distinct tra-jectories. While the Center Party began its journey with the Catholic Reforma-tion, bypassed the Enlightenment and classical antiquity, and continued through romanticism, the nineteenth-century Catholic ghetto, and the Kul-turkampf, Protestants took another path to the CDU—through the principali-ties, the Enlightenment and classical antiquity, nineteenth-century science and education, cultural Protestantism and nationalism, Nazi persecution, and the Confessing Church. These two paths, Dirks concluded, determined the "lasting elements" of the *"christlichen Abendlandes."*[251]

While Protestant Christian Democrats offered their own understanding of the German past, they also struck a different note in their critiques of the economic components of materialism. To be sure, they rejected Marxism,[252] which they, like their Catholic colleagues, linked to National Socialism as "two varieties of one and the same mechanistic-biological worldview."[253] But, in contrast to CDU Catholics, Protestants—most prominently, those from Rhenish Wuppertal, where former liberals such as Klaus Brauda and Hermann Lutze and liberal sympathizers such as Otto Schmidt were active—offered a defense of capitalism and its practitioners. In September 1946, Wuppertal Protestants argued that attacking "capitalists" in the postwar era was futile, since many bakers and butchers were now better off than the "capitalists"; moreover, not all officers or factory owners and manufacturers were "bad."[254] For his part, Otto Schmidt defended at length what Catholics condemned as materialist free-market capitalism. While "liberal, early capitalism" in no way provided for all those in need, Schmidt explained, "it should not and cannot be disputed that, in the given circumstances, the liberal economic principle achieved significant things. The living standard of wide sections [of the population] was, under the influence of liberal capitalism, far higher than in the age of the guild economy."[255]

The fact that the widespread Catholic condemnation of liberalism and its ideological affinities with capitalism was by no means echoed by liberal Protestants highlighted once again the fact that the antimaterialist consensus behind the CDU's call for a Christian state rested on confessionalized philosophical and historical assumptions. Not surprisingly, these philosophical differences would become pronounced as the construction of a Christian Democracy moved from a theoretical to a policymaking plane. Indeed, on issues of great ideological and political conflict—particularly the party's economic policies—Protestant and Catholic tensions shaped decisively the contours of CDU policy. Furthermore, as the history of political Catholicism consistently demonstrated, a common rejection of materialism and its various forms had never assured Catholic harmony; as the primary inheritor of the Center Party's personnel and ideology, the CDU revealed the Catholic Teilkultur's fractures as well.

Protestants' and Catholics' mutual embrace of antimaterialism as an explanation of National Socialism and a program for German recovery testified to the common Christian impulses in occupied Germany during the "Hour of the Church." Shared experiences under the Third Reich and belief in rechristianization as an antidote to Nazism inspired members of both Christian confessions to commit to a new political movement. But as their leaders' reliance on confessionalized interpretations of the German past and present combined with class tensions within and beyond the Catholic milieu, the development of a party platform would prove a highly conflictual process.

CHAPTER 5

Antimaterialism Applied:
Ideological Positions in the Early CDU

The translation of the CDU's vision of a Christian, antimaterialist state into a coherent political program constituted an ongoing process throughout the occupation years that would test the two confessions' commitment to an interconfessional union. Of the host of prescriptions Christian Democrats offered for the German future, the CDU's vision of a Christian state was manifest above all in the cultural and economic spheres. Germany's gender and family order, confessional schools, and economics were central pillars on which the CDU sought to construct a rechristianized state; consequently, these three case studies provide valuable insights into the birthing hour of Christian Democracy.

The patterns of the party's organization—the dominance of former Center Party and Christian Trade Union members and clergy over divided and smaller numbers of Protestants—necessarily shaped early CDU policy debates. While the Rhenish Catholics' ascendancy guaranteed continuity with the Cologne line of political Catholicism, pre-1933 traditions of Protestant-Catholic cooperation on cultural issues offered the prospect for pan-Christian communion. On the reconstruction of the German familial and gender order, Protestants and Catholics, male and female, revealed strong similarities. But as the Weimar-era relationship between the Center Party and the DNVP made clear, alliances between conservative Protestants and Catholics had been colored by tension and disappointment, particularly regarding confessional schools; the early CDU's experience would be no different. At the same time, the intraparty battle over Christian Socialism highlighted the resilience of class tensions within the Catholic milieu. In contrast to the Weimar years, however, Protestants would play an important role in this debate, as both Rhenish Protestants and Catholic opponents of Christian Socialism challenged trade union Catholics in the name of interconfessionalism.[1]

Cultural policies and economics were naturally not the only issues with which the early CDU grappled. Early Christian Democrats addressed numerous facets of the new state's organization, ranging from denazification to media restrictions to foreign and military policy. One notable position many party leaders took concerned the shape of the future state—democratic and, in a clear expression of the traditional Catholic rejection of Prussian centralism, federal. As Konrad Adenauer explained in March 1946, "We do not want a Bismarckian Reich under Prussian leadership. We do not want the centralized Germany of National Socialism. We do not want a German confederation [*Staatenbund*]."[2] Instead, Christian Democrats invoked Catholic German traditions to call for an explicitly federal Germany[3] that would operate as a "protective defense of freedom against excesses of centralized power."[4] Although some Protestant Christian Democrats supported a more centralized future government, this issue would remain secondary for the CDU until the Parliamentary Council, when the CDU's broad commitment to federalism would conflict with the CSU's greater demands for regional autonomy.[5]

More pressing for most early Christian Democrats was the call for a Christian ethos to infuse German economic and cultural reorganization. In the words of the Schwäbisch-Gmünd CDU, "We demand the organization of a Christian cultural state as an organism in which the separate areas of life such as religion, science, law, economics, technical science, and the arts are intertwined completely with one another to form a living whole."[6] As the British zone CDU explained in March 1947, "Culture means to us nothing less than the fashioning of God's creation according to the principle of God's order and based on the vital energies of Christianity. . . . The Christian Democratic Union wants a Christian culture and a Christian state order."[7] That same month, the Rhenish CDU put it succinctly: "Who votes CDU wants the public rule of the Ten Commandments in our *Heimat*."[8]

In keeping with "the recognition of Christian culture as the basis of the state,"[9] the organization of Germany's schools, family, and gender order constituted key elements of the CDU's Kulturpolitik. Already constituent features of Catholic and Protestant politics before 1933, these issues appeared all the more pressing in the wake of Nazism and unprecedented war. While Protestants and Catholics might differ on how to codify Christian cultural policies, particularly regarding schools, their underlying ideological accord was clear. In the earliest years of Christian Democracy, cultural policy served largely to highlight Christian antimaterialist commonalities.

Gender and Family Order in the Early CDU

The early postwar years saw the emergence of conflicting images of women, including those of the heroic "woman of the rubble" and the deviant fraternizer, but arguably the dominant motif, evident in the profusion of postwar images of mothers and Madonnas, was that of the victimized mother. The adoption of specifically female experiences, including rape, to represent national suffering necessarily implied the innocence of those victimized. At the same time, a traditional version of motherhood held broad appeal as a foundational ideal for the new state, even as the realities of women's lives challenged that archetype.[10]

Christians throughout occupied Germany contributed significantly to a discourse of unblemished maternalism through their proclamations about the German family. The loss of home and family members, desperate postwar conditions, the separation of spouses, unemployment, and "moral decay" all constituted primary concerns for clerics, who regarded the traditional family as the central organ for rechristianizing Germany.[11] Christian Democrats echoed clerical pronouncements, emphasizing the importance of anchoring German women and family within a traditional Christian social order; indeed, references to women and the family appeared in almost every early CDU statement or program.

With very few exceptions, CDU statements on women and the family began by delineating the devastating impact of the Nazi years on the moral fabric of German society. Consistent with the party's disregard for Christian complicity in the racialization of German sexual and familial ideals, Christian Democrats focused instead on the impact of Nazi policies on the sanctity of the family.[12] In a typical locution, the September 1945 Frankfurt Guiding Principles explained that "National Socialism talked a lot about the German family, but in reality it did everything to tear it apart." To win young people's unqualified loyalty, National Socialism alienated them from their families and "wrenched them out of their cultural, moral, and religious attachments." National Socialism above all needed soldiers: "That is why it tried to break the inner power of the family and to poison its spirit. That is why it undermined the authority of parents as well as the obedience of children, why it unscrupulously ripped families apart."[13] By subordinating the youth to the state and its aggression, National Socialism "seduced the youth, robbed them of their respect for parental and church authorities, and taught them to scoff at and deride the best values of the German past."[14]

At the same time National Socialism seized control of the family, it also, in the view of the CDU, degraded female morality through such policies as the 1938 reform permitting divorce on the grounds of incompatibility, infertility, or the refusal of intercourse.[15] Under the Nazis, according to Elfriede Nebgen, Germans married with "cynical flippancy" and divorced casually.[16] Reflecting the new Nazi culture of marriage, wives previously deemed satisfactory when the husbands had been "unimportant" had been pushed to the side; instead, men found younger women to "cut a fine figure."[17]

Beyond their abandonment for younger and more beautiful women, German women suffered most from Nazi Germany's regard for them as procreative machines. "The essential mission of the woman inside and outside marriage" was to "satisfy the National Socialist need for masses of people for waging war, for conquering other *Völker* and races."[18] That "the civic duty of the woman was seen almost exclusively in the fulfillment of her biological function"[19] now made it all the more important to restore German honor and morality by reestablishing traditional Christian familial relations and women's inherent morality as mothers.[20] "We want the family to become again the source of happiness and satisfaction," declared an August 1946 pamphlet *To All Women!*— "the family, in which the woman represents warmth and motherliness. We want women and girls to be esteemed, loved, and honored. . . . Dishonor and perfidy have become extensive through the war and Nazism in Germany. The esteem of women and girls is in danger! We want to call a halt here! Moral eradication must not be allowed to gain ground."[21]

Restoring "the dignity befitting the mothers of the nation" was all the more important, Christian Democrats argued, since female morality remained threatened under Allied occupation.[22] Absent husbands, sex and relationships with Allied soldiers, increased rates and tolerance of divorce and nonmarital births, and greater acceptance of single women and nontraditional living arrangements all contributed to a fear that the occupation years were only deepening the Nazi-induced family crisis.[23] According to the Berlin CDUD in June 1946, the era posed a "severe moral danger to female youth," demanding a new emphasis on "purity" and "respect for the dignity of the woman."[24] Maria Dietz expressed special concern about "women's mission . . . to protect the paradise of the family from every destructive power—no matter what it is called: open relationship—marriage for three—companionate marriage—matriarchy. In the family lies the most fertile ground out of which our state life can renew itself again."[25]

In Christian Democratic proposals of moral regeneration to overcome Nazism's legacies and face the challenges of occupation, women's role as educators and "guardians of the Christian family" underscored the centrality of the nuclear family.[26] Advancing a formulation adopted by numerous CDU programs throughout occupied Germany, the Rhenish CDU declared, "The family is the foundation of the social order. Its *Lebensraum* is holy and must stand under the special protection of the state. It has its own rights from nature, which stand under the special protection of the state."[27] That the CDU's emphasis on the family necessarily prescribed a traditional family order was clear: "We want marriage to become again the foundation of the life companionship between man and woman." Only then could Germany achieve "healing based on strength of character, on reverence for God, on authority before the parents!"[28] In the same way that the CDU privileged a certain kind of family, the party called on the new state to protect procreative marriages. As the Frankfurt Guiding Principles explained, marriage, "according to its inherent law of nature," was to begin with a "life covenant" and culminate in "a family blessed with children." To guarantee this "natural" development, the CDU suggested, "the state is to teach such a marriage and family in the school and to protect it in public and spiritual life. The state, through its wage and tax legislation and its housing policies, is to create the room that this family needs to be able to come into being and develop itself fully."[29]

The woman's place in the new Germany as wife and mother was affirmed by CDU descriptions of the role the man was to play as "head and father of a family."[30] A booklet published by the Düsseldorf CDU, *One Mind, One Way, One Goal,* explained, "Each family—indeed, this cannot be disputed—each family needs paternal power [*patria potestas*], a master who carries the burden of all the all-encompassing worry."[31] The Frankfurt Guiding Principles endorsed this point: "The man must be the head in the fullest sense; he can do that only when he is not the object, but the subject of his life; that means that the state—through its economic and social policies—grants him the possibility to nourish his family in honor; and, through its social and state constitution, [it offers him the possibility] to be a true fellow supporter of public responsibility. Only then will the woman as the heart of the family in inner freedom help to carry the responsibility of the man and be able to be the trusted mother of his children."[32]

While Catholics dominated Christian Democratic discourse on gender and the family and Catholic distinctiveness was evident in references to natural law, Protestants revealed no discernable difference of opinion on these issues. Reclaiming their shared commitment to patriarchy from the Weimar years, religious Protestants and Catholics alike regarded Christianity as the foundation for traditional family and female life. Protestant Theophil Kaufmann, for example, argued that Germany could develop healthily only when the life of the family, the "primordial cell" of society, functioned according to the "Commandments."[33] Esther-Maria von Coelln noted specifically that, in the new Germany, "We want to remain women and not become masculine or genderless creatures. Suffragettes or bluestockings are not our ideal."[34]

Indeed, in their discussion of the family and its centrality to the new, antimaterialist Germany, female Christian Democrats embraced the depiction of women's role as that of mother and wife without exception. As the party's Women's Working Group explained in 1947, the integrity of the family had been sorely tested over the past decades, especially "through materialism, through the delusion of National Socialism, through war and collapse."[35] Now, according to Christine Teusch, "The woman as the recipient and carrier of life will do justice best and most nobly to her calling within the natural order."[36]

The widespread party consensus regarding maternal virtue and familial authority would soon find itself translated into political action, first in the Parliamentary Council of 1948–49 and then, in the 1950s, in the Bundestag, when the CDU enjoyed considerable success in its efforts to legislate its vision for the new Germany's gender order.[37] In the future, female Christian Democrats, led by Helene Weber, would challenge their male colleagues on specific issues pertaining to women's roles in society; a less pronounced Protestant-Catholic split on these questions would also emerge. In the early years of Christian Democratic organization, however, family and gender politics largely united the party. That a functional consensus between Protestants and Catholics existed on these issues was crucial for the early CDU's cohesion; in a party fraught with confessionalized tension, such islands of agreement facilitated cooperation when other issues threatened the new party's antimaterialist alliance.

Confessional Schools in a Christian State

As they had cast their commitment to a Christian family, Christian Democrats referred directly to the Nazi dictatorship in framing their approach to pedagogy. Guaranteeing Christian influence over education was especially crucial in the wake of Nazi efforts to remake German education in the spirit of interior minister Wilhelm Frick's 1935 decree, Deconfessionalization of Public Life. Despite the 1933 concordat's guarantee of confessional schools, the Nazis had sought to remove clerics, religious instruction, and crucifixes from the schools and to introduce National Socialist teachings; by 1941, all confessional schools had been replaced by community schools.[38] After the war, Christian Democrats portrayed National Socialist educational policies as the result of a long process of secularization.[39] For many Catholics, the Nazi assault on their schools resembled a mid-twentieth-century Kulturkampf, one far worse than its nineteenth-century progenitor.[40]

In the eyes of Catholic Christian Democrats, the Nazis' violation of parents' "natural" rights to dictate their children's education seared above all else. According to Heinrich Krone, the Nazis' attempt to establish total control over German schools meant that "all education was geared toward this state, from the elementary school to the university. . . . How difficult it was for parents to fight for their own rights to their own children."[41] Referring to parental rights, Peter Altmeier argued that National Socialism "violated [*vergewaltigt*] this natural right. It disregarded and dismissed the parents' wishes when it forced the so-called community school on the German Volk."[42] In the words of Josef André, "The state's claim to totality means the violation [*Vergewaltigung*] of the Persönlichkeit and the annihilation of human dignity and is to be combated like every idolization of the state. The right of parents to the education of their children must be preserved."[43]

Immanent in their discussions of women as Christian educators, early Christian Democrats regarded Germany's schools as an extension of the Christian family and therefore crucial to the "creation of a Christian state and public life."[44] At the British zone CDU's first party congress, in August 1947, Christine Teusch, secretary of education and cultural affairs for North Rhine-Westphalia from 1947 to 1954, decried Weimar-era liberal school reforms, the Third Reich's nationalization of the school system, and contemporary socialist pedagogy. According to Teusch, the Christian Democratic belief in the value and freedom of the individual necessarily led inexorably to state recognition of parental rights. "Only then can children be provided the proper spiritual, moral, and religious upbringing. This then produces moral families, which are the nuclei [*Keimzellen*] of the new Germany."[45]

Catholic politicians' references to "parents' rights" highlighted a chief element of postwar Catholic discourse on education, the Elternrecht. They also raised a divisive question within the early CDU. Though the term *Elternrecht* sounded quite liberal in principle, in practice it implied state-funded, confessionally segregated public schools that enabled parents to guarantee that the content and culture of their children's school corresponded to their religious and cultural preferences. That the term and its philosophical underpinnings were grounded in Catholic natural law and a distinctly Catholic sacralization of the value and freedom of the individual was hardly lost on secular and Protestant Germans. Inherent in the notion of the Elternrecht was the Catholic teaching of subsidiarity, which dictates that the state not intervene at risk of compromising personalism unless community support of the individual were insufficient; in this case, the parent was designated the agent of authority to determine the religious character of German schools.[46]

The organization of public schools, already a controversial question during the Weimar Republic, would return in the Federal Republic to divide secular Germans from devout Christians, especially practicing Catholics. As other school models came into question, particularly the interconfessional community school with confessionally separate religious instruction (the *Gemeinschaftsschule,* previously referred to as the *Simultanschule*), the pedagogical issue would remain complicated for Catholic politicians. The passion with which many Catholics defended confessionally divided schools made clear the degree to which post–1945 Germany remained a society riven by confessional difference. How the issue was resolved in a party founded on a platform of interconfessionalism tells us much about the dynamics of early Christian Democracy.

As had long been the case, confessional schools represented to many Catholic voters and the Catholic priesthood a litmus test of the party's commitment to Catholicism. In the clerical view, education was fundamental to the larger project of rechristianization. Securing economic, political, and social reforms depended on the proper formation of the individual.[47] For many priests, the end of the Nazi dictatorship meant first and foremost the return of confessional schools.[48] Not only in Cologne did CDU organization depend on ecclesiastical approval of the party's platform on schools.[49] Clerical support was crucial to the CDU's battle with the postwar Center Party, which maintained that only confessional schools could fulfill parental rights under natural law as well as state law, including the concordat.[50]

Many CDU programs certainly called explicitly for confessional schools.[51] Nevertheless, the school issue was conflictual from the party's earliest days, not only between Protestants and Catholics but within each confessional community. In the first months of Rhenish and Westphalian party organization, Westphalian Christian Democrats challenged the Cologne Guiding Principles' openness to both confessional schools and Christian "community schools with confessional religious instruction." In September 1945, the Guiding Principles of the Christian Democratic Party in the Rhineland and Westphalia eschewed any specific reference to confessional or community schools, calling simply for consultation with the churches, separate confessional religious instruction, and the right to private schools.[52] Following continued negotiations throughout the fall between Rhenish and Westphalian representatives,[53] the December 1945 Bad Godesberg program demanded confessional schools while making no mention of community schools,[54] and in the coming years, the Rhenish CDU would call exclusively for confessional schools.[55]

The dissimilarity in early CDU programs on confessional schools was in part a function of Germany's pre-1945 regional traditions. While Article 146 of the Weimar Constitution had guaranteed a common primary school for all pupils, the article had never been enforced as a result of Center Party opposition; instead, each state determined the organization of its schools.[56] Accordingly, some CDU programs called for regional flexibility. According to the Mannheim CDU, for example, "The Christian community school with confessional instruction" was to be "ensured," but in areas desiring confessional schools, confessional schools were to be "recognized."[57] The Baden-Württemberg CDU called for honoring local desires in school organization,[58] while the Heidelberg CDU petitioned for "religious education" so that "the youth be raised in awe of God, seniority, and experience" but made no specific mention of confessional schools.[59] The Frankfurt program hewed a similar line.[60]

Protestants also differed among themselves on the organization of Christian education, not least because there was no Protestant equivalent to Catholic natural law or papal encyclicals providing a theological framework for pedagogy. In addition to regional variations, Protestant positions were marked by Reform and Lutheran Protestants' divergent understandings of the role of the state and social institutions. Lutherans who adhered to the doctrine of two kingdoms held the state responsible for worldly issues, including the organization of schools, while Reform Protestants stood closer to Catholic natural law's mandate to shape the secular order.[61] For this reason, Sebastian Müller-Rolli speaks in the plural of "*school political positions* in the Protestant Church" after World War II. In the British zone, for example, while the Catholic Church clearly demanded the reintroduction of confessional schools, Protestant Church leaders articulated a variety of stances;[62] those Protestant Church leaders who did endorse confessional schools sometimes did so against their own wishes under pressure from the Catholic Church.[63]

This disunity was clearly evident in early Protestant Christian Democratic programmatic statements. In contrast to the Rhenish Protestant Church, which endorsed community schools in the summer of 1945,[64] Rhenish Protestant Christian Democrats by and large supported confessional schools.[65] Wuppertal Protestants, for example, adopted the Cologne CDU's call for confessionally divided schools,[66] as did CDU Protestants from Württemberg.[67] Other Protestants, especially the liberal minority within the party, avoided explicit commitment.[68] On some occasions, particularly when former members of the DDP were involved, the school question significantly hindered Protestant and Catholic political cooperation.[69] Former conservatives were also not reliably committed to religious segregation. Schlange-Schöningen called for "the education of the German youth in a Christian sense at home, at school, and at church" but not for confessional schools;[70] other leading Protestants, including Robert Lehr, concurred.[71] Despite the range of their positions on the issue, Protestants shared a more distanced relationship to the question of confessional schools than that of Catholics, for whom it was an unmistakable priority. This was true not only within the party but more broadly throughout German society, as evident in British zone opinion polls conducted in 1947 and 1949.[72]

For the most part, the early CDU successfully papered over party nonuniformity on the issue. In large part, the school question remained in check during the early postwar period because the British and American occupiers, sympathetic to church demands and in keeping with the concordat, allowed parents to dictate school organization, while the French enjoyed limited success in imposing a strictly secular French pedagogical model on their zone.[73] Typical of the party's early malleability was the British zone CDU's February 1946 adoption of three different formulations on the school question, the first for party publications and the second and third—more flexibly worded—for party rallies and dealings with Baden,[74] the southern region of which had had confessionally mixed schools since 1868.[75]

The school question remained controversial, however, especially as states began to draft constitutions and could no longer rely on Allied decision making. Confessional differences fractured some local organizations, threatening to split parties between Catholic supporters of confessional schools and Protestant opponents. In March 1947 in Tübingen, for example, the party's Catholic majority faced serious conflict with its one-third Protestant minority over school organization.[76] Not only would the CDU's commitment to confessional schools emerge as a divisive issue for the party in the Parliamentary Council of 1948–49, but the 1950s would see a number of party and West German battles over confessional schools at the state level.[77]

Underlying this significant discord, however, was a strong consensus among Christian Democrats on the role of education in the new Germany. CDU members may have disagreed on whether Protestant and Catholic children should be coeducated, but no Christian Democrat ever suggested the removal of Christianity from the public schools. Although policy on confessional schools, much more so than that on women and the family, would strain party alliances, neither issue contested the fundamental Christian Democratic assumptions regarding the primacy of Christianity in the postwar state. By September 1948, when the Parliamentary Council began meeting and the party needed an operational platform, the CDU had resolved larger, more definitive, ideological battles to set itself on a clear, antimaterialist course. Defining *Christian* in party political terms would result in a sharp distinction between Christians on one side and materialists of all ilks on the other; the party's economic debate would make this divide indelible.

Economic Ideologies in the Early CDU

In light of the war's devastation, questions concerning economic recovery assumed for Germans and the Allies an urgency unequaled by any other aspect of postwar reconstruction.[78] Although the German economy was controlled by the occupying powers, CDU politicians wrote and spoke extensively on the form German economics should take. In so doing, early Christian Democrats articulated competing visions of a Christian, antimaterialist economy. While dissimilarities in economic policy existed clearly between Protestants and Catholics, different schools of political Catholicism evident before 1933 also resurfaced, producing significant policy differences within the post-1945 Catholic Teilkultur. Reflecting the personnel and ideological legacy of Rhenish and Westphalian political Catholicism, the development of the party's economic program took place primarily within the British zone, particularly in the Rhenish and Westphalian circles of the party's zonal leadership.[79]

In keeping with traditional Catholic teachings on economics, CDU Catholics stressed that human economic activity was subject to sacred restraints and prescriptions. While Josef Gockeln underscored that no aspect of life "may exist beyond the laws" of a "Christian life order,"[80] Heinrich Krone envisioned a "Christian life order" in which the "state, economy, and society" function as "the essence of man created by God and for God, [but] never as ends in and of themselves."[81] In November 1945, Catholic businessman Wilhelm Naegel introduced a speech on the "Christian Democratic Party and the Economy" by explaining that only a "materialistic worldview" would seek to operate economic activity according to its own rules.[82] Josef Kannengießer struck an analogous tone in September 1946: Because "we want nothing less than a Christian order in a Christian Volk," it is the CDU's "greatest and fundamental obligation" to create a state consistent with "God's order of the universe," characterized by "a righteous economic and property order."[83]

That CDU Catholics linked economic reconstruction to the realization of a Christian state was evident in their emphasis on personalism. Consistent with Catholic natural law, "neither the state, nor the economy, nor mass organizations"[84] but the individual was to assume "the center of the economy with both his responsibility as well as with his claims and demands, with his duties and privileges."[85] In its obligation to enable each individual to develop his God-given gifts as a Persönlichkeit,[86] the state necessarily sanctioned the "recognition and protection of private property."[87] In this respect, the formula, "The right to property will be guaranteed," as it appeared in the Cologne Guiding Principles, constituted one of the most frequently invoked principles of CDU economic policy.[88] As Karl Arnold explained in November 1945, personal responsibility, initiative, and the development of culture were all tied to the right to private property: "We affirm private property because we affirm the Persönlichkeit. Without private property, the Persönlichkeit and the family cannot develop."[89]

The Catholic conception of the Persönlichkeit did more than provide the foundation for the CDU's economic program; it also served to distinguish—both in intraparty discussions and for propaganda purposes—Christian Democratic economic ideals from those of liberals and Marxists. True, the Bad Godesberg program stressed the importance of "freedom, spontaneity, and independence" in the economic sphere, but it also emphasized that property and private initiative should no longer exist for their own purposes, as they had when "liberal methods of a past era" predominated.[90] Because the Christian individual was at all times constrained by the Gemeinschaft,[91] the right to private property was not absolute.[92] Quoting Pope Leo XIII's encyclical *Rerum Novarum,* Karl Zimmermann explained that Christian teachings judged private property necessary only to assure the livelihood of a man, his family, and especially his children.[93] Capitalism's "unbridled individualistic economic order," according to Wilhelm Naegel, was a consequence of the "unchristian" "development of mammonism," a development that led to the agglomeration of economic power and abuse of economic interests of "the entire Volk."[94]

Consistent with this critique of capitalism, Catholic postwar thought was widely unsympathetic to large industry and capitalism's by-product, depersonalization.[95] By destroying Germany's idealized Gemeinschaft and encouraging massification and atomization, Catholics claimed, urbanization represented "the most accursed legacy of the nineteenth century."[96] At the same time, in keeping with Catholic teachings, CDU Catholics distinguished sharply between the Catholic and Marxist understandings of the Gemeinschaft. By disregarding the centrality of private property, Marxism subjugated the Persönlichkeit to the Gemeinschaft; according to the Darmstadt CDU, the Marxist "materialist" and "degenerating" philosophy of the individual had inspired "Bolshevism," collective principles of economic organization, and atheism.[97] In contrast to the teachings and methods of Marx, Josef André explained in

"Property and Socialism," "The spirit of Christ and the teachings of Christ will restore order."[98]

Beyond the condemnation of Marxist socialism for its disregard of personal property, CDU Catholics linked Marxist economics directly to the materialist development of state power that Catholics believed they had opposed—particularly in the form of the Prussian state—for centuries. In the words of Konrad Adenauer, "The state has no unconditional right over the individual, and all functioning of the state must conform to the well-being of the individual. That holds true for the economy as well."[99] The role of the state in a Marxist economic order had in any case, in the view of the Catholic CDU, been definitively discredited by the experience of National Socialism. Consistent with their emphasis on the socialism of National Socialism,[100] Catholics described the Nazi years as a realization of "socialist," "collectivist" state-dominated economics.[101] Because Nazi "socialization" had led to an economy controlled by the "'National Socialist' state," the resulting economic system, which had no respect for God or, therefore, for the individual, had flouted the right to private property; the inevitable result, contended the Catholic CDU, had been unparalleled disaster.[102]

In rejecting both capitalism and socialism for their materialist understandings of the Persönlichkeit, the Gemeinschaft, and the state, CDU Catholics adhered consistently to the classic Catholic "middle way" between "free enterprise of a purely materialistic form" and "state-run economics."[103] In the words of Josef Kannengießer, "A new economic and societal order inspired by Christian principles must vanquish the liberal-capitalistic and the socialist class conflict endeavors."[104] Theodor Scharmitzel argued similarly that "neither Marxism nor capitalism, both materialistic worldviews, is capable of creating healthy, just social conditions. That is why we reject fundamentally and most emphatically both anti-Christian systems."[105] The main task of the CDU, concluded a September 1946 election pamphlet for North Rhine-Westphalia, was to work for the "protection of justly acquired private property and the preservation of private initiative in the economy" and against "rash socialization in the city and country, but also against every sort of freebooterism [*Freibeutertum*] in the economy."[106]

In light of the debates about economic policy that would soon overtake the party, it is notable that CDU Catholics agreed not only on the fundamental philosophical principles of economic reconstruction but to a significant degree on their implementation. While by no means as unqualified as that concerning philosophical bases for economic organization, the degree of accord within the early CDU on a practical economic program was striking. As a translation of the Catholic middle way between capitalism and socialism, the most important component of this consensus was the widely held support among Catholic Christian Democrats for state involvement in the form of "planned management" (*planvolle Lenkung*).[107]

The term *Lenkung* and other references to state involvement in Germany's economic reconstruction abounded in early Christian Democratic documents.[108] An early party program from the Wetzlar CDU suggested that although working people should be allowed to acquire property, the state should retain the right to intervene in the economy through social legislation and at times of economic crisis.[109] At the Bad Godesberg conference, the party's leaders argued that "Christian Democrats want as much freedom and sovereignty as possible, but also as much *planvolle Lenkung* as necessary."[110] And in a May 1946 speech, Adenauer explained that providing for the people's needs in such desperate times could be accomplished only through "planned government control of the economy."[111]

As CDU Catholics stressed the importance of an active governmental role in Germany's economic sphere, they also maintained that their "planned management of the economy" differed intrinsically from that of the Nazis and Marxists.[112] While tempering capitalism's obsession with profit through a "systematic management of the economy," it was, according to Anton Storch, essential to avoid a "state economy" similar to that under National Socialism.[113] As expressed in the Hesse-Palatinate CDU program, "The system of planned governmental control of the economy" must remain "filled and animated by the old abendländische idea of the free and responsible Persönlichkeit." The state, then, had a dual, but limited, obligation—the "*Bedarfsdeckung*," or "provision for the needs" of the German people, and the cultivation of the Persönlichkeit.[114]

Rooted in Catholic social teachings, the concept of *Bedarfsdeckung* had long signified in Catholic discourse a rejection of nineteenth-century economic liberalism, and its reappearance underscores the continuities in Catholic thought.[115] The ultimate goal of economic organization, as Konrad Adenauer formulated it, was not to create every possible opportunity to earn money, but to provide for the "Bedarfsdeckung of the entire Volk."[116] In a typical formulation found in numerous party programs and speeches, the Rhineland-Hesse-Nassau CDU demanded a state-controlled economy that would serve the "Bedarfsdeckung of the Volk" by meeting the "legitimate demands" of an "abendländisches civilized people." Only then could Germany march "Forward with God!"[117]

The Catholic ideological consensus on Lenkung and Bedarfsdeckung as fundaments of abendländische economics testified to the coherency of a Catholic vision of the postwar world. And yet, as the Catholic milieu transmitted a certain unity of vision, it also imparted class divides that had riven the Catholic world for decades. At the same time, Protestant Christian Democrats' emphasis on the economic rights and activities of the individual challenged this underlying Catholic consensus. Despite the early CDU's substantial concurrence on economic policy, confessional and class differences would conjoin to render economics the most contested arena in early Christian Democracy.

Christian Socialism

The concept of Christian Socialism took center stage in the wide-ranging debate over the CDU's official economic policy. In the search for a clearer definition of the Catholic middle way, many early CDU Catholics championed a socialist economic order inspired by Christian values. Attempts to reconcile Catholicism and socialism enjoyed an upsurge in popularity in the wake of World War I. Bolstered by the conviction that the Great Depression marked an end to the capitalist era, anticapitalist sentiment was even more widespread after World War II, as political observers throughout Europe agreed that the continent was entering a socialist age in which war-ravaged populations would vote in parties of the left committed to nationalizing all industry.[118] Absent a clear understanding of what socialism would entail, this broad European consensus concerning capitalism's contribution to global war and political extremism was intensified in occupied Germany by widespread deprivation, the black market, and food rationing.[119]

That the popularity of Christian Socialism within the early CDU reflected the zeitgeist of the postwar era should not obscure the fact that the Christian Democratic debate over Christian Socialism represented a continuous stage in the development of Catholic thought and history. Regarded by some as the dominant strain of Catholic social thought in post–1945 Germany,[120] Christian Socialism was but one manifestation of Left Catholicism, a larger Europe-wide postwar movement especially influential in France, Belgium, and Italy.[121] More closely associated with Catholic theoreticians than practitioners in the interwar years, Christian Socialism nevertheless claimed notable adherents among the politically active and the clergy. After the war, it would find its most committed supporters among the priests and Christian Trade Unionists who had played crucial roles in organizing the CDU.

While clerics would emerge as among the leading Christian Socialists, the priesthood was by no means univocal on Germany's economic future. Consistent with clerical divisions over interconfessionalism, clergymen disagreed on Christian Socialism for a number of reasons, including theology. Having historically embraced an economic philosophy oriented toward the Gemeinschaft, Dominicans found themselves more readily drawn to socialism; it was no surprise that Dominicans Eberhard Welty and Laurentius Siemer called for Christian Socialism. While Jesuit teachings also emphasized the common good, Jesuits supported market-oriented economics prioritizing the development of the Persönlichkeit, particularly in the form of solidarism, often explicitly associated with the Catholic middle way between capitalism and socialism.[122] Though it was unusual for Christian Democrats to refer to solidarism by name—Adolf Süsterhenn was an exception in this regard—its doctrines, linked before 1933 to the Cologne line, would inform the position of numerous Christian Democrats, including Konrad Adenauer.[123]

Although Christian Democrats certainly referred to papal encyclicals and church doctrine,[124] the general divide between supporters and opponents of Christian Socialism was by no means purely theological.[125] In a testament to the continuities of the Catholic milieu, the battle within the Catholic CDU over its economic program was fought to a large degree along class lines.[126] Reflecting the prominence of clergymen and former Christian Trade Unionists in the CDU's organization, the term *Christian Socialism*—or a related expression, *Socialism Based on Christian Responsibility* (*Sozialismus aus christlicher Verantwortung*)—appeared frequently in early CDU programs. Demanding "social justice and social love," the Cologne Guiding Principles declared, "So we plead for a true Christian Socialism, which has nothing in common with false collectivist objectives, which contradict fundamentally the essence of man."[127]

In a signal of the term's malleability, early Christian Democratic appeals for Christian Socialism were generally more impressionistic than particular. When Christian Socialists did translate Catholic support for Lenkung into a practical economic program, they focused primarily on those sectors of the economy to be nationalized. According to the Cologne CDU in June 1945, the postal service, railways, coal-mining industry, and energy production were to be fundamentally "affairs of the public service"; banks and insurance companies were also to be subject to state control.[128] The December 1945 Bad Godesberg program, which called for Socialism Based on Christian Responsibility, codified these demands.[129]

Indeed, in an indication of the widespread influence of trade unionists and clergy in the early CDU, Christian Socialism found broad support beyond the northern Rhineland. Whereas Jakob Diel in the Rhineland-Palatinate understood Christian Socialism simply as an emphasis on the common good over individual interests,[130] other party programs repeated the Cologne CDU's list of "social property" to be nationalized.[131] Josef Arndgen, for example, explained that transferring mineral resources to common ownership, rendering the big banks and insurance companies common property, and making energy production a common concern would prevent private property from becoming a public danger.[132] According to an early Stuttgart party program, the "transformation of the property order" and "nationalization of social property" were devastated Germany's only means of realizing the basic Christian commandment, "Love your neighbor as yourself."[133]

Among the leading exponents of Christian Socialism in the early CDU were Walter Dirks and Eugen Kogon, editors of the *Frankfurter Hefte,* one of the most influential journals in occupied Germany.[134] Dirks and Kogon called for Socialism Based on Christian Responsibility rather than Christian Socialism, perhaps out of sensitivity to Jewish Germans.[135] The Frankfurt understanding of socialism is often distinguished from that of Eberhard Welty and other Rhenish Catholics for its reliance on Marx, an association that Welty took pains to reject.[136] Dirks's and Kogon's political advocacy of socialism would in any case be largely limited to the Frankfurt program; they withdrew from active party work in early 1946 to devote themselves to the *Frankfurter Hefte.*[137] Thereafter, their interventions were largely journalistic. In "The Abendland and Socialism," Dirks called for a reconciliation of socialism and the values of the Abendland to provide the new spirit Germany needed to rebuild: "The Abendland will be socialist, or it will not be."[138]

Despite the support Christian Socialism enjoyed, it hardly represented an uncontested position within the party. Even at the first gatherings in the Rhineland, several Catholics opposed inscribing Christian Socialism into the new party's program.[139] Such nascent opposition—primarily from the ranks of middle-class Catholics—would soon burgeon. Especially after the Bad Godesberg meeting in December 1945, the divisions among CDU Catholics would be reinforced by a power struggle for the leadership of the west German CDU, as Christian Socialism became identified with Jakob Kaiser, while Adenauer, head of the British zone CDU, led the party's campaign against it.[140] More so than Kaiser, Adenauer was influenced by solidarism and was sympathetic to an individualistic societal and economic order.[141] As a product of the Catholic Rhenish bourgeoisie, Adenauer had always been resolutely antisocialist.[142]

Kaiser, in contrast, committed his party organization immediately and unequivocally to a socialist economy. Most strikingly, Berlin CDUD members did not speak uniformly of Christian Socialism or even Socialism Based on Christian Responsibility, but occasionally simply of socialism. According to the June 1945 CDUD founding program, "The state of the Volk cries out for socialism, for the utilization of the rest of the goods that remain for us, in the interest of all of the Volk. And we assent to all steps taken to allow for this demand. For us, socialism is no longer a theory or a dogma; instead, the realization of a practical socialism has become a lifesaving necessity for us."[143]

This departure from traditional Catholic discourse was above all evident in Jakob Kaiser's public statements. Even as he distinguished sharply his understanding of socialism from that of Marx and highlighted the centrality of the Persönlichkeit, Kaiser offered a unique frame for Socialism Based on Christian Responsibility. The CDU's socialism, he asserted, "follows from the recognition that, through the spiritual, social, and economic collapse of our Volk, we are faced with a completely new situation."[144] Historically, Kaiser explained, this situation could be traced directly to the collapse of the "bourgeois age" as it had existed since the French Revolution. Because the war had deprived so many Germans of their property and employment, the CDU bore responsibility for designing a novel anticapitalist program: While the *Communist Manifesto* had been a "brilliant achievement" (*geniale Leistung*) in its time, it was now incumbent on different authors to write its second half—this time for a classless society.[145]

Beyond situating Christian Socialism in the narrative of socialist economics, Kaiser distinguished his vision of a Christian Socialist Germany by casting it in an international context. Pairing economic recovery with Germany's future international relations, Kaiser declared that "at the same time we are seeking our own path toward a new social configuration," "we also have to be a bridge between East and West."[146] By positing a German moral obligation to serve as a "synthesis of East and West in the life of Europe," Kaiser's "bridge" theory raised what would become a prominent dissenting voice on Christian Democratic foreign policy.[147]

Kaiser's link of Christian Socialism to Germany's role in postwar Europe guaranteed that the party's socialism debate would extend well beyond economic questions. Indeed, by proposing an economic program for a Germany of eastern as well as western orientation, Kaiser challenged directly the Rhenish, Catholic, abendländische roots of Christian Democracy, including its orientation toward Western Europe. Economically, Kaiser's interpretation of the end of the "bourgeois age" and association of Christian Socialism with Marxism emphasized a strictly antiliberal rather than antisocialist interpretation of antimaterialism. In a party dependent on Protestants to remain interconfessional, this delineation would pose significant questions for Christian Democratic unity. In particular, Kaiser's Christian Socialism would challenge the traditional bases of interconfessional politics as practiced since the Volksverein—that is, Protestant-Catholic cooperation in opposition to socialism.

Protestant Economic Ideologies

Reflecting the absence of a coherent Protestant economic philosophy, Protestant economic positions were inherently heterogeneous. Nevertheless, because most Protestants adopted Protestant theology's stress on individual, ethical decision making, they instinctually disfavored doctrines emphasizing community.[148] That they were overwhelmingly members of the middle class certainly reinforced their reservations about socialism; this was true whether they had belonged to a liberal, conservative, or fascist party before 1933. Indeed, to a large degree, CDU Protestants were defined more by the economic policies of the parties they chose not to join than by any organic economic idea. This was evident in Schlange-Schöningen's characterization of the CDU as a home for all those to the "right of Social Democracy," a description Adenauer rejected by noting that the CDU also claimed manual laborers, including Protestant workers, among its members.[149] Nevertheless, while CDU Protestants clearly identified with middle-class concerns, they remained opponents of liberalism. Although the early FDP articulated a variety of positions on state planning, it was clearly oriented toward defending business interests and would by 1947 unadulteratedly embrace the free market.[150] As devout Christians or Christian sympathizers, CDU Protestants were generally suspicious of liberals' anticlericalism and traditional reservations regarding a social welfare agenda.[151] They joined the CDU for that reason.

Signaling the importance not only of the British zone within the larger CDU but also of the Rhineland within the British zone, Wuppertal Protestants came in many ways to articulate the Protestant voice in early Christian Democracy. Mirroring the demographics of Wuppertal's population at approximately 80 percent Protestant, the Wuppertal CDU posited a significant exception to the general trend of party Protestant underrepresentation. Better organized and more ideologically unified than their Protestant colleagues in northern Germany, Wuppertal Protestants launched a concerted campaign to increase Protestant influence on the party's leadership ranks.[152] In early December 1945, following an October proposal, Rhenish Protestants held the first of a series of meetings to discuss Protestant Christian Democratic issues. Beginning in 1947,

Rhenish CDU Protestants gathered every second month in Düsseldorf, providing a model for Westphalian Protestants, who organized in December of that year.[153]

Elected in early 1946 to represent Protestants in the Rhenish CDU State Executive Committee, Otto Schmidt was recognized by Protestants and Catholics as the foremost representative of Rhenish Protestant Christian Democracy.[154] Chair of the Wuppertal CDU, Schmidt enjoyed considerable influence with Konrad Adenauer as well as other leading Catholics in the British zone CDU on issues of economic and cultural policy.[155] Schmidt's relationship with Adenauer was nonetheless riddled with conflict, especially after Schmidt publicly supported Leo Schwering over Adenauer in January 1946 to chair the Rhenish CDU.[156]

Schmidt's proclamations concerning Christian Democratic economics were notable for their philosophical character. In an article subtitled "An Attempt at a Socioeconomic New Order," Schmidt argued that Germany's economic infrastructure was so weak that it would be impossible for liberal economic policies to render "orderly economic subsistence." At the same time that Schmidt invoked "Christian knowledge" to argue for a focus on both the community and the individual, his emphasis remained primarily on the rights of the individual. "The limit of the common good," Schmidt asserted, "is far more difficult to recognize than that of the individual good." This point, he noted, had been proven by National Socialists, who—in the name of the "common good"—had committed the most atrocious crimes. "In the true common good," Schmidt concluded, "the service for the individual must be identifiable."[157]

A similar concern with the individual in the economic reconstruction of Germany was evident among Schmidt's coreligionists. In an August 1945 flyer, Wuppertal Protestants argued that only a "Gemeinschaft order" that granted the "widest scope for a private initiative" could produce "healthy economics" and the best product at the most reasonable price.[158] Former conservatives concurred. Friedrich Holzapfel, deputy chair of the CDU Westphalian state association, noted that "the word *social* is not used in our party program,"[159] while Robert Lehr, in a speech at the founding of the Düsseldorf CDU in November 1945, made no mention of the nationalization of industries or restrictions on private ownership of property.[160]

In September 1945, Protestant members of the program commission charged with revising the Cologne Guiding Principles for publication as the Guiding Principles of the Christian Democratic Party in the Rhineland and Westphalia succeeded in excising the words *Christian Socialism* from the text.[161] Hermann Lutze, a DStP member before 1933, was joined by fellow

Protestants in arguing that the term *socialist* was too burdened by history to appear together with *Christian*. Although Lutze rejected demands to transfer certain basic industries and companies to common economic management,[162] the program still called for limits on big business and monopolies and for as much "common property" as served the public weal; as in the Cologne program of June 1945, the postal service, railways, coal-mining industry, and energy production were to be public concerns, while banks and insurance companies would fall under state control.[163]

While no coordinated Protestant position on the party's economic program existed, the majority of prominent Protestants in the early CDU—with the notable exception of a few individuals, mostly in Berlin—opposed unequivocally the notion of Christian Socialism. Indeed, while Protestant Christian Democrats signaled, through their rejection of a postwar liberal party, an apparent commitment to state intervention in the economic sphere, most stood closer to the liberal political and economic traditions than to those of the Social Democrats. Protestants' philosophical and political antisocialism would prove crucial to the CDU debate concerning Christian Socialism, which would have the broadest impact on the political construction of Christian Democracy. As the forge within which the party's ideology was hammered, the CDU dispute over Christian Socialism represented the most important step in charting Christian Democracy's antimaterialist path.

CHAPTER 6

Christian Democracy in Practice: Economic Discourse and Policy

More than any other controversy, the battle over Christian Socialism defined the interconfessional alliance at the heart of German Christian Democracy. By delineating the outlines for Christian Democratic economics, party members' discourse ultimately determined the boundaries of Christian Democratic anti-materialism. Widespread and yet in many ways undifferentiated, Christian Democratic support for Christian Socialism necessarily blurred the party's antimaterialist rejection of socialism—the historic foundation of Protestant-Catholic political cooperation. At the same time, the increasingly hostile international climate polarized all European exchanges about capitalism and communism. In short order, CDU economic policy found itself caught in the crosshairs of Protestant-Catholic relations and the Cold War, to the decisive detriment of Christian Socialists.

Early Opposition to Christian Socialism

The Christian Socialist debate took hold quickly after the December 1945 Bad Godesberg conference; by early 1946, the formation of two fronts within the party—one associated with Adenauer, the other with Kaiser—was so conspicuous that party members regarded support for one leader as a threat to their standing with the other.[1] In part a result of Adenauer's personal assumption of power, the conflict would also be sustained by the June 1946 founding of the Social Committees of the Christian Democratic Employees (Sozialausschüsse der christlich-demokratischen Arbeitnehmerschaft). Modeled on the workers' committees of the pre-1933 Center Party and based in Cologne, the Social Committees were tied closely to the Dominican clergy Siemer and Welty, who hosted educational courses for workers in the Walberberg cloister. Led primarily by Johannes Albers, the committees derived their early membership almost exclusively from Catholic North Rhine-Westphalians; despite electing those Protestants who joined to the Executive Committee, the committees never succeeded in attracting a significant Protestant following.[2]

In addition to Wuppertal Protestants, who argued that the Social Committees would exacerbate internal party tensions,[3] middle-class CDU Catholics resisted the organization of the Social Committees.[4] Equally concerned was DGB leader Hans Böckler; already uneasy that former Christian Trade Unionists were underrepresented in the Trade Union Federation, Böckler now feared that the former trade unionists, especially with their ties to Western European Christian Trade Unions, would refound their Christian union.[5] While the former trade unionists established the Social Committees, their adversaries gathered strength as well. After securing his command of the zonal and Rhenish CDU parties, Adenauer began immediately to put his personal stamp on the party's programmatic development. Accused by Otto Schmidt of the "application of the Führer principle," Adenauer brooked little opposition in crafting the British zone CDU's first official programmatic statement.[6] In large part a product of Adenauer's vision and political authority, the March 1, 1946, Neheim-Hüsten Program highlights the rootedness of Adenauer's early understanding of Christian Democracy in bourgeois Rhenish Catholicism.[7]

After insisting that Christian ethics inspire not only all aspects of state reconstruction but also the delimitation of state power, the program called for the "mixed socialization [*Vergesellschaftung*] of the mines" and "modest property for all honest workers" in the name of securing democracy. In addition, the Neheim-Hüsten program proposed banning the concentration of economic power in the hands of a few or large organizations to protect the freedom of the Persönlichkeit. Neheim-Hüsten opted specifically not to embrace the nationalization of industry, noting that "the question of socialization of elements of the economy is not practical, in that the German economy is not free. For its later regulation, economic and political criteria—above all the common good—will be determining."[8]

To be sure, the elision of Christian Socialism in Neheim-Hüsten reflected Adenauer's influence. But the decision to sidestep the socialization question also signaled the beginning of a shift within the western CDU against the politics and personages associated with Berlin.[9] In February 1946, Kaiser received word from Otto Lenz that anti-Berlin tendencies were taking hold in Frankfurt and the Rhineland; even as they supported Christian Socialism, members of the Frankfurt CDU condemned Kaiser's claim to represent the entire CDU as "Berlin centralism."[10] If western Christian Democrats had hitherto not publicly challenged the CDUD, Adenauer opined, they certainly did not recognize its authority.[11] Kaiser, for his part, was well aware of these tensions; he had articulated anti-Prussian sentiments during and after the war. In an attempt to remove from Berlin the onus of Prussianism, Kaiser insisted that, "Prussia belongs to the past, but Berlin lives."[12]

In addition to traditional western Catholic hostility toward Berlin and class tensions within the Catholic milieu, discomfort with the Berlin CDUD's advocacy of socialism was palpable within the party's Protestant ranks. In February 1946, Otto Schmidt wrote to Adenauer that the Berlin program had led "to the most grave misgivings against the CDU" among Protestants.[13] Two months later, Schmidt declared that he did not believe the British zone CDU should place itself under the "authority of Jakob Kaiser," who, in Schmidt's estimation, had not contributed to "an intellectual clarification of what is meant by Christian Socialism."[14]

Protestants were concerned with "socialist tendencies" in the CDU, particularly in the CDUD, as well as with the not unrelated political influence of Catholic trade unionists within the party. In March 1946, former DNVP sympathizer Emil Marx, expressing concern that the Christian Socialists' emphasis on Gemeinschaft might threaten "private initiative," informed Johannes Albers that trade unionists' calls for a "democratization of the economy" disturbed more than just the "capitalists" in the party: "We all want that which is meant with the expression 'democratization of the economy'—that is, the greatest possible good of all should be realized. Just that appears to me endangered, however, when the way for class rule is prepared."[15] In an early April 1946 letter to Adenauer, Klaus Brauda addressed specifically the influence of "former Christian Trade Union leaders whom we have in our ranks." In particular, Brauda criticized the western CDU for appearing prepared to accept as a "necessary evil" Kaiser's "attempt to transplant the radicalization of the east zone in the west zones." Were the party to adhere to this program of "Christian radicalism," he concluded, it would validate the Rhenish SPD's contention that little distinguished the policies of Social and Christian Democracy.[16]

By launching such personal attacks, Brauda and his colleagues not only registered their unwavering opposition to Kaiser and his vision of Christian Democracy but also highlighted the relevance of confession to the economic debate. Although party members of both confessions generally favored such appellations as *capitalists,* the *middle class,* and *businessmen,* euphemism could not conceal the extent to which Protestants perceived their position as confessional. This was nowhere more obvious than in their efforts to argue otherwise. In his March 1946 letter to Johannes Albers, for example, Marx hastened to conclude that his criticisms of Christian Socialism—in contradiction to the spirit and tone of his letter—were "in no way specifically evangelical or Protestant."[17] The following month, Brauda showed a similar defensiveness in an implicit but clear reference to the Protestants he represented, maintaining that the demands of Kaiser and his colleagues "will have very unpleasant electoral and opinion poll consequences for us": "We will not make a stand against the socialist parties by outdoing them in radicalism," Brauda concluded; "instead, we will combat them by seeking and finding in Christian realism . . . the synthesis and not the antithesis of the *Stände* [economic estates]."[18]

The fear that Christian Socialism could render the CDU less attractive to Protestant voters related directly to Protestants' concerns that their distinctive voice in Christian Democratic policymaking was being ignored. Their disquiet was heightened by negotiations between Christian Democratic and Center Party representatives, leading to fears that a fusion of the two Catholic-dominated parties threatened Protestants' already tenuous standing within the CDU.[19] This anxiety was demonstrated most dramatically by Otto Schmidt's sustained campaign of opposition to the Neheim-Hüsten Program.[20] As a result of the party's neglect of its confessional minority and Protestants' "theological reservations,"[21] Schmidt argued, certain phrases in the Neheim-Hüsten Program suggested an inadequate commitment to the inviolability of private property.[22] If the CDU did not intend to delineate *Christian* in practical terms, the Wuppertal CDU suggested, then the party should just as well use the term *Catholic.*[23]

While the Protestant perspective was indisputably critical of Christian Socialism, the other forum for the Christian Socialism debate remained that of the Catholic Teilkultur. The pivotal role of the trade unionists in the British zone and particularly the Rhineland was highlighted by increasing pressure placed on Kaiser by the Soviet authorities. Soon after assuming the CDUD's leadership in December 1945, Kaiser antagonized Soviet authorities by, among other things, criticizing the nationalization of the industrial sector and land reform.[24] Kaiser's anticipation of the April 1946 unification of the Communist and Social Democratic parties in the Soviet zone and his apprehensions concerning communist influence on the unified trade union movement were reinforced by various Soviet restrictions on his own activities.[25] Only in mid-March 1946, with the help of the British occupation authorities, did he manage to undertake his long-planned journey to western Germany.

Kaiser's first trip to the British zone sharpened considerably the existing tensions within the party between supporters and opponents of Christian Socialism. By reestablishing contact with longtime colleagues from the Christian

Trade Unions—he went first to Cologne, where he met Johannes Albers—Kaiser signaled his determination to forge a united front of western and eastern Christian Socialists.[26] In response, Adenauer organized an early April meeting in Stuttgart of representatives from the British zone CDU and the French and American zones' regional parties to which Kaiser was pointedly not invited. According to Adenauer's meeting minutes, leading western zone representatives objected formally to Kaiser's statements characterizing Berlin as a synthesis or bridge between east and west Germany, the *bürgerliche* age as having come to an end, and the *Communist Manifesto* as having been a "brilliant achievement." Most important, the council concluded, expressions such as "We are social" and references to Christian Socialism were insufficiently precise and could only lead to confusion and conflict within the party. Finally, western Christian Democrats expressed reservations about the CDUD's proposed interzonal party conference and the prospect of locating the future party seat in Berlin or the Soviet zone.[27]

After Kaiser and Adenauer's meeting some days later did little to mollify Kaiser's anger at his former colleagues' apparent acquiescence to Adenauer in Stuttgart,[28] Adenauer continued his offensive. He learned in late April that Christian Socialists planned to gather at the Walberberg cloister and sought to influence the proceedings.[29] The next month, Adenauer expended considerable effort to meet with Fathers Siemer and Welty. Welty's recent publication, "Christian Socialism," in *Die Neue Ordnung,* had served as a basis for the meeting. "I am also almost in complete agreement with Father Welty's comments," Adenauer wrote to Maria Sevenich, "except for the unfortunate term 'socialism.'" Using a "concept condemned to extinction" will only "scare off many people, far more than we attract with it."[30]

In light of Adenauer's power play in Stuttgart, the four-zonal party gathering in Berlin assumed magnified importance. While Kaiser went to great lengths to persuade friends and prominent CDU politicians from western and southern Germany to attend,[31] Adenauer downplayed the conference as a Soviet zone party assembly.[32] Responding to Kaiser's upset at Adenauer's polemics against Berlin and the CDUD,[33] Adenauer claimed support from "by far [the] largest number of Rhenish and influential southern German gentlemen in the CDU": "I ask you to believe me, very honored Mr. Kaiser, that both in the West as well as in the South there exist considerable misgivings about Berlin and also, to some extent, the course of the CDU in Berlin." Because the Berlin gathering had grown much larger than Kaiser initially had led him to believe, Adenauer informed Kaiser that he would not be attending.[34]

Kaiser's June 16, 1946, speech at the Berlin meeting made clear that he was well aware of the forces coalescing against him. After paying tribute to "west Germany" and especially the Rhenish "origins of German culture," Kaiser called specifically on "my friends from the workers of the West and South," including Karl Arnold, Heinrich Strunk, and Father Siemer, to reclaim the spirit of their shared resistance to Nazism and dedicate themselves to establishing a progressive, unified Germany. Kaiser defended passionately the program of socialism, which he distinguished carefully from materialist Marxism. Remaining wealth in the southern and western areas of the country should not distort the realities of Germany's destitution, Kaiser argued; only through a Christian-inspired socialism could Germans reclaim their "human dignity."[35]

Adenauer's calculated absence from the June 1946 party meeting in Berlin[36] and the final statement issued by the conference's Economic-Political Committee embracing Socialism Based on Christian Responsibility[37] only reinforced the widespread impression among political observers that the CDU was a party of two wings—one identified with Berlin and Kaiser, the other with the Rhineland and Adenauer. The personalization of the split appeared striking not only to the Allies and the party's political opponents but also to CDU members themselves.[38] When British zone party leaders loyal to Adenauer criticized the term *Christian Socialism* at a late June 1946 meeting in Neuenkirchen,[39] the former Christian Trade Unionist Heinrich Strunk objected, characterizing the resolution as "an affront against Jakob Kaiser."[40]

Strunk's protest notwithstanding, the Neuenkirchen statement underscored the degree to which western Christian Democrats were drawing an increasingly sharp distinction between their interpretation of Christian politics and that of Kaiser. It also revealed how protagonists within the Catholic Teilkultur had begun to use Protestants as referents. In a significant reflection of the changed dynamics of political Catholicism, western German Catholics framed their criticism of Christian Socialism in terms of interconfessionalism: "For the first time in the political life of the German Volk, the rich heritage and the tradition of the Christian social movement of both confessions has become politically operative in a large party. In this hour of Christian collectedness, a clear dismissal of and distinction from the materialistic and collectivistic conception of society is needed more than ever. The utilization of the term *Christian Socialism* or *Socialism Based on Christian Responsibility* as an expression of a social outlook and social will . . . is misleading."[41]

Not only did Christian Socialism pose potential ideological difficulties for the new movement of Christian Democracy, but CDU leaders were also clearly contemplating the electoral impact of Christian Socialism on rural Catholics and potential Protestant recruits for the party.[42] Echoing his earlier reflections to Maria Sevenich, Adenauer noted, "As for the expression *Christian Social-ism,* we are not dealing here with an apt combination of words. One should not—in the long run—accustom party supporters to seeing simply something tolerable in socialism. . . . With the word *socialism,* we win five people and twenty run away."[43]

Antimaterialism Deployed: National Socialism and Marxism

In addition to concern about party Protestants, growing reservations on the part of western German Catholics regarding Christian Socialism were reinforced by international and domestic politics. Although the Vatican and German bish-ops' staunch anticommunism as well as Soviet restrictions on political activity, church freedoms, and confessional schools had discredited socialist and Com-munist parties, especially in the eyes of Christians,[44] German anti-Marxism was by no means limited to religious antimaterialism, nor was it exclusively Christian Democratic. National Socialist anticommunist propaganda, Red Army invasion and occupation policies, and ultimately the Cold War all con-tributed to growing anticommunist sentiment in the future Federal Republic of Germany.[45] This organic anticommunism would come to play a critical role in postwar politics; within the CDU, it provided Adenauer with valuable ammuni-tion for his battle with Kaiser.

Adenauer stood at the vanguard of the effort to distinguish the CDU sharply from any form of socialism. While few early Christian Democrats cast their abandonment of the Center Party explicitly as an anti-Marxist strategy, Adenauer had from the earliest postwar days tied his embrace of Christian Democracy to defeating socialism and communism.[46] In August 1945, Ade-nauer linked Germany's salvation through Christianity to "strong resistance against the state system and ideology of the East—Russia—and a thoughtful and cultural and with that also a foreign policy alliance [*Anschluss*] with West-ern Europe." According to Adenauer, "Only this planned integration of all Christian and democratic forces can protect us from the dangers threatening from the East."[47]

While Adenauer's campaign to eliminate the slogan *socialism* from Chris-tian Democratic discourse drew on traditional Christian hostility to socialist materialism, it also clearly served party propaganda, especially as Christian Democrats stressed the common materialism animating the Nazis, Soviets, East German Communists, and West German Social Democrats. Opposing the Nazis was, after 1945, more discourse than deed, but contesting Marxist-based movements quickly emerged as a matter of postwar political survival. This was certainly patent in 1946 and 1947, when the SPD emerged from municipal and state elections as the CDU's major electoral threat.[48] By accusing the SPD of mimicking the Nazis, Christian Democrats practiced the association of the ideological left with National Socialism well before CDU rhetoric and politics moved onto the international stage. As the September 15, 1946, local elections in the British and French zones approached, Christian Democrats seized on their first opportunity to hone this tactic.

By the late spring of 1946, Adenauer focused on the inherent dangers of a "socialist" economic system in the era's "great battle between Christianity and materialistic Marxism."[49] Decrying materialist governments' inherent authoritarianism, Adenauer championed the CDU's protection of "the freedom and the dignity of the individual" from the threats posed by an economic or political concentration of power.[50] In portraying a variety of economic policies—including those of the Nazis and Allies—as prone to state control and the subordination of the Persönlichkeit to the Gemeinschaft, Adenauer highlighted the full rhetorical potential of the concepts of materialism and materialist state rule.[51] In a trifecta of antimaterialist indictment, Adenauer directly linked Prussian militarism to dictatorship and to the SPD, accusing the SPD of being even more obsessed with centralized power than had been the Nazis: "As a German, I can only with the greatest regret establish that the old Prussian spirit, that ruthless undemocratic aspiration to exclusive power, speaks through the official announcements of the SPD, in a way in which it has, up to now, only obsessed the Prussian Junkerdom."[52]

Indeed, Adenauer led CDU members in asserting that the SPD—by embodying the same destructive, explicitly anti-Christian materialism as had the Nazis—risked returning Germany to the path it had just traveled.[53] In August 1946, Karl Zimmermann explained that every "collectivist system," whether National Socialism or Marxism, idolized secular theories, such as the "national Gemeinschaft" or materialist economics, excluding "spiritual and religious values."[54] The following month, Josef Kannengießer argued that only a Christian legal order could guarantee the "personal freedom of man" endangered by Marxism's "collectivist state, economic, and societal order."[55] A pamphlet, *Why CDU?* declared that "the classical materialism of a Karl Marx and Friedrich Engels . . . leads inexorably to collectivism of the East, with all of its horrors. . . . National Socialism was no different. It too installed the Volk as God. What was the result? . . . It leads to dictatorship, of which one kind is the 'dictatorship of the proletariat.'"[56] Not surprisingly, CDU Protestants vigorously embraced the notion that the Marxists manifested Nazi-style anti-Christian materialism. In the words of a September 1946 Wuppertal publication, "As far as socialism leads to collectivism" and seeks to impose "the omnipotence of the state or a class" over that of individuals, "it is obsessed by the same evil that has plagued us for so long."[57]

The CDU found no better evidence of Marxism's materialist and dictatorial impulses than its hostility to religion. Less an analysis of how the state apparatus functioned or the use of arbitrary terror, the CDU's theory of totalitarianism identified National Socialism and communism first and foremost as godless.[58] For early Christian Democrats, the suppression of Christianity was not a by-product of totalitarian rule but its defining feature.[59] Adenauer linked the history of Social Democracy to National Socialism's "means to oppress and extirpate Christianity, which systematically dechristianized public life in Germany,"[60] while others in the CDU located Social Democracy's hostility to religion in its support for the separation of church and state. According to Josef Kannengießer, "We reject fundamentally the conception and the word and the attitude: politics and religion have nothing to do with each other. As is well known, the socialists say religion is a private thing. . . . National Socialism said that to us as well."[61]

Related to what they perceived as Marxist atheism, Catholic party members were equally outspoken about the SPD's "degradation of the family and motherhood" following the Nazis' assault on the "organic cell" of society.[62] In a September 1946 article, "The Christian Woman in Political Current Events," Christine Teusch argued that "for us today there is only the decision between Christianity and collectivism." In particular, communist and socialist policies regarding abortion and motherhood outside marriage denied the "most profound intrinsic value of the woman."[63]

Christian Socialism under Fire

Even as the CDU would persist in attacking the SPD for its "Nazi-like" persecution of religion[64] and "cultural Bolshevism,"[65] the role of Christian Socialism disunited early Christian Democracy. While other party groupings, including the Frankfurt CDU, continued to identify themselves with Christian Socialism throughout the spring and summer of 1946, the most important battleground remained that of the British zone Catholic milieu. Much of this discussion took place privately; in the priority it placed on Protestants, it revealed the transformation of political Catholicism. In July 1946, prominent trade unionist Anton Storch wrote to Johannes Albers that he now rejected using the terms *Christian Socialism* or *Socialism Based on Christian Responsibility* to describe the party's economic program because the expression *socialism* carried "a bitter aftertaste." With National Socialism in the past and the threat of "communist socialism" looming, it was difficult to determine exactly what Christian Socialism entailed. The most important thing, Storch maintained, was "to help the broad social strata, so that they can once again eat their fill and in the coming winter not freeze to death; [these] are the problems that we must now solve. It does not matter under which motto we do this."[66]

Moreover, Storch insisted, Christian politics had changed. The disadvantages of identifying the party with socialism, Storch continued, were dramatized by the importance of the party's interconfessional alliance to defending Germany against the threat posed by communism: "If I were not of the firm belief that we are in the position to bring encroaching communism to a standstill, I would decline every task in public life and as a journeyman carpenter let things take their course. I am certain, however, that we can do it. In the CDU, forces have come together that are truly in the position to give Germany a new character. We must only prevent our being maneuvered against one another." Above all else, Storch insisted, the CDU should not be allowed, through a debate about economic policy, to become divided into a right wing and a left wing. Clearly associating Protestants with the party's "right wing," Storch noted that he had "come to the conviction" that several Protestants he had met recently in Hamburg and Kiel "are very valuable people." In light of the long-standing confessional differences between Protestants and Catholics, Storch concluded, "It is small wonder many things in a new party have to get worked out."[67]

The Rhenish CDU seemed increasingly to share Storch's discomfort with the name *Christian Socialism* rather than with any specific measure implied by its program. The expression *Christian Socialism* did not appear in the July 1946 report from the Cologne meeting of the Social and Economic-Political Committee of the Rhenish CDU, which stressed instead the CDU's preference for "social-economic and cooperative forms."[68] As Adenauer explained in reference to the British zone's September 1946 elections, the Rhenish State Executive Committee had agreed to postpone the discussion of the "expediency of the use of the words *Christian Socialism* or *Socialism Based on Christian Responsibility*" until after the elections to avoid the appearance of internal divisions. The debate, he added, was "merely about the name and not about the thing itself."[69]

If Storch and some fellow trade unionists increasingly followed Adenauer's lead, other members of the Rhenish-Westphalian CDU continued to employ the expressions *Christian Socialism* or *Socialism Based on Christian Responsibility,* including in campaign materials.[70] In mid-June 1946, former Christian Trade Unionists in Cologne drafted the program of the now officially founded Social Committees. While intentionally sidestepping a commitment to specific measures of socialization, those present nevertheless declared that the CDU remained loyal to the December 1945 Bad Godesberg program, including the specific demand for Socialism Based on Christian Responsibility.[71] At an early August 1946 meeting in Krefeld, Johannes Albers called not only for the realization of Christian Socialism but for the overthrow of capitalism "as a sociological institution."[72] At the same meeting, Karl Zimmermann cited the papal encyclical *Quadragesimo anno* to assert that nationalization was compatible with Catholic natural law; socialization, Zimmermann argued, implied not a categorical nationalization but a mixed economy based on "cooperative organization."[73]

Yet signs of a shift in the ranks of the CDU's western trade unionists concerning the advisability of associating Christian Democracy with a socialist economic program accreted. Increasing numbers of former Christian Socialists in the British zone, among them Karl Arnold, began following Anton Storch in eschewing the word *socialism* while retaining their economic vision.[74] That trade unionists did not insist, as a bloc, on inserting a commitment to Christian Socialism into the British zone CDU's August 1946 Guiding Principles for Economic and Social Policy signaled a further softening on their part,[75] as did the fact that many of the program's specific measures were adopted directly from a speech Adenauer delivered in Essen on August 24.[76]

At the same time, the drumbeats against Kaiser grew louder. In an article published in the *Rheinischer Merkur* in late August 1946, Adolf Süsterhenn, minister of justice and education and cultural affairs and member of the CDU's Rhineland-Palatinate Landtag faction, cast doubt on Kaiser's renunciation of the "collectivism" apparent now in Berlin and "east Germany." While the Catholic social tradition had been committed since the nineteenth century to the "deproletarization of the proletariat" by protecting "moral freedom and human dignity" and rejecting "collectivistic depersonalization," its "new name," Christian Socialism, was in Süsterhenn's view inherently vague and confusing. Süsterhenn also resented Kaiser's claims to party leadership. In a letter to the editors of the *Rheinischer Merkur* in September 1946, Süsterhenn declared, "I would regard it as of the utmost importance if we succeeded in killing the

'Christian Socialism' of Jakob Kaiser and comrades. The prerequisites are completely obvious. . . . If Kaiser is forced to drop his Christian Socialism, it will mean a considerable loss of prestige for him and his position in the union. I have no doubt that Herr Kaiser, through very skillful emissaries, is systematically attempting to influence the southern and western German Christian Democrats in the spirit of Berlin centralism."[77]

If Süsterhenn's treatise signaled the liberty western Christian Democrats believed they enjoyed in attacking Kaiser, the early November meeting in Herne of the Social Committees from the southern Rhineland and Westphalia indicated that the tide against the CDUD was cresting. Former Christian Trade Unionists heaped praise on Kaiser—"For the Christian working class in the Rhineland and in Westphalia, Jakob Kaiser is its man"—and in a keynote address, Theodore Blank, a Dortmund trade unionist, identified himself completely with Kaiser and Socialism Based on Christian Responsibility, arguing that only a "socialist" order could replace capitalism now that it had been rendered "obsolete" by the destruction of the "*bürgerliche* order." But as a fellow trade unionist subsequently demanded from the audience, "Who could listen to it?" It was not the content of the speech but its formulation that created a fury; above all else, Blank's language was criticized as "severe."[78]

In a telling indication of the shifting attitudes within the trade union movement as a whole, Karl Zimmermann responded immediately by invoking Kaiser's authority to repudiate Christian Socialism. In a recent address in Düsseldorf to Christian trade union leaders, Zimmermann contended, Kaiser had conceded, "'When I speak to you here in the West of socialism, I know that for you this word sounds harsher than on Berlin soil for ears from the East.'" In fact, continued Zimmermann, in a clear illustration of the powerful rhetorical quality of this debate, "Only with difficulty can our ear become accustomed to this word 'socialism.'" That Blank had raised the issue of Christian Socialism nevertheless had its merit, Zimmermann maintained; as the ensuing discussion revealed, the assembly disagreed solely on the label, not the substance of economic policy. When Blank declared, "'In contrast to capitalism, socialism means purely and simply that man [and] his spiritual, moral, and economic welfare stand in the center of interest,'" Zimmermann asserted, "Then we can only say, matter-of-factly, yes to that." But because Marxism had far more aggressive goals and the "collectivist state economy" posed the most profound post–Nazi threat to Christian Germany, it was incumbent on Christian Democrats to label clearly their agenda. Zimmermann suggested the term *Christian social reform*.[79]

Protestants and Christian Socialism

As Zimmermann's linguistic deliberations reflected the Catholic Teilkultur's ongoing reconsideration of the CDU's relationship to Christian Socialism, Protestant Christian Democrats, with isolated exceptions, continued uncondi-tionally to reject Christian Socialism.[80] In August 1946, attendees at a Protes-tant Working Group of the CDU conference were sufficiently discontent with the current state of the debate that they resolved to meet with Adenauer. Argu-ing that natural law and Catholic social teachings did little to inspire Protes-tants, the group suggested that the CDU invoke the Reformation to awaken in Protestants a sense of social and political responsibility.[81]

Beyond the theological level, the Protestant discussion of the CDU's eco-nomic program consistently stressed the very real problem of attracting and retaining Protestant votes. In September 1946, a party leader in overwhelm-ingly Protestant Thuringia complained to Jakob Kaiser that the CDU's use of the word *socialism* had "driven a considerable portion of the party's potential supporters to the Liberal Democrats." "Christian Socialism," he asserted, "did not attract the votes of SPD people, on which we had really been counting"; instead, those Protestants who voted had shown more confidence in "capitalis-tic liberalism." To attract the Protestant electorate, the author concluded, the CDU must drop "the propaganda for Christian Socialism for the Landtag elec-tions."[82] Commenting on the September 15, 1946, municipal elections in the British and French zones, Wilhelm Lindner struck a similar chord, noting that the Westphalian CDU had done well because it was less entangled in "ideo-logical antagonism." "Christianity and socialism," Lindner opined, in clear ref-erence to the debate concerning Christian Socialism raging in the Rhenish CDU, "go together like fire and water."[83]

Protestant CDU election propaganda sounded similar themes. In October 1946 election brochures, the CDU of the predominantly Protestant town of Herford stressed that the party stood for "the right to work, just pay, and the possibility of professional advancement for all [as well as] for the protection of the rightfully acquired private property and the support of private initiative in the economy." Party officials assured voters that the CDU opposed "every sort of dictatorship, whether it be that of an individual, a party, or a class," as well as "overly hasty socialization."[84]

The Protestant campaign against the doctrine of Christian Socialism con-tinued unabated with the turn of the year. In January 1947, Emil Marx stressed that the CDU needed to establish a unified economic program in time for the first Landtag elections in April,[85] while Wilhelm Simpfendörfer declared publicly that socialism served merely to raise hopes that could never be fulfilled because "no one knows what socialization means and what it is seeking." At the same time, Simpfendörfer insisted, Marxism led necessarily to collectivism, as demonstrated by the Soviet Union and the Soviet occupation zone. Rejecting the accusation that the CDU was a party of capital simply because it refused to endorse nationalization, Simpfendörfer maintained that the CDU's abiding goal was to prevent both depersonalization and the development of an antidemocratic state bureaucracy.[86] In a speech delivered in Südwürttemberg-Hohenzollern in early 1947, Ulrich Steiner insisted, "At this point, it must be stressed once again that the CDU is by no means hostile to property but rather recognizes property that has been honestly acquired and productively administered for the community." As for measures of "socialization," Steiner continued, Germany was absolutely not in the position to afford any "ideological experiments." Instead, "We believe that, in the economic sphere, the entrepreneur's initiative and joyousness of responsibility are still the best pillars for a healthy economy."[87]

The Cold War and the CDUD

As 1947 began, the gap between Catholic discourse on Christian Democratic economics and the stalwart antisocialism of CDU Protestants remained. Moreover, much to Adenauer's chagrin,[88] the debate among Catholic CDU members and the rivalry between Kaiser and Adenauer continued to define much of the party's public image and internal politics.[89] Indeed, in a reflection of the palpable divisions within the larger party, Kaiser provoked Adenauer's criticism with a January 1947 article, "Deutscher Weg 1947,"[90] and the CDUD published yet another unequivocal endorsement of Socialism Based on Christian Responsibility.[91]

Nonetheless, the beginnings of a semantic and ideological compromise were manifest. That 1947 marked the real emergence of the Cold War tensions not surprisingly had direct consequence for the CDU's debate over Christian Socialism. Not only in the three western zones of Germany but throughout Western Europe, the heightened influence of the United States and the perceived belligerence of the Soviet Union discouraged support for communist and socialist domestic political forces. Especially after the failed Moscow conference of the Allied foreign ministers in late spring 1947, the SPD and other Western European socialist parties began conspicuously to lose domestic political support.[92] In Germany, the rise of American power at the expense of British authority would have a direct impact on state debates about nationalization.[93]

The Moscow negotiators' inability to establish an accord on reparations and the federal organization of Germany represented just one of Europe's numerous steps toward division. In January 1947, the Americans and British fused their occupation zones to create the Unified Economic Area, or Bizone; that March, the Truman administration promised financial assistance to countries threatened by foreign "totalitarian" aggression. In June, the introduction of the European Recovery Program, the Soviet delegation's departure from the Munich conference of minister-presidents, and the constitution of the Economic Council of the Bizone in Frankfurt further solidified the links of the three western zones of occupation to the anti-Soviet powers. Following the premature conclusion of the fifth conference of the foreign ministers in London in November–December 1947, the division of Germany into two completely separate states appeared conceivable if not likely.

For Berlin Christian Democrats, the political machinations of the Soviet occupation authorities considerably tightened limits on CDU political activity. After Soviet occupiers impeded non-SED parties' ability to campaign in the October 1946 Landtag elections, the SED collected 47.5 percent of the zone's votes to the CDU's 24.5 percent.[94] Beginning in mid-1947, tensions between Kaiser and the Soviet authorities increased after Kaiser set the CDUD on a more confrontational course.[95] At the same time, zonal authorities devoted considerable energy to sowing dissension within the party,[96] winning over Otto Nuschke and Reinhold Lobedanz.[97] While general discontent in the CDUD Executive Committee with Kaiser's leadership was exacerbated by confessional tensions—leading Protestants including von der Gablentz, Rudolf Pechel, and Robert Tillmanns felt marginalized by the inner circle of former Center Party members[98]—the majority of the party's members remained loyal to Kaiser,[99] even after the Soviets forced him and Ernst Lemmer to resign in mid-December 1947[100] and banned him from speaking in the Soviet zone.[101] In November 1947, Adenauer would complain to Albers that Kaiser had not yet seemed to grasp that "the coming age will not belong to socialism."[102] By the end of the year, Adenauer, by virtue of his command of the western zones, held solitary control of the CDU.[103]

In 1948, few questions remained about the freedom of Soviet zone Christian Democracy. Beginning in January, the Soviets began a purge of so-called reactionary Christian Democrats; when the CDUD decided to participate in the Second People's Congress in March 1948 in Berlin, dissenting party members were personally threatened.[104] None of these developments was lost on western

Christian Democrats, who anticipated Kaiser's eventual relocation.[105] The September 1948 election of Nuschke as first chair at the Erfurt Party Conference after the Soviets forbade other candidacies represented the final break for western Christian Democrats, who now resolved to cease cooperation with the CDUD and recognize Kaiser and Lemmer as the group's legitimate leaders.[106] While Adenauer did meet with Nuschke in March 1949 regarding the Parliamentary Council's work,[107] the western CDU's decision appeared confirmed as, under Nuschke, the CDUD pursued a course of compromise that quickly undermined the party's claim to independence. In October 1951, the CDUD officially replaced its program of Socialism Based on Christian Responsibility with one of Christian realism and committed the party to Marxist socialism.[108]

After his dismissal, Kaiser gathered those loyal to him within the CDUD and attempted, from the Christian Democratic Jakob Kaiser Office in West Berlin, to maintain contact with Christian Democrats throughout the Soviet zone. In September 1950, this group, which included Heinrich Krone, Elfriede Nebgen, Robert Tillmanns, and Emil Dovifat, constituted the Exile CDU. Kaiser's position within the larger party had been fundamentally undermined, however, and with it his campaign for Christian Socialism. As a result, the last skirmishes of the battle concerning the CDU's association with Christian Socialism were waged not between Berlin and western Germany but exclusively within the British zone.

The Ahlen Program and North Rhine-Westphalian Landtag Debates about Socialization

The last stage of the contestation concerning CDU economic policy took place not only within the British zone, but—highlighting the importance of the Rhineland and Westphalia—in the Landtag for North Rhine-Westphalia. Because economic reconstruction was the first and most pressing issue with which the Landtag deputies grappled, the CDU's contribution to the Landtag debates represented a crucial stage in the evolution of Christian Democratic economics; indeed, in a reflection of the authority of Rhenish-Westphalian Christian Democrats within the multizonal party, the CDU's policies in the North Rhine-Westphalia Landtag served as a model for other Christian Democratic parties in their own Landtag debates over West Germany's postwar economic order.[109]

Carved by the British out of the rump of the North Rhine Province (created by the division of the Prussian Rhine Province) and the province of Westphalia in July and August 1946, the *Land* North Rhine-Westphalia inaugurated its Landtag in October 1946. Distributed initially in accordance with 1932 election results, Landtag seats were adjusted after the September 1946 municipal elections and the October 1946 district elections to reflect the CDU's nearly three-to-two advantage over the SPD.[110] While Rudolf Amelunxen, who would soon join the Center Party, continued as minister-president, the British appointed Karl Arnold as deputy minister-president and minister for education and cultural affairs, social services, and justice. Despite having acknowledged the problematic associations of the term *socialism,* Karl Arnold remained clearly associated with the trade unionist challenge against Adenauer. In the interests of serving their own nationalization agenda, the British hoped his appointment would bolster what they regarded as the CDU's left wing.[111]

For Adenauer, leadership of the Landtag faction represented a "second stage" of political engagement in addition to heading the British zone CDU.[112] By participating in state governance beginning in early 1947, the CDU under Adenauer found itself for the first time in its short history compelled to coordinate a unified program adequate to political rule.[113] It did so against the backdrop of the devastatingly hard winter of 1946–47, which lent new urgency to economic planning while intensifying popular suspicions of capitalism.[114] After the British military government announced publicly its detailed plans to nationalize the Ruhr's heavy industries,[115] Schlange-Schöningen worried that the CDU would be too riven by internal divisions to muster an effective response. Adenauer's quick dismissal of his concerns notwithstanding,[116] Schlange-Schöningen's apprehensions appeared prescient. Absent clear decision-making mechanisms, rivalries among individuals and small groups with competing agendas frequently left the faction without a unified message.[117]

Indeed, the CDU sustained one of its most public rows over Christian Socialism at the beginning of the parliamentary session. In late January 1947, at the behest of British occupation officials (working closely with Jakob Kaiser), Karl Arnold, Johannes Albers, and Walter Strunk of the Social Committees endorsed an SPD proposal to transfer the coal, iron, and steel industries to a public body responsible to a national German government. Arnold also reportedly threatened the secession of trade unionists from the party should Adenauer not embrace such a statement as CDU policy.[118] As difficult as it is to imagine Arnold effecting a party split, some observers saw his maneuver as representing the first real opposition to Adenauer's course.[119] The gambit also presaged Arnold's continuing challenges to Adenauer's leadership.

Such collaboration with the British was all the more striking since Rhenish-Westphalian trade unionists had begun in late 1946 to distance themselves from their Berlin colleagues and Christian Socialism. In early January, Johannes Albers wrote to Adenauer to assure him that despite their previous reservations, former trade unionists now stood squarely behind their zonal party leader. Past misunderstandings, Adenauer replied, should now give way to the motto of the day, unity.[120] Even as the embers of Christian Socialism clearly continued to smolder, Adenauer's call for harmony would not go unheard, soon finding expression in the early February 1947 British zone CDU's Ahlen Program.

The Ahlen Program, officially titled, *CDU Overcomes Capitalism and Marxism: The Ahlen Economic and Social Program of the CDU,* has long been the most cited and discussed of the CDU's early statements.[121] Often examined out of context and interpreted as a radical break from preceding discussions within the CDU,[122] the Ahlen Program in fact codified widely held positions within the Rhenish-Westphalian CDU regarding Germany's future economic order. It also represented a clever political maneuver on the part of Adenauer, who invoked the Ahlen conference in part to delay a vote on the British resolution based on the SPD socialization proposal. By the end of the zonal conference, Adenauer had engineered a consensus supporting mixed ownership of industry over state-directed socialization, an important achievement in light of the forthcoming North Rhine-Westphalian Landtag elections.[123]

That the tensions between Adenauer and the trade unionists colored the formulation of the Ahlen Program was obvious in Johannes Albers's initial opposition to Adenauer's proposals. By the time of the program's public issuance, however, both Albers and the Protestants present at the deliberations supported it.[124] In this sense, Ahlen represented less a dramatic turn in the development of CDU economic policy than a token of the party's emergent consensus, both in its excision of Christian Socialism and its references to social justice and the individual. In a statement reflecting a sentiment that had never been challenged within the Catholic Teilkultur, the Ahlen Program commenced with a clear indictment of the injustices enacted in Germany by the "capitalist economic system." The program relied further on standard formulations in arguing that to achieve the "Bedarfsdeckung of the Volk," the economy was to serve the "development of the creative forces of the Persönlichkeit and the Gemeinschaft"; at the same time, the individual's freedom and property were to be respected and protected from the concentration of economic power.

The program's rootedness in Catholic CDU economic discourse was clearly evident in its concern with protecting the sanctity of the individual from the overweening power of the state. After the Nazi regime had effected a concentration of industrial concerns and granted economic leaders excessive political power, the Ahlen Program asserted, the renewed imposition of state control over the economy could only mark a return to authoritarianism: Now that "the age of unlimited rule of private capitalism is done with," the CDU bore responsibility for preventing the replacement of private capitalism by a form of "state capitalism."[125] In this regard, Christian Democrats understood Ahlen as future political propaganda—specifically, as a signpost of the CDU's differences from the SPD.[126]

The Ahlen Program as a blueprint for the protection of individual freedom was also evident in its policy measures. While the program eschewed the label *Christian Socialism,* it demanded that large concerns, particularly those whose power could threaten the freedom of individuals, be broken up through the institution of cartel laws. Both coal and large-scale iron-producing industries, for example, were to be nationalized, and employees were to participate in the management of sizable public concerns as long as the "necessary entrepreneur initiative" were protected. In this regard, Ahlen recognized the essentiality of planning and Lenkung of Germany's devastated economy; significantly, guidance was to be exercised by parliament-controlled economic bodies, not by the state.[127]

The success of the Ahlen Program in codifying both a substantive and a conceptual consensus within the party was underscored by the February 5–6, 1947, meeting of the party's state associations in Königstein. Marking only the second gathering of representatives from all four zones, the conference and its endorsement of the spirit and specifics of the Ahlen Program affirmed the developing party consensus on a Christian Democratic economy. That the program did not invoke Christian Socialism reflected agreement not only within the British zone but increasingly throughout the CDU that a just economic program need not carry the title *socialist.* As the northern Baden CDU explained at its second State Party Congress later that year, the fact that the term *Christian Socialism* had been sacrificed for pragmatic, propagandistic reasons hardly meant that supporters of Ahlen had abandoned Catholic-inspired economic justice; the era simply demanded rhetorical and ideological clarity.[128]

In a further indication of the party's shifting balance of power, Adenauer secured the site of the newly established Working Association of the CDU/CSU (Arbeitsgemeinschaft der CDU/CSU) in Frankfurt.[129] The significance of locating the party's first interzonal organizational center in western Germany rather than Berlin, as Kaiser and Lemmer had sought, was lost on no one,[130] least of all the CDU's Soviet zone leaders, whose relations with their "western" colleagues became yet more embittered.[131] Christian Socialism's fading fortunes were evident yet again at a late February 1947 meeting of the Social

Committees, where trade unionists conspicuously avoided the phrase *Christian Socialism* and speakers such as Josef Gockeln associated "socialism" directly with the horrors of a "totalitarian state economy." Kaiser steered clear of economics altogether, speaking on "The Union in the East Zone and Germany's Unity." As a final, dramatic signal of the trade union endorsement of Adenauer and his course, those present declared that Adenauer, who had addressed the assembly at length, "had won the heart of the Christian working *Volk*."[132]

The degree to which Adenauer sought to position the Ahlen Program as a resolution of intraparty differences was evident in a speech he delivered in mid-March 1947 at a meeting of the CDU's British Zonal Committee in Herford. Earlier in the month, while addressing the North Rhine-Westphalian Landtag, Adenauer acknowledged earlier dissension within the party but asserted that CDU members now were "unanimously agreed, one and all, regardless of which *Stand* [economic estate], regardless of whether entrepreneur or employee, factory owner, or farmer: we are all on the same footing."[133] In Herford, Adenauer underscored this point. Characterizing the Ahlen Program as "a very good achievement," Adenauer argued that the program provided excellent proof that, within the party, "there is no left and no right wing [and] that we are not reactionary"; even the head of the SPD faction, Adenauer noted, referred to left and right wings within the CDU as a "fairy tale." Instead, Adenauer declared, the program demonstrated that "we really are making the very earnest attempt to position the entire German economy on another social foundation from that on which it has hitherto stood."[134]

If Adenauer's proclamations were more rhetoric than reality, the CDU nonetheless approached the political test in the North Rhine-Westphalian Landtag emboldened by its burgeoning consensus. Drawing directly from the language and themes of the Ahlen Program, in early March 1947 the Rhenish and Westphalian Christian Democrats presented the Landtag with six motions regarding mixed ownership.[135] In a shift from the practical prescriptions of the Ahlen Program, the Landtag program stepped back from a specific call for the "mixed socialization" (*Vergesellschaftung*) of the mining, iron, and chemical industries in the British zone.[136] Instead, it demanded the "breakup" of basic industries—particularly iron, chemical, and mining—so that no one stockholder could control more than 10 percent of the portfolio, in keeping with "the planning and *Lenkung* of the economy."[137]

The CDU's concern with preventing the empowerment of the state or small groups of individuals extended further to its embrace of a "principle of dispersion of power." To protect individual workers from the excessive power of state capitalist concerns, the enforcement of workers' partnership in industry, or codetermination (*Mitbestimmungsrecht*), was considered as important as the employee's right to share in industry profits. Although codetermination in West German industry would not be legislated until the early 1950s, the CDU's call for a "new order of the relations between employer and employee" reflected clearly the influence of Catholic social teachings and antistate sentiment on early Christian Democratic policymaking.[138]

In the explanation accompanying the party's six motions, the CDU echoed much of the theoretical explication of the Ahlen Program.[139] Because the "capitalistic economic system" had proven itself inappropriate for the German Volk, a "capitalistic" drive for profit and power could no longer serve as the basis of the German economic order; the "past system of unlimited rule by private capitalism" was to be abandoned. To protect the individual from capitalism's concentration of economic and political influence in the hands of the very few, the CDU advocated a new "social economic" order devoted to individual rights and values.[140]

Indeed, in an address notable for its philosophical tone, Adenauer made clear the degree to which the CDU's policies reflected Christian Democratic ideology. In light of the fact that capitalism focused exclusively on profit as an "outward manifestation of the economy" was "done with," the CDU sought "a mixed-economic form of management." But the transitory "planning and *Lenkung*" urged by the CDU and that advocated by the SPD were, according to Adenauer, fundamentally dissimilar: "It is an important difference—whether I regard the planning and management as an end in itself or as a necessary evil. We are of the opinion that it is a necessary evil." While the CDU would prevent a centralization of both economic and government power, the KPD and SPD motions to nationalize the mining, iron, and steel-producing industries were potentially dangerous.[141] Drawing directly on the common "materialist" essence of socialism and Nazism, Adenauer characterized the SPD's call for state involvement in the economy as "exactly the recipe of National Socialism"—that is, the "rule of a party not only with political but also with economic means."[142] In a passionate coda to his parliamentary address, Adenauer conceded that "private initiative" had indeed brought much "harm" to Germans in the past. While the CDU concurred that "unimpeded" or "unrestrained" private initiative should be banned, Germans could not simply renounce this expression of the human spirit: The "freedom of the Persönlichkeit"—"man's most precious gift"—and its expression through the ownership of private property were to be restricted solely when their limitation served the better interests of the German people.[143]

Adenauer's endorsement of individual liberty and his indictment of "unrestrained" private initiative did more than confirm the contours of Catholicism's traditional middle way between liberal capitalism and Marxism. By accusing the overly powerful Marxist state of impinging on the sanctity of the Persönlichkeit, Adenauer and his colleagues underscored the political potential of rejecting Christian Socialism in the name of unconditional antimaterialism. In his address to the CDU Zonal Committee in Herford, Adenauer referred repeatedly to the forthcoming April 20 Landtag elections in North Rhine-Westphalia, Lower Saxony, and Schleswig-Holstein. In addition to disseminating the Ahlen Program, the six North Rhine-Westphalia Landtag motions,[144] and campaign posters stressing Christian unity and doctrine,[145] Adenauer instructed his fellow British zone Christian Democrats to highlight parallels between the SPD and the NSDAP with an emphasis on cultural policies, particularly schools, and the two parties' hunger for power.[146] The Rhenish CDU certainly took Adenauer at his word, predicting in one brochure that the SPD would make the economy a "stomping ground for bureaucrats and party bigwigs,"[147] while warning in another that "visibly satanic forces have dragged our Volk into the abyss. It was forced to prostrate itself on its knees before the idol of the state. The idol lies crushed on the ground, but the demons do not want to retreat. The expulsion of idols is the command of the hour."[148]

While the Christian Democratic program in the North Rhine-Westphalian Landtag helped set the party on its future ideological course, it also prefigured the party's political alliances. The FDP endorsement of the CDU's six motions concerning the "disclosure of the property relations in the mining, iron-producing as well as chemical large-scale industry" marked the sound defeat of the SPD's motion proposing a public opinion poll regarding the socialization of heavy industry;[149] at the same time, it represented a tactical victory by Adenauer over the British occupation forces, which had sought to pass socialization legislation with the support of the SPD and the CDU's trade union wing.[150] In the broader realm of political affinities, FDP support for the six motions would provide an important basis for political cooperation, reflecting and reinforcing Adenauer's clear preference for a CDU-FDP coalition in contrast to Karl Arnold's commitment to a coalition with the SPD.[151]

Karl Arnold's Challenge

While the landmark Ahlen Program and CDU policies in the North Rhine-Westphalia Landtag represented a significant degree of consensus within the party, dissension within the western Teilkultur nonetheless remained. Evident both in his continuing sympathy for Christian Socialism—even as he eschewed the term—and his reservations concerning categorical rejection of the SPD as a coalition partner, Karl Arnold continued to offer, although in muted form, an alternative vision of German Christian Democracy.[152] In his early March 1947 Landtag address following Adenauer's oration, Arnold reemphasized CDU support for the "breakup" of "private capitalist concerns and powerful organizations in the mining industry and in the large-scale industries" to establish a "social economy" with partnership in industry. In contrast to Adenauer's pointed attacks on the SPD and KPD plans for nationalization, Arnold maintained that the new social order could succeed only when inspired and supported by a wide variety of groups; Arnold also spoke favorably of measures of "socialization," although with the caveat "when we even want to so describe the measures for the new order of the economy."[153]

Through his challenge to the emergent paradigm of Christian Democracy, Arnold not only signaled lingering disharmony within the Catholic CDU but also demonstrated that the adjustment of political Catholicism to interconfessionalism had not yet come full course. The continued Protestant dismay with Christian Socialism, while heeded by the majority of CDU Catholics, had been heightened by Arnold's prominent role in the North-Rhine Westphalia Landtag. That tension intensified after the April 20, 1947 Landtag elections. While the Christian Democrats lost decisively to the SPD in Schleswig-Holstein and especially Lower Saxony, they retained their lead in North Rhine-Westphalia, albeit with 37.6 percent of the vote, a one-fifth decline from the preceding fall's local elections. Over Adenauer's opposition, Arnold remained the CDU candidate for minister-president.[154]

That Arnold and Adenauer's differences persisted, especially in light of Arnold's preference for a coalition including the SPD, was hardly a surprise.[155] As Adenauer communicated to Arnold in early June, the faction did not approve the May 26, 1947, position paper Arnold had sent the SPD, especially some of Arnold's economic proposals and his assertion that "the liberal capitalist economic system died out according to its own rules"; the Ahlen Program, Adenauer explained, sufficed.[156] The following day, Adenauer wrote to Carl Schröter that the CDU faction had overwhelmingly rejected the efforts of Arnold and several of his friends to deviate from the Ahlen Program in building the North Rhine-Westphalian government.[157]

Despite Adenauer's best efforts to undermine his position, Arnold led the CDU into a coalition government including all parties (the CDU, SPD, Center Party, and KPD) except the FDP.[158] In his June 17 address (*Regierungserklärung*) to the Landtag as minister-president, which Adenauer boycotted,

Arnold revisited the differences that distinguished his understanding of the CDU's economic program from that of the party's majority. After criticizing "the capitalistic economic system" that violated the "morally prescribed service to the Gemeinschaft," Arnold called for a "genuine social economy . . . in which the responsibility and initiative of the individual can take full effect." While he argued at length that "social economics does not mean bureaucratized state economics," Arnold nevertheless supported stronger measures against the British zone's major industries than did many of his colleagues, including Adenauer.[159] In a passage that immediately proved controversial within the North Rhine-Westphalian CDU, Arnold demanded that the "participation of private big business" in basic industries "be excluded."[160]

Arnold's call for the "exclusion" of private capital from all German industries extended beyond the provisions of the Ahlen Program, which envisioned private enterprise playing a role in some industries.[161] Not only did Arnold's declaration exacerbate his troubled relations with Adenauer,[162] but fallout from the speech underscored the profound gap that remained between Protestants and Catholics in the British zone and beyond. At an official gathering of CDU Protestants of the Northern Rhineland and Westphalia in mid-July 1947, Protestants led by Robert Lehr und Helmut Lauffs strongly condemned the CDU's coalition with Marxist politicians. Moreover, as Protestants concerned about the party's future direction, they demanded that the "thought of the Union of both Christian confessions be fertilized" in the development of CDU policy; the present "government and faction circles in the CDU" revealed a "dangerous inclination" to prioritize the "Marxist coalition partners" over the "principles of the party." In addition to the coalition alliance, they continued, Arnold's government policy statement "blurred the boundaries of our conception of the economy." If Arnold sought to attract workers from the SPD through an openness to "socialism," he ran the risk of alienating "wide circles of the middle class" and farmers without attracting the sought-after workers: "Through its approval of the government policy statement," the convention concluded, "the Landtag faction not only overstepped the boundaries, as far as it was concerned, of the Ahlen Program, but it . . . disregarded the guiding principles of the party congress."[163]

If the Protestant response to Arnold highlighted the confessional line running through early Christian Democracy, Arnold's reaction was equally revealing. Defending in impassioned language his long-standing commitment to the "true and genuine values of Christianity,"[164] Arnold expressed particular dismay at what he described to Lehr as the open confessionalization of the party's economic policy. Ignoring dynamics inherent in Christian Democratic politics from its inception, Arnold criticized Protestants for portraying CDU economic and coalition policy as a confessional issue: "To confuse general political questions with the thought of the confessional union and to handle them, in a way, as a Protestant problem, at a Protestant meeting, appears to me an objectively unnecessary encumbrance on the political cooperation between the confessions, which I, based on the spirit of the Union, deeply regret."[165]

At the same time that he attacked the party's Protestants for "confessionalizing" CDU policy, however, Arnold underscored through his own display of religious resentment the tensions coursing through the early CDU. Defending "Christian workers" as "the most active and devoted core" of the party, Arnold praised in particular "politically and ideologically well-trained Christian workers" for having displayed "in the Third Reich and also now, again, a maximum of immunity vis-à-vis Marxist, nationalistic, or other erroneous slogans." In a thinly veiled indictment of Protestants for greater susceptibility to "materialist" phenomena, Arnold concluded, "Not all of the circles represented in the CDU can lay claim to the same for themselves."[166]

While Arnold's rebuke of the Protestant dispatch provoked no immediate rejoinder, the Protestant critique of Arnold's speech from other sources continued unabated. In a June 25, 1947 circular letter, Emil Marx wrote that while the CDU had agreed that private capital could no longer play the dominant role in Germany's economy, "to exclude it completely" would meet with "considerable reservations on *our side.*"[167] As Germans in economic distress had called out in the past for a "Führer," a Wuppertal party brochure of June 1947 alleged, "today the slogan *socialization* . . . appears to be playing a similar role in the brains of many people." Because "Bolshevist communism" is "standing at our door," the brochure concluded, "old terms" such as *socialism* were no longer acceptable.[168]

The Debate Resolved? Recklinghausen in August 1947

As the CDU party congress in mid-August 1947 in Recklinghausen subsequently demonstrated, Arnold's deviation from the emerging consensus sounded more an echo than a call to arms. In his speech, Adenauer underscored the centrality of the "principle of the distribution of power" and the imprecision of the term *socialization*; while the CDU intended to prevent the "rule of private capital" in the mining and other basic industries, he explained, the concentrated economic power of these industries should under no circumstances be transferred to the state. Regarding Arnold's call for the "exclusion of big business" from such industries, Adenauer concluded that Arnold's formulation represented "only another expression of that which we already resolved in Ahlen and in the North Rhine-Westphalian Landtag in March of this year— namely, that no representative of private capital shall control directly or indirectly more than 10 percent of the votes; with that, big business is eo ipso excluded." At the same time that he sought to defuse the controversy with Arnold, Adenauer praised the CDU's successful integration of Protestants and Catholics, noting that cooperation across the confessional line had bred familiarity and appreciation. Protestants and Catholics had learned a great deal from each other, he added, above all that more united than divided them.[169]

Adenauer's deflection of Arnold's proposal and the otherwise harmonious proceedings at the Recklinghausen party congress signaled a probationary end to the party's economic dispute.[170] While by no means definitively over, the Christian Democratic battle for an ideological consensus was irrefragably beginning to resolve. Indeed, as the party's course in the near future would reveal, the basic contours of a German Christian Democratic program were now set: Christian Democracy entailed the rechristianization of German society in the spirit of unprecedented Protestant-Catholic cooperation. Devoted to the abendländische ethic of the freedom of the Persönlichkeit in the economic sphere, the CDU portrayed itself as Germany's salvation from materialism's resurgence in the guise of Marxism, specifically Social Democratic "economic control" (*Zwangsbewirtschaftung*).[171] Protestant as well as Catholic Christian Democrats could embrace an antimaterialist economic program as long as it delineated sharply between socialist economics and Christian economics. State intervention was necessary; the call for *planvolle Lenkung* in the service of Bedarfsdeckung dictated against unrestrained capitalism. By the late summer of 1947, the CDU emerged from its most protracted debate with a clear ideological and operational consensus. In 1948, the introduction of the social market economy and rise of Ludwig Erhard within the party, although contested, would give new expression to this accord constructed by Protestants and Catholics during Christian Democracy's first two years.

CHAPTER 7

The CDU in Council:
Forging Economic and Cultural Policy

The year 1948 provided the CDU with both unprecedented opportunities to translate its ideological compact into policy and significant political challenges. The party entered the year in a sustained confrontation with the refounded Center Party and a pitched battle with the SPD for political leadership of the future Federal Republic. Christian Democrats had won the 1946 and 1947 elections in the future state of Baden-Württemberg, retained their dominant position in North Rhine-Westphalia's April 1947 Landtag elections, and emerged victorious later that year in the Rhineland-Palatinate Landtag election. Hesse, Schleswig-Holstein, and Lower Saxony had all seen SPD victories in 1946 or 1947, however. Christian Democratic political hegemony was hardly self-evident.

Even as the debate over Christian Socialism appeared largely resolved, confessional tension continued to permeate intraparty dynamics. That the transformation of political Catholicism remained incomplete was underscored by the continued appeal of the Center Party and Protestant apprehensions regarding its possible merger with the CDU. Cultural policy also highlighted the consequence of confession. As Protestants and Catholics cast back to a pre-Nazi consensus on questions of family and gender, confessional schools divided them and forced a reckoning with the Catholic Church. Family and school policy would assume prominence in the Parliamentary Council, while Christian Democratic economic policy would be enacted in the Bizone's Economic Council, where the CDU sought to implement policies codified in the North Rhine-Westphalian Landtag. It was also in the Bizone that the CDU and Ludwig Erhard forged an alliance with enormous effect.

The association of Christian Democracy with social market economics in 1948 represented less a radical break in the party's ideological or economic development than an expression of the compromise already reached within the western zones, especially the British. The affiliation with Erhard was a clear product of external as well as internal dynamics. As the Cold War's rising hostilities cast a pall over parties and policies of the left across Western Europe, West Germans' wartime and postwar experiences reinforced suspicion of a planned economy. Ludwig Erhard's role within the CDU nevertheless tested the strength of the young party's accord on ideology and economics and laid bare the confessional and class lines crisscrossing early Christian Democracy.

Ludwig Erhard and Christian Democratic Confessionalism

Even as he would come to symbolize the social market economy within and beyond West Germany, Erhard's relationship to Christian Democracy was anything but straightforward. Erhard had played no role in the party's founding or its earliest debates, and although party records backdated his membership to 1949 and he would represent Ulm-Heidenheim in the Bundestag from 1949 until 1977, Erhard officially joined the party only in 1963, just before he was elected chancellor.[1] A Protestant Bavarian unpopular with the CSU, Erhard was hardly a likely candidate for Christian Democratic asendance. One historian described the process by which Erhard became the symbol of the CDU/CSU/FDP coalition in 1949 as occurring "almost overnight and under curious circumstances."[2]

For the CDU, alliance with Erhard would sharpen the emergent delineation of antimaterialism to stress antisocialism and the importance of the Persönlichkeit. At the same time, Erhard's Lutheran upbringing and family's politics located him firmly outside the Catholic milieu.[3] Considering his pre-1933 support for the DDP and his predominantly Protestant ministerial appointments, it is hardly surprising that many CDU Catholics observed the rise of this Kulturprotestant with deep skepticism.[4] If not all Catholics regarded Erhard as the embodiment of "Protestant liberalism, economic materialism, and political secularism,"[5] many detected underlying differences with their Protestant colleague on such fundamental questions as the relationship of the Persönlichkeit and the Gemeinschaft.[6] In particular, Karl Arnold, Johannes Albers, and Jakob Kaiser would campaign in 1948 and 1949 to undermine Erhard's authority within the western zones and CDU. Nevertheless, Erhard's economic training and thought help to explain why the overwhelming majority of CDU members recognized in the social market economy a model consistent with early CDU economic ideologies. Within these broad outlines, Erhard and the early CDU made common cause.

The Social Market Economy

The roots of the social market economy reach back into the Weimar Republic, when economists including Walter Eucken, Wilhelm Röpke, and Alexander Rüstow advocated a moral economic order grounded in the spirit of equal opportunity.[7] At odds on numerous counts, these thinkers nevertheless agreed that the state should control the economy to protect financial stability and more broadly democracy, human dignity, and individual freedom.[8] If the Great Depression made all too real the risks of laissez-faire capitalism,[9] Nazi economic policies had demonstrated the importance of a market economy. Rejecting high tariffs, monopolies, and cartelization, these economists advocated a progressive tax system with the specific goal of redistribution of income.[10]

The social market economy and its architects revealed clear Christian influences.[11] Both the Freiburg circle's devotion to the Christian principle of "brotherly love" and their rejection of nineteenth-century liberalism and Marxism were grounded in the long-standing tradition of Protestant social ethics reaching back to Adolf Stöcker.[12] At the same time, the social market economy drew on the Catholic teachings of solidarism and subsidiarity, permitting state intervention only to protect individual freedom.[13] Though he did not share all of these thinkers' cultural assumptions, including that of Christian reformism, as a student and economist Erhard would absorb the essence of their ideas,[14] known variously as ordo-liberalism or neoliberalism.[15]

Erhard outlined his postwar perspective in, among other places, an October 1946 article, "Free Economy and Planned Economy," in which he described the risks posed by excessive bureaucracy to the "values" of the Persönlichkeit. If the labels of *socialism* and *capitalism* were reductive and falsely dichotomous, Erhard asserted, one could nevertheless discern crucial differences between a "market economy with free price development and a nationalized command economy." Stressing that capitalism hardly excluded planning or social commitment, Erhard underscored the "social responsibility" of any new economic system.[16]

Politically, the social market economists initially affiliated with the FDP, and Erhard enjoyed far better relations with the Bavarian FDP than with the CSU. Not only did the Christian Socialists force Erhard to resign in January 1947 as Bavarian economics minister, but they joined the SPD to target him in postwar Germany's first parliamentary investigation.[17] For their part, Bavaria's postwar liberals endeavored to win Erhard to their side, and he did speak at their first party rally in Nuremberg in February 1946, advocating reconciliation between liberalism and socialism.[18] But while the FDP's southern branches eschewed laissez-faire capitalism to embrace ordo-liberalism,[19] the larger FDP constituency was unenthusiastic about redistributive taxation or restricting cartels; most neoliberal economic theorists ultimately joined the CDU. It was nonetheless through Bavarian FDP connections that in September 1947 Erhard was named head of the Special Bureau for Monetary and Currency Matters of the Economic Council and charged with developing a program for currency reform.[20] From this position and again with FDP support, he would win an even more prominent Bizonal role some months later that would bring him into direct contact with CDU leaders.

Erhard's Rise in the CDU

It was in the spring of 1948, in the wake of CSU Johannes Semler's January 1948 dismissal (for describing American aid as "chicken feed") that FDP politicians pushed Erhard's appointment as director of the Administration for Economics.[21] Not only was Erhard largely unknown in Germany, but his stock with the CDU leadership was limited at best.[22] In a May 1948 letter to Maria Meyer-Sevenich, Adenauer misspelled Erhard's name and characterized his reputation as "extraordinarily capable" but lacking in administrative experience;[23] their first meeting likely did not take place until the late spring of 1948.[24]

With Erhard's appointment, a cadre of leading social market economy theorists was named to the newly constituted advisory council of the Economic Administration; new members included Jesuit priest Oswald von Nell-Breuning, who would emerge as a leading West German voice on Catholic social teachings in the 1950s, and Otto Heinrich von der Gablentz.[25] Consistent with the wartime writings of the Freiburg circle, the advisory council began immediately to implement policies designed to engineer a free market with continued controls over food and housing.[26] On April 21, 1948, Erhard delivered his first major speech as economics director;[27] he and the advisory council soon would endorse the lifting of restrictions on foreign trade, monopoly control, the negotiation of wages, and the reduction of price controls.[28]

Despite implying to FDP leaders that he would join their party in exchange for nomination to the directorship, Erhard rapidly developed a political relationship with the CDU in 1948.[29] At the same time, the British zone CDU continued to hone its strictly antisocialist policy independent of Erhard's influence. In particular, the CDU whetted its antinationalization rhetoric and politics in the North Rhine-Westphalian Landtag. Characterizing the Social Democratic proposal for the socialization of the coal industry as "Russian," the CDU argued in August 1948 that, after "twelve years of state management of the economy," Germany could no longer afford an assault on the Persönlichkeit through increased state power.[30] When the SPD's bill passed with Center Party support, Karl Arnold engineered a Christian Democratic abstention (with one exception) on the vote. The ultimate political victory, however, belonged to Adenauer, who had achieved his larger goal that the CDU lend no support to state socialization or the SPD.[31]

Center Party–CDU Negotiations Redux

The ramifications of this vote—on what ironically became a moot issue after the British occupiers blocked the law's enforcement—were manifold.[32] The socialization denouement not only dashed Karl Arnold's hopes of an alliance with the SPD but ended a renewed CDU attempt at merger with the Center Party. The Zentrum had remained a thorn in the CDU's side, especially in North Rhine-Westphalia, where it scored almost 10 percent in the April 1947 Landtag elections despite a targeted CDU campaign against "wasted" Center Party votes.[33] After the CDU's clear electoral victories in September 1946, Adenauer had eschewed negotiations with his Catholic opponents in the hopes that their party would implode. When he acceded to clerical pressure to meet with new Center Party leader Johannes Brockmann before the 1947 British zone Landtag elections, the two men failed to reach any meaningful accord.[34]

The so-called Bottrop discussions in June–July 1948 were conducted confidentially by Karl Arnold and Karl Spiecker without the initial knowledge or approval of either party's chair, in part at the behest of Catholic clergy. After learning of the negotiations, Adenauer made clear his deep reservations, above all about removing the word *Christian* from the party's name and alienating party Protestants. The CDU's failure to integrate Protestants and Catholics in one party, Adenauer intoned, would be a "national disaster" with unforeseeable consequences.[35] Already in May of that year, Adenauer had called for the organization of a committee to facilitate resolution of Protestant-Catholic tensions within the party.[36] He now warned that a party merger would cost the North Rhine-Westphalian CDU its Protestant membership within a month; numerous Protestants, he reported, had already contacted him in distress.[37]

Despite offering a rousing defense of his strategy,[38] Arnold ended talks when the Center Party backed the SPD's proposal for socialization.[39] Although the two parties would reopen negotiations in January 1949, Arnold's decision represented a critical moment in the Center Party's history. While the refounded Zentrum continued to attract a loyal constituency, it remained riven over the degree to which it should portray itself as a party "without ideology" or as a party of social progressivism.[40] For the CDU, the episode highlighted the strained relations between Albers and Arnold on one hand and Adenauer on the other.[41] More broadly, it revealed the depths of Protestant insecurity and the immaturity of interconfessionalism. Adenauer's references to Protestant apprehension may well have been tactical, but Protestant antipathy to the Center Party was widespread, as was evident in Westphalian Protestants' fear that a "Center Party clique" (*Zentrumsklüngelei*) was working surreptitiously to bring together the Zentrum and the CDU.[42]

The Bizone Economic Council

Protestant discomfort was also palpable as the CDU's economic policies in North Rhine-Westphalia found their echo in the party's decision making on the interzonal level. British zone Christian Democrats largely dictated CDU Bizonal policy, beginning with the composition of the CDU's Bizone delegation.[43] In keeping with the dynamics of interconfessional politics, British zone Protestants were granted disproportionate representation on the Economic Council; consistent with their position on CDU economic policy, Wuppertal Protestants demanded that all representatives be committed firmly to an antisocialist course.[44]

When Friedrich Holzapfel was named head of the CDU faction in the Economic Council specifically because he was Protestant, his appointment recalled his initial designation as deputy chair of the Westphalian CDU and reflected the zonal committee's ongoing efforts to address Protestant complaints about confessional parity.[45] Indeed, establishing greater confessional balance had assumed heightened importance for party Protestants after the naming of overwhelmingly Catholic Landtag deputies in North Rhine-Westphalia.[46] Although a Landtag deputy position had been designated Protestant, Protestant members of the party complained that their constituency was sorely underrepresented, a protest they would make repeatedly into the next year.[47]

The fact that the Economic Council presented the first opportunity for different CDU state parties to forge a unified program was not lost on Adenauer. By seeking throughout late 1947 and into 1948 to coordinate the policies of the Economic Committee of the North Rhine-Westphalian Landtag faction with those of the Bizone's Economic Council, Adenauer imprinted on the

CDU's Bizonal policies the settlement established in the British zone.[48] At the same time, Adenauer called on British zonal leaders publicly to endorse CDU Bizonal policies.[49] Adenauer's maneuvering would have other long-term consequences: Specifically, the CDU's antisocialist economic and political strategy in the Frankfurt Economic Council set the stage for the party's future coalition with the FDP and CSU.[50]

As an essential step in this honing of economic and party politics, the CDU emerged in early 1948 as Erhard's biggest supporter in the Economic Council. Adenauer's role in this embrace is both clear and obscure.[51] Although he read and was influenced by Röpke's ideas, Adenauer was drawn to Erhard primarily for two reasons:[52] Erhard's contention that a free market would guarantee greater social justice than would centralized planning, and his preference for a CDU-FDP coalition that might include smaller parties of the right, such as the conservative Protestant German Party (Deutsche Partei [DP]).[53] Both considerations were consistent not only with Adenauer's personal predilections but also with a staunchly antisocialist rendering of Christian Democratic antimaterialism.

Erhard and the Social Committees

Adenauer began to engineer Erhard's acceptance within the CDU over the objections of the Social Committees and trade unionists.[54] In late May 1948, Adenauer charged men known primarily for their association with Erhard with developing the CDU's next program. Although Adenauer included Albers on the committee,[55] it was telling that the following year's *Düsseldorf Guiding Principles* emerged not from Albers's British zone Committee for Economic and Social Policy but from a Committee for Economics headed by Protestant Franz Etzel. In the words of Hugo Scharnberg, a leader of the program committee, "We want to renounce the centrally managed administrative economics and return to a market economy. . . . There should be a basis of trust established between employer and employee. At this stage, we need specialists."[56]

Especially in the wake of the June 20, 1948, currency reform and its apparent success in improving the distribution of food and goods, the CDU solidified its ties to "specialists" opposed to state control of the economy. Reflecting Erhard's growing influence within the party, Adenauer invited him to deliver the keynote address at the Second Party Congress of the British zone CDU in late August in Recklinghausen. As Adenauer increasingly identified himself and the CDU with Erhard, however, some former Christian Trade

Unionists within the party remained unpersuaded.[57] Their objections were hardly lost on Erhard, who before the Economic Council vote in mid-June 1948 on his Guiding Principles Law met with a small group of trade unionists headed by Theodor Blank to assuage their concerns.[58] Erhard's efforts were not in vain; he managed to win Social Committee representatives on the Economic Council in support of his proposal.[59]

Indeed, while the Social Committees would remain critical of Erhard, public protest was increasingly becoming the preserve of a few individuals. By August 1948, when Erhard survived another no-confidence vote on the Economic Council, his fortunes had become inextricably linked to those of the CDU/CSU and FDP.[60] He therefore entered Recklinghausen with a quickly constructed but intact party consensus behind him. In his speech, "Market Economics of a Modern Character," Erhard asserted that the social market economy corresponded completely to the bases of the Catholic-Protestant ideological consensus within the CDU. Free market economics did not imply unfettered competition, he insisted; only with a controlled degree of planning could the German state realize the advantages of market economics without falling into the "depersonalization of man" inherent in classic capitalism. Because "planned economics" led inexorably to state "economic control," the social market economy offered a necessary path between the oppressive state control of a "termite state" and the "junk room of liberalism": "The market economy of a modern character is not the free market economy of liberal exploitation from a past era, nor the 'free interplay of forces.' . . . Rather, the market economy of a modern character is the socially obligated market economy that allows again for the advantage of the single individual, prioritizes the value of the Persönlichkeit, [and] favors just accomplishment as well as earned reward."[61]

Although interrupted by frequent expressions of support and followed by praise from trade unionist Anton Storch, Erhard's presentation failed to mollify his remaining critics.[62] Johannes Albers pointed out that the "thunderous applause" for Erhard should not hide the difficult circumstances in which German workers found themselves; he praised in particular the policymaking contributions of former Christian Trade Unionists.[63] Jakob Kaiser, for his part, reminded party members that they were all committed to the same "principle of the christlichen Abendlandes"—an undogmatic principle, Kaiser added, that allowed for both liberal and—"let us say it calmly"—socialist measures, as long as they respected human dignity.[64]

Working hard to downplay such dissension, Adenauer stressed party unity in his closing address. He called out, "Where here is the talk of divisions, where of unbridgeable differences, where of tension between the confessions, where of right and left wings? There is no trace of it!"[65] But as Albers's and Kaiser's interventions made clear, leading members of the Social Committees remained instinctively suspicious of Erhard's commitment to the social component of the social market economy.[66] In November 1948, Kaiser would publicly protest trade unionists' lack of influence in the party,[67] while the Social Committees worked throughout that fall to anchor the social market economy's social character by petitioning Erhard about a variety of measures to ameliorate the impact of market economics on the western zones.[68]

This ongoing class-based dissension within the Catholic milieu would continue to tear at the party even as leaders of the British zone CDU and particularly its representatives in the Bizone throughout late 1948 increasingly supported Erhard's policies.[69] On one hand, the CDU deployed Erhard as an election speaker for October communal elections in North Rhine-Westphalia, a strategy seemingly affirmed by the CDU's victory there and in other local elections that season—Schleswig-Holstein in October, the French zone and Lower Saxony in November.[70] On the other hand, as prices climbed dramatically and he held wages firm, Erhard found himself under near continuous assault, not only from the trade unions and the SPD but from leaders of the CSU and CDU. Tensions between Karl Arnold and Erhard in particular boiled throughout the fall, punctuated by Arnold's public campaign for an Office for Price Controls.[71]

In response to the ongoing fractiousness, Adenauer called a meeting of CDU/CSU leaders for January 8–9, 1949, in Königswinter. The objective, Adenauer declared, was to forge a united front, especially important in light of the upcoming Bundestag elections:[72] "If the SPD together with the KPD receive a majority in the Bundestag, then Christian Germany is lost, then we are heading toward a Christianity-free if not a positively a-Christian Europe. So much is dependent on Germany for the preservation of Christianity that we all have the greatest responsibility."[73] In particular, Adenauer explained, with clear reference to Karl Arnold, the CDU/CSU faction in the Economic Council needed to cease publicly challenging Erhard.[74] If not entirely successful at squelching dissent, Adenauer's directive was largely effective. At Königswinter, except for a clash between Erhard and Albers, Christian Democrats generally honored Adenauer's plea and approved Erhard's motion supporting the "social market economy." (At the behest of Albers and Karl Arnold, the parties added a final line underscoring the importance of combating the gap between salaries and prices.)[75]

Despite the apparent compromise reached at the Königswinter meeting, Erhard's critics continued to discomfit party harmony. At the last meeting of the British zonal committee, in Königswinter on February 25, 1949, Erhard ascribed the economy's stabilization to the policies of the social market economy. Insisting that a planned economy would inevitably end in brutality, he portrayed economics as simply a means to a higher, ethical end and depicted the market economy, "which has nothing more to do with a liberalism of antediluvian character," as the only economic order capable of being social.[76]

While Erhard's speech was greeted with vigorous applause, it provoked immediate responses from Albers and Kaiser, both of whom objected to the constitution of a program committee charged with translating Erhard's speech into campaign propaganda. In contrast to the Ahlen Program, Albers complained, Erhard's approach represented "more or less the principle of liberal economics." When Jakob Kaiser added that Erhard was regarded by many people, including in the CDU, as a liberal, Albers interjected, "And he is one!"[77] Erhard's response was equally pointed: "You say that I have developed a liberal program so that I, so to speak, belong to the Democratic Party. Then I would like to ask, Why am I then sitting here with you?" Defending his allegiance to the CDU's moral principles, Erhard asserted, "I don't represent the interests of the entrepreneurs. I have no talents as a capitalist. . . . I own no house, no property, no securities. . . . I am as uncapitalist as it is possible to be." As far as his lack of party membership, he explained, somewhat facetiously, with clear reference to his difficulties with the CSU, "I come from Bavaria." Acknowledging his reputation as an "odd man out" (*Fremdkörper*) in the party, he concluded by stressing, "My party line is your party line. If that were not the case, then I would be honest and would not be standing here."[78]

Kaiser's and Albers's opposition, relentless as it was, represented a swan song for the former Christian Trade Unionists and their competing vision of a Christian Democratic economics. By early 1949, the overwhelming majority of Christian Socialists recognized that any deviation from a strictly antisocialist course was no longer feasible.[79] Theodor Blank had made this point clearly in early January 1949 in Königswinter, when he distanced himself from Johannes Albers;[80] indeed, Blank, who had caused a furor in November 1946 by supporting both Kaiser and Christian Socialism, had refused Kaiser's entreaties throughout 1948 to oppose the party's course.[81]

The trade unionists' protests were nonetheless significant because they signaled an incomplete consensus on the defining issue of early Christian Democracy. If Alfred Mierzejewski's assertion that Erhard "never enjoyed majority support within the CDU" overstates the discord,[82] the Social Committees' backing for Erhard clearly remained qualified.[83] Karl Arnold, for example, would stay committed to a vision of socialization until the 1950s,[84] while voices of

Left Catholicism, such as Walter Dirks's, were influential throughout the 1950s and 1960s.[85] But while the trade unionists remained organized in the Social Committees, later named the Christian Democratic Workers' Association (Christlich-Demokratische Arbeitnehmerschaft [CDA]), they had limited impact on the codetermination laws and the Works Council Act of 1952 and found their position weakened within the CDU by the battle between the refounded Christian Trade Unions of Germany (Christliche Gewerkschaften Deutschlands [CGD]) and the DGB. Although the CDA more directly asserted itself against the larger party after the 1957 election, for the most part former Christian Trade Unionists remained loyal if not unquestioning members of the CDU.[86]

Christian Democratic Embrace of the Social Market Economy

By 1949, then, the party's direction was clear. Underscoring again the influence of the British zonal organization within the broader CDU, Erhard's Königswinter speech was adopted as the basis for the CDU's electoral program.[87] Drafted in the British zone in mid-July 1949 by a committee headed by Franz Etzel in direct consultation with Erhard, the Düsseldorf Guiding Principles charted what Hermann Pünder described as the CDU's path "exactly through the middle"—between the authoritarian state of (National) Socialism and liberalism's outmoded glorification of the individual—to "a socially organized economic policy."[88] Rejecting "capitalist forms and old liberalism of an unsocial, monopolistic character," the program explicitly recognized the Ahlen Program's principles, although they were to be "expanded and developed further on the market economy side."[89] With the Düsseldorf program's commitment to achieve "a maximum amount of economic benefit and social justice for all," the Christian Democratic economic debate came to a definitive end.[90]

The fallout from the CDU's embrace of Erhard was minimal. Arguably the most prominent member of the CDU to leave the party over its association with Erhard (and Adenauer's opposition to grand coalitions) was Maria Meyer-Sevenich, who attested to her continuing allegiance to Christian Socialism in the 1948 publication *Face and Mask: Questions about the Economy*.[91] As a former communist, Sevenich was not bound to the CDU as were most Catholics; her influence in the party had, in any case, by this point largely dissipated.[92] Although Wilhelm Elfes would continue to protest both the CDU's economic and coalition policies, he did not leave the party until 1951, when he was expelled for cooperating with the KPD in opposing rearmament.[93] One of the few

Protestants who had supported Christian Socialism, Otto Heinrich von der Gablentz, would also later make clear his disappointment, but he remained a Christian Democrat until 1965.[94] As for Adenauer's erstwhile internal enemy, Jakob Kaiser, who had in May 1949 succeeded Johannes Albers as chair of the Social Committees and pleaded for a coalition with the SPD, repeatedly attacked the Social Democrats in the 1949 election campaign for their role in the Soviet occupation zone. Even as he made clear his continued preference for the Ahlen Program over the Düsseldorf Guiding Principles, Kaiser's support for Adenauer reflected the campaign cooperation of the Social Committees as a whole.[95]

The defeat of Christian Socialism cemented a Protestant-Catholic alliance in the name of antimaterialist antisocialism and addressed one major aspect of the CDU's broader goal of rechristianizing Germany. It did so consistent with the traditions of Rhenish middle-class Catholicism and its commitment to interconfessionalism. If economic policy commanded center stage in the party's early history, it did not overshadow Kulturpolitik. The traditional, patriarchal family and confessional schools figured prominently in CDU projections of the new Christian Germany. These issues would carry special political weight in 1948 and 1949, as the CDU and Center Party failed to resolve their differences; the confessional school issue in particular tested the CDU's commitment to traditional Catholic politics, its relationship to the church, and its interconfessionalism. As the scaffolding around the edifice of the future West German state, the Parliamentary Council provided the forum for these cases.

The Parliamentary Council

The Parliamentary Council, which began its work after a spring and summer of intensifying Cold War tensions, was in essence a function of those tensions. Two months after the February 1948 communist coup in Prague, the French opted to join their occupation zone to the Bizone. On July 1, the London Recommendations presented to the eleven German minister-presidents in the American headquarters of the I. G.-Farben-Haus in Frankfurt proposed a western constitutional assembly that would, in the hope of joining all four zones, nonetheless explicitly avoid the term *constitution*. In the interim, the Allied decision to introduce a new currency into the western zones provoked a dramatic escalation in Cold War hostilities, the Berlin blockade. Even throughout the last months of 1948, with the arrest of Catholic priests in Romania and, on Christmas Day, of the Hungarian primate, Cardinal Joseph Mindszenty, the Cold War continued to serve as the backdrop to the work of the Parliamentary Council.[96]

The most important preparatory work for the Parliamentary Council took place in August 1948 at the Herrenchiemsee Convention. There, a group of experts and politicians laid out the major issues to be resolved with majority and minority recommendations; their report would ultimately prescribe the debates of the Parliamentary Council and even language for some articles of the Basic Law.[97] With seventy members chosen from the Landtag delegates of the three western zones of occupation,[98] the Parliamentary Council would lay down the foundations for the new state through debate on questions ranging from the new state's name (the CDU initially suggested *Reich*) and flag (the CDU desired a design with a cross) to its bill of rights, the death penalty, the location of its capital, the outlines of its voting system, and its governing structure.[99] With the exception of the KPD delegates, all representatives endorsed Adenauer as president—apparently regarding this as his last hoorah, the SPD imagined Adenauer would restrict himself to presiding over the discussions—granting him a high-profile role as national representative vis-à-vis the Allies.[100] At age seventy-two, Adenauer was far from the only elderly member of the council.[101] Of the thirty-two delegates who represented the CDU/CSU, only three had been born after 1910. Two-thirds were Catholic, one-third Protestant; well over half had belonged to pre-1933 Catholic parties, while another half had suffered Nazi persecution.[102]

Much as had the Economic Council, the Parliamentary Council would represent a defining moment for Christian Democracy. Party officials attempted to seal the CDU's fissures on a number of issues—between the CDU and its fellow Christian party, the CSU; between party Catholics and Protestants; between party leaders and the Catholic clergy; and even between male and female Christian Democrats. As in the CDU faction in the North Rhine-Westphalian Landtag, internal divisions were exacerbated by the party's lack of coordination and organization. The Working Group of the CDU/CSU established in Frankfurt in early 1947 was essentially a gathering of state chairs, not a central party office, and the CDU commanded no other interzonal organization. Unsure whether CDU faction members represented their own or official party positions, CDU opponents often blamed delays in the council's work on the CDU/CSU's inability to establish internal party consensus.[103]

One of the party's first dilemmas concerned the new state's governing structure, an issue of special importance to the American occupiers.[104] As the CDU/CSU's April 1948 Principles for a German Federal Constitution demonstrated, the CDU's position—consistent with Catholic teachings of subsidiarity and traditional German Catholic suspicion of a strong state—was marked by strong support for federalism.[105] Nonetheless, at a meeting of southern Christian Democrats with CSU representatives more than a year earlier,[106] Bavarians had accused Adenauer of being "centralistic."[107] Indeed, the CDU and CSU entered the Parliamentary Council fundamentally divided on the issue. If southern and southwestern Christian Democrats demanded more state autonomy than did Christian Democrats from North Rhine-Westphalia,[108] the CSU sought even greater power and financial authority for the states,[109] leading to a public confrontation between CDU and CSU leaders and a delay in parliamentary debate in the name of what one newspaper referred to as "a Bavarian resistance movement."[110] Ultimately, despite Adenauer's concession to the CSU of an elected senate for a Bundesrat constituted by state governments, the Bavarian Christian Socialists, with two Franconian exceptions, would vote against the Basic Law.[111]

While federalism consumed the CDU in the early months of the Parliamentary Council and would remain a dominant issue, other divisive issues for the Catholic milieu soon emerged.[112] Although the council rebuffed CDU attempts to invoke God (the *Invocatio Dei*) and characterize constitutional rights as "God-given," the Basic Law's preamble did acknowledge "responsibility before God," and church interests in general fared well in the early months of the Parliamentary Council.[113] A push to separate church and state was rejected and the concordat question resolved through an early compromise that recognized not the 1933 concordat (with its guarantee of confessional schools) but the agreements between the states and the churches in place on May 8, 1945.[114] The CDU petition for continued recognition of the Weimar constitutional articles regulating church-state relations was also accepted, codifying the churches' pre-1933 rights, including the assessment of taxes.[115] Overall, as Hans-Otto Kleinmann has observed, the Basic Law revealed greater evidence of Christian influence than it did of socialist.[116]

Confessional Schools in the Parliamentary Council

Nonetheless, the tenor and substance of these church-related parliamentary discussions foreshadowed much of the widespread contentiousness that would surface on other religious issues. In late 1948, the debate over the concordat inspired press references to a renewed Kulturkampf;[117] in January 1949, SPD members criticized the concordat for mandating Catholic Church prayers for the National Socialist state.[118] For the CDU's part, Adolf Süsterhenn accused the SPD, KPD, and FDP of representing the "Soviet viewpoint" on matters of church and state.[119]

All of these tensions would be on even greater display during the debate about confessional schools. Securing religiously segregated schools was one of the primary concerns of millions of Germans as they constructed their new state, and the question dominated long stretches of Parliamentary Council business. While the CSU paid the issue little heed because the Bavarian constitution guaranteed confessional schools,[120] the question loomed large for the CDU. Confessional schools had been a defining issue for the pre-1933 Zentrum, and the Elternrecht remained a Center Party priority after 1945; for the CDU, supporting confessional schools had always appeared axiomatic for maintaining clerical support. Indeed, for many Christian Democrats, the school issue epitomized the clear divide between materialist socialists and liberals on one hand and Christians on the other.[121] But as the founding of the CDU revealed, Christian Democrats were divided on the issue, not only confessionally but within each religious faction of the party as well.[122]

The CDU was acutely aware of the potential propaganda coup the school issue represented for the Center Party, which, despite its two-person representation in the Parliamentary Council, wielded significant influence as a consequence of Johannes Brockmann's and Helene Wessel's eloquence and passion.[123] Led by Adolf Süsterhenn, the minister of justice and the minister of education and cultural affairs of the Rhineland-Palatinate and an inveterate defender of Catholic natural law,[124] the CDU framed its demand for confessional schools both in terms of personal freedom and human rights[125] and historically, by linking the Kulturkampf to post–World War I Prussian cultural policies (the so-called Hoffmann Commandments) and Nazism.[126] The SPD and FDP signaled their opposition early on. Noting that the war-related population dislocations had undermined the old "cujus regio, ejus religio" rule and that confessional schools would only marginalize expelled populations,[127] Theodor Heuss reminded Christian Democrats of their different positions on the school issue as a result of political realities and local traditions.[128]

Along with the trade unions and civil servant organizations, the Christian churches would constitute one of the leading interest groups pressuring the Parliamentary Council to codify rights desired or guaranteed these groups before 1933. Although both churches expressed strong support for the codification of the Elternrecht in the Basic Law, public discourse on the question was dominated by the Catholic Church.[129] In contrast to Catholics, who derived the Elternrecht from Catholic natural law, Protestants had no theological basis from which to demand confessionally segregated public schools; as Heuss would explain in the Parliamentary Council debates, the issue held a very different place in Protestant teachings and tradition than in those of the Catholic

Church.[130] As a result, differences among Protestants, especially between Lutheran and Reform leaders, left unclear which organ of the church represented Protestants vis-à-vis the Parliamentary Council on the question of schools. Only in early November, for example, did the EKD write to the council regarding a constitutionally protected Elternrecht.[131]

In contrast to the somewhat anemic engagement of the Protestant Church, Catholic clergy were united in their commitment to pressure CDU delegates on the school question, especially as other issues of importance to Catholic clergy, such as codetermination, were excluded from the Parliamentary Council.[132] Appointed by Cardinal Frings to represent the Bishops' Conference on school issues, Wilhelm Böhler would labor indefatigably, developing a lobbying organization specifically for the Parliamentary Council.[133] Having served from 1920 to 1935 as the general secretary of the Catholic School Organization of Germany and of the Bishops' Central Office for Religious Schools, Böhler had already gained postwar experience by representing the church in North Rhine-Westphalia's constitutional process. Though he occasionally cooperated with the Protestant Church, Böhler's most intimate connections by far were to Catholic politicians.[134] Indeed, after an early November meeting of the CDU/CSU faction devoted to reviewing the Protestant and especially Catholic churches' positions on church-related issues,[135] Böhler worked with Center and CDU politicians to formulate common demands; on November 10, Süsterhenn secured CDU faction approval of a document that drew on Cardinal Frings's late October letter to Adenauer and Center deputy Brockmann.[136]

Two weeks later, the Committee for Policy Issues, the group of twelve members charged with drafting articles to send to the High Committee, took up the CDU/CSU petition regarding protection of marriage and the family as well as the Elternrecht. Following private meetings with Adenauer and Süsterhenn in November and Böhler in December,[137] Heuss—whom Adenauer would later describe as "anticlerical"[138]—again led the opposition to the Elternrecht in the Committee for Policy Issues. Objecting that the Elternrecht could hardly be constituent for Catholics since it first emerged in the nineteenth century, Heuss also noted that subjects such as math defied confessionalism. Despite the passion of the CDU's arguments—Süsterhenn warned that the question would dictate the CDU/CSU stance on the Basic Law—the direction of the discussion was clear.[139] It was no surprise when the CDU/CSU petition was defeated in the first reading of the High Committee by a vote of eleven to ten, with the majority constituting SPD, FDP, and KPD delegates.[140]

The churches responded immediately to the rejection of the CDU/CSU petition. If Protestant Church officials remained divided on the issue—in contrast to Martin Niemöller,[141] more conservative Protestant leaders would speak out in support of the Elternrecht, including in an official statement from the EKD in early February[142]—the CDU's cooperation with a unified Catholic Church did much to reinforce the perception of their close collaboration. In mid-December 1948, Adenauer arranged a meeting between representatives of the Catholic and Protestant churches and council factions (with the exception of the KPD)[143] at which Böhler represented both the Catholic and Protestant churches.[144] A week after KPD delegate Heinz Renner accused the CDU of raising the confessional school issue solely at the behest of Cardinal Frings,[145] Helene Weber read aloud to the chamber a letter Frings had mailed in late November to every Parliamentary Council member.[146]

Inspired by the Center Party's post–World War I tenaciousness in asserting its cultural agenda, Böhler maintained an undiminished commitment to seeing through the confessional school issue.[147] In November and December 1948, letters and telegrams from Catholic priests, Catholic groups, and individual Catholic citizens poured in, demanding protection of the marriage and family, rights of the churches, and the Elternrecht.[148] (Heuss later remarked that he would have granted them greater due were they not mostly from the dioceses and identical in language.)[149] At the turn of the year, Catholic priests followed Frings's call to use their New Year's sermons to deliver an official German bishops' statement on the rejection of the Elternrecht in the High Committee.[150]

While the Catholic Church was univocal in its efforts to secure religiously segregated schools, confessional tensions began to tear at the CDU faction. In advance of the Parliamentary Council proceedings, CDU leaders doubted their Protestant colleagues' support for church-backed cultural questions.[151] That the confessional school question hardly enjoyed unanimous support was evident in the faction's early October divided vote[152] and party debates following the approval on November 10 of the document containing church demands.[153] After Walter Strauss and other CDU Protestants suggested elements of the party's proposal for church-state relations could be used in anti-CDU propaganda, Protestant Hermann von Mangoldt cited the Schleswig-Holstein Protestant Church's lack of support for confessional schools to justify his own objections.[154]

While the faction agreed, in a highly symbolic replacement of a Protestant by a Catholic, that Helene Weber would speak to the council in von Mangoldt's place, it was forced to confront the fact that fully half of its members had reservations about the current proposals for church-state relations and the Elternrecht. Dissenters included Protestant Theophil Kaufmann, who complained that the faction had pushed other parties into the opposition, when—considering its own disunity—it should have shown more flexibility.[155] In the end, Kaufmann and von Mangoldt would be joined by Strauss in withdrawing their support from the CDU's original demand to retain all the concordat articles, including the guarantee of confessional schools.[156]

While CDU Protestants signaled their growing disaffection, party Catholics forged onward. In mid-January, Helene Weber invoked the comparison of Nazism and socialism as she introduced a renewed petition for confessional schools on behalf of the CDU/CSU, the Center Party, and the German Party: "Now that we have the total state behind us, which brought us the community schools as it saw fit, now that we observe in the Russian-occupied area what the state would like to say, that the parents in their desire for education are simply oppressed [*vergewaltigt*], we are of the view that we must be utterly careful."[157] Weber's impassioned words effected no greater persuasion than previous CDU arguments, however, and FDP, SPD, and KPD delegates stood firm against codifying the Elternrecht in the Basic Law. The Catholic Church's commitment also remained unwavering. After writing to Adenauer in early February that he would mobilize Catholic parishioners should the Basic Law not include certain guarantees, including of confessional schools, Cardinal Frings publicly thanked the Center Party representatives for their advocacy of the Elternrecht.[158]

Frings's pointed intervention notwithstanding, after the failure of Süsterhenn's mid-February proposal to decide the school question by referendum, Adenauer decided to negotiate.[159] Adenauer had in fact already laid the groundwork for a strategic shift in December even as he pursued last-ditch efforts, including meeting with the three military governors, to influence the SPD.[160] In early December, Adenauer shared with the faction contingency plans should the CDU's original demands be rejected; on December 15, he called on the CDU/CSU to support the Basic Law with or without the Elternrecht. In a veiled reference to Protestant Christian Democratic opposition, Adenauer explained that in "the North," the question of the Elternrecht was simply not as important.[161] On February 1, Adenauer expressed his personal disappointment at the party's failure to win the Elternrecht and noted the political fodder this would grant the party's opposition—that is, the Center Party. He nonetheless urged the CDU faction to endorse the entirety of the Basic Law in the name of the forty-three million Germans who would otherwise have no state to represent them.[162] A week later, Adenauer outlined for the faction his tactic to contain the political damage, which was to issue a joint statement with the Center Party.[163]

With the failure to accomplish the codification of confessional schools, the CDU also negotiated a compromise.[164] The Basic Law would not guarantee the Elternrecht but would enshrine a provision for private, denominational, state-supervised schools in areas where interconfessional schools predominated. At the same time, the CDU would accept the Bremen Clause exempting from Basic Law provisions any state, like Bremen, that had enacted school laws before January 1, 1949. (This would allow Bremen to continue its practice of confessionally neutral religious instruction in schools.) In exchange, the Basic Law would mandate that religious instruction be taught in all schools except those deemed religion-free (*bekenntnisfrei*).[165] That Adenauer considered the Bremen Clause the resolution of the confessional school controversy was evident in his request at a February 22, 1949, CDU/CSU faction meeting that a Protestant member contact Bishop Lilje and Hans-Christoph Seebohm to persuade the German Party to withdraw its Elternrecht petition.[166]

Adenauer's decision to accede was not unanimously embraced within his party, however; indeed, few other issues pertaining to the Basic Law were as hotly debated within the CDU faction as confessional schools.[167] Among others, CDU Catholics Süsterhenn, Weber, Albert Finck, and Ernst Wirmer expressed dissatisfaction with the compromise language and sought to revise it, and the party's vote on the Bremen Clause in the High Committee was sharply divided.[168] In his report to the British zone CDU in Königswinter on February 25, 1949, Adenauer acknowledged that for some members of the CDU Parliamentary Council faction, supporting confessional schools at the risk of torpedoing the Basic Law was a matter of conscience.[169]

Yet Adenauer had compelling reasons to step back from the Elternrecht issue. Focused on constructing a strong West Germany safe from communist influence and free from Allied control, Adenauer saw acceptable cost in demonstrating Christian Democratic independence from the church, whose leaders he regarded as not always politically astute.[170] Adenauer also opted for conciliation to maintain party harmony between Protestants and Catholics and more broadly between the Catholic-dominated CDU and the Protestant-dominated FDP. Adenauer was publicly supported by CDU Protestants, who joined him in defending the Basic Law's larger accomplishments;[171] as CDU Protestant Walter Otto explained in late February 1949, confessional schools were hardly a priority for Protestant voters at a time of Cold War.[172]

Indeed, while most CDU Protestants were satisfied with Christian community schools, those devout Protestants who preferred confessional schools were generally less public in their support than were their Catholic colleagues.[173] As Josef Kannengießer underscored, the issue simply played a different role in Schleswig-Holstein than in the Rhineland or Westphalia.[174] Even Adolf Süsterhenn conceded that certain areas of Germany had significant numbers of CDU voters perfectly satisfied with interconfessional community schools with confessionally separate religious instruction.[175] Although Protestant Christian Democrats would not officially codify their support for Christian community schools until 1952,[176] that a confessional division on the question had been clear from the party's earlier days lay the CDU open to easy attack.[177] Regarding the Elternrecht debate, Social Democrat Walter Menzel asked ironically whether the CDU were truly a party of two confessions committed to the same goal: "Isn't it always the CDU, of all parties, that portrays as its party's special advantage that people of both confessions want [to work] together to achieve a political goal and political project?"[178]

Considering Catholic leaders' investment in securing confessional public schools, it was no surprise that they—Böhler and Frings in particular—were aggrieved at the CDU's unilateral decision to compromise.[179] On February 10, 1949, after Süsterhenn reported to the special Bishops' Conference called to discuss the Parliamentary Council debates,[180] the bishops issued a statement signaling their ongoing commitment to confessional schools: "The struggles and suffering of the past years would be for nothing" were the federal constitution not designed to prevent the "violation [*Vergewaltigung*] of Christian conscience," especially regarding the education of youth.[181] Church efforts to mobilize Catholic constituents produced, according to press reports, some eight hundred thousand petition signatures of supporters of the Elternrecht[182] and a firestorm of protest when Adenauer announced publicly that he would vote for the Basic Law even against the desires of church authorities.[183] In an early March church rally in the Mainz cathedral, the city's bishop, Dr. Albert Stohr, and Süsterhenn called on Catholics and the dioceses to engage themselves politically.[184] At the same time, Böhler reminded German Catholics of the Nazis' implementation of community schools and those schools' association with the "totalitarian state."[185]

Passions within the CDU did not abate quickly. Although forced in early February to acknowledge that the CDU had no means to secure the Elternrecht, Süsterhenn promised that the CDU would fight for Christians' "right" with all legally available means.[186] Only in early March 1949, after considerable internal party wrangling,[187] did Süsterhenn confirm that the CDU no longer regarded the Bremen Clause as a "casus belli."[188] But he and his party allies continued their campaign.[189] Members of the CDU/CSU, Center Party, and German Party attempted to insert the confessional school guarantee at the end of deliberations in the High Committee on May 5, 1949, and again three days later, when the Parliamentary Council voted to approve the Basic Law.[190] Helene Weber's insistence on advancing Süsterhenn's three petitions over the strong objections of Adenauer and Robert Lehr highlighted continued divisions within the faction;[191] during the fourth reading in the High Committee on May 5, some CDU delegates voted against various petitions, while others abstained.[192]

In the end, if CDU Catholics such as Süsterhenn had difficulty accepting defeat, members of the devout Catholic public expressed true outrage.[193] One aggrieved citizen characterized the sacrifice of confessional schools as evidence of the resurgent influence of "nationalism, liberalism, and socialism" in an "omnipotent total state" and in a thinly veiled attack on CDU Protestants condemned the "nationalist and liberal elements in the CDU" for having revealed their true inclination to "state monopoly over education."[194] Another detractor charged the Parliamentary Council with following an "uneradicated totalitarian course" in the new Germany that only pretended to effect the "salvation of abendländischen culture."[195] Newspapers sympathetic to the CDU/CSU printed articles demanding, "Who betrayed the Elternrecht?"[196] accusing the SPD of resurrecting "old-fashioned antipathies from the Kulturkampf era of the nineteenth century,"[197] and dishonoring Germany's "abendländischen inheritance."[198] Critics of the CDU were also quick to point out that the two Center Party and two DP representatives voted against the Basic Law to protest its failure to enshrine their desired cultural policies, including above all confessional schools.[199]

The question of the churches' response remained crucial. In early March, the EKD issued a statement signed by Hanns Lilje indicating Protestants' disappointment as well as their acceptance of the Basic Law as proposed on the assumption that state constitutions would fulfill their expectations regarding parental control over schools.[200] Following a late May statement of the German bishops expressing enormous regret at the failure to secure confessional schools,[201] Böhler declared that, despite reservations about the Basic Law, the church would not oppose it. He explained further that Cardinal Frings, who had joined the CDU in November 1948, had not left the party in May 1949 out of disgust with its failure to represent church interests, as was widely suspected;[202] Frings's decision, Böhler asserted, was simply in keeping with Article 32 of the concordat.[203] In fact, Frings, apparently in consort with the Vatican, had assured church support for the Basic Law after Münster bishop Michael Keller decried the CDU's failure to guarantee confessional schools as proof of the inherent relativism of interconfessionalism, calling for the bishops to reject the Basic Law and for any political vote to support it to be declared a sin.[204]

Not surprisingly, despite the CDU's final acceptance of the Bremen Clause, the Parliamentary Council's confessional school debate reinforced the new party's image of pugnacious Catholicism.[205] Maria Meyer-Sevenich charged her former party with unnecessarily creating religious antagonism by simply doing the Catholic Church's bidding.[206] Heuss accused Weber of allowing the Elternrecht issue to become a personal "question of prestige,"[207] while Communist delegate Renner characterized her as an *"ecclesia militans."*[208] As the Parliamentary Council voted to approve the Basic Law on May 8, 1949, Heuss noted that these had been his first experiences in the "atmosphere of Rhenish Catholicism."[209]

Yet against the backdrop of the longer history of political Catholicism, the Parliamentary Council debate over confessional schools demonstrated the precedence of political calculation for both the CDU and the church. If the CDU prioritized interconfessionalism, political compromise, and establishing independence from the Catholic Church, church leaders also demonstrated pragmatism. While Catholic clerics well recognized their limited influence over the Christian Democrats, the Center Party hardly offered a viable alternative, in part as a consequence of the church's earlier political choices. At the same time, largely because of Christian Democrats, the church had retained its privileges as outlined in the concordat. The CDU remained, then, the church's most powerful ally in its declared struggle against secularism and communism. For all of these reasons, clergymen maintained loyalty to the CDU even as it failed to do their bidding.[210]

The school issue certainly highlighted the tensions inherent in the transformation of confessional culture within postwar Germany. It was impossible to deny that Protestants, represented primarily in the SPD, KPD, and FDP, and Catholics, grouped disproportionately in the Center Party and CDU/CSU, had broadly split on the question in the Parliamentary Council. The invocation of the Kulturkampf and resentment of the Catholic Church's interventions made clear that German culture was still defined by a significant degree of Protestant-Catholic suspicion. On no occasion during parliamentary proceedings did Christian Democrats speak to the obvious contradiction of politicians committed to interconfessional cooperation seeking to segregate their children by religion, nor did they address explicitly the confessional line running through their party, although, as Walter Menzel's earlier statement and criticisms from Catholic citizens made clear, these internal divisions hardly escaped the notice of outside observers. In response to SPD delegate Gustav Zimmermann's accusation that confessional schools would only exacerbate Germany's confessional divide, Adolf Süsterhenn replied that the Third Reich had demonstrated where attempts to overcome the Protestant-Catholic division through state means, such as community schools, would lead.[211]

Only during the final day of debate concerning the Basic Law would a Catholic Christian Democrat, Albert Finck, speak directly to the confessionalized tenor of the debate. He did so at length: "There has been a lot of discussion of confessional division and confessional quarrels. Nothing could be more false. The leading representatives of the confessions have together demanded the Elternrecht. In this regard, then, there can be no talk of a dispute between Protestants and Catholics. Believe me, ladies and gentlemen, Protestants and Catholics, Christians, the devout Christian Volk, were never drawn so closely to one another as has been the case in these years, and we have good reason for that. Our experiences in the Third Reich, the shared experience in the concentration camps and in the prisons, the shared persecution of the Christian churches in the Third Reich, the persecution of Christians in the East . . . are for us cause enough that we must come together and build a unified front. Believe me: that which we have experienced in the Parliamentary Council has also compelled us, the devout, thinking Christian part of the population, to stand and fight together for our natural rights."[212]

Finck's address may have been singular, but it was striking. Disregarding completely the obvious confessional line that ran not only through the Parliamentary Council on this question but even through his own party, Finck reflexively invoked the Kirchenkampf paradigm from the party's founding ideology. He also implicitly compared opposition on the part of non-Christian parties to the Elternrecht to National Socialist and communist persecution of Christians. With this, he reminded listeners, including those in his own party, that, whatever the differences among them, religious Catholics and Protestants were ultimately united in their rejection of materialism and secularism and their commitment to rechristianizing the new German state. Other issues before the Parliamentary Council, particularly those pertaining to the family, would also recall for Christian Democrats their shared agenda.

Gender and the Family in the Parliamentary Council

There would be far less dissension within the CDU and the Parliamentary Council on questions of gender and the family, though these measures would also attract considerable public attention. While it would provoke a firestorm of protest from female West Germans, the parliamentary debate concerning women's place in the new Germany was carried out primarily by men. Just four

(6 percent) of the voting representatives to the Parliamentary Council were female. In addition to Frieda Nadig and Elisabeth Selbert from the SPD and Helene Wessel of the Center Party, only one female Christian Democrat, Helene Weber, belonged to the Parliamentary Council, despite various appeals from CDU/CSU women to party males to appoint women.[213] Compared to the 10 percent of female delegates in the Weimar National Assembly, the representation of women in the Parliamentary Council was hardly an encouraging indicator of the status of women in postwar politics.[214]

Although the party agreed to fund the Women's Association of the CDU/CSU (Frauenarbeitsgemeinschaft der CDU/CSU) founded in May 1948, female Christian Democrats complained repeatedly about party officials' disregard for the women's work.[215] In general, the CDU/CSU Parliamentary Council faction devoted minimal time to discussing gender- and family-related questions; Helene Weber was routinely the only member to raise them.[216] When Weber noted in a January 1949 faction meeting how little respect women in the party enjoyed, Adenauer responded that integrating youth should also be a priority.[217] It was not surprising that Weber would complain privately, "We women are at present accomplishing less in the party and in the press than before 1933."[218]

A strong consensus existed within the CDU that the reconstruction of Germany required a traditional family structure anchored by a Christian mother. As Weber put it, it was "unpleasant" for a husband to stay home and care for the children, so women should be free for family life.[219] Although this consensus was rarely contested within the party, it did occasionally break down along gender lines. Two issues framed the Parliamentary Council's work on women and the family: Article 3, paragraph 2, pertained to male and female equality, while Article 6 concerned state protection of the family, motherhood, and marriage. In contrast to the state constitutions promulgated in 1946 and 1947, all of which guaranteed equal pay for equal work and some of which promised greater equality within marriage, the Parliamentary Council restricted its concern to the political and legal spheres, in part out of deference to the Civil Code and in part because the parties had agreed to exclude social and economic rights from the Basic Law.[220] While the SPD certainly differed with the CDU on numerous aspects of these questions, Social and Christian Democrats shared fundamental assumptions about male and female difference and women's place in the home.[221] As a result, in comparison with the school issues, these measures of cultural policy would be relatively harmoniously resolved.[222]

The first debate focused on guaranteeing women rights—in particular, whether men and women should be described as "the same" in the Basic Law or recognized as different with a stipulation banning sex discrimination. Relying on the Weimar constitution as a model, the Herrenchiemsee draft submitted that "men and women have the same citizenship [*staatsbürgerlichen*] rights and responsibilities."[223] In keeping with her long-standing understanding of the roles of men and women in society, Helene Weber preferred language guaranteeing women equal pay for equal work but no rights beyond that.[224] Although Weber would ally herself on the pay issue with the SPD and KPD, the philosophical gulf between her and her Marxist female colleagues, whom she considered "completely radical," was fundamental.[225] In contrast to Weber's restricted definition of equality, at the end of November the SPD submitted a petition authored by Elisabeth Selbert that read simply, "Men and women have the same rights [*sind gleichberechtigt*]."[226]

As with the school issue, Christian Democrats invoked Cold War specters in their projections of a future Germany. Robert G. Moeller has demonstrated how much of the Christian Democratic discourse about the family in the Parliamentary Council and the 1950s was cast in terms of anticommunism;[227] this was certainly evident in early December 1948, when Protestant Christian Democrat Theophil Kaufmann decried a Soviet Union where men and women were considered equal with no consideration for their different biological or spiritual makeup.[228] The CDU/CSU and FDP also expressed considerable concern that a statement of gender equality would undermine the Civil Code. In early December 1948, the CDU/CSU and FDP joined to defeat the SPD proposal for equal rights in the High Committee.[229]

The rejection of the provision for equal rights for women precipitated a popular outcry comparable only to the public engagement on the school issue. A wave of public opposition, primarily from women in unions and on the political left but also from social and middle-class women's organizations, saw thousands and thousands of petitions pour into the Parliamentary Council offices.[230] Selbert personally involved delegates' wives, including those of CDU representatives, as well as other women.[231] At least one fellow female Christian Democrat protested to Helene Weber that, considering all that women had done during both wars, women deserved full equality with men.[232] Under public pressure, the CDU/CSU and FDP acknowledged that they had misjudged the situation, dismissed their earlier opposition as a misunderstanding, and signaled openness to the SPD measure. Despite many Christian Democrats' belief that the public had overreacted,[233] the party acceded, and in mid-January 1949 the SPD petition, which read, "Men and women have the same rights," passed unanimously, with the proviso that the Bundestag would revise the Civil Code by 1953.[234] While the CDU succeeded in adding one clarifying clause, its attempt to couple language describing women's "equal responsibilities" with the guarantee of "equal rights" was rejected.[235]

The CDU also acted pragmatically when it came to Article 2, which codified the "protection of life." Without internal dissent, the CDU/CSU joined a majority of delegates in the view that "seeds of a new life" (*das keimende Leben*) need not be cited specifically in the Basic Law because preexisting language concerning the "right to life and bodily integrity" encompassed an abortion ban. The clergy registered no notable protest on this issue, signaling that church leaders too endorsed this interpretation.[236] In contrast, the churches focused on Article 6, pertaining to the family—specifically parental rights and responsibilities and state protection of motherhood and marriage.[237] In December 1948, Cardinal Frings (as chair of the Fulda Bishops' Conference) and state bishop Theophil Wurm (as praeses of the EKD) jointly petitioned the Parliamentary Rat for, among other issues, constitutional safeguards for the family.[238]

In late November 1948, Süsterhenn spelled out the CDU demand for special protection of families based on marriage as the "permanent relationship of man and woman."[239] From the vantage point of the SPD and FDP, the Christian Democratic insistence on heterosexual marriage as the precedent and foundation of the family ignored the realities of widowhood and single parenthood in postwar Germany. The majority vote to amend the CDU proposal resulted in the guarantee of state protection of marriage and family with no specific delineation of the nature of marriage or its relationship to family.[240] The CDU also sought a clear legal distinction between children born into marriage and those born outside it.[241] According to Helene Weber, Germany may have had more women than men—she rejected the term *surplus* (*Frauenüberschuss*)—but no married woman had the right to conceive a child out of wedlock.[242] Nonmarital children deserved every necessary and practicable support and protection, but they were, in Weber's view, intrinsically different from those born within marriage.[243]

The parties most disagreed on this question of the status of children of single mothers. The SPD ultimately failed to win recognition of children registered in and outside marriage as legally equal,[244] although the SPD, CDU/CSU, and FDP agreed on language guaranteeing all children equal societal status and opportunities to develop.[245] This somewhat artful formulation left unclear whether unmarried mothers and nonmarital children were granted the state's protection,[246] leading to a situation whereby unmarried mothers had the "right and obligation" to care for their children without equal legal parental authority to married mothers.[247] (This question would not be resolved until 1969, when children born out of wedlock would gain full legal equality.)

In this realm of cultural policy, then, Christian Democrats largely achieved their aims. Indeed, the role of women in the family and the structure of the family had been consensus issues for Christian politicians since before World War II. The Parliamentary Council debates revealed no significant dissension between CDU Protestants and Catholics, nor did a confessional line run obviously through the Parliamentary Council as it had on the question of confessional schools. Moreover, female Christian Democrats advocated the same positions as did their male colleagues. On only one issue did the sole female CDU representative differ from her male colleagues. In the debate over female equality, Helene Weber joined SPD and KPD representatives in advocating constitutionally guaranteed equal wages, although she offered her own petition stressing equality of work opportunities and compensation when men and women performed the same labor.[248] She was nonetheless opposed directly and publicly by fellow party member Hermann von Mangoldt. Weber and the SPD ultimately would accept the exclusion of their petitions by the logic that particular social, economic, and cultural policies would remain the purview of the states and that a broader assertion of gender equality implied equality in female labor.[249]

Although the CDU/CSU had eventually supported the SPD motion regarding female rights, evidence indicated some confusion or discomfort in Catholic ranks with the Basic Law's strict guarantee of equality. It was not clear to all Catholic women how they were to reconcile traditional Catholic teachings with the notion of "the same wages for the same work" (which they, like Weber and the SPD, presumed was implied by the Basic Law's guarantee of gender equality),[250] and the Catholic Church later expressed concern that such legal equality threatened women's primary roles as housewives and mothers.[251] For her part, Weber, in anticipation of the 1949 Bundestag election, would describe the codification of male and female equality as "strictly a matter of formulation."[252]

Questions regarding women's roles ultimately would divide the party along confessional and gender lines. In the Bundestag, when Weber returned in December 1949 to calling for equal pay for equal work, she was countered again by a male colleague, who noted that the churches were discomforted by the Basic Law's codification of gender equality.[253] (Weber also caused a minor sensation in the Bundestag by referring, as did many other female Christian Democrats, to the Third Reich as a "Männerstaat.")[254] In the 1952 Bundestag debates concerning rewriting the Civil Code, Adenauer made clear that he, like the Catholic Church, embraced retaining patriarchal authority in a revised Civil Code. With this stance, he lost the support of the women's caucus within the CDU and the leadership of the Protestant clergy, although female Christian

Democrats were hardly unified; Helene Weber and her Protestant colleague Elisabeth Schwarzhaupt disagreed with each other on the issue even as they opposed Adenauer.[255]

At the same time, devout Catholics and Protestants would continue to find much that united them in the realm of Kulturpolitik. In the 1950s, for example, conservative Protestants and Catholics forged common cause through film censorship in campaigns to protect the Abendland from challenges to the patriarchal family and traditional motherhood.[256] Originating with Protestant clerics, the 1952 antipornography law was supported by Catholic leaders and laypeople.[257] When the Equal Rights Law finally passed in 1957 (after the Bundestag missed its 1953 deadline to revise the Civil Code in light of the Basic Law's equal rights provision), its endorsement of paternal authority over children was supported by leading Catholic and Protestant politicians and theologians before being overturned two years later by West Germany's Federal Constitutional Court.[258]

In 1948 and 1949, family and women's issues unified the CDU as they had religious Protestants and Catholics for the preceding half century. While the question of confessional schools tested the commitment of the church and devout Catholics to the party, the CDU continued to enjoy the support of the vast majority of the Catholic Teilkultur. Concurrently, the party's flexibility on the school issue allowed it to emerge with its Protestant-Catholic alliance strained but intact. That alliance, first secured over economic policy, remained conflictual, as did relations across the class line within the Catholic milieu. Nonetheless, as Christian Democrats headed into the Federal Republic's first parliamentary elections, they did so with a successful political track record in the Parliamentary and Economic Councils. There they codified the party's ideological profile, one of a religiously endowed antimaterialism that underlay antiliberal and antisocialist economics, traditional cultural politics, and an uncompromising anticommunism.

CHAPTER 8

Christian Democracy and Confessional Culture in the Federal Republic

Its major ideological and leadership struggles resolved, the CDU found itself on the eve of the August 14, 1949 Bundestag election in its strongest position to date. With its election victory, Christian Democrats would commence two decades of political leadership. Yet while the party could justifiably present itself as an unprecedented Protestant-Catholic alliance, the Catholic Teilkultur remained fractured and confessional tensions within the CDU were still potent, even as the Federal Republic would undergo far-reaching social transformations. The advent of individualism, consumerism, secularism, and deconfessionalization and the concurrent dissolution of the Catholic milieu would induce profound changes in the party and West German society. That Christian Democracy nevertheless remained marked by confessional difference testifies to the salience of religion in the Federal Republic.

The CDU and the Center Party

Considering the CDU's indelible association with Catholic Germany, it is perhaps ironic that the party's representation of the Catholic Teilkultur had never been undisputed. Especially as the CDU wrestled with the confessional school question in the Parliamentary Council, the Center Party remained an abiding concern for Christian Democrats, and party leaders resolved again to bridge the Catholic milieu's political gap. When Karl Arnold reinitiated discussions with Center Party leaders in January 1949, he did so with Adenauer's approval, even as Adenauer continued to highlight the risks of incurring Protestant ire by increasing Catholic influence within the party.[1] The failure of this round of negotiations would have especially dire consequences for the Zentrum. After fusion attempts foundered on the opposition of some Center Party organizations and leaders, including Helene Wessel, significant numbers of Center members followed Karl Spiecker to the CDU.[2]

Catholic priests threw the weight of the church behind their politics by denying Center Party members a platform at church meetings and in publications and even banning them from Catholic ancillary organizations.[3] The importance of clergy support for the CDU was not lost on Center Party stalwarts.[4] In February 1949, Wessel complained that the CDU/CSU was "exploiting" the religiosity of large numbers of voters "with the help of upper clergy and part of the middle and lower clergy" in order "to make this West Germany into a clerical-fascist state."[5] When Wilhelm Böhler attempted to forge an agreement between the CDU and Center Party banning political attacks, Adenauer balked at, among other things, the proposition that the clergy treat the CDU and Center Party equally.[6]

Indeed, political attacks between the two Catholic cousins continued unabated. In particular, the Center Party would exploit the CDU/CSU's failure to secure confessional schools and explicit protection of "seeds of a new life" in the Basic Law as evidence of Christian Democracy's incapacity to represent Catholic voters and their concerns.[7] Center Party propaganda made special mention of the number of Protestant delegates in the CDU faction,[8] while Center Party leaders needled CDU Protestants over their lack of influence within the party.[9] For his part, CDU representative Josef Schrage attacked unmarried Helene Wessel of the Center Party for advocating the Elternrecht while knowing nothing about raising children.[10]

The Center Party assault came as no surprise to the CDU, which with the passage of the Basic Law had resolved to develop a clear public relations line for the confessional school issue designed to account for the fact that "some members" had voted on the Bremen Clause with the SPD.[11] As the CDU prepared for the first federal elections, Adenauer advised party members to eschew the school issue as it could only hurt the CDU politically.[12] Helene Weber took a different tack, arguing that it was a mistake to imply that the Elternrecht had been left unprotected. Rather, only the "full Elternrecht," she maintained, had failed to win constitutional protection; the Elternrecht was covered under the marriage and family law, specifically Article 6, paragraph 2, which guaranteed parents the right to care for and raise their children. Moreover, Weber insisted, in contrast to the Center Party, which before 1933 had revealed divisions on this issue, CDU/CSU representatives "fought until the end of discussions for the full Elternrecht."[13] Weber was echoed by Paul Steup, who also rejected the Center Party's characterization of the CDU as unreliable in the larger "struggle for individual rights." Warning against sowing dissension within the

Christian world when the real enemy at hand was socialism, Steup stressed the importance of shoring up the Christian Abendland in the face of the SPD and KPD's atheism and state idolization.[14]

Bundestag Campaign in 1949

In its contraposition of Christianity with the all-powerful materialist state, Steup's discourse resonated with Erhard's critique of socialism and the paradigm of Christian Democracy that emerged in 1948 undergirding the social market economy. This theme of freedom versus state control, or "market" versus "planned," would serve as the dominant motif of the CDU's campaign for the Bundestag elections.[15] Because the CDU did not formally constitute as a national party until the Goslar party congress in October 1950, Adenauer led the CDU's campaign not as party chair but as head of the British zone CDU, still the only party branch organized on a zonal level.[16] The party's campaign slogans were nevertheless determined in early January 1949; organized by Bruno Dörpinghaus, general secretary of the Working Group of the CDU/CSU, but headed by Adenauer, the CDU election committee set up a press and propaganda committee to design and produce materials for the entire West German CDU campaign.[17]

Although Christian Democrats were yet to adopt the more sophisticated, American style of campaigning that would appear in future elections, they nonetheless understood the power of simple messages and illustrations. Christian Democratic posters depicted the success of the social market economy and the failings of the planned economy, while targeted appeals to the "Christian housewife" suggested that CDU/CSU economic policies would restore German family life.[18] CDU propaganda also focused to a notable degree on Adenauer as leader.[19] As the CDU began its campaign for the Federal Republic's first election, Christian Democrats left no doubt of the connection between the materialism of old and of new: "National Socialism and Marxism are closely related in their basic outlooks [and] completely consistent in their methodology."[20] Germans caught between the black market and the irregularities and insufficiencies of the state-regulated food rationing system were open to an economic program that appeared to build on the strengths of each system without risking its drawbacks.[21] The CDU also benefited from the increasingly palpable success of Erhard's policies. By mid-1949, prices had fallen and the number of jobs had increased, though so, too, had unemployment, with enormous numbers of returning POWs and refugees from the East.[22] Nonetheless, economic recovery appeared under way in the western zones.

The mantra of freedom versus oppression served the CDU in the foreign policy sphere as well. Tapping into the antimaterialist anticommunism intrinsic to abendländische Christian Democracy,[23] CDU members came to represent the Abendland essentially as a bastion of anticommunism and the Federal Republic as Western Europe's best defense against communist infiltration.[24] In their confessionalization of the Cold War, the CDU partook in a larger western discourse portraying the confrontation as an epic religious battle between the West and atheistic communism.[25] While U.S. President Harry S. Truman cast the struggle against the Soviet Union as a "crusade" to protect Western civilization from the threat of Soviet godlessness, British foreign secretary Ernest Bevin described the East-West power struggle as moral combat for the survival of Western values, like that against Nazi Germany.[26] The Vatican supported these transatlantic leaders' efforts, not only working closely with foreign governments to combat Soviet influence but also announcing the excommunication of all communist Catholics in July 1949.[27]

Evident already in the interwar years, an anti-Bolshevik rendering of the Abendland reached a crescendo during the Nazi years to justify the invasion of the Soviet Union, both on the part of Nazi propagandists and Catholic leaders such as Bishop Clemens August Graf von Galen. After World War II, but especially after 1948, the portrayal of the Abendland as a bulwark against communism enjoyed widespread use, including by Protestants in the German Party and even in the FDP.[28] Indeed, throughout the Cold War, many Christians, particularly Catholics, regarded the Abendland as the antipode to the Soviet Union, which was imagined to embody all the consequences of the Western European abandonment of medieval Catholicism for the radicalism of the Enlightenment and secularism.[29]

The contraposition of the western Abendland with the unchristian East was dramatized by the CDU's invocation of the term *Asian*. As early as in March 1946, Adenauer famously declared, "The danger is great. Asia is on the Elbe. Only an economically and spiritually healthy Western Europe under the leadership of England and France—a Western Europe including, as a western component, the part of Germany not occupied by Russia—can halt the further spiritual and powerful advance of Asia."[30] Consistent with Hans-Peter Schwarz's depiction of Adenauer's understanding of the Abendland as militant,[31] Adenauer explained in a May 1947 letter in which he described the KPD and SPD as "totalitarian" that there were only "two big fronts in Europe and the world": the "Christian-abendländische front, whose strongest support here in Germany is the CDU and the CSU, and the Asian front."[32] Echoing motifs of National Socialist propaganda, Adenauer identified in the "enormous power of Asia, represented through Russia and its satellite states," a "completely different spirit and way of thinking than [that of] abendländischen Europeans."[33]

Although striking for their passion, Adenauer's references to a battle between the Abendland and Asia were hardly isolated.[34] While Christine Teusch referred to "the heathen [*heidnischen*] Asian peoples with Russia at the top,"[35] Bruno Dörpinghaus argued in 1948 that the "Asian world of ideas" posed the biggest and most serious threat to "Christianity of the Abendland."[36] Only a common front of "Christian *Völker* of the West," maintained Dörpinghaus, could withstand the "danger of Marxism and, with it, that of communism."[37] Linus Kather, cofounder of the Hamburg CDU, saw the threat as even more pressing: "Asia stands on the borders of Lower Saxony and Bavaria! The danger is enormous."[38] Indeed, according to Clemens Münster, the Abendland had historically been "threatened from the East and South by Asian peoples."[39]

This Cold War adaptation of one of the CDU's ideological fundaments resonated not only in the international arena but also with the larger process of ideological transformation at work in the early party. Through its internal debate over Christian Socialism, the CDU had narrowed its conception of antimaterialism to imply anti-Marxism. By 1949, especially with the defeat of Jakob Kaiser's foreign policy vision of Germany as the bridge between East and West, allegiance to both antimaterialism and the Abendland signaled unadulterated anticommunism.[40] That the CDU would emerge from the Federal Republic's first elections as the governing party provided it the opportunity to instill this ideology into the new German state.

The 1949 Bundestag Election

With 78.5 percent of those eligible voting, West Germans gave the CDU and CSU a combined 31.0 percent of the vote, enabling them to edge out the SPD, which received 29.2 percent. As it had dominated the campaign, antisocialism would also dictate coalition negotiations for the Federal Republic's first government. Adenauer in particular maintained that the election results represented a referendum on the "planned" economy that must be honored.[41] While Karl Arnold, Josef Gockeln, Johannes Albers, and Peter Altmeier, among others, argued for a grand coalition, the SPD made clear that it would join the CDU only if Erhard were dismissed.[42] Adenauer, for his part, never wavered from his antipathy to cooperation with the SPD, and the Frankfurt Economic Council coalition of the CDU/CSU, FDP, and German Party was confirmed. On September 15, 1949, the seventy-three-year-old Adenauer was sworn in as the first chancellor of the Federal Republic of Germany by the new president of the Bundestag, FDP chair Theodor Heuss.

The CDU's affinity with the FDP was based above all else on the parties' shared hostility to socialism and communism. A highly fractious party clearly divided between left and right, the FDP enjoyed one position of consensus within the party—a rejection of Social Democratic economics. Some FDP members did reveal an openness to Christian ideas; Heuss had been one of a number of former liberals to contact former Center Party members in 1945 to explore founding an interconfessional party.[43] But as was dramatically evident in the Parliamentary Council, Heuss and his fellow liberals steadfastly opposed rechristianizing Germany and were especially suspicious of Catholic influence over the new state. At the same time, the FDP embraced a more liberal interpretation of the social market economy than did most Catholic Christian Democrats.[44]

Considering the FDP's cultural politics and its emphasis on the "market economy" within the social market economy, it is not surprising that some Catholic voters and clergymen, including Wilhelm Böhler, expressed deep reservations concerning the CDU-FDP agreement or that those fears compounded existing concerns within the Catholic Teilkultur about the new economics minister's sympathies for economic liberalism.[45] While Erhard conceded feeling drawn to the FDP, whose leaders offered him at least one spot on the party slate, he maintained that only through the CDU could he ensure the health of free market capitalism in West Germany.[46] Moreover, Erhard's commitment to Christian Democracy appeared repaid by popular support, as he campaigned nationally to large crowds and would win his first election as a Bundestag delegate in 1949 with 40 percent of the vote.[47]

As Catholic qualms about Erhard made clear, the now governing Christian Democrats had hardly overcome the legacy of Christian division. The CDU's integration of Protestants and Catholics necessarily related directly to the continued existence within the CDU and the Federal Republic of the Catholic Teilkultur.[48] That milieu was still sufficiently intact that the 1949 election has been commonly referred to as the Weimar Republic's last election; indeed, the results for the CDU/CSU mirrored those of the Center Party and BVP in July 1932.[49] The CDU won just 25 percent of Protestant votes in 1949 and carried only one Protestant region, Schleswig-Holstein, where the party enjoyed especially strong support from the Protestant Church.[50]

Electoral continuity was also evident in the gender breakdown of the CDU's support. Leading women in the CDU faced open sexism from male Christian Democrats[51] and complained repeatedly that the party neglected them and their activities until election time.[52] Yet for the CDU, inheriting the Center Party's electoral base meant relying not simply on Catholic backing but on female Catholic support, particularly in rural areas. While women voted at significantly lower rates than men before 1933, this was no longer the case after 1945 and especially in the late 1940s and early 1950s, when millions of men had been killed and many others eligible to vote were in POW camps or otherwise detained. Crucial to the CDU's electoral fortunes, Catholic women voted not only overwhelmingly for the CDU but at higher percentages than other German women.[53] This helps to explain how the CDU/CSU enjoyed almost twice the level of SPD female support (41 versus 21 percent) in 1949, leading Kurt Schumacher to blame West German women for Social Democracy's loss.[54]

The CDU's disproportionate reliance on Catholic voters—male and female—was also reflected in its leadership ranks, including the party's first federal cabinet and Bundestag faction, both of which were approximately two-thirds Catholic. While Protestants claimed a variety of party backgrounds, ranging from the DDP to the DVP, DNVP, NSDAP, and CSVD, no more than five members of the Bundestag fraction hailed from any one party, underscoring not only Protestants' lack of unity but also the CDU's success in appealing to bourgeois Protestants across the ideological spectrum. At the same time, the Bundestag faction was marked by anti–National Socialism; seventeen of its members had been arrested at some point during the Third Reich.[55] Although the number of leading Christian Democrats with National Socialist pasts would increase significantly over the coming years—including, most famously, state secretary Hans Globke—electorally the CDU would prove less the NSDAP successor party than the FDP, even in areas where the FDP adopted the profile of the liberal milieu party in continuation of the DDP tradition.[56]

While the CDU struggled to gain more than a foothold in Protestant West Germany, the party clearly succeeded in becoming the dominant political party in the Catholic milieu. In 1949, the Center received just over 3 percent of the federal vote (all ten of its seats were in North Rhine-Westphalia), and it would join the SPD in the opposition to the CDU.[57] Although the Center Party would do well in the 1950 North Rhine-Westphalian Landtag election in Münster, Detmold, and Arnsberg and in local elections in Münster Land and Paderborn Land into the 1950s, by 1957 it held no seats in the Bundestag and was reduced to "splinter status" even in its stronghold state of North Rhine-Westphalia.[58]

(Though still in existence today, with a federal leadership and active organizations in most *Länder,* the party's recently elected representatives are all on the local level.)[59]

But the CDU's success in establishing itself as the representative of the Catholic milieu was a doubled-edged sword. Some Protestants concerned about the loss of traditional Protestant dominance in Germany regarded the CDU simply as the better organized of the competing organs of political Catholicism.[60] This perception was part of many Protestants' larger sense that the new confessional balance in West Germany portended Catholic dominance for the first time in German history. Not unlike after World War I, even some Protestants committed to ecumenism feared Catholic political and demographic hegemony in the new state.[61] This sentiment was nowhere more famously expressed than by Martin Niemöller, who declared in December 1949, "The present West German government was conceived in the Vatican and born in Washington. The continuance of the West German state means the death of continental Protestantism."[62]

Niemöller's "conceived in the Vatican" accusation struck even some of the CDU's harshest critics as excessive, and it occasioned a broad discussion of the involvement of Protestant ministers in politics, including a warning on Adenauer's part against renewed confessional strife and clerical arrogance.[63] Objections to the role of the Catholic Church in West German politics were hardly unique to Niemöller, however. In his closing speech to the Parliamentary Council, Theodor Heuss had criticized at length the Catholic clergy's political engagement, particularly clerical warnings that Catholics could not in good conscience join the SPD or FDP.[64] Moreover, Frings's CDU membership confirmed what many party critics had long suspected about his influence over party policy and highlighted the CDU's hypocrisy in having fought for the concordat while a leading Catholic official violated its ban on clerical political activity.[65]

Confessionalism in the 1950s

Protestant fears would ease somewhat as Protestant votes for the CDU increased across the 1950s, as did overall support for Christian Democracy. In 1953, the CDU improved its performance dramatically, attracting 45.2 percent of the electorate as the party absorbed support from a number of smaller splinter parties, including those previously favored by Protestant middle-class conservatives. Most important for the party's goal of bridging the country's confessional divide, the CDU increased its appeal to Protestants to 34 percent.

While this represented only 22.4 percent of secularized Protestants, it constituted 53.6 percent of Protestants tied to the church.[66] In 1953, the party also made a concerted effort to balance its leadership, with the result of ten Catholics and eight Protestants in the federal cabinet and a higher percentage of Protestants in the CDU/CSU Bundestag faction than in either the party's membership or the electorate.[67] That this unwritten law of proportionality applied more broadly was evident in the widely understood formula guaranteeing confessional equilibrium between the positions of chancellor and West German president;[68] even the awarding of the Order of Merit of the Federal Republic of Germany attracted Adenauer's and Heuss's personal efforts to engineer confessional balance.[69]

Despite such attention to confessional harmony and growing Protestant goodwill toward the CDU, complaints about the influence of the Catholic Church over the CDU and the new German state resounded throughout the 1950s,[70] and opinion polls in the late 1950s and early 1960s revealed that public association of the party and its leaders with the Catholic Church remained undiminished. For critics, the clerical hierarchy's support for the CDU/CSU was nowhere more obvious than in the 1953 and 1957 federal elections, codified in the bishops' pastoral letters, in the electoral statements of the Central Committee of German Catholics (Das Zentralkomitee der deutschen Katholiken [ZdK]) and various other Catholic organizations, as well as in the church press.[71] CDU Catholics reinforced the CDU's Catholic image through their public statements heralding the arrival of Catholics in power,[72] while Adenauer's appointment after the 1953 election of Franz-Josef Wuermeling to direct the new Ministry of Family Affairs brought an unvarnished Catholic voice into national politics. Adenauer's famously authoritarian style of leadership, captured by the sobriquet *chancellor democracy,* also likely reinforced a perception of Catholic patriarchy, even as his authoritativeness reassured many, especially older voters, of the state's stability.[73]

The understanding of the CDU as a thoroughly Catholic party was reinforced by West German Protestant perceptions of the party's policies. While some Protestants regarded land reform and codetermination as Catholic strategies designed to deny Protestants their rights and wealth,[74] under Wuermling, many West Germans saw CDU family policies as church-sponsored attempts to imprint a Catholic vision of the family and women onto the new state.[75] Even foreign policy symbolized the confessionalized gap. Niemöller was not alone in portraying West German Cold War strategy as a Catholic ideological "crusade" designed to sacrifice the Protestant, eastern part of Germany. The

All-German People's Party (Gesamtdeutsche Volkspartei [GVP]), founded by former Christian Democrat Gustav Heinemann, employed boldly confessionalized language attacking West Germany as a Catholic state linked to Rome.[76] Even a 1955 FDP poster described German reunification under the CDU as ending with the "writing off of the Protestant population of the Soviet zone."[77] When in 1965 the EKD called for a diplomatic opening with Poland, it reinforced the perception of a distinctly Protestant West German foreign policy.[78]

The movement to European unity reinforced these apprehensions. In the immediate postwar years, the integration of western Germany into a European confederation enjoyed the support of the German clerical hierarchy and the Vatican.[79] Drawing directly on Catholic understandings of the Abendland, postwar organizers, including Adenauer, excluded Britain from their conceptions of Europe,[80] constructing the European Economic Community in accordance with Catholic political traditions, including federalism, personalism, solidarism, and subsidiarity.[81] Within the CDU, European integration found its greatest support among Catholics; Adenauer even excluded CDU Protestants from taking leading roles in advancing European unification.[82] For their part, Protestant-dominated parties made no secret of their suspicions: Social Democratic leader Kurt Schumacher decried European integration as a Catholic and clerical project,[83] while a 1953 GVP election flyer protested the sacrifice of East German Protestants on the altar of Catholic-led European unification, decrying, "No Protestant vote for the Catholic CDU!"[84]

For all of these reasons, some scholars have argued that Protestants had as much difficulty identifying with the early Federal Republic as did Catholics with the Protestant-dominated Weimar Republic.[85] The salience of religious culture in the 1950s Federal Republic was perhaps nowhere more evident than in the debates about confessional schools that percolated throughout the states. While less controversial in confessionally homogenous states—confessional schools were instituted in states with substantial Catholic populations, such as Bavaria and the Rhineland-Palatinate, while community schools predominated in majority Protestant areas such as Schleswig-Holstein—in the states with mixed populations, such as North Rhine-Westphalia, Lower Saxony, Hesse, and Baden-Württemberg, the issue provoked considerable dissension.[86] That educating Protestant and Catholic children together remained a defining question for many West German Catholics was underscored by the fact that not until the Second Vatican Council did the Pope grant community schools with separate religious instruction equal status to confessionally segregated public schools.[87]

Confessional Tensions within the CDU

If confessional disaffinity was evident in 1950s West Germany, it was clearly palpable within the CDU as well. As the confessional school issue devolved to the states, Protestant and Catholic Christian Democrats found their union tested again and again.[88] By the early 1950s, some CDU Catholics sought to adopt a new school policy in light of the fact that fewer and fewer Catholic parents were insisting on confessional schools. At the same time, party Protestants made clear that they interpreted the Elternrecht to imply recognition of parental desires for any type of school. As late as the early 1960s, Christine Teusch defended the CDU's endorsement of confessional schools against CDU Protestant attacks, while Adolf Süsterhenn found himself negotiating between Catholic Church officials and party Protestants regarding party policy.[89]

In the early 1950s, Adenauer would repeatedly warn the CDU/CSU Bundestag faction that interconfessional hostility threatened the German people's future.[90] That confessional difference remained marked was demonstrated by the March 1952 organization of Protestants within the party. In December 1945, CDU Rhenish Protestants had begun to meet regularly, with Westphalian Protestant conferences following in 1947.[91] Highlighting the prominence of Rhenish Protestants within the CDU, Wuppertal Protestants built on their earlier organization to found the intraparty Protestant Working Group (Evangelischer Arbeitskreis [EAK]).[92] Rhenish Protestants, including Otto Schmidt, Helmut Lauffs, and Emil Marx, would lead the new group.[93]

In a broader sense, the organization of the EAK emerged from the tensions inherent in Protestant Christian Democracy. As Otto Boelitz lamented to Friedrich Holzapfel regarding the development of CDU policy, "You are thoroughly acquainted with the difficulty associated with" this question. "On the one hand, we as Protestants may surrender nothing of the theological (as well as biblical) suppositions for our political actions; on the other hand, we must stress the Christian commonalities that bind us to the Catholics."[94] The desire to reconcile Protestant beliefs with the mandate of Christian unity was rendered more complicated by Protestants' long-standing concern about their minority status. Even as they acknowledged Catholic complaints concerning Protestant domination of the civil service, EAK members stressed their lack of representation in specific ministries and within the party more generally;[95] the dearth of Protestants was especially striking among female Christian Democrats.[96]

The more immediate origins of the EAK lay, however, in the conflict between Gustav Heinemann and Konrad Adenauer over West German rearmament and unification politics. When Heinemann, a founding member of the

CDU, broke with Adenauer to make common cause with Martin Niemöller, Bundestag president and leading CDU Protestant Hermann Ehlers grew sufficiently concerned about national Protestant opinion that he more formally organized Protestant Christian Democrats.[97] In seeking to increase Protestant electoral support for the CDU, EAK leaders continued to face the opposition of Protestant theologians who rejected in principle the pretext of a Christian party;[98] despite regular meetings with the "Protestant Academy" of the council of the EKD, CDU Protestants failed to overcome reservations in the EKD concerning the name and even existence of a Christian party.[99]

In an effort to demonstrate that the EAK posed no threat to party Catholics, the group's leaders invited Adenauer to address their first meeting, held in Siegen, a former stronghold of the CSVD and of the Pietist tradition of political Protestantism. Even as he stressed in his speech that all Christian Democrats shared political goals, above all defeating materialism, Adenauer acknowledged, "For many solutions, Protestants need other explanations than Catholics. That is why such special conferences are necessary. They bring no separation; instead, they are a fruitful action within the framework of the entire CDU."[100] Adenauer's address represented an unusually frank acknowledgment of the party's confessional differences, which the EAK would both channel and magnify.[101] Although its raison d'être was to support Adenauer's foreign policy, the EAK antagonized the chancellor by calling for intensified contacts with Protestant East Germany; in September 1952, the EAK endorsed Ehlers's decision to receive a delegation from the East German People's Chamber despite Adenauer's entreaties to cancel the event.[102]

Dechristianization, Deconfessionalization, and Dissolution of the Catholic Milieu

As fractious as Protestant-Catholic relations appeared both inside and beyond the CDU in the early postwar years, Christian conflicts nonetheless masked larger societal change that would, among other things, undermine the role of the church in West German politics and society and facilitate confessional harmony. Beginning in the late 1950s, a host of factors converged to remake dramatically West German political and religious life. Political stability, the introduction of new technologies, increased individualism, mobility, the breakdown of the Catholic ghetto, and Protestant-Catholic integration all contributed to the decreased authority in West Germany of such standard-bearers as church, school, and family.[103] Above all else, West German life was transformed by an economic recovery so dramatic that it has now taken on legendary proportions. Fueled by inexpensive labor, including eastern expellees and refugees, and by West German tax, cartel, and trade policies, the Federal Republic's economy expanded more than 8 percent a year across the 1950s.[104] With the advent of a newly individualized "ethic of consumption"[105] came a reinvestment of the sacred into everyday life, as evidenced by, among other things, the heightened importance attributed to love and sexual satisfaction.[106]

Olaf Blaschke has argued that the dissolution of the Catholic milieu by the mid-1960s was, in fact, a fifty-year-long process under way since World War I. Already apparent during the Weimar era in decreased Center Party support and church attendance, the fraying of the Teilkultur and processes of dechristianization received a significant boost from those refugees and expellees who felt alienated by their new churches. Barely discernable at the time as a consequence of the increase in absolute numbers of Catholics with the arrival of the expellees and refugees, church attendance began to fall as early as 1950. As the welfare state assumed functions previously provided by social organizations, the Catholic world of organizations, particularly professional organizations, contracted.[107] Male adolescents, for example, with some regional and occupational exceptions, began in the mid-1950s to abandon the youth groups that had long served as incubators for the Catholic milieu.[108] Indeed, for a generation coming of age in a West Germany governed by the CDU/CSU in coalition with the FDP, the traditional logic underlying the Catholic milieu—defensiveness against a Protestant state and liberalism—made little sense.[109]

The dynamics of secularization, dechristianization, and the decline of Christendom—the terms themselves are much debated—are far from understood and are clearly part of much larger continental phenomena.[110] Indeed, as Dagmar Herzog has noted, secularization and religious renewal seem inextricably and dialectically bound and at times difficult to disentangle.[111] If the postwar decline in church attendance has continued relatively unabated, its relationship to religious or spiritual life is hardly axiomatic. Even as declining church attendance led Jesuit theologian Karl Rahner in 1970 to declare West Germany a "pagan land with a Christian past and vestiges of Christianity,"[112] studies found that only 20 percent of West Germans in the 1960s held no religious beliefs.[113]

Interrogating the relationship between weakened church ties and religious identity, Ellen Lovell Evans warns us not to overstate the importance of secularization to deconfessionalization, highlighting instead the role of ecumenism in the dilution of Europe's Catholic milieus.[114] Here the Second Vatican Council of 1962–65 surely played a notable role, as its unprecedented openness to ecumenical initiatives marked a departure from the "alternative" Catholic society of the nineteenth century.[115] If their causes remain indefinite, the effects of secularization and ecumenicism on the lowering of the West German confessional barrier are broadly evident, whether in the rise of "mixed marriages" between Protestants and Catholics or in the shift from confessional to community schools.[116] For these reasons, Mark Ruff has aptly labeled the 1960s "the time of a second foundation of the Federal Republic," when "the social and cultural rifts that had plagued German society for nearly 100 years had finally been overcome."[117]

Christian Democracy both reflected and reinforced these profound shifts. Not only did the CDU's leadership become less Catholic, but so did the party's electoral support and membership, altering Christian Democracy's Protestant complexion. As Protestant electoral support for the CDU increased from 31.3 percent in 1953 to 42 percent in 1957 to approximately 50 percent in the mid-1970s, the CDU's Protestant constituency shifted distinctly rightward.[118] While the Confessing Church and CSVD incubated many first-hour CDU Protestants, those who remained in the party in the coming decades were largely prewar conservatives.[119] Michael Klein ascribes this phenomenon at least in part to Protestants' "antiparty mentality," whereby those unacculturated to party politics retreated or were marginalized following internal party setbacks: Such prominent early CDU Protestants as Otto Schmidt, Hans Schlange-Schöningen, Theodor Steltzer, Otto Heinrich von der Gablentz, and Friedrich Holzapfel all withdrew from political activity.[120] More important, perhaps, the CDU's virulent anticommunism and policies of Western alliance alienated many religious Protestants. The rearmament debate not only catalyzed intraparty Protestant organization but inspired liberal Protestants to abandon the party for the GVP and eventually the SPD, thereby reinforcing the conservatism of Protestant Christian Democracy.[121]

At the same time the party was becoming more Protestant and conservative, Catholic voters were increasingly joining liberal Protestants in defecting to the SPD.[122] In contrast to the Weimar Republic, when the SPD could be safely characterized as a Protestant party, fully one-third of the SPD's support in the early Federal Republic was Catholic. Following the SPD's initiative to improve relations with the Catholic Church and religious Germans more generally,[123] the 1969 election saw a breakthrough in Catholic working-class support for the SPD.[124] Although the CDU would continue into the 1980s to derive approximately one-third of its support from the Catholic working class, a clear pattern emerged correlating Catholics' distance from their church with their support for the SPD.[125]

The CDU's shifting electorate was also evident in diminished support from women, once heralded by Adenauer as "consistently our most loyal voters."[126] Indeed, in light of the 1957 election results—the CDU won 53.5 percent of female votes to the SPD's 28.9 percent—it is not an overstatement to suggest that the CDU owed its absolute majority to Catholic women.[127] While the CDU attracted 8–10 percent more of the female vote than other parties through 1969, in 1972 male and female voters distributed their support approximately evenly, and in 1980 the SPD received more female votes than male. Although this trend would reverse itself in 1983 and 1987, the CDU's advantage among women in those elections was significantly less than in the Federal Republic's first two decades.[128]

If the CDU's leadership and electorate mirrored the broader trend of deconfessionalization, Christian Democracy arguably played an active role in that process as well.[129] First and foremost, the CDU offered an unprecedented and self-conscious model of democratic cooperation among politicians of different faiths through the late 1960s, when the CDU ceased profiling itself as an avowedly interconfessional party.[130] At the same time, the CDU's public silence about confessional conflict and identity within the party—party officials never officially acknowledged their proportion policy and sought to deflect attention from their leaders' religious affiliations—contributed to what Frank Bösch has called the "public dethematizing of the confessional question."[131] Finally, by distancing the party from the Catholic Church on defining issues, Christian Democrats helped undermine the notion that the CDU operated at the behest of German priests. Significantly, in 1967, after years of pressure from CDU Protestants, the CDU/CSU finally removed the demand for confessional schools from the party program.[132]

Indeed, one clear effect of the transformation of West German religious life was a reconfiguration of the relationship between the party and the Catholic Church. If the election of 1957 marked a high point of identification between the CDU/CSU and the church's new Catholic Office, led by Wilhelm Böhler, less than a decade later the Catholic Church's electoral statements no longer directly or indirectly endorsed the CDU/CSU. While the church's 1961 pastoral letter accused the SPD of favoring Christianity only during electoral season, the 1965 declaration (*Erklärung*)—no longer a pastoral letter—exhorted Catholics simply to vote for candidates with a "religious attitude." By 1969, the church merely recommended that voters favor parties "open to the Christian view of man and society." The impact of these diluted endorsements was twofold: Catholic voter support for the CDU/CSU diminished, but so did the party's reputation as beholden to the church.[133]

Church leaders' motivations for this strategy varied. As dechristianization undermined the church's influence and political value to the CDU/CSU, ecclesiastical officials ironically sought their own distance. To stem the church's diminishing authority in politics, some priests argued for expanding their political connections beyond one party. In establishing links with the SPD, church leaders weakened both ties to the CDU/CSU and Catholic voters' resistance to Social Democracy.[134] At the same time, some clergy distanced themselves from what they perceived as an increasingly secular and Protestant CDU, particularly after Adenauer relinquished the chancellorship in 1963.[135]

Christian Democratic Ideology
Deconfessionalized: Materialism

The complex overlay of shifting dynamics of secularization and deconfessionalization not only altered the CDU's relationship with the church, electorate, and party leadership but also necessarily affected Christian Democratic ideology. In the 1950s, the CDU began consciously and unconsciously to abandon or reconfigure language and precepts specifically associated with the Catholic milieu. Most important, the foundation of German Christian Democracy—antimaterialism—underwent significant revision as materialism adopted new emphases with the emergence of West Germany's consumer society.[136] Having been honed through the debate over Christian Socialism, by the mid-1950s antimaterialism assumed yet another new configuration. In direct response to the successes of the social market economy, materialism began to function in CDU discourse as one of two variants—"dialectical" materialism (Marxism) or "practical" materialism (consumerism).

That materialism in CDU discourse had hitherto connoted neither material goods nor consumption is—considering the economic conditions of the late 1940s—not enormously surprising. But as West Germans began to enjoy the fruits of American-style consumerism, some Christians criticized what the CDU had wrought. The concerns were located primarily not with the former Christian Socialists, many of whom believed the social market economy was largely fulfilling its social mandate by compensating war losses through the 1952 "equalization of burdens" (*Lastenausgleich*) and, beginning in the late 1950s, with the construction of the welfare state. Indeed, with Anton Storch as minister of labor and Jakob Kaiser as minister for internal German affairs and vice chair of the CDU from 1950 to 1958, former advocates of Christian Socialism were well represented in the new government and party.[137]

Christian-inspired criticism of the social market economy would come instead from across the CDU and from Christian circles outside the party. As tremendous anxiety accompanied what conservative, religious West Germans, especially clergymen, decried as unrestrained acquisitive greed, conservative Germans reclaimed a societal critique that posited "Amerika" as the emblem of consumerism and "practical" materialism.[138] Specifically, many West Germans harboring moral scruples about the country's new wealth feared that consumerism would induce a form of collectivism inherent in Nazism and Stalinism. If a population's engagement in capitalist acquisition hardly seems to suggest its growing susceptibility to communism, from the Christian conservative point of view all materialist ideologies suffered the same fundamental flaw: they were anti-Christian.[139]

While "practical" materialism in CDU discourse could imply a rejection of Catholic political priorities, such as confessional schools, for the most part it connoted simply a consumerism that portended seduction by "dialectical materialism."[140] Pervasive in CDU discourse in the mid- to late 1950s,[141] this nexus between "practical" and "dialectical materialism" emerged as a particular theme for Adenauer, who repeatedly shared his fear that West Germans, who had fallen into "a spiritual lethargy" as a result of having earned and bought so much,[142] now failed to understand "that a much worse materialism than the National Socialist stands directly at our doors."[143] Indeed, in June 1955, Adenauer exhorted fellow Christian Democrats to persuade West Germans that "the variations of materialism from which we are suffering—that is, the overestimation of the ownership and consumption, and so on, of material goods—prepare the soil for welcoming this poison from the East."[144] In November 1956, Adenauer even blamed West Germans' lack of interest in the Hungarian uprising on the fact that "the German Volk appears to be almost sunken in materialism, not in the sense of communist materialism, but in naked materialism; they want to earn as much as possible, live as well as possible, and everything else is unimportant."[145]

While striking for the connection it proposed between valuation of material goods, soullessness, and communism, this discourse is also notable for what it did not include—an explicit linkage of materialism to the United States. Since the interwar era, "Amerika" had come for many Germans to symbolize all that was modern—from technology to advertising, democracy, and materialist consumption to cultural superficiality, greed, and female aggression.[146] In the 1950s, however, while many Christian elites disdained the United States for its liberalism, materialism, and Protestant-infused individualism,[147] Christian Democrats did not openly criticize the United States on these counts.[148] In this, national Christian Democrats departed from the larger conservative and religious West German rhetoric surrounding materialism that would have brought them into direct political conflict with their most important ally.[149]

This tension and the CDU's use of materialism not only paralleled and reflected the dynamics of dechristianization and deconfessionalization but would signal a momentous cultural and political shift in West German history. This complicated process had many roots, not least of which was the transformation and arguably modernization of West German political culture, in part occasioned and—in some respects, such as race—complicated by the negotiation of a newly intimate relationship with the United States.[150] In the late 1950s, West German Christian conservatives began to lose influence to Cold War liberals, who reconfigured the link between consumerism and communism to portray consumerism as fundamental to democracy. Articulated by Ludwig Erhard, this new discourse marked a radical reversal from the Catholic critique of "practical materialism" to embrace American cultural imports and consumption. Unexpectedly adept at American-inspired propaganda, the CDU's increasingly sophisticated electoral campaigns began to cast the satisfaction of personal desire as a means to secure societal stability, economically and in terms of gender roles; by portraying the freedom to consume as a political right, the CDU enabled the West German state to distinguish itself from its East German counterpart. In a national propaganda campaign in which consumption represented a form of "civic participation," Christian-inspired reservations about consumerism found no place.[151]

The new political and cultural CDU discourse that emerged in the late 1950s represented an increasingly liberal view of politics that from the perspective of Christian Democratic history also unmistakably reflected the rise of Protestant voices and the diminution of Catholic hegemony. After the organization of the Protestant Working Group in 1952, Protestants increasingly challenged what they perceived as CDU Catholics' arrogance and insensitivity. This Protestant pressure—"furor protestanticus," as Heuss put it to Adenauer—focused on, among other things, Protestant representation in the CDU's Bundestag faction and Catholic Christian Democrats' political language.[152] It would culminate in the transition of party leadership from the Catholic troika at the helm of the CDU since the mid-1950s—Adenauer, Heinrich Krone, and Hans Globke—to the "Protestant period" of the 1960s, when the CDU was dominated by Protestants Ludwig Erhard, Gerhard Schröder, and Kai-Uwe von Hassel. Protestant ascendancy was not lost on CDU Catholics, who in 1966 founded a Catholic counterpart to the Protestant Working Group in response to their discomfort with Protestant Christian Democrats' increased influence.[153]

Christian Democratic Ideology Deconfessionalized:
The Abendland

As the founding principle of Christian Democratic ideology, antimaterialism, underwent striking change in the 1950s and 1960s, so too did the fundament of the Abendland. The term *Abendland* was deployed repeatedly in the late 1940s to depict the Cold War as a battle between Western European Christians and Soviet heathens. As it had earlier in the century, the Abendland also figured in occupied Germany as an ideological framework for unified Europe. Visions of the Abendland buttressed Western European integration, particularly reconciliation with the French, as well as a newly Europeanized German national identity.[154] The term *Reich,* Adolf Süsterhenn explained in October 1948, was in essence another name for the "Christian Abendland"; in a modern sense, Süsterhenn observed, that would mean "European Union or European confederation."[155]

But even as German Christian Democrats recast the modern Abendland as a Western European political and economic union, use of the term began to fade with the modernization of West German society. Internally, pressure came from CDU Protestants—such as Gerstenmaier's earlier remonstrance that the "Christian Abendland" was not a "Catholic Abendland"[156]—while outwardly it emitted from alliance with the United States. Fashioned especially under the Third Reich as a rejection of both American and Soviet aggression, the Abendland after World War II conveyed a clear sense of cultural superiority over all non–Western Europeans, including Americans.[157] As the Federal Republic embedded itself under the American security umbrella, Christian Democrats were forced to negotiate the contradictions between traditional understandings of the Abendland and American cultural identity, particularly the evangelical Protestantism underlying American anticommunism.[158]

While some Germans sought to protect abendländische culture from the American way of life even as they regarded the U.S. alliance as a necessary evil,[159] others aimed explicitly to bridge the America-Abendland gap by emphasizing the Christian roots of the United States or by comparing the United States to ancient Rome or Greece.[160] However, as Konrad Adenauer and others revealed, even an overt inclusion of the United States in the Abendland remained ambivalent.[161] In a speech at the Recklinghausen party congress in 1948 in which he condemned the Morgenthau Plan as "an offense against humanity at least worthy of being placed alongside National Socialist crime," Adenauer grudgingly conceded that in a world divided between Asia and Abendland, "South and North America also belong to the European, abendländischen spirit." But Adenauer's quick reminder that Europe remained the "refuge and the source of the christlich-abendländischen spirit"[162] was consistent with his later ruminations that Europeans were products of Christian humanism, from which they derived notions of individual freedom, whereas the Anglo-Saxons had no real ideology.[163]

Such critiques of the United States, like those of American consumerism, remained consciously subdued within the CDU, and the challenge of integrating the United States into a Christian Democratic Abendland ultimately was resolved not by the reconfiguration of the Abendland but by its diminished relevance.[164] Just a decade after the founding of the Federal Republic, the prospect of rechristianization inherent in the Abendland offered declining appeal to secularizing West Germans, while the European Union movement delineated a Western Europe oriented toward the Atlantic. Consistent with broader processes of liberalization in West Germany, the Abendland was replaced throughout the 1950s in party and national discourse by notions of a democratic, pluralistic "Western Europe" or simply "Europe."[165] Part of the larger process of Westernization or liberalization of the Federal Republic,[166] this linguistic and ideological shift was most evident in CDU politicians' adoption of a new vocabulary of *antitotalitarianism, the West,* and the *Free World,* language far less distinctly German Catholic.[167]

As the term *Abendland* began to fade from national Christian Democratic discourse, it seeped farther right on the political spectrum to the Socialist Reich Party (Sozialistische Reichspartei Deutschland [SRP] and the First Legion, an organization characterized by Jakob Kaiser as "neofascist."[168] The rhetoric's real downfall came in 1955, when Christian Democrat Heinrich von Brentano, in his first public appearance as foreign minister, gave a highly charged address repeatedly comparing West Germany's defense of the Abendland against pagan communism to the thousand-year-old Catholic preservation of Europe against pagan (Muslim) incursion.[169] The hostile public reaction to the speech precipitated press attacks and ultimately a parliamentary investigation of the government-supported Abendländische Akademie for antidemocratic sympathies.[170] Only this can explain a previously unthinkable exchange: In a November 1956 meeting of the CDU's Executive Committee, Adenauer explicitly eschewed using the term *Abendland* in party propaganda.[171]

As the term Abendland's demise reflected a marked deconfessionalization of Christian Democratic discourse, its survival within the party testified to the unevenness of that process. While the Abendland disappeared from official party publications, it nonetheless continued to figure prominently within the CDU/CSU in the 1960s foreign policy debate between Gaullists, who preferred an independent European policy and looser Western alliance, and Atlanticists, who advocated a strong transatlantic alliance under American hege-mony.[172] The divide was marked both by language—Atlanticists favored the term *the West,* which included the United States and Great Britain, while Gaul-lists invoked the Abendland[173]—and confession. CDU Atlanticists were more likely to be Protestant; Gaullists were disproportionately Catholic and publicly linked to political and intellectual supporters of the Abendland. If Torsten Op-pelland is right to remind us that CDU Protestants and Catholics operated on the basis of two different, confessionally formed "mental maps," this Protestant-Catholic split hardly characterized the CDU alone.[174] The foreign policy con-fessional line ran across the party spectrum, as the SPD and FDP supported Atlanticism, while the CSU emerged as a bastion of Gaullism.[175]

Confessionalism's Legacies

Indeed, for all the changes occasioned by dechristianization and deconfession-alization, religious culture continued to color West German politics in signifi-cant ways. The CDU's Bundestag delegation remained almost two-thirds Cath-olic as late as 1969;[176] in 1971, the population of the Federal Republic was approximately 51 percent Protestant, but Protestants represented only 25 per-cent of CDU members.[177] Moreover, although it receded steadily beginning in the 1960s (with the exception of the 1980 election), the confessional line through the West German electorate remained intact from the 1950s through German unification.[178] Those Catholics most devoted to church rituals particu-larly preferred the CDU/CSU,[179] and even into the 1980s scholars described the CDU as a "predominantly Catholic Party,"[180] a characterization no doubt reinforced by the uninterrupted dominance of North Rhine-Westphalian mem-bers.[181] As Catholic religiosity mattered, so did Protestant. As previously noted, in 1953, over half of West Germany's religiously devout Protestants voted for the CDU/CSU, while less than a quarter of secular Protestants did so,[182] a pat-tern that would continue into the 1990s;[183] in unified Germany's former East German states, the small Protestant Church membership voted disproportion-ately for the CDU.[184] At the same time, Lutheran Protestants consistently fa-vored the CDU more than their brethren from the Reform or united churches, testifying to the continued importance of intra-Protestant divisions.[185]

The history of Christian Democracy in the early republic embodies the complexities of German confessional relations. Largely a Catholic enterprise at the dawn of West German history, the CDU imprinted its vision of foreign and domestic policy onto the new state. But within a decade, significant alterations were well under way in that state's culture. Catholic ideology, specifically the concept of the Abendland, helped birth a broader, dechristianized understanding of confrontation with the Soviet Union even as it gave way to a less religiously colored terminology. Antimaterialism was transformed from a pillar of Christian Democratic antisecularism to an ultimately moot critique of capitalist consumption. As West German society began to deconfessionalize and commercialize, Christian Democracy followed and catalyzed these complex trends by undergoing its own transformation. The Protestant Christian Democratic campaign for equal influence within the party was matched by a diminution of Catholic clerical participation in CDU affairs, marking a break in the age-old link between Church and Turm. Increasing levels of Protestant support for Christian Democracy underscored the transformation of political Catholicism into interconfessionalism. But religious difference hardly disappeared from German culture or politics. The Protestant-Catholic confessional line remained visible, both across the CDU and throughout West German society. Religious identity, critical to the formation of the Federal Republic, remained determinate.

Conclusion

The history of the Christian Democratic Union is tied inextricably to the evolution of German confessional relations. The party's origins as well as its success rested on the dismantling of the Catholic Turm and what Josef Kannengießer dubbed Germany's "centuries-old barrier" of confessional hostility. The end of the German "religious *Sonderweg*" was a clear function of the dramatic political, social, and demographic impact of World War II.[1] And yet the process of interconfessional accommodation would unfold over decades and involve innumerable twists and turns. Although in profoundly different ways than in the 1920s or 1950s, West Germany remained a confessionalized society. Even in the unified Germany of the twenty-first century, more Catholics continue to vote for the CDU than do Protestants, and religion classes in German public schools remain, with notable exceptions, confessionally divided.[2]

In today's Germany, however, it is difficult to find strong evidence of the influence of intra-Christian difference on the public sphere. When confessional complaints are raised, they fail to gain traction within broader society. In 1990, for example, some western Catholics expressed fears that German unification would return Germany to Protestant dominance; Rhenish Catholics would soon protest the return of the capital to "Prussian" Berlin.[3] Later that decade, former East Germans criticized the influx of (western) Catholic politicians—specifically, that four of the five new minister-presidents were Catholic—while other detractors speculated that the Vatican was directing unified Germany's politics.[4] But tensions between Catholics and Protestants hardly framed German unification, and confessionalized analyses of the process were striking for their dearth. When religion did enter public discussion, it was generally in reference to clashes between western German abortion and educational laws and practices and those of a formerly atheistic state; Brandenburg's abolition of religious instruction in public schools underscored that tension.[5]

In the present-day CDU/CSU, confessional differences have been largely elided, at least publicly. While committed to articulating a Protestant voice within the CDU, the EAK has little national profile.[6] The old proportionality system, by which Protestant and Catholic appointments were closely calibrated, is no longer practiced. Nevertheless, Sarah Elise Wiliarty argues, Chancellor Angela Merkel advanced within the CDU structure so quickly in part because she fulfilled an internal quota for Protestants (as well as for women and easterners).[7] Clear cultural differences also exist between CDU/CSU southern and western Catholics and Merkel, a woman raised in an East German Protestant minister's home who served in 1992–93 as chair of the EAK. Those differences were underlined in February 2009, when Merkel challenged the Pope over his handling of an antisemitic priest. Contrasting Merkel, "a remarried, divorced Protestant woman," with Konrad Adenauer, Catholic journalist Martin Lohmann accused her of "possibly having a deep-seated problem with the Catholic Church." He cited her refusal to support the (re)organization of a CDU Catholic Working Group to offset the EAK and the "eastern and more heathen" character of the Federal Republic after unification.[8]

In casting his critique in the categories of Christian and secular, Lohmann highlighted a difference in German society far greater than that between Protestants and Catholics—that is, the gap between Christians and non-Christians. While Catholics and Protestants are evenly divided in Germany today, both groups are smaller than those who describe themselves as having other religious affiliations or as having no religious affiliation;[9] Lohmann's ultimate success in founding in 2009 a Working Group of Engaged Catholics (Arbeitskreis Engagierter Katholiken [AEK]) signals the alienation traditional, practicing Catholics feel even within the CDU.[10] Indeed, the number of Germans currently attending weekly services at Christian churches is low and diminishes annually.[11] Elections in unified Germany demonstrate that religiously devout Protestant and more numerous Catholic churchgoers disproportionately support the CDU.[12] Politically and culturally, Protestants and Catholics who attend weekly services have more in common with each other than they do with secular Germans or, in the view of many Union members, with Muslims. CDU/CSU politicians now invoke their parties' Christian roots and profile primarily in debates concerning Islam in Germany; in an echo of von Brentano's controversial 1956 speech, some even contrast Islam with Germany's abendländische culture.[13]

That the centuries-old confessional divide in German history has been subsumed by a larger gulf between Christians and non-Christians ironically reflects the worldviews of the CDU's founders. Their goal to join Christian forces in an alliance against Christianity's perceived enemies has largely been realized, though at the cost of their agenda of rechristianization. Dating from the first decades of Catholic political organization, the desire to join devout Protestants and Catholics in a Christian front had remained an abiding and unrealized aspiration of the German Catholic Teilkultur. The Center Party's numbered and unsuccessful attempts to break out of the Turm—associated first with Bachem, then Brauns and Stegerwald—highlighted Catholics' desire to interconfessionalize their politics as well as the prohibitive confessional impediments to their efforts. Only in the wake of World War II and its revolutionary social, political, and demographic impact did Protestants and Catholics forge a political compact. That their cooperation remained conflictual well into the 1960s highlights the degree to which confession remained an influential factor in German history after 1945.

The construction of a Christian Democratic ideology and politics was among Germany's most important post–World War II developments. Marking the first time that German Protestants and Catholics embraced an avowedly interconfessional democratic party, the founding of the CDU augured the Allies' reconstitution of the German political system. The CDU's survival and success—and the parallel failure of the Center Party after 1945 to sustain exclusively Catholic politics—signaled both the end of established German political Catholicism and the beginning of a political consolidation of religious, conservative, and bourgeois Protestants, traditionally hostile to democratic and party politics but limited in their postwar options. The cooperation of Protestants and Catholics after 1945 took place within a tradition of political Catholic initiatives to Protestants—jointly to oppose socialism, as seen in the Volksverein and the Christian Trade Unions, and to promote shared conservative cultural politics, particularly pertaining to women and the family. Yet reclaiming issues of consensus from pre-1933 German history was a doubled-edged sword, as the CDU's confessional divisions over the Elternrecht revealed.

Indeed, in many ways—organizationally, culturally, electorally—political Catholicism in the late 1940s resembled that of the 1920s. The role of the Catholic clergy in the founding of the CDU, the rootedness of Christian Democratic leadership in the Catholic Teilkultur, the prominence of the Rhineland and Westphalia, the class tensions between Christian Trade Unionists and bourgeois Catholics, and party members' traditional language and ideological instincts all testified to the strong continuities across the Nazi era in Germany's Catholic milieu. At the same time, Catholic Christian Democrats' attentiveness to Protestant positions and the CDU's willingness to compromise with Protestant-dominated parties against church wishes in the Parliamentary Council made clear that the CDU was not the Center Party. If Bachem's cry, "We must come out of the tower!" was hardly realized by the end of Germany's occupation, the tower of German Catholicism no longer stood as tall.

Not only for their outreach to Protestants and sacrifices for interconfessionalism but for their commitment to democratic party politics and civil liberties, German Catholics have been credited by some scholars with having been the "true discoverers of the Federal Republic."[14] While many would challenge that statement, including Konrad H. Jarausch, the CDU indisputably played a central role in what Jarausch characterizes as the "gradual recovery of democracy's legitimacy during the postwar period."[15] In particular, Christian Democracy was essential to what Jarausch identifies as the development of a "culture of civility" in postwar Germany—the rejection of militarism and Nazism, the establishment of the rule of law, and the achievement of socially responsible economic prosperity.[16] Unlike the SPD, which contributed to the stability of the early Federal Republic through its participatory opposition, the CDU had the opportunity to imprint its ideology on the new body politic. While Christian Democrats failed to realize a new Christian state, West German culture, domestic and international policies, and public discourse in the 1950s certainly reflected the influence of Catholic authorities. Ideologically, the new republic would be antimaterialist in its rejection of classic liberalism, National Socialism, and Marxism. By opposing communist and Nazi enemies of Christian life, Protestant and Catholic Christian Democrats constructed their own doctrine of totalitarianism.

Of course, an antisocialist interpretation of antimaterialism dominated the Federal Republic. At the same time that anti-Marxism underlay the Federal Republic's raison d'être and foreign policy, it underwrote the social market economy. More than any other state course of action, Ludwig Erhard's economic policies defined the West German state for its new citizens. The social market economy, like Christian Democracy, was never simply anti-Marxist window dressing for laissez-faire economics.[17] The practical implications of Catholic anti-Marxism for German economic and social organization were not always self-evident, but, as James Van Hook argues, Christian Democrats were more consistent than not in their interpretation of the social market economy as a free market with strong social protections. While critics on the left often saw the social market economy as just a half step from capitalism, it retains to this day distinctive features reflecting its origins in Christian social thought. In a 2007 poll, only 21 percent of Germans agreed that the Christian Democratic Union was "a party of neoliberalism."[18]

Although cast in a Christian antisocialist, antimaterialist context, the social market economy, like all aspects of the early CDU platform, was confessionalized from its debut. The party's association with the so-called third way of economic organization between liberalism and Marxism emerged from a fractious process that required the subordination of left-wing Catholics in the name of ideological coherence and interconfessional cohesion. The antisocialist compact hammered out in 1946 and 1947 enabled Protestants and Catholics alike to carry the CDU banner into West Germany's first federal elections. That they held it aloft through the coming decades was one clear consequence of the social market economy's dramatic success. As declining deprivation quieted former Christian Trade Unionists and growing consumption secured interconfessional satisfaction, Protestants and Catholics could together celebrate German economic recovery. Indeed, according to Mark Spicka, the social market economy and specifically the party's nonreligious propaganda surrounding it enabled the CDU to break out of the Catholic Turm.[19]

Ultimately, as the backdrop to the early party's debate over Christian Socialism and adoption of the social market economy, the Cold War cemented the Protestant-Catholic antisocialist alliance. Konrad Adenauer in particular hewed an aggressive anticommunist line from the earliest days of Christian Democracy. Yet CDU foreign policy was hardly confessionally neutral. If it is an overstatement to suggest, as Volkhard Laitenberger does, that the Western alliance in the spirit of the Abendland was Adenauer's Catholic gift to the Federal Republic and the social market economy Ludwig Erhard's Protestant present,[20] Laitenberger justly recognizes the salience of religious difference. Even the ties that bound Protestants and Catholics to each other in Christian Democracy—economic and foreign policy—were interwoven with confessional difference. This was also true of cultural politics. While Protestants and Catholics largely agreed on the role women should play in the family and society, gendered and confessional differences would emerge, especially in the 1950s, on how to legislate that vision. Far more explicit were the differences the confessional school question laid bare.

Indeed, while tensions within the Catholic CDU would flare along class lines as they had since the beginning of Catholic politics, the party's internal cohesion remained most consistently vulnerable along the confessional line. Party leadership showed continuity with the old Center Party through the early 1960s; when that continuity ended, it marked the CDU's definitive break from the organized Catholic milieu.[21] That milieu itself underwent a dramatic transformation, reconfiguring the relationship of the Catholic clergy to party politics and more generally the role of Catholics in the state. While the CDU was far from achieving its stated goal of interconfessional politics in 1949, its history suggests that it and the Federal Republic have since traveled parallel paths of dechristianization and deconfessionalization.

Christian Democracy was born in an atmosphere of confessional continuity and change, as powerful currents of religiosity flowed through occupied Germany and the early Federal Republic. The project of rechristianizing Germany animated Christian Democracy's organizers as they worked to secure an interconfessional accord along antimaterialist lines, transforming political Catholicism as it had existed in Germany for a century. In forging Germany's first democratic interconfessional alliance, early Christian Democrats sought the "political unity of the Christian Volk" in "fulfillment of decades-long yearning."[22] By sustaining interconfessional cooperation, they established a political powerhouse that has shaped postwar Germany in unrivaled ways. That the Christian Democratic Union was founded and has governed in a context of confessionalism reminds us of the importance of religion and religious difference to twentieth-century German history.

Notes

INTRODUCTION

1. Geoffrey Pridham, "Christian Democracy in Italy and West Germany: A Comparative Analysis," in *Social and Political Movements in Western Europe,* ed. Martin Kolinsky and William E. Paterson (London, 1976), 146.

2. Claus Leggewie, "CDU—Integrationsmodell auf Widerruf? Die zwei Modernisierungen der deutschen Rechten nach 1945," *Blätter für deutsche und internationale Politik* 34 (1989): 294–308.

3. Richard Stöss, "Einleitung: Struktur und Entwicklung des Parteiensystems der Bundesrepublik—Eine Theorie," in *Parteien-Handbuch: Die Parteien der Bundesrepublik Deutschland, 1945–1980,* vol. 1, *AUD Bis EFP,* ed. Richard Stöss (Opladen, 1983), 121–45; Sarah Elise Wiliarty, *The CDU and the Politics of Gender in Germany: Bringing Women to the Party* (Cambridge, 2010), chapter 2.

4. Konrad H. Jarausch, *After Hitler: Recivilizing Germans, 1945–1955* (Oxford, 2006), vii–viii.

5. Wilfried Loth, *Katholiken im Kaiserreich: Der politische Katholizismus in der Krise des wilhelminischen Deutschlands* (Düsseldorf, 1984), 17.

6. Werner K. Blessing, "'Deutschland in Not, wir im Glauben' . . . Kirche und Kirchenvolk in einer katholischen Region, 1933–1949," in *Von Stalingrad zur Währungsreform: Zur Sozialgeschichte des Umbruchs in Deutschland,* ed. Martin Broszat, Klaus-Dietmar Henke, and Hans Woller, 3rd ed. (Munich, 1990), 15.

7. Gangolf Hübinger, *Kulturprotestantismus und Politik: Zum Verhältnis von Liberalismus und Protestantismus im wilhelminischen Deutschland* (Tübingen, 1994).

8. Olaf Blaschke, "Das 19. Jahrhundert: Ein Zweites Konfessionelles Zeitalter?" *Geschichte und Gesellschaft* 26 (2000): 38–75.

9. Ellen Lovell Evans, *The Cross and the Ballot: Catholic Political Parties in Germany, Switzerland, Austria, Belgium, and the Netherlands, 1785–1985* (Boston, 1999), 8.

10. M. Rainer Lepsius, "Parteiensystem und Sozialstruktur: Zum Problem der Demokratisierung der deutschen Gesellschaft," in *Deutsche Parteien vor 1918,* ed. Gerhard A. Ritter (Cologne, 1990), 56–80.

11. Karl Rohe, *Wahlen und Wählertraditionen in Deutschland: Kulturelle Grundlagen deutscher Parteien und Parteiensysteme im 19. und 20. Jahrhundert* (Frankfurt a.M., 1992).

12. Helmut Walser Smith and Chris Clark, "The Fate of Nathan," in *Protestants, Catholics, and Jews in Germany, 1800–1914*, ed. Helmut Walser Smith (Oxford, 2001), 29.

13. Detlef Lehnert and Klaus Megerle, introduction to *Politische Teilkulturen zwischen Integration und Polarisierung: Zur politischen Kultur in der Weimarer Republik*, ed. Detlef Lehnert and Klaus Megerle (Opladen, 1990), especially 10–11.

14. Rohe, *Wahlen*, 20–21.

15. Margaret Lavinia Anderson, "Living Apart and Together in Germany," in *Protestants, Catholics, and Jews*, ed. Smith, 320, 325–26.

16. Peter Lösche and Franz Walter, "Katholiken, Konservative, und Liberale: Milieus und Lebenswelten bürgerlicher Parteien in Deutschland während des 20. Jahrhunderts," *Geschichte und Gesellschaft* 26.3 (2000): 471; Arbeitskreis für kirchliche Zeitgeschichte (AKKZG), "Katholiken zwischen Tradition und Moderne: Das katholische Milieu als Forschungsaufgabe," *Westfälische Forschungen* 43 (1993): 588–654; Johannes Horstmann and Antonius Liedhegener, *Konfession, Milieu, Moderne: Konzeptionelle Positionen und Kontroversen zur Geschichte von Katholizismus und Kirche im 19. und 20. Jahrhundert* (Schwerte, 2001); Frank Bösch, *Das konservative Milieu: Vereinskultur und lokale Sammlungspolitik in ost- und westdeutschen Regionen (1900–1960)* (Göttingen, 2002); Mark Edward Ruff, "Katholische Jugendarbeit und junge Frauen in Nordrhein-Westfalen, 1945–1962: Ein Beitrag zur Diskussion über die Auflösung des katholischen Milieus," *Archiv für Sozialgeschichte* 38 (1998): 263–84; Mark Edward Ruff, "Der 'Bruderzwist' der DJK: 'Integralisten' und 'Modernisierer' in einem katholischen Sportverband," in *Katholiken und Protestanten in den Aufbaujahren der Bundesrepublik*, ed. Thomas Sauer (Stuttgart, 2000), 148–69; Mark Edward Ruff, *The Wayward Flock: Catholic Youth in Postwar West Germany, 1945–1965* (Chapel Hill, 2005).

17. Markus Köster, "'Betet um einen guten Ausgang der Wahl!' Kirche und Parteien im Bistum Münster zwischen Kapitulation und Konzil," in *Siegerin in Trümmern: Die Rolle der katholischen Kirche in der deutschen Nachkriegsgesellschaft*, ed. Joachim Köhler and Damian van Melis (Stuttgart, 1998), 103–24; Barbara Stambolis, "'Heilige Feste und Zeiten' zwischen Selbstvergewisserung und Auflösung des katholischen Milieus nach 1945," *Kirchliche Zeitgeschichte* 13.1 (2000): 178–216; Cornelia Quink, "Milieubedingungen des politischen Katholizismus in der Bundesrepublik," in *Politische Kultur in Deutschland: Bilanz und Perspektiven der Forschung*, ed. Dirk Berg-Schlosser and Jakob Schissler (Opladen, 1987), 309–21.

18. Beth A. Griech-Polelle, *Bishop von Galen: German Catholicism and National Socialism* (New Haven, 2002), 7.

19. Noel D. Cary, *The Path to Christian Democracy: German Catholics and the Party System from Windthorst to Adenauer* (Cambridge, 1996).

20. Hugh McLeod, *Religion and the People of Western Europe, 1789–1970*, 1st ed. (Oxford, 1981), 132.

21. Jean-Dominique Durand, *L'Europe de la Démocratie chrétienne* (Brussels, 1995), 229.

22. Martin Conway, introduction to *Political Catholicism in Europe, 1918–1965*, ed. Tom Buchanan and Martin Conway (Oxford, 1996), 1–3.

23. Literature on Christian Democracy includes Michael P. Fogarty, *Christian De-*

mocracy in Western Europe, 1820–1953 (Notre Dame, 1957); R. E. M. Irving, *The Christian Democratic Parties of Western Europe* (London, 1979); Karl Josef Hahn, *Die christliche Demokratie in Europa: Die europäische Volkspartei* (Rome, 1979); Jean-Marie Mayeur, *Des Partis catholiques à la démocratie chretienne* (Paris, 1980); Winfried Becker and Rudolf Morsey, eds., *Christliche Demokratie in Europa: Grundlagen und Entwicklungen seit dem 19. Jahrhundert* (Cologne, 1988); Günther Rüther, ed., *Geschichte der Christlich-Demokratischen und Christlich-Sozialen Bewegungen in Deutschland: Grundlagen, Unterrichtsmodelle, Quellen, und Arbeitshilfen für die politische Bildung* (Bonn, 1989); Durand, *Europe;* David Hanley, ed., *Christian Democracy in Europe: A Comparative Perspective* (London, 1994); Stathis N. Kalyvas, *The Rise of Christian Democracy in Europe* (Ithaca, 1996); Buchanan and Conway, *Political Catholicism;* Emiel Lamberts, ed., *Christian Democracy in the European Union (1945/1995)* (Leuven, 1997); Ellen Lovell Evans, *Cross and the Ballot;* Thomas Kselman and Joseph A. Buttigieg, eds., *European Christian Democracy: Historical Legacies and Comparative Perspectives* (Notre Dame, 2003); Michael Gehler and Wolfram Kaiser, eds., *Christian Democracy in Europe since 1945* (London, 2004); Wolfram Kaiser, "Christian Democracy in Twentieth-Century Europe," *Journal of Contemporary History* 39.1 (2004): 127–35; Wolfram Kaiser and Helmut Wohnout, eds., *Political Catholicism in Europe, 1918–1945* (London, 2004); Wolfram Kaiser, *Christian Democracy and the Origins of European Union* (Cambridge, 2007).

24. Works credited with opening up this field include David Blackbourn, *Class, Religion, and Politics in Wilhelmine Germany: The Center Party in Württemberg before 1914* (New Haven, 1980); Margaret Lavinia Anderson, *Windthorst: A Political Biography* (New York, 1981); Jonathan Sperber, *Popular Catholicism in Nineteenth-Century Germany* (Princeton, 1984); Richard Evans, "Religion and Society in Modern Germany," in *Rethinking German History: Nineteenth-Century Germany and the Origins of the Third Reich,* ed. Richard Evans (London, 1987), 125–55; Thomas Nipperdey, *Religion im Umbruch: Deutschland, 1870–1918* (Munich, 1988); David Blackbourn, *Marpingen: Apparitions of the Virgin Mary in Nineteenth-Century Germany* (New York, 1994). On the salience of religion to international relations, see Jonathan Fox, "Integrating Religion into International Relations Theory," in *Routledge Handbook of Religion and Politics,* ed. Jeffrey Haynes (London, 2009), 273–92. See also Stuart Woolf, "Europe and Its Historians," *Central European History* 12.3 (2003): 323. On American history, see Jon Butler, "Jack-in-the-Box Faith: The Religion Problem in Modern American History," *Journal of American History* 90 (2004): 1357–78; Kevin M. Schultz and Paul Harvey, "Everywhere and Nowhere: Recent Trends in American Religious History and Historiography," *Journal of the American Academy of Religion* 78.1 (2010): 129–62.

25. Thomas Albert Howard, "A 'Religious Turn' in Modern European Historiography?" *Historically Speaking* 4 (2003): 25–26; Jeffrey Cox, Thomas Albert Howard, Thomas Kselman, and George S. Williamson, "Modern European Historiography Forum," *Church History* 75.1 (2006): 120–62.

26. Wilfried Loth, "Katholizismus und Moderne: Überlegungen zu einem dialektischen Verhältnis," in *Zivilisation und Barbarei: Die widersprüchlichen Potentiale der Moderne: Detlev Peukert zum Gedenken,* ed. Frank Bajohr, Werner Johe, and Uwe Lohalm (Hamburg, 1991), 88; Karl-Egon Lönne, "Germany," in *Political Catholicism,* ed. Buchanan and Conway, 165.

27. William Patch, "The Catholic Church, the Third Reich, and the Origins of the Cold War: On the Utility and Limitations of Historical Evidence," *Journal of Modern History* 82.2 (June 2010): 396–433.

28. Recent works include Ruff, *Wayward Flock;* Monique Scheer, *Rosenkranz und Kriegsvisionen: Marienerscheinungskulte im 20. Jahrhundert* (Tübingen, 2006); Michael E. O'Sullivan, "West German Miracles: Catholic Mystics, Church Hierarchy, and Postwar Popular Culture," *Zeithistorische Forschungen* 6.1 (2009): 11–34.

29. Samuel Moyn, "The First Historian of Human Rights," *American Historical Review* 116.1 (2011): 58–79.

30. Mark Edward Ruff, "Integrating Religion into the Historical Mainstream: Recent Literature on Religion in the Federal Republic of Germany," *Central European History* 42.2 (2009): 307–37.

31. Hartmut Lehmann, "Von der Erforschung der Säkularisierung zur Erforschung von Prozessen der Dechristianisierung und der Rechristianisierung im neuzeitlichen Europa," in *Säkularisierung, Dechristianisierung, Rechristianisierung im neuzeitlichen Europa: Bilanz und Perspektiven der Forschung,* ed. Hartmut Lehmann (Göttingen, 1997), 11; Antonius Liedhegener, "Katholisches Milieu in einer industriellen Umwelt am Beispiel Bochum: Strukturen und Entwicklungslinien, 1830–1974," in *Politische Zäsuren und Gesellschaftlicher Wandel im 20. Jahrhundert: Regionale und vergleichende Perspektiven,* ed. Matthias Frese and Michael Prinz (Paderborn, 1996), 592; Detlef Pollack, "Funktionen von Religion und Kirche in den politischen Umbrüchen des 20. Jahrhunderts: Untersucht anhand der politischen Zäsuren von 1945 und 1989 in Deutschland," *Kirchliche Zeitgeschichte* 12.1 (1999): 67.

32. Andreas Holzem, "Dechristianisierung und Rechristianisierung: Der deutsche Katholizismus im europäischen Vergleich," *Kirchliche Zeitgeschichte* 11.1 (1998): 69–93.

33. Daniel Lois, "Wie verändert sich die Religiosität im Lebensverlauf? Eine Panelanalyse unter Berücksichtigung von Ost-West-Unterschieden," *Kölner Zeitschrift für Soziologie und Sozialpsychologie* 63 (2011): 83–110.

34. Oded Heilbronner, "From Ghetto to Ghetto: The Place of German Catholic Society in Recent Historiography," *Journal of Modern History* 72.2 (2000): 453–95; Mark Edward Ruff, "Catholic Elites, Gender, and Unintended Consequences in the 1950s: Toward a Reinterpretation of the Role of Conservatives in the Federal Republic," in *Conflict, Catastrophe, and Continuity: Essays on Modern German History,* ed. Frank Biess, Mark Roseman, and Hanna Schissler (New York, 2007), 254.

35. Kees van Kersbergen, "The Distinctiveness of Christian Democracy," in *Christian Democracy in Europe,* ed. Hanley, 31–32; Stathis N. Kalyvas, "Unsecular Politics and Religious Mobilization: Beyond Christian Democracy," in *European Christian Democracy,* ed. Kselman and Buttigieg, 295. Works that diminish either the Christian bases for Christian Democracy or the early party's ties to the Catholic milieu, especially the Catholic Church and clergy, include Helmuth Pütz, *Die CDU: Entwicklung, Aufbau, und Politik der Christlich Demokratischen Union Deutschlands,* 3rd ed. (Düsseldorf, 1978); Geoffrey Pridham, *Christian Democracy in Western Germany: The CDU/CSU in Government and Opposition, 1945–1976* (London, 1976); Irving, *Christian Democratic Parties;* Wulf Schönbohm, *Die CDU wird moderne Volkspartei: Selbstverständnis, Mitglieder, Organisation, und Apparat, 1950–1980* (Stuttgart, 1985); Horstwalter

Heitzer, *Die CDU in der britischen Zone, 1945–1949: Gründung, Organisation, Programm, und Politik* (Düsseldorf, 1988); Kalyvas, *Rise.* In the first volume of his definitive biography of Konrad Adenauer, Hans-Peter Schwarz minimizes Adenauer's rootedness in a Catholic world shaped by the Kulturkampf. See Hans-Peter Schwarz, *Konrad Adenauer: A German Politician and Statesman in a Period of War, Revolution, and Reconstruction,* vol. 1, *From the German Empire to the Federal Republic, 1876–1952,* trans. Louise Willmot (Providence, 1995). For a different emphasis, see Marie-Luise Recker, *Konrad Adenauer: Leben und Politik* (Munich, 2010). Accounts of the CDU that conflate "conservative" or "bourgeois" with Catholic or Christian, eliding the religious element, include Susanne Fuchs, *Frauen Bewältigen den Neuaufbau: Eine lokalgeschichtliche Analyse der unmittelbaren Nachkriegszeit am Beispiel Bonn* (Pfaffenweiler, 1993), 17, 73; Antje Späth, "Vielfältige Forderungen nach Gleichberechtigung und 'nur' ein Ergebnis: Artikel 3 Absatz 2 GG," in *Frauen in der Geschichte V: "Das Schicksal Deutschlands liegt in der Hand seiner Frauen"—Frauen in der deutschen Nachkriegsgeschichte,* ed. Anna-Elisabeth Freier and Annette Kuhn (Düsseldorf, 1984), 122–67; Jeffrey Herf, *War by Other Means: Soviet Power, West German Resistance, and the Battle of the Euromissiles* (New York, 1991), 14–21.

36. David Blackbourn, *Populists and Patricians: Essays in Modern German History* (London, 1987), 11; Margaret Lavinia Anderson, "Piety and Politics: Recent Work on German Catholicism," *Journal of Modern History* 63.4 (1991): 707.

37. Martin Conway, "The Age of Christian Democracy: The Frontiers of Success and Failure," in *European Christian Democracy,* ed. Kselman and Buttigieg, 44. Most early histories of the CDU's origins were written by German Catholics or those sympathetic to their subject, including Leo Schwering, *Vorgeschichte und Entstehung der CDU* (Cologne, 1952); Leo Schwering, *Frühgeschichte der Christlich-Demokratischen Union* (Recklinghausen, 1963); Ernst Deuerlein, *CDU-CSU, 1945–1957: Beiträge zur Zeitgeschichte* (Cologne, 1957); Pütz, *CDU;* Wulf Schönbohm, *CDU: Porträt einer Partei* (Munich, 1979); Winfried Becker, *CDU und CSU, 1945–1950: Vorläufer, Gründung, und regionale Entwicklung bis zum Entstehen der CDU-Bundespartei* (Mainz, 1987); Hans-Otto Kleinmann, *Geschichte der CDU: Von der Gründung bis 1990* (Stuttgart, 1992); Felix Becker, ed., *Kleine Geschichte der CDU* (Stuttgart, 1995); Hermann-Josef Arentz, "Die Anfänge der Christlich-Demokratische Union in Köln," in *Köln nach dem Nationalsozialismus: Der Beginn des gesellschaftlichen und politischen Lebens in den Jahren 1945/46,* ed. Otto Dan (Wuppertal, 1981); Marcus Holz, "Christliche Weltanschauung als Grundlage von Parteipolitik: Eine Analyse des genuin Christlichen in der frühen CDU/CSU (1945–50) aus der Betrachtung des christlichen Menschenbildes und seiner ideengeschichtlichen Hintergründe" (Ph.D. diss., Universität der Bundeswehr München, 1992); Rudolf Lill, "Über die Anfänge der CDU in Köln, 1945–1948," *Historisch-Politische Mitteilungen* 12 (2005): 157–72. Works that adopt a more critical perspective include Heitzer, *CDU;* Jean Julg, *La démocratie chrétienne en République fédérale allemande* (Paris, 1985).

38. A. R. L. Gurland, *Die CDU/CSU: Ursprünge und Entwicklung bis 1953,* ed. Dieter Emig (Frankfurt a.M., 1980); Gerhard Kraiker, *Politischer Katholizismus in der BRD: Eine ideologie-kritische Analyse* (Stuttgart, 1972).

39. Cary, *Path.*

40. Frank Bösch, *Die Adenauer-CDU: Gründung, Aufstieg, und Krise einer Erfolgs-*

partei, 1945–1969 (Stuttgart, 2001); Frank Bösch, *Macht und Machtverlust: Die Geschichte der CDU* (Stuttgart, 2002).

41. David Broughton, "The CDU-CSU in Germany: Is There Any Alternative?" in *Christian Democracy in Europe*, ed. Hanley, 101.

CHAPTER 1

1. Geraldine F. Grogan, *The Noblest Agitator: Daniel O'Connell and the German Catholic Movement, 1830–50* (Dublin, 1991); Hans Maier, *Revolution and Church: The Early History of Christian Democracy, 1789–1901* (Notre Dame, 1969), 9; Winfried Becker, "Staats- und Verfassungsverständnis der christlichen Demokratie von den Anfängen bis 1933," 105; Joseph N. Moody, introduction to *Church and Society: Catholic Social and Political Thought and Movements, 1789–1950*, ed. Joseph N. Moody (New York, 1953), 3.

2. Ellen Lovell Evans, *Cross and Ballot*, 2–14.

3. Wolfram Kaiser, *Christian Democracy*, 15–16; Christopher Clark and Wolfram Kaiser, eds., *Culture Wars: Secular-Catholic Conflict in Nineteenth-Century Europe* (Cambridge, 2003).

4. Dagmar Herzog, *Intimacy and Exclusion: Religious Politics in Pre-Revolutionary Baden* (Piscataway, 2007).

5. Ronald J. Ross, *The Failure of Bismarck's Kulturkampf: Catholicism and State Power in Imperial Germany* (Washington, 1998), 6.

6. Helmut Walser Smith, *German Nationalism and Religious Conflict: Culture, Ideology, Politics, 1870–1914* (Princeton, 1995), 20.

7. Michael B. Gross, *The War against Catholicism: Liberalism and the Anti-Catholic Imagination in Nineteenth-Century Germany* (Ann Arbor, 2004), 22–26.

8. Christoph Weber, *Kirchliche Politik zwischen Rom, Berlin, und Trier: Die Beilegung des preußischen Kulturkampfes, 1876–1888* (Mainz, 1970).

9. Ross, *Failure*, 7.

10. Smith, *German Nationalism*, 48.

11. Olaf Blaschke, ed., *Konfessionen im Konflikt: Deutschland zwischen 1800 und 1970: Ein zweites konfessionelles Zeitalter* (Göttingen, 2002).

12. AKKZG, "Katholiken zwischen Tradition und Moderne," 598.

13. Wolfgang Altgeld, *Katholizismus, Protestantismus, Judentum: Über religiös begründete Gegensätze und nationalreligiöse Ideen in der Geschichte des deutschen Nationalismus* (Mainz, 1992), 197–98; Blackbourn, *Marpingen*; Gross, *War against Catholicism*.

14. Christopher Clark, "The New Catholicism and the European Culture Wars," in *Culture Wars*, ed. Clark and Kaiser, 11–46. Cf. Margaret Lavinia Anderson, *Practicing Democracy: Elections and Political Culture in Imperial Germany* (Princeton, 2000).

15. Ellen Lovell Evans, *Cross and Ballot*, 14.

16. Heinz Hürten, *Kurze Geschichte des deutschen Katholizismus, 1800–1960* (Mainz, 1986), 150–59.

17. Smith, *German Nationalism*, 43; Anderson, *Windthorst*, 178; Ellen Lovell Evans, *Cross and Ballot*, 117, 216–17.

18. Sperber, *Popular Catholicism,* 150.

19. Doris Kaufmann, *Katholisches Milieu in Münster, 1928–1933: Politische Aktionsformen und gesellschaftsspezifische Verhaltensräume* (Düsseldorf, 1984), 26.

20. Rohe, *Wahlen,* 76–77.

21. Smith, *German Nationalism,* 92; Kaufmann, *Katholisches Milieu,* 27; Rudolf Morsey, ed., *Das Wahlverhalten der Deutschen Katholiken im Kaiserreich und in der Weimarer Republik: Untersuchungen aus dem Jahre 1928 von Johannes Schauff* (Mainz, 1975); Karl-Egon Lönne, *Politischer Katholizismus im 19. und 20. Jahrhundert* (Frankfurt, 1986), 217, 223; John K. Zeender, *The German Center Party, 1890–1906* (Philadelphia, 1976), 10; John H. Whyte, *Catholics in Western Democracies: A Study in Political Behavior* (New York, 1981), 50.

22. Heinrich Lutz, *Zwischen Habsburg und Preußen: Deutschland, 1815–1866* (Berlin, 1985), 127; Nipperdey, *Religion im Umbruch,* 9–19; Owen Chadwick, *The Secularization of the European Mind in the Nineteenth Century* (Cambridge, 1975), 111; Blackbourn, *Class, Religion, and Politics,* 46–53.

23. Anderson, *Windthorst,* 316–65; Olaf Blaschke, *Katholizismus und Antisemitismus im Deutschen Kaiserreich* (Göttingen, 1997), 56, 275; Irving, *Christian Democratic Parties,* 11–14.

24. Ronald J. Ross, *Beleaguered Tower: The Dilemma of Political Catholicism in Wilhelmine Germany* (Notre Dame, 1976), 44; Loth, *Katholiken im Kaiserreich,* 41–43.

25. Loth, *Katholiken im Kaiserreich,* 55; Zeender, *German Center Party,* 22–23.

26. Anderson, *Windthorst,* 142, 160, 256, 382; Lönne, *Politischer Katholizismus,* 162.

27. Hürten, *Kurze Geschichte,* 46, 63–64.

28. Ernst Rudolf Huber, *Deutsche Verfassungsgeschichte seit 1789,* vol. 2, *Der Kampf um Einheit und Freiheit, 1830–1850* (Stuttgart, 1960), 365.

29. Thomas Mergel, *Zwischen Klasse und Konfession: Katholisches Bürgertum im Rheinland, 1794–1914* (Göttingen, 1994).

30. Smith, *German Nationalism,* 75; Altgeld, *Katholizismus, Protestantismus, Judentum,* 203. Cf. Christoph Weber, *"Eine starke, enggeschlossene Phalanx": Der politische Katholizismus und die erste deutsche Reichstagswahl 1871* (Essen, 1992).

31. Zeender, *German Center Party,* 3; Ross, *Beleaguered Tower,* xiv; Mergel, *Zwischen Klasse und Konfession,* 5.

32. Ernst Rudolf Huber, *Deutsche Verfassungsgeschichte,* 358–59.

33. Edgar Alexander, "Church and Society in Germany: Social and Political Movements and Ideas in German and Austrian Catholicism (1789–1950)," in *Church and Society,* ed. Moody, 375.

34. Zeender, *German Center Party,* 3.

35. Martin Stankowski, *Linkskatholizismus nach 1945: Die Presse oppositioneller Katholiken in der Auseinandersetzung für eine demokratische und sozialistische Gesellschaft* (Cologne, 1976), 7.

36. Jürgen Kohns, *Konrad Adenauer und der Föderalismus* (Würzburg, 1987), 16, 113–14.

37. Lönne, *Politischer Katholizismus,* 176.

38. Mergel, *Zwischen Klasse und Konfession,* 14.

39. Sperber, *Popular Catholicism,* 259; Ross, *Beleaguered Tower,* 42.

40. Heinz Hürten, *Deutsche Katholiken, 1918 bis 1945* (Paderborn, 1992), 23.

41. Mergel, *Zwischen Klasse und Konfession,* 15.

42. Sperber, *Popular Catholicism,* 7, 288, 290.

43. Lönne, *Politischer Katholizismus,* 107; Alexander, "Church and Society," 445–47; Anderson, *Windthorst,* 136, 226; Rudolf Morsey, *Die Deutsche Zentrumspartei, 1917–1923* (Düsseldorf, 1966), 325.

44. Ross, *Beleaguered Tower,* 42–43; Ellen Lovell Evans, *The German Center Party, 1870–1933: A Study in Political Catholicism* (Carbondale, 1981), 103.

45. Helmut Langhoff and Veit Veltzke, "Im Westen viel Neues: Als Nordrhein-Westfalen preußisch war," in *Wir sind Preußen: Die preußischen Kerngebiete in Nordrhein-Westfalen, 1609–2009,* ed. Stephan Sensen, Eckhard Trox, Maria Perrefort, Gerhard Renda, and Veit Velzke (Essen, 2009), 61.

46. Blackbourn, *Class, Religion, and Politics,* 34–37; Loth, *Katholiken im Kaiserreich,* 39, 76; Anderson, *Windthorst,* 369.

47. Anne Fremantle, ed., *The Papal Encyclicals in Their Historical Context: The Teachings of the Popes* (New York, 1956), 166.

48. Alexander, "Church and Society," 407–34.

49. Loth, *Katholiken im Kaiserreich,* 82.

50. Michael Schneider, *Die Christlichen Gewerkschaften, 1894–1933* (Bonn, 1982), 212–13; Ute Schmidt, "Zentrumspartei oder Union—Zur Archäologie eines Parteienkonflikts nach 1945," in *Politische Zäsuren,* ed. Frese and Prinz, 652.

51. Hermann-Josef Grosse Kracht, "Religion in der Demokratisierungsfalle? Zum Verhältnis von traditioneller Religion und politische Moderne am Beispiel des deutschen Katholizismus im Kaiserreich," *Geschichte in Wissenschaft und Unterricht* 51 (2000): 149–53; Mergel, *Zwischen Klasse und Konfession,* 210.

52. Stanley Suval, *Electoral Politics in Wilhelmine Germany* (Chapel Hill, 1985), 74; Ursula Mittmann, *Fraktion und Partei: Ein Vergleich von Zentrum und Sozialdemokratie im Kaiserreich* (Düsseldorf, 1976), 7–16.

53. Mary E. Hobgood, *Catholic Social Teaching and Economic Theory: Paradigms in Conflict* (Philadelphia, 1991), 111.

54. Gotthard Klein, *Der Volksverein für das katholische Deutschland, 1890–1933* (Paderborn, 1996), 47, 116; Horstwalter Heitzer, *Der Volksverein für das katholische Deutschland im Kaiserreich, 1890–1918* (Mainz, 1979), 28–29, 55; Margaret Lavinia Anderson, "Interdenominationalism, Clericalism, Pluralism: The 'Zentrumsstreit' and the Dilemma of Catholicism in Wilhelmine Germany," *Central European History* 21.4 (1988): 364–65; Mergel, *Zwischen Klasse und Konfession,* 311; Suval, *Electoral Politics,* 73–74.

55. Schneider, *Christlichen Gewerkschaften,* 107, 222, 266, 268–70, 334, 569; Dirk H. Müller, *Arbeiter—Katholizismus—Staat: Der Volksverein für das katholische Deutschland und die katholischen Arbeiterorganisationen in der Weimarer Republik* (Bonn, 1966), 48; Julius Bachem, "Wir müssen aus dem Turm heraus!" *Historisch-Politische Blätter für das katholische Deutschland* 137.1 (1906): 378–86, in *Unter Wilhelm II: 1890–1918* (Darmstadt, 1982), ed. Hans Fenske, 238–40.

56. Bachem, "Wir müssen aus dem Turm heraus!"; Cary, *Path,* 32–34.

57. Martin Scharfe, *Die Religion des Volkes: Kleine Kultur- und Sozialgeschichte*

des Pietismus (Gütersloh, 1980), 162; Uriel Tal, *Christians and Jews in Germany: Religion, Politics, and Ideology in the Second Reich, 1870–1914,* trans. Noah Jonathan Jacobs (Ithaca, 1975), 121–53.

58. Martin Greschat, "'Rechristianisierung' und 'Säkularisierung': Anmerkungen zu einem europäischen interkonfessionellen Interpretationsmodell," in *Christentum und politische Verantwortung: Kirchen im Nachkriegsdeutschland,* ed. Jochen-Christoph Kaiser and Anselm Doering-Manteuffel (Stuttgart, 1990), 5–11.

59. Martin Greiffenhagen, *Das Dilemma des Konservatismus in Deutschland* (Frankfurt a.M., 1986), 41, 85, 89–91, 127–31, 157, 205.

60. Rohe, *Wahlen,* 70.

61. Erich Schmidt-Volkmar, *Der Kulturkampf in Deutschland, 1871–1890* (Göttingen, 1962), 113, 129.

62. Kurt Nowak, *Evangelische Kirche und Weimarer Republik: Zum politischen Weg des deutschen Protestantismus zwischen 1918 und 1932* (Weimar, 1981), 12.

63. Lucian Hölscher, Tillman Bendikowski, Claudia Enders, and Markus Hoppe, eds., *Datenatlas zur religiösen Geographie im protestantischen Deutschland: Von der Mitte des 19. Jahrhunderts bis zum Zweiten Weltkrieg,* 4 vols. (Berlin, 2001).

64. Ross, *Beleaguered Tower,* 135.

65. Ellen Lovell Evans, *German Center Party,* 201.

66. Anderson, "Interdenominationalism, Clericalism, Pluralism," 358. Cf. Horstwalter Heitzer, *Georg Kardinal Kopp und der Gewerkschaftsstreit, 1900–1914* (Cologne, 1983).

67. Anderson, "Interdenominationalism, Clericalism, Pluralism," 304; Heitzer, *Volksverein,* 22, 146, 151.

68. Felix von Löe, a leading member of the early Center Party, quoted in Zeender, *German Center Party,* 118. Cf. Clark, "New Catholicism," 45.

69. Nipperdey, *Religion im Umbruch,* 27; Blackbourn, *Class, Religion, and Politics,* 20.

70. Schneider, *Christlichen Gewerkschaften,* 180; Mergel, *Zwischen Klasse und Konfession,* 310.

71. Ross, *Beleaguered Tower,* 56, 68, 74; Ellen Lovell Evans, *German Center Party,* 104, 197.

72. Schneider, *Christlichen Gewerkschaften,* 181; Anderson, "Interdenominationalism, Clericalism, Pluralism," 367.

73. Morsey, *Deutsche Zentrumspartei,* 33–35.

74. Günther Grünthal, "'Zusammenschluß' oder 'Evangelisches Zentrum'? Ein Beitrag zur Geschichte der Deutschen Zentrumspartei in der Weimarer Republik," in *Staat und Gesellschaft im politischen Wandel: Beiträge zur Geschichte der modernen Welt,* ed. Werner Pöls (Stuttgart, 1979), 303.

75. Karsten Ruppert, *Im Dienst am Staat von Weimar: Das Zentrum als regierende Partei in der Weimarer Demokratie, 1923–1930* (Düsseldorf, 1992), 31.

76. Dirk H. Müller, *Arbeiter—Katholizismus—Staat,* 259.

77. Ruppert, *Im Dienst am Staat,* 32; Rohe, *Wahlen,* 150.

78. Rudolf Morsey, *Der Untergang des politischen Katholizismus: Die Zentrumspartei zwischen christlichem Selbstverständnis und "Nationaler Erhebung" 1932/33*

(Stuttgart, 1977), 14; Julia Sneeringer, *Winning Women's Votes: Propaganda and Politics in Weimar Germany* (Chapel Hill, 2002), 6; Gabriele Bremme, *Die Politische Rolle der Frau in Deutschland* (Göttingen, 1956), 111.

79. Ruppert, *Im Dienst am Staat,* 32.

80. Rohe, *Wahlen,* 109, 130.

81. Lönne, *Politischer Katholizismus,* 177, 186–87; Fogarty, *Christian Democracy,* 306.

82. Eric D. Kohler, "The Successful German Center-Left: Joseph Hess and the Prussian Center Party, 1908–32," *Central European History* 23.4 (1990): 322; Wilfried Loth, "Zwischen autoritärer und demokratischer Ordnung: Das Zentrum in der Krise des Wilhelminischen Reiches," in *Die Minderheit als Mitte: Die Deutsche Zentrumspartei in der Innenpolitik des Reiches, 1871–1933,* ed. Winfried Becker (Paderborn, 1986), 62–68.

83. Lönne, *Politischer Katholizismus,* 222; Cary, *Path,* 106.

84. Ellen Lovell Evans, *German Center Party,* 275–76; Morsey, *Deutsche Zentrumspartei,* 360–78.

85. Dirk H. Müller, *Arbeiter—Katholizismus—Staat,* 63–65, 199–200, 213, 254–57; Herbert Hömig, *Das preußische Zentrum in der Weimarer Republik* (Mainz, 1979), 285.

86. Morsey, *Deutsche Zentrumspartei,* 428–29.

87. Dietrich Orlow, *Weimar Prussia, 1918–1925: The Unlikely Rock of Democracy* (Pittsburgh, 1986); Dietrich Orlow, *Weimar Prussia, 1925–1933: The Illusion of Strength* (Pittsburgh, 1991).

88. Günther Grünthal, *Reichsschulgesetz und Zentrumspartei in der Weimarer Republik* (Düsseldorf, 1968), 36, 107.

89. Ruppert, *Im Dienst am Staat,* 34.

90. Gabriele Clemens, *Martin Spahn und der Rechtskatholizismus in der Weimarer Republik* (Mainz, 1983), 86, 103, 136.

91. Lönne, *Politischer Katholizismus,* 227–35.

92. Kaufmann, *Katholisches Milieu,* 34; Thomas M. Gauly, *Kirche und Politik in der Bundesrepublik Deutschland, 1945–1976* (Bonn, 1990), 67–68.

93. Michael J. Inacker, *Zwischen Transzendenz, Totalitarismus, und Demokratie: Die Entwicklung des kirchlichen Demokratieverständnisses von der Weimarer Republik bis zu den Anfängen der Bundesrepublik (1918–1959)* (Neukirchen-Vluyn, 1994), 75; Hugo Stehkämper, *Konrad Adenauer als Katholikentagspräsident 1922: Form und Grenze politischer Entscheidungsfreiheit im katholischen Raum* (Mainz, 1977).

94. Schwarz, *Konrad Adenauer: A German Politician,* 1:164; Stehkämper, *Konrad Adenauer,* 43–45.

95. Inacker, *Zwischen Transzendenz,* 42.

96. Ellen Lovell Evans, *German Center Party,* 223.

97. Hömig, *Preußische Zentrum,* 31–32; Grünthal, *Reichsschulgesetz,* 31; Morsey, *Deutsche Zentrumspartei,* 100, 134.

98. Cary, *Path,* 69–70, 201–34.

99. Lönne, *Politischer Katholizismus,* 223.

100. Ellen Lovell Evans, *German Center Party,* 224.

101. Kurt Weitzel, "Von der CSVP zur CDU: Die Gründung der CDU in Rheinhes-

sen 1945–1947" (Ph.D. diss., Johannes Gutenberg-Universität Mainz, 1980), 17. The party did lose a slight degree of support in the June 1920 Reichstag elections. See Morsey, *Deutsche Zentrumspartei,* 320.

102. Ellen Lovell Evans, *Cross and Ballot,* 205.

103. Lönne, *Politischer Katholizismus,* 224–25; Dirk H. Müller, *Arbeiter—Katholizismus—Staat,* 249; Ute Schmidt, "Zentrumspartei oder Union," 654.

104. Morsey, *Deutsche Zentrumspartei,* 155, 289, 583.

105. Rudolf Morsey, "Kirche und politische Parteien, 1848–1948/49," in *Kirche—Politik—Parteien,* ed. Anton Rauscher (Cologne, 1974), 25.

106. Grosse Kracht, "Religion in der Demokratisierungsfalle?" 145.

107. Morsey, *Deutsche Zentrumspartei,* 216.

108. Grünthal, *Reichsschulgesetz,* 142.

109. Karsten Ruppert, "Die Deutsche Zentrumspartei in der Mitverantwortung für die Weimarer Republik: Selbstverständnis und politische Leitideen einer konfessionellen Mittelpartei," in *Die Minderheit als Mitte: Die Deutsche Zentrumspartei in der Innenpolitik des Reiches, 1871–1933,* ed. Winfried Becker (Paderborn, 1986), 74.

110. Grünthal, *Reichsschulgesetz,* 108; Hellmut Becker and Gerhard Kluchert, *Die Bildung der Nation: Schule, Gesellschaft, und Politik vom Kaiserreich zur Weimarer Republik* (Stuttgart, 1993), 160.

111. Morsey, *Deutsche Zentrumspartei,* 619; Ellen Lovell Evans, *German Center Party,* 263.

112. Grünthal, *Reichsschulgesetz,* 74–78.

113. Dorothee Buchhaas, *Gesetzgebung im Wiederaufbau: Schulgesetz in Nordrhein-Westfalen und Betriebsverfassungsgesetz, 1945–1952* (Düsseldorf, 1985), 59.

114. Johann Baptist Müller, "Der deutsche Sozialkonservatismus," in *Konservatismus,* 2nd ed., ed. Hans-Gerd Schumann (Königstein/Ts., 1984), 199–221.

115. Sebastian Müller-Rolli, *Evangelische Schulpolitik in Deutschland, 1918–1958: Dokumente und Darstellung* (Göttingen, 1999), 57–63.

116. HAStK, 1187, 33, 37, 40/5. Cf. Sneeringer, *Winning Women's Votes,* 113–14, 160–62, 182.

117. Bremme, *Politische Rolle,* 70–77. The parties here were clearly operating within the context of the modern European "feminization of religion." See Michael P. Carroll, "Give Me That Ol' Time Hormonal Religion," *Journal for the Scientific Study of Religion* 43 (2004): 275–78.

118. The term *formalistische Gleichstellung* is Christine Teusch's. See Barbara Greven-Aschoff, *Die bürgerliche Frauenbewegung in Deutschland, 1894–1933* (Göttingen, 1981), 159–79.

119. Robert G. Moeller, *Protecting Motherhood: Women and the Family in the Politics of Postwar West Germany* (Berkeley, 1993), 47–49.

120. Atina Grossmann, *Reforming Sex: The German Movement for Birth Control and Abortion Reform, 1920–1950* (New York, 1995), 78–87.

121. Dagmar Herzog, *Sex after Fascism: Memory and Morality in Twentieth-Century Germany* (Princeton, 2005), 33, 55.

122. Cary, *Path,* 65–66.

123. Hömig, *Preußische Zentrum,* 196; Grünthal, *Reichsschulgesetz,* 196–97, 207; Ellen Lovell Evans, *Cross and Ballot,* 209.

124. Ruppert, *Im Dienst am Staat,* 414–16; Lönne, *Politischer Katholizismus,* 186; Ruppert, "Deutsche Zentrumspartei," 82–83.

125. Benno Haunhorst, "'Der Sozialismus als sittliche Idee': Theodor Steinbüchels Beitrag zu einer christlichen Sozialethik," in *Sozial- und Linkskatholizismus: Erinnerung—Orientierung—Befreiung,* ed. Heiner Ludwig and Wolfgang Schroeder (Frankfurt a.M., 1990), 75–100.

126. Some figures, including Theodor Steinbüchel, did maintain ties to members of the Volksverein and Christian Trade Unions. See Franz Focke, *Sozialismus aus christlicher Verantwortung: Die Idee eines christlichen Sozialismus in der katholisch-sozialen Bewegung und in der CDU* (Wuppertal, 1978), 295.

127. Alois Baumgartner, *Sehnsucht nach Gemeinschaft: Ideen und Strömungen im Sozialkatholizismus der Weimarer Republik* (Munich, 1977), 91; Bruno Lowitsch, "Der Frankfurter Katholizismus in der Weimarer Republik und die 'Rhein-Mainische Volkszeitung,'" in *Sozial- und Linkskatholizismus,* ed. Ludwig and Schroeder, 46–74. Cf. Karl Prümm, *Walter Dirks und Eugen Kogon als katholische Publizisten der Weimarer Republik* (Heidelberg, 1984).

128. Rudolf Uertz, *Christentum und Sozialismus in der frühen CDU: Grundlagen und Wirkungen der christlich-sozialen Ideen in der Union, 1945–1949* (Stuttgart, 1981), 18–19, 74; Ute Schmidt, "Die Christlich Demokratische Union Deutschlands," in *Parteien-Handbuch,* ed. Stoss, 1:520; Paul Misner, "Christian Democratic Social Policy: Precedents for Third-Way Thinking," in *European Christian Democracy,* ed. Kselman and Buttigieg, 68–92.

129. Ruppert, *Im Dienst am Staat,* 274–87.

130. By the end of the Weimar Republic, clerics would also be in charge of the Center Party state organizations in Prussia, Baden, and Saxony. See Dirk H. Müller, *Arbeiter—Katholizismus—Staat,* 74.

131. Rudolf Morsey, "Die Deutsche Zentrumspartei," in *Das Ende der Parteien,* ed. Erich Matthias and Rudolf Morsey (Düsseldorf, 1960), 301–2; Ellen Lovell Evans, *German Center Party,* 329–32.

132. Lönne, *Politischer Katholizismus,* 230.

133. Ellen Lovell Evans, *Cross and Ballot,* 224.

134. Lönne, *Politischer Katholizismus,* 232–36.

135. Karl Otmar von Aretin, "Der deutsche Widerstand gegen Hitler," in *Nation, Staat, und Demokratie in Deutschland: Ausgewählte Beiträge zur Zeitgeschichte,* ed. Andreas Kunz und Martin Vogt (Mainz, 1993), 213–14.

136. Hürten, *Deutsche Katholiken,* 182; Rohe, *Wahlen,* 158.

137. Morsey, "Deutsche Zentrumspartei," 356–64; Erich Kosthorst, *Jakob Kaiser: Der Arbeiterführer* (Stuttgart, 1967), 170–71. For an insightful account of how one Zentrum deputy, Friedrich Dessauer, was persuaded to accede, see Heinz Blankenberg, *Politischer Katholizismus in Frankfurt am Main, 1918–1933* (Mainz, 1981), 286–87.

138. Dirk H. Müller, *Arbeiter—Katholizismus—Staat,* 275; Winfried Becker, "Die Deutsche Zentrumspartei gegenüber dem Nationalsozialismus und dem Reichskonkordat, 1930–1933: Motivationsstrukturen und Situationszwänge," *Historisch-Politische Mitteilungen* 7 (2000): 1–37. Cf. Thomas Brechenmacher, ed., *Das Reichskonkordat 1933: Forschungsstand, Kontroversen, Dokumente* (Paderborn, 2007).

139. Lönne, *Politischer Katholizismus,* 238–42.

140. Morsey, *Untergang des politischen Katholizismus,* 52; Barbara Stambolis,

"'Fest soll mein Taufbund immer stehn': Jugendliche im katholischen Milieu oder die Grenzen der Gleichschaltung—Lebensweltlich geprägte Resistenzräume im Dritten Reich," *Geschichte in Wissenschaft und Unterricht* 51 (2000): 157–72.

141. Kurt Nowak, "Christentum in politischer Verantwortung: Zum Protestantismus in der Sowjetischen Besatzungszone (1945–1949)," in *Christentum und politische Verantwortung,* ed. Jochen-Christoph Kaiser and Doering-Manteuffel, 55.

142. J. R. C. Wright, *"Above Parties": The Political Attitudes of the German Protestant Church Leadership, 1918–1933* (Oxford, 1974), 54.

143. Dagmar Pöpping, *Abendland: Christliche Akademiker und die Utopie der Antimoderne, 1900–1945* (Berlin, 2002), 140.

144. Vanessa Conze, *Das Europa der Deutschen: Ideen von Europa in Deutschland zwischen Reichstradition und Westorientierung (1920–1970)* (Munich, 2006), 28–29.

145. Nowak, *Evangelische Kirche,* 287.

146. Inacker, *Zwischen Transzendenz,* 24, 40.

147. Eberhard Sammler, "Politische Strömungen im deutschen Protestantismus," in *Wirtschaftlicher Wandel, religiöser Wandel, und Wertwandel: Folgen für das politische Verhalten in der Bundesrepublik Deutschland,* ed. Dieter Oberndörfer, Hans Rattinger, and Karl Schmitt (Berlin, 1985), 238.

148. Karsten Ruppert, "Der Einfluß christlich-demokratischer wie christlich-sozialer Ideen und Parteien auf Geist und Politik in der Weimarer Zeit," in *Christliche Demokratie in Europa: Grundlagen und Entwicklungen seit dem 19. Jahrhundert,* ed. Winfried Becker and Rudolf Morsey (Cologne, 1988), 129.

149. Gottfried Niedhart, *Deutsche Geschichte, 1918–1933: Politik in der Weimarer Republik und der Sieg der Rechten,* 2nd ed. (Stuttgart, 1994), 116–27.

150. Hartmut Lehmann, *Pietismus und weltliche Ordnung in Württemberg vom 17. bis zum 20. Jahrhundert* (Stuttgart, 1969), 317 n. 54, 322.

151. Michael Klein, *Westdeutscher Protestantismus und politische Parteien: Anti-Parteien-Mentalität und parteipolitisches Engagement von 1945 bis 1963* (Tübingen, 2005), 35–36.

152. Friedrich Hartmannsgruber, "Die christlichen Volksparteien, 1848–1933: Ideen und Wirklichkeit," in *Geschichte,* ed. Rüther, 130–32.

153. Günter Opitz, *Der Christlich-soziale Volksdienst: Versuch einer protestantischen Partei in der Weimarer Republik* (Düsseldorf, 1969).

154. Michael Klein, *Westdeutscher Protestantismus,* 37; Lehmann, *Pietismus und weltliche Ordnung,* 315–17.

155. Peter Egen, "Die Entstehung des Evangelischen Arbeitskreises der CDU/CSU" (Ph.D. diss., Ruhr Universität Bochum, 1971), 9–11.

156. Lehmann, *Pietismus und weltliche Ordnung,* 320–27.

157. BAK, NL 114, 25, 216, Elfgen to Friedensburg, June 8, 1932.

158. Morsey, "Deutsche Zentrumspartei," 314 n. 49.

159. BAK, NL 114, 25, 130, Muhle to Friedensburg, May 20, 1930. See also BAK, NL 114, 25, 131, Friedensburg to Muhle, May 22, 1930; BAK, NL 114, 25, 137, Körber to Friedensburg, July 21, 1930; BAK, NL 114, 25, 220, Friedensburg to Spangenberg, October 15, 1932.

160. Niedhart, *Deutsche Geschichte,* 114–27; Ludwig Richter, *Die Deutsche Volkspartei, 1918–1933* (Düsseldorf, 2002), 16.

161. Richard Steigmann-Gall, *"The Holy Reich": Nazi Conceptions of Christianity,*

1919–1945 (Cambridge, 2003). Cf. "Discussion Forum—Richard Steigmann-Gall's *The Holy Reich,*" *Journal of Contemporary History* 42.1–2 (2007).

162. Shelley Baranowski, *The Sanctity of Rural Life: Nobility, Protestantism, and Nazism in Weimar Prussia* (Oxford, 1995), 9; Richard Steigmann-Gall, "Apostasy or Religiosity? The Cultural Meanings of the Protestant Vote for Hitler," *Social History* 25.3 (2000): 267–85.

163. Wright, *"Above Parties,"* 90. Cf. Luise Schorn-Schütte and Walter Sparn, eds., *Evangelische Pfarrer: Zur sozialen und politischen Rolle einer bürgerlichen Gruppe in der deutschen Gesellschaft des 18. bis 20. Jahrhunderts* (Stuttgart, 1997); Inacker, *Zwischen Transzendenz,* 199.

164. Steigmann-Gall, *"Holy Reich,"* 11.

165. Doris L. Bergen, *Twisted Cross: The German Christian Movement in the Third Reich* (Chapel Hill, 1996), 2–7; Gerhard Besier, *Die Kirchen und das Dritte Reich: Spaltungen und Abwehrkämpfe, 1934–1937* (Munich, 2001), 11–13.

166. Marcus Holz, "Christliche Weltanschauung," 52–53.

167. Gerhard Besier, "Zwischen Neuanfang und Restauration: Die evangelischen Kirchen in Deutschland nach dem Zweiten Weltkrieg," in *Ende des Dritten Reiches— Ende des Zweiten Weltkrieges: Eine perspektivische Rückschau,* ed. Hans-Erich Volk-mann (Munich, 1995), 709–12.

168. Besier, *Kirchen,* 14.

169. A. J. Nicholls, *Freedom with Responsibility: The Social Market Economy in Germany, 1918–1963* (Oxford, 1994), 103, 115–21; Inacker, *Zwischen Transzendenz,* 152–57.

170. Klaus Schardt, *Ludwig Erhard—Der Vater des Wirtschaftswunders* (Nurem-berg, 2000), 27; Alfred C. Mierzejewski, *Ludwig Erhard: A Biography* (Chapel Hill, 2004), 22; Mark E. Spicka, *Selling the Economic Miracle: Economic Reconstruction and Politics in West Germany, 1949–1957* (Providence, 2007), 34; Elmar Müller, *Wider-stand und Wirtschaftsordnung: Die wirtschaftspolitischen Konzepte der Widerstandsbe-wegung gegen das NS Regime und ihr Einfluß auf die Soziale Marktwirtschaft* (Frank-furt a.M., 1988), 105–48; Volker Hentschel, *Ludwig Erhard: Ein Politikerleben* (Berlin, 1998), 38.

171. Nicholls, *Freedom,* 96–97; Mark Eger, "Die Konzeption der Sozialen Markt-wirtschaft von Ludwig Erhard als Ergebnis soziologischen Denkens" (Ph.D. diss., Julius-Maximilians-Universität zu Würzburg, 1999), 103.

172. Karl-Joseph Hummel and Michael Kißener, eds., *Die Katholiken und das Dritte Reich: Kontroversen und Debatten* (Paderborn, 2009).

173. Hugo Stehkämper, "Protest, Opposition, und Widerstand im Umkreis der (un-tergegangenen) Zentrumspartei: Ein Überblick," in *Der Widerstand gegen den National-sozialismus: Die deutsche Gesellschaft und der Widerstand gegen Hitler,* ed. Jürgen Schmädeke and Peter Steinbach (Munich, 1985), 128; Hürten, *Deutsche Katholiken,* 572.

174. Ulrich von Hehl, *Katholische Kirche und National Socialism im Erzbistum Köln, 1933–1945* (Mainz, 1977), 16. Cf. Derek Hastings, *Catholicism and the Roots of Nazism: Religious Identity and National Socialism* (Oxford, 2010).

175. Lönne, *Politischer Katholizismus,* 237; Klaus Scholder, *Die Kirchen und das Dritte Reich,* vol. 2, *Das Jahr der Ernüchterung 1934* (Berlin, 1985), 221–68.

176. Stehkämper, "Protest, Opposition, und Widerstand," 907.

177. For a discussion of the various definitions of *resistance,* including a debate over the role of Catholic Church during the Nazi era, see Schmädeke and Steinbach, *Widerstand,* 1120–27.

178. Von Aretin, "Deutsche Widerstand," 227; Stambolis, "'Fest soll mein Taufbund immer stehn'"; Matthias Schulze, *Bund oder Schar—Verband oder Pfarrjugend? Katholische Jugendarbeit im Erzbistum Paderborn nach 1945* (Paderborn, 2001).

179. Konrad Repgen, "Die Deutschen Bischöfe und der Zweite Weltkrieg," *Historisches Jahrbuch* 115 (1995): 450. For a tiny subset of local priests' resistance to Nazi rule, see GStM, 76, IV, Sekt. 1, Abt. IX, 25, I, 1, 12, 14, 16, 21, 28, 77–82.

180. Inacker, *Zwischen Transzendenz,* 127. The experience and legacies of resistance would have much greater influence on postwar Christian Democratic politics in France and Italy than in Germany. See Wolfram Kaiser, *Christian Democracy,* 120.

181. Von Aretin, "Deutsche Widerstand," 219.

182. Günter Buchstab, Brigitte Kaff, and Hans-Otto Kleinmann, eds., *Christliche Demokraten gegen Hitler: Aus Verfolgung und Widerstand zur Union* (Freiburg i.B., 2004), 13–57.

183. Kosthorst, *Jakob Kaiser,* 178–84.

184. Buchstab, Kaff, and Kleinmann, *Christliche Demokraten,* 34–37; BAK, NL 5, 217, 3–4, Pünder to Portmann, June 26, 1946; BAK, NL 5, 664, 66.

185. Stehkämper, "Protest, Opposition, und Widerstand," 900.

186. Roman Bleistein, *Die Jesuiten im Kreisauer Kreis: Ihre Bedeutung für den Gesamtwiderstand gegen den Nationalsozialismus* (Passau, 1990).

187. Vera Bücker, "Die KAB-Zeitung und das Dritte Reich," *Kirchliche Zeitgeschichte* 14.1 (2001): 175–96; Jürgen Aretz, *Katholische Arbeiterbewegung und Nationalsozialismus: Der Verband Katholischer Arbeiter und Knappenvereine Westdeutschlands, 1923 bis 1945* (Mainz, 1977).

188. Participants included Johannes Albers, Karl Arnold, Wilhelm Elfes, Andreas Hermes, Christine Teusch, and Franz Thedieck. See Elfriede Nebgen, *Jakob Kaiser: Der Widerstandskämpfer* (Stuttgart, 1967), 42; Stefan Noethen, "Pläne für das vierte Reich: Der Widerstandskreis im Kölner Kettelerhaus, 1941–1944," *Geschichte in Köln* 39 (1996): 51–73. Cf. BAK, Kl. Erw. 345, 34; BAK, NL 18, 56, 76.

189. Heinz-Albert Raem, *Katholischer Gesellenverein und Deutsche Kolpingsfamilie in der Ära des Nationalsozialismus* (Mainz, 1982). For contacts between Unitas and Walberberg, see HAStK, 1193, 330–39.

190. Vera Bücker, "Der Kölner Kreis und seine Konzeption für ein Deutschland nach Hitler," *Historisch-Politische Mitteilungen* 2 (1995): 49.

191. In 1936, after former DDP and DStP member Ernst Lemmer offered to join the Zentrum in a post-Nazi Germany, Kaiser assured him that the Center Party would not be refounded. See Theodor Eschenburg, *Jahre der Besatzung, 1945–1949* (Stuttgart, 1983), 184–85.

192. Andreas Lienkamp, "Socialism Out of Christian Responsibility: The German Experiment of Left Catholicism (1945–1949)," in *Left Catholicism: Catholics and Society in Western Europe at the Point of Liberation, 1943–1955,* ed. Gerd-Rainer Horn and Emmanuel Gerard (Leuven, 2001), 202.

193. Nebgen, *Jakob Kaiser,* 187–89.

194. Buchstab, Kaff, and Kleinmann, *Christliche Demokraten,* 43–46.

CHAPTER 2

1. Joachim Köhler and Damian van Melis, introduction to *Siegerin in Trümmern,* ed. Köhler and Melis (Stuttgart, 1998), 11.

2. Alexander von Plato and Almut Leh, eds., *"Ein unglaublicher Frühling": Erfahrene Geschichte im Nachkriegsdeutschland, 1945–1948* (Bonn, 1997), 11, 15, 27.

3. Johannes-Dieter Steinert, "Die große Flucht und die Jahre danach: Flüchtlinge und Vertriebene in den vier Besatzungszonen," in *Ende des Dritten Reiches—Ende des Zweiten Weltkrieges: Eine Perspektivische Rückschau,* ed. Hans-Erich Volksmann (Munich, 1995), 557.

4. Gauly, *Kirche und Politik,* 71.

5. NA, OMGUS, RG 260, 368, Population of the U.S. Zone of Germany, Part I: Summary (November 1947), 7; Suval, *Electoral Politics,* 64. Cf. Sabine Voßkamp, *Katholische Kirche und Vertriebene in Westdeutschland: Integration, Identität und Ostpolitischer Diskurs, 1945–1972* (Stuttgart, 2007).

6. Franz Urban Pappi, "Die konfessionell-religiöse Konfliktlinie in der deutschen Wählerschaft: Entstehung, Stabilität und Wandel," in *Wirtschaftlicher Wandel,* ed. Oberndörfer, Rattinger, and Schmitt (Berlin, 1985), 283.

7. Joachim Beckmann, ed., *Kirchliches Jahrbuch für die Evangelische Kirche in Deutschland 1949* (Gütersloh, 1950), 538. See also Hans Braun, "Demographische Umschichtungen im Deutschen Katholizismus nach 1945," in *Kirche und Katholizismus, 1945–1949,* ed. Anton Rauscher (Munich, 1977), 9–25.

8. Pappi, "Konfessionell-religiöse Konfliktlinie," 283.

9. Thomas Kleinknecht, "Die westfälische Nachkriegsdiakonie vor der Flüchtlingsfrage: Kirchliche Fürsorge und der Prozess der Integration: Eine Forschungsskizze," in *Kontinuität und Neubeginn: Die rheinische und westfälische Kirche in der Nachkriegszeit (1945–1949),* ed. Bernd Hey and Günther van Norden (Bielefeld, 1996), 150–52.

10. Joachim Köhler and Rainer Bendel, "Bewährte Rezepte oder unkonventionelle Experimente? Zur Seelsorge an Flüchtlingen und Heimatvertriebenen: Anfragen an die und Impulse für die Katholizismusforschung," in *Siegerin in Trümmern,* ed. Köhler and van Melis, 203; Michael Schwartz, "'Zwangsheimat Deutschland': Vertriebene und Kernbevölkerung zwischen Gesellschaftskonflikt und Integrationspolitik," in *Nachkrieg in Deutschland,* ed. Klaus Naumann (Hamburg, 2001), 130–43.

11. Martin Greschat, "'Mit den Vertriebenen kam Kirche'? Anmerkungen zu einem unerledigten Thema," *Historisch-Politische Mitteilungen* 13 (2006): 50–51; Stambolis, "'Heilige Feste,'" 193–97.

12. Peter Waldmann, "Die Eingliederung der ostdeutschen Vertriebenen," in *Vorgeschichte der Bundesrepublik Deutschland: Zwischen Kapitulation und Grundgesetz,* ed. Josef Becker, Theo Stammen, and Peter Waldmann, 2nd ed. (Munich, 1987), 170.

13. Harry Noormann, "Neue Freiheit, vertagte Befreiung: Zur gesellschaftlichen Rolle der Kirchen in der Nachkriegszeit," in *Deutschland, 1945–1949: Ringvorlesung an der THD im Sommersemester 1985,* ed. Hans-Gerd Schumann (Darmstadt, 1989), 134; Paul Erker, "Revolution des Dorfes? Ländliche Bevölkerung zwischen Flüchtlingszustrom und landwirtschaftlichem Strukturwandel," in *Von Stalingrad zur Währungsreform,* ed. Broszat, Henke, and Woller, 382–83.

14. Braun, "Demographische Umschichtungen," 20.

15. Anne Martin, *Die Entstehung der CDU in Rheinland-Pfalz* (Munich, 1995), 88.

16. Adenauer to Weber, May 26, 1946, in *Briefe, 1945–1947*, 255–56. Adenauer wrote, "On the one hand, we need to be as good as possible toward them. On the other hand, we must not, as you rightly explain, plant the Prussian spirit in our Rhenish youth. We must attempt to assimilate them and instill in them our spiritual mind-set. Under no circumstances can we have increasing numbers of eastern refugees in leading positions." For similar sentiments, see Adenauer to Engels, June 3, 1946, in *Briefe, 1945–1947*, 257.

17. Frederic Spotts, *The Churches and Politics in Germany* (Middletown, 1973), 48–50.

18. Adolf M. Birke, "Katholische Kirche und Politik in der Phase des Neubeginns, 1945–1949," in *Die Zeit nach 1945 als Thema kirchlicher Zeitgeschichte: Referate der internationalen Tagung in Hünigen/Bern (Schweiz) 1985*, ed. Victor Conzemius, Martin Greschat, and Hermann Kocher (Göttingen, 1988), 185.

19. von Plato and Leh, *"Unglaublicher Frühling,"* 31.

20. Michael Hirschfeld, *Katholisches Milieu und Vertriebene: Eine Fallstudie am Beispiel des Oldenburger Landes, 1945–1965* (Cologne, 2002); Rainer Bendel, *Aufbruch aus dem Glauben? Katholische Heimatvertriebene in den gesellschaftlichen Transformationen der Nachkriegsjahre, 1945–1965* (Cologne, 2003).

21. Martin Greschat, "Die Kirchen in den beiden deutschen Staaten nach 1945," *Geschichte in Wissenschaft und Unterricht* 42.5 (1991): 267–84; Rudolf Morsey, "Der deutsche Katholizismus in den Jahren der Besatzungsherrschaft, 1945–1949," in *Von Windthorst bis Adenauer: Ausgewählte Aufsätze zu Politik, Verwaltung, und politischem Katholizismus im 19. und 20. Jahrhundert*, ed. Ulrich von Hehl, Hans Günter Hockerts, Horst Möller, and Martin Schumacher (Paderborn, 1997), 245.

22. "Religiöse Neugeburt in Deutschland," *Sunday Express,* May 19, 1946, in *"Unglaublicher Frühling,"* ed. von Plato and Leh, 344; NA, OMGUS, RG 260, 186, 000.3, Information and Security Section, Religious Affairs Branch, *Monthly Bulletin* 9 (January 1948).

23. Clemens Vollnhals, "Die Evangelische Kirche zwischen Traditionswahrung und Neuorientierung," in *Von Stalingrad zur Währungsreform,* ed. Broszat, Henke, and Woller, 115. Of all of Germany's institutional elites, the hierarchy of the Catholic Church was statistically the least tainted by National Socialism. See Wolfgang Zapf, *Wandlungen der deutschen Elite: Ein Zirkulationsmodell deutscher Führungsgruppen, 1919–1961* (Munich, 1965), 103; Damian van Melis, "Der katholische Episkopat und die Entnazifizierung," in *Siegerin in Trümmern,* ed. Köhler and van Melis, 49–50.

24. Griech-Polelle, *Bishop von Galen,* 5. Cf. Konrad Repgen, "Die Erfahrung des Dritten Reiches und das Selbstverständnis der deutschen Katholiken nach 1945," in *Zeit nach 1945,* ed. Conzemius, Greschat, and Kocher, 140.

25. Rebecca Boehling, *A Question of Priorities: Democratic Reform and Economic Recovery in Postwar Germany* (Providence, 1996), 64, 71–77, 203; Karl Herbert, *Kirche zwischen Aufbruch und Tradition: Entscheidungsjahre nach 1945* (Stuttgart, 1989), 15; Günter Baadte, "Grundfragen der politischen und gesellschaftlichen Neuordnung in den Hirtenbriefen der deutschen Bischöfe, 1945–1949," *Jahrbuch für christliche Sozialwissenschaften* 27 (1986): 96.

26. Karen Riechert, "Der Umgang der katholischen Kirche mit historischer und ju-

ristischer Schuld anlässlich der Nürnberger Kriegsverbrecherprozesse," in *Siegerin in Trümmern,* ed. Köhler and van Melis, 20.

27. Jerry Z. Muller, *The Other God That Failed: Hans Freyer and the Deradicalization of German Conservatism* (Princeton, 1987), 336.

28. Winfried Becker, "Grundlinien des Verhältnisses zwischen römisch-katholischer Kirche und Staat in Deutschland während des 19. und 20. Jahrhunderts," *Kirchliche Zeitgeschichte* 14:1 (2001): 91.

29. Köhler and Bendel, "Bewährte Rezepte oder unkonventionelle Experimente?" 216.

30. Helmut Gollwitzer, interview, in *"Unglaublicher Frühling,"* ed. von Plato and Leh, 345.

31. Muller, *Other God,* 336.

32. Peter Fäßler, *Badisch, Christlich, und Sozial: Zur Geschichte der BCSV/CDU im französisch besetzten Land Baden (1945–1952)* (Frankfurt a.M., 1995), 30, 37; Anthony Kauders, "Catholics, the Jews, and Democratization in Post-War Germany, Munich, 1945–65," *German History* 18.4 (2000): 468; Reinhard Scheerer, *Evangelische Kirche und Politik, 1945 bis 1949: Zur theologisch-politischen Ausgangslage in den ersten Jahren nach der Niederlage des "Dritten Reiches"* (Cologne, 1981), 83–85, 127; Heinz Hürten, "Beobachtungen zur Situation der katholischen Kirche in den drei westlichen Besatzungszonen Deutschlands," *Kirchliche Zeitgeschichte* 2.1 (1989): 205; Joachim Kuropka, "Britische Besatzungspolitik und Neubeginn des öffentlichen Lebens: Probleme des politischen Wiederaufbaus in der britischen Besatzungszone," in *Neubeginn 1945 zwischen Kontinuität und Wandel,* ed. Willigis Eckermann and Joachim Kuropka (Cloppenburg, 1988), 18.

33. NA, OMGUS, RG 260, 116, AG 000.1–3, Wurm to OMGUS, April 21, 1947.

34. Birke, "Katholische Kirche," 180–81.

35. NA, OMGUS, RG 260, 186, 000.3, Information and Security Section, Religious Affairs Branch, *Monthly Bulletin* 9 (January 1948). Cf. Ivo Zeiger, "Kirchliche Zwischenbilanz 1945: Bericht über die Informationsreise durch Deutschland und Österreich im Herbst 1945," ed. Ludwig Volk, *Stimmen der Zeit* 5 (1975): 297; Harry Noormann, *Protestantismus und politisches Mandat, 1945–1949,* vol. 2, *Dokumente und Kommentare* (Gütersloh, 1985), 21–22.

36. Schulze, *Bund oder Schar,* 171. After his fall 1945 tour, however, Zeiger reported no priest shortage. See Zeiger, "Kirchliche Zwischenbilanz," 303.

37. Ewald Frie, "Zwischen Amtskirche und Verbandswesen: Der deutsche Caritasverband, 1945–1949," in *Siegerin in Trümmern,* ed. Köhler and van Melis, 161–74.

38. In recognition of the crucial emergency services the churches provided, even the Soviets allowed them to operate relatively freely in the first months after the war. See Martin Onnasch, "Die Situation der Kirchen in der sowjetischen Besatzungszone, 1945–1949," *Kirchliche Zeitgeschichte* 2.1 (1989): 210–20; Christoph Kösters, ed., *Caritas in der SBZ/DDR, 1945–1989: Erinnerungen, Berichte, Forschungen* (Paderborn, 2001), 239; Ernst-Alfred Jauch and Gisela Helwig, "Katholische Kirche," in *Kirchen und Gesellschaft in beiden deutschen Staaten,* ed. Gisela Helwig and Detlef Urban (Cologne, 1987), 11.

39. van Melis, "Katholische Episkopat," 68.

40. Wolfgang Löhr, "Rechristianisierungsvorstellungen im deutschen Katholizis-

mus, 1945–1948," in *Christentum und politische Verantwortung,* ed. Jochen-Christoph Kaiser and Doering-Manteuffel, 33. As early as 1946, some observers noted that the religious renaissance was petering out. The Protestant Church experienced a wave of church joinings in 1945 and 1946, but by 1949, when twice as many people left the church as joined it, the entire postwar gain measured only seventy-five thousand. See Inacker, *Zwischen Transzendenz,* 242. In Mainz, Bishop Albert Stohr made repeated references in his 1946 and 1947 sermons to the diminished numbers of Catholics attending church or participating in Catholic organizations. See DDAM, 45, 1, 201.

41. Franz Walter, "Milieus und Parteien in der deutschen Gesellschaft: Zwischen Persistenz und Erosion," *Geschichte in Wissenschaft und Unterricht* 46 (1995): 488.

42. Eberhard Röhm and Jörg Thierfelder, *Juden, Christen, Deutsche, 1933–1945,* vol. 1, *1933 bis 1935,* 2nd ed. (Stuttgart, 2004), 65.

43. Müller-Rolli, *Evangelische Schulpolitik,* 46.

44. Bergen, *Twisted Cross,* chapter 6.

45. Michael F. Feldkamp, *Mitläufer, Feiglinge, Antisemiten? Katholische Kirche und Nationalsozialismus* (Augsburg, 2009), 101.

46. Franz Walter, "Milieus und Parteien," 490.

47. Stambolis, "'Heilige Feste,'" 178–216; Frank Nienhaus, "Transformations- und Erosionsprozessse des katholischen Milieus in einer ländlich-textilindustrialisierten Region: Das Westmünsterland, 1914–1968," in *Politische Zäsuren,* ed. Frese and Prinz, 616.

48. Thomas Grossmann, *Zwischen Kirche und Gesellschaft: Das Zentralkomitee der deutschen Katholiken, 1945–1970* (Mainz, 1991), 30–34.

49. Besier, *Kirchen,* 16; Kevin P. Spicer, *Hitler's Priests: Catholic Clergy and National Socialism* (DeKalb, 2008).

50. Klaus Tenfelde, "Historische Milieus—Erblichkeit und Konkurrenz," in *Nation und Gesellschaft in Deutschland: Historische Essays,* ed. Manfred Hettling and Paul Nolte (Munich, 1996), 263; Lösche and Walter, "Katholiken, Konservative, und Liberale," 484–85. For a contrary view, see Dirk Berg-Schlosser, "Die Konstituierung des Wirtschaftsssytem," in *Vorgeschichte der Bundesrepublik Deutschland,* ed. Josef Becker, Stammen, and Waldmann, 111–13.

51. Doris von der Brelie-Lewien, "Abendland und Sozialismus: Zur Kontinuität politisch-kultureller Denkhaltungen im Katholizismus von der Weimarer Republik zur frühen Nachkriegszeit," in *Politische Teilkulturen,* ed. Lehnert and Megerle, 188–218.

52. Bergen, *Twisted Cross,* 212; Torsten Oppelland, "Der Evangelische Arbeitskreis der CDU/CSU, 1952–1969," *Historisch-Politische Mitteilungen* 5 (1998): 108; Matthew D. Hockenos, *A Church Divided: German Protestants Confront the Nazi Past* (Bloomington, 2004), 42–45.

53. Benjamin Pearson, "The Pluralization of Protestant Politics: Public Responsibility, Rearmament, and Division at the 1950s *Kirchentage,*" *Central European History* 43.2 (2010): 281.

54. Martin Möller, *Evangelische Kirche und Sozialdemokratische Partei in den Jahren 1945–1950: Grundlagen der Verständigung und Beginn des Dialoges* (Göttingen, 1984), 189.

55. von Plato and Leh, *"Unglaublicher Frühling,"* 66–77.

56. Walther L. Bernecker, "Die Neugründung der Gewerkschaften in den West-

zonen," in *Vorgeschichte der Bundesrepublik Deutschland,* ed. Josef Becker, Stammen, and Waldmann, 270.

57. Daniel E. Rogers, *Politics after Hitler: The Western Allies and the German Party System* (London, 1995). Cf. NA, OMGUS (Hesse), RG 260, 1141, Newman to Wagner, May 14, 1948. The U.S. military government revoked the license for the CDU magazine, *Die Freiheit,* for criticizing the American occupiers.

58. Norbert Frei, "Die Besatzungsherrschaft als Zäsur?" in *Politische Zäsuren,* ed. Lehnert and Megerle, 785.

59. Rogers, *Politics after Hitler,* x, 20.

60. The British zone would encompass Westphalia, Lower Saxony, Hamburg, Schleswig-Holstein, and the Rhineland with the exception of the southern areas of the administrative districts of Koblenz and Trier, which were assigned to the French zone.

61. Heitzer, *CDU,* 747; Schönbohm, *CDU wird moderne Volkspartei,* 47.

62. BAK, NL 174, 50, Rhineland CDP, *Rundschreiben* 5, 45 (Cologne, October 27, 1945); Leo Schwering, *Frühgeschichte,* 13; HAStK, 1193, 401, 8, Schwering, speech (Brühl, Pulheim, July 14, 1946); StBKAH, 11.01, 243, 246, Adenauer to Albers, October 11, 1948; StBKAH, 11.01, 243, 246, Adenauer to Schaeven, October 29, 1948.

63. Adenauer to Silverberg, December 10, 1946, in *Briefe über Deutschland,* 56–59. Cf. *PRSU* (November 9, 1948), 143.

64. NA, OMGUS, RG 260, 368, Records of the Executive Office, the Control Office, Cf. Heitzer, *CDU,* 17, 36; Konrad Adenauer, *Erinnerungen, 1945–1953* (Stuttgart, 1965), 26–29; Leo Schwering, *Frühgeschichte,* 42–43, 46; BAK, NL 278, 142, CDU member in Bochum (unsigned) to Holzapfel, March 14, 1946; *DGG* (February 25, 1949), 821.

65. HAStK, 1193, 218,1, Lensing to Stricker, August 23, 1945; Gerhard Besier, "Die politische Rolle des Protestantismus in der Nachkriegszeit," *Aus Politik und Zeitgeschichte* B 50 (2000): 29. Hein argues that FDP complaints about British favoritism toward the SPD were unjustified. See Dieter Hein, *Zwischen liberaler Milieupartei und nationaler Sammlungsbewegung: Gründung, Entwicklung, und Struktur der Freien Demokratischen Partei, 1945–1949* (Düsseldorf, 1985), 208. Frank Bösch echoes this assessment with regard to the CDU. See Bösch, *Adenauer-CDU,* 34.

66. Rogers, *Politics after Hitler,* 23, 60–62.

67. At the same time, local officers could impede political activity. For British delays of Christian Democratic organization in Düsseldorf and Westphalia, see Heitzer, *CDU,* 54–55, 90.

68. The early chronology of the Christian Democratic Union in Cologne and the Rhineland has been recounted in many places. See, most recently, Günter Buchstab and Klaus Gotto, eds., *Die Gründung der Union: Tradition, Entwicklung, und Repräsentanten,* 2nd ed. (Munich, 1990); Günter Buchstab, "1945–1949," in *Lexikon der Christlichen Demokratie in Deutschland,* ed. Winfried Becker, Günter Buchstab, Anselm Doering-Manteuffel, and Rudolf Morsey (Paderborn, 2002), 53–64; Ulrich Soénius, "Neubeginn im zerstörten Köln," in *50 Jahre CDU Köln, 1945–1995: Festschrift zur 50. Wiederkehr des Gründungstage der Christlich Demokratischen Union,* ed. Christlich-Demokratischen Union Köln (Cologne, 1995), 8–15; Lill, "Über die Anfänge der CDU," 157–72. Cf. Winfried Herbers, *Der Verlust der Hegemonie: Die Kölner CDU, 1945/46–1964* (Düsseldorf, 2003).

69. Arentz, "Anfänge," 121–22.

70. Leo Schwering, *Frühgeschichte,* 9–11. Schwering addressed Ibach by the familiar form, "Du."

71. Leo Schwering, *Frühgeschichte,* 49. Other CDU founders would echo this reference. See BAK, NL 18, 136, 141–42, Kaiser, speech (Düsseldorf, March 29, 1946); BAK, NL 18, 420, 12, Bernoth to CDU workers (December 29, 1947); BAK, NL 18, 420, 16, "Deutsch, Christlich, Demokratisch, Sozial: Adam Stegerwalds politisches Vermächtnis," *Der Tag: Unabhängige Zeitung für Deutschland* (December 5, 1948); ACDPStA, I-208–5, André, speech (n.d.).

72. ACDPStA, I-056-1, Huber, Denkschrift (Stuttgart, September 12, 1945); ACDPStA, I-182-4/03, Neschen, "Weltanschauung und Politik" (August 1946); ACDP-StA, I-182-4/03, B. I.3, Kannengießer, flyer, "Katholiken—Seht die Gefahr!" (Osnabrück, September 1946); Josef Kannengießer, ed., "Entscheidung—aus christlicher Verantwortung (CDU oder neues Zentrum?)" (Dortmund, September 1946), 5.

73. ACDPStA, I-206-20, Adam Stegerwald, "Wohin gehen wir?" (Würzburg, November 5, 1945), 29. Cf. ACDPStA, I-182-6, B II.1.1, flyer (September 1945).

74. StBKAH, 08.06, 333, Strunk to Hamacher, November 21, 1945.

75. BAK, Z5/14, PRSB, October 21, 1948.

76. Leo Schwering, *Frühgeschichte,* 16; Lönne, "Germany," 177.

77. The Americans authorized German political activity on the district level on August 27, 1945, on the state level on November 23, 1945, and on the zonal level on February 28, 1946. The British followed closely behind, permitting district party organization after September 15, 1945, state organization after December 10, 1945, and zonal organization in early 1946.

78. Walter Först, *Geschichte Nordrhein-Westfalens,* vol. 1, *1945–1949* (Cologne, 1970), 36, 42–44.

79. Leo Schwering, *Frühgeschichte,* 13.

80. HAStK, 1193, 109, Schwering to Barzel, May 22, 1962. Schwering also described the Zentrum and the Catholic Church as "synonyms." See Leo Schwering, *Frühgeschichte,* 119.

81. BAK, NL 5, 218, 84, Elfgen to Pünder, October 27, 1945.

82. StBKAH, 08.51, 126, Henry to Adenauer, March 4, 1946.

83. Konrad Adenauer, "Rede des Ersten Vorsitzenden der Christlich Demokratischen Union für die britische Zone" (Düsseldorf, May 12, 1946), *Schriftenreihe der Christlich Demokratischen Union des Rheinlandes* 10 (Cologne, 1946), 7.

84. ACDPStA, I-182-7/1, Gormann to Lensing, September 21, 1945.

85. Helga Grebing, Peter Porzorski, and Rainer Schulze, eds., *Die Nachkriegsentwicklungen in Westdeutschland, 1945–1949,* vol. 2, *Politik und Gesellschaft* (Stuttgart, 1980), 68.

86. Leo Schwering, *Frühgeschichte,* 34–36.

87. HAStK, 1193, 421, 1–2, Bericht über die Gründungsversammlung der Christlich Demokratischen Partei des Rheinlandes (Cologne, September 2, 1945).

88. Arentz, "Anfänge," 123, 136.

89. HAStK, 1193, 521, 1–2.

90. HAStK, 1193, 205, 1, Schwering to Köhler, April 17, 1961. Cf. Leo Schwering, *Frühgeschichte,* 73–76; Reinhard Schmeer, *Volkskirchliche Hoffnungen und der Aufbau*

der Union: Evangelische Kirche und CDU/CSU in den ersten Nachkriegsjahren (Cologne, 2001), 49–51.

91. HAStK, 1193, 521, 1–2.

92. Leo Schwering, *Frühgeschichte,* 59–60, 72; Stefan Noethen, "Christlicher Sozialismus in der Stunde der Neuordnung 1945: Das Dominikanerkloster Walberberg und die Kölner Leitsätze der CDU," *Geschichte im Westen* 11 (1996): 48–71.

93. HAStK, 1193, 296, 9, Welty to Schwering, February 6, 1962; HAStK 1193, 296, 8, Welty to Schwering, January 11, 1962; Leo Schwering, *Frühgeschichte,* 58, 75–79, 82–83. For the text of *Was Nun?* see StBKAH, 08.06, 108–24.

94. Carolyn M. Warner, *Confessions of an Interest Group: The Catholic Church and Political Parties in Europe* (Princeton, 2000), 197.

95. H. G. Wieck, *Die Entstehung der CDU und die Wiedergründung des Zentrums im Jahre 1945* (Düsseldorf, 1953), 64.

96. HAStK, 1193, 345, 1.

97. Lill, "Über die Anfänge der CDU," 158.

98. HAStK, 1193, 330, 1–7.

99. Markus Schwering, "Leo Schwering (1883–1971)—Zur Biographie," in *Leo Schwering, In den Klauen der Gestapo: Tagebuchaufzeichnungen der Jahre 1944–1945,* ed. Markus Schwering (Cologne, 1988), 7–41.

100. HAStK, 1193, 330, 1–7.

101. BAK, Kl. Erw. 345, 34; BAK, NL 18, 56, 76; Stehkämper, "Protest, Opposition, und Widerstand," 141; Nebgen, *Jakob Kaiser,* 42. Cf. Raem, *Katholischer Gesellenverein.*

102. Leo Schwering, *Frühgeschichte,* 25; Cf. Leo Schwering, *In den Klauen der Gestapo.*

103. Winfried Herbers, "Leo Schwering (1873–1971)," in *Christliche Demokraten,* ed. Buchstab, Kaff, and Kleinmann, 457. Cf. Martin Brockhausen, "'Geboren im Widerstand': Zur Erinnerung an den Nationalsozialismus in der CDU, 1950–1990," *Zwischen Kriegs- und Diktaturerfahrung: Katholizismus und Protestantismus in der Nachkriegszeit,* ed. Andreas Holzem and Christoph Holzapfel (Stuttgart, 2005), 203–34.

104. BAK, NL 5, 476, 232; BAK, NL 5, 476, 211; BAK, NL 18, 61, 63, Kaiser, speech (Düsseldorf, March 30, 1946), in "Kaiser über den Sinn der Gewerkschaften," *Der Tagesspielgel* (March 31, 1946); BAK, NL 5, 219, 3; ACDPStA, I-208-5, André, speech (ca. summer 1946).

105. Robert Grosche, *Kölner Tagebuch, 1944–1946* (Cologne, 1969).

106. Bösch, *Adenauer-CDU,* 23 n.13.

107. BAK, Kl. Erw. 345, 34; BAK, NL 18, 56, 76; P. Laurentius Siemer, *Aufzeichnungen und Briefe* (Frankfurt a.M., 1957), 131–39.

108. The Americans offered Ibach the mayorship of Königswinter, but he rejected the offer. See Leo Schwering, *Frühgeschichte,* 10, 17–21.

109. Leo Schwering, *Frühgeschichte,* 85–86; Otto Dann, ed., *Köln nach dem Nationalsozialismus: Der Beginn des gesellschaftlichen und politischen Lebens in den Jahren 1945/46* (Wuppertal, 1981), 249; Först, *Geschichte Nordrhein-Westfalens,* 36. Siemer later asked the Christian politicians to meet elsewhere "because we cannot offer the cloister for partisan purposes." See Siemer, *Aufzeichnungen,* 157.

110. Bösch, *Adenauer-CDU*, 23.

111. Ute Schmidt, *Zentrum oder CDU: Politischer Katholizismus zwischen Tradition und Anpassung* (Opladen, 1987), 152.

112. Ludwig Volk, ed., *Akten deutscher Bischöfe über die Lage der Kirche, 1933–1945*, vol. 6, *1943–1945* (Mainz, 1985), (May 15, 1945), 487.

113. Heitzer, *CDU*, 685–90; Rudolf Morsey, "Zwischen Verwaltung und Politik: Hermann Pünder und die Gründung der CDU in Münster," in *Weltpolitik, Europagedanke, Regionalismus: Festschrift für Heinz Gollwitzer*, ed. Heinz Dollingen, Horst Gründer, and Alwin Hanschmidt (Münster, 1992), 531, 542 n. 29. For the August pastoral letter, see *DdB* (August 23, 1945), 40–45.

114. Paul E. Sigmund, "The Catholic Tradition and Modern Democracy," *Review of Politics* 49.4 (1987): 541.

115. Warner, *Confessions*, 196 n. 16.

116. Ute Schmidt, "Zentrumspartei oder Union," 652.

117. Gauly, *Kirche und Politik*, 152.

118. *DdB* (January 6, 1946), 62–66. See also *DdB* (June 21, 1945), 18–19.

119. Rudolf Morsey, "Prälaten auf der politischen Bühne: Zur Rolle geistlicher Parlamentarier im 19. und 20. Jahrhundert," in *Von Windthorst bis Adenauer*, 239; Klaus Gotto, "Gleiche Distanz zu allen Parteien? Die Kirche im Parteienstaat," in *Kehrt um und glaubt—Erneuert die Welt: 87: Deutscher Katholikentag vom 1. September–5. September 1982 in Düsseldorf, Die Vortragsreihen: Gestalten des Glaubens—Zeugen des Glaubens—Fragen zur Zeitgeschichte nach 1945*, ed. Zentralkomitee der deutschen Katholiken (Paderborn, 1982), 323; Heitzer, *CDU*, 687.

120. ACDPStA, I-182-7/1, Gormann to Lensing, September 21, 1945.

121. Leo Schwering, *Frühgeschichte*, 98; Ute Schmidt, *Zentrum oder CDU*, 149, 288–98.

122. ACDPStA, III-002-91, Father Marx to Bochum CDP, November 6, 1945.

123. Albert E. J. Hollaender, "Offiziere und Prälaten: Zur Fuldaer Bischofskonferenz, August 1945," *Mitteilungen des Österreichischen Staatsarchivs* 25 (1972): 201; Köster, "'Betet,'" 108; Heitzer, *CDU*, 685.

124. Frings to Hamacher, March 29, 1946, in Wieck, *Entstehung*, 66 n. 114b. Cf. Morsey, "Kirche und politische Parteien," 33; Warner, *Confessions*, 197.

125. Martin, *Entstehung der CDU*, 224.

126. Van Melis, "Katholische Episkopat," 60 n. 75.

127. Ulrike Marga Dahl-Keller, *Der Treueid der Bischöfe gegenüber dem Staat: Geschichtliche Entwicklung und gegenwärtige staatskirchenrechtliche Bedeutung* (Berlin, 1994), 157–58.

128. Konrad Repgen, "Der Konkordatsstreit der fünfziger Jahre: Von Bonn nach Karlsruhe (1949–1955/57)," *Kirchliche Zeitgeschichte* 3.1 (1990): 211–12.

129. Warner, *Confessions*, 191.

130. Volk, *Akten deutscher Bischöfe*, (May 15, 1945), 486. See also Volk, *Akten deutscher Bischöfe*, (August 21–23, 1945), 671–83; Boehling, *Question of Priorities*, 77.

131. Heitzer, *CDU*, 688–90.

132. Köster, "'Betet,'" 110.

133. Ute Schmidt, *Zentrum oder CDU*, 150.

134. Birke, "Katholische Kirche," 189; Heitzer, *CDU*, 688–96; Morsey, "Prälaten," 240–41.

135. Repgen, "Konkordatsstreit," 222.

136. Ute Schmidt, *Zentrum oder CDU*, 149.

137. Bösch, *Adenauer-CDU*, 23.

138. Martin, *Entstehung der CDU*, 222–23.

139. Martin, *Entstehung der CDU*, 227–28.

140. Bösch, *Adenauer-CDU*, 23.

141. For exceptions to the general pattern of priests abandoning political offices and candidacies, see Morsey, "Kirche und politische Parteien," 34–39; Markus Köster, *Katholizismus und Parteien in Münster, 1945–1953: Kontinuität und Wandel eines politisches Milieus* (Münster, 1993), 75; Siemer, *Aufzeichnungen*, 162.

142. Max Müller, "Zur Vorgeschichte der Gründung der badischen CDU in Freiburg/ Br.," in *Leo Wohleb—Der andere politische Kurs: Dokumente und Kommentare*, ed. Paul-Ludwig Weinacht (Freiburg i.B., 1975), 118–29.

143. Weitzel, "Von der CSVP zur CDU," 108–9.

144. Stegerwald declared, "The most serious struggles I had in my life were the almost two decades of continuous arguments with Catholic integralism." See ACDPStA, I-206-20; Adam Stegerwald, "Vor- und Nebenfragen zu dem Vortrag 'Wohin gehen wir?'" in *"Wohin gehen wir?"* (Würzburg, November 1945), 17, 61–62.

145. BAK, NL 391, 13, André, speech (Stuttgart, January 13, 1946).

146. Eugen Kogon, "Der Geistliche im öffentlichen Leben," *Frankfurter Hefte: Zeitschrift für Kultur und Politik* 1.9 (1946): 796–98; Eugen Kogon, "Klerus, Seelsorge, und Politik in Böhmen und im Rheinland," *Frankfurter Hefte: Zeitschrift für Kultur und Politik* 2.6 (1947): 535–38.

147. Martin, *Entstehung der CDU*, 91.

148. Ute Schmidt, "Christlich Demokratische Union," 493–94.

149. Adenauer to Scharnagl, August 21, 1945, in *Briefe über Deutschland*, 23–27.

150. ACDPStA, I-056-1, Adenauer, speech (Stuttgart, November 21, 1946).

151. Adenauer to Canon Jansen, April 29, 1946, in *Briefe 1945–1947*, 237–38. Adenauer sought as late as 1963 to persuade the Vatican to allow priests to engage politically. See Morsey, "Prälaten," 241.

152. StBKAH, 07.05, 50, Adenauer to Frings, November 1, 1948.

153. HAStK, 1193, 521, 1–2.

154. ACDPStA, I-208-005, André, speech (n.d.).

155. ACDPStA, I-182-4/03, B I.3, Rhineland CDP, "Offener Brief an alle katholischen Männer und Frauen des Rheinlandes!" ed. Hans Schreiber (Cologne, November 1945).

156. Walter Dirks, "Die Zweite Republik: Zum Ziel und zum Weg der deutschen Demokratie," *Frankfurter Hefte: Zeitschrift für Kultur und Politik* 1.1 (April 1946): 23.

157. Leo Schwering, *Frühgeschichte*, 133; Schwarz, *Konrad Adenauer: A German Politician*, 1:336.

158. Bösch, *Adenauer-CDU*, 46.

159. Hans Peter Mensing, "Adenauer und der Protestantismus," in *Adenauer und die Kirchen*, ed. Ulrich von Hehl (Bonn, 1999), 59.

160. Leo Schwering, *Frühgeschichte*, 12; Shelley Baranowsky, "Consent and Dissent: The Confessing Church and Conservative Opposition to National Socialism,"

Journal of Modern History 59.1 (1987): 53–78; Shelley Baranowsky, *The Confessing Church, Conservative Elites, and the Nazi State* (Lewiston, 1986).

161. ACDPStA, I-171-1/2, Dovifat, speech (Spandau, September 2, 1945).

162. BAK, NL 278, 239, CDUD, Sondermaterial (Berlin, n.d.), 7/I-8/I.

163. ACDPStA, I-182-8/03, B III.2, Bachem to Lensing, November 15, 1945. Cf. ACDPStA, I-182-8/03, B III.2, Steup to Kannengießer, November 20, 1945.

164. Dirks, "Zweite Republik," 23.

165. ACDPStA, I-182-7/1, Schopp to Kannengießer, August 20, 1945.

166. Bösch, *Adenauer-CDU,* 46.

167. Arentz, "Anfänge," 129.

168. Kurt Weitzel, *Vom Chaos zur Demokratie: Die Entstehung der Parteien in Rheinland-Pfalz, 1945–1947* (Mainz, 1989), 64, 71–72.

169. HAStK, 1193, 348, 10.

170. Winfried Becker, *CDU und CSU,* 110. On the CDU founding in Grevenbroich, see HAStK, 1193, 348, 5.

171. HAStK, 1193, 348, 2.

172. HAStK, 1193, 348, 4, Spiecker to Schwering, July 20, 1946.

173. Leo Schwering, *Frühgeschichte,* 105.

174. Wieck, *Entstehung,* 76.

175. Gurland, *CDU/CSU,* 23–24; Egen, "Entstehung," 20.

176. Joachim Beckmann, *Kirchliches Jahrbuch,* 548.

177. ACDPStA, III-002-91, Father Marx of Bödefeld to the Bochum CDP, November 6, 1945.

178. ACDPStA, I-182-008/03, B III.2, Schreiber to Kannengießer, November 28, 1945. Cf. BAK, NL 5, 218, 82, Pünder to Elfgen, December 5, 1945.

179. The influence of Rhenish events on the organization of Westphalian Christian Democracy was later a matter of dispute between Lensing and Schwering. See HAStK, 1193, 218, 6, Lensing to Schwering, May 8, 1962. The importance of August 1945 contacts between Rhenish and Westphalian former Zentrum members for the Westphalians' eventual decision appears to contradict Lensing's narrative. See HAStK, 1193, 359, 3; Lambert Lensing, "Wellenbrecher für Deutschland: Die Gründungstage der Christlich-Demokratischen Union Westfalens," *Westfalenpost* 38 (May 14, 1948).

180. Köster, *Katholizismus und Parteien,* 29.

181. BAK, NL 5 , 475, 111–17; BAK, NL 5, 220, 38, Pünder to Hermes, September 21, 1945; HAStK, 1304, 367, Pünder to Holtmann, October 24, 1945; HAStK, 1193, Jöstingmeier to Schwering, April 24, 1962. See also Susanne Leschinski, "Clemens August Kardinal von Galen in der Nachkriegszeit, 1945/46," in *Clemens August Graf von Galen: Neue Forschungen zum Leben und Wirken des Bischofs von Münster,* ed. Joachim Kuropka (Münster, 1992), 261.

182. Katrin Schmandt, "Die Christlich-Demokratische Partei in Paderborn: Gründung und Aufbau," in *Westfälische Zeitschrift: Zeitschrift für Vaterländische Geschichte und Altertumskunde,* ed. Verein für Geschichte und Altertumskunde Westfalens (Paderborn, 1996), 333–39. See also HAStK, 1193, 289, Tölle to Schwering, May 5, 1962.

183. ACDPStA, I-182-8/03, B III.2, Lensing to Kannengießer, September 5, 1945; ACDPStA, I-182-8/03, B III.2, Kannengießer to Lensing, November 2, 1945.

184. Winfried Becker, *CDU und CSU,* 20–21.

185. Leo Schwering, *Frühgeschichte,* 112–13.

186. HAStK, 1193, 218, 13, Lensing to Schwering, November 7, 1962, December 11, 1962; HAStK, 1193, 218, 17, Lensing to Schwering, December 21, 1962; HAStK, 1193, 218, 6, Lensing to Schwering, May 8, 1962. Here Lensing revises the chronology from his article, "Wellenbrecher für Deutschland: Die Gründungstage der Christlich-Demokratischen Union Westfalens," *Westfalenpost* 38 (May 14, 1948). Cf. Christopher Beckmann, "Lambert Lensing (1889–1965): Zeitungsverlegen, Mitgründer der CDU, Landesvorsitzender der CDU Westfalen-Lippe," *Historisch-Politischen Mitteilungen* 14 (2007): 153–86.

187. HAStK, 1193, 359, 3, Lensing, "Wellenbrecher für Deutschland: Die Gründungstage der Christlich-Demokratische Union Westfalens," *Westfalenpost* 38 (May 14, 1948).

188. Schmeer, *Volkskirchliche Hoffnungen,* 76–77.

189. Wieck, *Entstehung,* 105.

190. Schmeer, *Volkskirchliche Hoffnungen,* 199, 221–23.

191. Schmeer, *Volkskirchliche Hoffnungen,* 60, 184.

192. Heitzer, *CDU,* 58; Egen, "Entstehung," 19.

193. Schmeer, *Volkskirchliche Hoffnungen,* 116.

194. Gurland, *CDU/CSU,* 25.

195. Wieck, *Entstehung,* 92.

196. No representative from the French-occupied Rheinland (Koblenz or Trier) attended, at least not officially, but Otto Lenz participated as the "Courier from Berlin." See Leo Schwering, *Frühgeschichte,* 129; Wieck, *Entstehung,* 98, 102.

197. Cologners (Schwering, Adenauer, Albers, and Pferdmenges) held four of the seven Advisory Council seats; in the larger Executive Committee, Cologne Christian Democrats commanded ten of twenty-three additional seats. Catholic leaders intentionally deployed older, authoritative Center Party members as speakers to advocate for the new movement. For one example of the persuasive effects of Hugo Mönnig's speech, see HAStK, 1193, 348, 1, Henry to Schwering, April 6, 1954.

198. ACDPStA, I-182-6/01, B II.1.1, Schwering to Gilsing, September 6, 1945.

199. HAStK, 1193, 218,1, Lensing to Stricker, August 23, 1945.

200. HAStK, 1193, 359, 1, "Die Gründung der Christlich-Demokratischen Partei in Westdeutschland," *Ruhr-Zeitung* (September 8, 1945).

201. ACDPStA, I-182-6-1, B II.1.1, Lensing to Schwering, September 5, 1945.

202. BAK, NL 71, 21, 19, Holzapfel to Schlange-Schöningen, December 19, 1945.

203. HAStK, 1193, 348, 4, Spiecker to Schwering, July 20, 1946.

204. BAK, NL 178, 335, CDU-Herford, Kreispartei, Bericht über die Gründungsversammlung der CDP (November 24, 1945); BAK, NL 391, 13, Bericht über die Gründungsversammlung der Christlich-Sozialen Volkspartei (Göppingen, October 1, 1945); HAStK, 1193, 348, 4, Spiecker to Schwering, July 20, 1946. The CDP was founded on August 28, 1945 in Duisburg, where five of the thirty participants were Catholic priests.

205. Bösch, *Adenauer-CDU,* 53–54.

206. Winfried Becker, *CDU und CSU,* 142–44.

207. HAStK, 1193, 360, 2.

208. Bösch, *Adenauer-CDU,* 24–25.

209. Joseph Nietfeld, "Die Zentrumspartei: Geschichte und Struktur 1945–1958" (Ph.D. diss., Technische Universität Carolo-Wilhelmina zu Braunschweig, 1985), 165.

210. StBKAH, 08.55, 394, Informationsbrief der Zentrumspartei (British Zone, January 1946).

211. Cary, *Path,* 152–54, chapter 10.

212. ACDPStA, I-182-6/01, B II.1.1, Schwering to Lensing, September 14, 1945.

213. ACDPStA, I-182-8/03, B III.2, Schreiber to Kannengießer, September 28, 1945. See also ACDPStA, I-182-8/03, B III.2, Schreiber to Kannengießer, October 12, 1945.

214. Leo Schwering, *Frühgeschichte,* 95; ACDPStA, I-182-8/03, B. III.2, Lensing to Kannengießer, September 13, 1945.

215. ACDPStA, I-182-8/03, B III.2, Kannengießer to Schwering, October 14, 1945.

216. Nietfeld, "Zentrumspartei," 41.

217. Cary, *Path,* 158.

218. ACDPStA, I-182-7/1, Lensing to Schrage, October 25, 1945; HAStK, 1193, 422, 2; Leo Schwering, ed., *Christlich Demokratische Partei des Rheinlandes* 2.45 (Cologne, November 12, 1945); ACDPStA, I-182-008/03, B III.2, Kannengießer to Lensing, December 7, 1945; ACDPStA, I-182-8/03, B III.2, Lensing to Kannengießer, February 1, 1946.

219. ACDPStA, I-182-8/3, B III.2, Schreiber to Kannengießer, October 12, 1945. See also ACDPStA, I-182-008/03, B III.2, Kannengießer to Lensing, November 2, 1945.

220. ACDPStA, I-182-8/3, B III.2, Schreiber to Kannengießer, October 10, 1945.

221. HAStK, 1193, 191, Schwering to Ibach, October 4, 1945.

222. ACDPStA, I-182-8/03, B III.2, Schwering to Lensing, September 28, 1945; HAStK, 1193, 145,1, Schwering to Eckert, November 29, 1945. Cf. Leo Schwering, *Frühgeschichte,* 125.

223. ACDPStA, I-182-8/03, B III.2, Schreiber to Kannengießer, November 28, 1945.

224. ACDPStA, I-182-8/03, B III.2, Kannengießer to Schreiber, November 20, 1945.

225. ACDPStA, I-182-8/03, B III.2, Kannengießer to Steup, January 30, 1946.

226. HAStK, 1193, 251, 1, Schwering to Reichensperger, January 14, 1946.

227. StBKAH, 08.51, 126, Henry to Adenauer, March 4, 1946.

228. ACDPStA, I-182-8/03, B III.2, Kannengießer to Gronowski, June 6, 1946.

229. Adenauer to "leading Catholic clerics in Cologne," Grosche, Schreiber, Gickler, April 15, 1946, in *Briefe, 1945–1947,* 216.

230. Heitzer, *CDU,* 691–92; Gauly, *Kirche und Politik,* 151.

231. Adenauer to Frings, April 27, 1947, in *Briefe, 1945–1947,* 477.

232. BAK, Z5/188 F, 11, "Heimatlos," *Allgemeine Zeitung* 36 (February 12–13, 1949).

233. StBKAH, 08.55, 374, Moritz to Schönenborn, March 20, 1946.

234. StBKAH, 08.06, 333, Strunk to Hamacher, November 21, 1945.

235. Elisabeth Friese, "Helene Wessel (1898–1969)," in *Katholiken und Protestanten,* ed. Sauer, 210.

236. HAStK, 1193, 218, 1, Lensing to Stricker, August 23, 1945.

237. HAStK, 1193, 218, 29, Lensing to Schwering, July 11, 1963.

CHAPTER 3

1. Quoted in Christoph Kleßmann, *Die doppelte Staatsgründung: Deutsche Geschichte, 1945–1955* (Bonn, 1991), 143.

2. Wolfgang Benz, *Potsdam 1945: Besatzungsherrschaft und Neuaufbau im Vier-Zonen-Deutschland,* 4th ed. (Munich, 2005), 74, 80.

3. Raymond Poidevin, "Die französische Deutschlandpolitik, 1943–1949," in *Die Deutschlandpolitik Frankreichs und die Französische Zone, 1945–1949,* ed. Claus Scharf and Hans-Jürgen Schröder (Wiesbaden, 1983), 15–25.

4. Martin, *Entstehung der CDU,* 221; Hürten, "Beobachtungen," 209; Zeiger, "Kirchliche Zwischenbilanz," 300.

5. Morsey, "Kirche und politische Parteien," 35; Fäßler, *Badisch, Christlich, und Sozial,* 17–26.

6. Schmeer, *Volkskirchliche Hoffnungen,* 359–60, 394–95, 417, 424.

7. Plakat aus Baden-Württemberg (Bezirksverband Nord-Württemberg) aus der unmittelbaren Nachkriegszeit, in *Politik und Plakat: 50 Jahre Plakatgeschichte am Beispiel der CDU,* ed. Gerd Langguth (Bonn, 1995), 22, 207.

8. Josef Foschepoth, "Zur deutschen Reaktion auf Niederlage und Besatzung," in *Westdeutschland, 1945–1955: Unterwerfung, Kontrolle, Integration,* ed. Ludolf Herbst (Munich, 1986), 155.

9. Frank Häußler, "Ulrich Steiner und der Laupheimer Kreis: Ein konservatives Randphänomen in der Frühzeit der Bundesrepublik Deutschland," *Historisch-Politische Mitteilungen* 6 (1999): 191.

10. Presse- und Informationsdienste der Christlich-Demokratischen Union Deutschlands, ed., *Die Gründungsgeschichte der CDU im Trierer Land, 1945/46* (Bonn, 1966).

11. Martin, *Entstehung der CDU,* 67.

12. Finck wrote in his diary in 1944, "The history of the old parties—and with it also that of the Center Party and the Bavarian People's Party—is over and one must build a totally new party on interconfessional foundations." Quoted in Helmut Kohl, "Die politische Entwicklung in der Pfalz und das Wiedererstehen der Parteien nach 1945" (Ph.D. diss., Ruprecht-Karls-Universität zu Heidelberg, 1958), 62.

13. LHA, 700, 145, 688, 1. Cf. Martin, *Entstehung der CDU,* 68.

14. LHA, 700, 145, 687, 1.

15. Kohl, "Politische Entwicklung," 65–74.

16. Winfried Becker, *CDU und CSU,* 99.

17. HAStK, 1193, 302, 6, Wolff to Schwering, May 9, 1964.

18. Martin, *Entstehung der CDU,* 223.

19. Weitzel, "Von der CSVP zur CDU," 20–29; Morsey, "Kirche und politische Parteien," 25.

20. Weitzel, *Vom Chaos zur Demokratie,* 39–41.

21. Diethelm Prowe, "Democratization as Conservative Restabilization," in *American Policy and the Reconstruction of West Germany, 1945–1955,* ed. Jeffry M. Diefendorf, Axel Frohn, and Hermann-Josef Rupieper (Cambridge, 1993), 307–29; Adenauer, *Erinnerungen,* 19–26.

22. NA, OMGUS, RG 260, 95, Report by the Political Directorate on Part II of Section III: Democratisation (February 8, 1947). Cf. Erich J. Hahn, "U.S. Policy on a West

German Constitution, 1947–1949," in *American Policy,* ed. Diefendorf, Frohn, and Rupieper, 22.

23. A November 1947 American report, "Political Parties in Germany," dismissed suggestions that "the US authorities favor the CDU." See NA, OMGUS, Records of the Executive Office, the Control Office, RG 260, 368. This language was repeated in a similar report dated September 1948. Cf. Boehling, *Question of Priorities,* 119.

24. StBKAH, 08.05, 61.

25. Ulrich von Alemann, *Das Parteiensystem der Bundesrepublik Deutschland* (Bonn, 2001), 50–51. Cf. Alf Mintzel, *Die CSU: Anatomie einer konservativen Partei (1945–1972)* (Opladen, 1975); Alf Mintzel, *Geschichte der CSU: Ein Überblick* (Opladen, 1977); Konstanze Wolf, *CSU und Bayernpartei: Ein besonderes Konkurrenzverhältnis, 1948–1960* (Cologne, 1982); Klaus-Dietmar Henke and Hans Woller, eds., *Lehrjahre der CSU: Eine Nachkriegspartei im Spiegel vertraulicher Berichte an die amerikanische Militärregierung* (Stuttgart, 1984); Alf Mintzel, "Die Christlich-Soziale Union in Bayern," in *Parteien in der Bundesrepublik Deutschland,* ed. Alf Mintzel and Heinrich Oberreuter (Bonn, 1992); Barbara Fait, Alf Mintzel, and Thomas Schlemmer, eds., *Die CSU, 1945–1948: Protokolle und Materialien zur Frühgeschichte der Christlich-Sozialen Union,* 3 vols. (Munich, 1993); Christoph Henzler, "Die Christlich-Soziale Union in den ersten Nachkriegsjahren," in *Geschichte einer Volkspartei: 50 Jahre CSU—1945–1955,* ed. Hanns-Seidel Stiftung (Grünwald, 1995); Barbara Fait, *Die Anfänge der CSU, 1945–1948: Der holprige Weg zur Erfolgspartei* (Munich, 1995); Alf Mintzel, *Die CSU-Hegemonie in Bayern: Strategie und Erfolg, Gewinner, und Verlierer* (Passau, 1998); Thomas Schlemmer, *Aufbruch, Krise, und Erneuerung: Die Christlich-Soziale Union, 1945–1955* (Munich, 1998); Andreas Kießling, *Die CSU: Machterhalt und Machterneuerung* (Wiesbaden, 2004).

26. ACDPStA, I-056-2; Schmeer, *Volkskirchliche Hoffnungen,* 409–15; Winfried Becker, *CDU und CSU,* 67–73.

27. Winfried Becker, *CDU und CSU,* 136–37; Gurland, *CDU/CSU,* 42.

28. NA, OMGUS Hesse, RG 260, 471, Josef Ardngen et al. to Military Government, Frankfort o/Main, September 15, 1945. Cf. Joachim Rotberg, *Zwischen Linkskatholizismus und bürgerlicher Sammlung: Die Anfänge der CDU in Frankfurt am Main* (Frankfurt a.M., 1999), 80–101.

29. Ute Schmidt, "Hitler ist tot und Ulbricht lebt: Die CDU, der Nationalsozialismus, und der Holocaust," in *Der Umgang mit dem Nationalsozialismus und Antisemitismus in Österreich, der DDR, und der Bundesrepublik Deutschland,* ed. Werner Bergmann, Rainer Erb, and Albert Lichtblau (Frankfurt a.M., 1995), 81.

30. Winfried Becker, *CDU und CSU,* 89.

31. Franz Dietze, "Entscheidungsstrukturen und -prozesse in der Ost-CDU, 1945–1952," in *Die Ost-CDU: Beiträge zu ihrer Entstehung und Entwicklung,* ed. Michael Richter and Martin Rißmann (Weimar, 1995), 47–62.

32. Walrab von Buttlar, *Ziele und Zielkonflikte der sowjetischen Deutschlandpolitik, 1945–1947* (Stuttgart, 1980), 109–17; Norman M. Naimark, *The Russians in Germany: A History of the Soviet Zone of Occupation, 1945–1949* (Cambridge, 1995).

33. Gerhard Wettig, "Der Konflikt der Ost-CDU mit der Besatzungsmacht, 1945–1948, im Spiegel sowjetischer Akten," *Historisch-Politische Mitteilungen* 6 (1999): 113.

34. Ernst Lemmer, *Manches war doch anders: Erinnerungen eines deutschen Demokraten,* 1st ed. (Frankfurt a.M., 1968), 253; BAK, NL 18, 164a, 66, Kaiser to Albers, August 19, 1945; BAK, NL 18, 129, 259.

35. Bernecker, "Neugründung der Gewerkschaften," 272–76.

36. Wolfgang Schroeder, *Katholizismus und Einheitsgewerkschaft: Der Streit um den DGB und der Niedergang des Sozialkatholizismus in der Bundesrepublik bis 1960* (Bonn, 1992), 74–93.

37. Werner Conze, *Jakob Kaiser: Politiker zwischen Ost und West, 1945–1949* (Stuttgart, 1969), 11–12, 15, 19, 29–30.

38. Alexander Fischer, "Andreas Hermes und die gesamtdeutschen Anfänge der Union," in *Die CDU in der sowjetisch besetzten Zone/DDR, 1945–1952,* ed. Alexander Fischer and Manfred Agethen (Sankt Augustin, 1994), 8.

39. ACDPStA, I-090-15/1, Magistrat der Stadt Berlin, Abteilung für Ernährung, to Spranger, June 15, 1945.

40. Manfred Wilde, *Die SBZ-CDU, 1945–1947: Zwischen Kriegsende und kaltem Krieg* (Munich, 1998), 497–98. Cf. Ralf Thomas Baus, *Die Christlich-Demokratische Union Deutschlands in der sowjetisch besetzten Zone, 1945 bis 1948: Gründung—Programm—Politik* (Düsseldorf, 2001).

41. Manfred Agethen, "Der Widerstand der demokratischen Kräfte in der CDU gegen den Gleichschaltungsdruck von sowjetischer Besatzungsmacht und SED, 1945–1952," in *Die CDU,* ed. Fischer and Agethen, 22; Alexander Fischer, "Andreas Hermes," 9.

42. Wilde, *SBZ-CDU,* 498.

43. BAK, ZSg. 1-20/1 (11); Lemmer, *Manches,* 254–55; Christian Schwießelmann, "Norddeutsch, protestantisch, liberal—Gründerpersönlichkeiten der CDU in Mecklenburg-Vorpommern," *Historisch-Politische Mitteilungen* 13 (2006): 29. See also Christian Schwießelmann, *Die CDU in Mecklenburg und Vorpommern, 1945–1952: Von der Gründung bis zur Auflösung des Landesverbandes: Eine parteiengeschichtliche Darstellung* (Düsseldorf, 2010).

44. Katrin Baus and Ralf Thomas Baus, "Die Gründung der Christlich-Demokratischen Union Deutschlands in Brandenburg 1945," *Historisch-Politische Mitteilungen* 6 (1999): 79, 101–4.

45. Ralf Thomas Baus, "Die Gründung der Christlich-Demokratischen Union Deutschlands in Sachsen 1945," *Historisch-Politische Mitteilungen* 2 (1995): 87, 97–98.

46. Lemmer, *Manches,* 255, 271.

47. BAK, NL 18, 164a, 77, Albers to Kaiser, January 23, 1946.

48. BAK, NL 18, 164a, 159, Deutz to Kaiser, January 13, 1946.

49. BAK, NL 18, 164a, 158, Kaiser to Deutz, August 19, 1945.

50. BAK, Zsg. 1-17/1 (26), Lensing, speech (Bochum, September 2, 1945).

51. HAStK, 1193, 205, 1, Schwering to Köhler, April 17, 1961.

52. With the exception of the Saxon CDUD, which would use the longer version into the 1950s, the abbreviation CDU would largely replace CDUD in the Soviet Zone by 1947. See Sonja Zeidler, "Zwischen Anpassung und Selbstbehauptung: Die Ost-CDU und ihre Sprache in den Jahren, 1945–1957," *Historisch-Politische Mitteilungen* 6 (1999): 141.

53. Werner Conze, *Jakob Kaiser*, 21.

54. Wieck, *Entstehung*, 75.

55. BAK, NL 114, 27, 224, Hermes to Friedensburg, September 12, 1945.

56. Wettig, "Konflikt," 113–14.

57. Wilde, *SBZ-CDU*, 243–55.

58. ACDPStA, I-090-15/1, Hermes and Schreiber, eds., *Rundschreiben* (Berlin, December 20, 1945).

59. ACDPStA, I-182-7/01, B II.2, Horster to Lensing, October 15, 1945.

60. Michael Klein, "Der westdeutsche Protestantismus und die CDU bis zum Ende der Ära Adenauer," *Historisch Politische Mitteilungen* 14 (2007): 83.

61. Bösch, *Macht und Machtverlust*, 16. Cf. Pappi, "Konfessionell-religiöse Konfliktlinie," 283–87.

62. McLeod, *Religion*, 137.

63. Lothar Albertin, introduction to *Politischer Liberalismus in der britischen Besatzungszone, 1946–1948: Führungsorgane und Politik der FDP*, ed. Hans F. W. Gringmuth (Düsseldorf, 1995), xi–xii, xxii; Hein, *Zwischen liberaler Milieupartei*, 25–29, 121, 190–94.

64. Sabine Pfeffer, *Politischer Konservatismus in England und in der Bundesrepublik Deutschland nach 1945: Ein Vergleich konservativer Prinzipien* (Münster, 1989), 4.

65. Wolfgang Huber, "Protestantismus und Demokratie," in *Protestanten in der Demokratie: Positionen und Profil im Nachkriegsdeutschland*, ed. Wolfgang Huber (Munich, 1990), 26–27.

66. Rogers, *Politics after Hitler*, 51.

67. For one example of a CDU party's difficulties with Allied (in this case, British) approval of its membership, see BAK, NL 278, 142, Haley Major (Comd 226 Mil Gov Det), Political Activity—CDU (Siegen, February 22, 1946). The memorandum threatened that if two members were not "excluded from the party" by February 25, 1946, the Siegen CDU would lose its party authorization.

68. Michael Klein, *Westdeutscher Protestantismus*, 379; Reinhard Schmeer, "Die Evangelische Kirche im Rheinland und die CDU, 1945–1949," *Monatshefte für Evangelische Kirchengeschichte des Rheinlandes* 41 (1992): 316; Wolfgang Huber, "Protestantismus und Demokratie," 26–28; Johannes Kahle, *Evangelische Kirche und Demokratie: Der Einordnungsprozeß der Deutschen Evangelischen Kirche in das demokratische Funktionssystem der Nachkriegsära in den Westzonen* (Pfaffenweiler, 1988), 105.

69. Müller-Rolli, *Evangelische Schulpolitik*, 39.

70. Heitzer, *CDU*, 753.

71. Inacker, *Zwischen Transzendenz*, 207–25.

72. Pearson, "Pluralization," 280.

73. Harry Noormann, *Protestantismus und politisches Mandat, 1945–1949*, vol. 1, *Grundriß* (Gütersloh, 1985), 282; Werner Jochmann, "Evangelische Kirche und Politik in der Phase des Neubeginns, 1945–1950," in *Zeit nach 1945*, ed. Conzemius, Greschat, and Kocher, 202–3; Sammler, "Politische Strömungen," 238–40. Torsten Oppelland concurs but notes that Niemöller, Adenauer's leading critic, was Lutheran. See Torsten Oppelland, "Adenauers Kritiker aus dem Protestantismus," in *Adenauer und die Kirchen*, ed. von Hehl, 117.

74. Schmeer, "Evangelische Kirche," 339.

75. Pearson, "Pluralization," 279–80.

76. Friedrich Merzyn, ed., *Kundgebungen: Worte und Erklärungen der Evangelischen Kirche in Deutschland, 1945–1959* (Hanover, 1993), 4. On the resolutions' authenticity, see Schmeer, *Volkskirchliche Hoffnungen,* 38–40.

77. Morsey, "Prälaten," 241; Nowak, "Christentum," 49; Bösch, *Adenauer-CDU,* 36 n. 67, 46; Wieck, *Entstehung,* 117, 184; Heitzer, *CDU,* 699.

78. Mensing, "Adenauer," 51; Kahle, *Evangelische Kirche,* 108; Inacker, *Zwischen Transzendenz,* 306; Schmeer, *Volkskirchliche Hoffnungen,* 637.

79. BAK, NL 278, 139, Dietsch to Holzapfel, April 23, 1947; ACDPStA, III-002-058, Steup to Catholic Dean Bülten, November 3, 1945.

80. Dertinger to von der Gablentz, March 8, 1946, in Schmeer, *Volkskirchliche Hoffnung,* 316.

81. Heitzer, *CDU,* 699–700.

82. Martin, *Entstehung der CDU,* 91.

83. HAStK, 1193, 359, 6, Kannengießer, Zur Gründung der Chr. Dem. Union betr. Dr. Holzapfel (February 14, 1965).

84. HAStK, 1193, 417, 8.

85. HAStK, 1193, 417, 8. Cf. ACDPStA, I-182-004/01, B I.1; StBKAH, 08.54, 141, 238.

86. Bösch, *Adenauer-CDU,* 54.

87. HAStK, 1193, 417, 8. Cf. Wieck, *Entstehung,* 158.

88. John Farquharson, "The Consensus That Never Came: Hans Schlange-Schöningen and the CDU, 1945–9," *European History Quarterly* 19.3 (1989): 354–55.

89. BAK, NL 71, 21, 34–35, Schlange-Schöningen, *Rundbrief* (October 13, 1945).

90. Schlange-Schöningen had written Stegerwald as early as August 22, 1945 (although he was unable to dispatch the letter until September 15) about founding a "Protestant wing" to work with a reformed Zentrum. See ACDPStA, I-206-012/1, 1250–51, Schlange-Schöningen to Stegerwald, August 22, 1945 (revised September 14, 1945). Cf. Michael Klein, "Der westdeutsche Protestantismus," 84.

91. BAK, NL 71, 21, 6, Niederschrift über die politische Versammlung (October 30, 1945); BAK, NL 71, 21, 14, Schlange-Schöningen to Schröter, November 20, 1945.

92. Bösch, *Adenauer-CDU,* 45.

93. Bösch, *Adenauer-CDU,* 37.

94. Christopher Beckmann, "Adolf Blomeyer (1900–1969): Landwirt und Bürgermeister, Nordrhein-Westfalen," in *In Verantwortung vor Gott und den Menschen: Christliche Demokraten im Parlamentarischen Rat 1948/49,* ed. Günter Buchstab and Hans-Otto Kleinmann (Freiburg i.B., 2008), 113–21.

95. HAStK, 1193, 417, 8.

96. BAK, NL 71, 21, 47, Schlange-Schöningen, "Christliche Demokratie" (November 24, 1945).

97. StBKAH, 08.57, 159–61, Adenauer to Schlange-Schöningen, January 29, 1946.

98. ACDPStA, I-182-6/3, B II.1.3, Bericht über die Zusammenkunft des vorläufigen Vorstandes der Christlich-demokratischen Partei (Hamm, October 9, 1945).

99. BAK, NL 278, 138, Biermann to Holzapfel, March 25, 1946.

100. HStAD, RWN 119, 1, 48–51, Schmidt to Adenauer, March 9, 1946.

101. ACDPStA, I-182-7/1, CDP Ortsgruppe Meschede to Lensing, September 12, 1945.

102. BAK, NL 278, 142, Wenning to Holzapfel, July 3, 1946. Cf. BAK, NL 278, 142, Düsenberg to Holzapfel, January 25, 1946.

103. BAK, NL 278, 138, Loentz to Holzapfel, August 14, 1946.

104. Egen, "Entstehung," 33.

105. HAStK, 1187, 46, Vorläufige Vorstand der C-D Union Essen, flyer (Essen, n.d.).

106. Jakob Kaiser, "Deutschlands geschichtliche Aufgaben" (Berlin, February 13, 1946), in *Der Soziale Staat: Reden und Gedanken, Wege in die Neue Zeit* 2, 7; emphasis added.

107. For the example of Otto Rippel, see Michael Klein, *Westdeutscher Protestantismus,* 118 n. 125. On Theodor Steltzer's early sympathy for Nazism, see Pöpping, *Abendland,* 161–64.

108. Johannes Albers, "Die Aufgabe der Christlich Demokratischen Union im Leben des deutschen Volkes," *Schriftenreihe der Christlich Demokratischen Union des Rheinlandes* 2 (n.d.), 2. Cf. ACDPStA, I-182-4/03, "Was will die Christlich-Soziale Volkspartei?"

109. The significant number of former DNVP members in the CDU was evident already in 1947–50 in the composition of the CDU's North Rhine-Westphalian Landtag faction. See Ludwig Gruber, *Die CDU-Landtagsfraktion in Nordrhein-Westfalen, 1946–1980: Eine parlamentshistorische Untersuchung* (Düsseldorf, 1988), 71.

110. Schmeer, *Volkskirchliche Hoffnungen,* 449; Winfried Becker, *CDU und CSU,* 74.

111. Adam Stegerwald, "Wohin gehen wir?" (Würzburg, November 5, 1945), 65–66.

112. Jeffrey Herf, *Divided Memory: The Nazi Past in the Two Germanys* (Cambridge, 1997), 217.

113. Christopher Beckmann, "Lambert Lensing," 174–81.

114. BAK, ZSg. 1-17/1 (26), Lensing, speech (Bochum, September 2, 1945).

115. Rainer Salzmann, ed., *Die CDU/CSU im Frankfurter Wirtschaftsrat: Protokolle der Unionsfraktion, 1947–1949* (Düsseldorf, 1988), xxii n. 67.

116. Denazification proceedings against Beyerle concluded in 1947 that, although he had been a paying member of, among other Nazi organizations, the Allgemeine SS from 1934 to 1936, Beyerle had also proven his opposition to Nazism in speeches and publications that had occasioned the confiscation of his private papers, the arrest of his two sons, and a ten-day period of detention. See ACDPStA, I-056-022, Gross, "Spruchkammer Zentralgeschäftsstelle, Beglaubigte Abschrift" (Stuttgart, July 25, 1947).

117. Schroeder, *Katholizismus,* 294 n. 53.

118. Weitzel, *Vom Chaos zur Demokratie,* 201.

119. For the debate between Noel Cary and Ellen Lovell Evans on Stegerwald's role during the Nazi years, see Cary, "Political Catholicism and the Reform of the German Party System, 1900–1957" (Ph.D. diss., University of California, Berkeley, 1988), 584–99 and Cary, *Path,* 160–63.

120. Bösch, *Adenauer-CDU,* 31.

121. BAK, NL 18, 129, 200–202, Schlange-Schöningen, *Rundbrief* (Lütjenburg, October 31, 1945).

122. Allan Borup, *Demokratisierungsprozesse in der Nachkriegszeit: Die CDU in*

Schleswig-Holstein und die Integration demokratieskeptischer Wähler, trans. Detlef Siegfried (Bielefeld, 2010).

123. ACDPStA, I-182-8/02, B III.1, Engel to Kannengießer, March 28, 1946.

124. Dieter Fricke, Werner Fritsch, Herbert Gottwald, Siegfried Schmidt, and Manfred Weissbecker, eds., *Lexikon zur Parteiengeschichte: Die bürgerlichen und kleinbürgerlichen Parteien und Verbände in Deutschland (1789–1945),* vol. 2, *Deutsche Liga für Völkerbund—Gesamtverband der Christlichen Gewerkschaften Deutschlands* (Cologne, 1984), 476–86.

125. BAK, NL 18, 136, 289–300, Kaiser, speech (November 6, 1946). Cf. ACDPStA, I-056-1, Beyerle, speech outline (May 18, 1947).

126. ACDPStA, I-009-4/2, Sevenich, Speakers' Guidelines for the British Zone (ca. summer 1946).

127. BAK, NL 005, 8, 144, Pünder, speech (Cologne, July 7, 1946).

128. ACDPStA, I-009-4/2, Sevenich, Speakers' Guidelines for the British Zone (ca. summer 1946).

129. BAK, Z6 1/226, 2–4, Adenauer to Schlange-Schöningen, December 22, 1946. Cf. StBKAH, 8/18, 87–88.

130. BAK, Z6 1/226, 5–8, Schlange-Schöningen to Griffin, May 1946.

131. ACDPStA, I-182-7/1, Gormann to Steup, July 3, 1946. The letter was marked "Confidential!"

132. ACDPStA, III-002-91, Marx to Bochum CDP, November 6, 1945.

133. BAK, NL 278, 142, CDU Kreis Soest, flyer (September 1946).

134. ACDPStA, I-090-15/1, Bericht über die Sitzung der CDP (Frankfurt a.M., October 31, 1945); Hein, *Zwischen liberaler Milieupartei,* 179.

135. Walter Dirks, "Die Zweite Republik: Zum Ziel und zum Weg der deutschen Demokratie," *Frankfurter Hefte: Zeitschrift für Kultur und Politik* 1.1 (April 1946): 23.

136. HAStK, 1187, 41, Christlich-Demokratische Union oder Zentrumspartei? (ca. August 1946).

137. ACDPStA, I-155-30/1, Dovifat, speech (January 1946).

138. ACDPStA, I-90-15/1, Nebgen, speech (November 10, 1945).

139. BAK, NL 5, 476, 220–21, Lemmer, speech (July 7, 1946).

140. ACDPStA, I-208-4/1, Lemmer, speech (Berlin, June 16, 1946).

141. ACDPStA, I-071-2/5, Kaufmann, speech (n.d.); emphasis added.

142. Hans Süssmuth, *Kleine Geschichte der CDU-Frauen-Union: Erfolge und Rückschläge, 1948–1990* (Baden-Baden, 1990).

143. HAStK, 1187, 21; HAStK, 1187, 1. Cf. Julg, *Démocratie chrétienne,* 220.

144. IZG, ED 160; Moeller, *Protecting Motherhood,* 64.

145. Ingrid Langer, "Maria Meyer-Sevenich, geb. Sevenich, CDU (1907–1970)," in *Alibi-Frauen? Hessische Poltikerinnen,* vol. 1, *In den Vorparlamenten, 1946–1950,* ed. Ingrid Langer (Frankfurt a.M., 1994), 129–66.

146. Sevenich generally hyphenated her last name after her July 1947 marriage to Dr. Werner Meyer, who was elected in May 1947 as the head of Lower Saxony's Christian Democratic Young Union.

147. HAStK, 1193, 124, von Brentano to Schwering, September 29, 1964.

148. ACDPStA, I-182-9/2, Kannengießer to Barlage, August 5, 1946; ACDPStA, I-182-10/1, Ballhausen to Sevenich, July 9, 1946; ACDPStA, I-155-30/2, von der Ga-

blentz Bericht über die Reise nach Frankfurt/Main, Darmstadt, Marburg (September 21–October 8, 1945); ACDPStA, I-105-45, DI/2, Binder to Sevenich, October 16, 1946.

149. BAK, NL 278, 335, CDU Herford, *Rundschreiben* 1 (n.d.).

150. BAK, NL 18, 129, 348–50, Aktennotiz betreffend Reise Herrn Hummel nach dem Westen; ACDPStA, I-208-5, André to the American Military Government (Stuttgart, November 5, 1946).

151. Gurland, *CDU/CSU,* 42 n. 99.

152. ACDPStA, I-247-4/1, Erklärung der Jungen Union (Detmold, November 12, 1946); BAK NL 278, 313, Sevenich to Junge Union, November 29, 1946.

153. For two of many examples, see BAK, NL 278, 313, Sevenich to Holzapfel, March 3, 1947; BAK, NL 278, 313, Sevenich to Adenauer, October 28, 1946.

154. ACDPStA, I-182-9/02, B III.5, Sevenich to the Headquarters of the British Occupying Authorities (October 19, 1946); ACDPStA, I-009-4/4, CDU-Pressedienst (December 7, 1947). In an interview, Adenauer made clear that Sevenich's hunger strike was not endorsed by the CDU, although he later praised her. See ACDPStA, VII-004-13/3, *Südost Kurier* (November 9, 1946); ACDPStA, I-182-9/02, B III.5, Adenauer, speech (Lippstadt, December 17, 1946). Others in the party more clearly supported her protest. See HStAD, RWN 119, 2, 207, Schmidt to Sevenich, January 16, 1947; ACDPStA, I-182-9/02, Kannengießer to Sevenich, December 9, 1946.

155. ACDPStA, I-182-8/03, B III.2, Schreiber to Kannengießer, November 28, 1945; ACDPStA, I-182-8/03, B III.2, Kannengießer to Schreiber, November 29, 1945; ACDPStA, I-182-8/03, B III.2, Kannengießer to Lensing, December 7, 1945; HAStK, 1187, 36/4, Hermes, *Rundschreiben* (November 21, 1945); BAK, NL 18, 129, 206, Dertiger, *Rundschreiben* (on behalf of Hermes) (November 24, 1945).

156. Schwering described how "after only a few sentences, Maria Sevenich put the assembly under her spell until she left the rostrum an hour and a half later to frenzied applause." Leo Schwering, *Frühgeschichte,* 152–56, quote on 152. Cf. NA, OMGUS (Hesse), RG 260, 471, An die Militaerregierung z. Hd. Herrn Oberstleutnant Sheehan.

157. BAK, NL 18, 129, 207, Nebgen to Hermes, December 12, 1945. Cf. ACDPStA, I-182-8/03, B. III.2, Kannengießer to Lensing, December 7, 1945.

158. ACDPStA, I-182-8/03, B III.2, Kannengießer to Lensing, December 7, 1945.

159. Karl Zimmermann, "Erste Reichstagung der Christlich Demokratischen Union," in *Schriftenreihe der Christlich Demokratischen Union des Rheinlandes* 5 (Cologne, 1945), 5.

160. Werner Conze, *Jakob Kaiser,* 42.

161. Hermes's speech was read by two professors who circumvented the Soviet travel ban with the aid of British military officials. See Alexander Fischer, "Andreas Hermes," 17. In January 1946, the British also transported to their zone the chief editor of the CDU paper *Neue Zeit* after he came into conflict with Soviet authorities. See NA, OMGUS, RG 260, 1, AG 000.1, Colonel T. F. Bogart to Deputy Military Governor (January 24, 1946).

162. Benz, *Potsdam 1945,* 141. The same conditions had applied to the SPD conference outside of Hanover in October, which the Allies also allowed to take place.

163. Zimmermann, "Erste Reichstagung," 4–7; Leo Schwering, *Frühgeschichte,* 173.

164. Alexander Fischer, "Andreas Hermes," 19.

165. Toni Diederich, "Adenauer als Kölner Oberbürgermeister von Mai bis Oktober

1945," in *Konrad Adenauer: Oberbürgermeister von Köln: Festgabe der Stadt Köln zum 100. Geburtstag ihres Ehrenbürgers am 5. Januar 1976,* ed. Hugo Stehkämper (Cologne, 1976), 525–28.

166. Schwarz, *Konrad Adenauer: A German Politician,* 1:320–27.

167. StBKAH, 08.09/1, 6, Mönnig to Adenauer, May 15, 1945; StBKAH, 08.05, 54–56, Schwering and Scharmitzel to Adenauer, July 16, 1945; BAK, NL 18, 89, 1, Kaiser to Adenauer, August 19, 1945; BAK, NL 18, 89, 2, Adenauer to Kaiser, August 30, 1945; StBKAH, 08.05, 21b, Schwering to Adenauer, August 30, 1945; StBKAH, 08.05, 66, Schwering to Adenauer, August 30, 1945; StBKAH, 08.05, 27, Schwering to Adenauer, September 4, 1945; StBKAH, 08.05, 28, Adenauer to Schwering, September 7, 1945; StBKAH, 08.05, 13, Pfad to Adenauer, September 5, 1945; StBKAH, 08.05, 14, Adenauer to Pfad, September 8, 1945; StBKAH, 08.05, 9, Adenauer to Hamacher, September 14, 1945; HAStK, 1193, 286,4, Teusch to Schwering, May 6, 1963; StBKAH, 08.05, 1, Adenauer to Boden, August 16, 1945; StBKAH, 08.05, 2, Adenauer to Boden, August 18, 1945; StBKAH, 08.05, 4, Adenauer to van Eyck, September 25, 1945. In late summer 1945, Adenauer invited Siemer to his home to discuss the CDU program. Adenauer later visited the Walberberg monastery but was unable to see Siemer. See Siemer, *Aufzeichnungen,* 161–62. Siemer and Adenauer nevertheless remained in contact. See StBKAH, 08.09, 65, Siemer to Adenauer, September 14, 1945.

168. Adenauer to Schwering, October 16, 1945, in *Briefe 1945–1947,* 127.

169. The story of Adenauer's ascension to power has been told in many places, among them Marie-Luise Recker, *Konrad Adenauer, 1876–1967: Parteipolitiker, Bundeskanzler, Europäischer Staatsmann* (Pforzheim, 2001); Rudolf Morsey, "Konrad Adenauer und der Weg zur Bundesrepublik Deutschland, 1946–1949," in *Rhöndorfer Gespräche,* vol. 3, *Konrad Adenauer und die Gründung der Bundesrepublik Deutschland,* ed. Rudolf Morsey (Stuttgart, 1979); Arentz, "Anfänge," 133–35. For the documentation, see HAStK, 1193, 412, 16; StBKAH, 08.54, 266–67, Adenauer to Albers, Teusch, Franken, von Gumppenberg, Arnold, Strunk, and Rott, January 6, 1946; ACDPStA, I-182-8/03, B III.2, Kannengießer to Schreiber, January 11, 1945; StBKAH, 08.54, 265, Christlich Demokratische Union des Rheinlandes, Niederschrift über die Sitzung des Landesvorstands (Düsseldorf, January 21, 1946); StBKAH, 08.57, 216, Adenauer to Hermes, January 25, 1946; ACDPStA, I-182-1/3, Kannengießer to Schreiber, January 26, 1946; ACDPStA, I-182-1/3, Kannengießer to Hermes, January 26, 1946; ACDPStA, I-182-008/03, B III.2, Kannengießer to Steup, January 30, 1946; ACDPStA, I-182-008/02, B III.1, Hermes to Kannengießer, January 31, 1946; HAStK, 1193, 99, 1, Schwering to Albers, February 6, 1946; ACDPStA, I-182-010/3, Steup to Kannengießer, February 7, 1946; BAK, NL 18, 44, 481–82, Rott to Kaiser, February 14, 1946; HAStK, 1193, 218, Lensing to Schwering, February 22, 1963; ACDPStA, I-182-10/3, Kannengießer to Lensing, February 21, 1946.

170. Rudolf Morsey, "Der Beginn der 'Gleichschaltung' in Preussen: Adenauers Haltung in der Sitzung des 'Dreimännerkollegiums' am 6. Februar 1933," *Vierteljahrshefte für Zeitgeschichte* 11 (1963): 85–97; Konrad Adenauer, "Konrad Adenauer als Präsident des Preussischen Staatsrates," in *Konrad Adenauer,* ed. Stehkämper, 355–404; Stehkämper, "Protest, Opposition, und Widerstand," 113–50.

171. Schwarz, *Konrad Adenauer: A German Politician,* 1:235–38.

172. On the political ties of the Maria Laach abbey to conservative Catholics and the

Nazis, see Marcel Albert, *Die Benediktinerabtei Maria Laach und der Nationalsozialismus* (Paderborn, 2004); Pöpping, *Abendland,* 166–82; Ute Schmidt, "Linkskatholische Positionen nach 1945 zu Katholizismus und Kirche im NS-Staat," in *Sozial- und Linkskatholizismus: Erinnerung—Orientierung—Befreiung,* ed. Heiner Ludwig and Wolfgang Schroeder (Frankfurt a.M., 1990), 139–40. Adenauer knew the head of the abbey, Ildefons Herwegen, from the Apostel Gymnasium in Cologne. See Walter Först, *In Köln: Kleine Stadtgeschichte im 20. Jahrhundert,* vol. 1, *1918–1936* (Düsseldorf, 1982), 114.

173. Elmar Müller, *Widerstand,* 145.

174. Schwarz, *Konrad Adenauer: A German Politician,* 1:283.

CHAPTER 4

1. BAK, ZSg. 1-17/1 (9). Karl Zimmermann, "Treuebekenntnis ehemaliger christlicher Gewerkschaftler zur CDP," *Christlich Demokratische Partei des Rheinlandes* 4.45 (Cologne, November 15, 1945).

2. Helmut König, *Die Zukunft der Vergangenheit: Der Nationalsozialismus im politischen Bewusstsein der Bundesrepublik* (Frankfurt a.M., 2003), 19–24. Cf. Anselm Doering-Manteuffel, "Die 'Frommen' und die 'Linken' vor der Wiederherstellung des bürgerlichen Staats: Integrationsprobleme und Interkonfessionalismus in der frühen CDU," in *Christentum und politische Verantwortung,* ed. Jochen-Christoph Kaiser and Doering-Manteuffel, 91.

3. Maria Mitchell, "Materialism and Secularism: CDU Politicians and National Socialism, 1945–1949," *Journal of Modern History* 67.2 (1995): 278–308.

4. Quoted in Dorothee Buchhaas and Herbert Kühr, "Von der Volkskirche zur Volkspartei—Ein analytisches Stenogramm zum Wandel der CDU im rheinischen Ruhrgebiet," in *Vom Milieu zur Volkspartei: Funktionen und Wandlungen der Parteien im kommunalen und regionalen Bereich,* ed. Herbert Kühr (Königstein, 1979), 159.

5. Adenauer to Schmitz, June 18, 1945, in *Briefe über Deutschland,* 16–17; Adenauer to Heile, February 14, 1946, in *Briefe, 1945–1947,* 159–61; Ulrich von Hehl, introduction to *Adenauer und die Kirchen,* ed. von Hehl, 25.

6. Michael L. Hughes, "'Through No Fault of Our Own': West Germans Remember Their War Losses," *German History* 18.2 (2000): 193–213; Robert G. Moeller, *War Stories: The Search for a Usable Past in the Federal Republic of Germany* (Berkeley, 2001).

7. Damian van Melis, "'Ganz Deutschland war ein einziges großes Konzentrationslager': Die katholische Kirche und die Frage der deutschen Kollektivschuld," in *Vergangenheitsbewältigung: Modelle der politischen und sozialen Integration in der bundesdeutschen Nachkriegsgeschichte,* ed. Gary S. Schaal and Andras Wöll (Baden-Baden, 1997), 129–46.

8. Christoph Kösters, "Kirche und Glaube an der 'Heimatfront,'" in *Kirchen im Krieg: Europa, 1939–1945,* ed. Karl-Joseph Hummel and Christoph Kösters (Paderborn, 2007), 390–91.

9. BAK, NL 278, 139, CDU, Kreis Detmold, "Aufruf!" (ca. spring 1946).

10. Michael Klein, "Der westdeutsche Protestantismus," 87; Günter Buchstab,

"Konrad Adenauer: Wertgrundlagen und Politikverständnis," in *Zum Ideologieproblem in der Geschichte: Herbert Hömig zum 65. Geburtstag,* ed. Erik Gieseking (Lauf an der Pegnitz, 2006), 279–94.

11. Hermann Lübbe, *Säkularisierung: Geschichte eines ideenpolitischen Begriffs* (Freiburg, 1965), 112.

12. BAK, Z5/12a, PRSB, September 1, 1948.

13. Lydia Bendel-Maidl and Rainer Bendel, "Schlaglichter auf den Umgang der deutschen Bischöfe mit der nationalsozialistichen Vergangenheit," in *Die Katholische Schuld? Katholizismus im Dritten Reich—Zwischen Arrangement und Widerstand,* ed. Rainer Bendel, 2nd ed. (Münster, 2004), 247.

14. ACDPStA, I-293-1/3, Elfes, speech (M. Gladbach, September 25, 1946). Cf. Stephen Brockmann, "Germany as Occident at the Zero Hour," *German Studies Review* 25.3 (2002): 489.

15. For a selection of the numerous examples of such statements by both CDU and church leaders, see BAK, ZSg. 1-17/1 (4), Pfad, speech (November 18, 1945), 6; ACDPStA, I-182-6, B II.1.1, Lensing, speech (Bochum, September 2, 1945); ACDPStA, I-208-3/1, Ersing, speech (Stuttgart, January 13, 1946); Sevenich, speech (Wiesbaden, March 11, 1946), 10; ACDPStA, I-105-45/2, Maria Sevenich, "Neue Wege in der Politik," in *Schriftenreihe "Neue Politik" Stuttgart* 1 (Württemberg, October 1946), 10–11; ACDPStA, I-208-3/1, Hermes, speech (Stuttgart, January 13, 1946); BAK, NL 391, 14, Christlich-Soziale Volkspartei, "Deutsches Volk!" (Stuttgart, December 1945); ACDPStA, I-208-5, André, speech (n.d.); BAK, NL 391, 13, Simpfendörfer, speech (Stuttgart, November 10, 1945); *GvG* (October 22, 1945), 1238–39; *DdB* (December 25, 1945), 59. Cf. Foschepoth, "Deutschen Reaktion," 152; Barbara Marshall, "German Attitudes to British Military Government, 1945–1947," *Journal of Contemporary History* 15.4 (1980): 655–84.

16. George L. Mosse, *Toward the Final Solution: A History of European Racism,* 2nd ed. (Madison, 1985), 106, 116, 131, 149.

17. Blaschke, *Katholizismus und Antisemitismus,* 49–50, 54; Tal, *Christians and Jews,* 96–98; Michael Burleigh and Wolfgang Wippermann, *The Racial State: Germany, 1933–1945* (Cambridge, 1991), 36; Baranowski, *Sanctity,* 71, 102, 169.

18. Herzog, *Sex after Fascism,* 26; Bergen, *Twisted Cross,* 32, 161.

19. Kauders, "Catholics," 476; John Connelly, "Catholic Racism and Its Opponents," *Journal of Modern History* 79.4 (2007): 813–47.

20. Frank Stern, *Im Anfang war Auschwitz: Antisemitismus und Philosemitismus im deutschen Nachkrieg* (Gerlingen, 1991), 14.

21. The few references would include HAStK, 1187, 40, brochure (January 1946); BAK NL 174, 50, CDU, *Vertrauliche Mitteilungen* 2.46 (Siegburg, April 26, 1946), 4; BAK, NL 391, 13, Bausch, speech (December 15, 1945); ACDPStA, I-208-4/1, Lemmer, speech (Berlin, June 16, 1946); ACDPStA, I-059-2/3, Christlich-Soziale Volkspartei, flyer (December 1945). Cf. Leo Schwering, *Frühgeschichte,* 161; Kauders, "Catholics," 469.

22. ACDPStA, I-206-16/4, Stegerwald to Ew. Herrn Geistl. Rat Rüdemann, August 2, 1945.

23. Eike Wolgast, *Die Wahrnehmung des Dritten Reiches in der unmittelbaren Nachkriegszeit (1945/46)* (Heidelberg, 2001), 68–70.

24. NA, OMGUS (Hesse), RG 260, 471, party program (Frankfurt a.m., November 1945).

25. BAK, NL 5, 476, Adenauer, speech (Cologne, March 24, 1946). Adenauer referred to Jews as "influential" (*maßgebend*) in big business. Cf. BAK, NL 278, 335, Wilhelm Lindner, ed., CDU Evangelische Verbindungsstelle, *Rundbrief* (May 1946); BAK, NL 278, 313, Freiherr Senfft von Pilsach, *Rundbrief* "Sammelantwort" (March 27, 1946); ACDPStA, I-155-2/3, von der Gablentz, speech (Berlin-Frohnau, May 11, 1945). Cf. Karin Walter, *Neubeginn—Nationalsozialismus—Widerstand: Die politisch-theoretische Diskussion der Neuordnung in CDU und SPD, 1945–1948* (Bonn, 1987), 86.

26. BAK, Kl. Erw. 855, 14, "Warum Christlich? Warum Union?" *Neue Zeit* 1.2 (July 24, 1945).

27. BAK, ZSg. 1-19/4 (1950), *Politisches Jahrbuch—CDU/CSU—1950,* 188. Cf. Wilde, *SBZ-CDU,* 512.

28. BAK, NL 278, 239, CDUD, Sondermaterial (Berlin, n.d.), 3/I.

29. Ulrich Steiner joined the Nazi Party in 1931. Because Steiner's father had converted to Christianity from Judaism, Steiner was categorized in 1933 as a "Mischling 1. Klasse," expelled from the party, and forced to end his studies. In 1944, he was arrested with his mother; he survived the end of the war in a satellite camp of Buchenwald. In June 1946, Steiner was named deputy chair of the Süd-Württemberg CDU. Before 1933, Klaus Brauda had been a member of the DVP and DStP. Labeled a "non-Aryan Christian" by the Nazis, Brauda survived until 1945 with the help of friends. He had been baptized Protestant and became devout during his years of persecution; Föhse's description of him as a "Jude" is, therefore, inaccurate. See Ulrich Föhse, *Entstehung und Entwicklung der Christlich-Demokratischen Union in Wuppertal, 1945–1950* (Hausarbeit zur Ersten Staatsprüfung für das Lehramt an der Grund- und Hauptschule, Pädagogische Hochschule Rheinland, Abteilung Wuppertal, April 1970), 1–25.

30. Schmeer, *Volkskirchliche Hoffnungen,* 303–4. For example, Walter Strauß, a co-founder of the Berlin CDUD, was a Protestant convert from Judaism.

31. Bösch, *Adenauer-CDU,* 350.

32. Greschat, "'Rechristianisierung,'" 6.

33. Michael Phayer, "The German Catholic Church after the Holocaust," *Holocaust and Genocide Studies* 10.2 (1996): 154.

34. Suzanne Brown-Fleming, *The Holocaust and Catholic Conscience: Cardinal Aloisius Muench and the Guilt Question in Germany* (Notre Dame, 2006).

35. For the construction of von Galen's image as a resister, see Griech-Polelle, *Bishop von Galen,* 136–64.

36. *GvG* (January 21, 1946), 1279.

37. *GvG* (February 17, 1946), 1300.

38. *GvG* (October 22, 1945), 1238. See also Ludwig Volk, ed., *Akten Kardinal Michael v. Faulhabers, 1917–1945,* vol. 2, *1935–1945* (Mainz, 1978) (June 28, 1945), 1082; Volk, *Akten Kardinal Michael v. Faulhabers* (June 18, 1945), 1072; Volk, *Akten Kardinal Michael v. Faulhabers* (June 28, 1945), 1083; *DdB* (June 28, 1945), 31; *GvG* (October 7, 1945), 1233; *GvG* (October 19, 1945), 1235; *DdB* (June 29, 1945), 37.

39. Frank M. Buscher and Michael Phayer, "German Catholic Bishops and the Holocaust, 1940–1952," *German Studies Review* 11.3 (1988): 470–73. For a recently dis-

covered document presumably drafted for the Pope by Archbishop Jaeger of Paderborn that suggests a more self-critical stance on the part of the West German bishops, see Ulrich Helbach, "'Es hätte unserer Kirche und unserem Volk mehr gedient, wenn wir weniger geschwiegen hätten . . .'—Die 'Schuldfrage' im Frühjahr 1945 im Lichte eines neuen Quellenfundes: Eingabe der westdeutschen Bischöfe an Papst Pius XII," in *Rheinisch—Kölnisch—Katholisch: Beiträge zur Kirchen- und Landesgeschichte sowie zur Geschichte des Buch- und Bibliothekswesens der Rheinlande: Festschrift für Heinz Finger zum 60. Geburtstag,* ed. Siegfried Schmidt (Cologne, 2008), 341–72. Cf. Ulrich Helbach, ed., *Akten Deutscher Bischöfe seit 1945: Westzonen, 1945–1947* (Paderborn, 2008). On Berlin bishop Konrad Graf von Preysing's critique of the church's role in the Third Reich, see Bendel-Maidl and Bendel, "Schlaglichter," 245–51.

40. Karin Walter, *Neubeginn,* 64–65. Cf. Repgen, "Erfahrung," 138, 142, 151–53.

41. Merzyn, *Kundgebungen,* 14.

42. Martin Greschat, introduction to *Im Zeichen der Schuld: 40 Jahre Stuttgarter Schuldbekenntnis: eine Dokumentation,* ed. Martin Greschat (Neukirchen-Vluyn, 1985), 19, 33.

43. Merzyn, *Kundgebungen,* 6, 9, 12, 15, 18–19.

44. Gerhard Besier and Gerhard Sauter, *Wie Christen ihre Schuld bekennen: Die Stuttgarter Erklärung 1945* (Göttingen, 1985); Besier, "Zwischen Neuanfang und Restauration," 728.

45. Hockenos, *Church Divided,* 42–63, 121–22.

46. BAK, NL 18, 129, 200–202, Schlange-Schöningen, *Rundbrief* (Lütjenburg, October 31, 1945).

47. BAK, NL 71, 21, 6, Schlange-Schöningen, speech (Plönstadtheide, October 30, 1945).

48. See, among others, Adam Stegerwald, "Wohin gehen wir?" (Würzburg, November 5, 1945), 63; StBKAH, 08.54, 281, Arnold, speech (Düsseldorf, November 24, 1945); ACDPStA, I-208-3/1, Hermes, speech (Stuttgart, January 13, 1946); Hermes, speech (Berlin-Schöneberg, April 11, 1948); ACDPStA, I-155-2/3, von der Gablentz, speech (Frohnau, August 12, 1945); ACDPStA, I-056-1, Bausch, speech (Fellbach, October 13, 1946); ACDPStA, I-028-1/1, Krone, speech (Berlin, May 7, 1948); BAK, NL 391, 13, André, speech (Stuttgart, January 13, 1946); BAK, NL 278, 139, "Generalpardon für die Jugend? Bewährung in der Krisis—Feste Grundlagen der Zukunft," *Niedersächsische Rundschau: Wochenschrift der Christlich-Demokratischen Union, Landesverband Hannover* 1.4 (Hanover, June 7, 1946); Johannes Albers, "Die Aufgabe der Christlich Demokratischen Union im Leben des deutschen Volkes," *Schriftenreihe der Christlich Demokratischen Union des Rheinlandes* 2 (Cologne, 1945), 3.

49. Carl Klinkhammer, "Die deutschen Katholiken und die Schuldfrage," *Neues Abendland* 1 (1946): 12–16, in *Nachkriegsdeutschland: 1945–1949,* ed. Peter Bucher (Darmstadt, 1990), 214–21.

50. Nevertheless, Dirks, like many leading interwar Catholics, referred to Judaism as a "race." See Connelly, "Catholic Racism," 818 n. 23. Cf. Barbro Eberan, *Luther? Friedrich "der Große?" Wagner? Nietzsche? . . . ? . . . ? Wer war an Hitler schuld? Die Debatte um die Schuldfrage, 1945–1949,* 2nd ed. (Munich, 1985), 171; Moeller, *War Stories,* 4; Ute Schmidt, "Linkskatholische Positionen," 130–47.

51. Eugen Kogon, "Kirchliche Kundgebungen von politischer Bedeutung," *Frankfurter Hefte* 2.7 (1947): 633–38. Cf. Karen Riechert, "Umgang," 41.

52. Kaiser, speech (Berlin, June 16, 1946), in *Nachkriegsdeutschland,* ed. Bucher, 182, 190. More typical was Peter Altmeier, who suggested that denazification in the Palatinate resembled a "political persecution of Christians." See Altmeier, speech (Koblenz, December 6, 1946), in *Peter Altmeier: Reden, 1946–1951,* ed. Karl Martin Graß and Franz-Josef Heyen (Boppard a.R, 1979), 14.

53. Hans Meiser, "Der Nationalsozialismus und seine Bewältigung im Spiegel der Lizenzpresse der Britischen Besatzungszone von 1946–1949" (Ph.D. diss., Universität Osnabrück, 1980), 272.

54. StBKAH, 07.01, 145, Adenauer to Pastor Custodis, February 23, 1946. Cf. Repgen, "Erfahrung," 157–60.

55. Karin Walter, *Neubeginn,* 39; Martin Greschat, "Kontinuität und Diskontinuität im deutschen Protestantismus nach 1945," *Monatshefte für Evangelische Kirchengeschichte des Rheinlandes* 41 (1992): 270–72.

56. Volk, *Akten Kardinal Michael v. Faulhabers* (June 28, 1945), 1082.

57. GvG (January 25, 1946), 1285. Cf. *DdB* (June 21, 1945), 17; *DdB* (September 21, 1945), 51; *DdB* (February 8, 1946), 87–89.

58. BAK, Z5/59. PRSB, December 9, 1948; *DdB* (June 21, 1945), 54. Cf. *DdB* (August 23, 1945), 41; *DdB* (September 21, 1945), 48; *GvG* (October 7, 1945), 1232.

59. NA, OMGUS (Hesse), RG 260, 471, CDU flyer (Sachsenhausen, ca. March 1946). Von Arnim's statement was reproduced in an advertisement for a speech by Erich Köhler, deputy chair of the Gross-Hessen CDU, in the Sachsenhausen district of Frankfurt a.M., on March 17, 1946. Von Arnim was co-organizer of the Berlin CDUD and *Oberkonsistorialpräsident* of the Altpreußische Union (the unified Prussian Protestant Church).

60. BAK, NL 391, 12, Bausch, Bestätigung (December 10, 1948) for Baron Wilhelm von Hahn, whom Bausch knew through Moral Re-Armament. Bausch had made the same claim in a certificate for *Oberregierungsrat* Ernst Lauer (November 30, 1946) and on behalf of his sister-in-law, who belonged to the CSVD (December 5, 1946).

61. Kaiser, speech (Berlin, June 16, 1946), in *Nachkriegsdeutschland,* ed. Bucher, 181. Cf. BAK, NL 18, 129, 167, Kaiser, speech (Berlin, June 22, 1945); Sevenich, speech (Wiesbaden, March 11, 1946), 15.

62. BAK, NL 278, 139, "Rückblick und Ausblick," *Niedersächsische Rundschau: Wochenschrift der Christlich-Demokratischen Union, Landesverband Hannover* 1.3 (Hanover, June 1, 1946).

63. Karl Zimmermann, "Das politisch-soziale Weltbild des christlichen Arbeiters" (Krefeld, August 8, 1946), 5.

64. Marcus Holz, "Christliche Weltanschauung," 135.

65. Bergen, *Twisted Cross,* 12.

66. Kannengießer, "Entscheidung," 5–6.

67. ACDPStA, I-056-1, Christlich-Soziale Union flyer (Heidelberg, November 29, 1945). Cf. Lill, "Über die Anfänge der CDU," 166; Morsey, "Zwischen Verwaltung."

68. ACDPStA, I-182-7/1, CDP Program (Bockum-Hövel, November 1945).

69. ACDPStA, I-182-4/03, "Was will die Christlich-Soziale Volkspartei?"

70. ACDPStA, I-90-15/1, Nebgen, speech (November 10, 1945).

71. BAK, NL 5, 476, 230–32, Pünder, speech (July 7, 1946).

72. BAK, ZSg. 1-17/1 (26), Lensing, speech (Bochum, September 2, 1945).

73. HAStK, 1193, 422, 1, Karl Zimmermann, ed., *Christlich Demokratische Partei des Rheinlandes Rundbrief* 1.45 (Cologne, October 23, 1945).

74. BAK, ZSg. 1-17/1 (5), Cillien, speech (Hanover, November 18, 1945), 1–2. Cf. StBKAH, 07.11, Peter Lütsches, "Ein offenes Wort an alle!" (October 1946); BAK, ZSg. 1-20/1 (11), "Christliche Politik?" *Neue Zeit* (September 6, 1946); Augustin Rösch, *Kampf gegen den Nationalsozialismus,* ed. Roman Bleistein (Frankfurt a.M., 1985), 279.

75. *DGG* (August 3, 1948), 555. Even decades later, in an address celebrating the thirtieth anniversary of the founding of the Rhenish CDU, Otto Schmidt located the CDU's origins in the shared persecution of Christians under National Socialism. See Otto Schmidt, "Anspruch und Antwort: Gedanken zur Geschichte der Christlich Demokratischen Union Rheinland," in *Festvortrag gehalten am 5. September 1975 zur Erinnerung an die Gründung der rheinischen CDU vor 30 Jahren in Köln* (Cologne, 1975), 9.

76. StBKAH, 08.54, 275–76, Lehr, speech (Düsseldorf, November 24, 1945).

77. BAK, NL 18, 129, 53, Steltzer, speech (Berlin, June 17, 1945).

78. Walter Dirks, "Die geistige Aufgabe des deutschen Katholizismus," *Frankfurter Hefte: Zeitschrift für Kultur und Politik* 1.2 (1946): 45.

79. BAK, NL 391, 13, Simpfendörfer, speech (Stuttgart, November 10, 1945).

80. Heinz Joachim Held, "Ökumene in der Nachkriegszeit," in *Kontinuität und Neubeginn,* ed. Hey and van Norden, 287–316.

81. Griech-Polelle, *Bishop von Galen,* 79–93; Jürgen Kampmann, "Bischof von Galen und die evangelischen Christen," in *Streitfall Galen: Clemens August Graf von Galen under Nationalsozialismus: Studien und Dokumente,* ed. Joachim Kuropka, 2nd ed. (Münster, 2007), 79–94.

82. Martin Niemöller even debated converting to Catholicism during his years of imprisonment. See Axel Schildt, "Ökumene wider den Liberalismus: Zum politischen Engagement konservativer protestantischer Theologen im Umkreis der Abendländischen Akademie nach dem Zweiten Weltkrieg," in *Katholiken und Protestanten,* ed. Sauer, 190–94. See also Annelise Thimme, ed., *Friedrich Thimme 1868–1938: Ein politischer Historiker, Publizist, und Schriftsteller in seinen Briefen* (Boppard a.R., 1994), 386–87.

83. Moyn, "First Historian," 67.

84. NA, OMGUS (Hesse), RG 260, 471, CDU flyer (Sachsenhausen, ca. March 1946).

85. David M. Thompson, "Ecumenicism," in *The Cambridge History of Christianity: World Christianities c. 1914–c. 2000,* ed. Hugh McLeod (Cambridge, 2006), 50–70; Daniel Gorman, "Ecumenical Internationalism: Willoughby Dickinson, the League of Nations, and the World Alliance for Promoting International Friendship through the Churches," *Journal of Contemporary History* 45 (2010): 57–58; Robert A. Krieg, "Joseph Lortz and Max Metzger on Ecumenism and Hitler," in *In God's Hands: Essays in Honour of Michael A. Fahey,* ed. Michael Andrew Fahey, Jaroslav Z. Skira, and Michael S. Attridge (Leuven, 2006), 89–108. On the World Council of Churches, see Armin

Boyens, "Der Ökumenische Rat der Kirchen im Zweiten Weltkreig," in *Kirchen im Krieg,* ed. Hummel and Kösters, 47–66; Andreas Lindt, *Das Zeitalter des Totalitarismus: Politische Heilslehren und ökumenischer Aufbruch* (Stuttgart, 1981), 31–32, 40–49.

86. Held, "Ökumene," 287–316.

87. Riechert, "Umgang," 22.

88. Kösters, *Caritas,* 93; Gauly, *Kirche und Politik,* 78–97; Hürten, "Beobachtungen," 205; van Melis, "Katholische Episkopat," 42–69.

89. NA, OMGUS, RG 260, AG 1948, 325, AG 000.1–AG 000.5. This station was established in Bamberg in 1948.

90. Walter Dirks, "Evangelisch-katholisches Gespräch," *Frankfurter Hefte: Zeitschrift für Kultur und Politik* 2.1 (1947): 13–14.

91. Gauly, *Kirche und Politik,* 75–76; Thomas Fandel, "Konfessionalismus und Nationalsozialismus," in *Konfessionen im Konflikt: Deutschland zwischen 1800 und 1970: Ein zweites konfessionelles Zeitalter,* ed. Olaf Blaschke (Göttingen, 2002), 299–334.

92. Andrew Chandler, "Catholicism and Protestantism in the Second World War in Europe," in *Cambridge History,* ed. McLeod, 283.

93. Dirks, "Geistige Aufgabe," 45.

94. ACDPStA, I-90-15/1, Nebgen, speech (November 10, 1945); BAK, NL 278, 239, CDUD, Sondermaterial (Berlin, n.d.), 6/I; Maria Sevenich, "Unser Gesicht: Abhandlung über Christlichen und Marxistischen Sozialismus," *Politik aus Christlicher Verantwortung* 1 (Bad Godesberg, December 14–16, 1945), 2; BAK, NL 391, 13, Bausch, speech (Plochingen, December 15, 1945); BAK, NL 114, 27, 313, Friedensburg to von der Gablentz, November 1, 1945; *DGG* (August 28–29, 1948), 655; Zonenausschuss der CDU in der britischen Zone, ed., "Was ist—Was will die CDU? Gedanken zur politischen Arbeit der Christlich-Demokratischen Union" (1948), 6.

95. Adenauer, "Rede," 6.

96. Martin Greschat, "Konfessionelle Spannungen in der Ära Adenauer," in *Katholiken und Protestanten,* ed. Sauer, 28.

97. Blessing, "'Deutschland,'" 67, 95.

98. ACDPStA, I-056-19, Beyerle, speech (Ulm, February 24, 1946).

99. Adenauer to Heile, March 29, 1946, in *Briefe, 1945–1947,* 195–96.

100. Wolfgang Lück, *Das Ende der Nachkriegszeit: Eine Untersuchung zur Funktion des Begriffs der Säkularisierung in der "Kirchentheorie" Westdeutschlands, 1945–1965* (Bonn, 1976), 165.

101. Damian van Melis, "'Strengthened and Purified through Ordeal by Fire': Ecclesiastical Triumphalism in the Ruins of Europe," in *Life after Death: Approaches to a Cultural and Social History of Europe During the 1940s and 1950s,* ed. Richard Bessel and Dirk Schumann (Cambridge, 2003), 231–41.

102. Greschat, "'Rechristianisierung,'" 3–4.

103. Besier, "Politische Rolle," 29.

104. A striking number of CDU/CSU politicians, including Karl Arnold, Konrad Adenauer, Helene Weber, and Paul Bausch, were involved in MRA efforts to facilitate postwar reconciliation. Adenauer, for example, visited Caux in 1948. For the organization's American evangelical roots and context, see David Sack, *Moral Re-Armament: The Reinventions of an American Religious Movement* (New York, 2009). On the role of

MRA in France and West Germany after the war, see Edward Luttwack, "Franco-German Reconciliation: The Overlooked Role of the Moral Re-Armament Movement," in *Religion: The Mission Dimension in Statecraft,* ed. Douglas Johnston and Cynthia Sampson (New York, 1994), 37–57. For two of numerous references to Christian Democrats' support for MRA, see BAK, NL 391, 12, Bausch, Bestätigung (November 30, 1946); NA, OMGUS, RG 260, 186, 000.3.

105. NA, OMGUS (Hesse), RG 260, 471, CDU (Rödelheim, December 1945).

106. StBKAH, 08.54, 393–98, Ein Ruf zur Sammlung des deutschen Volkes: Vorläufiger Entwurf zu einem Programm der Christlichen Demokraten Deutschlands, Vorgelegt von den Christlichen Demokraten Köln im Juni 1945 (Cologne, June 1945).

107. StBKAH, 08.05, 77–78, Karl Arnold, Anton Betz, Maximilian Freiherr von Gumppenberg, eds., *Christliche Volkspartei Deutschlands vorbereitender Ausschuss,* "An die Bevölkerung Düsseldorfs!" (Düsseldorf, ca. August 1945).

108. StBKAH, 08.54, 399–403, Leitsätze der Christlich-Demokratischen Partei in Rheinland und Westfalen (Cologne, Bochum, Düsseldorf, September 1945).

109. Südwürttemberg-Hohenzollern CDU, program (June 23, 1946), in Ossip K. Flechtheim, ed., *Dokumente zur parteipolitischen Entwicklung in Deutschland seit 1945,* vol. 2, *Programmatik der deutschen Parteien* (Berlin, 1963), 47–48.

110. ACDPStA, I-206-12/1, 1250, Schlange-Schöningen to Stegerwald, August 22, 1945.

111. BAK, NL 278, 335, CDU Evangelische Verbindungsstelle, *Rundbrief* 2 (Herford, May 1946). Cf. Besier, "Politische Rolle," 29.

112. BAK, NL 391, 13, Bausch, speech (Plochingen, December 15, 1945).

113. ACDPStA, I-009-5/4, 13, Steiner, speech (Biberach, March 30, 1947).

114. BAK, NL 71, 21, 6, Niederschrift über die politische Versammlung (October 30, 1945).

115. Greschat, "'Rechristianisierung,'" 11.

116. The age structure of the CDU's faction in the North Rhine-Westphalian Landtag from 1947 to 1950 underscores the pattern evident in biographies of the early party's leaders: Only 6 percent of the party's delegates were under forty, while 70 percent were between forty and sixty and 24 percent were over sixty. See Gruber, *CDU-Landtagsfraktion,* 59.

117. Hans-Gerd Eward, *Die gescheiterte Republik: Idee und Programm einer "Zweiten Republik" in den Frankfurter Heften (1946–1950)* (Frankfurt a.M., 1988).

118. Werner Weidenfeld, *Konrad Adenauer und Europa: Die geistigen Grundlagen der westeuropäischen Integrationspolitik des ersten Bonner Bundeskanzlers* (Bonn, 1976), 44–46.

119. Mosse, *Toward the Final Solution,* 106, 116, 131, 149.

120. Wolfgang Altgeld, "Christentum, Revolution, Nation: Geschichtliche und Zeitgeschichtliche Auseinandersetzungen in der Formierung des deutschen Katholizismus," *Historisches Jahrbuch* 121 (2001): 503; Altgeld, *Katholizismus, Protestantismus, Judentum,* 164.

121. Hans-Peter Schwarz, ed., *Konrad Adenauer: Reden, 1917–1967: Eine Auswahl,* 45–46.

122. For two of many examples, see BAK, R43I/2658, 95, "Neun Jahre Zentrumspolitik: Leistung und Aufgabe," *Flugschriften der Deutschen Zentrumspartei* (1928):

15; BAK, R45II/62, Maximilian Pfeiffer, ed., "Zentrum und politische Neuordnung: Ein Programm," *Flugschriften der Deutschen Zentrumspartei* 2.12 (1918): 4, 30.

123. Lübbe, *Säkularisierung*, 26–34, 40–68, 74–77, 90, 106.

124. Pöpping, *Abendland*, 87; Vanessa Conze, *Europa*, 33.

125. Albrecht Langner, "Wirtschaftliche Ordnungsvorstellungen im deutschen Katholizismus, 1945–1963," in *Katholizismus, Wirtschaftsordnung, und Sozialpolitik, 1945–1963*, ed. Albrecht Langner (Paderborn, 1980), 79.

126. BAK, NL 391, 13, André, speech (Stuttgart, January 13, 1946); Adam Stegerwald, "Wo stehen wir?" (Würzburg, August 21, 1945), 9–10; HAStK, 1193, 421, 1–2, Bericht über die Gründungsversammlung der Christlich Demokratischen Partei des Rheinlandes am Sonntag (Cologne, September 2, 1945), 6; BAK, Kl. Erw. 640, 11, 22; Theodor Scharmitzel, "Die Christlich-Demokratische Union Deutschlands: Ihr Wesen und Wollen," *Schriftenreihe der Christlich-Demokratische Union Deutschlands, Landesverband Rheinland* 1 (Cologne, March 25, 1946): 4.

127. Ute Schmidt, "Linkskatholische Positionen," 146.

128. ACDPStA, I-90-15/1, Nebgen, speech (November 10, 1945); ACDPStA, I-105-45, DI/I, Tübingen CDU, outline for "Principles of our Social Program" (Tübingen, May 6, 1947). Cf. Klaus Epstein, *The Genesis of German Conservatism* (Princeton, 1966), 55–59; Lönne, *Politischer Katholizismus*, 49.

129. Scharmitzel, "Christlich-Demokratische Union Deutschlands," 9.

130. ACDPStA, I-028-1/1 Krone, radio address (*Nordwestdeutscher Rundfunk*, October 3, 1946).

131. ACDPStA, I-028-1/1, Krone, speech (Schöneberg, July 6, 1947).

132. Vera Bücker, *Die Schulddiskussion im deutschen Katholizismus nach 1945* (Bochum, 1989), 227–29.

133. ACDPStA, I-009-5/7, 5, CDU Landesverband Baden, "Vom Sinn und Wesen der Kultur," *Flugschriften der Union* (Heidelberg, February 9–10, 1946). Cf. ACDPStA, I-059-2/3, Grundsätzliches zum Programm der christlich-sozialen Volkspartei (Zentrale Schwäbisch Gmünd); BAK, NL 391, 13, André, speech (Stuttgart, January 13, 1946); Stegerwald, "Wo stehen wir?" 8–12.

134. Sevenich, "Unser Gesicht," 6.

135. Altgeld, *Katholizismus, Protestantismus, Judentum*, 75.

136. Alexander Schwan, "Humanismen und Christentum," in *Enzyklopädische Bibliothek in 30 Teilbänden: Christlicher Glaube in moderner Gesellschaft*, ed. Franz Böckle, Franz-Xaver Kaufmann, Karl Rahner, Bernhard Welte, and Robert Scherer (Basel, 1981), 19:52–54; Ulrich Matz, "Zum Einfluß des Christentums auf das politische Denken der Neuzeit," in *Geschichte*, ed. Rüther, 35–36.

137. ACDPStA, I-171-1/1, Emil Dovifat, "Liberalismus" (n.d.).

138. BAK, ZSg. 1-17/1 (8), Arnold, speech (Düsseldorf, November 24, 1945), 22.

139. Clemens, *Martin Spahn*, 120.

140. Zimmermann, "Das politisch-soziale Weltbild," 7.

141. ACDPStA, I-208-5, André, speech (n.d.).

142. Kaiser, speech (Berlin, June 16, 1946), in *Nachkriegsdeutschland*, ed. Bucher, 180.

143. ACDPStA, I-171-1/1, Dovifat, speech (n.d.).

144. Adenauer, "Rede," 5–6.

145. BAK, NL 391, 13, André, speech (Stuttgart, January 13, 1946).

146. Bücker, *Schulddiskussion,* 251; Eberan, *Luther?* 141.

147. ACDPStA, I-059-2/3, Grundsätzliches zum Programm der christlich-sozialen Volkspartei (Zentrale Schwäbisch Gmünd).

148. Maria Sevenich, "Die Christlich-Demokratische Union in der Not der Zeit" (Stuttgart, February 23, 1946), 16–17.

149. StBKAH, 08.54, 404, Programm der Christlich-Demokratischen Union der britischen Zone (Neheim-Hüsten, March 1, 1946).

150. Judith A. Dwyer, ed., *The New Dictionary of Catholic Social Thought* (Collegeville, 1994), 724–38. I am grateful to Paul Misner for this reference.

151. Karin Walter, *Neubeginn,* 58; Marcus Holz, "Christliche Weltanschauung," 18; Connelly, "Catholic Racism," 826–27.

152. StBKAH, 08.09/1, 152–53, Adenauer, speech (Bonn, April 7, 1946).

153. StBKAH, 08.54, 393–98, Ein Ruf zur Sammlung des deutschen Volkes: Vorläufiger Entwurf zu einem Programm der Christlichen Demokraten Deutschlands, Vorgelegt von den Christlichen Demokraten Köln im Juni 1945 (Cologne, June 1945).

154. ACDPStA, I-208-5, André, speech (Gerabronn, Langenburg, ca. November 1946).

155. Sigmund, "Catholic Tradition," 541.

156. StBKAH, 08.54, 281, Arnold, speech (Düsseldorf, November 24, 1945).

157. StBKAH, 08.54, 404, Programm der Christlich-Demokratischen Union der britischen Zone (Neheim-Hüsten, March 1, 1946).

158. ACDPStA, I-90-15/1, Nebgen, speech (November 10, 1945).

159. Stegerwald, "Wo stehen wir?" 24.

160. Artur Ketterer, ed., "Das innere Gesetz der 'Union' (CDU) und seine politischen Folgerungen," *Politik aus christlicher Verantwortung* 2 (1946): 7–8. Cf. NA, OMGUS (Württemberg-Baden), RG 260, 311.

161. StBKAH, 08.54, 281, Arnold, speech (Düsseldorf, November 24, 1945).

162. Focke, *Sozialismus,* 30–31; Ruppert, "Deutsche Zentrumspartei," 76.

163. StBKAH, 08.09/1, 151–52, Adenauer, speech (Bonn, April 7, 1946). Cf. HAStK, 1187, 41, Teusch, speech (Ehrenfeld, September 22, 1946).

164. Hans-Peter Schwarz, "Konrad Adenauer—Abendländer oder Europäer? Zur Bedeutung des Christlichen in seiner auswärtigen Politik," in *Adenauer und die Kirchen,* ed. von Hehl, 106.

165. Vanessa Conze, *Europa,* 20–35, 59–60, 119–20; Doris von der Brelie-Lewien, *Katholische Zeitschriften in den Westzonen, 1945–1949: Ein Beitrag zur politischen Kultur der Nachkriegszeit* (Göttingen, 1986), 139–40; Richard Faber, *Abendland: Ein "politischer Kampfbegriff"* (Hildesheim, 1979), 12, 16–30, 133; Paul Kluke, "Nationalsozialistische Europaideologie," *Vierteljahreshefte für Zeitgeschichte* 3.3 (1955): 240–75; Axel Schildt, "Eine Ideologie im Kalten Krieg—Ambivalenzen der abendländischen Gedankenwelt im ersten Jahrzehnt nach dem Zweiten Weltkrieg," in *Von der Kriegskultur zur Friedenskultur? Zum Mentalitätswandel in Deutschland seit 1945,* ed. Thomas Kühne (Hamburg, 2000), 50–51.

166. Schwarz, "Abendländer oder Europäer?" 106. Pöpping argues unpersuasively that the importance resistance movements such as July 20, 1944 accorded the Abendland rendered it ideologically unproblematic after the war. See Pöpping, *Abendland,* 268.

167. Vanessa Conze, *Europa,* 124, 148–50.

168. Dieter Felbick, *Schlagwörter der Nachkriegszeit, 1945–1949* (Berlin, 2003), 105.

169. ACDPStA, I-182-4/01, B I.1, Dr. Fr. Wagner, ed., program outline (Gelsenkirchen, July 21, 1945).

170. ACDPStA, I-105-45, Württemberg/Hohenzollern CDU, program (April 26, 1948).

171. Maria Sevenich, "Das Werden der neuen deutschen Demokratie!" (Wiesbaden, March 11, 1946)," 11.

172. ACDPStA, I-182-10/01, Zimmermann, speech (Rhineland, September 9, 1945), in *Rundschreiben* 5.45 (Cologne, October 27, 1945).

173. ACDPStA, I-206-12/1, 1252, Hermes, speech (ca. Berlin, July 22, 1945).

174. HAStK, 1187, 424, Maria Meyer-Sevenich, "Die Union als Gottesarbeit im Dienst am Kreuz," *Schriftenreihe der Christlich Demokratischen Union des Rheinlandes* 4 (Cologne, December 1945), 8.

175. Walter Dirks, "Das Abendland und der Sozialismus," *Frankfurter Hefte* 1.3 (1946): 68.

176. StBKAH, 08.54, 393–98, Ein Ruf zur Sammlung des deutschen Volkes: Vorläufiger Entwurf zu einem Programm der Christlichen Demokraten Deutschlands, Vorgelegt von den Christlichen Demokraten Köln im Juni 1945 (Cologne, June 1945); Zimmermann, "Erste Reichstagung," 11.

177. ACDPStA, I-182-10/01, Zimmermann, speech (Rhineland, September 9, 1945), in *Rundschreiben* 5.45 (Cologne, October 27, 1945). Cf. Württemberg-Hohenzollern CDU, program (January 6, 1946), in *Dokumente,* ed. Flechtheim, 46.

178. ACDPStA, I-206-20, "Programm der Christlich-Sozialen Union für Würzburg-Stadt und -Land," in Stegerwald, "Wohin gehen wir?" 65.

179. ACDPStA, I-208-5, André, radio address (May 17, 1946).

180. Alexander, "Church and Society," 347.

181. Faber, *Abendland,* 172. For one notable exception to this trend, see Pöpping, *Abendland,* 124–30.

182. Schildt, "Ideologie," 56.

183. Eberan, *Luther?* 24.

184. Bücker, *Schulddiskussion,* 265.

185. NA, OMGUS (Württemberg-Baden), RG 260, 707, program (Mosbach, December 12, 1945); Eugen Kogon, "Das Dritte Reich und die preußisch-deutsche Geschichte," *Frankfurter Hefte: Zeitschrift für Kultur und Politik* 1.3 (1946), 54; Bücker, *Schulddiskussion,* 307; von der Brelie-Lewien, *Katholische Zeitschriften,* 136.

186. James J. Sheehan, *German History 1770–1866* (Oxford, 1989), 561; Lutz, *Zwischen Habsburg und Preußen,* 127.

187. Ross, *Beleaguered Tower,* 9.

188. Sperber, *Popular Catholicism,* 10–11, 55. Cf. James M. Brophy, *Popular Culture and the Public Sphere in the Rhineland* (Cambridge, 2007).

189. Gordon A. Craig, *Germany, 1866–1945* (Oxford, 1980), 14.

190. Vanessa Conze, *Europa,* 38.

191. Hömig, *Preussische Zentrum,* 67; Morsey, *Deutsche Zentrumspartei,* 115–17; Faber, *Abendland,* 178; Langhoff and Veltzke, "Im Westen viel Neues," 83.

192. Kogon, "Das Dritte Reich," 46.

193. StBKAH, 08.09/1, 152–53, Adenauer, speech (Bonn, April 7, 1946). See also ACDPStA, I-009-4/2, Adenauer, radio address (*Nordwestdeutscher Rundfunk,* March 6, 1946).

194. Adenauer to Schmitt, December 22, 1946, in *Briefe über Deutschland,* 59–60.

195. *PRSU* (September 28, 1948), 598.

196. Sevenich, "Werden," 3. Cf. Eberan, *Luther?* 130; Bücker, *Schulddiskussion,* 241.

197. Sevenich, "Unser Gesicht," 18.

198. Stegerwald, "Wo stehen wir?" 18–19. Bernhard Pfad echoed Stegerwald almost word for word. See BAK, NL 278, 139, Pfad, "Volk in Not: Marxismus ist Militarismus in Zivil—Christen denkt um!" (Duderstadt, n.d.), *Niedersächsische Rundschau: Wochenschrift der Christlich-Demokratischen Union, Landesverband Hannover* 1.3 (Hanover, June 1, 1946).

199. HAStK, 1187, 42, 162–63, Altmeier, speech (Koblenz, November 22, 1945).

200. Blessing, "'Deutschland,'" 16; Stegerwald, "Wo stehen wir?" 29.

201. BAK, NL 5, 476, Adenauer, speech (Cologne, March 24, 1946).

202. *PRSU* (November 9, 1948), 143–44. Adenauer amended this position later that month, suggesting that the CDU should not give up on the prospect of winning eastern votes were the Soviets to pull out. See *PRSU* (November 25, 1948), 201.

203. Adenauer to Schmitt, December 22, 1946, in *Briefe über Deutschland,* 59–60.

204. Adenauer to Scharnagl, February 7, 1946, in *Briefe 1945–1947,* 152–54; ACDP-StA, I-182-4/01, Hessen-Pfalz CDU, program.

205. BAK, NL 18, Adenauer, December 12, 1946, quoted in "Ein Neues Preußen?" *Die Zeit* (December 3, 1953).

206. BAK, NL 18, 56, 78, 80–81.

207. BAK, NL 278, 265, Lotz, speech (November 22, 1946).

208. HAStK, 1187, 42, 162–63, Altmeier, speech (Koblenz, November 22, 1945). Altmeier repeated this language two weeks later. See Altmeier, speech (Koblenz, December 6, 1946), in *Peter Altmeier,* ed. Grass and Heyen, 18.

209. Kogon, "Das Dritte Reich," 53.

210. Stegerwald, "Wohin gehen wir?" 52–53.

211. Kogon, "Das Dritte Reich," 49.

212. Eugen Kogon, "Gericht und Gewissen," *Frankfurter Hefte: Zeitschrift für Kultur und Politik* 1.1 (1946), 33.

213. Martin, *Entstehung der CDU,* 88.

214. Adenauer to van Cauwelaert, June 18, 1946, in *Briefe über Deutschland,* 51. Cf. ACDPStA, I-208-3/02, Stuttgart CDU, brochure (n.d.); ACDPStA, I-009-25/1, *Union/Dienst* 2.3 (1947).

215. BAK, NL 5, 476, Adenauer, speech (Cologne, March 24, 1946). Cf. BAK, NL 5, 48, Bayental-Martenburg CDU, Wählerversammlung (April 11, 1947). The electoral district Cologne-Aachen posted the country's lowest percentage of support for the NSDAP in March 1933—just over 30 percent. See Lill, "Über die Anfänge der CDU," 162–64.

216. Wolfram Kaiser, *Christian Democracy,* 215–17.

217. Gerhard Besier, "'Christliche Parteipolitik' und Konfession: Zur Entstehung des Evangelischen Arbeitskreises der CDU/CSU," *Kirchliche Zeitgeschichte* 3 (1990): 168.

218. Oppelland, "Der Evangelische Arbeitskreis," 109.

219. Egen, "Entstehung," 97–98; Michael Klein, "Der Westdeutsche Protestantismus," 93.

220. NA, OMGUS (Hesse), RG 260, 471, CDU flyer (Sachsenhausen, presumably March 1946).

221. Schlange-Schöningen, speech (November 27, 1947), in Helmut Stubbe-Da Luz, "Union der Christen—Splittergruppe—Integrationspartei: Wurzeln und Anfänge der Hamburger CDU bis Ende 1946" (Ph.D. diss., Universität Hamburg, 1989), 401.

222. *DGG* (August 3, 1948), 559, 569.

223. Marcus Holz, "Christliche Weltanschauung," 64; Lück, *Ende der Nachkriegszeit,* 53, 165; Vollnhals, "Evangelische Kirche," 145.

224. BAK, NL 391, 13, Simpfendörfer, speech (Stuttgart, November 10, 1945).

225. Otto Schmidt, "Christlicher Realismus—Ein Versuch zu sozialwirtchaftlicher Neuordnung," *Schriftenreihe der Christlich Demokratischen Union des Rheinlandes* 7 (Cologne, 1946): 4–6. Cf. Günther van Norden, "Der schwierige Neubeginn," in *Kontinuität und Neubeginn,* ed. Hey and van Norden, 18.

226. Otto Boelitz, "Erziehung und Schule im Christlich-Demokratischen Staat: Das Bildungsideal und das Schulprogramm der CDU," *Politik aus Christlicher Verantwortung* 7 (Recklinghausen, 1946), 7.

227. Moyn, "First Historian," 71.

228. StBKAH, 08.54, 273–74, Lehr, speech (Düsseldorf, November 24, 1945).

229. BAK, NL 5, 108, Wuppertal CDU, "Das neue Weltbild und die politischen Zielsetzungen" (Wuppertal, September 1946).

230. Nowak, "Christentum," 46.

231. Brockmann, "Germany"; Moyn, "First Historian," 63–64.

232. ACDPStA, I-056-3, Simpfendörfer, speech (n.d.).

233. StBKAH, 08.29, 92, von der Gablentz, speech (Berlin, June 1945).

234. HStAD, RWN 119, 2, 121, Aschmann to Schmidt, October 7, 1946; HStAD, RWN 119, 2, 122, Schmidt to Aschmann, October 16, 1946; HStAD, RWN 119, 2, 84, Lutze to Freund, September 3, 1946. Cf. Eberan, *Luther?* 117–19; Kogon, "Das Dritte Reich," 44.

235. ACDPStA, I-155-2/3, von der Gablentz, speech (Frohnau, August 12, 1945).

236. ACDPStA, I-155-3/2, von der Gablentz, speech (June 10, 1948).

237. BAK Z5/126, 1, 30, Theodor Steltzer, "Diskussionsbeitrag zum deutschen Verfassungsproblem" (n.d.).

238. Pöpping, *Abendland,* 159–61.

239. BAK, Z5/12b, PRSB, September 9, 1948.

240. Clemens Münster, "Grenzen des Abendlandes," *Frankfurter Hefte: Zeitschrift für Kultur und Politik* 2.8 (1947): 777. Cf. Vanessa Conze, *Europa,* 39.

241. Kogon, "Das Dritte Reich," 48, 52. When Catholics did refer to Slavs, they subordinated them to "Romans and Teutons." See Dirks, "Abendland," 68. According to Clemens Münster, Slavs belonged to the "indogermanischen Völkerfamilie." See Münster, "Grenzen," 783. Cf. Voßkamp, *Katholische Kirche,* 227.

242. Schwarz also included in this list Judaism and the Enlightenment. See Schwarz, "Abendländer oder Europäer?" 106.

243. Schildt, "Ideologie," 54; Pöpping, *Abendland,* 248–64; Brockmann, "Germany."

244. ACDPStA, I-155-3/2, von der Gablentz, speech (June 10, 1948).

245. BAK, NL 5, 108, Wuppertal CDU, "Das neue Weltbild und die politischen Zielsetzungen" (Wuppertal, September 1946); BAK, NL 5, 114, Wuppertal CDU, "Ein neuer Anfang im politischen Leben Deutschlands? Ein Wort zum Nachdenken für junge Menschen und solche, die sich die Aufgeschlossenheit und Spannkraft eines jungen Herzens bewahrt haben" (Wuppertal, September 1946); BAK, NL 278, 335, Friedrich Holzapfel, ed., Herford CDU, *Rundschreiben* 5 (December 7, 1946); BAK, NL 278, 335, Herford CDU, brochure (June 1948); BAK, NL 71, 21, 20, Christlich-Demokratische Aufbaupartei, flyer (January 30, 1946); BAK, NL 391, 13, Bausch, speech (Plochingen, December 15, 1945); ACDPStA, I-009-5/4, 13, Steiner, speech (Biberach, March 30, 1947). Cf. Langner, "Wirtschaftliche Ordnungsvorstellungen," 86; Ingrid Laurien, *Politisch-kulturelle Zeitschriften in den Westzonen, 1945–1949: Ein Beitrag zur politischen Kultur der Nachkriegszeit* (Frankfurt a.M., 1991), 194–97; Faber, *Abendland,* 115–17; Heinz Hürten, "Der Topos vom christlichen Abendland in Literatur und Publizistik nach den beiden Weltkriegen," in *Katholizismus, nationaler Gedanke, und Europa seit 1800,* ed. Albrecht Langner (Paderborn, 1985), 149.

246. Thomas Ruster, *Die verlorene Nützlichkeit der Religion: Katholizismus und Moderne in der Weimarer Republik,* 2nd ed. (Paderborn, 1997), 144.

247. Tim Geiger, *Atlantiker gegen Gaullisten: Außenpolitischer Konflikt und innerparteilicher Machtkampf in der CDU/CSU, 1958–1969* (Munich, 2008), 52.

248. Axel Schildt, *Zwischen Abendland und Amerika: Studien zur westdeutschen Ideenlandschaft der 50er Jahre* (Munich, 1999), 21–61; Schildt, "Ökumene," 187–205. Cf. von der Brelie-Lewien, *Katholische Zeitschriften,* 152; Karin Walter, *Neubeginn,* 114; Faber, *Abendland,* 115–17; Hürten, "Topos."

249. Felbick, *Schlagwörter,* 105.

250. Schildt, *Zwischen Abendland und Amerika,* 36–37. Cf. Dorothee Buchhaas, *Die Volkspartei: Programmatische Entwicklung der CDU, 1950–1973* (Düsseldorf, 1981), 210–16.

251. Walter Dirks, "Das christliche Abendland: Sein Nachwirken in den Konfessionen der Bundesrepublik," in *Christlicher Glaube und Ideologie,* ed. Klaus von Bismarck and Walter Dirks (Stuttgart, 1964), 121.

252. BAK, NL 5, 108, Wuppertal CDU, "Das neue Weltbild und die politischen Zielsetzungen" (Wuppertal, September 1946).

253. Quoted in Schmeer, *Volkskirchliche Hoffnungen,* 226–27. Cf. Marcus Holz, "Christliche Weltanschauung," 66; van Norden, "Schwierige Neubeginn," 18.

254. BAK, NL 5, 112, Wuppertal CDU, "Ein neuer Anfang im politischen Leben Deutschlands? Ein Wort zum Nachdenken für junge Menschen und solche, die sich die Aufgeschlossenheit und Spannkraft eines jungen Herzens bewahrt haben" (Wuppertal, September 1946).

255. Otto Schmidt, "Christlicher Realismus," 4–6.

CHAPTER 5

1. Michael Klein, "Der westdeutsche Protestantismus," 83.

2. BAK, NL 5, 476, Adenauer, speech (Cologne, March 24, 1946).

3. BAK, NL 278, 139, Hamburger Geschäftsstelle der CDU, "Die Grundsätze der Christlich-Demokratischen Union" (Hamburg, February 1946).

4. ACDPStA, I-182-4/01, CDU Hessen-Pfalz, Grundsätze and Arbeitsprogramm (Gekürzte Fassung).

5. Bösch, *Adenauer-CDU*, 43.

6. ACDPStA, I-059-2/3, Grundsätzliches zum Programm der christlich-sozialen Volkspartei (Zentrale Schwäbisch-Gmünd).

7. HStAD, RWN 119, 3, 119, Muster L7: "Unser Warnung, unser Ruf," in Hans Schreiber, ed., *Rundschreiben* 18 (Cologne, March 25, 1947).

8. HStAD, RWN 119, 3, 110, Rhenish CDU, "Christlich oder was sonst?" in Schreiber, *Rundschreiben.*

9. BAK, NL 18 , 420, 16, "Deutsch, Christlich, Demokratisch, Sozial: Adam Stegerwalds politisches Vermächtnis," *Der Tag: Unabhängige Zeitung für Deutschland* (December 5, 1948).

10. Mariatte C. Denman, "Visualizing the Nation: Madonnas and Mourning Mothers in Postwar Germany," in *Gender and Germanness: Cultural Productions of a Nation,* ed. Patricia Herminghouse and Magda Hueller (Providence, 1997); Elizabeth Heineman, "The Hour of the Woman: Memories of Germany's 'Crisis Years' and West German National Identity," *American Historical Review* 101.2 (1996): 354–95.

11. Lukas Rölli-Alkemper, *Familie im Wiederaufbau: Katholizismus und bürgerliches Familienideal in der Bundesrepublik Deutschland, 1945–1965* (Paderborn, 2000), 59–65.

12. Herzog, *Sex after Fascism,* 10, 43.

13. BAK, NL 5, 475, 118–26, Frankfurter Leitsätze (Frankfurt a.M., September 1945).

14. BAK, NL 5, 475, 120, Pünder, speech (Frankfurt a.M., 1945).

15. BAK, NL 5, 475, 118–26, Frankfurter Leitsäzte (Frankfurt a.M., September 1945). Cf. Herzog, *Sex after Fascism,* 62.

16. ACDPStA, I-90-15/1, Elfriede Nebgen, "Christlich-Demokratische Union und Frauenprobleme der Gegenwart" (December 1945).

17. "Frauen im Männerstaat," in *Frauen Gestern und Heute: Wege in die Neue Zeit* 3 (Berlin, 1946): 42–44.

18. ACDPStA, I-90-15/1, Elfriede Nebgen, "Christlich-Demokratische Union und Frauenprobleme der Gegenwart" (December 1945).

19. Christine Teusch, "Die christliche Frau im politischen Zeitgeschehen," *Schriftenreihe der Christlich-Demokratischen Union Westfalen-Lippe* 2 (September 1946): 5.

20. Gelnhausen CDU, "An Dich, Deutsche Frau und Mutter" (Gelnhausen, February 1946), in Heinrich Rüschenschmidt, "Die Entstehung der hessischen CDU, 1945/46: Lokale Gründungsvorgänge und Willensbildung im Landesverband" (Staatsexamen, Philipps-Universität Marburg, 1979), 6; Teusch, "Christliche Frau," 7; HAStK, 1193, 287.

21. HAStK, 1187, 41, "An alle Frauen!" (Dortmund, August 1946).

22. ACDPStA, I-009-5/7, 5.

23. Elizabeth D. Heineman, *What Difference Does a Husband Make? Women and Marital Status in Nazi and Postwar Germany* (Berkeley, 1999), 108–36.

24. NA, OMGUS, Manpower Division, RG 260, 93.

25. ACDPStA, I-448-2/6, Maria Dietz, speech (ca. 1947).

26. Plakat zur Kommunalwahl in Nordrhein-Westfalen am 15.9.1946, in *Politik und Plakat,* ed. Langguth, 53.

27. StBKAH, 08.54, 393–98, Ein Ruf zur Sammlung des deutschen Volkes: Vorläufiger Entwurf zu einem Programm der Christlichen Demokraten Deutschlands, Vorgelegt von den Christlichen Demokraten Köln im Juni 1945 (Cologne, June 1945); ACDPStA, I-208-3/2, Mannheim CDU, draft party program (Mannheim, n.d.); NA, OMGUS (Württemberg-Baden), RG 260, 707; BAK, NL 391, 13, Grundsätzliches zum Programm der christlich-sozialen Volkspartei (Christliche Union) (Stuttgart, October 1945).

28. HAStK, 1187, 41, "An alle Frauen!" (August 1946).

29. BAK, NL 5, 475, 118–26, Frankfurter Leitsätze (Frankfurt a.M., September 1945); HAStK, 1187, 496; HAStK, 1187, 41, "An alle Frauen!" (August 1946).

30. Zimmermann, "Das politisch-soziale Weltbild," 10. Cf. StBKAH, 08.54, 404–10, British Zone CDU, program (Neheim-Hüsten, March 1946). Cf. Gurland, *CDU/CSU,* 116; Theodor Scharmitzel, "Christliche Demokratie im neuen Deutschland," *Schriftenreihe der Christlich Demokratischen Union des Rheinlandes* 1 (Cologne, 1945): 492.

31. ACDPStA, I-194-1-9, CDU, "Ein Sinn, ein Weg, ein Ziel" (Düsseldorf, n.d.).

32. BAK, NL 5, 475, 118–26, Frankfurter Leitsäzte (Frankfurt a.M., September 1945).

33. ACDPStA, I-071-2/5, Kaufmann, speech (n.d.).

34. ACDPStA, I-331-1/1, Esther-Maria von Coelln, "Frau, Politik, und Friede," *Thueringer Tageblatt* (Weimar, March 22, 1947).

35. ACDPStA, I-152-1/3, Entschliessungsentwurf der Frauenarbeitsgemeinschaft zur 2. Jahrestagung der Union (Berlin, 1947). Cf. ACDPStA, I-016-5/2, radio address, "Abschnitt, Ehe, und Familie" (March 1947).

36. Teusch, "Christliche Frau," 7.

37. Maria Höhn, "Frau im Haus und Girl im *Spiegel:* Discourse on Women in the Interregnum Period of 1945–1949 and the Question of German Identity," *Central European History* 26.1 (1993): 57–90; Elizabeth D. Heineman, "Complete Families, Half Families, No Families at All: Female-Headed Households and the Reconstruction of the Family in the Early Federal Republic," *Central European History* 29.1 (1996): 19–60; Moeller, *Protecting Motherhood.*

38. Guenter Lewy, *The Catholic Church and Nazi Germany* (Boulder, 2000), 52; Müller-Rolli, *Evangelische Schulpolitik,* 109–11; Feldkampf, *Mitläufer,* 92, 102–11; Ian Kershaw, *Popular Opinion and Political Dissent in the Third Reich: Bavaria, 1933–1945* (Oxford, 2002); Joachim Kuropka, ed., *Zur Sache—Das Kreuz! Untersuchungen zur Geschichte des Konflikts um Kreuz und Lutherbild in den schulen Oldenburgs, zur Wirkungsgeschichte eines Massenprotests und zum Problem nationalsozialistischer Herrschaft in einer agrarisch-katholischen Region* (Vechta, 1986).

39. *DGG* (August 28–29, 1948), 653.

40. Franz Sonnenberger, "Der neue 'Kulturkampf': Die Gemeinschaftsschule und ihre historischen Voraussetzungen," in *Bayern in der NS-Zeit,* vol. 3, *Herrschaft und Gesellschaft im Konflikt,* ed. Martin Broszat, Elke Fröhlich, and Anton Grossmann (Munich, 1981), 236–37.

41. ACDPStA, I-028-1/1, Krone, radio address (*Nordwestdeutscher Rundfunk,* October 3, 1946).

42. Altmeier, speech (Koblenz, December 6, 1946), in *Peter Altmeier,* ed. Grass und Heyen, 16.

43. ACDPStA, I-208-5, André, radio address (May 17, 1946).

44. ACDPStA, I-208-5. André, radio address (June 29, 1946).

45. *DGG* (August 14–15, 1947), 413–14.

46. Müller-Rolli, *Evangelische Schulpolitik,* 50, 499–500, 634–37.

47. Ludwig Lemhöfer, "Die Katholiken in der Stunde Null: Restauration des Abendlandes oder radikaler Neubeginn?" in *Katholische Kirche und NS-Staat: Aus der Vergangenheit lernen?* ed. Monika Kringels-Kemen and Ludwig Lemhöfer, 3rd ed. (Frankfurt a.M., 1983), 108.

48. Martin, *Entstehung der CDU,* 224.

49. HAStK, 1193, 348, 4, Spiecker to Schwering, July 20, 1946. Cf. BAK, NL 278, 138, Dempwolf to Holzapfel, February 24, 1946.

50. StBKAH, 08.55, 395.

51. Typical here was Südwürttemberg-Hohenzollern CDU, program (June 23, 1946), in *Dokumente,* ed. Flechtheim, 47.

52. *DGG* (September 1945), 110.

53. ACDPStA, I-082-8/3, B III.2, Schwering to Lensing, October 1, 1945.

54. Zimmermann, "Erste Reichstagung," 11.

55. HStAD, RWN 119, 3, 120, Muster L7: "Unser Warnung, unser Ruf," in Schreiber, *Rundschreiben.*

56. Bösch, *Adenauer-CDU,* 129.

57. ACDPStA, I-208-3/2, Mannheim CDU, draft party program (Mannheim, n.d.).

58. ACDPStA, I-056-1, CDU Landesverband Württemberg and Landesverband Baden, flyer (November 1946).

59. ACDPStA, I-056-1, Christlich-Soziale Union, flyer (Heidelberg, November 29, 1945).

60. BAK, NL 5, 475, 118–26, Frankfurter Leitsäzte (Frankfurt a.M., September 1945). See also NA, OMGUS (Hesse), RG 260, 471, party program (Frankfurt a.M., November 1945).

61. Buchhaas, *Gesetzgebung im Wiederaufbau,* 84–86, 90.

62. Müller-Rolli, *Evangelische Schulpolitik,* 36–38, 107–8, 297–308, 369.

63. Buchhaas, *Gesetzgebung im Wiederaufbau,* 107.

64. Helmuth Pütz, *Innerparteiliche Willensbildung: Empirische Untersuchung zum bildungspolitischen Willensbildungsprozeß in der CDU* (Mainz, 1974), 57. Cf. Burkhard van Schewick, *Die katholische Kirche und die Entstehung der Verfassungen in Westdeutschland, 1945–1950* (Mainz, 1980), 47.

65. Friedrich Holzapfel, for example, supported confessionally segregated schools. See BAK, NL 278, 138, Holzapfel to Dempwolf, March 12, 1946.

66. ACDPStA, I-172-95/1-2, Wuppertal CDU, flyer (August 27, 1945).

67. Bösch, *Adenauer-CDU,* 129.

68. ACDPStA, I-090-15/1, Lemmer, speech (n.d.).

69. Weitzel, "Von der CSVP zur CDU," 55; Wieck, *Entstehung,* 66.

70. ACDPStA, I-206-012/1, 1250–51, Schlange-Schöningen to Stegerwald, August 22, 1945 (revised September 14, 1945).

71. StBKAH, 08.54, 276–77, Lehr, speech (Düsseldorf, November 24, 1945).

72. Buchhaas, *Gesetzgebung im Wiederaufbau,* 86, 105–8.

73. Bösch, *Adenauer-CDU,* 130; Müller-Rolli, *Evangelische Schulpolitik,* 347–83.

74. ACDPStA, I-208-3/2, Bausch to André, February 20, 1946.

75. Thomas Ellwein, *Klerikalismus in der deutschen Politik* (Munich, 1955), 117–18.

76. ACDPStA, I-009-5/7, 35, Vertraulich! v.M. Bericht Nr. 3 (Tübingen, February 22, March 22, 26, 1947).

77. Bösch, *Adenauer-CDU,* 131.

78. Indeed, in anticipation of the opportunity for reconstruction, many leading Germans had devised economic recovery plans during the Nazi years. See Elmar Müller, *Widerstand;* Christine Blumenberg-Lampe, ed., *Der Weg in die Soziale Marktwirtschaft: Referate, Protokolle, Gutachten der Arbeitsgemeinschaft Erwin von Beckerath, 1943–1947* (Stuttgart, 1986).

79. Rhineland-Palatinate politicians, for example, were largely uninvolved in the debate over Christian Socialism. See Martin, *Entstehung der CDU,* 268–69. Cf. Heitzer, *CDU,* 46 n. 46.

80. ACDPStA, I-194-1-9, Gockeln, speech, in *Auszüge aus Reden des Verbandsvorsitzenden Josef Gockeln* (Cologne, 1947).

81. ACDPStA, I-028-1/1, Krone, speech (Schöneberg, July 6, 1947).

82. StBKAH, 08.57, 178, Naegel, speech (Hanover, November 18, 1945).

83. Kannengießer, "Entscheidung," 7.

84. ACDPStA, I-182-4/01, B I.1, pamphlet, "Was ist die CDU" (n.d.).

85. StBKAH, 08.57, 178, Naegel, speech (Hanover, November 18, 1945).

86. ACDPStA, I-056-1, CDU Landesverband Württemberg and Landesverband Baden, flyer (November 1946).

87. StBKAH, 08.57, 178, Naegel, speech (Hanover, November 18, 1945). Cf. ACDPStA, I-009-5/4, 9, Heinrich von Brentano, ed., Christlich-Demokratische Union Deutsche Aufbau-Bewegung (Darmstadt, n.d.).

88. StBKAH, 08.54, 393–98, Ein Ruf zur Sammlung des deutschen Volkes.

89. StBKAH, 08.54, 283–84, Arnold, speech (Düsseldorf, November 24, 1945).

90. Zimmermann, "Erste Reichstagung," 8; StBKAH, 08.54, 283–84, Arnold, speech (Düsseldorf, November 24, 1945).

91. ACDPStA, I-009-5/1, 5, CDUD, party program (Berlin, June 26, 1945).

92. ACDPStA, I-090-15/1, Emil Dovifat, party program outline (ca. 1945).

93. Zimmermann, "Das politisch-soziale Weltbild," 8–9.

94. StBKAH, 08.57, 178, Naegel, speech (Hanover, November 18, 1945).

95. Bücker, *Schulddiskussion,* 309, 367–68.

96. BAK, ZSg. 1-20/1, "Christliche Politik?" *Neue Zeit* (September 6, 1946). Cf. Maria Sevenich, "Um Schuld und Not unserer Zeit: Realpolitische Erwägungen über Kollektiv- und Individualschuld und das christliche Menschenbild," *Politik aus christlicher Verantwortung* 2 (Recklinghausen, 1946), 22; Stegerwald, "Wo stehen wir?" 10–11.

97. ACDPStA, I-009-5/4, 9, von Brentano, Christlich-Demokratische Union Deutsche Aufbau-Bewegung.

98. ACDPStA, I-208-5, André, speech (n.d.).

99. Adenauer, "Rede," 8–9.

100. As Jeffrey Herf observes, Christian Democrats consistently referred to the Third Reich as "National *Socialism*" rather than Nazism to imply links between Hitler and

Marx, while Walter Ulbricht and Kurt Schumacher studiously avoided the term. See Herf, *Divided Memory,* 219.

101. Zimmermann, "Erste Reichstagung," 8; Arentz, "Anfänge," 127.

102. StBKAH, 08.57, 178, Naegel, speech (Hanover, November 18, 1945).

103. StBKAH, 08.57, 178, Naegel, speech (Hanover, November 18, 1945).

104. Kannengießer, "Entscheidung," 7. Cf. StBKAH, 08.57, 178.

105. Scharmitzel, "Wesen und Wollen," 18.

106. ACDPStA, I-182-4/03, flyer (North Rhine-Westphalia, September 1946).

107. Nicholls, *Freedom,* 264 n. 36. Nicholls suggests the French *dirigisme* is the best translation for *Lenkung.*

108. For a typical example, see Rhine-Hessen CDU, program (January 1947), in Weitzel, *Vom Chaos zur Demokratie,* 34–35.

109. ACDPStA, I-009-5/4, 11, Christlich-Demokratische Partei für Stadt und Kreis Wetzlar (Wetzlar, December 20, 1945).

110. Zimmermann, "Erste Reichstagung," 8.

111. Adenauer, "Rede," 8–9.

112. ACDPStA, I-105-45/2, Maria Sevenich, "Neue Wege in der Politik," *Schriftenreihe "Neue Politik" Stuttgart* 1 (Württemberg, October 1946), 18–19.

113. BAK, ZSg. 1-17/1 (3), Storch, speech (Hanover, November 18, 1945). Cf. BAK, NL 278, 139, Bernhard Pfad, "Volk in Not: Marxismus ist Militarismus in Zivil—Christen denkt um!" *Niedersächsische Rundschau: Wochenschrift der Christlich-Demokratischen Union, Landesverband Hannover* 1.3 (Hanover, June 1, 1946).

114. ACDPStA, I-182-4/01, Hessen-Pfalz CDU, Grundsätze and Arbeitsprogramm (Gekürzte Fassung). Cf. Albers, "Aufgabe," 5.

115. Karin Walter, *Neubeginn,* 103–4.

116. Adenauer, "Rede," 8–9.

117. Rhineland-Hesse-Nassau CDU, program (n.d.), in Weitzel, *Vom Chaos zur Demokratie,* 62–63.

118. Diethelm Prowe, "Economic Democracy in Post–World War II Germany: Corporatist Crisis Response, 1945–1948," *Journal of Modern History* 57.3 (1985): 455.

119. Von Plato and Leh, *"Unglaublicher Frühling,"* 40.

120. Focke, *Sozialismus,* 197; Langner, "Wirtschaftliche Ordnungsvorstellungen," 28–29.

121. Emmanuel Gerard and Gerd-Rainer Horn, introduction to *Left Catholicism: Catholics and Society in Western Europe at the Point of Liberation, 1943–1955,* ed. Gerd-Rainer Horn and Emmanuel Gerard (Leuven, 2001), 9.

122. Karl-Egon Lönne, "Katholizismus 1945: Zwischen gequälter Selbstbehauptung gegenüber dem Nationalsozialismus und Öffnung zur pluralistischen Gesellschaft," in *Ende des Dritten Reiches,* ed. Volkmann, 763–64. Cf. Oswald von Nell-Breuning, "Die politische Verwirklichung der christlichen Soziallehre," in *Wirtschaft und Gesellschaft heute,* vol. 3, *Zeitfragen, 1955–1959* (Freiburg i.B., 1960), 11–24.

123. Martin, *Entstehung der CDU,* 270.

124. Franz Graf von Galen, brother of the bishop of Münster, Clemens August Graf von Galen, quoted *Quadragesimo anno* to support his claim that Christian Socialism was an oxymoron. The teachings of the Catholic Church, Galen concluded, rendered it "impossible to be a good Catholic and a true socialist at the same time." See ACDPStA,

I-293-1/3, von Galen, open letter, September 11, 1946. A month earlier, von Galen cited Leo XIII's maxim that an unequal distribution of the gifts of earth's treasures was grounded in nature and therefore intended by God. See ACDPStA, I-293-1/3, von Galen to Hamacher, August 10, 1946.

125. That Catholic social teachings represented to many Catholic politicians more revered tradition or theoretical doctrine than practical economic program is suggested by Adenauer's review of a pamphlet written by the influential Jesuit priest, Oswald von Nell-Breuning. Forwarded to Adenauer by Cardinal Frings of Cologne, the pamphlet struck him as "speculative theories that in no way take into account the actual economic situation." Although he attended a gathering at the Dominican Walberberg monastery in early February 1946, von Nell-Breuning appears to have had little direct contact with CDU leaders before 1949. See StBKAH, 07.14, 87, Adenauer to Frings, April 27, 1947; cf. ACDPStA, I-182-7/1, Deist to Kannengießer, February 11, 1946.

126. If leading proponents of Christian Socialism were largely associated with the working class, they were also, with very few exceptions, male. Martin Conway, "Left Catholicism in Europe in the 1940s: Elements of an Interpretation," in *Left Catholicism,* ed. Horn and Gerard, 276.

127. StBKAH, 08.54, 393–98, Ein Ruf zur Sammlung des deutschen Volkes.

128. StBKAH, 08.54, 393–98, Ein Ruf zur Sammlung des deutschen Volkes.

129. Zimmermann, "Erste Reichstagung," 13.

130. Martin, *Entstehung der CDU,* 270.

131. ACDPStA, I-206-20, Programm der Christlich-Sozialen Union für Würzburg-Stadt und -Land, in Stegerwald, "Wohin gehen wir?" 68; ACDPStA, I-182-4/01, Hessen-Pfalz CDU, Grundsätze and Arbeitsprogramm (Gekürzte Fassung).

132. ACDPStA, I-343-4/1, Arndgen, speech (n.d.).

133. BAK, NL 391, 13, Grundsätzliches zum Programm der christlich-sozialen Volkspartei (Christliche Union) (Stuttgart, October 1945).

134. Lönne, "Katholizismus," 763–64.

135. Wilhelm Damberg, "Kritiker Adenauers aus dem Katholizismus," in *Adenauer und die Kirchen,* ed. von Hehl, 149. Although there is no evidence that other early Christian Democrats distinguished between the two terms for that or any other reason, some scholars do identify Socialism Based on Christian Responsibility more closely with the Frankfurt CDU. See Damian van Melis, "Europapolitik oder Abendlandideologie? Die Dominikanerzeitschrift Neue Ordnung in den ersten Jahrzehnten der BRD," in *Katholiken und Protestanten,* ed. Sauer, 177, 186; Horst-Albert Kukuck, "Etappen im Ringen um eine Wirtschaftskonzeption der CDU, 1945–1949," in *Politische Parteien auf dem Weg zur parlamentarischen Demokratie in Deutschland: Entwicklungslinie bis zur Gegenwart,* ed. Lothar Albertin and Werner Link (Düsseldorf, 1981), 241. Cf. Ute Schmidt, "Hitler," 81; Rotberg, *Zwischen Linkskatholizismus,* 111–12.

136. Lienkamp, "Socialism," 214–22; Walter Euchner, Helga Grebing, Franz-Josef Stegmann, Peter Langhorst, Traugott Jähnichen, and Norbert Friedrich, eds., *Geschichte der sozialen Ideen in Deutschland: Sozialismus—Katholische Soziallehre—Protestantische Sozialethik: Ein Handbuch,* 2nd ed. (Wiesbaden, 2005), 778.

137. Damberg, "Kritiker," 151.

138. Dirks, "Abendland," 76.

139. Leo Schwering, *Frühgeschichte,* 17.

140. Focke, *Sozialismus,* 245.

141. Doering-Manteuffel, "'Frommen,'" 93.

142. Gerald Ambrosius, *Die Durchsetzung der Sozialen Marktwirtschaft in West-deutschland, 1945–1949* (Stuttgart, 1977), 28.

143. BAK, NL 18, 129, 34.

144. Jakob Kaiser, "Deutschlands geschichtliche Aufgaben" (Berlin, February 13, 1946), *Der Soziale Staat: Reden und Gedanken, Wege in die Neue Zeit* 2, 9.

145. BAK, NL 18, 88, 24.

146. Jakob Kaiser, "Deutschlands geschichtliche Aufgaben," 8.

147. Jakob Kaiser, "Deutschlands geschichtliche Aufgaben," 17; Rainer Zitelmann, *Adenauers Gegner: Streiter für die Einheit* (Erlangen, 1991).

148. Doering-Manteuffel, "'Frommen,'" 92.

149. StBKAH, 08.57, 159–61, Adenauer to Schlange-Schöningen, January 29, 1946; Adenauer to Scharnagl, February 7, 1946, in *Briefe, 1945–1947,* 152–54.

150. Nicholls, *Freedom,* 117–19.

151. Schmeer, *Volkskirchliche Hoffnungen,* 110.

152. HStAD, RWN 119, 2, 297, Schmidt to Schütz, January 10, 1947. Cf. Ute Schmidt, "Christlich Demokratische Union," 499.

153. HStAD, RWN 119, 3, 200, Boelitz to Schmidt, May 16, 1947. See also Schmeer, "Evangelische Kirche," 300–337; Egen, "Entstehung," 21–29, 45; Wieck, *Entstehung,* 97–98.

154. HStAD, RWN 119, 3, 219, Marx to Schmidt, June 12, 1947; HAStK, 1193, 134, 2, Schwering to Schaeven, May 20, 1946. Cf. Schmeer, "Evangelische Kirche," 322.

155. For the voluminous correspondence between Adenauer and Schmidt, see HStAD, RWN 119, 1.

156. StBKAH, 08.54, 265, Christlich Demokratische Union des Rheinlandes: Niederschrift über die Sitzung des Landesvorstands (Düsseldorf, January 21, 1946).

157. Otto Schmidt, "Christlicher Realismus," 5–8.

158. ACDPStA, I-172-95/1-2, flyer (Wuppertal, August 27, 1945).

159. BAK, NL 278, 139, Holzapfel, speech (Buer, September 1, 1946).

160. StBKAH, 08.54, 273-74, Lehr, speech (Düsseldorf, November 24, 1945).

161. Siegfried Heimann, "Christlicher Sozialismus in der CDU," in *Lexikon des Sozialismus,* ed. Thomas Meyer, Karl-Heinz Klär, Susanne Miller, Klaus Novy, and Heinz Timmermann (Cologne, 1986), 114.

162. Wieck, *Entstehung,* 95; Schmeer, *Volkskirchliche Hoffnungen,* 108.

163. *DGG* (September 1945), 109–13.

CHAPTER 6

1. BAK, NL 18, 44, 481–82, Rott to Kaiser, February 14, 1946.

2. Schroeder, *Katholizismus,* 287–91.

3. Egen, "Entstehung," 38.

4. Karl Zimmermann, "Herner Tagung der Sozialausschüsse der CDU von Niederrhein-Westfalen" (Herne, November 8–9, 1946); Adenauer to Gockeln, June 12, 1946, in *Briefe, 1945–1947,* 264. In April 1947, Adenauer acknowledged his initial

reservations concerning Albers's work but claimed now to support him. See Adenauer to Albers, April 8, 1947, in *Briefe, 1945–1947,* 460–61.

5. Schroeder, *Katholizismus,* 84–85, 92.

6. HStAD, RWN 119, 1, 38–45, Schmidt to Adenauer, March 2, 1946; Adenauer to Schmidt, March 9, 1946, in *Briefe, 1945–1947,* 183–84. Cf. Bösch, *Adenauer-CDU,* 64.

7. Leo Schwering, *Frühgeschichte,* 182; Rudolf Morsey, "Vom Kommunalpolitiker zum Kanzler: Die politische Rolle Adenauers in der Zeit der Weimarer Republik und in der Ära der Besatzungsherrschaft (1919–1949)," in *Konrad Adenauer: Ziele und Wege, 3 Beispiele,* ed. Konrad-Adenauer-Stiftung (Mainz, 1972), 48.

8. StBKAH, 08.54, 404, Neheim-Hüsten Program (March 1, 1946).

9. Adenauer to Sevenich, March 9, 1946, in *Briefe, 1945–1947,* 184. Cf. BAK, NL 174, 50, Thedieck to Elfgen, February 25, 1946.

10. Werner Conze, *Jakob Kaiser,* 69–70; Focke, *Sozialismus,* 271.

11. Adenauer to Scharnagl, February 7, 1946, in *Briefe, 1945–1947,* 152–54.

12. Jakob Kaiser, "Europa und Deutschland," *Der Soziale Staat: Reden und Gedanken, Wege in die Neue Zeit* 2 (Berlin, January 30, 1946): 23–24.

13. HStAD, RWN 119, 1, 31, Schmidt to Adenauer, February 26, 1946.

14. HAStD, RWN 119, 1, 68–70, Schmidt to Adenauer, April 2, 1946.

15. HAStD, RWN 119, 1, 63, Marx to Albers, March 25, 1946. Marx's comments are especially noteworthy considering he had served before 1933 as chair of the Gutenberg-Bund, a Christian trade union.

16. HStAD, RWN 119, 1, 72, Brauda to Adenauer, April 8, 1946.

17. HAStD, RWN 119, 1, 63, Marx to Albers, March 25, 1946.

18. HStAD, RWN 119, 1, 72, Brauda to Adenauer, April 8, 1946.

19. Adenauer to Schmidt, March 23, 1946, in *Briefe, 1945–1947,* 194. Cf. Cary, *Path,* 186.

20. Adenauer to Schmidt, February 23, 1946, in *Briefe, 1945–1947,* 174–75; Adenauer to Schmidt, March 2, 1946, in *Briefe, 1945–1947,* 182. Cf. Schmeer, *Volkskirchliche Hoffnungen,* 92–94. Schmidt protested in particular Neheim-Hüsten's rejection of a sentence, "God is the ruler of history, Christ the strength and law of our lives," which had appeared in the Rhineland-Westphalia Guiding Principles on which Schmidt had worked in the fall of 1945.

21. HAStD, RWN 119, 1, 38–45, Schmidt to Adenauer, March 2, 1946.

22. HStAD, RWN 119, 1, 31, Schmidt to Adenauer, February 26, 1946.

23. BAK, NL 278, 142, H. von Lassaulx and Otto Schmidt, eds., Christlich Demokratische Union, Kreis Wuppertal, Kritische Ueberlegungen zum Aufruf und zum Programm der Christlich Demokratische Union für die Britische Zone vom 1.3.1946 (Wuppertal, March 3, 1946). The document is headed, "Confidential! Intended Personally for the Recipient Only." See also HStAD, RWN 119, 1, 21, Schmidt to Adenauer, February 20, 1946; RWN 119, 1, 31, Schmidt to Adenauer, February 26, 1946. Adenauer and Schmidt's confessionalized battle over programmatic language continued into May 1946, when Adenauer met with the executive committee of the Wuppertal Christian Democratic Party. See StBKAH, 08.54, 245, Aktennotiz (May 5, 1946). See StBKAH, 08.54, 247 for the Wuppertal CDU's proposed revisions. Schmidt would ultimately pull back from CDU party work after this conflict. See Bösch, *Adenauer-CDU,* 64. Even thirty years later, Schmidt complained that Protestant theological consider-

ations had been sacrificed to Catholic natural law. See Otto Schmidt, "Anspruch und Antwort: Gedanken zur Geschichte der Christlich Demokratischen Union Rheinland," *Festvortrag gehalten am 5. September 1975 zur Erinnerung an die Gründung der rheinischen CDU vor 30 Jahren in Köln* (Cologne, 1975), 10.

24. Wettig, "Konflikt," 121.

25. BAK, NL 278, 239, Kaiser, speech (February 2–3, 1946).

26. Werner Conze, *Jakob Kaiser,* 54–56, 71; Detlev Hüwel, *Karl Arnold: Eine politische Biographie* (Wuppertal, 1980), 75.

27. StBKAH, 08.05, 110.

28. ACDPStA, I-208-04/1, Kaiser to André, April 19, 1946. Cf. Werner Conze, *Jakob Kaiser,* 79–80.

29. Adenauer to Pferdmenges, April 22, 1946, in *Briefe, 1945–1947,* 230–31. Cf. Uertz, *Christentum und Sozialismus,* 91.

30. Adenauer to Sevenich, May 26, 1946, in *Briefe, 1945–1947,* 254–55.

31. ACDPStA, I-208-04/1, Kaiser to André, May 5, 1946. Cf. Werner Conze, *Jakob Kaiser,* 89.

32. StBKAH, 08.09/1, 179, Adenauer, speech (Wuppertal, May 5, 1946). Cf. Adenauer to Thomas, April 15, 1946, in *Briefe, 1945–1947,* 220–22.

33. ACDPStA, I-009-05/1, 9, Kaiser to Adenauer, May 5, 1946.

34. ACDPStA, I-009-05/1, 10, Adenauer to Kaiser, May 24, 1946.

35. Kaiser, speech (June 16, 1946), in *Nachkriegsdeutschland,* ed. Bucher, 179–91.

36. Numerous other representatives of the western zones, including Friedrich Holzapfel, Helene Weber, Karl Arnold, Josef André, and Gustav Heinemann, did attend the meeting. See Werner Conze, *Jakob Kaiser,* 92.

37. BAK, NL 278, 239, *Der Tagesspiegel* 136 (June 14, 1946).

38. NA, OMGUS, RG 260, 1, AG 000.1, U.S. Headquarters, Berlin District, Louis Glaser, Lt. Col, Chief, Civil Administration Branch, OMG BD, Special Report of Civil Administration Branch, Berlin Elections: Political Opinion and Summary (June 10, 1946), 9–10.

39. ACDPStA, I-182-10/3, Zonal Committee of the CDU for the British Zone (Neuenkirchen, June 27–28, 1946).

40. Werner Conze, *Jakob Kaiser,* 97; Hüwel, *Karl Arnold,* 76.

41. ACDPStA, I-182-10/3, Zonal Committee of the CDU for the British Zone (Neuenkirchen, June 27–28, 1946).

42. Martin Conway reminds us that Left Catholicism in postwar Europe was an urban phenomenon whose advocates failed to address rural concerns. See Conway, "Left Catholicism," 276.

43. *DGG* (June 26–28, 1946), 149–50.

44. Marie-Emmanuelle Reytier, "Die deutschen Katholiken und der Gedanke der europäischen Einigung, 1945–1949: Wende oder Kontinuität?" *Jahrbuch für europäische Geschichte* 3 (2002): 178.

45. Lothar Rolke, *Protestbewegungen in der Bundesrepublik: Eine analytische Sozialgeschichte des politischen Widerspruchs* (Opladen, 1987), 138.

46. Adenauer was joined in this regard by Bernhard Pfad. See Bösch, *Adenauer-CDU,* 21, 27–28.

47. Adenauer to Scharnagl, August 21, 1945, in *Briefe über Deutschland,* 23–27.

48. Buchhaas, *Volkspartei,* 176.

49. Adenauer to Canon Jansen, April 29, 1946, in *Briefe, 1945–1947,* 237–38.

50. StBKAH, 08.09/1, 151–52, Adenauer, speech (Bonn, April 7, 1946). Cf. Adenauer, "Rede," 8–9.

51. *DGG* (June 26–28, 1946), 149–50.

52. BAK, NL 5, 476, Adenauer, speech (Cologne, March 24, 1946).

53. ACDPStA, I-056-01, Adenauer, speech (Stuttgart, November 21, 1946); *DGG* (December 17, 1946), 277–78. Wolgast argues that CDU members risked violating the ban on polemicizing against the (Soviet) Allies when comparing directly Nazism and communism. See Wolgast, *Wahrnehmung,* 135 n. 85.

54. Zimmermann, "Das politisch-soziale Weltbild," 4.

55. Kannengießer, "Entscheidung," 7.

56. HAStK, 1187, 41, *Warum CDU?* (September 1946).

57. BAK, NL 5, 110, "Das neue Weltbild und die politischen Zielsetzungen" (Wuppertal, September 1946).

58. BAK, NL 18, 420, 16, Eduard Bernoth, "Deutsch, Christlich, Demokratisch, Sozial: Adam Stegerwalds politisches Vermächtnis," *Der Tag* (December 5, 1948).

59. HAStK, 44, flyer, "Deutsche Christliche Frau!" (n.d.). Cf. Lübbe, *Säkularisierung,* 113–14; Faber, *Abendland,* 15–36; Ingrid Laurien, "Die Verarbeitung von Nationalsozialismus und Krieg in politisch-kulturellen Zeitschriften der Westzonen, 1945–1949," *Geschichte in Wissenschaft und Unterricht* 39 (1988): 220–37.

60. StBKAH, 08.09/1, 152–53, Adenauer, speech (Bonn, April 7, 1946).

61. Kannengießer, "Entscheidung," 6.

62. HAStK, 1187, 41, flyer, "An alle Frauen!" (August 1946).

63. Teusch, "Christliche Frau," 7. In 1947, the Soviet zone would temporarily abolish paragraph 218 of the German criminal code pertaining to abortion. See Atina Grossmann, *Reforming Sex,* 197.

64. HStAD, RWN 119, 3, 110, Rhenish CDU, "Christlich oder was sonst?" in Hans Schreiber, ed., *Rundschreiben* 18 (Cologne, March 25, 1947); ACDPStA, I-182-04/03, Paul Steup, "Ein ernstes Wort in schwerer Zeit" (May 1949).

65. ACDPStA, I-105-45, Programm der CDU Württemberg/Hohenzollern (April 26, 1948).

66. ACDPStA, I-182-08/02, B III.1, Storch to Albers, July 24, 1946.

67. ACDPStA, I-182-08/02, B III.1, Storch to Albers, July 24, 1946. Ironically, Josef Löns had complained a month earlier that "a certain unity propaganda of the Marxist trade union variety" had left its mark on Storch. See BAK, NL 278, 267, Löns to Holzapfel, June 14, 1946.

68. HAStK, 1187, 43, 118, Entschließung des Sozial- und Wirtschaftspolitischen Ausschusses der CDU des Rheinlandes (Cologne, July 23, 1946).

69. Adenauer to Betz, July 27, 1946, in *Briefe, 1945–1947,* 293.

70. Plakat zur Kommunalwahl in Nordrhein-Westfalen am 15.9.1946, in *Politik und Plakat,* ed. Langguth, 50. See also Hüwel, *Karl Arnold,* 76–77.

71. BAK, NL 278, 268, Johannes Albers, ed., "Was ist und was soll der Sozialausschuß?" (Cologne, June 15, 1946).

72. HAStK, 1187, 41, Albers, *Rundbrief* (Cologne, September 20, 1946).

73. Zimmermann, "Das politisch-soziale Weltbild," 7–12.

74. Hüwel maintains that Arnold used the word *socialism* only once after mid-1946—in a speech in Berlin in September 1947. See Hüwel, *Karl Arnold,* 77.

75. The program explicitly stated, "Mixed economic and cooperative forms of management are preferred to attempts to nationalize. The CDU is of the opinion that the mining industry, for example, can be managed in this way." See ACDPStA, I-182-10/02, Leitsätze für die Wirtschafts- und Sozialpolitik (Cologne, August 26, 1946).

76. StBKAH, 08.59, 22–23, Adenauer, speech (Essen, August 24, 1946).

77. Adolf Süsterhenn, "Christlicher Sozialismus?" *Rheinischer Merkur* 48 (August 27, 1946) and "Solidarismus statt Sozialismus," *Rheinischer Merkur* 52 (September 10, 1946), in *Adolf Süsterhenn: Schriften zum Natur-, Staats-, und Verfassungsrecht,* ed. Peter Bucher (Mainz, 1991), 40–48.

78. Zimmermann, "Herner Tagung."

79. Zimmermann, "Herner Tagung."

80. The major exceptions to the otherwise seemingly monolithic Protestant rejection of Christian Socialism were Paul Bausch and Otto Heinrich von der Gablentz. Cf. ACDPStA, I-208-003/2, Paul Bausch, "Christlicher Sozialismus überwindet die Not" (Kaltental, November 1946); ACDPStA, I-155-03/1, Otto Heinrich von der Gablentz, "Warum sind wir Sozialisten?" (Berlin, January 24, 1947). Ulrich Steiner also initially called for Christian Socialism. See Schmeer, *Volkskirchliche Hoffnungen,* 478.

81. Quoted in Egen, "Enstehung," 43–44.

82. ACDPStA, I-155-30/5, Müller-Jabusch to Kaiser, September 19, 1946.

83. BAK, NL 278, 335, Wilhelm Lindner, ed., Christlich-Demokratische Union Evangelische Verbindungsstelle, *Rundbrief* 4 (Herford, September 1946).

84. BAK, NL 278, 335, brochures (Herford, October 1946).

85. HStAD, RWN 119, 3, 5, Marx to Schmidt, January 7, 1947.

86. Simpfendörfer, speech (ca. late 1946–early 1947), in Schmeer, *Volkskirchliche Hoffnungen,* 449–52; quotation on 451.

87. ACDPStA, I-172-95/1, Steiner, speech (Biberach, March 30, 1947).

88. Adenauer to Kaiser, January 13, 1947, in *Briefe, 1945–1947,* 416–17.

89. NA, OMGUS, Manpower Division, RG 260, 94, Welter to Landahl and Lemmer, April 11, 1947; BAK, NL 5, 476, 100, Ernst Lemmer, "Ein ordnendes Wort," *Neue Zeit* (Berlin, November 24, 1946). See also BAK, NL 18, 160, 120, Kaiser to Arnold, January 1, 1947; ACDPStA, I-009-04/4, CDU-Pressedienst, Confidential Information (December 18, 1946).

90. Adenauer to Kaiser, January 13, 1947, in *Briefe, 1945–1947,* 416–17.

91. HAStK, 1187, 46, Mitteilungen der CDU (Berlin, January 1, 1947).

92. Bernd Uhl, *Die Idee des christlichen Sozialismus in Deutschland, 1945–1947* (Mainz, 1975), 56.

93. Peter Van Kemseke, "From Permission to Prohibition: The Impact of the Changing International Context on Left Catholicism in Europe," in *Left Catholicism,* ed. Horn and Gerard, 267.

94. Von Plato and Leh, *"Unglaublicher Frühling,"* 70.

95. Wilde, *SBZ-CDU,* 503–4.

96. Ralf Thomas Baus, *Christlich,* 379–86.

97. Schwießelmann, "Norddeutsch," 30.

98. Wilde, *SBZ-CDU,* 73.

99. Wettig, "Konflikt," 129.

100. NA, OMGUS, RG 260, 116, AG 000.1–AG 000.3. File No: AG 337 (CA), Subject: CDU/CSU Coordinating Committee Conference in Berlin, 28–29 December 1947. Cf. Agethen, "Widerstand," 27–28.

101. Cary, *Path,* 202.

102. StBKAH, 08.11, 48, Adenauer to Albers, November 2, 1947. Cf. ACDPStA, I-009-05/2, 81, Mitteilungen der Presseabteilung der CDU (Berlin, January 7, 1947).

103. Michael Richter, *Die Ost-CDU, 1948–1952: Zwischen Widerstand und Gleichschaltung* (Düsseldorf, 1991), 32.

104. Soviet authorities had already fired the editor in chief of the Soviet-licensed Christian Democratic newspaper, *Neue Zeit,* in December 1947 for resisting censorship. See NA, OMGUS, RG 260, 116, AG 000.1–AG 000.3. Cf. Ralf Thomas Baus, *Christlich,* 433.

105. Cary, *Path,* 203.

106. Wilde, *SBZ-CDU,* 496. This decision was made on September 21, 1948 by the executive committee of the Working Group of the CDU/CSU.

107. Michael F. Feldkamp, *Der Parlamentarischer Rat, 1948–1949: Die Entstehung des Grundgesetzes* (Göttingen, 2008), 159.

108. Ralf Thomas Baus, *Christlich,* 454–57.

109. This was especially the case in Lower Saxony and Württemberg-Baden. See Ambrosius, *Durchsetzung,* 46.

110. NA, OMGUS, Manpower Division, RG 260, 95, Report by the Political Directorate on Part II of Section III: Democratisation. Cf. Gruber, *CDU-Landtagsfraktion,* 296 n. 6, 297.

111. James C. Van Hook, *Rebuilding Germany: The Creation of the Social Market Economy, 1945–1957* (Cambridge, 2004), 73–74.

112. Recker, *Konrad Adenauer: Leben und Politik,* 36.

113. Michael Alfred Kanther, ed., *Die Kabinettsprotokolle der Landesregierung von Nordrhein-Westfalen, 1946 bis 1950,* vol. 1, *Einleitung, Dokumente 1–207* (Siegburg, 1992), 1–22, 39–40; Gurland, *CDU/CSU,* 243–51.

114. Kukuck, "Etappen," 248.

115. Josef Foschepoth and Rolf Steininger, eds., *Britische Deutschland- und Besatzungspolitik, 1945–1949* (Paderborn, 1985); Van Hook, *Rebuilding Germany.*

116. StBKAH, 8/18, 87–88, Adenauer to Schlange-Schöningen, December 22, 1946. Adenauer dismissed Schlange-Schöningen's concerns that the British plans would create significant difficulties within the CDU, assuring him that the party would forge a unified stance. Cf. BAK, Z6 1/226, 2–4.

117. Gruber, *CDU-Landtagsfraktion,* 86.

118. Hüwel, *Karl Arnold,* 129–31.

119. Kukuck, "Etappen," 249.

120. StBKAH, 07.01, 41, Albers to Adenauer, January 4, 1947; StBKAH, 07.01, 41, Adenauer to Albers, January 13, 1947.

121. Herbert Reichel, "Das 'Ahlener Programm' der CDU—Ein fortwirkender Auftrag und seine Grenzen," *Jahrbuch für christliche Sozialwissenschaften* 17 (1976): 243.

122. For a typical characterization of the Ahlen Program, see Mary Fulbrook, *History of Germany, 1918–2008: The Divided Nation,* 3rd ed. (Chichester, 2009), 120.

123. Van Hook, *Rebuilding Germany,* 76.

124. HStAD, RWN 119, 3, 5, Marx to Schmidt, January 7, 1947.

125. Hans Schreiber, ed., "Neuordnung der industriellen Wirtschaft," in *Was will die CDU? Das Parteiprogramm und die ergänzenden programmatischen Erklärungen der CDU der britischen Zone* (Cologne, 1948).

126. BAK, ZSg. 1-17/4 (4). Adenauer sent a copy of the Ahlen Program to general counsel Maurice W. Altaffer with the explanation that it was directed in particular against the SPD's "efforts at nationalization." See Adenauer to Altaffer, June 5, 1947, in *Briefe, 1945–1947,* 512.

127. Kukuck, "Etappen," 249.

128. Reichel, "'Ahlener Programm,'" 250.

129. Wiliarty, *CDU,* 60.

130. Van Hook, *Rebuilding Germany,* 147.

131. Lemmer, *Manches,* 289–96.

132. Karl Zimmermann, ed., "Erbe und Aufgabe: Bericht über die Tagung der Sozialausschüsse der CDU der britischen Zone" (Herne, February 21–22, 1947).

133. LNWSB (March 4–6, 1947), 20.

134. *DGG* (March 18, 1947), 289.

135. Drucksachen des Landtages Nordrhein-Westfalen, I-109-I-114. The CDU motions read, "1. On the breakup of the mining industry, iron-producing and chemical large-scale industry; 2. on the alteration of relations of ownership and power in the economy; 3. on the new order of the relations between employer and employee; 4. on the planning and management [*Lenkung*] of the economy; 5. on the disclosure of the property relations in the mining, iron-producing, as well as chemical large-scale industry; 6. on the transfer of the corresponding jurisdictions to the German legislation."

136. See Van Hook, *Rebuilding Germany,* 54 n. 2, 74 for an excellent discussion of the complex and varied meanings of the term *Sozialisierung.* Van Hook contrasts mixed ownership (*Vergesellschaftung*) with a statist version of socialization (*Verstaatlichung*).

137. Drucksachen des Landtages Nordrhein-Westfalen, I-109-I-114.

138. Drucksachen des Landtages Nordrhein-Westfalen, I-109-I-114. Cf. Uertz, *Christentum und Sozialismus,* 189–90. On *Mitbestimmungsrecht,* see Gloria Müller, *Mitbestimmung in der Nachkriegszeit: Britische Besatzungsmacht—Unternehmen—Gewerkschaften* (Düsseldorf, 1987); Horst Thum, *Wirtschaftsdemokratie und Mitbestimmung: Von den Anfängen 1916 bis zum Mitbestimmungsgesetz 1976* (Cologne, 1991).

139. Elmar Müller, *Widerstand,* 143.

140. Drucksachen des Landtages Nordrhein-Westfalen, I-109-I-114.

141. LNWSB (March 4–6, 1947), 20–22.

142. LNWSB (March 4–6, 1947), 80–83.

143. LNWSB (March 4–6, 1947), 21–22.

144. Typical in this regard was HStAD, RWN 119, 3, 98–113, CDU des Rheinlandes, *Rundschreiben* 13 (Cologne, March 12, 1947).

145. Plakat zur Landtagswahl in Nordrhein-Westfalen am 20.4.1947, in *Politik und Plakat,* ed. Langguth, 31, 33.

146. *DGG* (March 18, 1947), 288–90. Cf. Bösch, *Adenauer-CDU,* 85.

147. HStAD, RWN 119, 3, 110, Rhenish CDU, flyer Entwurf L3, "Christlich oder was sonst?"

148. HStAD, RWN 119, 3, 112, Muster L4, "Wähler von Nord-Rhein/Westfalen!" in *Rundschreiben,* ed. Schreiber.

149. LNWSB (March 4–6, 1947), 62–63. Cf. Adenauer to Lizenträger der *Köln-ischen Rundschau,* March 7, 1947, in *Briefe, 1945–1947,* 443.

150. Van Hook, *Rebuilding Germany,* 75–76.

151. Andreas Metz, *Die ungleichen Gründerväter: Adenauers und Erhards langer Weg an die Spitze der Bundesrepublik* (Konstanz, 1998), 93.

152. Uertz, *Christentum und Sozialismus,* 190–91.

153. LNWSB (March 4–6, 1947), 28.

154. The CDU won 37.6 percent of the vote, while the SPD recorded 32 percent of the vote, the Center 9.8 percent, the FDP 5.9 percent, and the KPD 14 percent. See Claus A. Fischer, ed., *Wahlhandbuch für die Bundesrepublik Deutschland: Daten zu Bundestags-, Landtags-, und Europawahlen in der Bundesrepublik Deutschland, in den Ländern, und in den Kreisen, 1946–1989* (Paderborn, 1990), 1:832. Cf. Gruber, *CDU Landtagsfraktion,* 300.

155. Adenauer to Arnold, May 23, 1947, in *Briefe, 1945–1947,* 498–99.

156. Adenauer to Arnold, June 3, 1947, in *Briefe, 1945–1947,* 509–10. Cf. Gruber, *CDU-Landtagsfraktion,* 302 n. 33.

157. Adenauer to Schröter, June 4, 1947, in *Briefe, 1945–1947,* 512.

158. LNWSB (June 17, 1947), 6. See also Gurland, *CDU/CSU,* 273–77, 291.

159. Hüwel, *Karl Arnold,* 132.

160. LNWSB (June 17, 1947), 8–15.

161. Uertz, *Christentum und Sozialismus,* 191.

162. Cary, *Path,* 191.

163. HStAD, RWN 122, 2, 152, Robert Lehr and Helmut Lauffs, eds., Evangelische Tagung (Düsseldorf, July 16, 1947).

164. HStAD, RWN 122, 2, 153, Arnold to Lehr, July 23, 1947.

165. HStAD, RWN 122, 2, 158–60, Arnold to Lehr, July 31, 1947.

166. HStAD, RWN 122, 2, 158–60, Arnold to Lehr, July 31, 1947.

167. HStAD, RWN 119, 3, 238–40, Emil Marx, ed., CDU Kreis Wuppertal, *Rundbrief,* "An unsere Mitarbeiter! Lieber Freunde!" (Wuppertal, June 25, 1947); emphasis added.

168. HStAD, RWN 119, 3, 217–18, CDU Kreisverein, brochure (Wuppertal, June 1947). Cf. ACDPStA, I-014-01/1, campaign flyer (Göttingen, 1947).

169. StBKAH, 08.55, 8–28, Adenauer, speech (Recklinghausen, August 14, 1947).

170. Friedrich-Wilhelm Henning, "Konrad Adenauer und die Soziale Marktwirtschaft bis 1956," in *Adenauers Verhältnis zu Wirtschaft und Gesellschaft,* ed. Hans Pohl (Bonn, 1992), 22.

171. BAK, NL 278, 335, flyer (Herford, October 1948).

CHAPTER 7

1. Nicholls, *Freedom,* 242; Hentschel, *Ludwig Erhard,* 107; Bösch, *Adenauer-CDU,* 366.

2. Metz, *Ungleichen Gründerväter,* 12. Cf. *DGG* (January 24–25, 1949), 838–62.

3. Schardt, *Ludwig Erhard,* 10.

4. Buchhaas, *Volkspartei,* 288.

5. Thomas Grossmann, *Zwischen Kirche,* 289.

6. Karin Walter, *Neubeginn,* 109–10.

7. Spicka, *Selling,* 31.

8. Siegfried G. Karsten, "Eucken's 'Social Market Economy' and Its Test in Post–War West Germany: The Economist as Social Philosopher Developed Ideas That Parallelled Progressive Thought in America," *American Journal of Economics and Sociology* 44.2 (1985): 175.

9. Eger, "Konzeption," 60–64.

10. Nicholls, *Freedom,* 44, 48, 57–59, 101, 115.

11. Inacker, *Zwischen Transzendenz,* 246–54.

12. Helmut Thielicke, ed., *In der Stunde Null: Die Denkschrift des Freiburger "Bonhoeffer-Kreises": Politischen Nöten unserer Zeit* (Tübingen, 1979), 144–54; Günter Brakelmann and Traugott Jähnichen, eds., *Die protestantischen Wurzeln der Sozialen Marktwirtschaft: Ein Quellenband* (Gütersloh, 1994).

13. Eger, "Konzeption," 108–33; Heimann, "Christlicher Sozialismus," 113.

14. Mierzejewski, *Ludwig Erhard,* 7–19, 31; Hentschel, *Ludwig Erhard,* 15, 25–26, 75–77.

15. Nicholls explains that the differences between neoliberalism, a term Rüstow invented in 1938, and social market economy were negligible. Eger argues that there is little difference between neoliberalism, represented by the Chicago School and followers at the London School of Economics of John Maynard Keynes, and ordo-liberalism; he consigns the Freiburg School to the neoliberal camp but notes that the terms can be used interchangeably. See Nicholls, *Freedom,* 12 n. 5, 96–97, 143; Eger, "Konzeption," 56–57.

16. Ludwig Erhard, "Freie Wirtschaft und Planwirtschaft," *Die Neue Zeitung* (October 14, 1946), in Peter Gillies, Daniel Koerfer, and Udo Wengst, *Ludwig Erhard* (Berlin, 2010), 160–63.

17. The investigation concluded that Erhard had committed no crime but lacked administrative experience. See Andreas Metz, "Gemeinschaft mit beschränkter Haltbarkeit: Adenauer und Erhard, 1948/49," *Historisch-Politische Mitteilungen* 5 (1998): 51–52.

18. Metz, *Ungleichen Gründerväter,* 55.

19. Elmar Müller, *Widerstand,* 150.

20. Nicholls, *Freedom,* 148, 156–57.

21. Van Hook, *Rebuilding Germany,* 159.

22. Had Adenauer not been consumed with the ill health and subsequent death of his wife, the post would likely have gone to his preferred candidate, Hans-Christoph Seebohm. Moreover, the SPD's forty-nine blank votes (to the CDU's forty and the FDP's eight) were counted as abstentions instead of as *no* votes. See Mierzejewski, *Ludwig Erhard,* 61–62.

23. Adenauer to Meyer-Sevenich, May 2, 1948, in *Briefe, 1947–1949,* 224. Adenauer referred to "Ehrhardt."

24. Metz, *Ungleichen Gründerväter,* 132.

25. Wolfgang Schroeder, "Oswald von Nell-Breuning contra Viktor Agartz: Ein

entscheidender Konflikt um das Selbstverständnis der Einheitsgewerkschaft," in *Sozial- und Linkskatholizismus: Erinnerung—Orientierung—Befreiung,* ed. Ludwig and Schroeder, 212. This inclusion of von Nell-Breuning marked the real debut of his collaboration with the CDU. Although von Nell-Bruening met with Albers and other Christian Trade Unionists in 1946, they apparently discussed only confessional schools.

26. Nicholls, *Freedom,* 196, 205.

27. Ludwig Erhard, speech (Frankfurt, April 21, 1948), in Ludwig Erhard, *Deutsche Wirtschaftspolitik: Der Weg der Sozialen Marktwirtschaft* (Düsseldorf, 1962), 38–61. Cf. Volkhard Laitenberger, "Ludwig Erhard—Konzeption und Durchsetzung der Sozialen Marktwirtschaft," in *Markt oder Plan: Wirtschaftsordnungen in Deutschland, 1945–1961,* ed. Haus der Geschichte der Bundesrepublik Deutschland (Frankfurt a.M., 1997), 124.

28. Jarausch, *After Hitler,* 83–84; Spicka, *Selling,* 39, 44.

29. Mierzejewski, *Ludwig Erhard,* 60; Uertz, *Christentum und Sozialismus,* 56.

30. LNWSB (August 8, 1948), 969–71, 981–88.

31. Hüwel, *Karl Arnold,* 136.

32. The British military government maintained that such an important question should be left to an elected federal German parliament as agreed at the Washington Coal Conference of August–September 1947. That the Allies' decision came as no surprise was evident in an August 1948 CDU flyer noting "the SPD knows for a fact that the military government will not approve the law"; indeed, the prevailing wisdom was that the SPD had engineered the vote for domestic political gain. See BAK, NL 278, 335, flyer (Dortmund, August 1948). Cf. Albert Diegmann, "American Deconcentration Policy in the Ruhr Coal Industry," in *American Policy,* ed. Diefendorf, Frohn, and Rupieper, 202. Invoking a similar rationale as in North Rhine-Westphalia, the U.S. government suspended Article 41 of Hesse's constitution, the Implementation Act for Article 160 of the Bavarian constitution, and the socialization law passed by the Schleswig-Holstein Landtag in late 1947. See Berg-Schlosser, "Konstituierung," 106–7.

33. Plakat zur Landtagswahl in Nordrhein-Westfalen am 20.4.1947, in *Politik und Plakat,* ed. Langguth, 36.

34. Cary, *Path,* 184–90.

35. *DGG* (August 3, 1948), 546–49.

36. *DGG* (May 19–20, 1948), 494.

37. *DGG* (August 3, 1948), 543–45, 554.

38. *DGG* (August 3, 1948), 548–52.

39. Cary, *Path,* chapter 11.

40. Cary, *Path,* chapter 10.

41. *DGG* (August 3, 1948), 570.

42. *DGG* (August 3, 1948), 560.

43. StBKAH, 08.57, 251, Adenauer, *Rundbrief,* June 6, 1947.

44. Focke, *Sozialismus,* 278–79.

45. HStAD, RWN 119, 2, 256, Lehr to Adenauer, December 5, 1946. Cf. Salzmann, *CDU/CSU,* 20.

46. Gruber, *CDU-Landtagsfraktion,* 61.

47. HStAD, RW 260, 19, Lütsches to Gockeln, May 14, 1947. Lütsches enclosed a copy of his May 14, 1947 letter to Adenauer. Cf. HStAD, RWN 119, 2, 186, Theill to

Schmidt, November 5, 1946; HStAD, RWN 119, 4, 27, Schmidt to Löns, February 23, 1948; HStAD, RWN 119, 4, 28, König to Schmidt, February 23, 1948; HStAD, RWN 119, 4, 29, Schmidt to König, March 12, 1948; HStAD, RWN 119, 4, 30, Krueger to Schmidt, March 27, 1948.

48. StBKAH, 08.61, 194, Adenauer to Holzapfel, May 5, 1948.

49. *DGG* (February 13–14, 1948), 478–80.

50. Ambrosius, *Durchsetzung,* 10.

51. Henning, "Konrad Adenauer," 30.

52. Metz, *Ungleichen Gründerväter,* 103.

53. StBKAH, 08.12, 10–23, Adenauer to Elfes, October 19, 1948. Cf. Nicholls, *Freedom,* 234–35, 246.

54. StBKAH, 08.11, 18, Albers to Adenauer, April 7, 1948; StBKAH, 08.11, 19, Adenauer to Albers, April 4, 1948.

55. *DGG* (May 19–20, 1948), 494.

56. *DGG* (May 19–20, 1948), 499–500.

57. Heitzer, *CDU,* 509–10.

58. Metz, "Gemeinschaft," 64.

59. For their dispute over whether Jakob Kaiser traveled from Berlin in an attempt to rally opposition to Erhard's election as economic director, see Hentschel, *Ludwig Erhard,* 64–65; Metz, *Ungleichen Gründerväter,* 112. Cf. Elmar Müller, *Widerstand,* 150–51.

60. Metz, "Gemeinschaft," 66.

61. *DGG* (August 28–29, 1948), 657–78; quotation on 658.

62. *DGG* (August 28–29, 1948), 691–99.

63. *DGG* (August 28–29, 1948), 700–703.

64. *DGG* (August 28–29, 1948), 709.

65. *DGG* (August 28–29, 1948), 710–12.

66. Uertz, *Christentum und Sozialismus,* 199.

67. BAK, NL 278, 316, brochure (Königswinter, November 6, 1948).

68. BAK, NL 278, 145, Albers to Holzapfel, October 15, 1948. Albers enclosed a copy of his October 14, 1948 letter to Erhard. Cf. BAK, NL 278, 145, Albers, press conference (Cologne, July 15, 1949); Ute Schmidt, "Christlich Demokratische Union," 521.

69. Rainer Salzmann, ed., *Die CDU/CSU im Frankfurter Wirtschaftsrat: Protokolle der Unionsfraktion, 1947–1949* (Düsseldorf, 1988) (September 26, 1948), 268. Cf. BAK, NL 278, 335, Friedrich Holzapfel, ed., flyer (Herford, October 11, 1948).

70. Metz, *Ungleichen Gründerväter,* 140.

71. *DGG* (October 28–29, 1948), 734–40.

72. Brigitte Kaff, ed., *Die Unionsparteien, 1946–1950: Protokolle der Arbeitsgemeinschaft der CDU/CSU Deutschlands und der Konferenenzen der Landesvorsitzenden* (Düsseldorf, 1991), 252–366.

73. Adenauer then complained that Catholics would have a difficult time persuading the Parliamentary Council not to meet on Three Kings' Day, "for us in our diocese a highly religious holiday." See *PRSU* (January 4, 1949), 313.

74. *PRSU* (January 6, 1949), 329.

75. *PRSU* (January 9, 1949), 73.

76. *DGG* (February 24–25, 1949), 842.

77. *DGG* (February 24–25, 1949), 838–62.

78. *DGG* (February 24–25, 1949), 863.

79. Uertz, *Christentum und Sozialismus*, 200.

80. Metz, "Gemeinschaft," 74.

81. Uertz, *Christentum und Sozialismus*, 196.

82. Mierzejewski, *Ludwig Erhard*, 87.

83. BAK, Z5/201F, "Gewerkshaftler der CDU waren unter sich," *Westfälische Rundschau* (August 30, 1949).

84. Hüwel, *Karl Arnold*, 137.

85. Lienkamp, "Socialism," 227.

86. William Patch, "The Legend of Compulsory Unification: The Catholic Clergy and the Revival of Trade Unionism in West Germany after the Second World War," *Journal of Modern History* 79 (2007): 848–80. Cf. Schroeder, *Katholizismus*, 82–83, 94, 124–25, 181–84, 295–96.

87. *DGG* (February 24–25, 1949), 854–57.

88. BAK, NL 5, 256, 91–105, Hermann Pünder, "Die Frankfurter Wirtschaftspolitik im Frühjahr 1949" (Frankfurt a.M., March 1949). Cf. StBKAH, 08.61, 198–204, Pünder, speech (Frankfurt, March 16, 1948); BAK, NL 5, 245, Pünder, speech (Caux, July 5, 1949).

89. *DGG* (July 15, 1949), 866–80.

90. There was, however, apparently protracted debate whether to adopt the term *controlled economy* or *planned economy*. See Spicka, *Selling*, 61.

91. After Sevenich left the CDU in May 1948, she served as a delegate for the SPD in the Lower Saxony Landtag until she rejoined the CDU to protest Willy Brandt's Ostpolitik shortly before her death in 1970.

92. Adenauer to Meyer-Sevenich, April 19, 1948, in *Briefe, 1947–1949*, 212–13; Adenauer to Meyer-Sevenich, May 2, 1948, in *Briefe, 1947–1949*, 224–25; StBKAH, 07.23, 334–40, Meyer-Sevenich to Adenauer, May 14, 1948; StBKAH, 07.23, 341–46, Meyer-Sevenich to the Landesverband Hannover der CDU, May 14, 1948; StBKAH, 07.27, 173–74, Bericht über die Diskussion der CDU-Meschede mit Frau Maria Meyer-Sevenich (Meschede, December 13, 1948); StBKAH, 07.17, 11, Maria Sevenich, "Die Berichtigung—Eine Humoreske aus Ernster Veranlassung."

93. Albert Eßer, "Wilhelm Elfes (1884–1969): Oberbürgermeister von Mönchengladbach," in *Christliche Demokraten*, ed. Buchstab, Kaff, and Kleinmann, 162.

94. Von der Gablentz would later publish a book, *Die versäumte Reform: Zur Kritik der westdeutschen Politik* (Cologne, 1960).

95. Wengst notes that Kaiser's support may have been aided by Adenauer's promise of a ministry. See Udo Wengst, "Die CDU/CSU im Bundestagswahlkampf 1949," *Vierteljahrshefte für Zeitgeschichte* 34.1 (1986): 16, 32–33, 46–47, 52.

96. Feldkamp, *Parlamentarischer Rat*, 19–21.

97. Johannes Volker Wager, ed., *Der Parlamentarische Rat, 1948–1949: Akten und Protokolle*, vol. 1, *Vorgeschichte* (Boppard a.R., 1975), lv–lvi.

98. Twenty-seven members belonged to the CDU/CSU (who forged a cooperative agreement), twenty-seven to the SPD, five to the Liberals, and two each to the KPD, DP,

and the Center, with five additional nonvoting representatives from Berlin (three SPD, one CDU, one FDP).

99. BAK, Z5/179F, 2, "'Reich' oder 'Bund'?" *Westdeutsche Rundschau* (October 7, 1948); BAK Z5/179F, 2, "Vorschlag für den neuen Staat: 'Republik Deutschland,'" *Neues Tageblatt* (October 9, 1948). An official Flag Committee was appointed when the Committee for Policy Issues could not achieve consensus. See Feldkamp, *Parlamentarischer Rat*, 78, 191.

100. Metz, *Ungleichen Gründerväter*, 153.

101. Christoph Möllers, *Das Grundgesetz: Geschichte und Inhalt* (Munich, 2009), 23.

102. Salzmann, *CDU/CSU*, xxi; Hans-Otto Kleinmann, "'Wahren, pflegen, ausbauen': Das Werk des Parlamentarischen Rates zwischen Grundgesetzgebung und Erneuerungsdiskurs," in *In Verantwortung*, ed. Buchstab and Kleinmann, 25–27.

103. Günter Buchstab, "Felix Walter (1890–1949): Ministerialrat, Württemberg-Baden," in *In Verantwortung*, ed. Buchstab and Kleinmann, 370; Kleinmann, "'Wahren, pflegen, ausbauen,'" 31–34.

104. Hahn, "U.S. Policy," 21–44.

105. BAK, Z5/57, PRSB, November 30, 1948; BAK, Z5/191F, Adolf Süsterhenn, "Ein offenes Gespräch," *Rheinischer Merkur* (March 12, 1949).

106. Wolfgang Benz, "Föderalistische Politik in der CDU/CSU: Die Verfassungsdiskussion im 'Ellwanger Kreis,' 1947/48," *Vierteljahreshefte für Zeitgeschichte* 25.4 (1977): 776–820.

107. StBKAH, 08.57, 331, Adenauer to Pfeiffer, January 25, 1947.

108. BAK, Z5/182F, 5, "Die CDU vor der Entscheidung," *Niederdeutsche Zeitung* (November 23, 1948); BAK, Z5/178 F, "Für Föderalisten wenig Hoffnung," *Westdeutsche Zeitung* (September 24, 1948); BAK, Z5/178 F, "Hie Zentralismus—Hie Föderalismus: Fortschritt der Arbeiten in Bonn," *Deutsche Volkszeitung* (September 30, 1948); BAK, Z5/179F, 2, "CDU: Teils—Teils . . . ," *Rheinisch-Pfälzische Rundschau* (October 9, 1948); BAK Z5/179F, 2, "Bonn für 'Republik Deutschland,'" *Die Neue Zeitung* (October 9, 1948).

109. BAK, Z5/26, 1–215, Sitzungen des Ausschusses für Finanzfragen, Manuskripte der wörtlichen Protokolle, Bd. 3., 10. Sitzung (September 30, 1948). Cf. BAK, Z5/77, PRSB, January 20, 1949; BAK, Z5/180F, 3, "Abschluß in Bonn unbestimmt: Spannungen innerhalb der Fraktionen," *Nordsee-Zeitung* (October 16, 1948); BAK, Z5/180F, 3, "Angleichung der Auffassungen möglich: Süsterhenn über die strittigen Fragen in Bonn," *Allgemeine Zeitung* (Mainz, October 29, 1948); BAK, Z5/180F, 3, "CDU und CSU werden sich nicht einig," *Westdeutsche Allgemeine* (October 30, 1948); BAK, Z5/181F, 4 (3f), "Entscheidung gefordert," *Rhein Echo* (November 2, 1948); BAK, Z5/181, "Die 'neuralgischen Punkte' in Bonn," *Süddeutsche Zeitung* (November 2, 1948); BAK, Z5/181, "Die CSU gegen einen Senat," *Badisches Zeitung* (November 10, 1948); BAK, Z5/181, "Bonn und die Bayern," *Rheinische Post* (November 10, 1948); BAK, Z5/182F, "CSU bleibt starr," *Westdeutsche Rundschau* (November 27, 1948). Cf. Wolfgang Benz, *Zwischen Hitler und Adenauer: Studien zur deutschen Nachkriegsgesellschaft* (Frankfurt a.M., 1991), 15–16, 36.

110. BAK, Z5/181F, 4 (3f), "Eine bayerische Widerstandsbewegung," *Die Kurier*

(November 2, 1948); See also BAK, Z5/181, "Wahrrechtsausschuß bricht Beratungen ab, Uneinige CDU/CSU-Fraktion will Zeit gewinnen," *Neuer Vorwärts* (November 6, 1948).

111. BAK, Z5/187F, "Die Sicherung des Föderalismus," *Der gerade Weg* (February 11, 1949); BAK, Z5/186F, "Dr. Ehard mit Bonn unzufrieden," *Frankfurter Rundschau* (January 31, 1949); BAK, Z5/185F, "CDU richtet sich nach der CSU aus," *Westdeutsche Allgemeine* (January 11, 1949); BAK, Z5/185F, "Von Ellwangen nach Königswinter," *Rheinisch-Pfälzische Rundschau* (January 11, 1949); BAK, Z5/181F, 4, "CDU/CSU in Bonn gespalten," *Die Neue Zeitung* (November 2, 1948). Cf. Richard Ley, *Föderalismusdiskussion innerhalb der CDU/CSU von der Parteigründung bis zu der Verabschiedung des Grundgesetzes* (Mainz, 1978).

112. *DGG* (October 28–29, 1948), 713–34; Christian Bommarius, *Das Grundgesetz: Eine Biographie* (Berlin, 2009), 204–14.

113. BAK, Z5/65, PRSB, January 18, 1949; BAK, Z5/18, PRSB, May 8, 1949; BAK, Z5/180F, 3, "Das 'Reich' ist Vergangenheit," *Kölnische Rundschau* (October 21, 1948). Cf. Rudolf Uertz, "Christlich-demokratische Wertvorstellungen im Parlamentarischen Rat, 1948/49," *Historisch-Politische Mitteilungen* 15 (2008): 115.

114. BAK, Z5/184F, Dr. F.-H. Pielmeyer, "Die Konkordatsfrage," *Rhenischer Merkur* (December 18, 1948); BAK, Z5/186F, "Kampf um das Elternrecht: Zweite Lesung in Bonn beendet—Konkordatsfrage zurückgestellt," *Rheinische Post* (January 22, 1949); BAK, Z5/186F, "Reichskonkordat?" *Rheinische Zeitung* (January 26, 1949); BAK, Z5/184F; BAK, Z5/188F, Adolf Süsterhenn, "'Das Konkordat gilt noch': Kirche und Staat im neuen Deutschland," *Die Welt* 19 (February 15, 1949).

115. BAK, Z5/59, PRSB, December 7, 1948; BAK, Z5/64, PRSB, January 14, 1949; BAK, Z5/183F, "SPD, FDP, und KPD lehnen Schul-Bestimmungsrecht der Eltern ab," *Aachener Volkszeitung* (December 11, 1948); BAK, Z5/184F, "Die Kirchen zum Bonner Grundgesetz," *Süddeutsche Zeitung* (December 28, 1948).

116. Kleinmann, "'Wahren, pflegen, ausbauen,'" 35.

117. BAK, Z5/183F, "Bruderstreit und 'Kulturkampf,'" *Münchner Merkur* (December 10, 1948); BAK, Z5/183F, "'Kulturkampf' geistert in Bonn: Das Verhältnis zwischen Kirche und Staat vor dem Hauptausschuß," *Die Rheinpfalz* (December 11, 1948); BAK, Z5/184F, "Wird es Kulturkampf in Bonn geben?" *Die Neue Zeitung* (December 16, 1948); BAK, Z5/184F, "Die Kirche im Verfassungskampf," *Nordeutsches Echo* (December 16, 1948).

118. BAK, Z5/65, PRSB, January 19, 1949.

119. BAK, Z5/60, PRSB, December 15, 1948.

120. BAK, Z5/190F, Thomas Dehler, "Das Elternrecht," *Der Demokrat* 5 (March 1949).

121. Van Schewick, *Katholische Kirche,* 27.

122. Müller-Rolli, *Evangelische Schulpolitik,* 497.

123. BAK, Z5/13, PRSB, October 20, 1948. Cf. BAK, Z5/18, PRSB, May 8, 1949; BAK, Z5/183F, 6, 3f, "Für Bayern unannehmbar," *Die Rheinpfalz* (December 2, 1948).

124. Uertz, "Christlich," 112.

125. BAK, Z5/12a, PRSB, September 8, 1948.

126. BAK, Z5/59, PRSB, December 7, 1948.

127. BAK, Z5/12 b, PRSB, September 9, 1948; BAK, Z18, PRSB, May 8, 1949.

128. BAK, Z5/35, PRSB, December 4, 1948; BAK, Z5/59, PRSB, December 7, 1948.

129. Feldkamp, *Parlamentarischer Rat*, 125–26.

130. Müller-Rolli, *Evangelische Schulpolitik*, 527–41, 634–37.

131. BAK, Z5/108, 2, 57. Cf. BAK, Z5/108, 132, Rat der Evangelischen Kirche in Deutschland an den Parlamentarischen Rat (November 9, 1948); ACDPStA, I-293-01/3, Josef Rösing, "Das Elternrecht und seine Behandlung im Parlamentarischen Rat," 1–8.

132. Müller-Rolli, *Evangelische Schulpolitik*, 497, 501, 504–5, 512–15.

133. Norbert Trippen, "Von den Fuldaer 'Bischofskonferenzen' zur 'Deutschen Bischofskonferenz,' 1945–1976," *Historisches Jahrbuch* 121 (2001): 309; van Schewick, *Katholische Kirche*, 22–23, 30, 49.

134. BAK, Z5/182F, "Alliierte Hinweise 'zur Kenntnis genommen,'" *Süddeutsche Zeitung* (November 27, 1948); ACDPStA, I-293-01/3, Rösing, "Elternrecht," 8–14. Cf. Besier, "Politische Rolle," 34–35.

135. *DGG* (November 3, 1948), 118–20.

136. Van Schewick, *Katholische Kirche*, 84–85.

137. *DGG* (December 17, 1948), 297; Feldkamp, *Parlamentarischer Rat*, 77.

138. *DGG* (February 25, 1949), 799.

139. Müller-Rolli, *Evangelische Schulpolitik*, 542–65.

140. BAK, Z5/35, PRSB, December 7, 1948. On the FDP, see BAK, Z5/185, Hermann Höpker Aschoff, "Bonn und die christlichen Kirchen," *Die Zeit* (January 6, 1949).

141. BAK, Z5/128, 384, 219, Niemöller, Arbeitsgemeinschaft christlicher Kirchen in Deutschland (Wiesbaden, December 8, 1948); BAK, Z5/184F, "Niemöller zum Grundgesetz," *Westfalenpost* (December 29, 1948).

142. BAK, Z5/183F, *Rheinischer Merkur* (December 11, 1948); BAK, Z5/183F, Albert Finck, "Für oder wider Christus?" *Südwestdeutsche Volkszeitung* (December 6, 1948); BAK, Z5/183F, Albert Finck, "Für oder wider Christus?" *Aachener Volkszeitung* (December 8, 1948); BAK, Z5 189F, Adam Vollhardt, "Auch evangelische Kirche fordert Elternrecht," *Westdeutsche Allgemeine* (February 22, 1949).

143. BAK, Z5/184F, "In Bonn herrscht politische Hochspannung," *Neue Volks-Zeitung* (December 15, 1948); BAK, Z5/184F, "Die Vertrauensfrage für den Bund," *Kölnische Rundschau* 145.3 (December 16, 1948); BAK, Z5/184F, "Kirchenvertreter in Bonn," *Hessische Nachrichten* (December 15, 1948).

144. *PRSU* (December 13, 1948), 278.

145. BAK, Z5/59, PRSB, December 7, 1948.

146. BAK, Z5/35, PRSB, December 16, 1948.

147. BAK, Z5/183F, Domkapitular Wilhelm Böhler, "Verfassung und Volk," *Allgemeine Kölnische Rundschau* (December 10, 1948).

148. For examples, see BAK, Z5/108, 213, 222, 233, 237; BAK, Z5/109, 14, 22, 90, 95, 116, 119, 123, 149, 152, 160, 164, 167, 193, 194; BAK, Z5/110, 4, 7, 19, 22, 29, 49, 68, 154, 175, 217, 221, 222, 223, 224, 225, 227, 256, 247, 251, 263, 272, 281. Cf. BAK, Z5/182F, "Katholiken-Ausschüsse fordern Grundrechte," *Allgemeine Kölnische Rundschau* (November 17, 1948). It was later reported that 2,690 of the total 5,131 petitions received by the Parliamentary Council (51.5 percent) pertained to the Elternrecht. See BAK, Z5/199F, "An den Rand geschrieben," *Rhein-Ruhr-Zeitung* (May 28, 1949).

149. BAK, Z5/65, PRSB, January 18, 1949.

150. BAK, Z5/185F, "Erklärung der deutschen Bischöfe zur Schulfrage: Das Eltern-recht nachdrücklichst gefordert—Ein Appell an den Parlamentarischen Rat," *Aachener Volkszeitung* (January 3, 1949).

151. Van Schewick, *Katholische Kirche*, 49–53, 71.

152. *PRSU* (October 6, 1948), 55.

153. *PRSU* (November 17, 1948), 163.

154. *PRSU* (November 30, 1948), 243.

155. *PRSU* (December 6, 1948), 258–59; *PRSU* (December 13, 1948), 273. Kaufmann argued again the following month that the CDU was unnecessarily antago-nizing the FDP and that the confessional school measure had no chance of passing. See *DGG* (January 6, 1949), 330.

156. *PRSU* (January 21, 1949), 359.

157. BAK, Z5/65, PRSB, January 18, 1949.

158. ACDPStA, I-293-01/3, Rösing, "Elternrecht," 17–26; BAK, Z5/187, 10, "Kar-dinal Frings dankt dem Zentrum: Bonner 'Kompromiß' über Eltern- und Kirchenrechte bedenklich," *Neuer Westfälischer Kurier* (February 4, 1949); BAK, Z5/187F, "Kampf von der Kanzel?" *Hessische Nachrichten* (February 11, 1949).

159. BAK, Z5/188F, "Das Volk soll entscheiden!" *Rheinische Post* (February 16, 1949); BAK, Z5/188F, "CDU beantragt Schulrecht-Volksentscheid," *Westdeutsche Allgemeine* (February 17, 1949).

160. Adenauer reportedly threatened Menzel and Schmid that the CDU intended to let the Basic Law fail if it did not guarantee the Elternrecht. In the "Frankfurt Affair," Adenauer met on December 16 with the three military governors, Marie-Pierre Koenig, Lucius Clay, and Brian Hubert Robertson, in what his opponents saw as an attempt to solicit Allied intervention in the High Committee's ongoing conflicts, an act that led in January to a failed vote of no confidence against Adenauer. For a summary of the Frank-furt Affair, which cost Adenauer considerable political capital publicly and with the SPD and FDP, see Feldkamp, *Parlamentarischer Rat*, 131–38.

161. *PRSU* (December 15, 1948), 283.

162. *PRSU* (February 1, 1949), 369–70.

163. *PRSU* (February 8, 1949), 390.

164. BAK, Z5/65, PRSB, February 10, 1949.

165. ACDPStA, I-293-01/3, Rösing, "Elternrecht," 47; *PRSU* (February 1, 1949), 372 n. 8.

166. *PRSU* (February 22, 1949), 412.

167. Bösch, *Adenauer-CDU*, 131.

168. According to a Center Party flyer, the High Committee passed the Bremen Clause by a vote of twelve to five. The twelve positive votes included one CDU mem-ber; three Christian Democrats voted against it, while four abstained. See Cary, *Path*, 255. The stenographic report does not record how individual representatives voted but lists the present and voting Catholic CDU/CSU members as Heinrich von Brentano, Hermann Fecht, Wilhelm Laforet, Anton Pfeiffer, and Felix Walter; Protestant present and voting Christian Democrats were Robert Lehr, Hermann von Mangoldt, and Walter Strauß. See BAK, Z5/65, PRSB, February 10, 1949. Cf. van Schewick, *Katholische Kirche*, 113.

169. *DGG* (February 25, 1949), 805–6.

170. Years later, Adenauer would tell the CDU faction that Böhler had "no understanding of the reality of the world and what it's about." See *PBV* (April 26, 1954),
145.

171. BAK, Z5/188F, "'Bonner Verfassung besser als die von Weimar,'" *Mannheimer
Morgen* (February 2, 1949); *DGG* (February 25, 1949), 832.

172. *DGG* (February 25, 1949), 818–19.

173. Bösch, *Adenauer-CDU,* 129–30.

174. *DGG* (February 25, 1949), 825.

175. BAK, Z5/59, PRSB, December 7, 1948.

176. Egen, "Entstehung," 105–6.

177. BAK, Z5/186F, "Hilfe von Himmel," *Neuer Vorwärts* (January 29, 1949).

178. BAK, Z5/189F, "Demagogie mit 'Elternrechten,'" *Neuer Vorwärts* (January 29,
1949).

179. *PRSU* (February 9, 1949), 395.

180. ACDPStA, I-293-01/3, Rösing, "Elternrecht," 28–29.

181. BAK, Z5/188F, 11, Erklärung der deutschen Bischöfe zum geplanten Grundgesetz (Pützchen, February 11, 1949). Cf. BAK, Z5/187F, 10, "Konflikt um Ehe- und
Schulparagraph: Kirchlicher Protest gegen Bestimmungen des Bonner Grundgesetzes,"
Hamburger Allgemeine (February 9, 1949); BAK, Z5/187F, "Dem Abschluß in Bonn
entgegen," *Die Rheinpfalz* (February 8, 1949); ACDPStA, I-293-01/3, Rösing, "Elternrecht," 28–29.

182. The press reported that more than six hundred thousand Bavarians and two hundred thousand Rhine-Hessians had signed the petitions for Elternrecht. See BAK,
Z5/187F, "600,000 Eltern protestieren gegen Bonn," *Münchner Merkur* (February 7,
1949); BAK, Z5/187F, "Klerus hat Einwände gegen Bonn: Entscheidung des Hauptaus-
schusses über Elternrecht soll korrigiert werden," *Rhein-Echo* (February 10, 1949);
BAK, Z5/189, "Demokratie ohne Volk," *Rheinischer Merkur* (February 19, 1949). Cf.
Feldkamp, *Parlamentarischer Rat,* 128.

183. BAK, Z5/188F, 11, "'Bremer Klaus' mit Hilfe der CDU: Adenauer für Grundgesetz 'auch gegen die kirchlichen Stellen,'" *Neuer Westfälischer Kurier* (February 11,
1949); BAK, Z5/188F, "Endkampf um das Grundgesetz: Noch kurz vor Schluß neue
Krise in Bonn?" *Neues Tageblatt* (February 15, 1949); BAK, Z5/187F, "Schneller Fort-
gang der dritten Lesung," *Die Rheinpfalz* (February 18, 1949).

184. BAK, Z5/190F, 13, "Für die Konfessions-Schule," *Allgemeine Zeitung* (Mainz,
March 7, 1949).

185. BAK, Z5/190F, Domkapitular Wilhelm Böhler, "Die 'streitende Kirche,'"
Allgemeine Kölnische Rundschau (March 2, 1949).

186. Müller-Rolli, *Evangelische Schulpolitik,* 593.

187. *PRSU* (February 10, 1949), 399; *PRSU* (February 11, 1949), 401; *PRSU* (February 17, 1949), 408.

188. BAK, Z5 Anhang/12, 40.

189. *PRSU* (May 2, 1949), 529.

190. BAK, Z5/18, PRSB, May 8, 1949. Cf. Rösing, "Elternrecht," 30–32.

191. BAK, Z5/136, 755, 95, Antrag der CDU vom 2. Mai 1949, betr. Art. 7b. See also
PRSU (April 27, 1949), 522; *PRSU* (April 29, 1949), 527.

192. BAK, Z5/197, "Gegen undurchsichtige Geldzuwendungen an die Partei," *Neuer*

Westfälischer Kurier (May 5, 1949). Cf. BAK, Z5/198F, 21, "Tragödie eines Grundrechtes und ihre Akteure," *Neuer Westfälischer Kurier* (May 9, 1949); BAK, Z5/199F, 22, "Reiche Erfahrung," *Rhein-Ruhr-Zeitung* (May 16, 1949).

193. ACDPStA, I-293-01/3, Rösing, "Elternrecht," 27–28.

194. BAK, Z5/199F, "Staat gegen Eltern," *Neuer Westfälischer Kurier* (May 16, 1949).

195. BAK, Z5/198F, "Grundgesetz und Elternrecht," *Neuer Westfälischer Kurier* (May 11, 1949).

196. BAK, Z5/192F, "Wer verriet das Elternrecht?" *Neuer Westfälischer Kurier* (March 30, 1949). Cf. BAK, Z5180F, 3, Dr. Erwein Frhr. v. Aretin, "Gottlose Grundrechte," *Münchner Allgemeine* 7 (October 17, 1948); BAK, Z5/198F, 21, "Wo sind die Löwen?" *Neues Tagesblatt* (May 12, 1949).

197. BAK, Z5/183F, "Kulturkampfstimmung im Parlamentarischen Rat," *Rhein-Ruhr-Zeitung* (December 10, 1948). Cf. BAK, Z5/183F, "Sprachverwirrung in Bonn," *Rheinisicher Merkur* (December 11, 1948).

198. BAK, Z5/195F, "Anti-christliche Kräfte demaskieren sich: Die wahren Gründe für das Verhalten der SPD—Verneinung des abendländischen Erbes," *Westfalenpost* (April 23, 1949).

199. BAK, Z5/200F, 23, "Gegen Bruderkampf: Das Nein des Zentrums in Bonn darf zu keiner Zersplitterung im christlichen Lager mißbraucht werden," *Rheinisch-Pfälzische Landeszeitung* (June 13, 1949); ACDPStA, I-293-01/3, Rösing, "Elternrecht," 33–47.

200. The statement did not use the word Elternrecht. See Müller-Rolli, *Evangelische Politik,* 599–601. See also BAK, Z5/190F, "Evangelische Kirche macht Bedenken geltend," *Neues Tageblatt* (March 8, 1949); BAK, Z5/189F, 12, Landesbischof D. Dr. Hanns Lilje, "Die künftige Gestalt der Schule: Worum geht es in Bonn?" *Sonntagsblatt* (February 20, 1949); Besier, "Politische Rolle," 35.

201. BAK, Z5/199F, "Erklärung der deutschen Bischöfe: Eine Stellungnahme des Episkopats zum Grundgesetz der Deutschen Bundesrepublik," *Rheinischer Merkur* (May 28, 1949). Cf. ACDPStA, I-085-46/1, Böhler, radio address (June 12, 1949).

202. BAK, Z5/199F, "Unsere Meinung: Frings und die CDU," *Welt am Sonntag* (May 29, 1949). Adenauer made an official announcement to the CDU/CSU faction when Frings joined the party. See *PRSU* (November 10, 1948), 153.

203. BAK, Z5/200F, "Trotz Kritik positive Mitarbeit," *Allgemeine Kölnische Rundschau* (June 13, 1949); BAK Z5/199F, 22, "Der Kardinal gegen Wahllüge," *Rheinische Pfälzische Landeszeitung* (May 30, 1949); BAK, Z5/199F, "Um Kardinal Frings und Dr. Süsterhenn," *Trierische Volkszeitung* (May 30, 1949); BAK, Z5/199F, "Kardinale Wendung," *Rheinische Zeitung* (May 30, 1949). Ironically, an SPD delegate had noted in January that Cardinal Frings's CDU membership violated the concordat's ban on party activity. See BAK, Z5/65, PRSB, January 19, 1949.

204. BAK, Z5 Anhang/12, 88. Cf. Feldkamp, *Parlamentarischer Rat,* 128; Wilhelm Damberg, "Milieu und Konzil: Zum Paradigmenwechsel konfessionellen Bewußtseins im Katholizismus der frühen Bundesrepublik Deutschland," in *Konfessionen,* ed. Blaschke, 342; Bommarius, *Grundgesetz,* 193.

205. BAK, Z5/184F, "Kein Kultur- und Sozialkampf," *Westdeutsche Rundschau* (De-

cember 16, 1948). Cf. BAK, Z5/184F, "Für den Schulfreidenk," *Badische Zeitung* (December 18, 1948); BAK, Z5/187F, 10, "'Kulturkampf erwünscht?'" *Lübecker Freie Presse* (February 8, 1949); BAK, Z5/189F, 12, "Volkstag—Wahlkampf mit Kulturkampfparolen," *Neuer Vorwärts* (February 19, 1949); BAK, Z5/197F, 20, "Elternrecht," *Der Tag* (May 5, 1949); BAK, Z5/190F, "Das Kardinal-Hindernis," *Telegraf* (March 1, 1949).

206. BAK, Z5/191F, "Das Naturrecht," *Neuer Vorwärts* (March 12, 1949).

207. BAK, Z5/59, PRSB, December 7, 1948.

208. BAK, Z5/65, PRSB, January 18, 1949.

209. Quoted in Müller-Rolli, *Evangelische Schulpolitik,* 620.

210. Van Schewick, *Katholische Kirche,* 77; Warner, *Confessions,* 200–202.

211. BAK, Z5/59, PRSB, December 7, 1948.

212. BAK, Z5/18, PRSB, May 8, 1949.

213. On efforts to appoint Weber to the Parliamentary Council, see Petra Holz, *Zwischen Tradition und Emanzipation: CDU-Politikerinnen in der Zeit von 1946 bis 1960* (Königstein, 2004), 122. See also IZG, ED 160/10, 82, Lang-Brumann to Weber, August 27, 1948; IZG, ED 160/7, 66, Stephy Roeger, Frauenarbeitsgemeinschaft der CDU/CSU, *Die Geschäftsführung* (Stuttgart, July 14, 1948).

214. Moeller, *Protecting Motherhood,* 45.

215. Wiliarty, *CDU,* 73–74.

216. *PRSU* (December 6, 1948), 259.

217. *PRSU* (January 6, 1949), 330.

218. IZG, ED 160/10, 83, Weber to Lang-Brumann, September 6, 1948.

219. BAK, Z5/34, PRSB, November 30, 1948.

220. Eva Kolinsky, *Women in Contemporary Germany: Life, Work, and Politics,* 2nd ed. (Oxford, 1993), 44.

221. Hanna Schissler, "Social Democratic Gender Policies, the Working-Class Milieu, and the Culture of Domesticity in West Germany in the 1950s and 1960s," in *Between Reform and Revolution: German Socialism and Communism from 1840 to 1990,* ed. David E. Barclay and Eric D. Weitz (Providence, 1998), 511–15.

222. ACDPStA, I-293-01/3, Rösing, "Elternrecht," 14.

223. Petra Holz, *Zwischen Tradition,* 119.

224. *PRSU* (November 4, 1948), 128.

225. *PRSU* (April 12, 1949), 479.

226. Ines Reich-Hilweg, *Männer und Frauen sind gleichberechtigt: Der Gleichberechtigungsgrundsatz (Art. 3 Abs. 2 GG) in der parlamentarischen Auseinandersetzung, 1948–1957, und in der Rechtssprechung des Bundesverfassungsgerichts, 1953–1975* (Frankfurt a.M., 1979), 18–19.

227. Moeller, *Protecting Motherhood,* 104–5.

228. BAK, Z5/58, PRSB, December 3, 1948. Cf. ACDPStA, I-071-29/1.

229. Bommarius, *Grundgesetz,* 180–82.

230. BAK, Z5/65, PRSB, January 18, 1949. For a list of the petitions submitted, see Reich-Hilweg, *Männer,* 21 n. 26.

231. Bommarius, *Grundgesetz,* 183.

232. Petra Holz, *Zwischen Tradition,* 127.

233. Feldkamp, *Parlamentarischer Rat,* 74.

234. Späth, "Vielfältige Forderungen," 122–67; Moeller, *Protecting Motherhood,* chapter 2.

235. BAK, Z5/128, 376, 214, Antrag der Fraktion der CDU/CSU, dem Artikel 4, Abschnitt 2 (December 14, 1948); BAK Z5/65, PRSB, January 18, 1949.

236. *PRSU* (February 22, 1949), 411; BAK, Z5/65, PRSB, November 11, 1948; ACDPStA, VII-004-127/4, Helene Weber, Niederschrift über die Tagung der Frauenarbeitsgemeinschaft der CDU/CSU Deutschlands (Königswinter, May 25–26, 1949); BAK, Z5/65, PRSB, May 8, 1949. Cf. Rainer Beckmann, "Der parlamentarische Rat und das 'keimende Leben,'" *Der Staat* 47.4 (2008): 552, 558–61.

237. ACDPStA, I-293-01/3, Rösing, "Elternrecht," 9.

238. BAK, Z5/183F, *Rheinischer Merkur* (December 11, 1948).

239. BAK Z5/34, PRSB, November 30, 1948.

240. Heineman, *What Difference,* 143.

241. BAK, Z5/128, 302, 4, Antrag der CDU/CSU Fraktion zur Aufnahme folgender Grundrechtsartikel (November 24, 1948). Cf. BAK, Z5/59, PRSB, December 7, 1948; BAK, Z5/18, PRSB, May 8, 1949.

242. Weber explained, "We are no surplus because we haven't married." See BAK, Z5/35, PRSB, December 4, 1948.

243. BAK, Z5/184F, Helene Weber, "Ehe, Familie, und Elternrecht," *Süddeutsche Zeitung* (December 15, 1948).

244. BAK, Z5 Anhang/12, 41.

245. ACDPStA, I-293-01/3, Rösing, "Elternrecht," 14.

246. BAK, Z5/128, 341, 117, Ausschuß für Grundsatzfragen (December 4, 1948); BAK, Z5/128, 359, 152; Moeller, *Protecting Motherhood,* chapter 2.

247. BAK, Z5/187F, 10, "Gesetzbuch-Reform zugunsten der Frauen," *Süddeutsche Zeitung* (February 5, 1949).

248. IZG, ED 160/7, 66–68, Roeger to Weber, July 14, 1948.

249. BAK, Z5/65, PRSB, January 18, 1949. Cf. Reich-Hilweg, *Männer,* 25–29.

250. IZG, ED 160/31, 31, Koelmann to Weber, September 14, 1949.

251. Kolinsky, *Women,* 46.

252. ACDPStA, VII-004-127/4, Helene Weber, Niederschrift über die Tagung der Frauenarbeitsgemeinschaft der CDU/CSU Deutschlands (Königswinter, May 25–26, 1949).

253. Reich-Hilweg, *Männer,* 31–32.

254. Süssmuth, *Kleine Geschichte,* 81. For other examples of CDU women decrying the Third Reich as a "Männerstaat," see ACDPStA, I-90-15/1, Elfriede Nebgen, speech (presumably Berlin, November 10, 1945); Teusch, "Christliche Frau," 4; "Frauen," 42–44.

255. Moeller, *Protecting Motherhood,* 95–96, 105; Reich-Hilweg, *Männer,* 34–37.

256. Heide Fehrenbach, "The Fight for the 'Christian West': German Film Control, the Churches, and the Reconstruction of Civil Society in the Early Bonn Republic," *German Studies Review* 14.1 (1991): 39–63.

257. Herzog, *Sex after Fascism,* 113.

258. Herzog, *Sex after Fascism,* 118–19. For a perceptive analysis of shifting gender norms within the 1950s Catholic milieu, see Ruff, "Catholic Elites."

CHAPTER 8

1. *PRSU* (January 14, 1949), 345.

2. BAK, Z5/187F, "Spiecker Ausgeschlossen," *Allgemeine Zeitung* (February 12–13, 1949). Wessel would remain the most prominent member of the Center Party until she left the Zentrum in 1952 to found with Gustav Heinemann the All-German People's Party (Gesamtdeutsche Volkspartei [GVP]). In 1957, she joined the SPD. See Friese, "Helene Wessel," 210; Cary, *Path,* 241–71.

3. Warner, *Confessions,* 198–99.

4. BAK, Z5/200F, 23, "Wille zur Macht über den vorparlamentarischen Raum," *Frankfurter Rundschau* (June 15, 1949).

5. BAK, Z5/65, PRSB, February 22, 1949.

6. IZG, ED 160/12, Böhler to Weber, August 4, 1949. Cf. Cary, *Path,* 256–58.

7. ACDPStA, VII-004-127/4, Helene Weber, Niederschrift über die Tagung der Frauenarbeitsgemeinschaft der CDU/CSU Deutschlands (Königswinter, May 25–26, 1949).

8. BAK, Z5/190F, German Center Party, "Die Niederlage von Bonn!" (Münster, April 6, 1949).

9. BAK, Z5/65, PRSB, February 22, 1949.

10. BAK, Z5/199F, "An den Rand geschrieben," *Rhein-Ruhr-Zeitung* (May 28, 1949).

11. *PRSU* (May 11, 1949), 565. The voting record suggests that only one CDU delegate may have supported the Bremen Clause. See chapter 7.

12. Bösch, *Adenauer-CDU,* 134.

13. ACDPStA, VII-004-127/4, Helene Weber, Niederschrift über die Tagung der Frauenarbeitsgemeinschaft der CDU/CSU Deutschlands (Königswinter, May 25–26, 1949).

14. ACDPStA, I-182-04/03, Paul Steup, "Ein ernstes Wort in schwerer Zeit" (May 1949).

15. StBKAH, 12.01, 44–46, Adenauer, speech (Heidelberg, July 21, 1949).

16. Susan E. Scarrow, *Parties and Their Members: Organizing for Victory in Britain and Germany* (Oxford, 1996), 64.

17. *PRSU* (January 6, 1949), 329.

18. Die Wahl zum ersten Deutschen Bundestag am 14. August 1949, in *Politik und Plakat,* ed. Langguth, 75–76, 84–85. Cf. Spicka, *Selling,* 58–60, 74–75.

19. Thomas Mergel, *Propaganda nach Hitler: Eine Kulturgeschichte des Wahlkampfs in der Bundesrepublik, 1949–1990* (Göttingen, 2010), 211–14.

20. ACDPStA, I-182-04/03, Paul Steup, "Ein ernstes Wort in schwerer Zeit" (May 1949).

21. Von Plato and Leh, *"Unglaublicher Frühling,"* 40.

22. Nicholls, *Freedom,* 236, 243.

23. Sevenich, "Schuld," 23; ACDPStA, I-014-01/1, brochure (Göttingen, 1947); BAK, NL 278, 335, brochure, "Zur Aufklärung!" (October 1946).

24. Altmeier, speech (Koblenz, April 7, 1948), in *Peter Altmeier,* ed. Graß und Heyen, 106; Zonal Committee of the CDU in the British Zone, ed., "Was ist," 4.

25. Dianne Kirby, "Christian Faith, Communist Faith: Some Aspects of the Relationship between the Foreign Office Information Research Department and the Church of England Council on Foreign Relations, 1950–1953," *Kirchliche Zeitgeschichte* 13.1 (2000), 217. See also William Inboden III, *Religion and American Foreign Policy, 1945–1960: The Soul of Containment* (Cambridge, 2008).

26. Dianne Kirby, "Divinely Sanctioned: The Anglo-American Cold War Alliance and the Defence of Western Civilization and Christianity, 1945–48," *Journal of Contemporary History* 35.3 (2000): 385–412.

27. Dianne Kirby, "The Cold War, the Hegemony of the United States, and the Golden Age of Christian Democracy," in *Cambridge History*, ed. McLeod, 287–93.

28. Vanessa Conze, *Europa*, 43; Faber, *Abendland*, 27–29; Brockmann, "Germany," 485–89; Schildt, "Ideologie," 50–53, 56. Of those who stressed the anticommunism inherent in the Abendland during the Weimar Republic, the most prominent was Otto Dibelius. See Pöpping, *Abendland*, 141, 150.

29. Dirks, "Christliche Abendland," 125.

30. Adenauer to Sollmann, March 16, 1946, in *Briefe über Deutschland*, 42–43.

31. Schwarz, "Abendländer oder Europäer?" 100.

32. Adenauer to Silverberg, May 30, 1947, in *Briefe über Deutschland*, 64–68.

33. StBKAH, 08.55, 8–28, Adenauer, speech (Recklinghausen, 1948).

34. Weidenfeld, *Konrad Adenauer*, 150.

35. BAK, ZSg. 1-19/4 (1950), Christine Teusch, "Das christliche Bildungsideal," *Politisches Jahrbuch—CDU/CSU—1950*, 31.

36. ACDPStA, I-009-06/2, 305. Dörpinghaus to Nitsch, August 25, 1948.

37. HAStK, 1187, 41, flyer, "Warum CDU?" (September 1946).

38. *DGG* (August 28–29, 1948), 605.

39. Münster, "Grenzen," 777.

40. BAK, ZSg. 1-19/1, 122, Ausgabe A (August 4, 1948), 3.

41. Wengst, "CDU/CSU," 52.

42. BAK, Z5/201 F, 24, "Christliche Gewerkschaftler opponieren gegen Adenauer-Kurs," *Frankfurter Rundschau* (August 29, 1949); BAK, Z5/201F, "Gewerkschaften für Große Koalition," *Frankfurter Neue Presse* (August 30, 1949).

43. Hein, *Zwischen liberaler Milieupartei*, 47–48, 348, 352–53.

44. BAK, Z5/200F, "Die Regierungsbildung," *Ruhr Nachrichten* (August 24, 1949).

45. IZG, ED 160/12, Böhler to Weber (August 4, 1949).

46. Van Hook, *Rebuilding Germany*, 188.

47. Mierzejewski, *Ludwig Erhard*, 86; Spicka, *Selling*, 63–64.

48. Stöss, *Parteien-Handbuch*, 121–45.

49. Rohe, *Wahlen*, 164–66, 171.

50. Bosch, *Adenauer-CDU*, 325; Ute Schmidt, "Christlich Demokratische Union," 572–73.

51. Although he acceded when the faction voted for her, Adenauer openly opposed the appointment of Christine Teusch as minister of education and cultural affairs in North Rhine-Westphalia in 1947, in part because she was female. See Gruber, *CDU-Landtagsfraktion*, 306.

52. IZG, ED 160/11, 133, Weber to Pesch, March 25, 1949. Cf. Adenauer to Zimmer, July 24, 1950, in *Briefe über Deutschland*, 92–93.

53. Bremme, *Politische Rolle,* 31–32, 36–38, 90–92, 253, Tabelle V.

54. Metz, *Ungleichen Gründervater,* 224; Schissler, "Social Democratic Gender Policies," 514.

55. Helge Heidemeyer, ed., *Die CDU/CSU-Fraktion im Deutschen Bundestag: Sitzungsprotokolle, 1949–1953* (Düsseldorf, 1998), xvi–xxvi.

56. Rohe, *Wahlen,* 167–68. See also Kristian Buchna, *Nationale Sammlung an Rhein und Ruhr: Friedrich Middelhauve und die nordrhein-westfälische FDP, 1945–1953* (Munich, 2010).

57. Cary, *Path,* 257–59.

58. Ute Schmidt, "Zentrumspartei oder Union," 658; Warner, *Confessions,* 201 n. 20.

59. http://www.zentrumspartei.de/.

60. Thomas Sauer, "Der Kronberger Kreis: Christlich-Konservative Positionen in der Bundesrepublik Deutschland," in *Katholiken und Protestanten,* ed. Sauer, 121.

61. Ulrich von Hehl, "Konfessionelle Irritationen in der frühen Bundesrepublik," *Historisch-Politische Mitteilungen* 6 (1999): 176.

62. Quoted in *New York Herald Tribune* (December 14, 1949), in Oppelland, "Adenauers Kritiker," 131–33.

63. Mensing, "Adenauer," 50.

64. BAK, Z5/18, PRSB, May 8, 1949.

65. BAK, Z5/192F, "Politik der Kirche," *Neue Ruhr-Zeitung* 4.39 (March 30, 1949); BAK, Z5/13, PRSB, October 20, 1948; BAK, Z5/62, PRSB, January 8, 1949.

66. Rohe, *Wahlen,* 164–66, 171.

67. Von Hehl, "Konfessionelle Irritationen," 169.

68. Ellwein, *Klerikalismus,* 84.

69. Heuss to Adenauer, January 30, 1952, in *Unserem Vaterland zugute: Der Briefwechsel Theodor Heuss/Konrad Adenauer,* ed. Hans Peter Mensing (Berlin, 1989), 103–4.

70. Ellwein, *Klerikalismus,* 108.

71. Bösch, *Adenauer-CDU,* 118, 322.

72. Ellwein, *Klerikalismus,* 91.

73. Jarausch, *After Hitler,* 139.

74. Frank Bösch, "'Zu katholisch': Die Durchsetzung der CDU und das schwierige Zusammengehen der Konfessionen in der Bundesrepublik Deutschland," in *Solidargemeinschaft und fragmentierte Gesellschaft: Parteien, Milieus, und Verbände im Vergleich: Festschrift zum 60. Geburtstag von Peter Lösche,* edited by Tobias Dürr and Franz Walter (Opladen, 1999), 399–400.

75. Moeller, *Protecting Motherhood,* 101–8.

76. Von Hehl, "Konfessionelle Irritationen," 175–79.

77. Quoted in Bösch, "'Zu katholisch,'" 399–400.

78. Bösch, *Adenauer-CDU,* 340.

79. Reytier, "Deutschen Katholiken," 179–81.

80. Wolfram Kaiser, *Christian Democracy,* 232–33, 241. For a different perspective on Adenauer's views on this issue, see Hans-Peter Schwarz's claim that Adenauer always considered Britain part of the Abendland; Schwarz does concede that most people believed Adenauer imagined a map of the Carolingian Empire when he talked about

Europa. See Schwarz, "Abendländer oder Europäer?" 103–6, 110. Cf. Weidenfeld, *Konrad Adenauer,* 54–55.

81. Michael Burgess, "Politischer Katholizismus, Europäische Einigung, und der Aufstieg der Christdemokratie," in *Die Christen und die Entstehung der Europäischen Gemeinschaft,* ed. Martin Greschat and Wilfried Loth (Stuttgart, 1994), 125–37. Cf. Heinz Hürten, "Der Beitrag Christlicher Demokraten zum geistigen und politischen Wiederaufbau und zur europäischen Integration nach 1945: Bundesrepublik Deutschland," in *Christliche Demokratie,* ed. Winfried Becker and Morsey, 213–23.

82. Wolfram Kaiser, *Christian Democracy,* 232–33, 241–44.

83. Dietrich Orlow, "Delayed Reaction: Democracy, Nationalism, and the SPD, 1945–1966," *German Studies Review* 16.1 (1993): 87–90.

84. Egen, "Entstehung," il–l. The flyer provoked especially strong criticism from Adenauer. See *PBV* (September 10, 1953), 4.

85. Dorothee Buchhaas-Birkholz, ed., *"Zum politischen Weg unseres Volkes": Politische Leitbilder und Vorstellungen im deutschen Protestantismus, 1945–1952: Eine Dokumentation* (Düsseldorf, 1989), 14.

86. Ernst Christian Helmreich, *Religious Education in German Schools: An Historical Approach* (Cambridge, 1959), 237–41.

87. Ellen Lovell Evans, *Cross and Ballot,* 14; van Schewick, *Katholische Kirche,* 54.

88. Buchhaas, *Gesetzgebung im Wiederaufbau,* 79.

89. Pütz, *Innerparteiliche Willensbildung,* 56–69.

90. Fraktionssitzung (August 8, 1951), in *CDU/CSU-Fraktion,* ed. Heidemeyer, 330. See also Greschat, "Konfessionelle Spannungen," 31.

91. Oppelland, "Evangelische Arbeitskreis," 106.

92. Besier, "'Christliche Parteipolitik.'"

93. Egen, "Entstehung," 64 n. 1, 75.

94. BAK, NL 278, 141, Boelitz to Holzapfel, June 12, 1948.

95. Egen, "Entstehung," 120, 127.

96. IZG, ED 160/7, 137–38, Weber to Roeger, May 28, 1949. Cf. IZG, ED 160/31, 77, Weber et al. to Held, September 20, 1948; IZG, ED 160/12, 60, Arbeitsgemeinschaft katholischer Frauen to Adenauer, June 24, 1949.

97. Oppelland, "Evangelische Arbeitskreis," 108–9. Cf. Andreas Hillgruber, "Heinemanns evangelisch-christlich begründete Opposition gegen Adenauers Politik, 1950–1952," in *Politik und Konfession: Festschrift für Konrad Repgen zum 60. Geburtstag,* ed. Dieter Albrecht (Berlin, 1983).

98. Ehlers, speech (Bremen, March 10, 1952), in *Reden zur politischen Verantwortung: Schriften des Evangelischen Arbeitskreises für kulturelle Fragen,* ed. Hermann Ehlers (Bremen, 1956), 5–8.

99. Egen, "Entstehung," 48–61.

100. Quoted in Egen, "Entstehung," 93 n. 1, 106–7.

101. Oppelland, "Der Evangelische Arbeitskreis," 105, 121.

102. Egen, "Entstehung," 123–25.

103. Klaus Gotto, "Wandlungen des politischen Katholizismus seit 1945," in *Wirtschaftlicher Wandel,* ed. Oberndörfer, Rattinger, and Schmitt, 228.

104. Jarausch, *After Hitler,* 87–89.

105. Ruff, *Wayward Flock*, 4.
106. Herzog, *Sex after Fascism*, 30.
107. Hirschfeld, *Katholisches Milieu;* Damberg, "Milieu," 345–47, 335–50.
108. Ruff, *Wayward Flock*, 189–90.
109. Lösche and Walter, "Katholiken, Konservative, und Liberale," 487.
110. Jeffrey Cox, "Secularization and Other Master Narratives of Religion in Modern Europe," *Kirchliche Zeitgeschichte* 14.1 (2001): 24–35. Cf. Callum G. Brown, "The Secularization Decade: What the 1960s Have Done to the Study of Religious History," in *The Decline of Christendom in Western Europe, 1750–2000*, ed. Hugh McLeod and Werner Ustorf (Cambridge, 2003), 29–46.
111. Herzog, *Intimacy*, xi.
112. Spotts, *Churches*, x.
113. Buchhaas and Kühr, "Von der Volkskirche," 154.
114. Ellen Lovell Evans, *Cross and Ballot*, 14.
115. Damberg, "Milieu," 345–47.
116. For figures on mixed marriages, see Franz Greiner, "Die Katholiken in der technischen Gesellschaft der Nachkriegszeit," in *Deutscher Katholizismus nach 1945: Kirche, Gesellschaft, Geschichte*, ed. Hans Maier (Munich, 1964), 104. While 1982 data reveal that almost 80 percent of West German marriages were confessionally homogenous, the incidence of "mixed marriages" was clearly tied to dechristianization: The less frequently West Germans visited church, the more likely they were to marry outside their religious tradition. See Pappi, "Konfessionell-religiöse Konfliktlinie," 263–90. Cf. Rölli-Alkemper, *Familie*, 190–91; Müller-Rolli, *Evangelische Schulpolitik*, 44; Ellen Lovell Evans, *Cross and Ballot*, 271–72.
117. Ruff, *Wayward Flock*, 8–9.
118. Christof Wolf, "Konfessionelle versus religiöse Konfliktslinie in der deutschen Wählerschaft," *Politische Vierteljahresschrift* 37.4 (1996): 714.
119. Besier, "'Christliche Parteipolitik,'" 167; Bösch, *Adenauer-CDU*, 46.
120. Michael Klein, "Der westdeutsche Protestantismus," 86. Cf. Stefan Marx, "Robert Lehr (1883–1956): Landtagsabgeordneter, Nordrhein-Westfalen," in *In Verantwortung*, ed. Buchstab and Kleinmann, 259–60; Christopher Beckmann, "Adolf Blomeyer," 121. Less typical of this phenomenon was Ulrich Steiner, who left Christian Democratic politics after 1948 for a variety of reasons, including the revelation of his Nazi past. See Häußler, "Ulrich Steiner," 191.
121. Pearson, "Pluralization."
122. Buchhaas and Kühr, "Von der Volkskirche," 138, 151.
123. Kurt Klotzbach, "SPD und katholische Kirche nach 1945—Belastungen, Mißverständnisse und Neuanfänge," *Archiv für Sozialgeschichte* 29 (1989): 37–47.
124. Ute Schmidt, "Christlich Demokratische Union," 581.
125. Ellen Lovell Evans, *Cross and Ballot*, 270; Broughton, "CDU-CSU," 108.
126. Quoted in Otto Hermann Bolesch, ed., *Adenauer für alle Lebenslagen: Eine deutsche Fibel* (Munich, 1968), 24.
127. Claus A. Fischer, *Wahlhandbuch*, 1:12.
128. Süssmuth, *Kleine Geschichte*, 82, 130.
129. Kees van Kersbergen, "The Christian Democratic Phoenix and Modern Unsecular Politics," *Party Politics* 24.3 (2008): 264. Cf. Kalyvas, "Unsecular Politics."

130. Ulrich Lappenküper, "Between Concentration Movement and People's Party: The Christian Democratic Union in Germany," in *Christian Democracy in Europe since 1945,* ed. Michael Gehler and Wolfram Kaiser (London, 2004), 31.

131. Bösch, "'Zu katholisch,'" 406.

132. Pütz, *Innerparteiliche Willensbildung,* 67–68.

133. Bösch, *Adenauer-CDU,* 349; Gotto, "Wandlungen," 227–30.

134. Buchhaas and Kühr, "Von der Volkskirche," 150–51.

135. Oppelland, "Adenauers Kritiker," 147–48.

136. Axel Schildt, *Moderne Zeiten: Freizeit, Massenmedien, und "Zeitgeist" in der Bundesrepublik der 50er Jahre* (Hamburg, 1995), 351.

137. Kleinmann, "'Wahren, pflegen, ausbauen,'" 52. For the definitive history of *Lastenausgleich,* see Michael L. Hughes, *Shouldering the Burdens of Defeat: West Germany and the Reconstruction of Social Justice* (Chapel Hill, 1999).

138. S. Jonathan Wiesen, *West German Industry and the Challenge of the Nazi Past, 1945–1955* (Chapel Hill, 2001), 163–65. See also Maria Höhn, *GIs and Frauleins: The German-American Encounter in 1950s West Germany* (Chapel Hill, 2002); Uta G. Poiger, *Jazz, Rock, and Rebels: Cold War Politics and American Culture in a Divided Germany* (Berkeley, 2000); Heide Fehrenbach, *Cinema in Democratizing Germany: Reconstructing National Identity after Hitler* (Chapel Hill, 1995).

139. Schildt, *Moderne Zeiten,* 360.

140. *PBV* (September 10, 1953), 21 n. 69.

141. For representative examples, see *PBV* (June 3, 1955), 576–78; *PBV* (November 23, 1956), 1143–44.

142. *PBV* (January 13, 1956), 732–33.

143. *PBV* (May 2, 1955), 429–30; *PBV* (July 12, 1956), 939.

144. *PBV* (June 3, 1955), 570.

145. *PBV* (November 23, 1956), 1109.

146. Philipp Gassert, *Amerika im Dritten Reich: Ideologie, Propaganda, und Volksmeinung, 1933–1945* (Stuttgart, 1997), 13–14; Poiger, *Jazz,* 13.

147. Wolfram Kaiser, "Trigger-Happy Protestant Materialists? The European Christian Democrats and the United States," in *Between Empire and Alliance: America and Europe during the Cold War,* ed. Marc Trachtenberg (Lanham, 2003), 65.

148. CDU criticisms of the United States did emerge in the 1960s. See Eugen Gerstenmaier, *Reden und Aufsätze,* ed. Evangelischen Verlagswerk (Stuttgart, 1962), 2:93–94; Hans-Jürgen Grabbe, *Unionsparteien, Sozialdemokratie, und Vereinigte Staaten von Amerika, 1945–1966* (Düsseldorf, 1983), 41.

149. Geiger, *Atlantiker,* 50.

150. Spicka, *Selling,* 14–15; Höhn, *GIs;* Heide Fehrenbach, *Race after Hitler: Black Occupation Children in Postwar Germany and America* (Princeton, 2007).

151. Poiger, *Jazz,* 7–11, 206–19; Spicka, *Selling.* On the housewife as the paradigm of the new consuming citizen, see Erica Carter, *How German Is She? Postwar West German Reconstruction and the Consuming Woman* (Ann Arbor, 1997).

152. Mensing, "Adenauer," 59.

153. Torsten Oppelland, "'Politik aus christlicher Verantwortung': Der Evangelische Arbeitskreis der CDU/CSU in der Ära Adenauer," in *Katholiken und Protestanten,* ed. Sauer, 50, 60.

154. Hürten, "Topos," 149, 153–54; Michael Bosch, "Ideelle Aspekte der Westintegration der Bundesrepublik bei Konrad Adenauer," in *Wege in die Zeitgeschichte: Festschrift zum 65. Geburtstag von Gerhard Schulz,* ed. Jürgen Heideking, Gerhard Hufnagel, and Franz Knipping (Berlin, 1989), 191; Weidenfeld, *Konrad Adenauer.*

155. BAK, Z5/13, PRSB, October 20, 1948.

156. Schildt, *Zwischen Abendland und Amerika,* 36–37. Cf. Buchhaas, *Volkspartei,* 210–16.

157. Pöpping, *Abendland,* 218–19.

158. Wolfram Kaiser, "Trigger-Happy Protestant Materialists," 73.

159. Vanessa Conze, *Europa,* 137. Cf. Schildt, *Moderne Zeiten,* 333; Schildt, *Zwischen Abendland und Amerika,* 42–49.

160. DGG (August 28–29, 1948), 639–53; Adenauer, speech (Goslar, October 20, 1950), in *Christliche Demokratie in Deutschland: Analysen und Dokumente zur Geschichte und Programmatik der Christlich Demokratischen Union Deutschlands und der Jungen Union Deutschlands,* ed. Konrad-Adenauer-Stiftung (Melle, 1978), 55. Cf. Schildt, *Zwischen Abendland und Amerika,* 36; Faber, *Abendland,* 95–96.

161. Geiger, *Atlantiker,* 33, 54; Schwarz, "Abendländer oder Europäer?" 110; Schwarz, *Konrad Adenauer: A German Politician,* 1:393.

162. StBKAH, 08.55, 8–28, Adenauer, speech (Recklinghausen, 1948).

163. Ronald J. Granieri, *The Ambivalent Alliance: Konrad Adenauer, the CDU/CSU, and the West, 1949–1966* (Providence, 2003), 154, 167.

164. For example, while in the CDU's October 1950 Goslar program from the first Bundesparteitag of the party, party officials defined the "political struggle of the present" as the "preservation of Christian abendländischen culture and the salvaging of human freedom from the dangers of totalitarian state control and collectivistic depersonalization," the party's 1953 Hamburg Program made no reference to the Abendland. See Konrad-Adenauer-Stiftung, *Christliche Demokratie,* 53–62, 775.

165. Hürten, "Topos," 137, 146; Vanessa Conze, *Europa,* 5–13, 121–22, 138, 170, 385.

166. Anselm Doering-Manteuffel, *Wie westlich sind die Deutschen? Amerikanisierung und Westernisierung im 20. Jahrhundert* (Göttingen, 1999); Axel Schildt, *Ankunft im Westen: Ein Essay zur Erfolgsgeschichte der Bundesrepublik* (Frankfurt, 1999); Ulrich Herbert, ed., *Wandlungsprozesse in Westdeutschland: Belastung, Integration, Liberalisierung, 1945–1980* (Göttingen, 2002).

167. I am grateful to Volker Berghahn for directing my attention to the CDU's use of the term *totalitarianism.* For two of many examples, see ACDPStA, I-171-01/1, Dovifat, speech (27th anniversary of X. Congress of the Christian Trade Unions of Germany, ca. 1947); BAK, Z5/13, PRSB, October 20, 1948. Cf. Jean Solchany, "Vom Antimodernismus zum Antitotalitarismus: Konservative Interpretationen des Nationalsozialismus in Deutschland, 1945–1949," *Vierteljahrshefte für Zeitgeschichte* 44.3 (1996): 373–94.

168. Günter Buchstab, ed., *"Es mußte alles neu gemacht werden": Die Protokolle des CDU-Bundesvorstandes, 1950–1953,* 2nd ed. (Stuttgart, 1986), 11; Vanessa Conze, *Europa,* 159; Schildt, *Zwischen Abendland und Amerika,* 34 n. 62.

169. Von Brentano's analogy was prefigured in 1948 by Georges Bidault, who likened Soviet Communism to medieval Islam threatening Europe. See Wolfram Kaiser,

"Trigger-Happy Protestant Materialists," 68. Cf. Faber, *Abendland,* 37–38; Vanessa Conze, *Europa,* 162–67.

170. The initial inquiry from the Bundestag came from SPD representative Helmut Schmidt. See Schildt, *Zwischen Abendland und Amerika,* 68–77; Schildt, "Ideologie," 59.

171. *PBV* (November 23, 1956), 1178–80.

172. Vanessa Conze, *Europa,* 139, 389, 188–92, 400.

173. Granieri, *Ambivalent Alliance,* 2, 205.

174. Oppelland, "Adenauers Kritiker," 147–48.

175. Geiger, *Atlantiker,* 52, 59–60.

176. Bösch, *Adenauer-CDU,* 322.

177. Pütz, *CDU,* 37–43.

178. Andreas Engel, "Regionale politische Traditionen und die Entwicklung der CDU/CSU," in *Parteien und regionale politische Traditionen in der Bundesrepublik Deutschland,* ed. Dieter Oberndörfer and Karl Schmitt (Berlin, 1991), 120–21; Rohe, *Wahlen,* 174.

179. Pappi, "Konfessionell-religiöse Konfliktlinie," 263–90.

180. Karl Schmitt, *Konfession und Wahlverhalten in der Bundesrepublik Deutschland* (Berlin, 1989), 213.

181. Throughout West German history, more than a third of all CDU members hailed from North Rhine-Westphalia. See Corinna Franz and Oliver Gnad, eds., *Handbuch zur Statistik der Parlamente und Parteien in den westlichen Besatzungszonen und in der Bundesrepublik Deutschland,* vol. 2, *CDU und CSU: Mitgliedschaft und Sozialstruktur, 1945–1990* (Düsseldorf, 2005), 93–95.

182. Schmitt, *Konfession,* 122.

183. Christof Wolf, "Konfessionelle," 731.

184. Wolfgang G. Gibowski, "Germany's General Election in 1994: Who Voted for Whom?" in *Germany's New Politics,* ed. David P. Conradt, Gerald R. Kleinfeld, George K. Romoser, and Christian Søe (Tempe, 1995), 106–7.

185. Rohe, *Wahlen,* 167–68.

CONCLUSION

1. George S. Williamson, "A Religious Sonderweg? Reflections on the Sacred and the Secular in the Historiography of Modern Germany," *Church History* 75 (2006): 139–56.

2. Dieter Roth and Andreas Wüst, "Abwahl ohne Machtwechsel? Die Bundestagswahl 2005 im Lichte langfristiger Entwicklungen," in *Bilanz der Bundestagswahl 2005: Voraussetzungen, Ergebnisse, Folgen,* ed. Eckhard Jesse and Roland Sturm (Wiesbaden, 2006), 54; Sigrid Roßteutscher, "CDU-Wahl 2005: Katholiken, Kirchgänger, und eine protestantische Spitzenkandidatin aus dem Osten," in *Die Bundestagswahl 2005: Analyse des Wahlkampfes und der Wahlergebnisse,* ed. Frank Brettschneider, Oskar Niedermayer, and Bernhard Wessels (Wiesbaden, 2007), 321; Karl-Rudolf Korte, ed., *Die Bundestagswahl 2009: Analysen der Wahl-, Parteien-, Kommunikations-, und Regierungsforschung* (Wiesbaden, 2010).

3. Von Hehl, "Konfessionelle Irritationen," 187.

4. Von Hehl, *Adenauer und die Kirchen,* 228.

5. René Rémond, *Religion and Society in Modern Europe* (Oxford, 1999), 209–10.

6. http://www.eak-cducsu.de/web/index.php.

7. Wiliarty, *CDU,* 2, chapter 7.

8. Martin Lohmann, *Das Kreuz mit dem C: Wie christlich ist die Union?* (Kevelaer, 2009), 11, 131. Lohmann specifically contrasts Bonn with the new German capital, Berlin, where he argues that one must look harder to discover "Christian culture" (32–33).

9. A 2005 study by the EKD lists 29.4 million Germans as "of other belief or confessionless"; 25.7 million Protestants; 25.9 million Catholics; and 1.4 million Orthodox and belonging to other Christian churches. See *Der Spiegel* 29/2007, 35.

10. http://www.aek-online.de/.

11. By the late 1980s, the West German Protestant rate of weekly church attendance was a startling 4 percent. See Broughton, "CDU-CSU," 109. Mark Ruff cites a 1996 figure for weekly Catholic Church attendance of 18 percent. See Ruff, *Wayward Flock,* 1, 201. Cf. Lois, "Wie verändert sich die Religiosität."

12. Ellen Lovell Evans, *Cross and Ballot,* 277.

13. Hartmut Lehmann's introduction to his edited volume on coexistence and conflict of religions in unified Europe focuses on the Islam-Christian divide in Europe, with no reference to intra-Christian differences. See Hartmut Lehmann, "Zur Einführung: Koexistenz und Konflikt von Religionen in Europa," in *Koexistenz und Konflikt von Religionen im vereinten Europa,* ed. Hartmut Lehmann (Göttingen, 2004), 7–11.

14. Gerhard Schmidtchen, *Protestanten und Katholiken: Soziologische Analyse konfessioneller Kultur* (Bern, 1973), 245.

15. Jarausch, *After Hitler,* 132.

16. Jarausch, *After Hitler,* 98.

17. Nicholls, *Freedom,* 12; Mierzejewski, *Ludwig Erhard,* 41.

18. *Der Spiegel* 25/2007, 42.

19. Spicka, *Selling,* 51.

20. Laitenberger, "Ludwig Erhard," 118.

21. Buchhaas and Kühr, "Von der Volkskirche," 217–18.

22. Plakat zur Kommunalwahl in Nordrhein-Westfalen am 15.9.1946, in *Politik und Plakat,* ed., Langguth, 50.

Works Cited

PRIMARY SOURCES (1945–48)

Adenauer, Konrad. "Rede des Ersten Vorsitzenden der Christlich Demokratischen Union für die britische Zone" (Düsseldorf, May 12, 1946). *Schriftenreihe der Christlich Demokratischen Union des Rheinlandes* 10 (Cologne, 1946).

Albers, Johannes. "Die Aufgabe der Christlich Demokratischen Union im Leben des deutschen Volkes." *Schriftenreihe der Christlich Demokratischen Union des Rheinlandes* 2 (Cologne, 1945).

Boelitz, Otto. "Erziehung und Schule im Christlich-Demokratischen Staat: Das Bildungsideal und das Schulprogramm der CDU." *Politik aus Christlicher Verantwortung* 7 (Recklinghausen, 1946).

Dirks, Walter. "Das Abendland und der Sozialismus." *Frankfurter Hefte: Zeitschrift für Kultur und Politik* 1.3 (1946): 67–76.

Dirks, Walter. "Evangelisch-katholisches Gespräch." *Frankfurter Hefte: Zeitschrift für Kultur und Politik* 2.1 (1947): 13–16.

Dirks, Walter. "Die geistige Aufgabe des deutschen Katholizismus." *Frankfurter Hefte: Zeitschrift für Kultur und Politik* 1.2 (1946): 38–52.

"Frauen im Männerstaat." In *Frauen Gestern und Heute: Wege in die Neue Zeit*. Berlin, 1946.

Kaiser, Jakob. "Deutschlands geschichtliche Aufgaben." *Der Soziale Staat: Reden und Gedanken, Wege in die Neue Zeit* 2 (Berlin, February 13, 1946).

Kaiser, Jakob. "Europa und Deutschland." *Der Soziale Staat: Reden und Gedanken, Wege in die Neue Zeit* 2 (Berlin, January 30, 1946).

Kannengießer, Josef, ed. "Entscheidung—Aus christlicher Verantwortung (CDU oder neues Zentrum?)" (Dortmund, September 1946).

Ketterer, Artur, ed. "Das innere Gesetz der 'Union' (CDU) und seine politischen Folgerungen." *Politik aus christlicher Verantwortung* 2 (1946).

Kogon, Eugen. "Das Dritte Reich und die preussisch-deutsche Geschichte." *Frankfurter Hefte: Zeitschrift für Kultur und Politik* 1.3 (1946): 44–57.

Kogon, Eugen. "Der Geistliche im öffentlichen Leben." *Frankfurter Hefte: Zeitschrift für Kultur und Politik* 1.9 (1946): 796–98.

Kogon, Eugen. "Gericht und Gewissen." *Frankfurter Hefte: Zeitschrift für Kultur und Politik* 1.1 (1946): 25–37.

Kogon, Eugen. "Kirchliche Kundgebungen von politischer Bedeutung." *Frankfurter Hefte: Zeitschrift für Kultur und Politik* 2.7 (1947): 633–38.

Kogon, Eugen. "Klerus, Seelsorge, und Politik in Böhmen und im Rheinland." *Frankfurter Hefte: Zeitschrift für Kultur und Politik* 2.6 (1947): 535–38.

Münster, Clemens. "Grenzen des Abendlandes." *Frankfurter Hefte: Zeitschrift für Kultur und Politik* 2.8 (1947): 776–87.

Scharmitzel, Theodor. "Die Christlich-Demokratische Union Deutschlands: Ihr Wesen und Wollen." *Schriftenreihe der Christlich-Demokratische Union Deutschlands, Landesverband Rheinland* 1 (Cologne, March 25, 1946).

Scharmitzel, Theodor. "Christliche Demokratie im neuen Deutschland." *Schriftenreihe der Christlich Demokratischen Union des Rheinlandes* 1 (Cologne, 1945).

Schmidt, Otto. "Christlicher Realismus—Ein Versuch zu sozialwirtchaftlicher Neuordnung." *Schriftenreihe der Christlich Demokratischen Union des Rheinlandes* 7 (Cologne, 1946).

Schreiber, Hans, ed. "Neuordnung der industriellen Wirtschaft." In *Was will die CDU? Das Parteiprogramm und die ergänzenden programmatischen Erklärungen der CDU der britischen Zone.* Cologne, 1948.

Sevenich, Maria. "Die Christlich-Demokratische Union in der Not der Zeit" (Stuttgart, February 23, 1946).

Sevenich, Maria. "Um Schuld und Not unserer Zeit: Realpolitische Erwägungen über Kollektiv- und Individualschuld und das christliche Menschenbild." *Politik aus christlicher Verantwortung* 2 (Recklinghausen, 1946).

Sevenich, Maria. "Unser Gesicht: Abhandlung über Christlichen und Marxistischen Sozialismus." *Politik aus Christlicher Verantwortung* 1 (Bad Godesberg, December 14–16, 1945).

Sevenich, Maria. "Das Werden der neuen deutschen Demokratie!" (Wiesbaden, March 11, 1946).

Stegerwald, Adam. "Wo stehen wir?" (Würzburg, August 21, 1945).

Stegerwald, Adam. "Wohin gehen wir?" (Würzburg, November 5, 1945).

Teusch, Christine. "Die christliche Frau im politischen Zeitgeschehen." *Schriftenreihe der Christlich-Demokratischen Union Westfalen-Lippe* 2 (September 1946).

Zimmermann, Karl, ed. "Erbe und Aufgabe: Bericht über die Tagung der Sozialausschüsse der CDU der britischen Zone" (Herne, February 21–22, 1947).

Zimmermann, Karl. "Erste Reichstagung der Christlich Demokratischen Union." *Schriftenreihe der Christlich Demokratischen Union des Rheinlandes* 5 (Cologne, 1945).

Zimmermann, Karl. "Herner Tagung der Sozialausschüsse der CDU von Niederrhein-Westfalen" (Herne, November 8–9, 1946).

Zimmermann, Karl. "Das politisch-soziale Weltbild des christlichen Arbeiters" (Krefeld, August 8, 1946).

Zonenausschuss der CDU in der britischen Zone, ed. "Was ist—Was will die CDU? Gedanken zur politischen Arbeit der Christlich-Demokratischen Union" (1948).

PUBLISHED SOURCES

Adenauer, Konrad. *Erinnerungen, 1945–1953.* Stuttgart, 1965.

Adenauer, Konrad. "Konrad Adenauer als Präsident des Preussischen Staatsrates." In

Konrad Adenauer, Oberbürgermeister von Köln, edited by Hugo Stehkämper. Cologne, 1976.

Agethen, Manfred. "Der Widerstand der demokratischen Kräfte in der CDU gegen den Gleichschaltungsdruck von sowjetischer Besatzungsmacht und SED, 1945–1952." In *Die CDU in der sowjetisch besetzten Zone/DDR, 1945–1952,* edited by Alexander Fischer and Manfred Agethen. Sankt Augustin, 1994.

Albert, Marcel. *Die Benediktinerabtei Maria Laach und der Nationalsozialismus.* Paderborn, 2004.

Albertin, Lothar. *Politischer Liberalismus in der britischen Besatzungszone, 1946–1948: Führungsorgane und Politik der FDP,* edited by Hans F. W. Gringmuth. Düsseldorf, 1995.

Alexander, Edgar. "Church and Society in Germany: Social and Political Movements and Ideas in German and Austrian Catholicism (1789–1950)." In *Church and Society: Catholic Social and Political Thought and Movements, 1789–1950,* edited by J. N. Moody. New York, 1953.

Altgeld, Wolfgang. "Christentum, Revolution, Nation: Geschichtliche und Zeitgeschichtliche Auseinandersetzungen in der Formierung des deutschen Katholizismus." *Historisches Jahrbuch* 121 (2001): 501–12.

Altgeld, Wolfgang. *Katholizismus, Protestantismus, Judentum: Über religiös begründete Gegensätze und nationalreligiöse Ideen in der Geschichte des deutschen Nationalismus.* Mainz, 1992.

Ambrosius, Gerold. *Die Durchsetzung der Sozialen Marktwirtschaft in Westdeutschland, 1945–1949.* Stuttgart, 1977.

Anderson, Margaret Lavinia. "Interdenominationalism, Clericalism, Pluralism: The 'Zentrumsstreit' and the Dilemma of Catholicism in Wilhelmine Germany." *Central European History* 21.4 (1988): 350–78.

Anderson, Margaret Lavinia. "Living Apart and Together in Germany." In *Protestants, Catholics, and Jews in Germany, 1800–1914,* edited by Helmut Walser Smith. Oxford, 2001.

Anderson, Margaret Lavinia. "Piety and Politics: Recent Work on German Catholicism." *Journal of Modern History* 63.4 (1991): 681–716.

Anderson, Margaret Lavinia. *Practicing Democracy: Elections and Political Culture in Imperial Germany.* Princeton, 2000.

Anderson, Margaret Lavinia. *Windthorst: A Political Biography.* New York, 1981.

Arbeitskreis für kirchliche Zeitgeschichte (AKKZG). "Katholiken zwischen Tradition und Moderne: Das katholische Milieu als Forschungsaufgabe." *Westfälische Forschungen* 43 (1993): 588–654.

Arentz, Hermann-Josef. "Die Anfänge der Christlich-Demokratische Union in Köln." In *Köln nach dem Nationalsozialismus: Der Beginn des gesellschaftlichen und politischen Lebens in den Jahren 1945/46,* edited by Otto Dan. Wuppertal, 1981.

Aretz, Jürgen. *Katholische Arbeiterbewegung und Nationalsozialismus: Der Verband Katholischer Arbeiter und Knappenvereine Westdeutschlands, 1923 bis 1945.* Mainz, 1977.

Baadte, Günter. "Grundfragen der politischen und gesellschaftlichen Neuordnung in den Hirtenbriefen der deutschen Bischöfe, 1945–1949." *Jahrbuch für christliche Sozialwissenschaften* 27 (1986): 95–113.

Baranowski, Shelley. *The Sanctity of Rural Life: Nobility, Protestantism, and Nazism in Weimar Prussia.* Oxford, 1995.

Baranowsky, Shelley. *The Confessing Church, Conservative Elites, and the Nazi State.* Lewiston, 1986.

Baranowsky, Shelley. "Consent and Dissent: The Confessing Church and Conservative Opposition to National Socialism." *Journal of Modern History* 59.1 (1987): 53–78.

Baumgartner, Alois. *Sehnsucht nach Gemeinschaft: Ideen und Strömungen im Sozial-katholizismus der Weimarer Republik.* Munich, 1977.

Baus, Katrin, and Ralf Thomas Baus. "Die Gründung der Christlich-Demokratischen Union Deutschlands in Brandenburg 1945." *Historisch-Politische Mitteilungen* 6 (1999): 79–108.

Baus, Ralf Thomas. *Die Christlich-Demokratische Union Deutschlands in der sowjetisch besetzten Zone, 1945 bis 1948: Gründung—Programm—Politik.* Düsseldorf, 2001.

Baus, Ralf Thomas. "Die Gründung der Christlich-Demokratischen Union Deutschlands in Sachsen 1945." *Historisch-Politische Mitteilungen* 2 (1995): 83–117.

Becker, Felix, ed. *Kleine Geschichte der CDU.* Stuttgart, 1995.

Becker, Hellmut, and Gerhard Kluchert. *Die Bildung der Nation: Schule, Gesellschaft, und Politik vom Kaiserreich zur Weimarer Republik.* Stuttgart, 1993.

Becker, Winfried. *CDU und CSU, 1945–1950: Vorläufer, Gründung, und regionale Entwicklung bis zum Entstehen der CDU-Bundespartei.* Mainz, 1987.

Becker, Winfried. "Die Deutsche Zentrumspartei gegenüber dem Nationalsozialismus und dem Reichskonkordat, 1930–1933: Motivationsstrukturen und Situationszwänge." *Historisch-Politische Mitteilungen* 7 (2000): 1–37.

Becker, Winfried. "Grundlinien des Verhältnisses zwischen römisch-katholischer Kirche und Staat in Deutschland während des 19. und 20. Jahrhunderts." *Kirchliche Zeitgeschichte* 14.1 (2001): 77–95.

Becker, Winfried. "Staats- und Verfassungsverständnis der christlichen Demokratie von den Anfängen bis 1933." In *Geschichte der Christlich-Demokratischen und Christlich-Sozialen Bewegungen in Deutschland,* edited by Günther Rüther. 3rd ed. Bonn, 1989.

Becker, Winfried, and Rudolf Morsey, eds. *Christliche Demokratie in Europa: Grundlagen und Entwicklungen seit dem 19. Jahrhundert.* Cologne, 1988.

Beckmann, Christopher. "Adolf Blomeyer (1900–1969): Landwirt und Bürgermeister, Nordrhein-Westfalen." In *In Verantwortung vor Gott und den Menschen: Christliche Demokraten im Parlamentarischen Rat, 1948/49,* edited by Günter Buchstab and Hans-Otto Kleinmann. Freiburg i.B., 2008.

Beckmann, Christopher. "Lambert Lensing (1889–1965): Zeitungsverlegen, Mitgründer der CDU, Landesvorsitzender der CDU Westfalen-Lippe." *Historisch-Politische Mitteilungen* 14 (2007): 153–86.

Beckmann, Joachim, ed. *Kirchliches Jahrbuch für die Evangelische Kirche in Deutschland 1949.* Gütersloh, 1950.

Beckmann, Rainer. "Der parlamentarische Rat und das 'keimende Leben.'" *Der Staat* 47.4 (2008): 551–72.

Bendel, Rainer. *Aufbruch aus dem Glauben? Katholische Heimatvertriebene in den gesellschaftlichen Transformationen der Nachkriegsjahre, 1945–1965.* Cologne, 2003.

Bendel-Maidl, Lydia, and Rainer Bendel. "Schlaglichter auf den Umgang der deutschen Bischöfe mit der nationalsozialistichen Vergangenheit." In *Die Katholische Schuld? Katholizismus im Dritten Reich—Zwischen Arrangement und Widerstand,* edited by Rainer Bendel. 2nd ed. Münster, 2004.

Benz, Wolfgang. "Föderalistische Politik in der CDU/CSU: Die Verfassungsdiskussion im 'Ellwanger Kreis,' 1947/48." *Vierteljahreshefte für Zeitgeschichte* 25.4 (1977): 776–820.

Benz, Wolfgang. *Potsdam 1945: Besatzungsherrschaft und Neuaufbau im Vier-Zonen-Deutschland.* 4th ed. Munich, 2005.

Benz, Wolfgang. *Zwischen Hitler und Adenauer: Studien zur deutschen Nachkriegsgesellschaft.* Frankfurt a.M., 1991.

Berg-Schlosser, Dirk. "Die Konstituierung des Wirtschaftssssytem." In *Vorgeschichte der Bundesrepublik Deutschland: Zwischen Kapitulation und Grundgesetz,* edited by Josef Becker, Theo Stammen, and Peter Waldmann. 2nd ed. Munich, 1987.

Bergen, Doris L. *Twisted Cross: The German Christian Movement in the Third Reich.* Chapel Hill, 1996.

Bernecker, Walther L. "Die Neugründung der Gewerkschaften in den Westzonen." In *Vorgeschichte der Bundesrepublik Deutschland: Zwischen Kapitulation und Grundgesetz,* edited by Josef Becker, Theo Stammen, and Peter Waldmann. 2nd ed. Munich, 1987.

Besier, Gerhard. "'Christliche Parteipolitik' und Konfession: Zur Entstehung des Evangelischen Arbeitskreises der CDU/CSU." *Kirchliche Zeitgeschichte* 3 (1990): 166–87.

Besier, Gerhard. *Die Kirchen und das Dritte Reich: Spaltungen und Abwehrkämpfe, 1934–1937.* Munich, 2001.

Besier, Gerhard. "Die politische Rolle des Protestantismus in der Nachkriegszeit." *Aus Politik und Zeitgeschichte* B 50 (2000): 29–38.

Besier, Gerhard. "Zwischen Neuanfang und Restauration: Die evangelischen Kirchen in Deutschland nach dem Zweiten Weltkrieg." In *Ende des Dritten Reiches—Ende des Zweiten Weltkrieges: Eine perspektivische Rückschau,* edited by Hans-Erich Volkmann. Munich, 1995.

Besier, Gerhard, and Gerhard Sauter. *Wie Christen ihre Schuld bekennen: Die Stuttgarter Erklärung 1945.* Göttingen, 1985.

Birke, Adolf M. "Katholische Kirche und Politik in der Phase des Neubeginns, 1945–1949." In *Die Zeit nach 1945 als Thema kirchlicher Zeitgeschichte: Referate der internationalen Tagung in Hünigen/Bern (Schweiz) 1985,* edited by Victor Conzemius, Martin Greschat, and Hermann Kocher. Göttingen, 1988.

Blackbourn, David. *Class, Religion, and Politics in Wilhelmine Germany: The Center Party in Württemberg before 1914.* New Haven, 1980.

Blackbourn, David. *Marpingen: Apparitions of the Virgin Mary in Nineteenth-Century Germany.* New York, 1994.

Blackbourn, David. *Populists and Patricians: Essays in Modern German History.* London, 1987.

Blankenberg, Heinz. *Politischer Katholizismus in Frankfurt am Main, 1918–1933.* Mainz, 1981.

Blaschke, Olaf. "Das 19. Jahrhundert: Ein Zweites Konfessionelles Zeitalter?" *Geschichte und Gesellschaft* 26 (2000): 38–75.

Blaschke, Olaf. *Katholizismus und Antisemitismus im Deutschen Kaiserreich.* Göttingen, 1997.

Blaschke, Olaf, ed. *Konfessionen im Konflikt: Deutschland zwischen 1800 und 1970: Ein zweites konfessionelles Zeitalter.* Göttingen, 2002.

Bleistein, Roman. *Die Jesuiten im Kreisauer Kreis: Ihre Bedeutung für den Gesamtwiderstand gegen den Nationalsozialismus.* Passau, 1990.

Blessing, Werner K. "'Deutschland in Not, wir im Glauben' . . . Kirche und Kirchenvolk in einer katholischen Region, 1933–1949." In *Von Stalingrad zur Währungsreform: Zur Sozialgeschichte des Umbruchs in Deutschland,* edited by Martin Broszat, Klaus-Dietmar Henke, and Hans Woller. 3rd ed. Munich, 1990.

Blessing, Werner K. *Staat und Kirche in der Gesellschaft: Institutionelle Autorität und mentaler Wandel in Bayern während des 19. Jahrhunderts.* Göttingen, 1982.

Blumenberg-Lampe, Christine, ed. *Der Weg in die Soziale Marktwirtschaft: Referate, Protokolle, Gutachten der Arbeitsgemeinschaft Erwin von Beckerath, 1943–1947.* Stuttgart, 1986.

Boehling, Rebecca. *A Question of Priorities: Democratic Reform and Economic Recovery in Postwar Germany.* Providence, 1996.

Bolesch, Otto Hermann, ed. *Adenauer für alle Lebenslagen: Eine deutsche Fibel.* Munich, 1968.

Bommarius, Christian. *Das Grundgesetz: Eine Biographie.* Berlin, 2009.

Borup, Allan. *Demokratisierungsprozesse in der Nachkriegszeit: Die CDU in Schleswig-Holstein und die Integration demokratieskeptischer Wähler.* Translated by Detlef Siegfried. Bielefeld, 2010.

Bösch, Frank. *Die Adenauer-CDU: Gründung, Aufstieg, und Krise einer Erfolgspartei, 1945–1969.* Stuttgart, 2001.

Bösch, Frank. *Das konservative Milieu: Vereinskultur und lokale Sammlungspolitik in ost- und westdeutschen Regionen (1900–1960).* Göttingen, 2002.

Bösch, Frank. *Macht und Machtverlust: Die Geschichte der CDU.* Stuttgart, 2002.

Bösch, Frank. "'Zu katholisch': Die Durchsetzung der CDU und das schwierige Zusammengehen der Konfessionen in der Bundesrepublik Deutschland." In *Solidargemeinschaft und fragmentierte Gesellschaft: Parteien, Milieus, und Verbände im Vergleich: Festschrift zum 60. Geburtstag von Peter Lösche,* edited by Tobias Dürr and Franz Walter. Opladen, 1999.

Bosch, Michael. "Ideelle Aspekte der Westintegration der Bundesrepublik bei Konrad Adenauer." In *Wege in die Zeitgeschichte: Festschrift zum 65. Geburtstag von Gerhard Schulz,* edited by Jürgen Heideking, Gerhard Hufnagel, and Franz Knipping. Berlin, 1989.

Boyens, Armin. "Der Ökumenische Rat der Kirchen im Zweiten Weltkrieg." In *Kirchen im Krieg: Europa, 1939–1945,* edited by Karl-Joseph Hummel and Christoph Kösters. Paderborn, 2007.

Brakelmann, Günter, and Traugott Jähnichen, eds. *Die protestantischen Wurzeln der Sozialen Marktwirtschaft: Ein Quellenband.* Gütersloh, 1994.

Braun, Hans. "Demographische Umschichtungen im Deutschen Katholizismus nach 1945." In *Kirche und Katholizismus, 1945–1949,* edited by Anton Rauscher. Munich, 1977.

Brechenmacher, Thomas, ed. *Das Reichskonkordat 1933: Forschungsstand, Kontroversen, Dokumente.* Paderborn, 2007.

Bremme, Gabriele. *Die Politische Rolle der Frau in Deutschland.* Göttingen, 1956.

Brockhausen, Martin. "'Geboren im Widerstand': Zur Erinnerung an den Nationalsozialismus in der CDU, 1950–1990." In *Zwischen Kriegs- und Diktaturerfahrung: Katholizismus und Protestantismus in der Nachkriegszeit,* edited by Andreas Holzem and Christoph Holzapfel. Stuttgart, 2005.

Brockmann, Stephen. "Germany as Occident at the Zero Hour." *German Studies Review* 25.3 (2002): 477–96.

Brophy, James M. *Popular Culture and the Public Sphere in the Rhineland.* Cambridge, 2007.

Broughton, David. "The CDU-CSU in Germany: Is There Any Alternative?" In *Christian Democracy in Europe: A Comparative Perspective,* edited by David Hanley. London, 1994.

Brown, Callum G. "The Secularization Decade: What the 1960s Have Done to the Study of Religious History." In *The Decline of Christendom in Western Europe, 1750–2000,* edited by Hugh McLeod and Werner Ustorf. Cambridge, 2003.

Brown-Fleming, Suzanne. *The Holocaust and Catholic Conscience: Cardinal Aloisius Muench and the Guilt Question in Germany.* Notre Dame, 2006.

Buchanan, Tom, and Martin Conway, eds. *Political Catholicism in Europe, 1918–1965.* Oxford, 1996.

Bucher, Peter, ed. *Adolf Süsterhenn: Schriften zum Natur-, Staats-, und Verfassungsrecht.* Mainz, 1991.

Bucher, Peter, ed. *Nachkriegsdeutschland: 1945–1949.* Darmstadt, 1990.

Buchhaas, Dorothee. *Gesetzgebung im Wiederaufbau: Schulgesetz in Nordrhein-Westfalen und Betriebsverfassungsgesetz, 1945–1952.* Düsseldorf, 1985.

Buchhaas, Dorothee. *Die Volkspartei: Programmatische Entwicklung der CDU, 1950–1973.* Düsseldorf, 1981.

Buchhaas, Dorothee, and Herbert Kühr. "Von der Volkskirche zur Volkspartei—Ein analytisches Stenogramm zum Wandel der CDU im rheinischen Ruhrgebiet." In *Vom Milieu zur Volkspartei: Funktionen und Wandlungen der Parteien im kommunalen und regionalen Bereich,* edited by Herbert Kühr. Königstein, 1979.

Buchhaas-Birkholz, Dorothee, ed. *"Zum politischen Weg unseres Volkes": Politische Leitbilder und Vorstellungen im deutschen Protestantismus, 1945–1952: Eine Dokumentation.* Düsseldorf, 1989.

Buchna, Kristian. *Nationale Sammlung an Rhein und Ruhr: Friedrich Middelhauve und die nordrhein-westfälische FDP, 1945–1953.* Munich, 2010.

Buchstab, Günter. "1945–1949." In *Lexikon der Christlichen Demokratie in Deutschland,* edited by Winfried Becker, Günter Buchstab, Anselm Doering-Manteuffel, and Rudolf Morsey. Paderborn, 2002.

Buchstab, Günter, ed. *Adenauer: "Wir haben wirklich etwas geschaffen": Die Protokolle des CDU-Bundesvorstand, 1953–1957.* Düsseldorf, 1990.

Buchstab, Günter, ed. *"Es musste alles neu gemacht werden": Die Protokolle des CDU-Bundesvorstandes, 1950–1953.* 2nd ed. Stuttgart, 1986.

Buchstab, Günter. "Felix Walter (1890–1949): Ministerialrat, Württemberg-Baden." In *In Verantwortung vor Gott und den Menschen: Christliche Demokraten im Parlamentarischen Rat, 1948/49,* edited by Günter Buchstab and Hans-Otto Kleinmann. Freiburg i.B., 2008.

Buchstab, Günter. "Konrad Adenauer: Wertgrundlagen und Politikverständnis." In *Zum Ideologieproblem in der Geschichte: Herbert Hömig zum 65. Geburtstag,* edited by Erik Gieseking. Lauf an der Pegnitz, 2006.

Buchstab, Günter, and Klaus Gotto, eds. *Die Gründung der Union: Tradition, Entstehung und Repräsentanten.* 2nd ed. Munich, 1990.

Buchstab, Günter, Brigitte Kaff, and Hans-Otto Kleinmann, eds. *Christliche Demokraten gegen Hitler: Aus Verfolgung und Widerstand zur Union.* Freiburg i.B., 2004.

Buchstab, Günter, and Hans-Otto Kleinmann, eds. *In Verantwortung vor Gott und den Menschen: Christliche Demokraten im Parlamentarischen Rat, 1948/49.* Freiburg i.B., 2008.

Bücker, Vera. "Die KAB-Zeitung und das Dritte Reich." *Kirchliche Zeitgeschichte* 14.1 (2001): 175–96.

Bücker, Vera. "Der Kölner Kreis und seine Konzeption für ein Deutschland nach Hitler." *Historisch-Politische Mitteilungen* 2 (1995): 49–82.

Bücker, Vera. *Die Schulddiskussion im deutschen Katholizismus nach 1945.* Bochum, 1989.

Burgess, Michael. "Politischer Katholizismus, Europäische Einigung, und der Aufstieg der Christdemokratie." In *Die Christen und die Entstehung der Europäischen Gemeinschaft,* edited by Martin Greschat and Wilfried Loth. Stuttgart, 1994.

Burleigh, Michael, and Wolfgang Wippermann. *The Racial State: Germany, 1933–1945.* Cambridge, 1991.

Buscher, Frank M., and Michael Phayer. "German Catholic Bishops and the Holocaust, 1940–1952." *German Studies Review* 11.3 (1988): 463–85.

Butler, Jon. "Jack-in-the-Box Faith: The Religion Problem in Modern American History." *Journal of American History* 90 (2004): 1357–78.

Carroll, Michael P. "Give Me That Ol' Time Hormonal Religion." *Journal for the Scientific Study of Religion* 43 (2004): 275–78.

Carter, Erica. *How German Is She? Postwar West German Reconstruction and the Consuming Woman.* Ann Arbor, 1997.

Cary, Noel D. *The Path to Christian Democracy: German Catholics and the Party System from Windthorst to Adenauer.* Cambridge, 1996.

Cary, Noel. "Political Catholicism and the Reform of the German Party System, 1900–1957." Ph.D. diss., University of California, Berkeley, 1988.

Chadwick, Owen. *The Secularization of the European Mind in the Nineteenth Century.* Cambridge, 1975.

Chandler, Andrew. "Catholicism and Protestantism in the Second World War in Europe." In *The Cambridge History of Christianity: World Christianities c. 1914–c. 2000,* edited by Hugh McLeod. Cambridge, 2006.

Clark, Christopher. "The New Catholicism and the European Culture Wars." In *Culture Wars: Secular-Catholic Conflict in Nineteenth-Century Europe,* edited by Christopher Clark and Wolfram Kaiser. Cambridge, 2003.

Clark, Christopher, and Wolfram Kaiser, eds. *Culture Wars: Secular-Catholic Conflict in Nineteenth-Century Europe.* Cambridge, 2003.

Clemens, Gabriele. *Martin Spahn und der Rechtskatholizismus in der Weimarer Republik.* Mainz, 1983.

Connelly, John. "Catholic Racism and Its Opponents." *Journal of Modern History* 79.4 (2007): 813–47.

Conway, Martin. "The Age of Christian Democracy: The Frontiers of Success and Failure." In *European Christian Democracy: Historical Legacies and Comparative Perspectives,* edited by Thomas Kselman and Joseph A. Buttigieg. Notre Dame, 2003.

Conway, Martin. Introduction to *Political Catholicism in Europe, 1918–1965,* edited by Tom Buchanan and Martin Conway. Oxford, 1996.

Conway, Martin. "Left Catholicism in Europe in the 1940s: Elements of an Interpretation." In *Left Catholicism: Catholics and Society in Western Europe at the Point of Liberation, 1943–1955,* edited by Gerd-Rainer Horn and Emmanuel Gerard. Leuven, 2001.

Conze, Vanessa. *Das Europa der Deutschen: Ideen von Europa in Deutschland zwischen Reichstradition und Westorientierung (1920–1970).* Munich, 2006.

Conze, Werner. *Jakob Kaiser: Politiker zwischen Ost und West, 1945–1949.* Stuttgart, 1969.

Cox, Jeffrey. "Secularization and Other Master Narratives of Religion in Modern Europe." *Kirchliche Zeitgeschichte* 14.1 (2001): 24–35.

Cox, Jeffrey, Thomas Albert Howard, Thomas Kselman, and George S. Williamson. "Modern European Historiography Forum." *Church History* 75.1 (2006): 120–62.

Craig, Gordon A. *Germany, 1866–1945.* Oxford, 1980.

Dahl-Keller, Ulrike Marga. *Der Treueid der Bischöfe gegenüber dem Staat: Geschichtliche Entwicklung und gegenwärtige staatskirchenrechtliche Bedeutung.* Berlin, 1994.

Damberg, Wilhelm. "Kritiker Adenauers aus dem Katholizismus." In *Adenauer und die Kirchen,* edited by Ulrich von Hehl. Bonn, 1999.

Damberg, Wilhelm. "Milieu und Konzil: Zum Paradigmenwechsel konfessionellen Bewußtseins im Katholizismus der frühen Bundesrepublik Deutschland." In *Konfessionen im Konflikt: Deutschland zwischen 1800 und 1970: Ein zweites konfessionelles Zeitalter,* edited by Olaf Blaschke. Göttingen, 2002.

Dann, Otto, ed. *Köln nach dem Nationalsozialismus: Der Beginn des gesellschaftlichen und politischen Lebens in den Jahren 1945/46.* Wuppertal, 1981.

Denman, Mariatte C. "Visualizing the Nation: Madonnas and Mourning Mothers in Postwar Germany." In *Gender and Germanness: Cultural Productions of a Nation,* edited by Patricia Herminghouse and Magda Hueller. Providence, 1997.

Deuerlein, Ernst. *CDU-CSU, 1945–1957: Beiträge zur Zeitgeschichte.* Cologne, 1957.

Diederich, Toni. "Adenauer als Kölner Oberbürgermeister von Mai bis Oktober 1945." In *Konrad Adenauer: Oberbürgermeister von Köln: Festgabe der Stadt Köln zum 100. Geburtstag ihres Ehrenbürgers am 5. Januar 1976,* edited by Hugo Stehkämper. Cologne, 1976.

Diegmann, Albert. "American Deconcentration Policy in the Ruhr Coal Industry." In *American Policy and the Reconstruction of West Germany, 1945–1955,* edited by Jeffry M. Diefendorf, Axel Frohn, and Hermann-Josef Rupieper. Cambridge, 1993.

Dietze, Franz. "Entscheidungsstrukturen und -prozesse in der Ost-CDU, 1945–1952." In *Die Ost-CDU: Beiträge zu ihrer Entstehung und Entwicklung,* edited by Michael Richter and Martin Rißmann. Weimar, 1995.

Dirks, Walter. "Das christliche Abendland: Sein Nachwirken in den Konfessionen der

Bundesrepublik." In *Christlicher Glaube und Ideologie,* edited by Klaus von Bismarck and Walter Dirks. Stuttgart, 1964.

"Discussion Forum—Richard Steigmann-Gall's *The Holy Reich.*" *Journal of Contemporary History* 42.1–2 (2007).

Doering-Manteuffel, Anselm. "Die 'Frommen' und die 'Linken' vor der Wiederherstellung des bürgerlichen Staats: Integrationsprobleme und Interkonfessionalismus in der frühen CDU." In *Christentum und politische Verantwortung: Kirchen im Nachkriegsdeutschland,* edited by Jochen-Christoph Kaiser and Anselm Doering-Manteuffel. Stuttgart, 1990.

Doering-Manteuffel, Anselm. *Wie westlich sind die Deutschen? Amerikanisierung und Westernisierung im 20. Jahrhundert.* Göttingen, 1999.

Durand, Jean-Dominique. *L'Europe de la Démocratie chrétienne.* Brussels, 1995.

Dwyer, Judith A., ed. *The New Dictionary of Catholic Social Thought.* Collegeville, 1994.

Eberan, Barbro. *Luther? Friedrich 'der Große?' Wagner? Nietzsche? . . . ? . . . ? Wer war an Hitler schuld? Die Debatte um die Schuldfrage, 1945–1949.* 2nd ed. Munich, 1985.

Egen, Peter. "Die Entstehung des Evangelischen Arbeitskreises der CDU/CSU." Ph.D. diss., Ruhr Universität Bochum, 1971.

Eger, Mark. "Die Konzeption der Sozialen Marktwirtschaft von Ludwig Erhard als Ergebnis soziologischen Denkens." Ph.D. diss., Julius-Maximilians-Universität zu Würzburg, 1999.

Ehlers, Hermann. *Reden zur politischen Verantwortung: Schriften des Evangelischen Arbeitskreises für kulturelle Fragen.* Bremen, 1956.

Ellwein, Thomas. *Klerikalismus in der deutschen Politik.* Munich, 1955.

Engel, Andreas. "Regionale politische Traditionen und die Entwicklung der CDU/CSU." In *Parteien und regionale politische Traditionen in der Bundesrepublik Deutschland,* edited by Dieter Oberndörfer and Karl Schmitt. Berlin, 1991.

Epstein, Klaus. *The Genesis of German Conservatism.* Princeton, 1966.

Erhard, Ludwig. *Deutsche Wirtschaftspolitik: Der Weg der Sozialen Marktwirtschaft.* Düsseldorf, 1962.

Erker, Paul. "Revolution des Dorfes? Ländliche Bevölkerung zwischen Flüchtlingszustrom und landwirtschaftlichem Strukturwandel." In *Von Stalingrad zur Währungsreform: Zur Sozialgeschichte des Umbruchs in Deutschland,* edited by Martin Broszat, Klaus-Dietmar Henke, and Hans Woller. 3rd ed. Oldenbourg, 1990.

Eschenburg, Theodor. *Jahre der Besatzung, 1945–1949.* Stuttgart, 1983.

Eßer, Albert. "Wilhelm Elfes (1884–1969): Oberbürgermeister von Mönchengladbach." In *Christliche Demokraten gegen Hitler: Aus Verfolgung und Widerstand zur Union,* edited by Günter Buchstab, Brigitte Kaff, and Hans-Otto Kleinmann. Freiburg i.B., 2004.

Euchner, Walter, Helga Grebing, Franz-Josef Stegmann, Peter Langhorst, Traugott Jähnichen, and Norbert Friedrich, eds. *Geschichte der sozialen Ideen in Deutschland: Sozialismus—Katholische Soziallehre—Protestantische Sozialethik: Ein Handbuch.* 2nd ed. Wiesbaden, 2005.

Evans, Ellen Lovell. *The Cross and the Ballot: Catholic Political Parties in Germany, Switzerland, Austria, Belgium, and the Netherlands, 1785–1985.* Boston, 1999.

Evans, Ellen Lovell. *The German Center Party, 1870–1933: A Study in Political Catholicism.* Carbondale, 1981.

Evans, Richard. "Religion and Society in Modern Germany." In *Rethinking German History: Nineteenth-Century Germany and the Origins of the Third Reich*, edited by Richard Evans. London, 1987.

Eward, Hans-Gerd. *Die gescheiterte Republik: Idee und Programm einer "Zweiten Republik" in den Frankfurter Heften (1946–1950)*. Frankfurt a.M., 1988.

Faber, Richard. *Abendland: Ein "politischer Kampfbegriff."* Hildesheim, 1979.

Fäßler, Peter. *Badisch, Christlich, und Sozial: Zur Geschichte der BCSV/CDU im französisch besetzten Land Baden (1945–1952)*. Frankfurt a.M., 1995.

Fandel, Thomas. "Konfessionalismus und Nationalsozialismus." In *Konfessionen im Konflikt: Deutschland zwischen 1800 und 1970: Ein zweites konfessionelles Zeitalter,* edited by Olaf Blaschke. Göttingen, 2002.

Farquharson, John. "The Consensus That Never Came: Hans Schlange-Schöningen and the CDU, 1945–9." *European History Quarterly* 19.3 (1989): 353–83.

Fehrenbach, Heide. *Cinema in Democratizing Germany: Reconstructing National Identity after Hitler.* Chapel Hill, 1995.

Fehrenbach, Heide. "The Fight for the 'Christian West': German Film Control, the Churches, and the Reconstruction of Civil Society in the Early Bonn Republic." *German Studies Review* 14.1 (1991): 39–63.

Fehrenbach, Heide. *Race after Hitler: Black Occupation Children in Postwar Germany and America.* Princeton, 2007.

Felbick, Dieter. *Schlagwörter der Nachkriegszeit, 1945–1949.* Berlin, 2003.

Feldkamp, Michael F. *Mitläufer, Feiglinge, Antisemiten? Katholische Kirche und Nationalsozialismus.* Augsburg, 2009.

Feldkamp, Michael F. *Der Parlamentarischer Rat, 1948–1949: Die Entstehung des Grundgesetzes.* Göttingen, 2008.

Fenske, Hans, ed. *Unter Wilhelm II: 1890–1918.* Darmstadt, 1982.

Fischer, Alexander. "Andreas Hermes und die gesamtdeutschen Anfänge der Union." In *Die CDU in der sowjetisch besetzten Zone/DDR, 1945–1952,* edited by Alexander Fischer and Manfred Agethen. Sankt Augustin, 1994.

Fischer, Claus A., ed. *Wahlhandbuch für die Bundesrepublik Deutschland: Daten zu Bundestags-, Landtags- und Europawahlen in der Bundesrepublik Deutschland, in den Ländern, und in den Kreisen, 1946–1989.* 2 vols. Paderborn, 1990.

Flechtheim, Ossip K., ed. *Dokumente zur parteipolitischen Entwicklung in Deutschland seit 1945.* Vol. 2, *Programmatik der deutschen Parteien.* Berlin, 1963.

Focke, Franz. *Sozialismus aus christlicher Verantwortung: Die Idee eines christlichen Sozialismus in der katholisch-sozialen Bewegung und in der CDU.* Wuppertal, 1978.

Fogarty, Michael P. *Christian Democracy in Western Europe, 1820–1953.* Notre Dame, 1957.

Föhse, Ulrich. *Entstehung und Entwicklung der Christlich-Demokratischen Union in Wuppertal, 1945–1950.* Hausarbeit zur Ersten Staatsprüfung für das Lehramt an der Grund- und Hauptschule, Pädagogische Hochschule Rheinland, Abteilung Wuppertal, April 1970.

Först, Walter. *Geschichte Nordrhein-Westfalens.* Vol. 1, *1945–1949.* Cologne, 1970.

Först, Walter. *In Köln: Kleine Stadtgeschichte im 20. Jahrhundert.* Vol. 1, *1918–1936.* Düsseldorf, 1982.

Foschepoth, Josef. "Zur deutschen Reaktion auf Niederlage und Besatzung." In *West-*

deutschland, 1945–1955: Unterwerfung, Kontrolle, Integration, edited by Ludolf Herbst. Munich, 1986.

Foschepoth, Josef, and Rolf Steininger, eds. *Britische Deutschland- und Besatzungs-politik, 1945–1949.* Paderborn, 1985.

Fox, Jonathan. "Integrating Religion into International Relations Theory." In *Routledge Handbook of Religion and Politics,* edited by Jeffrey Haynes. London, 2009.

Franz, Corinna, and Oliver Gnad, eds. *Handbuch zur Statistik der Parlamente und Parteien in den westlichen Besatzungszonen und in der Bundesrepublik Deutschland.* Vol. 2, *CDU und CSU: Mitgliedschaft und Sozialstruktur, 1945–1990.* Düsseldorf, 2005.

Frei, Norbert. "Die Besatzungsherrschaft als Zäsur?" In *Politische Zäsuren und gesellschaftlicher Wandel im 20. Jahrhundert: Regionale und vergleichende Perspektiven,* edited by Matthias Frese and Michael Prinz. Paderborn, 1996.

Fremantle, Anne, ed. *The Papal Encyclicals in Their Historical Context: The Teachings of the Popes.* New York, 1956.

Fricke, Dieter, Werner Fritsch, Herbert Gottwald, Siegfried Schmidt, and Manfred Weißbecker, eds. *Lexikon zur Parteiengeschichte: Die bürgerlichen und klein-bürgerlichen Parteien und Verbände in Deutschland (1789–1945).* Vol. 2, *Deutsche Liga für Völkerbund—Gesamtverband der Christlichen Gewerkschaften Deutsch-lands.* Cologne, 1984.

Frie, Ewald. "Zwischen Amtskirche und Verbandswesen: Der deutsche Caritasverband, 1945–1949." In *Siegerin in Trümmern: Die Rolle der katholischen Kirche in der deutschen Nachkriegsgesellschaft,* edited by Joachim Köhler and Damian van Melis. Stuttgart, 1998.

Friese, Elisabeth. "Helene Wessel (1898–1969)." In *Katholiken und Protestanten in den Aufbaujahren der Bundesrepublik,* edited by Thomas Sauer. Stuttgart, 2000.

Fuchs, Susanne. *Frauen Bewältigen den Neuaufbau: Eine lokalgeschichtliche Analyse der unmittelbaren Nachkriegszeit am Beispiel Bonn.* Pfaffenweiler, 1993.

Fulbrook, Mary. *History of Germany, 1918–2008: The Divided Nation.* 3rd ed. Chich-ester, 2009.

Gassert, Philipp. *Amerika im Dritten Reich: Ideologie, Propaganda, und Volksmeinung, 1933–1945.* Stuttgart, 1997.

Gauly, Thomas M. *Kirche und Politik in der Bundesrepublik Deutschland, 1945–1976.* Bonn, 1990.

Gehler, Michael, and Wolfram Kaiser, eds. *Christian Democracy in Europe since 1945.* London, 2004.

Geiger, Tim. *Atlantiker gegen Gaullisten: Außenpolitischer Konflikt und innerparteili-cher Machtkampf in der CDU/CSU, 1958–1969.* Munich, 2008.

Gerard, Emmanuel, and Gerd-Rainer Horn. Introduction to *Left Catholicism: Catholics and Society in Western Europe at the Point of Liberation, 1943–1955,* edited by Gerd-Rainer Horn and Emmanuel Gerard. Leuven, 2001.

Gerstenmaier, Eugen. *Reden und Aufsätze.* Vol. 2. Edited by Evangelischen Verlags-werk. Stuttgart, 1962.

Gibowski, Wolfgang G. "Germany's General Election in 1994: Who Voted for Whom?" In *Germany's New Politics,* edited by David P. Conradt, Gerald R. Kleinfeld, George K. Romoser, and Christian Søe. Tempe, 1995.

Gillies, Peter, Daniel Koerfer, and Udo Wengst. *Ludwig Erhard.* Berlin, 2010.

Gorman, Daniel. "Ecumenical Internationalism: Willoughby Dickinson, the League of Nations, and the World Alliance for Promoting International Friendship through the Churches." *Journal of Contemporary History* 45.1 (2010): 51–73.

Gotto, Klaus. "Gleiche Distanz zu allen Parteien? Die Kirche im Parteienstaat." In *Kehrt um und glaubt—Erneuert die Welt: 87. Deutscher Katholikentag vom 1. September–5. September 1982 in Düsseldorf, Die Vortragsreihen: Gestalten des Glaubens—Zeugen des Glaubens—Fragen zur Zeitgeschichte nach 1945,* edited by Zentralkomitee der deutschen Katholiken. Paderborn, 1982.

Gotto, Klaus. "Wandlungen des politischen Katholizismus seit 1945." In *Wirtschaftlicher Wandel, religiöser Wandel und Wertwandel: Folgen für das politische Verhalten in der Bundesrepublik Deutschland,* edited by Dieter Oberndörfer, Hans Rattinger, and Karl Schmitt. Berlin, 1985.

Grabbe, Hans-Jürgen. *Unionsparteien, Sozialdemokratie, und Vereinigte Staaten von Amerika, 1945–1966.* Düsseldorf, 1983.

Granieri, Ronald J. *The Ambivalent Alliance: Konrad Adenauer, the CDU/CSU, and the West, 1949–1966.* Providence, 2003.

Graß, Karl Martin, and Franz-Josef Heyen, eds. *Peter Altmeier: Reden, 1946–1951.* Boppard a.R., 1979.

Grebing, Helga, Peter Porzorski, and Rainer Schulze, eds. *Die Nachkriegsentwicklungen in Westdeutschland, 1945–1949.* Vol. 2, *Politik und Gesellschaft.* Stuttgart, 1980.

Greiffenhagen, Martin. *Das Dilemma des Konservatismus in Deutschland.* Frankfurt a.M., 1986.

Greiner, Franz. "Die Katholiken in der technischen Gesellschaft der Nachkriegszeit." In *Deutscher Katholizismus nach 1945: Kirche, Gesellschaft, Geschichte,* edited by Hans Maier. Munich, 1964.

Greschat, Martin. "Einleitung." In *Im Zeichen der Schuld: 40 Jahre Stuttgarter Schuldbekenntnis: Eine Dokumentation,* edited by Martin Greschat. Neukirchen-Vluyn, 1985.

Greschat, Martin. "Die Kirchen in den beiden deutschen Staaten nach 1945." *Geschichte in Wissenschaft und Unterricht* 42.5 (1991): 267–84.

Greschat, Martin. "Konfessionelle Spannungen in der Ära Adenauer." In *Katholiken und Protestanten in den Aufbaujahren der Bundesrepublik,* edited by Thomas Sauer. Stuttgart, 2000.

Greschat, Martin. "Kontinuität und Diskontinuität im deutschen Protestantismus nach 1945." *Monatshefte für Evangelische Kirchengeschichte des Rheinlandes* 41 (1992): 255–72.

Greschat, Martin. "'Mit den Vertriebenen kam Kirche'? Anmerkungen zu einem unerledigten Thema." *Historisch-Politische Mitteilungen* 13 (2006): 47–76.

Greschat, Martin. "'Rechristianisierung' und 'Säkularisierung': Anmerkungen zu einem europäischen interkonfessionellen Interpretationsmodell." In *Christentum und politische Verantwortung: Kirchen im Nachkriegsdeutschland,* edited by Jochen-Christoph Kaiser and Anselm Doering-Manteuffel. Stuttgart, 1990.

Greven-Aschoff, Barbara. *Die bürgerliche Frauenbewegung in Deutschland, 1894–1933.* Göttingen, 1981.

Griech-Polelle, Beth A. *Bishop von Galen: German Catholicism and National Socialism.* New Haven, 2002.

Grogan, Geraldine F. *The Noblest Agitator: Daniel O'Connell and the German Catholic Movement, 1830–50.* Dublin, 1991.

Grosche, Robert. *Kölner Tagebuch, 1944–1946.* Cologne, 1969.

Gross, Michael B. *The War against Catholicism: Liberalism and the Anti-Catholic Imagination in Nineteenth-Century Germany.* Ann Arbor, 2004.

Grosse Kracht, Hermann-Josef. "Religion in der Demokratisierungsfalle? Zum Verhältnis von traditioneller Religion und politische Moderne am Beispiel des deutschen Katholizismus im Kaiserreich." *Geschichte in Wissenschaft und Unterricht* 51 (2000): 149–53.

Grossmann, Atina. *Reforming Sex: The German Movement for Birth Control and Abortion Reform, 1920–1950.* New York, 1995.

Grossmann, Thomas. *Zwischen Kirche und Gesellschaft: Das Zentralkomitee der deutschen Katholiken, 1945–1970.* Mainz, 1991.

Gruber, Ludwig. *Die CDU-Landtagsfraktion in Nordrhein-Westfalen, 1946–1980: Eine parlamentshistorische Untersuchung.* Düsseldorf, 1988.

Grünthal, Günther. *Reichsschulgesetz und Zentrumspartei in der Weimarer Republik.* Düsseldorf, 1968.

Grünthal, Günther. "'Zusammenschluß' oder 'Evangelisches Zentrum'? Ein Beitrag zur Geschichte der Deutschen Zentrumspartei in der Weimarer Republik." In *Staat und Gesellschaft im politischen Wandel: Beiträge zur Geschichte der modernen Welt,* edited by Werner Pöls. Stuttgart, 1979.

Gurland, A. R. L. *Die CDU/CSU: Ursprünge und Entwicklung bis 1953.* Edited by Dieter Emig. Frankfurt a.M., 1980.

Hahn, Erich J. "U.S. Policy on a West German Constitution, 1947–1949." In *American Policy and the Reconstruction of West Germany, 1945–1955,* edited by Jeffry M. Diefendorf, Axel Frohn, and Hermann-Josef Rupieper. Cambridge, 1993.

Hahn, Karl Josef. *Die christliche Demokratie in Europa: Die europäische Volkspartei.* Rome, 1979.

Hanley, David, ed. *Christian Democracy in Europe: A Comparative Perspective.* London, 1994.

Hartmannsgruber, Friedrich. "Die christlichen Volksparteien, 1848–1933: Ideen und Wirklichkeit." In *Geschichte der Christlich-Demokratischen und Christlich-Sozialen Bewegungen in Deutschland,* edited by Günther Rüther. 3rd ed. Bonn, 1989.

Hastings, Derek. *Catholicism and the Roots of Nazism: Religious Identity and National Socialism.* Oxford, 2010.

Haunhorst, Benno. "'Der Sozialismus als sittliche Idee': Theodor Steinbüchels Beitrag zu einer christlichen Sozialethik." In *Sozial- und Linkskatholizismus: Erinnerung—Orientierung—Befreiung,* edited by Heiner Ludwig and Wolfgang Schroeder. Frankfurt a.M., 1990.

Häussler, Frank. "Ulrich Steiner und der Laupheimer Kreis: Ein konservatives Randphänomen in der Frühzeit der Bundesrepublik Deutschland." *Historisch-Politische Mitteilungen* 6 (1999): 189–205.

Heidemeyer, Helge, ed. *Die CDU/CSU-Fraktion im Deutschen Bundestag: Sitzungsprotokolle, 1949–1953.* Düsseldorf, 1998.

Heilbronner, Oded. "From Ghetto to Ghetto: The Place of German Catholic Society in Recent Historiography." *Journal of Modern History* 72.2 (2000): 453–95.

Heimann, Siegfried. "Christlicher Sozialismus in der CDU." In *Lexikon des Sozialismus,* edited by Thomas Meyer, Karl-Heinz Klär, Susanne Miller, Klaus Novy, and Heinz Timmermann. Cologne, 1986.

Hein, Dieter. *Zwischen liberaler Milieupartei und nationaler Sammlungsbewegung: Gründung, Entwicklung, und Struktur der Freien Demokratischen Partei, 1945–1949.* Düsseldorf, 1985.

Heineman, Elizabeth. "The Hour of the Woman: Memories of Germany's 'Crisis Years' and West German National Identity." *American Historical Review* 101.2 (1996): 354–95.

Heineman, Elizabeth D. "Complete Families, Half Families, No Families at All: Female-Headed Households and the Reconstruction of the Family in the Early Federal Republic." *Central European History* 29.1 (1996): 19–60.

Heineman, Elizabeth D. *What Difference Does a Husband Make? Women and Marital Status in Nazi and Postwar Germany.* Berkeley, 1999.

Heitzer, Horstwalter. *Die CDU in der britischen Zone, 1945–1949: Gründung, Organisation, Programm, und Politik.* Düsseldorf, 1988.

Heitzer, Horstwalter. *Georg Kardinal Kopp und der Gewerkschaftsstreit, 1900–1914.* Cologne, 1983.

Heitzer, Horstwalter. *Der Volksverein für das katholische Deutschland im Kaiserreich, 1890–1918.* Mainz, 1979.

Helbach, Ulrich, ed. *Akten Deutscher Bischöfe seit 1945: Westzonen, 1945–1947.* Paderborn, 2008.

Helbach, Ulrich. "'Es hätte unserer Kirche und unserem Volk mehr gedient, wenn wir weniger geschwiegen hätten . . .'—Die 'Schuldfrage' im Frühjahr 1945 im Lichte eines neuen Quellenfundes: Eingabe der westdeutschen Bischöfe an Papst Pius XII." In *Rheinisch—Kölnisch—Katholisch: Beiträge zur Kirchen- und Landesgeschichte sowie zur Geschichte des Buch- und Bibliothekswesens der Rheinlande: Festschrift für Heinz Finger zum 60. Geburtstag,* edited by Siegfried Schmidt. Cologne, 2008.

Held, Heinz Joachim. "Ökumene in der Nachkriegszeit." In *Kontinuität und Neubeginn: Die rheinische und westfälische Kirche in der Nachkriegszeit (1945–1949),* edited by Bernd Hey and Günther van Norden. Bielefeld, 1996.

Helmreich, Ernst Christian. *Religious Education in German Schools: An Historical Approach.* Cambridge, 1959.

Henning, Friedrich-Wilhelm. "Konrad Adenauer und die Soziale Marktwirtschaft bis 1956." In *Adenauers Verhältnis zu Wirtschaft und Gesellschaft,* edited by Hans Pohl. Bonn, 1992.

Hentschel, Volker. *Ludwig Erhard: Ein Politikerleben.* Berlin, 1998.

Herbers, Winfried. "Leo Schwering (1873–1971)." In *Christliche Demokraten gegen Hitler: Aus Verfolgung und Widerstand zur Union,* edited by Günter Buchstab, Brigitte Kaff, and Hans-Otto Kleinmann. Freiburg i.B., 2004.

Herbers, Winfried. *Der Verlust der Hegemonie: Die Kölner CDU, 1945/46–1964.* Düsseldorf, 2003.

Herbert, Karl. *Kirche zwischen Aufbruch und Tradition: Entscheidungsjahre nach 1945.* Stuttgart, 1989.

Herbert, Ulrich, ed. *Wandlungsprozesse in Westdeutschland: Belastung, Integration, Liberalisierung, 1945–1980.* Göttingen, 2002.

Herf, Jeffrey. *Divided Memory: The Nazi Past in the Two Germanys.* Cambridge, 1997.

Herf, Jeffrey. "Multiple Restorations: German Political Traditions and the Interpretation of Nazism, 1945–1946." *Central European History* 26.1 (1993): 21–55.

Herf, Jeffrey. *War by Other Means: Soviet Power, West German Resistance, and the Battle of the Euromissiles.* New York, 1991.

Herzog, Dagmar. *Intimacy and Exclusion: Religious Politics in Pre-Revolutionary Baden.* Piscataway, 2007.

Herzog, Dagmar. *Sex after Fascism: Memory and Morality in Twentieth-Century Germany.* Princeton, 2005.

Hillgruber, Andreas. "Heinemanns evangelisch-christlich begründete Opposition gegen Adenauers Politik, 1950–1952." In *Politik und Konfession: Festschrift für Konrad Repgen zum 60. Geburtstag,* edited by Dieter Albrecht, Hans Günter Hockerts, Paul Mikat, and Rudolf Morsey. Berlin, 1983.

Hirschfeld, Michael. *Katholisches Milieu und Vertriebene: Eine Fallstudie am Beispiel des Oldenburger Landes, 1945–1965.* Cologne, 2002.

Hobgood, Mary E. *Catholic Social Teaching and Economic Theory: Paradigms in Conflict.* Philadelphia, 1991.

Hockenos, Matthew D. *A Church Divided: German Protestants Confront the Nazi Past.* Bloomington, 2004.

Höhn, Maria. "Frau im Haus und Girl im *Spiegel:* Discourse on Women in the Interregnum Period of 1945–1949 and the Question of German Identity." *Central European History* 26.1 (1993): 57–90.

Höhn, Maria. *GIs and Frauleins: The German-American Encounter in 1950s West Germany.* Chapel Hill, 2002.

Hollaender, Albert E. J. "Offiziere und Prälaten: Zur Fuldaer Bischofskonferenz, August 1945." *Mitteilungen des Österreichischen Staatsarchivs* 25 (1972): 185–206.

Hölscher, Lucian, Tillman Bendikowski, Claudia Enders, and Markus Hoppe, eds. *Datenatlas zur religiösen Geographie im protestantischen Deutschland: Von der Mitte des 19. Jahrhunderts bis zum Zweiten Weltkrieg.* 4 vols. Berlin, 2001.

Holz, Marcus. "Christliche Weltanschauung als Grundlage von Parteipolitik: Eine Analyse des genuin Christlichen in der frühen CDU/CSU (1945–50) aus der Betrachtung des christlichen Menschenbildes und seiner ideengeschichtlichen Hintergründe." Ph.D. diss., Universität der Bundeswehr München, 1992.

Holz, Petra. *Zwischen Tradition und Emanzipation: CDU-Politikerinnen in der Zeit von 1946 bis 1960.* Königstein, 2004.

Holzem, Andreas. "Dechristianisierung und Rechristianisierung: Der deutsche Katholizismus im europäischen Vergleich." *Kirchliche Zeitgeschichte* 11.1 (1998): 69–93.

Hömig, Herbert. *Das preussische Zentrum in der Weimarer Republik.* Mainz, 1979.

Horstmann, Johannes, and Antonius Liedhegener. *Konfession, Milieu, Moderne: Konzeptionelle Positionen und Kontroversen zur Geschichte von Katholizismus und Kirche im 19. und 20. Jahrhundert.* Schwerte, 2001.

Howard, Thomas Albert. "A 'Religious Turn' in Modern European Historiography?" *Historically Speaking* 4 (2003): 25–26.

Huber, Ernst Rudolf. *Deutsche Verfassungsgeschichte seit 1789.* Vol. 2, *Der Kampf um Einheit und Freiheit, 1830–1850.* Stuttgart, 1960.

Huber, Wolfgang. "Protestantismus und Demokratie." In *Protestanten in der Demokratie: Positionen und Profil im Nachkriegsdeutschland,* edited by Wolfgang Huber. Munich, 1990.

Hübinger, Gangolf. *Kulturprotestantismus und Politik: Zum Verhältnis von Liberalismus und Protestantismus im wilhelminischen Deutschland.* Tübingen, 1994.

Hughes, Michael L. "'Through No Fault of Our Own': West Germans Remember Their War Losses." *German History* 18.2 (2000): 193–213.

Hughes, Michael L. *Shouldering the Burdens of Defeat: West Germany and the Reconstruction of Social Justice.* Chapel Hill, 1999.

Hummel, Karl-Joseph, and Michael Kissener, eds. *Die Katholiken und das Dritte Reich: Kontroversen und Debatten.* Paderborn, 2009.

Hürten, Heinz. "Der Beitrag Christlicher Demokraten zum geistigen und politischen Wiederaufbau und zur europäischen Integration nach 1945: Bundesrepublik Deutschland." In *Christliche Demokratie in Europa: Grundlagen und Entwicklungen seit dem 19. Jahrhundert,* edited by Winfried Becker and Rudolf Morsey. Cologne, 1988.

Hürten, Heinz. "Beobachtungen zur Situation der katholischen Kirche in den drei westlichen Besatzungszonen Deutschlands." *Kirchliche Zeitgeschichte* 2.1 (1989): 203–10.

Hürten, Heinz. *Deutsche Katholiken, 1918 bis 1945.* Paderborn, 1992.

Hürten, Heinz. *Kurze Geschichte des deutschen Katholizismus, 1800–1960.* Mainz, 1986.

Hürten, Heinz. "Der Topos vom christlichen Abendland in Literatur und Publizistik nach den beiden Weltkriegen." In *Katholizismus, nationaler Gedanke, und Europa seit 1800,* edited by Albrecht Langner. Paderborn, 1985.

Hüwel, Detlev. *Karl Arnold: Eine politische Biographie.* Wuppertal, 1980.

Inacker, Michael J. *Zwischen Transzendenz, Totalitarismus, und Demokratie: Die Entwicklung des kirchlichen Demokratieverständnisses von der Weimarer Republik bis zu den Anfängen der Bundesrepublik (1918–1959).* Neukirchen-Vluyn, 1994.

Inboden, William, III. *Religion and American Foreign Policy, 1945–1960: The Soul of Containment.* Cambridge, 2008.

Irving, R. E. M. *The Christian Democratic Parties of Western Europe.* London, 1979.

Jarausch, Konrad H. *After Hitler: Recivilizing Germans, 1945–1955.* Oxford, 2006.

Jauch, Ernst-Alfred, and Gisela Helwig. "Katholische Kirche." In *Kirchen und Gesellschaft in beiden deutschen Staaten,* edited by Gisela Helwig and Detlef Urban. Cologne, 1987.

Jochmann, Werner. "Evangelische Kirche und Politik in der Phase des Neubeginns, 1945–1950." In *Die Zeit nach 1945 als Thema kirchlicher Zeitgeschichte: Referate der internationalen Tagung in Hünigen/Bern (Schweiz) 1985,* edited by Victor Conzemius, Martin Greschat, and Hermann Kocher. Göttingen, 1988.

Julg, Jean. *La démocratie chrétienne en République fédérale allemande.* Paris, 1985.

Kaff, Brigitte, ed. *Die Unionsparteien, 1946–1950: Protokolle der Arbeitsgemeinschaft der CDU/CSU Deutschlands und der Konferenenzen der Landesvorsitzenden.* Düsseldorf, 1991.

Kahle, Johannes. *Evangelische Kirche und Demokratie: Der Einordnungsprozeß der Deutschen Evangelischen Kirche in das demokratische Funktionssystem der Nachkriegsära in den Westzonen.* Pfaffenweiler, 1988.

Kaiser, Wolfram. *Christian Democracy and the Origins of European Union.* Cambridge, 2007.

Kaiser, Wolfram. "Christian Democracy in Twentieth-Century Europe." *Journal of Contemporary History* 39.1 (2004): 127–35.

Kaiser, Wolfram. "Trigger-Happy Protestant Materialists? The European Christian Democrats and the United States." In *Between Empire and Alliance: America and Europe during the Cold War,* edited by Marc Trachtenberg. Lanham, 2003.

Kaiser, Wolfram, and Helmut Wohnout, eds. *Political Catholicism in Europe, 1918–1945.* London, 2004.

Kalyvas, Stathis N. *The Rise of Christian Democracy in Europe.* Ithaca, 1996.

Kalyvas, Stathis N. "Unsecular Politics and Religious Mobilization: Beyond Christian Democracy." In *European Christian Democracy: Historical Legacies and Comparative Perspectives,* edited by Thomas Kselman and Joseph A. Buttigieg. Notre Dame, 2003.

Kampmann, Jürgen. "Bischof von Galen und die evangelischen Christen." In *Streitfall Galen: Clemens August Graf von Galen under Nationalsozialismus: Studien und Dokumente,* edited by Joachim Kuropka. 2nd ed. Münster, 2007.

Kanther, Michael Alfred, ed. *Die Kabinettsprotokolle der Landesregierung von Nordrhein-Westfalen, 1946 bis 1950.* Vol. 1, *Einleitung, Dokumente 1–207.* Siegburg, 1992.

Karsten, Siegfried G. "Eucken's 'Social Market Economy' and Its Test in Post-War West Germany: The Economist as Social Philosopher Developed Ideas That Paralleled Progressive Thought in America." *American Journal of Economics and Sociology* 44.2 (1985): 169–83.

Kauders, Anthony D. "Catholics, the Jews, and Democratization in Post-War Germany, Munich, 1945–65." *German History* 18.4 (2000): 461–84.

Kaufmann, Doris. *Katholisches Milieu in Münster, 1928–1933: Politische Aktionsformen und gesellschaftsspezifische Verhaltensräume.* Düsseldorf, 1984.

Kershaw, Ian. *Popular Opinion and Political Dissent in the Third Reich: Bavaria, 1933–1945.* Oxford, 2002.

Kirby, Dianne. "Christian Faith, Communist Faith: Some Aspects of the Relationship between the Foreign Office Information Research Department and the Church of England Council on Foreign Relations, 1950–1953." *Kirchliche Zeitgeschichte* 13.1 (2000): 217–41.

Kirby, Dianne. "The Cold War, the Hegemony of the United States, and the Golden Age of Christian Democracy." In *The Cambridge History of Christianity: World Christianities, c. 1914–c. 2000,* edited by Hugh McLeod. Cambridge, 2006.

Kirby, Dianne. "Divinely Sanctioned: The Anglo-American Cold War Alliance and the Defence of Western Civilization and Christianity, 1945–48." *Journal of Contemporary History* 35.3 (2000): 385–412.

Klein, Gotthard. *Der Volksverein für das katholische Deutschland, 1890–1933.* Paderborn, 1996.

Klein, Michael. "Der westdeutsche Protestantismus und die CDU bis zum Ende der Ära Adenauer." *Historisch Politische Mitteilungen* 14 (2007): 79–98.

Klein, Michael. *Westdeutscher Protestantismus und politische Parteien: Anti-Parteien-Mentalität und parteipolitisches Engagement von 1945 bis 1963.* Tübingen, 2005.

Kleinknecht, Thomas. "Die westfälische Nachkriegsdiakonie vor der Flüchtlingsfrage: Kirchliche Fürsorge und der Prozess der Integration. Eine Forschungsskizze." In *Kontinuität und Neubeginn: Die rheinische und westfälische Kirche in der Nachkriegszeit (1945–1949)*, edited by Bernd Hey and Günther van Norden. Bielefeld, 1996.

Kleinmann, Hans-Otto. *Geschichte der CDU: Von der Gründung bis 1990*. Stuttgart, 1992.

Kleinmann, Hans-Otto. "'Wahren, pflegen, ausbauen': Das Werk des Parlamentarischen Rates zwischen Grundgesetzgebung und Erneuerungsdiskurs." In *In Verantwortung vor Gott und den Menschen: Christliche Demokraten im Parlamentarischen Rat, 1948/49*, edited by Günter Buchstab and Hans-Otto Kleinmann. Freiburg i.B., 2008.

Kleßmann, Christoph. *Die doppelte Staatsgründung: Deutsche Geschichte, 1945–1955*. Bonn, 1991.

Klotzbach, Kurt. "SPD und katholische Kirche nach 1945—Belastungen, Mißverständnisse, und Neuanfänge." *Archiv für Sozialgeschichte* 29 (1989): 37–47.

Kluke, Paul. "Nationalsozialistische Europaideologie." *Vierteljahreshefte für Zeitgeschichte* 3.3 (1955): 240–75.

Kohl, Helmut. "Die politische Entwicklung in der Pfalz und das Wiedererstehen der Parteien nach 1945." Ph.D. diss., Ruprecht-Karls-Universität zu Heidelberg, 1958.

Kohler, Eric D. "The Successful German Center-Left: Joseph Hess and the Prussian Center Party, 1908–32." *Central European History* 23.4 (1990): 313–48.

Köhler, Joachim, and Rainer Bendel. "Bewährte Rezepte oder unkonventionelle Experimente? Zur Seelsorge an Flüchtlingen und Heimatvertriebenen: Anfragen an die und Impulse für die Katholizismusforschung." In *Siegerin in Trümmern: Die Rolle der katholischen Kirche in der deutschen Nachkriegsgesellschaft*, edited by Joachim Köhler and Damian van Melis. Stuttgart, 1998.

Köhler, Joachim, and Damian van Melis. Introduction to *Siegerin in Trümmern: Die Rolle der katholischen Kirche in der deutschen Nachkriegsgesellschaft*, edited by Joachim Köhler and Damian van Melis. Stuttgart, 1998.

Kohns, Jürgen. *Konrad Adenauer und der Föderalismus*. Würzburg, 1987.

Kolinsky, Eva. *Women in Contemporary Germany: Life, Work, and Politics*. 2nd ed. Providence, 1993.

König, Helmut. *Die Zukunft der Vergangenheit: Der Nationalsozialismus im politischen Bewusstsein der Bundesrepublik*. Frankfurt a.M., 2003.

Konrad-Adenauer-Stiftung, ed. *Christliche Demokratie in Deutschland: Analysen und Dokumente zur Geschichte und Programmatik der Christlich Demokratischen Union Deutschlands und der Jungen Union Deutschlands*. Melle, 1978.

Korte, Karl-Rudolf, ed. *Die Bundestagswahl 2009: Analysen der Wahl-, Parteien-, Kommunikations-, und Regierungsforschung*. Wiesbaden, 2010.

Köster, Markus. "'Betet um einen guten Ausgang der Wahl!' Kirche und Parteien im Bistum Münster zwischen Kapitulation und Konzil." In *Siegerin in Trümmern: Die Rolle der katholischen Kirche in der deutschen Nachkriegsgesellschaft*, edited by Joachim Köhler and Damian van Melis. Stuttgart, 1998.

Köster, Markus. *Katholizismus und Parteien in Münster, 1945–1953: Kontinuität und Wandel eines politisches Milieus*. Münster, 1993.

Kösters, Christoph, ed. *Caritas in der SBZ/DDR, 1945–1989: Erinnerungen, Berichte, Forschungen*. Paderborn, 2001.

Kösters, Christoph. "Kirche und Glaube an der 'Heimatfront.'" In *Kirchen im Krieg: Europa, 1939–1945,* edited by Karl-Joseph Hummel and Christoph Kösters. Paderborn, 2007.

Kosthorst, Erich. *Jakob Kaiser: Der Arbeiterführer.* Stuttgart, 1967.

Kraiker, Gerhard. *Politischer Katholizismus in der BRD: Eine ideologie-kritische Analyse.* Stuttgart, 1972.

Krieg, Robert A. "Joseph Lortz and Max Metzger on Ecumenism and Hitler." In *In God's Hands: Essays in Honour of Michael A. Fahey,* edited by Michael Andrew Fahey, Jaroslav Z. Skira, and Michael S. Attridge. Leuven, 2006.

Kselman, Thomas, and Joseph A. Buttigieg, eds. *European Christian Democracy: Historical Legacies and Comparative Perspectives.* Notre Dame, 2003.

Kukuck, Horst-Albert. "Etappen im Ringen um eine Wirtschaftskonzeption der CDU, 1945–1949." In *Politische Parteien auf dem Weg zur parlamentarischen Demokratie in Deutschland: Entwicklungslinie bis zur Gegenwart,* edited by Lothar Albertin and Werner Link. Düsseldorf, 1981.

Kuropka, Joachim. "Britische Besatzungspolitik und Neubeginn des öffentlichen Lebens: Probleme des politischen Wiederaufbaus in der britischen Besatzungszone." In *Neubeginn 1945 zwischen Kontinuität und Wandel,* edited by Willigis Eckermann and Joachim Kuropka. Cloppenburg, 1988.

Kuropka, Joachim, ed. *Zur Sache—Das Kreuz! Untersuchungen zur Geschichte des Konflikts um Kreuz und Lutherbild in den schulen Oldenburgs, zur Wirkungsgeschichte eines Massenprotests, und zum Problem nationalsozialistischer Herrschaft in einer agrarisch-katholischen Region.* Vechta, 1986.

Laitenberger, Volkhard. "Ludwig Erhard—Konzeption und Durchsetzung der Sozialen Marktwirtschaft." In *Markt oder Plan: Wirtschaftsordnungen in Deutschland, 1945–1961,* edited by Haus der Geschichte der Bundesrepublik Deutschland. Frankfurt a.M., 1997.

Lamberts, Emile, ed. *Christian Democracy in the European Union (1945/1995).* Leuven, 1997.

Langer, Ingrid. "Maria Meyer-Sevenich, geb. Sevenich, CDU (1907–1970)." In *Alibi-Frauen? Hessische Poltikerinnen,* vol. 1, *In den Vorparlamenten, 1946–1950,* edited by Ingrid Langer. Frankfurt a.M., 1994.

Langguth, Gerd, ed. *Politik und Plakat: 50 Jahre Plakatgeschichte am Beispiel der CDU.* Bonn, 1995.

Langhoff, Helmut, and Veit Veltzke. "Im Westen viel Neues: Als Nordrhein-Westfalen preußisch war." In *Wir sind Preußen: Die preußischen Kerngebiete in Nordrhein-Westfalen, 1609–2009,* edited by Stephan Sensen, Eckhard Trox, Maria Perrefort, Gerhard Renda, and Veit Velzke. Essen, 2009.

Langner, Albrecht. "Wirtschaftliche Ordnungsvorstellungen im deutschen Katholizismus, 1945–1963." In *Katholizismus, Wirtschaftsordnung, und Sozialpolitik, 1945–1963,* edited by Albrecht Langner. Paderborn, 1980.

Lappenküper, Ulrich. "Between Concentration Movement and People's Party: The Christian Democratic Union in Germany." In *Christian Democracy in Europe since 1945,* edited by Michael Gehler and Wolfram Kaiser. London, 2004.

Laurien, Ingrid. *Politisch-kulturelle Zeitschriften in den Westzonen, 1945–1949: Ein Beitrag zur politischen Kultur der Nachkriegszeit.* Frankfurt a.M., 1991.

Laurien, Ingrid. "Die Verarbeitung von Nationalsozialismus und Krieg in politisch-kulturellen Zeitschriften der Westzonen, 1945–1949." *Geschichte in Wissenschaft und Unterricht* 39 (1988): 220–37.

Leggewie, Claus. "CDU—Integrationsmodell auf Widerruf? Die zwei Modernisierungen der deutschen Rechten nach 1945." *Blätter für deutsche und internationale Politik* 34 (1989): 294–308.

Lehmann, Hartmut. *Pietismus und weltliche Ordnung in Württemberg vom 17. bis zum 20. Jahrhundert.* Stuttgart, 1969.

Lehmann, Hartmut, ed. *Säkularisierung, Dechristianisierung, Rechristianisierung im neuzeitlichen Europa: Bilanz und Perspektiven der Forschung.* Göttingen, 1997.

Lehmann, Hartmut. "Von der Erforschung der Säkularisierung zur Erforschung von Prozessen der Dechristianisierung und der Rechristianisierung im neuzeitlichen Europa." In *Säkularisierung, Dechristianisierung, Rechristianisierung im neuzeitlichen Europa: Bilanz und Perspektiven der Forschung,* edited by Hartmut Lehmann. Göttingen, 1997.

Lehmann, Hartmut. "Zur Einführung: Koexistenz und Konflikt von Religionen in Europa." In *Koexistenz und Konflikt von Religionen im vereinten Europa,* edited by Hartmut Lehman. Göttingen, 2004.

Lehnert, Detlef, and Klaus Megerle, eds. *Politische Teilkulturen zwischen Integration und Polarisierung: Zur politischen Kultur in der Weimarer Republik.* Opladen, 1990.

Lemhöfer, Ludwig. "Die Katholiken in der Stunde Null: Restauration des Abendlandes oder radikaler Neubeginn?" In *Katholische Kirche und NS-Staat: Aus der Vergangenheit lernen?* edited by Monika Kringels-Kemen and Ludwig Lemhöfer. 3rd ed. Frankfurt a.M., 1983.

Lemmer, Ernst. *Manches war doch anders: Erinnerungen eines deutschen Demokraten.* 1st ed. Frankfurt a.M., 1968.

Lepsius, M. Rainer. "Parteiensystem und Sozialstruktur: Zum Problem der Demokratisierung der deutschen Gesellschaft." In *Deutsche Parteien vor 1918,* edited by Gerhard A. Ritter. Cologne, 1990.

Leschinski, Susanne. "Clemens August Kardinal von Galen in der Nachkriegszeit, 1945/46." In *Clemens August Graf von Galen: Neue Forschungen zum Leben und Wirken des Bischofs von Münster,* edited by Joachim Kuropka. Münster, 1992.

Lewy, Guenter. *The Catholic Church and Nazi Germany.* Boulder, 2000.

Ley, Richard. *Föderalismusdiskussion innerhalb der CDU/CSU von der Parteigründung bis zu der Verabschiedung des Grundgesetzes.* Mainz, 1978.

Liedhegener, Antonius. "Katholisches Milieu in einer industriellen Umwelt am Beispiel Bochum: Strukturen und Entwicklungslinien, 1830–1974." In *Politische Zäsuren und Gesellschaftlicher Wandel im 20. Jahrhundert: Regionale und vergleichende Perspektiven,* edited by Matthias Frese and Michael Prinz. Paderborn, 1996.

Lienkamp, Andreas. "Socialism Out of Christian Responsibility: The German Experiment of Left Catholicism (1945–1949)." In *Left Catholicism: Catholics and Society in Western Europe at the Point of Liberation, 1943–1955,* edited by Gerd-Rainer Horn and Emmanuel Gerard. Leuven, 2001.

Lill, Rudolf. "Über die Anfänge der CDU in Köln, 1945–1948." *Historisch-Politische Mitteilungen* 12 (2005): 157–72.

Lindt, Andreas. *Das Zeitalter des Totalitarismus: Politische Heilslehren und ökumen-ischer Aufbruch.* Stuttgart, 1981.

Löffler, Peter, ed. *Bischof Clemens August Graf von Galen: Akten, Briefe, und Predig-ten, 1933–1946.* Vol. 2, *1939–1946.* Mainz, 1988.

Lohmann, Martin. *Das Kreuz mit dem C: Wie christlich ist die Union?* Kevelaer, 2009.

Löhr, Wolfgang. *Dokumente deutscher Bischöfe.* Vol. 1, *Hirtenbriefe und Ansprachen zu Gesellschaft und Politik, 1945–1949.* Würzburg, 1985.

Löhr, Wolfgang, ed. *Hirtenbriefe und Ansprachen zu Gesellschaft und Politik, 1945–1949.* Würzburg, 1985.

Löhr, Wolfgang. "Rechristianisierungsvorstellungen im deutschen Katholizismus, 1945–1948." In *Christentum und politische Verantwortung: Kirchen im Nachkriegs-deutschland,* edited by Jochen-Christoph Kaiser and Anselm Doering-Manteuffel. Stuttgart, 1990.

Lois, Daniel. "Wie verändert sich die Religiosität im Lebensverlauf? Eine Panelanalyse unter Berücksichtigung von Ost-West-Unterschieden." *Kölner Zeitschrift für Sozi-ologie und Sozialpsychologie* 63 (2011): 83–110.

Lönne, Karl-Egon. "Germany." In *Political Catholicism in Europe, 1918–1965,* edited by Tom Buchanan and Martin Conway. Oxford, 1996.

Lönne, Karl-Egon. "Katholizismus 1945: Zwischen gequälter Selbstbehauptung ge-genüber dem Nationalsozialismus und Öffnung zur pluralistischen Gesellschaft." In *Ende des Dritten Reiches—Ende des Zweiten Weltkriegs: Eine perspektivische Rückschau,* edited by Hans-Erich Volkmann. Munich, 1995.

Lönne, Karl-Egon. *Politischer Katholizismus im 19. und 20. Jahrhundert.* Frankfurt a.M., 1986.

Lösche, Peter, and Franz Walter. "Katholiken, Konservative, und Liberale: Milieus und Lebenswelten bürgerlicher Parteien in Deutschland während des 20. Jahrhunderts." *Geschichte und Gesellschaft* 26.3 (2000): 471–92.

Loth, Wilfried. *Katholiken im Kaiserreich: Der politische Katholizismus in der Krise des wilhelminischen Deutschlands.* Düsseldorf, 1984.

Loth, Wilfried. "Katholizismus und Moderne: Überlegungen zu einem dialektischen Verhältnis." In *Zivilisation und Barbarei: Die widersprüchlichen Potentiale der Moderne: Detlev Peukert zum Gedenken,* edited by Frank Bajohr, Werner Johe, and Uwe Lohalm. Hamburg, 1991.

Loth, Wilfried. "Soziale Bewegungen im Katholizismus des Kaiserreichs." *Geschichte und Gesellschaft* 17 (1991): 279–310.

Loth, Wilfried. "Zwischen autoritärer und demokratischer Ordnung: Das Zentrum in der Krise des Wilhelminischen Reiches." In *Die Minderheit als Mitte: Die Deutsche Zentrumspartei in der Innenpolitik des Reiches, 1871–1933,* edited by Winfried Becker. Paderborn, 1986.

Lowitsch, Bruno. "Der Frankfurter Katholizismus in der Weimarer Republik und die 'Rhein-Mainische Volkszeitung.'" In *Sozial- und Linkskatholizismus: Erinnerung—Orientierung—Befreiung,* edited by Heiner Ludwig and Wolfgang Schroeder. Frankfurt a.M., 1990.

Lübbe, Hermann. *Säkularisierung: Geschichte eines ideenpolitischen Begriffs.* Freiburg, 1965.

Lück, Wolfgang. *Das Ende der Nachkriegszeit: Eine Untersuchung zur Funktion des*

Begriffs der Säkularisierung in der "Kirchentheorie" Westdeutschlands, 1945–1965. Bonn, 1976.

Luttwack, Edward. "Franco-German Reconciliation: The Overlooked Role of the Moral Re-Armament Movement." In *Religion: The Mission Dimension in Statecraft,* edited by Douglas Johnston and Cynthia Sampson. New York, 1994.

Lutz, Heinrich. *Zwischen Habsburg und Preußen: Deutschland, 1815–1866.* Berlin, 1985.

Maier, Hans. *Revolution and Church: The Early History of Christian Democracy, 1789–1901.* Notre Dame, 1969.

Marshall, Barbara. "German Attitudes to British Military Government, 1945–1947." *Journal of Contemporary History* 15.4 (1980): 655–84.

Martin, Anne. *Die Entstehung der CDU in Rheinland-Pfalz.* Munich, 1995.

Marx, Stefan. "Robert Lehr (1883–1956): Landtagsabgeordneter, Nordrhein-Westfalen." In *In Verantwortung vor Gott und den Menschen: Christliche Demokraten im Parlamentarischen Rat, 1948/49,* edited by Günter Buchstab and Hans-Otto Kleinmann. Freiburg i.B., 2008.

Matz, Ulrich. "Zum Einfluß des Christentums auf das politische Denken der Neuzeit." In *Geschichte der Christlich-Demokratischen und Christlich-Sozialen Bewegungen in Deutschland,* edited by Günther Rüther. 3rd ed. Bonn, 1989.

Mayeur, Jean-Marie. *Des Partis catholiques à la démocratie chretienne.* Paris, 1980.

McLeod, Hugh. *Religion and the People of Western Europe, 1789–1970.* 1st ed. Oxford, 1981.

Meiser, Hans. "Der Nationalsozialismus und seine Bewältigung im Spiegel der Lizenzpresse der Britischen Besatzungszone von 1946–1949." Ph.D. diss., Universität Osnabrück, 1980.

Mensing, Hans Peter, ed. *Adenauer Briefe, 1945–1947.* Berlin, 1983.

Mensing, Hans Peter, ed. *Adenauer Briefe, 1947–1949.* Berlin, 1984.

Mensing, Hans Peter. "Adenauer und der Protestantismus." In *Adenauer und die Kirchen,* edited by Ulrich von Hehl. Bonn, 1999.

Mensing, Hans Peter, ed. *Konrad Adenauer Briefe über Deutschland, 1945–1955.* Berlin, 1999.

Mensing, Hans Peter, ed. *Unserem Vaterland zugute: Der Briefwechsel Theodor Heuss/ Konrad Adenauer.* Berlin, 1989.

Mergel, Thomas. *Propaganda nach Hitler: Eine Kulturgeschichte des Wahlkampfs in der Bundesrepublik, 1949–1990.* Göttingen, 2010.

Mergel, Thomas. *Zwischen Klasse und Konfession: Katholisches Bürgertum im Rheinland, 1794–1914.* Göttingen, 1994.

Merzyn, Friedrich, ed. *Kundgebungen: Worte und Erklärungen der Evangelischen Kirche in Deutschland, 1945–1959.* Hanover, 1993.

Metz, Andreas. "Gemeinschaft mit beschränkter Haltbarkeit: Adenauer und Erhard, 1948/49." *Historisch-Politische Mitteilungen* 5 (1998): 49–81.

Metz, Andreas. *Die ungleichen Gründerväter: Adenauers und Erhards langer Weg an die Spitze der Bundesrepublik.* Konstanz, 1998.

Mierzejewski, Alfred C. *Ludwig Erhard: A Biography.* Chapel Hill, 2004.

Misner, Paul. "Christian Democratic Social Policy: Precedents for Third-Way Thinking." In *European Christian Democracy: Historical Legacies and Comparative Perspectives,* edited by Thomas Kselman and Joseph A. Buttigieg. Notre Dame, 2003.

Mitchell, Maria. "Materialism and Secularism: CDU Politicians and National Socialism, 1945–1949." *Journal of Modern History* 67.2 (1995): 278–308.

Mittmann, Ursula. *Fraktion und Partei: Ein Vergleich von Zentrum und Sozialdemokratie im Kaiserreich.* Düsseldorf, 1976.

Moeller, Robert G. *Protecting Motherhood: Women and the Family in the Politics of Postwar West Germany.* Berkeley, 1993.

Moeller, Robert G. *War Stories: The Search for a Usable Past in the Federal Republic of Germany.* Berkeley, 2001.

Möller, Martin. *Evangelische Kirche und Sozialdemokratische Partei in den Jahren 1945–1950: Grundlagen der Verständigung und Beginn des Dialoges.* Göttingen, 1984.

Möllers, Christoph. *Das Grundgesetz: Geschichte und Inhalt.* Munich, 2009.

Moody, Joseph N., ed. *Church and Society: Catholic Social and Political Thought and Movements, 1789–1950.* New York, 1953.

Morsey, Rudolf. "Der Beginn der 'Gleichschaltung' in Preussen: Adenauers Haltung in der Sitzung des 'Dreimännerkollegiums' am 6. Februar 1933." *Vierteljahrshefte für Zeitgeschichte* 11 (1963): 85–97.

Morsey, Rudolf. "Der deutsche Katholizismus in den Jahren der Besatzungsherrschaft, 1945–1949." In *Von Windthorst bis Adenauer: Ausgewählte Aufsätze zu Politik, Verwaltung, und politischem Katholizismus im 19. und 20. Jahrhundert,* edited by Ulrich von Hehl, Hans Günter Hockerts, Horst Möller, and Martin Schumacher. Paderborn, 1997.

Morsey, Rudolf. "Die Deutsche Zentrumspartei." In *Das Ende der Parteien,* edited by Erich Matthias and Rudolf Morsey. Düsseldorf, 1960.

Morsey, Rudolf. *Die Deutsche Zentrumspartei, 1917–1923.* Düsseldorf, 1966.

Morsey, Rudolf. "Kirche und politische Parteien, 1848–1948/49." In *Kirche—Politik—Parteien,* edited by Anton Rauscher. Cologne, 1974.

Morsey, Rudolf. "Konrad Adenauer und der Weg zur Bundesrepublik Deutschland, 1946–1949." In *Rhöndorfer Gespräche,* vol. 3, *Konrad Adenauer und die Gründung der Bundesrepublik Deutschland,* edited by Rudolf Morsey. Stuttgart, 1979.

Morsey, Rudolf. "Prälaten auf der politischen Bühne: Zur Rolle geistlicher Parlamentarier im 19. und 20. Jahrhundert." In *Von Windthorst bis Adenauer: Ausgewählte Aufsätze zu Politik, Verwaltung, und politischem Katholizismus im 19. und 20. Jahrhundert,* edited by Ulrich von Hehl, Hans Günter Hockerts, Horst Möller, and Martin Schumacher. Paderborn, 1997.

Morsey, Rudolf. *Der Untergang des politischen Katholizismus: Die Zentrumspartei zwischen christlichem Selbstverständnis und "Nationaler Erhebung," 1932/33.* Stuttgart, 1977.

Morsey, Rudolf. "Vom Kommunalpolitiker zum Kanzler: Die politische Rolle Adenauers in der Zeit der Weimarer Republik und in der Ära der Besatzungsherrschaft (1919–1949)." In *Konrad Adenauer: Ziele und Wege, 3 Beispiele,* edited by Konrad-Adenauer-Stiftung. Mainz, 1972.

Morsey, Rudolf, ed. *Das Wahlverhalten der Deutschen Katholiken im Kaiserreich und in der Weimarer Republik: Untersuchungen aus dem Jahre 1928 von Johannes Schauff.* Mainz, 1975.

Morsey, Rudolf. "Zwischen Verwaltung und Politik: Hermann Pünder und die Gründung der CDU in Münster." In *Weltpolitik, Europagedanke, Regionalismus: Fest-*

schrift für Heinz Gollwitzer, edited by Heinz Dollingen, Horst Gründer, and Alwin Hanschmidt. Münster, 1992.

Mosse, George L. *Toward the Final Solution: A History of European Racism.* 2nd ed. Madison, 1985.

Moyn, Samuel. "The First Historian of Human Rights." *American Historical Review* 116.1 (2011): 58–79.

Müller, Dirk H. *Arbeiter—Katholizismus—Staat: Der Volksverein für das katholische Deutschland und die katholischen Arbeiterorganisationen in der Weimarer Republik.* Bonn, 1966.

Müller, Elmar. *Widerstand und Wirtschaftsordnung: Die wirtschaftspolitischen Konzepte der Widerstandsbewegung gegen das NS Regime und ihr Einfluß auf die Soziale Marktwirtschaft.* Frankfurt a.M., 1988.

Müller, Gloria. *Mitbestimmung in der Nachkriegszeit: Britische Besatzungsmacht—Unternehmen—Gewerkschaften.* Düsseldorf, 1987.

Muller, Jerry Z. *The Other God That Failed: Hans Freyer and the Deradicalization of German Conservatism.* Princeton, 1987.

Müller, Max. "Zur Vorgeschichte der Gründung der badischen CDU in Freiburg/Br." In *Leo Wohleb—Der andere politische Kurs: Dokumente und Kommentare,* edited by Paul-Ludwig Weinacht. Freiburg i.B., 1975.

Müller-Rolli, Sebastian. *Evangelische Schulpolitik in Deutschland, 1918–1958: Dokumente und Darstellung.* Göttingen, 1999.

Naimark, Norman M. *The Russians in Germany: A History of the Soviet Zone of Occupation, 1945–1949.* Cambridge, 1995.

Nebgen, Elfriede. *Jakob Kaiser: Der Widerstandskämpfer.* Stuttgart, 1967.

Niedhart, Gottfried. *Deutsche Geschichte, 1918–1933: Politik in der Weimarer Republik und der Sieg der Rechten.* 2nd ed. Stuttgart, 1994.

Nietfeld, Joseph. "Die Zentrumspartei: Geschichte und Struktur, 1945–1958." Ph.D. diss., Technische Universität Carolo-Wilhelmina zu Braunschweig, 1985.

Nicholls, A. J. *Freedom with Responsibility: The Social Market Economy in Germany, 1918–1963.* Oxford, 1994.

Nienhaus, Frank. "Transformations- und Erosionsprozessse des katholischen Milieus in einer ländlich-textilindustrialisierten Region: Das Westmünsterland, 1914–1968." In *Politische Zäsuren und Gesellschaftlicher Wandel im 20. Jahrhundert: Regionale und vergleichende Perspektiven,* edited by Matthias Frese and Michael Prinz. Paderborn, 1996.

Nipperdey, Thomas. *Religion im Umbruch: Deutschland, 1870–1918.* Munich, 1988.

Noethen, Stefan. "Christlicher Sozialismus in der Stunde der Neuordnung 1945: Das Dominikanerkloster Walberberg und die Kölner Leitsätze der CDU." *Geschichte im Westen* 11 (1996): 48–71.

Noethen, Stefan. "Pläne für das vierte Reich: Der Widerstandskreis im Kölner Kettelerhaus, 1941–1944." *Geschichte in Köln* 39 (1996): 51–73.

Noormann, Harry. "Neue Freiheit, vertagte Befreiung: Zur gesellschaftlichen Rolle der Kirchen in der Nachkriegszeit." In *Deutschland, 1945–1949: Ringvorlesung an der THD im Sommersemester 1985,* edited by Hans-Gerd Schumann. Darmstadt, 1989.

Noormann, Harry. *Protestantismus und politisches Mandat, 1945–1949.* Vol. 1, *Grundriß.* Gütersloh, 1985.

Noormann, Harry. *Protestantismus und politisches Mandat, 1945–1949*. Vol. 2, *Dokumente und Kommentare*. Gütersloh, 1985.

Nowak, Kurt. "Christentum in politischer Verantwortung: Zum Protestantismus in der Sowjetischen Besatzungszone (1945–1949)." In *Christentum und politische Verantwortung: Kirchen im Nachkriegsdeutschland,* edited by Jochen-Christoph Kaiser and Anselm Doering-Manteuffel. Stuttgart, 1990.

Nowak, Kurt. *Evangelische Kirche und Weimarer Republik: Zum politischen Weg des deutschen Protestantismus zwischen 1918 und 1932*. Weimar, 1981.

Onnasch, Martin. "Die Situation der Kirchen in der sowjetischen Besatzungszone, 1945–1949." *Kirchliche Zeitgeschichte* 2.1 (1989): 210–20.

Opitz, Günter. *Der Christlich-soziale Volksdienst: Versuch einer protestantischen Partei in der Weimarer Republik*. Düsseldorf, 1969.

Oppelland, Torsten. "Adenauers Kritiker aus dem Protestantismus." In *Adenauer und die Kirchen,* edited by Ulrich von Hehl. Bonn, 1999.

Oppelland, Torsten. "Der Evangelische Arbeitskreis der CDU/CSU, 1952–1969." *Historisch-Politische Mitteilungen* 5 (1998): 105–43.

Oppelland, Torsten. "'Politik aus christlicher Verantwortung': Der Evangelische Arbeitskreis der CDU/CSU in der Ära Adenauer." In *Katholiken und Protestanten in den Aufbaujahren der Bundesrepublik,* edited by Thomas Sauer. Stuttgart, 2000.

Orlow, Dietrich. "Delayed Reaction: Democracy, Nationalism, and the SPD, 1945–1966." *German Studies Review* 16.1 (1993): 77–102.

Orlow, Dietrich. *Weimar Prussia, 1918–1925: The Unlikely Rock of Democracy*. Pittsburgh, 1986.

Orlow, Dietrich. *Weimar Prussia, 1925–1933: The Illusion of Strength*. Pittsburgh, 1991.

O'Sullivan, Michael E. "West German Miracles: Catholic Mystics, Church Hierarchy, and Postwar Popular Culture." *Zeithistorische Forschungen* 6.1 (2009): 11–34.

Pappi, Franz Urban. "Die konfessionell-religiöse Konfliktlinie in der deutschen Wählerschaft: Entstehung, Stabilität, und Wandel." In *Wirtschaftlicher Wandel, religiöser Wandel, und Wertwandel: Folgen für das politische Verhalten in der Bundesrepublik Deutschland,* edited by Dieter Oberndörfer, Hans Rattinger, and Karl Schmitt. Berlin, 1985.

Patch, William. "The Catholic Church, the Third Reich, and the Origins of the Cold War: On the Utility and Limitations of Historical Evidence." *Journal of Modern History* 82.2 (2010): 396–433.

Pearson, Benjamin. "The Pluralization of Protestant Politics: Public Responsibility, Rearmament, and Division at the 1950s *Kirchentage.*" *Central European History* 43.2 (2010): 270–300.

Pfeffer, Sabine. *Politischer Konservatismus in England und in der Bundesrepublik Deutschland nach 1945: Ein Vergleich konservativer Prinzipien*. Münster, 1989.

Phayer, Michael. "The German Catholic Church after the Holocaust." *Holocaust and Genocide Studies* 10.2 (1996): 151–67.

Poidevin, Raymond. "Die französische Deutschlandpolitik, 1943–1949." In *Die Deutschlandpolitik Frankreichs und die Französische Zone, 1945–1949,* edited by Claus Scharf and Hans-Jürgen Schröder. Wiesbaden, 1983.

Poiger, Uta G. *Jazz, Rock, and Rebels: Cold War Politics and American Culture in a Divided Germany.* Berkeley, 2000.

Pollack, Detlef. "Funktionen von Religion und Kirche in den politischen Umbrüchen des 20. Jahrhunderts: Untersucht anhand der politischen Zäsuren von 1945 und 1989 in Deutschland." *Kirchliche Zeitgeschichte* 12.1 (1999): 64–94.

Pöpping, Dagmar. *Abendland: Christliche Akademiker und die Utopie der Antimoderne, 1900–1945.* Berlin, 2002.

Presse- und Informationsdienste der Christlich-Demokratischen Union Deutchlands, ed. *Die Gründungsgeschichte der CDU im Trierer Land, 1945/46.* Bonn, 1966.

Pridham, Geoffrey. "Christian Democracy in Italy and West Germany: A Comparative Analysis." In *Social and Political Movements in Western Europe,* edited by Martin Kolinsky and William E. Paterson. London, 1976.

Pridham, Geoffrey. *Christian Democracy in Western Germany: The CDU/CSU in Government and Opposition, 1945–1976.* London, 1976.

Prowe, Diethelm. "Democratization as Conservative Restabilization." In *American Policy and the Reconstruction of West Germany, 1945–1955,* edited by Jeffry M. Diefendorf, Axel Frohn, and Hermann-Josef Rupieper. Cambridge, 1993.

Prowe, Diethelm. "Economic Democracy in Post–World War II Germany: Corporatist Crisis Response, 1945–1948." *Journal of Modern History* 57.3 (1985): 451–82.

Prümm, Karl. *Walter Dirks und Eugen Kogon als katholische Publizisten der Weimarer Republik.* Heidelberg, 1984.

Pütz, Helmuth. *Die CDU: Entwicklung, Aufbau, und Politik der Christlich-Demokratischen Union Deutschlands.* 3rd ed. Düsseldorf, 1978.

Pütz, Helmuth. *Innerparteiliche Willensbildung: Empirische Untersuchung zum bildungspolitischen Willensbildungsprozeß in der CDU.* Mainz, 1974.

Pütz, Helmuth, ed. *Konrad Adenauer und die CDU der britischen Besatzungszone, 1946–1949: Dokumente zur Gründungsgeschichte der CDU Deutschlands.* Bonn, 1975.

Quink, Cornelia. "Milieubedingungen des politischen Katholizismus in der Bundesrepublik." In *Politische Kultur in Deutschland: Bilanz und Perspektiven der Forschung,* edited by Dirk Berg-Schlosser and Jakob Schissler. Opladen, 1987.

Raem, Heinz-Albert. *Katholischer Gesellenverein und Deutsche Kolpingsfamilie in der Ära des Nationalsozialismus.* Mainz, 1982.

Recker, Marie-Luise. *Konrad Adenauer: Leben und Politik.* Munich, 2010.

Reich-Hilweg, Ines. *Männer und Frauen sind gleichberechtigt: Der Gleichberechtigungsgrundsatz (Art. 3 Abs. 2 GG) in der parlamentarischen Auseinandersetzung, 1948–1957, und in der Rechtssprechung des Bundesverfassungsgerichts, 1953–1975.* Frankfurt a.M., 1979.

Reichel, Herbert. "Das 'Ahlener Programm' der CDU—Ein fortwirkender Auftrag und seine Grenzen." *Jahrbuch für christliche Sozialwissenschaften* 17 (1976): 243–64.

Rémond, René. *Religion and Society in Modern Europe.* Oxford, 1999.

Repgen, Konrad. "Die Deutschen Bischöfe und der Zweite Weltkrieg." *Historisches Jahrbuch* 115 (1995): 411–52.

Repgen, Konrad. "Die Erfahrung des Dritten Reiches und das Selbstverständnis der deutschen Katholiken nach 1945." In *Die Zeit nach 1945 als Thema kirchlicher Zeit-*

geschichte: Referate der internationalen Tagung in Hünigen/Bern (Schweiz) 1985, edited by Victor Conzemius, Martin Greschat, and Hermann Kocher. Göttingen, 1998.

Repgen, Konrad. "Der Konkordatsstreit der fünfziger Jahre: Von Bonn nach Karlsruhe (1949–1955/57)." *Kirchliche Zeitgeschichte* 3.1 (1990): 201–45.

Reytier, Marie-Emmanuelle. "Die deutschen Katholiken und der Gedanke der europäischen Einigung, 1945–1949: Wende oder Kontinuität?" *Jahrbuch für europäische Geschichte* 3 (2002): 163–84.

Richter, Ludwig. *Die Deutsche Volkspartei, 1918–1933.* Düsseldorf, 2002.

Richter, Michael. *Die Ost-CDU, 1948–1952: Zwischen Widerstand und Gleichschaltung.* Düsseldorf, 1991.

Riechert, Karen. "Der Umgang der katholischen Kirche mit historischer und juristischer Schuld anlässlich der Nürnberger Kriegsverbrecherprozesse." In *Siegerin in Trümmern: Die Rolle der katholischen Kirche in der deutschen Nachkriegsgesellschaft,* edited by Joachim Köhler and Damian van Melis. Stuttgart, 1998.

Rogers, Daniel E. *Politics after Hitler: The Western Allies and the German Party System.* London, 1995.

Rohe, Karl. *Wahlen und Wählertraditionen in Deutschland: Kulturelle Grundlagen deutscher Parteien und Parteiensysteme im 19. und 20. Jahrhundert.* Frankfurt a.M., 1992.

Röhm, Eberhard, and Jörg Thierfelder. *Juden, Christen, Deutsche, 1933–1945.* Vol. 1, *1933 bis 1935.* 2nd ed. Stuttgart, 2004.

Rolke, Lothar. *Protestbewegungen in der Bundesrepublik: Eine analytische Sozialgeschichte des politischen Widerspruchs.* Opladen, 1987.

Rölli-Alkemper, Lukas. *Familie im Wiederaufbau: Katholizismus und bürgerliches Familienideal in der Bundesrepublik Deutschland, 1945–1965.* Paderborn, 2000.

Rösch, Augustin. *Kampf gegen den Nationalsozialismus.* Edited by Roman Bleistein. Frankfurt a.M., 1985.

Ross, Ronald J. *Beleaguered Tower: The Dilemma of Political Catholicism in Wilhelmine Germany.* Notre Dame, 1976.

Ross, Ronald J. *The Failure of Bismarck's Kulturkampf: Catholicism and State Power in Imperial Germany.* Washington, 1998.

Roßteutscher, Sigrid. "CDU-Wahl 2005: Katholiken, Kirchgänger, und eine protestantische Spitzenkandidatin aus dem Osten." In *Die Bundestagswahl 2005: Analyse des Wahlkampfes und der Wahlergebnisse,* edited by Frank Brettschneider, Oskar Niedermayer, and Bernhard Weßels. Wiesbaden, 2007.

Rotberg, Joachim. *Zwischen Linkskatholizismus und bürgerlicher Sammlung: Die Anfänge der CDU in Frankfurt am Main.* Frankfurt a.M., 1999.

Roth, Dieter, and Andreas Wüst. "Abwahl ohne Machtwechsel? Die Bundestagswahl 2005 im Lichte langfristiger Entwicklungen." In *Bilanz der Bundestagswahl 2005: Voraussetzungen, Ergebnisse, Folgen,* edited by Eckhard Jesse and Roland Sturm. Wiesbaden, 2006.

Ruff, Mark Edward. "Der 'Bruderzwist' der DJK: 'Integralisten' und 'Modernisierer' in einem katholischen Sportverband." In *Katholiken und Protestanten in den Aufbaujahren der Bundesrepublik,* edited by Thomas Sauer. Stuttgart, 2000.

Ruff, Mark Edward. "Catholic Elites, Gender, and Unintended Consequences in the

1950s: Toward a Reinterpretation of the Role of Conservatives in the Federal Republic." In *Conflict, Catastrophe, and Continuity: Essays on Modern German History,* edited by Frank Biess, Mark Roseman, and Hanna Schissler. New York, 2007.

Ruff, Mark Edward. "Integrating Religion into the Historical Mainstream: Recent Literature on Religion in the Federal Republic of Germany." *Central European History* 42.2 (2009): 307–37.

Ruff, Mark Edward. "Katholische Jugendarbeit und junge Frauen in Nordrhein-Westfalen, 1945–1962: Ein Beitrag zur Diskussion über die Auflösung des katholischen Milieus." *Archiv für Sozialgeschichte* 38 (1998): 263–84.

Ruff, Mark Edward. *The Wayward Flock: Catholic Youth in Postwar West Germany, 1945–1965.* Chapel Hill, 2005.

Ruppert, Karsten. "Die Deutsche Zentrumspartei in der Mitverantwortung für die Weimarer Republik: Selbstverständnis und politische Leitideen einer konfessionellen Mittelpartei." In *Die Minderheit als Mitte: Die Deutsche Zentrumspartei in der Innenpolitik des Reiches, 1871–1933,* edited by Winfried Becker. Paderborn, 1986.

Ruppert, Karsten. *Im Dienst am Staat von Weimar: Das Zentrum als regierende Partei in der Weimarer Demokratie, 1923–1930.* Düsseldorf, 1992.

Ruppert, Karsten. "Der Einfluß christlich-demokratischer wie christlich-sozialer Ideen und Parteien auf Geist und Politik in der Weimarer Zeit." In *Christliche Demokratie in Europa: Grundlagen und Entwicklungen seit dem 19. Jahrhundert,* edited by Winfried Becker and Rudolf Morsey. Cologne, 1988.

Rüschenschmidt, Heinrich. "Die Entstehung der hessischen CDU, 1945/46: Lokale Gründungsvorgänge und Willensbildung im Landesverband." Staatsexamen, Philipps-Universität Marburg, 1979.

Ruster, Thomas. *Die verlorene Nützlichkeit der Religion: Katholizismus und Moderne in der Weimarer Republik.* 2nd ed. Paderborn, 1997.

Rüther, Günther, ed. *Geschichte der Christlich-Demokratischen und Christlich-Sozialen Bewegungen in Deutschland: Grundlagen, Unterrichtsmodelle, Quellen, und Arbeitshilfen für die politische Bildung.* 3rd ed. Bonn, 1989.

Sack, David. *Moral Re-Armament: The Reinventions of an American Religious Movement.* New York, 2009.

Salzmann, Rainer, ed. *Die CDU/CSU im Frankfurter Wirtschaftsrat: Protokolle der Unionsfraktion, 1947–1949.* Düsseldorf, 1988.

Salzmann, Rainer, ed. *Die CDU/CSU im Parlamentarischen Rat: Sitzungsprotokolle der Unionsfraktion.* Vol. 2, *Die CDU/CSU im Parlamentarischen Rat.* Stuttgart, 1981.

Sammler, Eberhard. "Politische Strömungen im deutschen Protestantismus." In *Wirtschaftlicher Wandel, religiöser Wandel, und Wertwandel: Folgen für das politische Verhalten in der Bundesrepublik Deutschland,* edited by Dieter Oberndörfer, Hans Rattinger, and Karl Schmitt. Berlin, 1985.

Sauer, Thomas. "Der Kronberger Kreis: Christlich-Konservative Positionen in der Bundesrepublik Deutschland." In *Katholiken und Protestanten in den Aufbaujahren der Bundesrepublik,* edited by Thomas Sauer. Stuttgart, 2000.

Scarrow, Susan E. *Parties and Their Members: Organizing for Victory in Britain and Germany.* Oxford, 1996.

Schardt, Klaus. *Ludwig Erhard—Der Vater des Wirtschaftswunders.* Nuremberg, 2000.

Scharfe, Martin. *Die Religion des Volkes: Kleine Kultur- und Sozialgeschichte des Pietismus.* Gütersloh, 1980.

Scheer, Monique. *Rosenkranz und Kriegsvisionen: Marienerscheinungskulte im 20. Jahrhundert.* Tübingen, 2006.

Scheerer, Reinhard. *Evangelische Kirche und Politik, 1945 bis 1949: Zur theologisch-politischen Ausgangslage in den ersten Jahren nach der Niederlage des "Dritten Reiches."* Cologne, 1981.

Schildt, Axel. *Ankunft im Westen: Ein Essay zur Erfolgsgeschichte der Bundesrepublik.* Frankfurt, 1999.

Schildt, Axel. "Eine Ideologie im Kalten Krieg—Ambivalenzen der abendländischen Gedankenwelt im ersten Jahrzehnt nach dem Zweiten Weltkrieg." In *Von der Kriegskultur zur Friedenskultur? Zum Mentalitätswandel in Deutschland seit 1945,* edited by Thomas Kühne. Hamburg, 2000.

Schildt, Axel. *Moderne Zeiten: Freizeit, Massenmedien und "Zeitgeist" in der Bundesrepublik der 50er Jahre.* Hamburg, 1995.

Schildt, Axel. "Ökumene wider den Liberalismus: Zum politischen Engagement konservativer protestantischer Theologen im Umkreis der Abendländischen Akademie nach dem Zweiten Weltkrieg." In *Katholiken und Protestanten in den Aufbaujahren der Bundesrepublik,* edited by Thomas Sauer. Stuttgart, 2000.

Schildt, Axel. *Zwischen Abendland und Amerika: Studien zur westdeutschen Ideenlandschaft der 50er Jahre.* Munich, 1999.

Schissler, Hanna. "Social Democratic Gender Policies, the Working-Class Milieu, and the Culture of Domesticity in West Germany in the 1950s and 1960s." In *Between Reform and Revolution: German Socialism and Communism from 1840 to 1990,* edited by David E. Barclay and Eric D. Weitz. Providence, 1998.

Schmädeke, Jürgen, and Peter Steinbach, eds. *Der Widerstand gegen den Nationalsozialismus: Die deutsche Gesellschaft und der Widerstand gegen Hitler.* Munich, 1986.

Schmandt, Katrin. "Die Christlich-Demokratische Partei in Paderborn: Gründung und Aufbau." In *Westfälische Zeitschrift: Zeitschrift fur Vaterländische Geschichte und Altertumskunde,* edited by Verein für Geschichte und Altertumskunde Westfalens. Paderborn, 1996.

Schmeer, Reinhard. "Die Evangelische Kirche im Rheinland und die CDU, 1945–1949." *Monatshefte für Evangelische Kirchengeschichte des Rheinlandes* 41 (1992): 315–41.

Schmeer, Reinhard. *Volkskirchliche Hoffnungen und der Aufbau der Union: Evangelische Kirche und CDU/CSU in den ersten Nachkriegsjahren.* Cologne, 2001.

Schmidt, Otto. *Anspruch und Antwort: Gedanken zur Geschichte der Christlich Demokratischen Union Rheinland.* Cologne, 1975.

Schmidt, Ute. "Die Christlich Demokratische Union Deutschlands." In *Parteien-Handbuch: Die Parteien der Bundesrepublik Deutschland, 1945–1980,* vol. 1, *AUD Bis EFP,* edited by Richard Stöss. Opladen, 1983.

Schmidt, Ute. "Hitler ist tot und Ulbricht lebt: Die CDU, der Nationalsozialismus, und der Holocaust." In *Der Umgang mit dem Nationalsozialismus und Antisemitismus in Österreich, der DDR, und der Bundesrepublik Deutschland,* edited by Werner Bergmann, Rainer Erb, and Albert Lichtblau. Frankfurt a.M., 1995.

Schmidt, Ute. "Linkskatholische Positionen nach 1945 zu Katholizismus und Kirche im NS-Staat." In *Sozial- und Linkskatholizismus: Erinnerung—Orientierung—Befreiung,* edited by Heiner Ludwig and Wolfgang Schroeder. Frankfurt a.M., 1990.

Schmidt, Ute. *Zentrum oder CDU: Politischer Katholizismus zwischen Tradition und Anpassung.* Opladen, 1987.

Schmidt, Ute. "Zentrumspartei oder Union—Zur Archäologie eines Parteienkonflikts nach 1945." In *Politische Zäsuren und Gesellschaftlicher Wandel im 20. Jahrhundert: Regionale und vergleichende Perspektiven,* edited by Matthias Frese and Michael Prinz. Paderborn, 1996.

Schmidt-Volkmar, Erich. *Der Kulturkampf in Deutschland, 1871–1890.* Göttingen, 1962.

Schmidtchen, Gerhard. *Protestanten und Katholiken: Soziologische Analyse konfessioneller Kultur.* Bern, 1973.

Schmitt, Karl. *Konfession und Wahlverhalten in der Bundesrepublik Deutschland.* Berlin, 1989.

Schneider, Michael. *Die Christlichen Gewerkschaften, 1894–1933.* Bonn, 1982.

Scholder, Klaus. *Die Kirchen und das Dritte Reich.* Vol. 2, *Das Jahr der Ernüchterung 1934.* Berlin, 1985.

Schönbohm, Wulf. *CDU: Porträt einer Partei.* Munich, 1979.

Schönbohm, Wulf. *Die CDU wird moderne Volkspartei: Selbstverständnis, Mitglieder, Organisation, und Apparat, 1950–1980.* Stuttgart, 1985.

Schorn-Schütte, Luise, and Walter Sparn, eds. *Evangelische Pfarrer: Zur sozialen und politischen Rolle einer bürgerlichen Gruppe in der deutschen Gesellschaft des 18. bis 20. Jahrhunderts.* Stuttgart, 1997.

Schroeder, Wolfgang. *Katholizismus und Einheitsgewerkschaft: Der Streit um den DGB und der Niedergang des Sozialkatholizismus in der Bundesrepublik bis 1960.* Bonn, 1992.

Schroeder, Wolfgang. "Oswald von Nell-Breuning contra Viktor Agartz: Ein entscheidender Konflikt um das Selbstverständnis der Einheitsgewerkschaft." In *Sozial- und Linkskatholizismus: Erinnerung—Orientierung—Befreiung,* edited by Heiner Ludwig and Wolfgang Schroeder. Frankfurt a.M., 1990.

Schultz, Kevin M., and Paul Harvey. "Everywhere and Nowhere: Recent Trends in American Religious History and Historiography." *Journal of the American Academy of Religion* 78.1 (2010): 129–62.

Schulze, Matthias. *Bund oder Schar—Verband oder Pfarrjugend? Katholische Jugendarbeit im Erzbistum Paderborn nach 1945.* Paderborn, 2001.

Schwan, Alexander. "Humanismen und Christentum." In *Enzyklopädische Bibliothek in 30 Teilbänden: Christlicher Glaube in moderner Gesellschaft,* edited by Franz Böckle, Franz-Xaver Kaufmann, Karl Rahner, Bernhard Welte, and Robert Scherer. Basel, 1981.

Schwarz, Hans-Peter. "Konrad Adenauer—Abendländer oder Europäer? Zur Bedeutung des Christlichen in seiner auswärtigen Politik." In *Adenauer und die Kirchen,* edited by Ulrich von Hehl. Bonn, 1999.

Schwarz, Hans-Peter. *Konrad Adenauer: A German Politician and Statesman in a Period of War, Revolution, and Reconstruction.* Vol. 1, *From the German Empire to the Federal Republic, 1876–1952.* Translated by Louise Willmot. Providence, 1995.

Schwarz, Hans-Peter, ed. *Konrad Adenauer: Reden, 1917–1967: Eine Auswahl.* Stuttgart, 1975.

Schwartz, Michael. "'Zwangsheimat Deutschland': Vertriebene und Kernbevölkerung zwischen Gesellschaftskonflikt und Integrationspolitik." In *Nachkrieg in Deutschland,* edited by Klaus Naumann. Hamburg, 2001.

Schweisselmann, Christian. *Die CDU in Mecklenburg und Vorpommern, 1945–1952: Von der Gründung bis zur Auflösung des Landesverbandes: Eine parteiengeschichtliche Darstellung.* Düsseldorf, 2010.

Schwießelmann, Christian. "Norddeutsch, protestantisch, liberal—Gründerpersönlichkeiten der CDU in Mecklenburg-Vorpommern." *Historisch-Politische Mitteilungen* 13 (2006): 25–46.

Schwering, Leo. *Frühgeschichte der Christlich-Demokratischen Union.* Recklinghausen, 1963.

Schwering, Leo. *In den Klauen der Gestapo: Tagebuchaufzeichnungen der Jahre 1944–1945.* Edited by Markus Schwering. Cologne, 1988.

Schwering, Leo. *Vorgeschichte und Entstehung der CDU.* Cologne, 1952.

Schwering, Markus. "Leo Schwering (1883–1971)—Zur Biographie." In Leo Schwering, *In den Klauen der Gestapo: Tagebuchaufzeichnungen der Jahre 1944–1945,* edited by Markus Schwering. Cologne, 1988.

Sheehan, James J. *German History, 1770–1866.* Oxford, 1989.

Siemer, P. Laurentius. *Aufzeichnungen und Briefe.* Frankfurt a.M., 1957.

Sigmund, Paul E. "The Catholic Tradition and Modern Democracy." *Review of Politics* 49.4 (1987): 530–48.

Smith, Helmut Walser. *German Nationalism and Religious Conflict: Culture, Ideology, Politics, 1870–1914.* Princeton, 1995.

Smith, Helmut Walser, and Chris Clark. "The Fate of Nathan." In *Protestants, Catholics, and Jews in Germany, 1800–1914,* edited by Helmut Walser Smith. Oxford, 2001.

Sneeringer, Julia. *Winning Women's Votes: Propaganda and Politics in Weimar Germany.* Chapel Hill, 2002.

Soénius, Ulrich. "Neubeginn im zerstörten Köln." In *50 Jahre CDU Köln, 1945–1995: Festschrift zur 50. Wiederkehr des Gründungstage der Christlich Demokratischen Union,* edited by Christlich-Demokratischen Union Köln. Cologne, 1995.

Solchany, Jean. "Vom Antimodernismus zum Antitotalitarismus: Konservative Interpretationen des Nationalsozialismus in Deutschland, 1945–1949." *Vierteljahrshefte für Zeitgeschichte* 44.3 (1996): 373–94.

Sonnenberger, Franz. "Der neue 'Kulturkampf': Die Gemeinschaftsschule und ihre historischen Voraussetzungen." In *Bayern in der NS-Zeit,* vol. 3, *Herrschaft und Gesellschaft im Konflikt,* edited by Martin Broszat, Elke Fröhlich, and Anton Grossmann. Munich, 1981.

Späth, Antje. "Vielfältige Forderungen nach Gleichberechtigung und 'nur' ein Ergebnis: Artikel 3 Absatz 2 GG." In *Frauen in der Geschichte V: "Das Schicksal Deutschlands liegt in der Hand seiner Frauen"—Frauen in der deutschen Nachkriegsgeschichte,* edited by Anna-Elisabeth Freier and Annette Kuhn. Düsseldorf, 1984.

Sperber, Jonathan. *Popular Catholicism in Nineteenth-Century Germany.* Princeton, 1984.

Sperber, Jonathan. *Rhineland Radicals: The Democratic Movement and the Revolution of 1848–1849.* Princeton, 1991.

Spicer, Kevin P. *Hitler's Priests: Catholic Clergy and National Socialism.* DeKalb, 2008.

Spicka, Mark E. *Selling the Economic Miracle: Economic Reconstruction and Politics in West Germany, 1949–1957.* Providence, 2007.

Spotts, Frederic. *The Churches and Politics in Germany.* Middletown, 1973.

Stambolis, Barbara. "'Fest soll mein Taufbund immer stehn': Jugendliche im katholischen Milieu oder die Grenzen der Gleichschaltung—Lebensweltlich geprägte Resistenzräume im Dritten Reich." *Geschichte in Wissenschaft und Unterricht* 51 (2000): 157–72.

Stambolis, Barbara. "'Heilige Feste und Zeiten' zwischen Selbstvergewisserung und Auflösung des katholischen Milieus nach 1945." *Kirchliche Zeitgeschichte* 13.1 (2000): 178–216.

Stankowski, Martin. *Linkskatholizismus nach 1945: Die Presse oppositioneller Katholiken in der Auseinandersetzung für eine demokratische und sozialistische Gesellschaft.* Cologne, 1976.

Stehkämper, Hugo. *Konrad Adenauer als Katholikentagspräsident 1922: Form und Grenze politischer Entscheidungsfreiheit im katholischen Raum.* Mainz, 1977.

Stehkämper, Hugo. "Protest, Opposition, und Widerstand im Umkreis der (untergegangenen) Zentrumspartei: Ein Überblick." In *Der Widerstand gegen den Nationalsozialismus: Die deutsche Gesellschaft und der Widerstand gegen Hitler,* edited by Jürgen Schmädeke and Peter Steinbach. Munich, 1985.

Steigmann-Gall, Richard. "Apostasy or Religiosity? The Cultural Meanings of the Protestant Vote for Hitler." *Social History* 25.3 (2000): 267–85.

Steigmann-Gall, Richard. *"The Holy Reich": Nazi Conceptions of Christianity, 1919–1945.* Cambridge, 2003.

Steinert, Johannes-Dieter. "Die große Flucht und die Jahre danach: Flüchtlinge und Vertriebene in den vier Besatzungszonen." In *Ende des Dritten Reiches—Ende des Zweiten Weltkrieges: Eine Perspektivische Rückschau,* edited by Hans-Erich Volksmann. Munich, 1995.

Stern, Frank. *Im Anfang war Auschwitz: Antisemitismus und Philosemitismus im deutschen Nachkrieg.* Gerlingen, 1991.

Stöss, Richard, ed. *Parteien-Handbuch: Die Parteien der Bundesrepublik Deutschland, 1945–1980.* Vol. 1, *AUD Bis EFP.* Opladen, 1983.

Stubbe-Da Luz, Helmut. "Union der Christen—Splittergruppe—Integrationspartei: Wurzeln und Anfänge der Hamburger CDU bis Ende 1946." Ph.D. diss., Universität Hamburg, 1989.

Süssmuth, Hans. *Kleine Geschichte der CDU-Frauen-Union: Erfolge und Rückschläge, 1948–1990.* Baden-Baden, 1990.

Suval, Stanley. *Electoral Politics in Wilhelmine Germany.* Chapel Hill, 1985.

Tal, Uriel. *Christians and Jews in Germany: Religion, Politics, and Ideology in the Second Reich, 1870–1914.* Translated by Noah Jonathan Jacobs. Ithaca, 1975.

Tenfelde, Klaus. "Historische Milieus—Erblichkeit und Konkurrenz." In *Nation und Gesellschaft in Deutschland: Historische Essays,* edited by Manfred Hettling and Paul Nolte. Munich, 1996.

Thielicke, Helmut, ed. *In der Stunde Null: Die Denkschrift des Freiburger "Bonhoeffer-Kreises": Politischen Nöten unserer Zeit.* Tübingen, 1979.

Thimme, Annelise, ed. *Friedrich Thimme, 1868–1938: Ein politischer Historiker, Publizist, und Schriftsteller in seinen Briefen.* Boppard a.R., 1994.

Thompson, David M. "Ecumenicism." In *The Cambridge History of Christianity: World Christianities c. 1914–c. 2000,* edited by Hugh McLeod. Cambridge, 2006.

Thum, Horst. *Wirtschaftsdemokratie und Mitbestimmung: Von den Anfängen 1916 bis zum Mitbestimmungsgesetz 1976.* Cologne, 1991.

Trippen, Norbert. "Von den Fuldaer 'Bischofskonferenzen' zur 'Deutschen Bischofskonferenz,' 1945–1976." *Historisches Jahrbuch* 121 (2001): 304–19.

Uertz, Rudolf. *Christentum und Sozialismus in der frühen CDU: Grundlagen und Wirkungen der christlich-sozialen Ideen in der Union, 1945–1949.* Stuttgart, 1981.

Uertz, Rudolf. "Christlich-demokratische Wertvorstellungen im Parlamentarischen Rat, 1948/49." *Historisch-Politische Mitteilungen* 15 (2008): 103–23.

Uhl, Bernd. *Die Idee des christlichen Sozialismus in Deutschland, 1945–1947.* Mainz, 1975.

Van Hook, James C. *Rebuilding Germany: The Creation of the Social Market Economy, 1945–1957.* Cambridge, 2004.

Van Kemseke, Peter. "From Permission to Prohibition: The Impact of the Changing International Context on Left Catholicism in Europe." In *Left Catholicism: Catholics and Society in Western Europe at the Point of Liberation, 1943–1955,* edited by Gerd-Rainer Horn and Emmanuel Gerard. Leuven, 2001.

Van Kersbergen, Kees. "The Christian Democratic Phoenix and Modern Unsecular Politics." *Party Politics* 24.3 (2008): 259–79.

Van Kersbergen, Kees. "The Distinctiveness of Christian Democracy." In *Christian Democracy in Europe: A Comparative Perspective,* edited by David Hanley. London, 1994.

Van Melis, Damian. "Europapolitik oder Abendlandideologie? Die Dominikanerzeitschrift Neue Ordnung in den ersten Jahrzehnten der BRD." In *Katholiken und Protestanten in den Aufbaujahren der Bundesrepublik,* edited by Thomas Sauer. Stuttgart, 2000.

Van Melis, Damian. "'Ganz Deutschland war ein einziges großes Konzentrationslager': Die katholische Kirche und die Frage der deutschen Kollektivschuld." In *Vergangenheitsbewältigung: Modelle der politischen und sozialen Integration in der bundesdeutschen Nachkriegsgeschichte,* edited by Gary S. Schaal and Andras Wöll. Baden-Baden, 1997.

Van Melis, Damian. "Der katholische Episkopat und die Entnazifizierung." In *Siegerin in Trümmern: Die Rolle der katholischen Kirche in der deutschen Nachkriegsgesellschaft,* edited by Joachim Köhler and Damian van Melis. Stuttgart, 1998.

Van Melis, Damian. "'Strengthened and Purified through Ordeal by Fire': Ecclesiastical Triumphalism in the Ruins of Europe." In *Life after Death: Approaches to a Cultural and Social History of Europe during the 1940s and 1950s,* edited by Richard Bessel and Dirk Schumann. Cambridge, 2003.

Van Norden, Günther. "Der schwierige Neubeginn." In *Kontinuität und Neubeginn: Die rheinische und westfälische Kirche in der Nachkriegszeit (1945–1949),* edited by Bernd Hey and Günther van Norden. Bielefeld, 1996.

Van Schewick, Burkhard. *Die katholische Kirche und die Entstehung der Verfassungen in Westdeutschland, 1945–1950.* Mainz, 1980.

Volk, Ludwig, ed. *Akten deutscher Bischöfe über die Lage der Kirche, 1933–1945.* Vol. 6, *1943–1945.* Mainz, 1985.

Vollnhals, Clemens. "Die Evangelische Kirche zwischen Traditionswahrung und Neuorientierung." In *Von Stalingrad zur Währungsreform: Zur Sozialgeschichte des Umbruchs in Deutschland,* edited by Martin Broszat, Klaus-Dietmar Henke, and Hans Woller. 3rd ed. Munich, 1990.

Von Aretin, Karl Otmar. "Der deutsche Widerstand gegen Hitler." In *Nation, Staat, und Demokratie in Deutschland: Ausgewählte Beiträge zur Zeitgeschichte,* edited by Andreas Kunz and Martin Vogt. Mainz, 1993.

Von Buttlar, Walrab. *Ziele und Zielkonflikte der sowjetischen Deutschlandpolitik, 1945–1947.* Stuttgart, 1980.

Von der Brelie-Lewien, Doris. "Abendland und Sozialismus: Zur Kontinuität politisch-kultureller Denkhaltungen im Katholizismus von der Weimarer Republik zur frühen Nachkriegszeit." In *Politische Teilkulturen zwischen Integration und Polarisierung: Zur politischen Kultur in der Weimarer Republik,* edited by Detlef Lehnert and Klaus Megerle. Opladen, 1990.

Von der Brelie-Lewien, Doris. *Katholische Zeitschriften in den Westzonen, 1945–1949: Ein Beitrag zur politischen Kultur der Nachkriegszeit.* Göttingen, 1986.

Von der Gablentz, Otto Heinrich. *Die versäumte Reform: Zur Kritik der westdeutschen Politik.* Cologne, 1960.

Von Hehl, Ulrich, ed. *Adenauer und die Kirchen.* Bonn, 1999.

Von Hehl, Ulrich. *Katholische Kirche und National Sozialism im Erzbistum Köln, 1933–1945.* Mainz, 1977.

Von Hehl, Ulrich. "Konfessionelle Irritationen in der frühen Bundesrepublik." *Historisch-Politische Mitteilungen* 6 (1999): 167–87.

Von Nell-Breuning, Oswald. "Die politische Verwirklichung der christlichen Soziallehre." In *Wirtschaft und Gesellschaft heute,* vol. 3, *Zeitfragen, 1955–1959.* Freiburg i.B., 1960.

Von Plato, Alexander, and Almut Leh, eds. *"Ein unglaublicher Frühling": Erfahrene Geschichte im Nachkriegsdeutschland, 1945–1948.* Bonn, 1997.

Von Sternberg, Wilhelm. *Adenauer: Eine deutsche Legende.* Berlin, 2001.

Voßkamp, Sabine. *Katholische Kirche und Vertriebene in Westdeutschland: Integration, Identität, und Ostpolitischer Diskurs, 1945–1972.* Stuttgart, 2007.

Wager, Johannes Volker, ed. *Der Parlamentarische Rat, 1948–1949: Akten und Protokolle.* Vol. 1, *Vorgeschichte.* Boppard a.R., 1975.

Waldmann, Peter. "Die Eingliederung der ostdeutschen Vertriebenen." In *Vorgeschichte der Bundesrepublik Deutschland: Zwischen Kapitulation und Grundgesetz,* edited by Josef Becker, Theo Stammen, and Peter Waldmann. 2nd ed. Munich, 1987.

Walter, Franz. "Milieus und Parteien in der deutschen Gesellschaft: Zwischen Persistenz und Erosion." *Geschichte in Wissenschaft und Unterricht* 46 (1995): 479–93.

Walter, Karin. *Neubeginn—Nationalsozialismus—Widerstand: Die politisch-theoretische Diskussion der Neuordnung in CDU und SPD, 1945–1948.* Bonn, 1987.

Warner, Carolyn M. *Confessions of an Interest Group: The Catholic Church and Political Parties in Europe.* Princeton, 2000.

Weber, Christoph. *"Eine starke, enggeschlossene Phalanx": Der politische Katholizismus und die erste deutsche Reichstagswahl 1871.* Essen, 1992.

Weber, Christoph. *Kirchliche Politik zwischen Rom, Berlin, und Trier: Die Beilegung des preußischen Kulturkampfes, 1876–1888.* Mainz, 1970.

Weidenfeld, Werner. *Konrad Adenauer und Europa: Die geistigen Grundlagen der westeuropäischen Integrationspolitik des ersten Bonner Bundeskanzlers.* Bonn, 1976.

Weitzel, Kurt. "Von der CSVP zur CDU: Die Gründung der CDU in Rheinhessen, 1945–1947." Ph.D. diss., Johannes Gutenberg-Universität Mainz, 1980.

Weitzel, Kurt. *Vom Chaos zur Demokratie: Die Entstehung der Parteien in Rheinland-Pfalz, 1945–1947.* Mainz, 1989.

Wengst, Udo. "Die CDU/CSU im Bundestagswahlkampf 1949." *Vierteljahrshefte für Zeitgeschichte* 34.1 (1986): 1–52.

Wettig, Gerhard. "Der Konflikt der Ost-CDU mit der Besatzungsmacht, 1945–1948, im Spiegel sowjetischer Akten." *Historisch-Politische Mitteilungen* 6 (1999): 109–37.

Whyte, John H. *Catholics in Western Democracies: A Study in Political Behavior.* New York, 1981.

Wieck, H. G. *Die Entstehung der CDU und die Wiedergründung des Zentrums im Jahre 1945.* Düsseldorf, 1953.

Wiesen, S. Jonathan. *West German Industry and the Challenge of the Nazi Past, 1945–1955.* Chapel Hill, 2001.

Wilde, Manfred. *Die SBZ-CDU, 1945–1947: Zwischen Kriegsende und kaltem Krieg.* Munich, 1998.

Wiliarty, Sarah Elise. *The CDU and the Politics of Gender in Germany: Bringing Women to the Party.* Cambridge, 2010.

Williamson, George S. "A Religious Sonderweg? Reflections on the Sacred and the Secular in the Historiography of Modern Germany." *Church History* 75.1 (2006): 139–56.

Wolf, Christof. "Konfessionelle versus religiöse Konfliktslinie in der deutschen Wählerschaft." *Politische Vierteljahresschrift* 37.4 (1996): 713–34.

Wolgast, Eike. *Die Wahrnehmung des Dritten Reiches in der unmittelbaren Nachkriegszeit (1945/46).* Heidelberg, 2001.

Woolf, Stuart. "Europe and Its Historians." *Central European History* 12.3 (2003): 323–37.

Wright, J. R. C. *"Above Parties": The Political Attitudes of the German Protestant Church Leadership, 1918–1933.* Oxford, 1974.

Zapf, Wolfgang. *Wandlungen der deutschen Elite: Ein Zirkulationsmodell deutscher Führungsgruppen, 1919–1961.* Munich, 1965.

Zeender, John K. *The German Center Party, 1890–1906.* Philadelphia, 1976.

Zeidler, Sonja. "Zwischen Anpassung und Selbstbehauptung: Die Ost-CDU und ihre Sprache in den Jahren, 1945–1957." *Historisch-Politische Mitteilungen* 6 (1999): 139–66.

Zeiger, Ivo. "Kirchliche Zwischenbilanz 1945: Bericht über die Informationsreise durch Deutschland und Österreich im Herbst 1945." Edited by Ludwig Volk. *Stimmen der Zeit* 5 (1975): 293–312.

Zitelmann, Rainer. *Adenauers Gegner: Streiter für die Einheit.* Erlangen, 1991.

Index